MW00639024

Nicholas Needham's landmark history of Christianity continues with expert treatment of an era charged with change. As he assesses the European Enlightenment, evangelical revivals throughout the Atlantic region, and developments within Roman Catholicism and Eastern Orthodoxy from his consistently Reformed perspective, Needham provides illuminating reading for those who share that perspective, but perhaps even more for those who do not.

MARK NOLL
Recent author of *America's Book: The Rise and Decline of a Bible Civilization, 1794-1911*

Nick Needham has done it again. His series, *2000 Years of Christ's Power,* has for some time been indispensable for students and teachers of church history, In this volume, Needham tackles the 18th century, and he does so with deftness and skill. As always, Needham remains attentive to the big picture, yet he also manages to maintain a grasp of the lesser known details throughout. Especially notable is Needham's inclusion of the Eastern and Russian Orthodox Church. Since the publication of volume 3, I have recommended *2000 Years of Christ's Power* as the best place to start for a survey of church history. Now I would add that volume 5 may be the best place to start to gain an understanding of the sweep of the 18th century. Highly recommended.

JONATHAN L. MASTER
President,
Greenville Presbyterian Theological Seminary

Martyn Lloyd-Jones used to describe himself as 'an eighteenth-century man'. As to why this might be so, this latest volume by Nick Needham in his comprehensive church history series may well explain. This volume is focused on the eighteenth-century Christian world, which necessarily entails the enviable task of detailing the Great Awakening and its magnificent aftershocks, and thus one might well understand why Lloyd-Jones was drawn to this period in the history of the Church. However, Needham not only details this remarkable move of God in this new study; he also helpfully delineates the variegated state of professing Christendom in this crucial era with magisterial vim and verve. Highly recommended!

MICHAEL A. G. HAYKIN
Chair and Professor of Church History,
The Southern Baptist Theological Seminary.

Dr Nick Needham's volumes on the history of the Christian church have been widely and enthusiastically received, and with good reason. Dr Needham writes with an engaging clarity and penetrating insight, bringing to life the risings and fallings, the struggles and triumphs, of the church of Christ throughout the past 2000 years. The latest volume in the series, *2000 Years of Christ's Power: The Age of Enlightenment and Awakening*, is yet another 'tour de force'. These volumes should be compulsory reading, first for pastors and elders called to teach and defend the faith, but also for Christians in general who desire to deepen their knowledge of the Saviour's power throughout the church's history. Commended with enthusiasm.

Ian Hamilton
President of Westminster Presbyterian Theological Seminary

NICK NEEDHAM

2000 YEARS OF CHRIST'S POWER

VOLUME

5

THE AGE OF ENLIGHTENMENT AND AWAKENING

CHRISTIAN FOCUS

paperback ISBN 978-1-5271-0973-5
ebook ISBN 978-1-5271-1025-0

10 9 8 7 6 5 4 3 2 1

Published in 2023
by
Christian Focus Publications Ltd,
Geanies House, Fearn, Ross-shire,
IV20 1TW, Great Britain.

www.christianfocus.com

and

Grace Publications Trust
7 Arlington Way
London, EC1R 1XA, England.

www.gracepublications.co.uk

Cover design by
Daniel van Straaten

Printed by Bell & Bain, Glasgow

MIX
Paper | Supporting responsible forestry
FSC® C007785
FSC www.fsc.org

Contents

List of illustrations and maps

Introduction

This volume is devoted to the story of the Church in the 18th century. However, each chapter has its own timeframe, which may slip back into the 17th century, or tiptoe into the 19th, depending on the topic

The 18th century was a dynamic and epoch-making era. It embraced:

- the intellectual and cultural paradigm-shift of the Enlightenment, the 'Age of Reason,' from whose transforming impact on society and religion – for good or ill or both – Europe and the world have never escaped;
- the dawn of the 'Age of the Machine' in the Industrial Revolution, which C. S. Lewis thought was the true dividing line separating the ancient and modern worlds;
- the birth of modern, secular, democratic politics in the French Revolution of 1789 – revolutionary democracy as political salvation – whose spiritual children we all are (who among us now questions that democracy is the proper form of government, to be fought for and even imposed?), together with the ensuing Revolutionary and Napoleonic wars that convulsed all Europe and Russia for the better part of three decades;
- the founding of the independent nation of America, when the thirteen British Colonies broke away from the British Empire in the war of 1775–83, taking a new, young nation on the first step of a long and painful journey to world superpower status;

- the golden fire of the Evangelical Revival in Britain and Great Awakening in America, which created a whole new set of expectations about what vital Protestant Christianity ought to be …

One hardly knows where to stop. All these, and other events and movements, acted and reacted on one another with potency. This is the narrative the present volume seeks to tell.

In many ways, I confess I do not feel especially at home in the 18th Century. My personal spiritual roots are far more among the early Church Fathers and the Protestant Reformers. I certainly have no great love for the Enlightenment, and I dislike the entire political trajectory on which the French Revolution set Europe and ultimately the world. The 18th Century was also a meagre age in producing great Christian thinkers. Apart from Jonathan Edwards in Colonial America, one is hard pressed to name a truly first-class mind surrendered to the Queen of the Sciences (theology!). However, England's Andrew Fuller, unjustly neglected by those outside his own tradition, certainly deserves a very honourable mention for his creative work of theological renewal, among a Calvinistic Baptist community that had largely lost its way amid the dark, tangled forests of an ugly anti-revival bigotry, and the fearfully chill winds of Hyper-Calvinism.[1] Still, I gladly admit I cannot help feeling my heart kindled as I read about the mighty deeds wrought in, by, and through the Evangelical preachers of that age of Revival and Awakening. Whatever their failings, these were religious heroes of quality and choice, who often endured fierce mob persecution and sneering establishment hostility, yet rose above it all to proclaim a self-evidently life-transforming message that brought new purpose, new life, hope, mental quickening, and the experience of positive community, to unguessed multitudes. When the Protestant world ceases to acknowledge, understand, and reverence John and Charles

1. There is of course the profound Schleiermacher, but I am reserving my detailed treatment of this genuinely epoch-making giant of a theologian for the next volume. His influence lies in the 19th century, although his first great theological treatise was published in 1799.

Wesley, George Whitefield, Howell Harris, Daniel Rowland, Gilbert Tennent, Samuel Davies, and others of the same spirit, it will have shown itself lost in distractions and deviations that could prove its utter undoing. If this volume can do anything to revitalise appreciation for these men and their associates, and their works (the works of God through them, as they would have affirmed), it will have served a useful purpose.

I conclude my introduction with a quotation from Jonathan Edwards on the religious awakening in Northampton, Massachusetts, in 1734–35, that so captivated many Protestant readers in his day who longed for better things:

> When this work first appeared and was so extraordinarily carried on amongst us in the winter, others round about us seemed not to know what to make of it. Many scoffed at and ridiculed it; and some compared what we called conversion, to certain distempers.[2] But it was very observable of many, who occasionally came amongst us from abroad with disregardful hearts, that what they saw here cured them of such a temper of mind. Strangers were generally surprised to find things so much beyond what they had heard, and were wont to tell others that the state of the town could not be conceived of by those who had not seen it.
>
> The notice that was taken of it by the people who came to town on occasion of the court that sat here in the beginning of March, was very observable. And those who came from the neighbourhood to our public lectures were for the most part remarkably affected. Many who came to town, on one occasion or other, had their consciences smitten, and awakened; and went home with wounded hearts, and with those impressions that never wore off till they had hopefully a saving issue; and those who before had serious thoughts, had their awakenings and convictions greatly increased. There were many instances of persons who came from abroad on visits, or on business, who had not been long here, before, to all appearances, they were savingly wrought upon,[3] and partook of that shower

2. Mental abberations.

3. God worked salvation in them.

of divine blessing which God rained down here, and went home rejoicing; till at length the same work began evidently to appear and prevail in several other towns in the county.

Acknowledgements

I wish to thank the following for the help given during the writing of this volume, whether by finding source material, giving direction, reading through drafts, or general encouragement: Phil Arthur, Alan Howe, Michael Haykin, James White, John McPherson, Joanna Cook, Bobby Grow, Father Alexis of the St Edward Brotherhood, Bill Graham, Laurence Price, Dieter Schneider, Russell Phillips, Tom Thrower, Jonathan Master, and others probably too numerous to mention.

Chapter 1

The Enlightenment

Introduction

The 18th Century was a century of paradox. On the one hand, it was the era of the Enlightenment, or the Age of Reason, as it is sometimes called. The Enlightenment was characterised by a Europe-wide philosophical questioning (at best) and sceptical rejection (at worst) of traditional Christian faith, as incompatible with reason – or at least requiring new rational and philosophical foundations, if some version of Christianity was to be worthy of Enlightened Man's belief. On the other hand, the same century was also the era of the Evangelical Revival, as it is known in Britain, or Great Awakening, as it is known in America, in which untold myriads were brought out of spiritual darkness into the True Light. The paradox is intensified by the way that these two phenomena acted and reacted on each other. The greatest philosopher of the Enlightenment, the German 'sage of *Königsberg*', Immanuel Kant, was clearly impacted and influenced by Christianity; the greatest theologian of the Great Awakening, Jonathan Edwards, was clearly impacted and influenced by the Enlightenment.[1] In this opening Chapter, we shall consider the Enlightenment and its various manifestations as the necessary backdrop to any credible account of religion in the 18th Century.

1. For Kant, see Part 3 of the present Chapter. For Jonathan Edwards, see Chapter 4, Part 2, section 3.

1
The scientific revolution and its effects

In significant ways, the Enlightenment (in German, the *Aufklärung*) grew out of the Western world's 'scientific revolution' of the 16th and 17th Centuries.[1] Historians have endlessly debated the origins of that revolution, and of the rise of modern science. One of the most creative thinkers about these issues, the eminent philosopher-mathematician Alfred North Whitehead (1861–1947), argued that Western science arose as a compelling and productive synthesis between (a) the devotion to reason among ancient Greek philosophers and (b) the Christian view of the universe as the creation of a wise, orderly God. This may be so, but it leaves unsettled the question of why that synthesis should have arisen with such force specifically in the 16th Century. Other historians have contended that the Protestant Reformation had a galvanizing effect on the scientific enterprise; and yet this leaves unexplained why so many of the pioneer modern scientists were Roman Catholics (such as da Vinci, Castelli, Copernicus, Descartes, Falloppio, Galileo, Garzoni, Gassendi, Kircher, Pascal, Steno, Torricelli, and others). This particular debate continues.

What we can say with some certainty is that the modern scientific enterprise in the West had its roots in the closing

1. This is not to deny the existence of Islamic science in the Eastern world. This Chapter is concerned with the rise and consequences of Western science.

centuries of the medieval period, with trailblazers such as Robert Grosseteste (1168–1253), Roger Bacon (1214–94), Jean Buridan (1300–1358), and Nicholas of Cusa (1401–64).[2] However, it was in the 16th and 17th Centuries that the scientific spirit and method ignited a culture-transfiguring flame, manifested in the life and work of such revered figures in science's Hall of Fame as Leonardo da Vinci (1452–1519), Nicolaus Copernicus (1473–1543), Galileo Galilei (1564–1642), Johannes Kepler (1571–1630), Evangelista Torricelli (1608–47), and Sir Isaac Newton (1643–1726).[3]

As the adventure of modern science developed in the Western world, thinkers were increasingly impressed by its power to understand and manipulate nature through rational investigation. This in turn began to encourage a sense (in many minds, though not in all) that human reason was perhaps sufficient to answer *all* the meaningful questions of life. Less and less deference was paid to the established views of tradition and authority, which in scientific matters had all too often proved inadequate and defective. Famously, the ancient Greek philosopher Aristotle (384–22 B.C.) – the pre-eminent thinker of all time, in the estimation of most educated Westerners of the 16th and 17th Centuries – had provided most of the previous two millennia's science; and yet he was weighed in the new scientific balance and found sadly wanting. This generated yet another paradox: while Protestant theologians were enthroning Aristotle within theology as the supreme mentor of human thinking (after the Bible), in the new 'scholasticism' of the

2. For Grosseteste and Bacon, see Volume 2, Chapter 7, section 3, under **Robert Grosseteste**. For Nicholas of Cusa, see Volume 2, Chapter 10, section 3.

3. Leonardo da Vinci, although chiefly famous as an artist, pursued many scientific interests with great ability, such as geology, botany, zoology, anatomy, optics, and engineering. Copernicus and Galileo were the architects of the 'heliocentric' theory of the solar system (that the earth and the other planets orbit the sun). Kepler worked out the principles governing the patterns of planetary movement, set forth as 'the laws of planetary motion'. Torricelli invented the barometer. Newton is most celebrated for formulating the theory of gravity.

post-Luther and post-Calvin world, scientists by contrast were dethroning him as an unsafe guide.[4]

Two decisive examples of the intellectual revolution accomplished by the rise of science can be given here. First, there was the new astronomy. The age-old 'geocentric' theory of the solar system – that the universe orbited around a fixed earth – was supplanted by the new, and more effectively explanatory, 'heliocentric' theory – that the earth is not fixed but orbits the sun, as do the other planets. Heliocentrism was championed by Polish astronomer Copernicus and Italian astronomer Galileo. Then there was the new physics, notably although not exclusively its investigations into optics and its theory of gravity. The new physics was championed above all by the pre-eminent English scientist Isaac Newton, who became the supreme icon of science. This was captured well in some humorous lines by the 18th Century English poet Alexander Pope (1688–1744):

> Nature and Nature's laws lay hid in night;
> God said, 'Let Newton be!' and all was light.

Newton enjoyed his iconic status within science until the 20th Century, when he was replaced by Albert Einstein.

Rather than looking to the inherited wisdom of the past, then, the scientific endeavour taught people to think and explore nature for themselves, utilizing reason, observation, experiment. The expectation was that unceasing progress would be made to an ever more accurate understanding of the universe. As the 17th Century moved toward its close and the 18th Century got under way, this attitude slid very easily into a much more comprehensive confidence in reason to map reality in every area of existence, including beliefs about spiritual reality. If rational thinkers no longer gave uncritical deference to ancient texts written by Aristotle in the sphere of science, why should they give uncritical deference to equally ancient texts such as the Bible in the sphere of religion? As Immanuel Kant affirmed, the

4. For the rise of the Aristotelian scholastic method in Protestant theology, see Volume 4, Chapter 1, Part 2.

watchword and war-cry of the Enlightenment was, 'Dare to use your own understanding!'

1. Scientific Optimism: Francis Bacon (1561–1626)

Often regarded as the first to extol the new science as offering vast positive potential for human progress, the London-born Francis Bacon (1561–1626) was an English politician who achieved high office under King James I (1603–25), as (successively) Solicitor General, Attorney General, Lord Keeper of the Great Seal, and Lord Chancellor. He was also instrumental in helping establish some of the new British Colonies on the American continent – Virginia, North and South Carolina, Newfoundland.

It is not, however, for his political career that Bacon is remembered, but as a philosopher, particularly a scientific thinker and publicist. His eloquent advocacy of scientific method – observation, gathering data, performing experiments, forming explanatory hypotheses – is found most fully and famously in his *Novum Organum* ('new method') of 1620. Bacon's treatise set out, in a wide-ranging and impactful way, the methodology of the scientific enterprise. The method is often called 'induction' (or even, in a previous generation, 'Baconian induction'). In this perspective, the 'inductive' method of observation and experiment to discover new truth is held in contrast with the 'deductive' method (where basic truths or principles are *already* known, and one simply teases out their hidden assumptions).

Yet Bacon did more than merely advocate scientific inductive method, however forcefully. He wedded this to an optimistic outlook on the benefits of science to humanity. This optimism is best seen in Bacon's novel *The New Atlantis* (1626), in which he envisages a new society flourishing on the basis of science. Bacon's fictional society has at its heart a college, Solomon's House, devoted to the scientific exploration and conquest of nature. Its purpose is described thus: 'The end [goal] of our foundation [college] is the knowledge of causes, and secret motions of things; and the enlarging of the bounds of human empire, to the effecting of all things possible.' This entitles *The*

New Atlantis to be considered the first of the various scientific utopias to be imagined in fiction.

Something akin to Solomon's House, inspired directly by Bacon's writings, would come into existence in the form of Britain's 'Royal Society', officially founded in 1660 as 'The Royal Society of London for Improving Natural Knowledge'. In the Royal Society, Bacon's notion of cooperative effort toward scientific understanding and mastery of the natural universe found a real-world embodiment. The Society would stand at the forefront of British scientific endeavour in the dawning age of Enlightenment.

Bacon's unbounded optimism about human progress through science became one of the key ingredients of the 18th Century Enlightenment, although for Bacon it was not divorced from a Christian worldview. Others, however, found it easy to accomplish that divorce, replacing faith in the Christian God with faith in human reason and scientific advance.

2. The Autonomy of Reason: René Descartes (1596–1650)

In some ways, the philosophical father of the Enlightenment and its exaltation of human reason was the influential French Catholic thinker, René Descartes (1596–1650). The son of a lawyer from Châtellerault in central France (although Descartes was born in nearby La Haye), and educated by Jesuits, the young philosopher trained as a lawyer, but was soon living off a private income from the sale of inherited property. He developed into a wandering scholar, eventually settling in the Dutch Republic. There was, however, intense controversy over his published ideas – the leading Dutch Reformed theologian Gisbert Voetius (1589–1676) declared an all-out intellectual war on Descartes, accusing him of being a closet atheist.[5] This prompted the Frenchman at last to move to Sweden, under the patronage of its young, unconventional, and pro-science queen, Christina (reigned 1644–54, then abdicated, died 1689). Descartes had never enjoyed good health, becoming a virtual vegetarian in

---

5. For Voetius, see Volume 4, Chapter 2, Part 1, section 6.

pursuit of a life-enhancing diet; but the fierce Swedish winter overwhelmed him, and he died of pneumonia in 1650.

Descartes has a merited place in the development of science, through his contributions to mathematical theory (geometry and algebra) and optics, and his efforts toward formulating an overall scientific philosophy. In the realm of epistemology (the theory of knowledge), however, his legacy was more questionable. Plagued by doubts about the certainty of human knowledge, Descartes made a famous (or infamous) intellectual experiment in 1619 of subjecting to doubt everything that could possibly be doubted. Once the acid of this universal solvent of doubt had done its work, Descartes found himself left with only one certain belief – that he himself existed. The whole world of the senses, after all, might be one vast hallucination. Yet no matter how deceived he might be in his various beliefs, Descartes could at least know with certainty that he was *thinking about the things he believed* (even if his beliefs were mistaken). One cannot believe without thinking. Therefore, Descartes could be certain he was thinking. And if he was thinking, he must exist as a thinker. 'I think, therefore I am (I exist)' – in Latin, *cogito ergo sum*. I must exist in order to think, even if I am thinking wrongly.

Descartes' philosophy of certainty-through-radical-doubt, expressed in his momentous *Discourse on Method* (1637), gave human reason the supreme priority in knowing truth. From the basic certainty of his own existence supplied by his own reason, Descartes then tried to prove the existence both of God and the external world (he demonstrated God, to his own satisfaction, by reviving a form of Anselm of Canterbury's 'ontological' argument – God is the Perfect Being, but He would not be perfect if He lacked existence). Even so, the 'God' thus demonstrated by Descartes' reason bore little resemblance to the God in whom Descartes' religion taught him to believe, the Christian Trinity made known in Jesus Christ, the crucified and risen God-Man. Descartes had opened a pathway to a reason-constructed view of God that was only a hair's-breadth away from the de-Christianised 'Supreme Being' of Enlightenment thought – the rational or natural religion of Deism.

2
Enlightenment religion

1. Deism and Lord Herbert of Cherbury

The Enlightenment gave birth to two tendencies in religion. The first is known as Deism. This was a variety of theism that built its convictions, not on supposed revelations in religious texts (whether the Bible, the Qur'an, or any other), but on the power of pure reason. Deists conceived of God as the 'Supreme Being' rather than the Trinity of Christian revelation: a God who was rather like a cosmic scientist, designing and creating the universe to run like clockwork. Having brought this perfect clockwork cosmos into existence, the Deist God then had (probably) nothing more to do but passively watch it ticking through its preordained motions.[1] Deists therefore rejected supernatural miracles as needless 'interference' in a world that already worked perfectly. As for salvation, all that was necessary was to observe the moral laws known to reason. God would reward the virtuous in the hereafter, and punish the unrepentant. No Saviour was required. In the Deist scheme, Jesus was reduced to a mere teacher who reminded people of moral truths that reason could discover by itself. Deists referred to their reason-based beliefs and piety as 'natural religion'.

1. 'Probably' because some Deists still wanted, in some sense, to affirm a meaningful providential care exercised by God over creation. Others, like Voltaire in his Deist novel *Candide*, mocked the whole idea. For Voltaire, see section 3.

Deism originated in England with Anglo-Welsh politician, soldier, and philosopher Lord Herbert of Cherbury (1582–1648), older brother of the celebrated Christian poet George Herbert (1593–1633).[2] Lord Herbert fought for the Protestant Dutch against their would-be Spanish masters from 1610, became British ambassador to the French court in 1619, and after returning to England served King Charles I until the outbreak of the English Civil War in 1642.[3] At that point he refused to answer Charles' summons to join him on the battlefield, and submitted at length to parliament, surrendering his castle of Montgomery to parliamentary forces.

Herbert was driven by a quest for religious truth in a Europe convulsed by ideological and military conflict between Roman Catholics, Lutherans, and Calvinists (especially in the savage Thirty Years' War of 1618–48, which involved almost all the European powers).[4] His study of non-Christian religion increased Herbert's perplexities. The ultimate outcome of this quest for truth amidst religious diversity was to prompt Herbert to distil a fundamental essence of all religion, in five points:

(i) There is one supreme God.
(ii) Humans owe worship to this God.
(iii) The most important ingredients of worship are virtue and piety.
(iv) Humans must repent if they do wrong.
(v) God will reward the virtuous and punish the impenitent in an afterlife.

We could call these the 'five points of Deism', and they have earned Herbert the title 'the father of Deism'. His Deistic philosophy of religion is expressed in his 1624 treatise *De Veritate* ('Concerning Truth'). Yet Herbert was always a strange type of Deist, believing not only in prayer (a Deist commonplace), but also in direct personal guidance from his God in various signs.

2. For George Herbert, see Volume 4, Chapter 3, Part 5, section 3.
3. For the English Civil War, see Volume 4, Chapter 3, Part 5.
4. For the Thirty Years' War, see Volume 4, Chapter 1, Part 3.

This belief in personal guidance through signs stands out most vividly in Herbert's decision to publish *De Veritate*:

> Being thus doubtful in my chamber, one fair day in the summer, my casement [window] being opened towards the south, the sun shining clear and no wind stirring, I took my book, *De Veritate*, in my hand, and, kneeling on my knees, devoutly said these words: 'O Thou eternal God, Author of the light which now shines upon me, and Giver of all inward illuminations, I do beseech Thee, of Thy infinite goodness, to pardon a greater request than a sinner ought to make; I am not satisfied enough whether I shall publish this book, *De Veritate*; if it be for Thy glory, I beseech Thee give me some sign from heaven; if not, I shall suppress it.' I had no sooner spoken these words, but a loud though yet gentle noise came from the heavens (for it was like nothing on earth) which did so comfort and cheer me, that I took my petition as granted, and that I had the sign I demanded, whereupon also I resolved to print my book.

We should note, incidentally, that Deists could pray very eloquent prayers to the Supreme Being, as Herbert demonstrates here. Eloquence in prayer to 'God' was no proof of Christian faith in the age of Enlightenment.

2. English Semi-Deism: John Locke (1632–1704)

Lord Herbert's ground-breaking Deism was the signpost toward a rich blossoming of Deist belief and literature in England in the period 1690–1740. England became the European capital of Deism; other countries, notably France and Germany, derived their Deist inspiration from England.[5] But Herbert did not stand alone. Another contributor to the growth of Deism was the premier English philosopher, John Locke (1632–1704). Locke was born the son of a lawyer in 1632 in Wrighton, in the county of Somerset. His years as a teenager and young man were lived during the English Civil War and its aftermath – his father fought for parliament. After studying at Oxford

5. For the flourishing of Deism in England in the period 1690–1740, see the more detailed account in Chapter 2, Part 1, section 3.

University, and then teaching logic, philosophy, and classics there, Locke's life from 1666 onwards became intimately and colourfully entwined with that of Anthony Ashley Cooper (Lord Shaftesbury, 1621–83), one of the founders of the Whig (or Liberal) party in English politics. Shaftesbury appointed Locke as his household physician – Locke had studied medicine quite intensively at Oxford.

Thereafter, Locke shared in Shaftesbury's long and bitter struggle as head of the Whig party in parliament against the perceived misrule of King Charles II (1660–85), in which Shaftesbury championed Protestantism and parliamentary government against royal autocracy and Charles' Catholic leanings.[6] The Whig cause was temporarily defeated in the closing years of Charles II's reign, and Locke and Shaftesbury fled into exile in the Dutch Republic. However, the Whigs re-emerged triumphant in the downfall of Charles' Catholic brother, King James II, in 1688, and the accession to the English throne at parliament's behest of Dutch Protestant leader, William of Orange, in 1689 (events known collectively as the 'Glorious Revolution').[7]

These graphic experiences formed Locke into a profound political philosopher who devoted his energies to justifying everything the Glorious Revolution stood for: a limited rather than absolute monarchy, a Protestant constitution, parliamentary government, individual rights, and religious freedom. Locke expounded this Whig philosophy in his epoch-making *Two Treatises of Government* (1690) and *Three Letters Concerning Toleration* (1689–92). Locke's words against the inhuman folly of religious coercion, and the sacredness of individual personal faith, rang with a Congregationalist or Baptist style conviction:

> No way whatsoever that I shall walk in, against the dictates of my conscience, will ever bring me to the mansions of the blessed. I may grow rich by an art that I take not delight in;

---

6. For the struggle of Shaftesbury and his Whig allies against Charles II, see Volume 4, Chapter 4, Part 1, section 5.

7. See Volume 4, Chapter 4, Part 2, sections 4 and 5, for the Glorious Revolution.

> I may be cured of some disease by remedies that I have not faith in; but I cannot be saved by a religion that I distrust, and by a worship that I abhor ... Faith only, and inward sincerity, are the things that procure acceptance with God.

However, Locke's religious beliefs were far from those of England's historic Congregationalists or Baptists. He was a Unitarian, disbelieving in the deity of Christ. Most of the time Locke seems to have been a 'Socinian', holding Jesus to have been merely human, although there were times when he veered more towards Arianism, viz. that Christ pre-existed His human birth as the first and greatest of God's creations. In his classic 1695 treatise *The Reasonableness of Christianity,* Locke reduced the whole of saving faith to giving mental assent to one proposition, 'Jesus is the Messiah'. Anything more than this he tended to regard as pointless complication introduced by malign theologians. Locke's reductionist attitude to faith both favoured and fostered a comparative indifference to theology, a characteristic that fed into the 'Latitudinarian' school of thought that came to dominate the Church of England post-1689.[8] His Unitarianism and radical doctrinal simplification of Christian belief also encouraged a slide into Deism among his many disciples.

What we might term Locke's semi-Deism was also evident in his theory of knowledge or epistemology, classically expressed in his *Essay Concerning Human Understanding* (1689). In this area of philosophy, Locke is usually contrasted with Descartes. This is because the French thinker took the autonomous or self-governing reason of the human mind as his final authority, whereas the English thinker's final authority was experience (or to be more exact, sense-experience, the experiences mediated by sense-perception). Yet in his own way, Locke also enthroned reason; he simply took sense-experience as the 'material' on which reason worked.

Locke's goal was to account for the origin of the mind's ideas. In his own day, many thinkers believed that certain ideas were 'innate', woven into the innermost fibres of the mind as part of its basic makeup – notably the ideas of God and moral law. Locke,

---

8. See Chapter 2, Part 1, section 1 for Latitudinarianism.

however, distrusted the whole concept of innate ideas. He argued instead that the human mind, when it first entered the world, was like a 'blank slate' (a famous Lockean phrase: in Latin, a *tabula rasa*). The mind's ideas originated as its blank slate was bombarded by sense-experience. Reason then sifted and organised all this by 'reflecting' on the many and various ideas generated by experience.

There were several consequences of Locke's approach. First, it meant for Locke that the actual object of the mind's knowledge was its own sense-produced ideas, rather than the objective realities of the external world. Second, God was not part of sense-experience (we do not 'see' Him); therefore, in Locke's philosophy, we can have knowledge of God's existence only by reasoning *from* sense-experience, 'demonstrating' God by argument. In the *Essay Concerning Human Understanding*, Locke offered a complex argument from our self-perception that there must be a Creator, since a perceived object cannot have come into being out of nothing. Therefore there must be an invisible, uncreated entity – a God – who stood behind the perceived world as its ultimate cause. However, Locke admitted that the argument was lengthy and elaborate, requiring close, sustained, logical attention. By weakening the connection of the mind with objective reality in this way, and by categorising God as a product of difficult and demanding rational argument, Locke's theory of knowledge made the mind far less intimate with God than it had been. For many who absorbed his outlook, this became a doorway out of the specifics of Christianity into a vaguer, less dogmatic Deism.

3. French Deism: Voltaire (1694–1778)

From England, Deism made its way to Continental Europe, where it was articulated with greater literary power than any English writer ever achieved. Key Deist thinkers of the Enlightenment era in Continental Europe were the highly influential French-speaking philosophers Voltaire (1694–1778) and Jean-Jacques Rousseau (1712–78). Although their names are often coupled – 'Voltaire and Rousseau' – as summing up the Enlightenment, they were very different men in spirit. Both, however, were antagonistic to orthodox Christianity.

Voltaire (a self-chosen pseudonym: his real name was François-Marie Arouet) was born in Paris, to a prosperous lawyer who belonged to the lower levels of the French aristocracy. From his teenage years, Voltaire conceived it as his life-mission to be a writer, despite his father's hostility (he wanted his son to follow in his footsteps as a lawyer). Voltaire went his own way, and in a long literary career succeeded in producing works in every genre – essays, poems, novels, plays, historical writings, and scientific treatises. These have given him a secure place in the pantheon of French literature. He was also an early European champion of coffee, drinking fifty cups a day according to some reports.

Voltaire's clashes with French tradition and authority began in his relatively young adulthood, resulting at the age of thirty-one in a two-and-a-half year exile in England, in 1726–28. In his land of exile, he learned to appreciate the English 'constitutional monarchy' (monarchy counterbalanced by a strong representative parliament, and unable to override laws duly enacted through parliament), in contrast to the absolute monarchy of his native France. Likewise, he approved of England's greater measure of civil and religious freedoms than France enjoyed. This experience helped to propel Voltaire along a path of campaigning political reform when he returned to his motherland.

From roughly the mid-1730s, Voltaire turned decisively against Christianity and embraced Deism. Thereafter he mingled his advocacy of civil and religious liberty, and historical and scientific investigations, with increasingly bitter attacks on the Christian religion. His most famous work, the short novel *Candide* (1759), was a half-humorous critique of the Christian faith in God's providential ordering of, and care for, creation. It narrates the life-story of a young man, Candide, who is educated by a Christian philosopher named Professor Pangloss.[9] The oft-repeated maxim of Pangloss, based on his belief in the perfect wisdom and goodness of God exercised in

9. Pangloss is derived from the Greek for (literally) 'all tongue'. It may suggest that Professor Pangloss, when faced with the anguished problems of life, is 'all words' – an endless stream of glib phrases which do nothing to shed any genuine light or comfort on the problem or the sufferer.

providence, is that 'all is for the best in the best of all possible worlds'.

However, as Candide travels the world, and encounters varieties of deep suffering, in himself and in others (including the notorious Lisbon earthquake of 1755, in which up to fifty thousand people may have died), the words of Pangloss begin to ring increasingly hollow. By the novel's end, Candide has rejected the optimistic providential faith-outlook of Pangloss, although there is no consensus among the novel's readers concerning what exactly Candide (and through him, Voltaire) puts in its place. Roman Catholics and Protestants alike regarded the novel as religiously subversive, and it was banned in both Catholic Paris and Calvinist Geneva.

If we turn to Voltaire's positive creed, his Deism, it was a philosophical affair of the intellect, but harnessed in the service of a passionate all-out war on Christianity. The Christianity against which Voltaire fought took the shape of French Catholicism; however, he attacked beliefs common to both Roman Catholics and Protestants. One of Voltaire's most eloquent Deist assaults on Christian belief is found in his *Sermon of the Fifty* (1762). This was a fictional work describing a group of fifty Deists who meet in secret every Sunday for a meal, prayer, and a discourse. Voltaire provided the anti-Christian discourse:

> ... when people come to realise that the Christian sect is in reality just a corruption of natural religion; when reason, liberated from its chains, will teach people that there is but one God, and that this God is the universal Father of all men, who are therefore brothers; that these human brothers must be kind and just towards each other, and follow all the virtues; that since God is just, He is bound to reward virtue and punish misdeeds – surely, my brothers, men will be better for acknowledging this, and less given to superstition [i.e. Christianity]. We are taking the first step on this path by setting this example secretly, and we dare to hope that it will be imitated publicly. May this great God, who hears my words, this God who surely cannot have been born of a young woman, nor died on a cross, nor be eaten in a morsel of bread, nor have inspired these Scriptures which are stuffed

with contradictions, insanity, and vileness – may this God, the Creator of all worlds, have mercy on the Christian sect that so blasphemes Him! May He bring them back to the holy natural religion, and cast His blessings upon our endeavours that He should be truly worshipped! Amen.

4. Deism of the Heart: Jean-Jacques Rousseau (1712–78)

Jean-Jacques Rousseau, the other great French-speaking Deist, was a native of Switzerland, born in Geneva in 1712, son of a clockmaker. It is often noted with irony that the two most famous citizens of Geneva, John Calvin and Jean-Jacques Rousseau, represent polar opposites in their beliefs, attitudes, and impact on society. In Calvin, we hear the voice of the Bible, the church fathers, and the call to Gospel-inspired Reformation; in Rousseau, we hear the voice of modern 'enlightened' humanity, no longer under the yoke of Christ, seeking to remake itself on the basis of its own autonomous reason and feelings.

After his father left Geneva as the result of a quarrel with a wealthy landowner, a teenaged Rousseau ended up in the Duchy of Savoy, nestling between France, Switzerland, and Italy. Here he embraced Roman Catholicism; he had an older Catholic lover, Françoise-Louise de Warens, who influenced him in this direction. (She was the first of several mistresses in Rousseau's life.) Rousseau's Catholicism, however, was not to endure, and he drifted into Deism. At length, having acquired a good education through de Warens' generosity, Rousseau ended up in Paris in 1742, where he cooperated with Denis Diderot in producing early portions of the famous Enlightenment project, the *Encyclopédie* (see below for Diderot and the *Encyclopédie*).

Rousseau's fame arrived with the publication in 1750 of his *Discourse on the Sciences and the Arts*, in which he argued for the corrupting effects of 'civilisation' on natural human goodness. Rousseau's vision of the innate goodness of human nature signified a fundamental rupture with his Calvinist upbringing and its view of humanity's radical evil. This treatise was followed by his *Discourse on the Origins of Inequality Among Men* (1754), in which Rousseau's philosophy of human perfectibility within a properly ordered society took shape.

This philosophy achieved classic formulation in Rousseau's *Social Contract* (1762), which opened with some of the most celebrated words in European literature: 'Man is born free, and everywhere he is in chains.' Human flourishing in community, Rousseau maintained, depended on all the community's members surrendering their rights to a communal government, representing all its members (embodying the 'general will'); from this political embodiment of the general will, there flow forth the life-enhancing rights of all citizens. Rousseau thought that some form of 'civil religion' would be necessary in this ideal society, but doubted that Christianity could fulfill that function; his suggestions for what a good civil religion would look like amount to Deism. The *Social Contract* would be deeply influential on the politics and religious experiments of the French Revolution of 1789.[10]

Rousseau's Deism was more romantic and emotional than Voltaire's – a 'Deism of the heart'. He offered it to the world most effectively in his novel *Emile: or, On Education* (1762), a piece of writing considered by Rousseau to be his best and most significant work. Like Voltaire's *Candide*, *Emile* would win the impartial honour of being banned in both Paris and Geneva. In the novel, Rousseau introduced the figure of a Savoyard priest (i.e., a priest from the Duchy of Savoy), who sets out his personal and feelings-based Deist creed with disarming eloquence:

> This Being who wills things, and can carry out His will – this Being who works by His own power – this Being, whoever He might be, who animates the universe, and brings harmony to all things – this is what I call God. To this name of 'God', I add the notions of mind, power, will, which I have gathered from the order of the universe, and the notion of benevolence which is their essential result. Even so, I know nothing further of the Being to whom I attribute these things. He hides Himself both from my senses and my reason. The more I think of

10. For the French Revolution, see Part 6 of this Chapter.

> Him, the more confused I become. I know very well that He exists, and that He exists as the Uncreated One; I know that my existence depends on His, and that every other created thing also depends on Him. I see the Deity everywhere in His works; I feel Him within me; I behold Him in all of creation around me. But if I try to contemplate Him in His own being, if I seek to discover where He is, what He is, what is His essence, then He eludes my grasp, and my anxious spirit finds nothing. Convinced of my mind's feebleness, therefore, I will never enter into arguments about God's nature, unless I am forced to it by the feeling of His relationship with myself.

The Savoyard priest (and through him, Rousseau) goes on to dismiss any text of any scripture as a basis for knowing God:

> In all of these three revelations [Judaism, Christianity, Islam], the holy books are written in languages unknown to the people who have faith in them. The Jews do not understand Hebrew any longer; the Christians do not understand Greek or Hebrew; the Turks and Persians do not understand Arabic, and even the very Arabs of today do not speak the language of Muhammad. Is not this a very foolish way of instructing humanity, by always speaking to them in a language they do not understand? But, someone will respond, these books have been translated! This is a very inadequate answer. Who can give me the assurance that they have been translated reliably, or that they could even have been so translated? Who can give me any good reason why God, when He wishes to speak to humankind, should require any interpreter? I could never think that what everyone needs to know can be shut up in these books! Nor can I think that he who cannot understand them, or cannot understand the persons who explain them, will be punished by God for an involuntary ignorance. Yet we are forever vexing ourselves with books. What a madness!

For Rousseau, all that was needed for human faith in deity was the immediate feeling of the heart that there is a God (by which Rousseau meant the Supreme Being of Deism, not the Trinity of Christian revelation). This 'romantic Deism' captivated Rousseau's generation. In part, this captivating influence was owing to Rousseau's own celebrity status as a writer and personality, the two elements combining in his honest but hardly edifying autobiography, the *Confessions* (published posthumously in 1782). The title may echo Augustine's masterpiece, but the content was notably devoid of any story of encounter with Christ or a life of faith. It was much more a bare-it-all self-exposé on Rousseau's part, sparing the reader none of the unsavoury details.

5. Revolutionary Deism: Thomas Paine (1737–1809)

Although Deism had begun in England in the mid-17th Century with Lord Herbert of Cherbury, producing its most abundant bloom of English literature in 1690–1740, it then passed its torch to Continental European thinkers like Voltaire and Rousseau. It was not until the period of the American and French Revolutions, toward the close of the 18th Century (America in 1775, France in 1789), that Deism found its most forceful and effective English voice. This was in the highly influential, politically radical thinker and propagandist for militant and revolutionary democracy, Thomas Paine (1737–1809).

Paine was born in Thetford, Norfolk, the son of a Quaker father and Anglican mother. After various attempts at a career, he emigrated to Pennsylvania, America, in 1774. Here at last he found his true talent as a publicist for radical causes – in this case, American independence from the British crown, in his treatise *Common Sense, Addressed to the Inhabitants of America* (1776), which made a widespread impact on the Americans who fought for independence from Britain in the Revolutionary War of 1775–83.[11] Paine, however, went beyond the comparatively conservative social and political outlook of most of the revolutionaries; he argued for a radical democracy in which voting rights would have no connection with property ownership. This radicalism heralded his sympathy for the more left-wing French Revolution of 1789.[12]

---

11. For more on the American Revolution, or War of Independence (or Revolutionary War of Independence!), see Chapter 4.
12. See Part 6.

Back in England in 1787, Paine soon became fascinated by the unfolding revolutionary drama in France, whose secular and democratic ideals he defended with aggressive eloquence in his *Rights of Man* (1791). However, Britain at this point was ruled by the anti-revolutionary Tory (conservative) government of William Pitt the Younger (1759–1806); and Pitt orchestrated a serious clamp-down on civil liberties and freedom of expression, in order to prevent the spread of revolutionary sentiment among the British. Owing to the *Rights of Man*, Paine became one of Pitt's targets, forcing Paine to flee to France, where he was welcomed and elected to the revolutionary National Assembly.

Unfortunately, the French revolutionaries were faction-ridden and beginning to turn on each other, and Paine's faction (the Girondins) became subject to persecution from the more powerful Montagnards, led by France's most well-known revolutionary, Maximilien Robespierre.[13] Consequently, Paine was arrested and imprisoned in 1793. In prison he worked on his masterpiece, *The Age of Reason* (published in three parts, 1794, 1795, and 1807). After Robespierre's fall from power and execution in 1794, Paine was released from captivity at the intercession of American diplomat James Monroe (who would be America's fifth president in 1817–25), enabling him to resume his French political career. At first, Paine cooperated with Napoleon Bonaparte on his seizure of political supremacy in 1799, advising him on plans for the invasion of Britain. By 1802, however, Paine was disillusioned with Napoleon, concluding that he was interested only in personal power, and returned to America, where he died in 1809.

Paine's *Age of Reason* was a Deist epic. As we have seen, 'Age of Reason' was a self-description of the Enlightenment, and Paine championed the Enlightenment's 'natural religion' of Deism with outspoken fervour. The subtitle of the work was *Being an Investigation into True and Fabulous Theology*. By 'true theology' he meant Deism; by 'fabulous theology' he meant the fictitious fables of Christianity. Paine subjected the Bible to

13. For Robespierre, see Part 6, section 2.

withering criticism, as 'more like the word of a demon than the Word of God', 'a book of lies, wickedness, and blasphemy'.

> The opinions I have advanced are the effect of the most clear and long-established conviction that the Bible and the Testament are impositions upon the world, that the fall of man, the account of Jesus Christ being the Son of God, and of his dying to appease the wrath of God, and of salvation by that strange means, are all fabulous inventions, dishonourable to the wisdom and power of the Almighty; that the only true religion is Deism, by which I then meant, and mean now, the belief of one God, and an imitation of his moral character, or the practice of what are called moral virtues – and that it was upon this only (so far as religion is concerned) that I rested all my hopes of happiness hereafter.

Paine illustrates vividly how anti-Christian Deism, and militant activism on behalf of radical political reform and secular democracy, could so easily coalesce in the ideological currents of the Enlightenment, in the English-speaking world as much as anywhere else.

6. Christian response to Deism: Joseph Butler (1692–1752)

The most significant Christian intellectual response to Deism came from the pen of Joseph Butler, Anglican Bishop of Durham. He is remembered (even studied) to this day as a Christian philosopher and apologist, who made an enduring contribution to the Deist controversy in his *Analogy of Religion, Natural and Revealed, to the Constitution and Course of Nature* (1736). In this logically acute treatise, Butler accomplished an unusual and thought-provoking assault on what had become the foundational outlook of Deism. It was a Deist commonplace that the Bible was full of immorality, arbitrariness, and absurdity on the part of its God, whereas the contemplation of nature revealed the rationally and morally superior God of Deism, the 'Supreme Being'.

Butler turned this contention on its head by arguing that the 'nature' to which Deists appealed was as problematic as scripture. Did the natural world not present its observer with a jagged and challenging vision of the struggle of living creatures to survive, amid violence, predation, accident, earthquake, volcanic eruption, flood, famine, illness, and death? How did nature boast any superiority over scripture in supposedly revealing a more rational or benevolent deity? Deists objected when the biblical God commanded Israel to slaughter the Canaanites; yet the God of nature, worshiped by Deists, equally slaughtered millions through natural calamities!

There was in fact, Butler suggested, an 'analogy' between nature and scripture in this regard; they corresponded to each other, rather than (as in Deist thinking) conflicted. Nature and scripture alike had enough light and evidence to invite the human mind and will to faith in God, yet enough darkness and difficulty to test that faith, giving it its very character as *faith* – justified trust – rather than some easy and obvious 'reasonable' perception of a simplistic deity. Moreover, since nature and scripture were so analogous to each other, probability determined that the same God was author of both, which thus vindicated Christianity. Rational probability was the safest guide, Butler argued, and it stood on the side of 'revealed religion'. Butler's *Analogy of Religion* was long regarded among English-speaking Christians as an admirably serious and substantial critique of the philosophically shallow rhetoric of Deism.

7. Enlightenment non-religion: Atheism

Deism was the first religious tendency linked to the Enlightenment. The other was pure atheism. This was the minority report – most of the non-Christian 'enlightened' thinkers of the 18th Century wanted to retain some minimal respect for religious belief, in the shape of Deism. However, for the first time in the history of Europe since the conversion of Constantine, first of the Christian emperors of Rome, atheism now enjoyed its distinguished European philosophical proponents. The most heavyweight were the French thinkers Denis Diderot (1713–84) and Jean-Baptiste le Rond d'Alembert (1717–83), and the Franco-German Paul Heinrich Dietrich, Baron d'Holbach (1723–89).

Denis Diderot was born in Langres, in the county of Champagne, educated in a Jesuit school, and had thoughts of the priesthood, which however he abandoned in favour of law. Although in 1743 he married a devout Catholic, Antoinette Champion, this prevented neither a number of extra-marital affairs on Diderot's part, nor an intellectual leaning first towards Deism, and then latterly towards atheism. His adoption of atheism found literary expression in *The Sceptic's Walk* (1747), a dialogue between a Deist, a pantheist, and an atheist.[14] Fear of Catholic harassment, however, held Diderot back from publishing this work (it finally saw the light in 1830). Nonetheless, other published works – fiction, scientific and philosophical writings – flowed from Diderot's pen, including what has been categorised as an early exposition of evolutionary biological theory (including natural selection) in his *Letter on the Blind* (1749).[15] Diderot's mature atheism made him unpopular with Deists, such as Jean-Jacques Rousseau who had at first collaborated with Diderot on the *Encyclopédie* (see below).

Jean-Baptiste le Rond d'Alembert was a Parisian, son of an artillery officer. He studied at a Jansenist school, but had no taste for theology, soon developing into a brilliant mathematician and scientist, known for his work in optics, fluid mechanics, and wave equations. He has also earned a place in the history of music theory. D'Alembert was less of an atheist than Diderot – perhaps 'sceptical agnostic' might be a fair description – but he had, even so, moved beyond the attenuated religiosity of Deism into something more godless.

Baron d'Holbach was German by birth, from Edesheim in the Rhenish Palatinate, but settled in France where he spent

---

14. Pantheism is the view that God and the universe are identical.

15. Forms of evolutionary theory were around long before Charles Darwin's *Origin of Species* (1859). What Darwin did was give huge and enduring popularity to a proposed mechanism – natural selection – in order to explain the more general idea of evolution (that all present life-forms are modified descendants of previous ones). The more general idea had been around for a century or more, popularised in the English-speaking world by Robert Chambers' *Vestiges of the Natural History of Creation* in 1844, fifteen years before Darwin's treatise.

much of his life as a wealthy salon-owner in Paris. He published anonymously the key atheistic writings of the Enlightenment, such as *Christianity Unmasked* (1761), *The System of Nature* (1770), *The Social System* (1773), *Natural Politics* (1773–74), and *Universal Morality* (1776). In these treatises, d'Holbach combined his atheism with materialism (physical matter is all that exists) and a moral system based on the individual's pursuit of enlightened self-interest. Once again, as it was with Diderot, d'Holbach's advanced atheism ran into some stiff Deistic opposition from other Enlightenment thinkers; Voltaire, for example, expressed his disgust at d'Holbach's atheism which ran so counter to Voltaire's own convinced Deism.

Together, Diderot and d'Alembert edited the hugely impactful *Encyclopédie*, published in multiple volumes between 1751 and 1772. Baron d'Holbach was one of the chief article-writers. The subtitle of the *Encyclopédie* was *A Systematic Dictionary of the Sciences, Arts, and Crafts*, and its aim was to spread far and wide the concepts and values of the Enlightenment. French Enlightenment intellectuals indeed were sometimes simply called 'Encyclopedists'. The contributors to the *Encyclopédie* were not all atheists, agnostics, or materialists – the arch-Deist Rousseau was among their number, at least initially; but the *Encyclopédie* massively helped to 'secularize' knowledge, by situating it outside any traditional Christian worldview.

3
The philosopher of the Enlightenment: Immanuel Kant (1724–1804)

1. Kant's life

As mentioned earlier, the acknowledged supreme philosopher of the Enlightenment was Immanuel Kant (1724–1804), who taught in the University of Königsberg (modern Kaliningrad) in Prussia. (The region today is part of Russia, but in the 18th Century it belonged to the German territory of East Prussia, in north-eastern Germany.) Kant was born in Königsberg, the son of a harness-maker. His parents were devout Lutherans who had embraced the Pietist renewal movement within German Lutheranism, and they sent the young Immanuel to a Pietist school.[1] This did not turn out well; Kant reacted strongly against the school's attempts to instil Pietist faith and spirituality into its students. Although he continued to have affection and admiration for his parents, he did not embrace their religious commitments, and the mature Kant would be a Deist.

Kant pursued an academic career, eventually becoming a tutor in Königsberg University in 1755 until his retirement in 1796. From 1770, he held a senior position in the university, lecturing in logic and metaphysics (philosophy). Intellectually, Kant was in many ways a disciple of Jean-Jacques Rousseau, although the

1. For Pietism, see Volume 4, Chapter 1, Part 4.

greatest single influence on him was German Enlightenment philosopher Christian Wolff (1679–1754). Wolff was himself an ardent disciple of Lutheran philosopher-theologian, Gottfried Wilhelm Leibniz (1646–1716);[2] Wolff's thinking (like that of Leibniz) ranged over almost every topic. Philosophically, Wolff was a rationalist of sorts. He took mathematics as supplying the blueprint for all sound thinking; correct definition of terms and rigorous proof were principles that permeated his philosophy. As applied to God, this took the form of 'natural theology', in which Wolff sought to offer purely logical proofs both of God's existence and attributes. He was strongly criticised by German Pietists for ascribing excessive power to human reason at the expense of divine revelation in the realm of theology. Wolff's brilliance created the first ever German 'school' of philosophy – school in the sense of a movement with a distinctive outlook and a body of followers. Wolffianism was the most prominent philosophical perspective in the world of German thought, until displaced by Kant's own philosophy.

Immanuel Kant

Kant was a Wolffian for many years, until he encountered – sometime between the late 1750s and 1770s – the writings of the great Scottish sceptical philosopher David Hume (1711–76). It was Kant's friend, the Christian philosopher Johann Georg Hamann (1730–88), who introduced Kant to Hume.[3] The writings of Hume were like an intellectual earthquake in Kant's

2. For Leibniz, see Chapter 5, Part 3.

3. For Hamann, see Chapter 5, Part 5, section 2.

mind; he famously affirmed that reading Hume had 'awakened him from his dogmatic slumbers', forcing upon him his major philosophical life's work. This was Kant's search to provide a positive alternative to Hume's acidic scepticism about truth and knowledge. Hume denied, for example, that reason could discover a 'self' at the centre of human thoughts and feelings; all reason can do is perceive a succession of thoughts and feelings, but no organising principle of selfhood behind or beneath them. Hume also denied that reason could discern any principle of causality in the way things happen in the world; reason could only discover a principle of sequence – after A happened, B then happened – but not that A caused B. This line of thinking, most famously laid out in Hume's *Enquiry concerning Human Understanding* (1748), of course struck at the very foundations of science.

2. Kant's Copernican revolution

Kant was provoked by Hume's scepticism to articulate an alternative philosophy that would set human knowledge on a sure foundation. This alternative Kant proceeded to map out in a series of epoch-making treatises: *Prolegomena to Any Future Metaphysics That Will Be Able to Present Itself as a Science* (1783), *An Answer to the Question: What is Enlightenment?* (1784), *Groundwork of the Metaphysics of Morals* (1785), *Metaphysical Foundations of Natural Science* (1786), *Critique of Pure Reason* (1787, a serious revision of an earlier work), *Critique of Practical Reason* (1788), *Critique of the Power of Judgment* (1790), and *Religion within the Bounds of Reason Alone* (1793).

In these writings, Kant embodied a watershed in Enlightenment thought, and indeed in Western philosophy as a whole. Kant himself believed that his philosophy was a 'Copernican revolution' in human thinking. In other words, as astronomer Nicolaus Copernicus had made the sun, not the earth, the centre of the solar system, thus overthrowing thousands of years of geocentric (earth-centred) thought, so Kant revolutionised philosophy by positing the human mind, instead of the objective structures of the universe, as the source of meaning and truth. Rather than the human mind 'revolving' around the larger, self-revealing reality of a divinely created cosmos, reality for Kant revolved around the human mind, which in a sense created what it knew. The mind did this by imposing on its experience its own mind-generated forms of meaning – such as the category of causality, and even the categories of space and time which (Kant held) were mental and subjective, not external and objective in nature.

This Kantian revolution had far-reaching theological implications, and much of post-Kantian theology ever since has been formulated in response to Kant: sometimes by absorbing his ideas, sometimes by critically rejecting them, sometimes charting a middle path. If we limit ourselves to Kant's huge theological impact, the key issues are the following.

First, Kant subjected all traditional arguments for God's existence to a devastating critique – the argument from design (apparent design in nature points to a designer), the cosmological argument (finite things require a transcendent cause), the ontological argument (the very concept of God as the maximally perfect being demands that He must actually exist). None of these arguments could satisfy Kant's probing intellect; he demolished them all – at least he did so in his own reckoning, and in that of many others. As far as Kant was concerned, human reason, as it reflected on the world, could find no knowledge of a God.

Second, Kant maintained that all human knowledge is 'filtered' through our mental and sensory equipment. Consequently, we can only ever know things as they seem or appear to us, once they have been thus filtered. Kant called the filtered appearances 'phenomena'. Things as they truly are in themselves, however, in their own objective reality (which Kant called 'noumena'), remain beyond all human grasp. This stance obviously affected in a serious way the human capacity to have any non-subjective knowledge of God.

Third, and in spite of the above, Kant remained a theist (of a Deistic sort). He claimed that human reason, considered practically, imposed a 'moral law' on human conduct. (Kant thus asserted the human autonomy of morality: it originated in human reason, not divine will.) This moral law gave human beings the framework in which to live their lives. Kant could wax very lyrical about the moral law; he said the only two things that moved him to awe and reverence were 'the starry skies above and the moral law within'. In order to make sense of this moral law, Kant argued, we must make three 'postulates' (a postulate is something akin to a theoretical assumption): (i) human freedom, (ii) human immortality, and (iii) the existence of God as the ultimate sanction behind the moral law. We must postulate human freedom, Kant affirmed, despite the absence of any scientific evidence for it, so as to give a practical incentive to people to strive after obedience to the moral law. We must postulate human immortality in order to satisfy our sense that moral virtue and happiness should ultimately coincide in an afterlife (as they do not in this present life). And finally we must postulate God (the Deistic God, not the Christian Trinity) as the perfect judge, who by His knowledge and power will ensure that virtue is rightly rewarded and evil properly punished in the hereafter.

Kant, then, denied that God could in any sense be objectively known, but retained Him as a necessary 'postulate' of the mind's self-imposed moral law. This approach may well have given a whole new lease on life to moral arguments for God's existence, which have figured so strongly in post-Kantian Christian apologetics (e.g., very famously in John Henry Newman and C. S. Lewis). In his own view, Kant had done good service to religion: he had 'denied knowledge to make room for faith'. Conservative-minded theologians, however, were not so sure. They asked whether in the Bible, faith in God was really a mere postulate devoid of real substantial knowledge.

Kant's ambiguous relationship to religion is shown in two other facets of his life and thought. First, almost in spite of himself and his Enlightenment optimism about the power of reason, Kant was compelled, in his rational investigation of the moral law, to confess something very much like the Christian doctrine of original sin. There was, he granted, a deep flaw in human nature, a mysterious susceptibility to evil, that continually undermined human efforts toward goodness. Other Enlightenment thinkers were outraged by this element in Kant's philosophy, seeing it as a sell-out to Christian dogma. It may more generously be ascribed to Kant's intellectual honesty about the human condition.

Second, Kant preserved a high moral reverence for the figure of Jesus. He was not, for Kant, the Son of God or Redeemer of sinners; but by virtue of His profound teaching and influence, Jesus was the founder of a new moral kingdom in the world. Kant made a bold attempt to denude Christianity of all its supernatural aspects, reinterpreting it in a strictly moral (and moralistic) way. We find this in his treatise *Religion within the Bounds of Reason Alone* (1793), which was to be the inspiration for many a form of 'liberal' theology.

Kant's philosophy transformed forever the intellectual landscape of Europe. No philosopher or theologian could henceforth seriously do his work, if he failed to engage with the enormous challenges thrown down by Kant. In that sense, to this very day all Western philosophy and theology is post-Kantian in character.

4
The Enlightenment and Scripture

1. Origins of Biblical Criticism: Benedict Spinoza (1632–77)

It was the Enlightenment that initiated the historical-critical study of the Bible. The meaning of this perhaps dubious phrase is that the Bible, as a historical artefact, was now subjected to methods of investigation detached from any belief in its character as a divine revelation; its text was treated in the same way a literary historian would treat the text (say) of Homer's *Iliad*. A true, rational scholar must approach the Bible with an attitude of religious neutrality. The overall results were distinctly corrosive of traditional Christian beliefs about the Church's sacred book.

The outstanding pioneer of this new, critical approach to scripture was one of the formative thinkers of the early Enlightenment, the Dutch Jewish philosopher, Benedict Spinoza (1632–77). Spinoza is more often remembered for his rich and entrancing espousal of pantheism – the view that God and the universe are identical. To be more accurate, Spinoza held that the universe is a manifestation of God, rather than a distinct creation. It was more a case of Spinoza losing the universe in God, rather than reducing God into nothing more than the universe; he was a 'God-intoxicated' man rather than a godless materialist. His pantheistic worldview would deeply influence many future Enlightenment leaders of thought (Fichte, Schelling, Hegel, Schleiermacher, Schopenhauer), who saw Spinoza's system as so brilliantly argued, it needed either to be adopted or adapted. However, we shall be considering Spinoza as a biblical critic, not a pantheistic philosopher.

Spinoza was the son of a Jewish merchant, part of an émigré Portuguese Jewish community that had settled in Amsterdam in the late 16th Century, seeking religious freedom in the tolerant Dutch Republic. The young Spinoza was an intellectual prodigy, and – inspired by the philosophy of Descartes – soon departed from the boundaries of traditional Jewish belief about God and the Hebrew scriptures. At the age of twenty-three, he was excommunicated from the synagogue for his unorthodoxy, and shunned by his own family. He then spent his brief life (he died aged forty-four) writing philosophy while making money by grinding optical lenses. Among Spinoza's impact-making writings were his *Short Treatise on God, Man, and Man's Wellbeing* (1662), *René Descartes's Principles of Philosophy* (1663), *Theologico-Political Treatise* (1670), *Treatise on the Emendation of the Intellect* (1677), and his masterpiece, *Ethics* (1677).

Spinoza's historical scepticism about the Bible is found in his *Theologico-Political Treatise*. His main contention was that scholars should study the Bible with an attitude of religious detachment, as they would study any item of ancient literature. This detachment entailed disbelieving (or at least suspending judgment on) the claim of the Bible, or its religious communities (Judaism, the Church), concerning the Bible's extraordinary attributes – its inspiration, its character as revelation, its supernatural content, its preservation from error. Spinoza's 'naturalistic' approach to scripture also involved other serious consequences for traditional faith, e.g., non-belief in predictive prophecy in scripture (since truly predictive prophecy would be supernatural, above and beyond rational nature).

Spinoza's more specific conclusions about scripture were expressed in a number of ways. He reasoned from the Pentateuch itself that its Mosaic authorship was unwarranted and indeed disprovable. He dismissed the historicity of the Genesis account of human origins, on the grounds that the geographically widespread and ethnically diverse nature of humanity required more than a single 'Adam' as humankind's progenitor. He denied that the Jewish history recorded in the Old Testament was any more special in quality than any other people's history – one could not rationally 'privilege' one people's history over another's. He argued that the substance of Old Testament Jewish law, ceremony, and ethics was determined by the varying historical situations and needs of Israel, not by any divine revelation. Despite not majoring on the topic, he applied the same lines of sceptical reasoning to the New Testament.

As we may discern from all this, Spinoza's ultimate authority was autonomous human reason, as he had learned from his intellectual mentor Descartes. Although he was a pantheist rather than a Deist, Spinoza's belief in God was thus a variety of the Enlightenment's 'rational religion'. He believed in a deity solely because his reason led him to such belief. He needed no revelation, and certainly no revelation imprisoned within past history and allegedly recorded in questionable ancient texts.

Spinoza's historical-critical attitude to the Bible was to become a commonplace of Enlightenment thought. He was not wholly original in his approach; other thinkers were already beginning to travel the same road. For example, in his sceptical treatment of Genesis, Spinoza relied on a treatise by French Catholic scholar Isaac La Peyrère (1596–1676), entitled *Prae-Adamitae* (1655), in which La Peyrère argued that Adam was the biological father only of the 'chosen line' culminating in Abraham and Israel; the Gentile nations – the bulk of humanity – were not descended from Adam. This position became known as 'polygenism' (multiple biological origins for the human race) as against 'monogenism' (one origin, Adam). Such ideas, it seems, were 'in the air' in the second part of the 17th Century. Spinoza, however, articulated them with unusual clarity and force.

2. Origins of Biblical Criticism: Richard Simon (1638–1712)

Influenced both by La Peyrère and Spinoza, Richard Simon (1638–1712) was another of the founders of the historical-critical study of scripture. He is often called 'the father of biblical criticism', although Spinoza may dispute that title with him. Simon, a French Oratorian priest and learned humanist scholar, made waves in 1678 with his *Critical History of the Old Testament*. In this treatise, he rejected the Mosaic authorship of large portions of the Pentateuch, and threw doubt on the historical integrity of the traditional Hebrew text of the Old Testament. This was too controversial for the French Catholic authorities, who suppressed the work; nearly all copies of the *Critical History* were destroyed in France, under the stern, orthodox eye of Jacques-Bénigne Bossuet of Meaux, France's most illustrious bishop and preacher.[1] However, a few copies of the *Critical History* crossed the English Channel into Britain, where the treatise was translated into English in 1682, becoming part of the budding British Enlightenment.

As a result of the controversy over the *Critical History*, Simon himself was expelled from the Oratorian order, retiring into the obscurity of a parish appointment as the curé of Bolleville in Normandy. Despite the negative reaction to his work in France, Simon nonetheless had the courage of his convictions, and carried on producing historical-critical writings on the Bible. In 1685 he issued a new, revised and expanded edition of the *Critical History* in the Dutch Republic, where French censorship could not touch it. In 1689 he published his *Critical History of the Text of the New Testament*, in which he undertook a detailed exploration into the historical origin and character of each New Testament document, the type of Greek in which they were written, the New Testament's use of the Old, and the various Greek manuscripts on which current New Testaments were based. The following year, 1690, came his *Critical History of the Versions of the New Testament*, where he surveyed New Testament translations from the patristic period down to his own day. In 1693 he gave the world his *Critical History of the Chief Commentators on the New Testament from the Beginning of Christianity to Our Own Times*.

In all these works, one way or another, Simon advanced the radical thesis that the original text of scripture had been entirely

1. For Bossuet, see Volume 4, Chapter 6, Part 3, section 5.

lost. All that remained in the Church's hands was a malleable text that had changed and developed over time. The historical-critical scholar, therefore, must use the tools of textual, linguistic, and historical investigation to try to reconstruct (as far as possible) what the original lost text might have been. Traditional Catholic and Protestant belief alike perceived Simon's project as a basic assault on the trustworthiness and truth of sacred scripture, and thus an attack on the very foundations of Christianity.

Despite the opposition of Catholic and Protestant orthodoxy, the historical-critical approach to the Bible, advocated with such power, eloquence, and erudition by Spinoza and Simon, made huge headway in the century of Enlightenment. We cannot tell the story here in any depth; other outstanding scholars such as Jean Leclerc (1657–1736), Jean Astruc (1684–1766), Johann Michaelis (1717–91), Johann Semler (1725–91), and Johann Gottfried Eichhorn (1752–1827) would have to be taken into account in a detailed survey.[2] Certainly by the close of the 18th Century, the historical-critical method had triumphed in Europe's greatest centres of Christian learning, namely, the German Lutheran universities, from where it streamed out into the rest of the European Christian world.

---

2. For Michaelis, see Chapter 5, Part 5, section 1.

5
The Enlightenment, history, and faith

1. Reimarus and Lessing: The Wolfenbüttel Fragments

The new currents of non-Christian thought that were flowing in Enlightenment philosophy found one of their most poignant expressions in the life and work of the pivotal German thinker Gotthold Ephraim Lessing (1729–81), sometimes hailed as 'the father of the German Enlightenment'. Lessing was born in Kamenz, Saxony, the son of a Lutheran pastor. After studying theology and medicine, he took up a literary vocation; he wrote for the stage and advised the fledgling German National Theatre in Hamburg, championing both ancient Greek drama and Shakespeare against the contemporary French theatre. Philosophically, he fell deeply under the influence of Voltaire, which set the scene for his own mature religious thought.

In 1770 Lessing became curator of the library of the Duke of Wolfenbüttel. Forming in this capacity a close relationship with the Reimarus family, he discovered in their possession an unpublished manuscript by a recently deceased family member, the Deist philosopher Hermann Samuel Reimarus (1694–1768). In this manuscript, Reimarus severely questioned the relationship between the historical Jesus and the theology found in the New Testament Epistles. An honest and judicious reading of the Gospels, Reimarus argued, revealed Jesus as simply a Jewish man of His times, a preacher of a coming kingdom of

God that would soon break into and terminate human history. By contrast, the Epistles present a completely different Jesus, a theologically complex construction who bears little relation to the actual Jesus of history. The apostles, therefore, not Jesus, were the founders of Christianity and the Church, creating a new religion by conscious fraud; Jesus, however, had been nothing more than a faithful Jew in life and death (and had not risen from the dead).

Moreover, the whole Bible – according to Reimarus – was shot through with historical error, irrationality, immorality, and religious superstition and folly. Reimarus measured biblical religion against what he believed were the pure and rational standards of Deism, and found the Bible lacking in almost every way. The most the Bible could do was produce a Christian sect of limited appeal; it could not serve as the basis for a universal religion grounded in common human reason – in other words, the Enlightenment religion of Deism.

Lessing decided to publish Reimarus' explosive manuscript in seven instalments (1774–78), under the title *The Wolfenbüttel Fragments*. Fierce controversy with orthodox Lutheran theologians ensued; ultimately Lessing lost this battle and was silenced by law. Even so, the ideas he had put into circulation were taken up by others, including Christian academics, and had extensive impact. Reimarus' understanding of the relationship between Jesus and the apostles still has wide currency today.

2. Lessing in his own right: The ugly broad ditch

Lessing himself felt the anguished tensions between Christianity and the Enlightenment concept of sovereign and universal reason. He voiced these tensions in his *On the Proof of the Spirit and of Power* (1777). In this celebrated treatise, Lessing argued that Christianity, by its very nature as a historical religion, created insuperable difficulties for a rational person. Reason, if it is to assent to truth-claims, requires those truths to be accessible *to* reason – to have the character of universal, necessary, intelligible truth. But Christianity, Lessing complained, precisely lacked this; it based itself on past events in history. A historical event is not like a necessary rational truth, since events can always be conceived as happening differently from how they did happen. Julius Caesar turned right on a particular day at a certain juncture; but he might have turned left, and that difference might have changed history.

Because historical events have this non-necessary or contingent character, Lessing called them 'accidental truths'. He proceeded to argue that such accidental truths could not constitute the proper foundation for belief in the universal and necessary truths of reason (among which he included belief in God – Lessing remained a theist). As he famously put it, 'The accidental truths of history can never become the proof of the necessary truths of reason.'

Lessing proposed a further problem. In order to validate its historical truth-claims, Christianity had traditionally urged the sanction of miracles. Jesus could be known to be the Son of God because of His miracles, ultimately the miracle of His resurrection. But these miracles themselves, Lessing protested, were distant events of past history. All we have is copies of copies of records of long-dead people who *allegedly* saw miracles. Those miracles were as inherently questionable, therefore, as any other claim about what had happened in the (to us) inaccessible past. Consequently, there was no sure pathway from open-to-question claims about historically far-off events, like the miracles associated with Jesus, to universal, first-order philosophical truths like God's existence. This historical gulf separating present reason from Christian truth-claims lodged in a remote past, Lessing called 'the ugly broad ditch'.

> This is the ugly broad ditch that I am unable to cross, no matter how often and how seriously I have endeavoured to make such a leap.

Lessing's problem here passed into the mainstream of European religious and philosophical thinking under the nickname 'Lessing's Ditch'. How can less-than-objectively-certain claims about historical events in a faraway past provide a genuine basis of rational certainty for such ultimate beliefs as God and the soul's immortality? Any attempted appeal to the Bible as God's infallible Word, which itself verified the historical Jesus and His miracles, had been fatally undercut for Lessing by the historical-critical approach to scripture. Traditionally minded theologians would wrestle with the problem of Lessing's Ditch for generations to come.

Lessing's alternative to orthodox Christian faith was set out in his play *Nathan the Wise* (1779). The religious heart of the play is a parable told by the character Nathan, a prosperous Jewish businessman, to Saladin, Sultan of Jerusalem during the Third Crusade (1189–92). The parable concerns Judaism, Christianity, and Islam. In response to Saladin's question which of the three religions is true, Nathan relates a story about a magic ring that makes its wearer beautiful in the sight of God and man. The ring has been passed down in a certain family from father to best-loved son over generations. But the time comes when a father who has three sons promises the ring to each of them. To keep his promise, he has two perfect duplicates made, and on his deathbed he gives the three rings, one to each son. The three sons argue over which is the genuine ring. But a discerning judge tells them it is impossible to know, and that perhaps all three rings are replicas of a now lost original. All the sons can do is live in such a way that they become beautiful in the sight of God and man, just as if each had the magic ring. If they do this, it will not matter whether they have it or not: they will already have everything the ring promised.

Nathan's parable suggests that no particular religion is the right religion, but that every person's religion has value relative to his ability to think and live in harmony with an 'ideal humanity'. Lessing further saw Christianity as capable of evolving beyond its historically limited origin into a more complete religion of perfected humanity and rational autonomy, where God would be envisaged along Deist lines. In Lessing, therefore, we discover in bold colours the Enlightenment's tendency to embrace relativism about different world-faiths, and an evolutionary perspective on particular faiths – their capacity for progress and development beyond their ostensibly imperfect and primitive origins, into something more like the Enlightenment's 'rational religion' of Deism. These attitudes entered into the cultural bloodstream of European thinking about religion, helping form the basis for religious relativism and ideas about particular religions (like Christianity) needing to make progress in order to keep in step with modernity and its superior values.

6
The Enlightenment and politics: the French Revolution

1. The dawn of modernity?

A strong argument can be made that the dawn of the modern world occurred in the year 1789. This was the first year of the French Revolution, an event whose significance spread far beyond the borders of France, reverberating throughout the whole of Europe. It was, in a sense, the Enlightenment seizing the political high ground of French and European civilisation. A bloody death-blow was dealt to the *ancien regime* – the life-system that had prevailed in Europe since the Christianisation of the Roman Empire in the 4th Century.

Not infrequently, historians may and do restrict the term *ancien regime* specifically to France and its forms of socio-political existence, from the later Middle Ages to 1789. However, when the Revolution destroyed those forms, there is no doubt that this was seen at the time as an assault on a far wider life-system, entrenched across Europe. It is in that broader Europe-wide sense that we shall be considering it. The *ancien regime* had functioned on a basis of Christianity as the accepted religion of society, propagated and enforced in and through the various institutions of culture (government, education, family life, public religion via state-established churches); and intimately integrated with this religious basis, the *ancien regime* had supported social power-structures that normally had their apex in a monarchy and (beneath it) a privileged aristocracy.

This life-system would now be comprehensively swept away by the French Revolution. In its place stepped forth a new, secular, militant democracy, rooted and grounded not in the revealed will of the Christian God but the natural 'Rights of Man', and preaching itself as Europe's new gospel of cultural salvation. The French Revolutionary armies became the new missionaries, exporting this vision across Europe. Since we today are spiritually children of the French Revolution, we take these values for granted, and it is hard for us to imagine how novel and convulsive they were at the close of the 18th Century.

2. Beginnings and development of the Revolution

By 1789, France's middle classes or *bourgeoisie* had, in large measure, been won over to the ideals of the Enlightenment; their land, however, was still governed by an old-style absolute monarchy – the Capetian dynasty, which had ruled France for eight hundred years, since 987– in alliance with a wealthy landowning aristocracy and the all-pervasive, state-sponsored Catholic Church. The opportunity for the French *bourgeoisie* to enact sweeping social and political reform came when King Louis XVI (1775–93) summoned the 'Estates General' in May 1789. This was an assembly of the so-called Three Estates of the realm – the clergy, the aristocracy, and the commons (the commons were the rest of society, although effectively the *bourgeoisie*). Louis felt that the Three Estates, which had not met since 1614, was the only body invested with sufficient national authority for raising the taxes necessary to stave off catastrophic bankruptcy, threatening his government and country. This looming financial disaster was partly owing to the vast amount of resources France had expended in helping the American revolutionaries achieve independence from the British crown in America's War of Independence, in 1775–83.[1] That very war in America, however, had inflamed French radical opinion: perhaps Frenchmen could now accomplish a similar feat in their own country, throwing off the yoke of its ancient

1. For more about the American War of Independence, see Chapter 4.

and top-heavy monarchy in favour of a more representative form of government, as the Americans had done.

When the Estates General met on May 1st 1789, events spiralled swiftly out of Louis XVI's control. The Third Estate of the commons was determined to reform France, not raise taxes, and on June 17th its members unilaterally declared themselves to be the National Assembly of France – in effect, the sovereign parliament of the body politic. When Louis refused to accept their aspirations, the National Assembly took the famous Tennis Court Oath on June 20th not to disband, despite any and all opposition, until the political reconstruction of France was completed.

It is not for us to follow the story in detail. However, when the French revolutionaries began to reshape their country in earnest, the outcomes included the abolition of the monarchy in 1792 (Louis XVI was publicly executed in January 1793), the destruction of the aristocracy, a new basis for society in the *Declaration of the Rights of Man and of the Citizen* which owed much to the political philosophy of Jean-Jacques Rousseau (Christianity and the Bible were conspicuously absent), and the enthronement of Deism as the new civil religion. From 1792 onwards, it also involved a radically secular 'dechristianisation' programme that sought to eliminate all vestiges of Christianity from French national life: many French Catholic priests were killed or deported to penal colonies, and almost all France's Catholic churches were closed down, sold, or reassigned to new uses.[2] The proud anti-Christian self-consciousness of the French Enlightenment was manifest in its adoption of a new calendar, in which 1792 was now Year 1 (the year when the French monarchy was overthrown and France was proclaimed a republic); time was to be marked by the birth, not of Man's Redeemer, but of Revolutionary Man.[3] An increasing paranoia

---

2. For more about the dechristianisation campaign and the suffering of religious believers in Revolutionary France, see Chapter 6, Part 2, section 1.

3. The Revolutionary calendar also abolished the Christian seven-day week, with its one day in seven devoted to rest and worship, replacing it

also gripped the Revolution, notoriously resulting in the execution by guillotine of myriads of real or alleged traitors – the 'Reign of Terror'.

The most heroic or villainous revolutionary (depending on one's perspective) working toward these goals was Maximilien Robespierre (1758–94), an ardent Deist and disciple of Rousseau. Robespierre, son of a lawyer from Arras, himself tumbled from power in July 1794 amid the continual in-fighting among the revolutionaries, and ironically followed many of his victims to the Paris guillotine. While he lived, however, Robespierre incarnated more than any other individual the spirit of the Revolution, with his devotion to producing a 'republic of virtue' in the new France. For Robespierre, the Revolution itself was the world-force for the regeneration of society and individuals, and all who resisted it were enemies of humanity to be shown no mercy.

3. Reception of the Revolution

The French Revolution was at first welcomed by all progressive opinion in Europe. In Britain, the new young Romantic poet, William Wordsworth (1770–1850), was electrified; he captured the sense felt by many that the Revolution was nothing less than the rebirth of human civilisation, a paradise regained of liberty and happiness:

> Bliss was it in that dawn to be alive,
> But to be young was very heaven! – Oh! times,
> In which the meagre, stale, forbidding ways
> Of custom, law, and statute, took at once
> The attraction of a country in romance!
> When Reason seemed the most to assert her rights,
> When most intent on making of herself
> A prime Enchantress – to assist the work
> Which then was going forward in her name!

---

with a new ten-day week. The months were all renamed, the new names reflecting the seasonal qualities of each month. The Revolutionary calendar was finally abandoned on January 1st 1806 under Napoleon, who restored the traditional calendar.

> Not favoured spots alone, but the whole earth,
> The beauty wore of promise.

Wordsworth later changed his mind and turned against France's Revolution, but his poetry expresses the initial optimism aroused by the Revolution in a multitude of hearts and minds. In Germany, the eminent philosopher G. W. F. Hegel (1770–1831) articulated Wordsworth's feelings more prosaically but no less rousingly:

> Not since the sun had stood in the heavens, and the planets orbited around it, had men perceived that humanity's very existence centres in its own mind, i.e., in human thought, inspired by which we construct the world of reality. Anaxagoras had been the first man to declare that reason governs the universe; but not until the Revolution did humanity advance to recognise the principle that reason ought to govern Man's spiritual universe. The Revolution was thus a magnificent mental dawn. All who were capable of thought shared in the triumphant joy of this epoch. Emotions of an exalted character enthused people's minds at that time; a spiritual passion thrilled through the world, as if the reconciliation between heaven and earth was now at last made real.

Hegel, like Wordsworth, also changed his mind. The British poet and the German philosopher became disillusioned when the Revolution, which had promised heaven on earth, degenerated into the Reign of Terror under Robespierre, and had to be saved from itself in 1799 by the military dictatorship of Napoleon Bonaparte (who outraged British and German patriotism alike with his actual or threatened invasions). The 'Napoleonic Code' of 1804, Napoleon's influential legal summary of many of the Revolution's 'rights of man and of the citizen', seemed less attractive to many British and German lovers of their land when offered at the point of a sword. The Scottish Christian thinker, Thomas Erskine of Linlathen (1788–1870), wryly observed that the French Revolution's creed seemed to be, 'We believe in human brotherhood: join us, or we shall kill you!'

The French Revolutionary experiment ended with Napoleon's military defeat in 1815 at the battle of Waterloo, in Belgium, by a coalition of (chiefly) Britain, Prussia, Austria, the Netherlands, Sweden, and Russia. Then followed the restoration of the Capetian monarchy in France, in the person of the brother of the executed Louis XVI. However, what the revolutionaries had done in 1789 could not be psychologically undone, and was never forgotten. It remained an inspiration and rallying-cry for generations to come, across the whole of Europe, ever bursting forth afresh – as in 1848, the 'year of revolutions', which like a Europe-wide political earthquake struck and shook conservative governments in many capital cities. The Enlightenment ideals of rational democracy, popular sovereignty, and social dechristianisation, were in the world to stay.

7

A final paradox: machines and music

One last word on the 18th Century background. It is another paradox. On the one side, the 18th Century was the period that witnessed the beginnings of the Industrial Revolution: the birth of the machine age, with its vastly life-changing impact on society and human thought-patterns. C.S.Lewis once argued that this was the single biggest mental, emotional, and social divide separating the pre-modern and modern era – the world before machines and the world after their coming.

The Industrial Revolution began in Britain; its origin is customarily dated to approximately the 1760s, and most historians judge that it lasted in substance until around 1830–40. It involved the socially and economically transformative exploitation of new materials such as iron and steel, and of new energy sources such as coal, petroleum, electricity (the electric motor), a new method of using water-power in the steam engine, the development of novel devices to enable swift mass-production of textiles (cotton, linen, wool), and an ever-expanding utilisation of science in the service of industry. From Britain, the Industrial Revolution eventually spread to the rest of Europe and to America in the first half of the 19th Century.

The Industrial Revolution and its new technology generated wealth and power on a previously undreamt-of scale, and made the world a smaller place as new, faster, mechanised forms of transportation and communication were invented (the steam locomotive, steamship, telegraph). However, it also meant a degrading 'industrial slavery' for many workers in the new machine-factories – the 'dark Satanic mills' (steam-powered flour factories) of William Blake's famous protest poem *Jerusalem*.[1]

> And did those feet in ancient time
> Walk upon England's mountains green?
> And was the holy Lamb of God
> On England's pleasant pastures seen?
> And did the Countenance Divine
> Shine forth upon our clouded hills?
> And was Jerusalem builded here
> Among these dark Satanic mills?[2]

On the other side, it was roughly the same 'age of the machine' that witnessed an outpouring of creative musical genius perhaps unsurpassed in history: Johann Sebastian Bach (1685–1750), George Frideric Handel (1685–1759), Joseph Haydn (1732–1809), Wolfgang Amadeus Mozart (1756–91), Ludwig van Beethoven (1770–1827), Franz Schubert (1797–1828), Robert Schumann (1810–56) – music would never quite be the same again. These composers were not necessarily Christians in authentic belief or piety; but their music stood as a sublime expression of human inspiration and vision in the creation of beauty, in contrast to the increasingly dehumanised and automated factory-world of the machine age. Many of their works are explicitly Christian in content (however conventional their personal Christianity might have been), providing spiritual as well as aesthetic inspiration to millions. 20th Century Swiss theologian Karl Barth captured this inspiration in a beautiful if half-humorous saying: 'When the angels play music for God, they play Bach. When they play for themselves, they play Mozart.'

---

1. This is the general interpretation of the 'dark Satanic mills'. Another sees it as a possible metaphor for the oppressive cultural institutions of the British state, established Church, and university education. Perhaps Blake intended both meanings.

2. The hymn version says *those* dark Satanic mills, but Blake wrote *these*.

PRIMARY SOURCE MATERIAL

Francis Bacon: foundations of scientific thinking – the four idols of unreason that must be overthrown

XXXIX. Four types of idols trouble the human mind. To these (for the sake of distinguishing them) we have given names, calling the first *Idols of the Tribe*, the second *Idols of the Cave*, the third *Idols of the Marketplace*, the fourth *Idols of the Theatre*.

XL. The only proper way to keep at bay and drive out these idols is by forming our ideas and axioms on the basis of true induction. Even so, it is very useful to point the idols out; for the teaching about the idols has the same relationship to the interpretation of nature as the disproof of false arguments to common logic.

XLI. The *Idols of the Tribe* are inborn in human nature and in the human tribe or race as such. For man's senses are falsely claimed to be the measure of things. Quite the reverse, all our perceptions (both of the senses and the mind) have reference to man, not to the world. The human mind is like those distorted mirrors that give their own properties to different things that reflect light, twisting and disfiguring them.

XLII. The *Idols of the Cave* are those peculiar to each individual. In addition to the mistakes common to the human race, each person has his own individual den or cavern, which diverts and corrupts the light of nature. This corruption comes about from the individual's own distinctive and unique outlook, or from his education and association with others, or from the things he reads, and from the authority acquired over him by the people he respects and admires, or from the various impressions made on his mind as it happens to be preoccupied and affected, or calm and peaceful, and so forth. Consequently, the human spirit (according to its numerous dispositions) is changeable, confused, and (so to speak) stimulated by chance. Heraclitus rightly said that people search for knowledge in their own smaller worlds, not in the larger or shared world.

XLIII. There are also idols created by the give-and-take fellowship and society of people with each other, which we call *Idols of the Marketplace*. These idols arise from the mutual dealings and association of human beings one with another. For men communicate through language. But words develop according to the will of the majority; and from a bad and inappropriate formation of words, there comes about an astonishing hindrance to the mind. The definitions and explanations of words with which educated people are accustomed to safeguard and protect their understanding will not always provide a total remedy; words still plainly force the mind, confuse everything, and propel humanity into futile and countless disputes and fallacies.

XLIV. Lastly, there are idols which have sneaked into people's minds from the different dogmas of distinctive systems of philosophy, and also from perverted standards of proof. These we call *Idols of the Theatre*. For we look upon all the systems of philosophy previously accepted or invented, as resembling so many theatrical plays brought forth and performed, creating fictitious and imaginary worlds. We are not speaking merely of current systems, nor indeed the philosophy and philosophical sects of antiquity, since many other plays of a similar kind can still be invented in the future, and made to harmonize with each other. For the causes of the most contradictory errors are usually identical. Again, we are not referring merely to general systems of philosophy, but also to many aspects and axioms of the sciences which have become hardened against all correction, through force of tradition, through unquestioning acceptance, and through careless neglect. We must, however, discuss each type of idol more fully and clearly, in order to protect the human mind against them.

Francis Bacon
***Novum Organum*, Book I**

Descartes: I think, therefore I am

I previously observed that, concerning practical matters, it is sometimes necessary to embrace as beyond doubt certain opinions which we perceive to be very uncertain. However, since I subsequently wished to devote my attention purely to the quest for truth, I thought that a precisely opposite procedure was demanded, and that I should reject as totally false all opinions concerning which I was able to conceive the slightest ground for doubt. In this way, I would determine whether, after that, there might remain anything in my belief that was completely beyond possibility of doubt. For that reason, because our senses sometimes mislead us, I was ready to suppose that nothing really existed as presented to us by our senses.

Again, because some people make mistakes in reasoning, and fall into illogical arguments, even on the most simple matters of geometry, I rejected as false all the chains of reasoning I had previously accepted as demonstrative proofs, convinced that I was as prone to error as anyone else. Lastly, I reflected that the very same perceptions we experience when awake, we may also experience when asleep, during which time none of those perceptions are real. So I posited that all the perceptions that had ever come into my mind when awake, possessed no more truth than the fantasies of my dreams.

But immediately upon so thinking, I observed that, whereas I was thus willing to think that everything in my mind was false, it was absolutely necessary that I myself, who was thinking such a sceptical thought, should possess some kind of existence. And so I observed this truth: 'I think, therefore I am.' I saw that this truth was so certain, possessing such evidence, that no basis of doubt, no matter how overstated, could be brought forward by sceptics that would have the power to shake it. I therefore concluded that I might, without hesitation, embrace this as the first principle of the philosophy I was seeking.

René Descartes
Discourse on Method, Part Four

John Locke: The simplicity and reasonableness of Christianity – 'Jesus is the Messiah'

Can there be any thing more absurd than to say, there are several fundamental articles [of belief], each of which every man must explicitly believe, upon pain of damnation, and yet not be able to say, which they be? ... This, as great an absurdity as it is, cannot be otherwise, whilst men will take upon them to alter the terms of the gospel; and when it is evident, that our Saviour and his apostles received men into the church, and pronounced them believers, for taking him to be the Messiah, their King and deliverer, sent by God, [orthodox Trinitarian theologians] have a boldness to say, 'this is not enough.' But, when you would know of them, what then is enough, they cannot tell you ...

Hence come those endless and unreasonable contentions about fundamentals, whilst each censures the defect, redundancy, or falsehood of what others require, as necessary to be believed: and yet he himself gives not a catalogue of his own fundamentals, which he will say is sufficient and complete. Nor is it to be wondered; since, in this way, it is impossible to stop short of putting every proposition, divinely revealed, into the list of fundamentals; all of them being of divine, and so of equal authority ...

It is no wonder, therefore, there have been such fierce contests, and such cruel havock made amongst Christians about fundamentals; whilst everyone would set up his system, upon pain of fire and faggot in this, and hellfire in the other world. Though, at the same time, whilst he is exercising the utmost barbarities against others, to prove himself a true Christian, he professes himself so ignorant, that he cannot tell, or so uncharitable, that he will not tell, what articles are absolutely necessary and sufficient to make a man a Christian. If there be any such fundamentals, as it is certain there are, it is as certain they must be very plain.

Why then does every one urge and make a stir about fundamentals, and nobody give a list of them? but because (as I have said) upon the usual grounds, they cannot: for I will be bold to say, that everyone who considers the matter, will see, that only the article of his being the Messiah their King, which alone our Saviour and his apostles preached to the unconverted world, and received those that believed it into the church, is the only necessary article to be believed by an atheist, to make him a Christian.

John Locke

A Second Vindication of the Reasonableness of Christianity

Voltaire: *Candide*

Baron Thunderton-Gibberish was one of the mightiest nobles in Westphalia, since his castle did not just have a gate, but windows too. His great hall was adorned with tapestries. All his farmyard dogs could be made into a pack of hounds whenever the need arose; his grooms were his huntsmen; and the village curate was his chief distributor of charities. They referred to him as 'My lord', and laughed at all his tales.

The Baron's wife weighed about three hundred and fifty pounds, and was therefore someone of weighty importance, and she carried out the ceremonial duties of the house with a dignity that compelled even weightier respect. Her daughter Cunegonde was seventeen, fresh-complexioned, beautiful, well-built, and desirable. The Baron's son seemed in every way worthy of his father. The tutor Pangloss was the family sage, and young Candide listened to his teaching with all the trustfulness of his youth and character.

Pangloss was a Professor of Metaphysico-theologico-cosmolo-imbecility. He gave admirable proof that no effect can arise without a cause; likewise he proved that since this is the best of all possible worlds, the Baron's castle was therefore the most resplendent of castles, and his wife the best of all possible Baronesses.

'Rationality proves,' said Pangloss, 'that everything must be precisely as it is. Because everything has been created for a purpose, all is necessarily for the best purpose. Take note that the nose has been formed to wear spectacles: therefore we have spectacles. Legs are manifestly designed to wear stockings: therefore we have stockings. Stones were created to be hewn, and to build castles: therefore my lord has a resplendent castle. After all, the greatest baron in the land should be the best housed. Pigs were created to be eaten: therefore we eat pork all year long. It follows that those who affirm that "all is well" have spoken foolishly; they should have said "all is for the best".'

Voltaire
Candide, Chapter One

Rousseau: Christianity cannot be the universal, reasonable religion

Let us posit that the missionaries of the Gospel are in fact present and preaching in the most remote nations of the earth. How can they reasonably expect to be believed merely on their own testimony, and not realise that their listeners will carefully demand some proof of the teaching? Any of these listeners might very reasonably say to these preachers:

'You tell me about a God who was born and put to death almost two thousand years ago, in another part of the world, in some utterly unknown city. You assure me that everyone who does not believe in this strange story is lost forever. Well, these are things too outlandish to be swiftly believed on the mere authority of a man like yourself who is a perfect stranger to me. Why did your God bring about those events, of which He requires me to be informed, at such a great distance? Is it a crime not to know what happens on the other side of the world? Was it possible for me to intuit that there existed, in the opposite hemisphere, a nation called the Jews, and a city called

Jerusalem? I might as well be expected to know what happens on the moon!

'Ah but, you say, you have now come to inform me! Yes, but why didn't you come sooner to inform my father? Why do you send that blameless man to hell merely because he knew nothing of this matter? Must he be punished forever for your delay in coming? He who was so fair-minded, so kindly, and so eager to know the truth! Be honest. Put yourself in my place. Do you really think that I can believe, upon your solitary testimony, all these far-fetched things you tell me? Do you think I can reconcile the great injustice of your God's methods with His allegedly just character which you claim to make known?

'Please let me first go and see this far-off country where so many miracles have occurred about which we know absolutely nothing here. Let me go there and be well-informed why the citizens of that "Jerusalem" of which you speak had the audacity to treat God as a thief or murderer. Oh but, you say, they did not acknowledge that He was God. Then how can I? I mean, I never even heard of Him except from you!

'You further add, behold how these Jews were punished, scattered, and taken into captivity. None of them ever went back to their former city. Certainly, they merited all this: but the present occupants of the city – what do they say about the unbelief, the murder of God, that marked their predecessors? Do they not deny it? Do they not confess His divinity as little as did the city's ancient residents? [The "present residents" being Muslims who deny Christ's deity.] Amazing! In the same city where your God was put to death, neither the ancient nor the present residents confess His divinity! And yet you would have *me* believe it, when I was born almost two thousand years after the event, and two thousand leagues distant from the place where it happened!

'Do you not see that, before I can believe this Bible of yours, which you claim is sacred but of which I know nothing, I need to be informed by others concerning when and by whom it was written; how it has been preserved and handed down to you; what they say about it in the region where it originated; and what reasons are given by those who reject it, even though they know as well as you all the things you have told me about? You must understand, then, the necessity that compels me to travel first to Europe, then Asia, and finally Palestine, to investigate and check out this matter for myself, and that I must be a complete idiot to stand here listening to you before I have undertaken this investigation.'

Such a speech as this seems to me very reasonable, and indeed I assert that every sensible person should, under such circumstances, speak in this way, and send the missionary about his business. He was in too much haste to instruct and baptize the heathen before he had sufficiently established the credentials of his mission.

Jean-Jacques Rousseau

Creed of a Savoyard Priest*, in *Emile: or, On Education

Thomas Paine: Deist contempt for the Bible

Whenever we read the obscene stories, the voluptuous debaucheries, the cruel and torturous executions, the unrelenting vindictiveness, with which more than half the Bible is filled, it would be more consistent that we called it the word of a demon, than the Word of God. It is a history of wickedness, that has served to corrupt and brutalize mankind; and, for my own part, I sincerely detest it, as I detest everything that is cruel. We scarcely meet with anything, a few phrases excepted, but what deserves either our abhorrence or our contempt, till we come to the miscellaneous parts of the Bible. In the anonymous publications, the Psalms, and the Book of Job, more particularly in the latter, we find a great deal of elevated sentiment reverentially expressed of the power and benignity of the Almighty; but they stand on no higher rank than many other compositions on similar subjects, as well before that time as since ...

Did the book called the Bible excel in purity of ideas and expression all the books now extant in the world, I would not take it for my rule of faith, as being the Word of God; because the possibility would nevertheless exist of my being imposed upon. But when I see throughout the greatest part of this book scarcely anything but a history of the grossest vices, and a collection of the most paltry and contemptible tales, I cannot dishonour my Creator by calling it by his name.

But some perhaps will say – Are we to have no word of God – no revelation? I answer yes. There is a Word of God; there is a revelation. The Word of God is the Creation we behold: And it is in this word, which no human invention can counterfeit or alter, that God speaketh universally to man …

It is only in the Creation that all our ideas and conceptions of a word of God can unite. The Creation speaketh a universal language, independently of human speech or human language, multiplied and various as they be. It is an ever existing original, which every man can read. It cannot be forged; it cannot be counterfeited; it cannot be lost; it cannot be altered; it cannot be suppressed. It does not depend upon the will of man whether it shall be published or not; it publishes itself from one end of the earth to the other. It preaches to all nations and to all worlds; and this word of God reveals to man all that is necessary for man to know of God. Do we want to contemplate his power? We see it in the immensity of the creation. Do we want to contemplate his wisdom? We see it in the unchangeable order by which the incomprehensible Whole is governed. Do we want to contemplate his munificence? We see it in the abundance with which he fills the earth. Do we want to contemplate his mercy? We see it in his not withholding that abundance even from the unthankful. In fine, do we want to know what God is? Search not the book called the scripture, which any human hand might make, but the scripture called the Creation.

Thomas Paine
***The Age of Reason*, Part One, Chs.7–9**

David Hume: Scepticism about cause and effect

When we look about us towards external objects, and consider the operation of causes, we are never able, in a single instance, to discover any power or necessary connexion; any quality, which binds the effect to the cause, and renders the one an infallible consequence of the other. We only find, that the one does actually, in fact, follow the other. The impulse of one billiard-ball is attended with motion in the second. This is the whole that appears to the outward senses. The mind feels no sentiment or inward impression from this succession of objects: Consequently, there is not, in any single, particular instance of cause and effect, anything which can suggest the idea of power or necessary connexion.

David Hume

***Enquiry concerning Human Understanding*, section 50**

Immanuel Kant: The right and rational way to believe in the Trinity

The Christian Faith teaches us these propositions:

(i) We must look upon the Supreme Lawgiver neither as soft, and therefore indulgent, to the weakness of humankind, nor as tyrannical, harshly commanding by naked right of His absolute and categorical authority. Likewise, we must not regard His commands as arbitrary, unrelated to our concepts of morality, but rather as concerned directly with the betterment of our nature.

(ii) We must not locate His benevolence in an unconditional good-will toward His creatures, as if He did not first assess the morality of their attitudes. Only after this assessment, in proportion to how well-pleased He is with their lives, does He make good their inability to measure up to His holiness.

(iii) In administering His justice, we cannot picture Him as requiring us to remove His condemnation by our entreaties, since that would be to entertain something illogical. But equally He cannot sit in judgment clothed only with the holiness of the Lawgiver, since no one then could ever be justified. Rather, we should look upon His righteousness as a principle which limits and restrains the exercise of His benevolence according to the aforementioned condition of our obedience to His holy law, to the extent that we sons of men are capable of meeting its demands.

In summary, we must serve God under this trio of distinct moral aspects. To signify this, the name of a threefold personality of the same single Being is no improper use of language. This Trinitarian symbolism may suitably suggest to us the pure moral religion in its entirety. Apart from this threefold division, religion might easily collapse into a mere dust-licking creation of a God in our own image, for human beings are extremely prone to think of the Deity more-or-less as they do an earthly king. This reduction of Deity to an earthly level happens, whenever these threefold functions are not properly separated, but clumsily mixed up and muddled.

On the other hand, if we took this belief in a triune God, not as purely descriptive of a practical moral idea, but rather as setting forth what God actually is in Himself, it would then be an enigma transcending all comprehension of thought; it would be quite incapable of being made intelligible (even by revelation) to our reason. In that case, the Trinity would rightly be considered as simply an absurd and unthinkable riddle. To believe such a tenet as though it added to someone's theoretical knowledge of the divine nature, could only be a confession of an utterly incoherent Church Creed. If anyone thinks he understands it, then he professes an article of ecclesiastical faith [based on nothing but a literal view of scripture] in which God has been imagined in manmade categories. Such a belief cannot benefit his moral improvement in the slightest.

Immanuel Kant
Religion Within the Bounds of Reason Alone,
Book 3, Apotome 1, section 7

Lessing: How can reason believe in a historical religion?

Had I been alive in the time of Christ, then naturally the fulfilment of prophecies in His person would have compelled me to give Him great consideration. And had I actually witnessed Him doing miracles, and found no reason to doubt that these were miracles indeed, then in such a miracle-worker marked out ahead of time by prophecies, I would have acquired strong confidence. I would have gladly submitted my intellect to His; I would have believed Him in everything He said, except where other equally unquestionable experiences counted against His words.

Or suppose that still today I were actually experiencing the fulfilment of prophecies concerning Christ or Christianity – prophecies I had long been certain were made ages ago, fulfilled in a way that left no room for dispute. Or suppose that right now, faithful Christians were doing miracles which I simply had to accept as genuine. What then could stop me from acknowledging this 'proof of the spirit and of power' as the apostle calls it (1 Cor. 2:4)? ...

But I live in the eighteenth century; and miracles do not take place any more. What would the problem be, if I today have qualms about believing the proof of Christianity supplied by 'the spirit and the power' of miracles, given that I can instead believe on the basis of other arguments more suitable to the time in which I live?

Here is the problem: this 'proof of the spirit and the power' doesn't have any spirit or power any longer. It has deteriorated into mere human testimonies *about* spirit and power.

The problem is that reports about the fulfilment of prophecies are not themselves fulfilled prophecies. And reports about miracles are not themselves miracles. If prophecies are fulfilled before my very eyes, or I see miracles with my own eyes, the effect is instantaneous. But mere *reports* about fulfilled prophecies and miracles have to come to me through a second-hand channel that robs them of all their proper impact ...

Is it always true that what I read in 'reputable historians' has the same certainty for me as what I experience myself? I am not aware that anyone has ever affirmed this. All that is affirmed is that our reports of these prophecies and miracles are as reliable as *historical* truths can ever be. And then this qualification is added: historical truths can never be proved with objective certainty. Yet (we are told) we must believe these historical truths with as much firmness as truths that have been proved with objective certainty.

My reply: first of all, who denies that these reports of miracles and prophecies are as reliable as historical truths can ever be?

I do not deny this. But if this is the only level of reliability the reports have, why are they treated as though they had infinitely greater reliability? In what way, you ask? In this way: something very different and far greater is based on these reports than may properly be based on truths that only have a historical level of proof.

If historical truth cannot be proved with objective certainty, then no truth can be proved with objective certainty on the *basis* of historical truths.

In other words: the accidental truths of history can never become the proof of the necessary truths of reason.

Gotthold Ephraim Lessing
On the Proof of the Spirit and of Power

The French Revolution: The Rights of Man

Declaration of the Rights of Man and of the Citizen
Approved by the National Assembly of France, August 26, 1789

The representatives of the people of France, gathered together as a National Assembly, holding that ignorance or neglect of, or scorn for, the rights of Man are the single source of public misfortunes and the corruption of governments, have resolved to publish in a formal and earnest declaration the natural, inalienable, and sacred rights of Man, so that this declaration, set continually before all the members of the body of society, shall at all times remind them of their rights and duties; so that the acts of the legislative authority, and also those of the executive, may be at any moment set alongside the goals and purposes for which all political institutions exist, and thus earn greater respect; and finally, so that the complaints of the citizens, based from this time forth on simple and indisputable principles, shall work for the preservation of the constitution and result in the wellbeing of all. Therefore, the National Assembly acknowledges and pronounces, in the presence and under the patronage of the Supreme Being[3] these following rights of Man and of the citizen:

---

3. We note the religious reference to the Enlightenment deity, the Supreme Being. *The Rights of Man* is a religious but not a Christian document.

Articles:

1. Human beings are born, and remain, free and equal with regard to their rights. Social distinctions may be established only on the basis of society's general good.
2. The purpose of all political association is to maintain the natural rights of Man which exist independently of human laws. These rights are liberty, property, security, and the right to resist tyranny.
3. The principle of all political sovereignty rests fundamentally in the nation. No group nor individual may exercise any authority within the nation which does not originate directly from the nation itself.
4. Liberty consists in the individual's freedom to do anything that harms no one else. Thus the exercise of each person's natural rights has no limits save those which guarantee to the other members of society the enjoyment of the same rights. These limits can be decided and established only by law.
5. The law can forbid only those actions that are harmful to society. No group or person may prevent that which is not forbidden by the law, and no one may be compelled to do anything not established by the law.
6. The law is the expression of society's general will. Every citizen has a right to take part either personally, or through a representative, in law-making. The law must be the same for all, both when it defends and when it punishes. Since all citizens are equal in the eyes of the law, they are all equally eligible for all ranks, positions, and occupations in public life, according to their abilities, and without discrimination save on the basis of virtues and talents.
7. No one may be accused, arrested, or imprisoned, save in those cases established by the law, and in harmony with the procedures determined by the law. If anyone solicits, transmits, carries out, or causes to be carried out, any unlawful order, he shall be punished. However, if any citizen is lawfully summoned or arrested, he must submit without obstruction, since in that case resistance is an offence.

8. The law shall determine only those punishments that are absolutely and obviously necessary. No one shall be punished unless the punishment is lawfully imposed, on the basis of a law passed and published before the offence was committed.
9. Everyone shall be regarded as innocent until officially found guilty. Therefore, if their arrest is deemed necessary, any harsh treatment not essential to securing the prisoner's person shall be sternly suppressed by law.
10. No one shall be disturbed by the government merely on account of his opinions, including his religious views, as long as his outward manifestation of those opinions does not disrupt public order as established by the law.
11. The free sharing of ideas and opinions is among the most precious of the rights of Man. In keeping with this, every citizen shall enjoy freedom of speech, writing, and printing. However, he shall bear the responsibility for abuses of this freedom as defined by the law.
12. Public armed forces are necessary to secure the rights of Man and of the citizen. These forces are, therefore, established for the benefit of all citizens, not for the personal gain of those given positions of military leadership.
13. In order to maintain public armed forces and to pay for the cost of government, a general tax is necessary. However, this tax should be fairly shared by all the citizens in accordance with their individual means.
14. All citizens have the right to decide, either personally or through their representatives, concerning the necessity of the public taxation; to vote on this freely; to know the uses to which it has been put; and to determine the amount, the method of assessment, the collection, and the duration of said taxes.
15. Society has the right to demand that every public agent shall give an account of his management of affairs.
16. A society in which observance of the law is not secured, and the separation of government powers not defined [legislative, executive, judicial], has no constitution at all.

17. Property ownership is an inviolable and sacred right. Therefore no one shall be deprived of his property save when public necessity, properly determined by law, shall unmistakably require it. Even then, it shall take place only on condition that the property owner must have previously been given just compensation.

Chapter 2

The Evangelical Revival in England and Wales

Introduction
'Evangelical' – what's in a word?

Historians debate whether the Evangelical movement in 18th Century Britain and America was substantially different from the types of Protestantism that preceded it. This debate is ongoing. Perhaps it would be relatively safe to say that there were elements of continuity and discontinuity. On the continuity side, the content of the Gospel proclaimed by 18th Century Evangelical Calvinists did not differ from the Reformation or Puritan message, unless by way of some nuances. 18th Century Gospel preachers and writers were steeped in the 'godly literature' of the Reformation and Puritan eras. Justification by faith alone in Christ alone, a Christ who was both very God and very Man, whose death was a penal substitutionary atonement for humanity's sin, and whose resurrection constituted Him a living and present Saviour who outpoured His Spirit on His people, bringing them new birth and sanctification: these basic doctrinal themes were common to the 16th, 17th, and 18th centuries.

Of course, the Evangelical Arminianism of John and Charles Wesley represented a serious departure from the mainstream British Reformed Protestantism of the 16th and 17th centuries. Not that Arminianism did not exist in 17th Century England; but in the Church of England, it had taken forms very different from the fervent Evangelical Arminianism of the Wesleys. There was the Arminianism of 'High Church' Anglicanism, otherwise known as 'Caroline divinity', from the Latin *Carolus*, Charles – the reference is to King Charles I (1625–49), the royal patron of this tradition. This type of Arminianism had emphasised sacramental grace flowing through the 'apostolic succession' of episcopal church order. Then there was the Arminianism, so to call it, of the Cambridge Platonists, rooted more in the Greek fathers of the early Church and their synergism, with a heavy dose of Platonic and Neoplatonic thought. Among the Latitudinarian party, which dominated Anglican theology in the era of the Revival, there was a rationalistic Arminianism, deriving from a philosophical assessment of human nature and its powers, which owed much to John Locke.

The distinctive contribution of the Wesleys was to refashion Arminianism into a Word-centred theology and piety of popular proclamation, aimed at leading people to immediate conversion, and allied to a far clearer recognition and appropriation of a Reformation doctrine of justification by faith than these other Anglican schools of thought possessed. This was something new in Anglicanism. It was not so new outside Anglicanism, however, since the General Baptists had long been Evangelical Arminians of this sort. However, their Protestant witness had become almost extinct in the 18th Century – for the most part, General Baptists had embraced Unitarianism by then (see below).

On the side of discontinuity, the emotionally intense and dramatic manner adopted by many 18th Century revival preachers (though not by all) fostered new expectations among listeners, including formally established congregations – not just open-air crowds – that preachers and ministers should be dynamic, experience-mediating orators, rather than simply well-educated expositors of scripture. The new sense of urgency felt in the Revival to communicate the Gospel to the unconverted masses also gave rise to a subtle shift in the perception of the preacher's task, and of the purpose of church gatherings. As one modern historian has put it, the passion for souls now began to eclipse the passion for truth. The purpose of church gatherings began to be seen as 'producing conversions' rather than worshiping the triune God.

The actual word 'Evangelical', which has become inescapably attached to the 18th Century Revival, does not in itself connote anything new. Deriving from 'Evangel', it has its linguistic roots in the Greek word for Gospel or good news, εὐαγγέλιον, which in Latin became *evangelium*, with its adjective *evangelicus*. 'Evangelical' certainly had a distinguished history prior to the 18th Century. John Wycliffe (c.1330–84), England's 'Morning Star of the Reformation', had been known as the Evangelical Doctor, according to the medieval custom of nicknaming great theological teachers (doctors) – Bernard of Clairvaux was the Mellifluous or Honey-Dripping Doctor, Thomas Aquinas the Angelic Doctor, Duns Scotus the Subtle Doctor, and so forth. Wycliffe's status as the Evangelical Doctor was based on his commitment to popular preaching, grounded in holy scripture as the Word of God and the Church's only infallible source of truth, as the primary and essential task of ministry.

In the 16th Century, the entire Lutheran wing of the German Reformation was known as *evangelisch* – essentially, Gospel-confessing – alongside the more popular label 'Lutheran'. Later in Lutheran history, *evangelisch* came to mean little more than historically and denominationally 'Protestant' in a very loose sense; but in the 16th and 17th Centuries, it retained a robustly theological significance. In the English language, 'evangelical' in the Reformation era simply meant 'adhering to the basic truth of the Gospel' (as understood by confessional Lutherans and Calvinists). For example, John Owen (1616–83), the prince of Puritan divines, repeatedly used the word 'evangelical' to describe the truth of the Gospel, especially justification by faith, in his classic treatise on that subject (*The Doctrine of Justification by Faith through the Imputation of the Righteousness of Christ; Explained, Confirmed, and Vindicated*, 1677). It would not, however, be until the early 19th Century that the noun 'Evangelicalism' was coined.

Although, then, in deference to tradition, we connect the term 'Evangelical' in a particular way to the 18th Century Revival, this is not to suggest that the present writer thinks a wholly novel religious movement was born in that century, separated by an unbridgeable chasm from everything that went before. It was rather more a case of the Reformation message being adapted and repackaged for the Age of Enlightenment.[1]

1. It is strongly arguable that the differences between Reformation and Puritan Evangelicalism, and 18th Century Revival Evangelicalism, were more pronounced in America than in Britain. See Chapter 4, Part 3.

1
The Background of the Evangelical Revival in England

Luke Tyerman, the great 19th Century biographer of John Wesley, lamented that 'Christian England' had never witnessed a century in its long history so destitute of soul and faith, as the period stretching from the accession to the throne of Queen Anne (1702), up to the reign of George II (1727–60). Tyerman may, of course, have been exaggerating in order to magnify the effect of Wesley's preaching. But the evidence suggests he was not *greatly* exaggerating. Let us, then, consider the backdrop to the Evangelical Revival.

1. Loss of faith: The Anglican Church

The Evangelical Revival of the 18th Century is one of the great defining experiences of the Church in England. So much English Christian thinking and expectation have their roots in the Revival, to this very day. Even so, perhaps one thing we are apt to forget is the sheerly unprecedented nature of the 18th Century movement. There was nothing in English society to suggest that it was on the verge of a major revitalisation of its Churches. In almost all ways, from a historic Protestant standpoint, the background to the Revival was one of deep moral and spiritual darkness.

As a culture, England had largely abandoned its Reformation religious heritage in the period 1690–1740. The Anglican Church (the cradle of the Revival) had its overwhelming theological mood set by the dominant Latitudinarian party. Their 'Latitudinarian' nickname stemmed from their insistence that a person needed to believe very little in order to be a Christian: one could tolerate a wide latitude of beliefs, as long as the bare fundamentals were accepted. The Latitudinarian conception of Christianity was marked by an exaltation of reason, a relative indifference to doctrinal specifics, and a preaching of little more than the platitudes of common-sense morality (albeit perhaps eloquently) from Anglican pulpits. The theological and philosophical hero of Latitudinarians was likely to be the semi-Deist thinker John Locke. Locke – we recollect – was a Unitarian who had made human reason and sense-experience the touchstones of truth, the sphere of religious truth included (rather than God's self-revelation in Christ), and stripped down the whole of Christian theology to the single proposition 'Jesus is the Messiah'. Locke's semi-Deism injected into Latitudinarianism a strain of what, at its most non-Christian, we can only characterise as a theology, preaching, and piety that sat strangely light to Trinitarian faith in God as manifest in the person and work of Jesus Christ. There was much talk of 'God' and 'virtue', but surprisingly little of Christ as traditionally confessed.

Latitudinarians were conspicuous in the Church of England's episcopal hierarchy over this half-century and beyond. Their bishops included John Tillotson (1631–94), Archbishop of Canterbury from 1691–94; Thomas Tenison (1636–1713), Archbishop of Canterbury from 1694–1714; John Moore (1646–1714), Bishop of Norwich and Ely (successively); White Kennet (1660–1728), Bishop of Peterborough; Benjamin Hoadly (1676–1761), Bishop of Bangor, Hereford, Salisbury, and Winchester (successively); Joseph Butler (1692–1752), Bishop of Durham; Edmund Law (1703–87), Bishop of Carlisle; Jonathan Shipley (1714–88), Bishop of Llandaff and St Asaph (successively); John Hinchliffe (1731–94), Bishop of Peterborough; and Richard Watson (1737–1816), Bishop of Llandaff. Of these Latitudinarian bishops, the most intellectually and spiritually noteworthy was Bishop Joseph Butler of Durham, whose strong contribution to the Deist controversy was examined in the previous Chapter.

Aside from the Anglican bishops, other prominent Latitudinarian clergy in the Church of England who did not hold episcopal office included Samuel Clarke (1675–1729), whose *Scripture Doctrine of the Trinity* (1712) caused a storm of controversy by arguing that supreme worship should be given to the Father alone (a sort of 'High Arianism'); John Jackson (1686–1763), prolific literary defender of Clarke's anti-Trinitarianism; William Whiston (1667–1752), who held various positions in the Church and Cambridge University, and was another anti-Trinitarian, finally leaving the Church of England in 1747 to become a (still Trinity-denying) Baptist; Francis Blackburne (1705–87), famous campaigner against the Church of England's 39 Articles of Religion as restrictive and unnecessary; and Christopher Wyvill (1740–1822), militant (bordering on revolutionary) political reformer, and opponent of British war with France after its 1789 Revolution.

The dominance of Latitudinarianism, then, in the Church of England, with its tendencies to semi-Deist rationalism and its potential for anti-Trinitarianism, did not seem to presage any resurgence of Reformation theology or piety. Wherever a Latitudinarian strain of theology and preaching prevailed among the clergy, its tendency was to instill into parishioners a sense that Christianity was little more than a belief in a Supreme Being (with a more or less Christian tincture) coupled with decent moral conduct – or at least lip-service to these. Such theology and preaching proved powerless as agents of spiritual and moral transformation. There even developed a view among the upper classes that Christianity was all very well for the lower social orders – they needed its teaching about future rewards and punishments to encourage them to behave morally – but no educated person could believe such absurdities. The Christianity in which the lower orders were instructed, however, was not likely to rise far above a vaguely Christianised Deism and a morality without roots in the Gospel.

2. Loss of faith: The Dissenting Churches

If we shift our attention from Anglicanism to English Nonconformity or Dissent, things were not much more promising. Dissent too had strayed far afield from its previous standards of orthodoxy, since attaining religious freedom in the Glorious Revolution of 1688–89. Its Presbyterian churches, once the home of such towering Puritan luminaries as Richard Baxter, John Flavel, and John Howe, had drifted deep into anti-Trinitarianism. The General or Arminian Baptists had gone the same way. Here was the effective birth of English Unitarianism (although Unitarians at that time were known as 'rational Dissenters'). The anti-Trinitarian shape of doctrinal change among Presbyterians and General Baptists once again confronts us with the spectre of Deism or semi-Deism. It can hardly be a historical accident that the period when so many Dissenters lost their faith in the Trinity of biblical revelation was the Age of Deism, when the 'Supreme Being', allegedly known by human reason, reigned over His clockwork universe.

We may discern the public signs of this Dissenting anti-Trinitarianism in the Salters Hall controversy of 1719. This was sparked by the case of two Presbyterian ministers, Joseph Hallet and James Peirce of Exeter in Devon, who (under the influence of the anti-Trinitarian Latitudinarian, William Whiston) had embraced a Christology that left no room for Christ's true deity. Their unorthodoxy soon became widely suspected – a misgiving that spilled over to include other Presbyterian ministers in the locality. Concerned parties, therefore, asked a number of the Presbyterian clergy of Exeter and its environs to gather, so that a body of lay Presbyterian deputies might assess how well-grounded the suspicions were. When the deputies requested the clergy to affirm their Trinitarian orthodoxy in the words of the Anglican Church's 39 Articles of Religion, the clergy refused, arguing that no human creed could function as a test of sound doctrine: scripture alone was the Church's confession of faith.

This anti-confessional stance was a huge departure from traditional Protestantism, and it did not augur well for the survival of a recognizable Reformation faith rooted both in scripture and the ecumenical creeds of the early Church (especially the Nicene Creed and the Creed or Formula of Chalcedon). When the lay deputies pressed the clergy to inform them how they themselves understood the teaching of scripture – in effect, what their own creed was – the clergy again declined the proposal. The result was a number of congregational splits, as the Presbyterian laity took sides for and against their theologically dubious ministers.

At this point, the distressed Presbyterians of Devon appealed to their more illustrious brethren in the capital city, London, to step in and provide guidance. Since there was now a fear that anti-Trinitarianism might be spreading more widely among Dissenters, London Presbyterians cooperated with Congregationalists and Baptists on a committee of inquiry. This committee called a more general meeting of Dissenters from London and elsewhere to convene at London's Salters Hall (in St Swithin's Lane) in February 1719.

One hundred and ten ministers were present at Salters Hall. The purpose of the meeting, however, was swiftly derailed, when it became a debate – not about belief in the Trinity – but about whether pastors and preachers could legitimately be required to subscribe to any human creed or confession above and beyond the Bible. When a vote was taken, a majority decided in favour of the Bible alone (fifty-seven votes to fifty-three). Most of the Presbyterians and Arminian Baptists voted against creeds and confessions, whereas most Congregationalists and Calvinistic Baptists voted in favour. This does not mean that all the anti-creedal Presbyterians and Baptists were necessarily anti-Trinitarian; but their refusal to utilise any tests of Trinitarian orthodoxy opened wide the floodgates of Unitarianism in their churches.

As this narrative makes clear, English Congregationalists and Calvinistic or Particular Baptists kept hold on their Trinitarian orthodoxy, unlike Presbyterians and Arminian Baptists. However, this did not carry the implication that all was well, doctrinally or spiritually, with the Congregationalists and Particular Baptists. They now felt the chilling wind of a novel variety of Calvinism, usually dubbed 'Hyper-Calvinism', stemming from the writings of Congregationalist Joseph Hussey (1660–1726) and Particular Baptist John Skepp (1675–1721).[1] Hyper-Calvinism was characterised by its refusal to 'offer' Christ as Saviour to sinners in general, on the basis that He was Saviour for the elect alone, for whom alone He had died. This had the effect of opening up a rather chilly gulf, theologically and emotionally, between Christ as preached and the listening congregation, who went away too often with the impression that He who was extolled as 'Saviour' might have no relevance to them, unless they could first discern whether they were among the elect. The brilliant Particular Baptist pastor-theologian of late 18th Century, Andrew Fuller (1754–1815), would describe the sadly debilitating impact that such Hyper-Calvinist preaching made on his young soul.[2]

3. The influence of Deism

If we turn from the narrower confines of church life to English society at large, the educated classes had drunk a significant dose of Deism. Such Deist-influenced piety, among those with any smattering of culture, tended to dwell on proving God's existence rationally through the 'design' argument, and seeking to inculcate the moral virtues by exhortation. (The similarities with Latitudinarianism are plain.) A classical specimen of semi-Deist piety can be found in the 'hymn of the starry skies' by illustrious Anglican essay-writer, dramatist, and politician, Joseph Addison (1672–1719):

> The spacious firmament on high,
> With all the blue ethereal sky,
> And spangled heavens, a shining frame,
> Their great Original proclaim.
> Th'unwearied sun from day to day

---

1. It has been argued that classical Hyper-Calvinism derives more from the disciples of Hussey and Skepp than from the men themselves or their writings.
2. For Andrew Fuller, see Part 6, section 2.

Does his Creator's power display,
And publishes to every land
The work of an Almighty hand.

What though in solemn silence all
Move round the dark terrestrial ball?
What though no real voice nor sound
Amid their radiant orbs be found?
In Reason's ear they all rejoice,
And utter forth a glorious voice,
For ever singing as they shine,
'The hand that made us is Divine!'

No doubt Addison's hymn was meant to be a gloss on Psalm 19:1-6, but the intrusive reference to 'reason' lets slip the Deistic flavour. We are not a million miles away from Immanuel Kant: 'the starry skies above and the moral law within', rather than God-in-the-flesh crucified for humanity's transgressions.

There was a publishing flood of Deist writings in England at this period (1690–1740), as some of its most influential treatises mounted a long drawn-out and impact-making assault on Christian belief: Charles Blount's *The Oracles of Reason* (1693); John Toland's *Christianity Not Mysterious* (1696); Anthony Collins' *A Discourse of Freethinking* (1713) and *Discourse of the Grounds and Reasons of the Christian Religion* (1724); Matthew Tindal's *Christianity as Old as the Creation; or, the Gospel a Republication of the Religion of Nature* (1730), sometimes called 'the Bible of Deism'; the multitudinous works of the productive Thomas Chubb, such as his *Discourse concerning Reason ... [proving that] reason is, or else that it ought to be, a sufficient guide in matters of Religion* (1731); and Thomas Morgan's three-volume *The Moral Philosopher* (1737 onward), which summed up the Deist position in dialogue form (the Christian Theophanes against the Deist Philalethes – the latter of course getting the better of the argument).

There were other prominent English Deists who did not necessarily advocate their beliefs so publicly or explicitly, but gave Deism a more indirect credence in society. Among these were the two distinguished politicians, Whig leader Anthony

Ashley-Cooper (Lord Shaftesbury, 1671–1713) and Tory leader Henry St John (Viscount Bolingbroke, 1678–1751); the famous painter William Hogarth (1697–1764), whose satirical depictions of 18th Century life still entrance; Mark Akenside (1721–70), learned physician, and (in his own day) fashionable poet; and a little later, England's most celebrated historian, Edward Gibbon (1737–94), author of *Decline and Fall of the Roman Empire*.

The combined results of all this on England's public faith in Christianity were little short of devastating, as contemporary testimonies illustrate. The French Enlightenment philosopher, the Deist-inclined Charles-Louis de Secondat, Baron Montesquieu (1689–1755), who visited England in 1729–31, commented in his *Notes on England:*

> There is no religion in England: only four or five members of the House of Commons go to communion or to a sermon in the House. Whenever anyone refers to religion, everybody starts laughing. When one man said, in my presence, 'I believe this as an article of faith', everyone began to laugh.

By 'religion', Montesquieu meant Christianity. Bishop Joseph Butler of Durham lamented:

> It has come, I know not how, to be taken for granted by many persons that Christianity is no longer a subject of inquiry; but that it is now at length discovered to be fictitious. And accordingly, it is treated as if, in the present age, this were an agreed point among all persons of discernment, and nothing remained but to set it up as a principal subject for mirth and ridicule, as it were, by way of reprisals for having so long interrupted the pleasures of the world.

Bishop Thomas Secker of Bristol (who would become Archbishop of Canterbury in 1758) said much the same:

> An open and professed disregard to religion is become, through a variety of unhappy causes, the distinguishing character of the present age; that this evil is grown to a great height of the nation and is daily spreading through every part of it.

Voltaire, based on his experience of life in England, commented on the morality of many Anglican clerics:

> the Anglican clergymen haunt the ale-houses, because custom endorses it, and if they get drunk, they do it seriously and it brings them no shame.

For the Dissenters, Presbyterian Matthew Henry (1662–1714), author of the famous Bible commentary, spoke in a similar vein as the 18th Century began:

> The low condition of the church of God ought to be greatly lamented; the Protestant interest small, very small; a decay of piety; attempts for reformation ineffectual. Help, Lord! There are but few who are truly religious; who believe the report of the Gospel, and who are willing to take the pains, and run the hazards of religion. Many make a fair show in the flesh, but few only walk closely with God. Where is he that engageth his heart, or that stirs up himself to take hold of his Maker?

A popular joke during that era was that a bill was being prepared in parliament to have the word 'not' taken out of the Ten Commandments and inserted into the Creeds. John Wesley would soon say: 'What is the present characteristic of the English nation? It is ungodliness. Ungodliness is our universal, our constant, our peculiar character.' Wesley's experience in Continental Europe burned into him a sense of how uniquely blasphemous in speech and irreverent in attitude the English were: 'I never heard one of them [in Germany] take the name of God in vain, or saw any one laugh when anything of religion was mentioned. So that I believe the glory of sporting with sacred things is peculiar to the English nation!'

There were some Christian lights amid the prevailing unbelief. The most well-known was Congregationalist minister and pioneer hymn-writer Isaac Watts (1674–1748). Watts pastored a flourishing Independent (Congregationalist) church in London (it changed its premises a number of times: Mark Lane, Pinners Hall, Bury Street). The 'godly remnant' of Trinitarian Dissenters in the pre-Revival period looked upon Watts as the model preacher. In many ways, we may perceive him as holding aloft the torch of Reformation and Puritan faith and proclamation, amid a surrounding social environment of blended apathy and hostility. It was not given to Watts, however, to shed any illumination into that larger darkness.[3]

3. For Watts' revolutionary contribution to English hymnody, see Part 7.

2
The Beginnings of the Evangelical Revival in England

1. Origins of the revival

The stirrings of reinvigorated faith in England began among a diverse group of individuals, most of whom became personally connected through Oxford University. The key figure, in terms of the widespread extent and effect of his public preaching, was George Whitefield[1] (1714–70). It will be convenient, therefore, to take Whitefield as an entry-point into the narrative, both humanising it, and simplifying (but not unduly) its complexities.

Whitefield was a native of Gloucester, where his parents ran the Bell Inn. Contemporaries inform us that he always retained his Gloucestershire accent, for instance pronouncing 'Christ' as 'Chroist'. He grew into a religiously inclined teenager: he fasted, prayed, sometimes devoted entire nights to reading his Bible, although as yet Whitefield was no Evangelical. He also discovered a talent for acting, which in a sense would reappear later in his 'theatrical' manner of preaching. In 1732, at the age of eighteen, he went to Oxford University, where he brought probably unwanted attention upon himself by his unwillingness to participate in various student activities he regarded as immoral or irreligious. However, this godly free-spiritedness drew Whitefield to the notice of an existing student-group in Oxford nicknamed the Holy Club.

1. Pronounced Whit-field, not White-field.

This little body of devout students had been founded in 1728 by Charles Wesley (1707–88), Robert Kirkham (dates unknown), and William Morgan (died 1732). The group also had the pejorative nicknames of the Bible Bigots, Bible Moths, the Godly Club, the Enthusiasts (18th Century jargon for 'self-deluded fanatics'), the Sacramentarians (because they took Anglican Holy Communion every week, rather than once a term as the university required[2]), and the Methodists (because they practised their piety in a 'methodical' way, that is, according to strict routines and disciplines). Prior to the Revival, the name 'Holy Club' is the one commonly employed to designate the group.

From 1729 onwards, the Holy Club fell under the personal sway and organising genius of Charles Wesley's slightly older brother John (1703–91), always something of a dominating character. John and Charles were sons of Samuel Wesley (1662–1735), the pious Anglican rector of Epworth, Lincolnshire, although Samuel's abundantly gifted wife Susanna (1669–1742) had a more deeply formative influence on John and Charles. She was the Anthusa to their Chrysostom, the Monica to their Augustine.[3]

At its zenith, the Holy Club had some ten or eleven dedicated members, and another ten or eleven less committed associates. Other members of note besides Whitefield and the Wesley brothers included James Hervey (1714–58), who went on to write some of the most significant spiritual literature of the early Revival[4]; Benjamin Ingham (1712–72), later a Moravian

---

2. Anglicans alone were allowed to study at Oxford or Cambridge, England's only two universities at that time. The universities were regarded as belonging to the Anglican establishment.

3. Samuel and Susanna Wesley had a less than ideal marriage, both being strong-minded persons who on occasion went their own way. In 1701 Susanna embraced the Jacobite cause (the belief that Britain's deposed Stuart dynasty was the rightful ruling house), which caused such marital disruption that she and Samuel separated for eight months. Samuel held that the Stuarts had lost the right to rule Britain when their last king, James II, had fled the country in 1688. See Chapter 3, Part 4, for the Jacobite cause in the 18th Century.

4. See Part 4, section 2 for more about Hervey.

evangelist in Yorkshire[5]; and John Gambold (died 1771), who became a Moravian bishop and hymnwriter.[6]

The 'methodical' spirituality of the Holy Club involved living in voluntary poverty, visiting prisoners and the poor, and distributing food, clothing, Bibles, and Anglican Prayer Books. They studied the classic literature of piety: Thomas a Kempis' *Imitation of Christ*, the writings of Anglicanism's 'spiritual Shakespeare' Jeremy Taylor (1613–67), and the more recent yet highly esteemed works of the Nonjuror William Law (1686–1761), such as Law's *Serious Call to a Devout and Holy Life* and *Christian Perfection*.[7] On a daily basis, Holy Club members followed a rigorous religious routine: on Mondays, Wednesdays, Fridays, and Saturdays, they engaged in prayer at noon; every day of the week, they prayed at 9 am, 12 midday, and 3 pm, using one of the Anglican Prayer Book's 'collects'[8]; on Wednesdays and Fridays they fasted, and between midday

---

5. See Chapter 5, Part Two for a full account of the Moravians.
6. Gambold's most famous hymn was his *O tell me no more of this world's vain store*, with its stanza:

    And when I'm to die
    'Receive me!' I'll cry,
    For Jesus hath loved me, I cannot tell why;
    But this I do find,
    We two are so joined,
    He'll not live in heaven and leave me behind.

7. The Non-jurors were Anglicans who had quarrelled with their mother Church after the Glorious Revolution of 1688–9, which had removed James II from the throne, replacing him with William of Orange. Most Anglican clergy had been willing to swear allegiance to William and pray for him as England's lawful king, but a minority had refused, believing that their oath of loyalty to James II and his descendants (of the Stuart dynasty) was inviolable. Some of these Non-jurors went into a state of schism against the Church of England, and the Nonjuring schism lasted until the end of the 18th Century. Many Non-jurors were very pious and learned men. William Law (1686–1761) had the widest influence, through his devotional writings. See Volume 4, Chapter 4, Part 2, section 6.
8. A collect is a 'gathering together' prayer, from the Latin *collecta*. The idea is that the prayer 'gathers together' into a single, short, comprehensive prayer the prayers of the congregation on a particular topic.

and 1 pm, they meditated on the cross; on Sundays between 3 and 4 pm, they meditated on Kempis' *Imitation of Christ*; they partook of Holy Communion every Sunday; and they fasted during Lent, during which they ate no meat.

It will be noted that at this early stage, the Holy Club Methodists were High Church Anglicans, rather than Calvinists or Puritans, in their religious attitudes. In some ways, this High Church Anglicanism would carry over into their very Evangelicalism, such as in the partisan devotion to the Church of England that marked some of them –including George Whitefield in the earlier part of his evangelistic career (Isaac Watts would accuse him of being an Anglican bigot), and John Wesley's lifelong refusal to break with Anglicanism in spite of its official hostility to his preaching.

Whitefield's membership in the Holy Club proved life-changing. As he immersed himself in the Club's 'literature of piety', he encountered the Scottish classic, *The Life of God in the Soul of Man*, by 17th Century Scottish Episcopalian, Henry Scougal (1650–78). Its impact on Whitefield was profound, especially its teaching on the necessity of the new birth. In Whitefield's words:

> God showed me that I must be born again, or be damned! I learned that a man may go to church, say his prayers, receive the sacrament, and yet not be a Christian. How did my heart rise and shudder, like a poor man that is afraid to look into his account-book, lest he should find himself a bankrupt. 'Shall I burn this book [i.e. *The Life of God in the Soul of Man*]? Shall I throw it down? Or shall I search it?' I did search it; and, holding the book in my hand, thus addressed the God of heaven and earth: 'Lord, if I am not a Christian, or if I am not a real one, for Jesus Christ's sake, show me what Christianity is that I may not be damned at last!' God soon showed me, for in reading a few lines further, that 'true religion is a union of the soul with God, and Christ formed within us', a ray of divine light was instantaneously darted in upon my soul, and from that moment, but not till then, did I know that I must become a new creature.

Whitefield went on to read William Law's *Serious Call,* and (significantly) three Puritan classics – Richard Baxter's *Call to the Unconverted,* Joseph Alleine's *Alarm to Unconverted Sinners,* and Matthew Henry's *Commentary on the Bible.* In this literary transition to the old Puritanism of 17th Century England, we see the Evangelicalism of the 18th Century taking form. Whitefield again records:

> Above all, my mind being now more opened and enlarged, I began to read the Holy Scriptures upon my knees, laying aside all other books, and praying over, if possible, every line and word. This proved meat indeed and drink indeed to my soul. I daily received fresh life, light, and power from above. I got more true knowledge from reading the book of God in one month than I could ever have acquired from all the writings of men.

Whitefield describes the moment of his eventual Evangelical conversion thus:

> One day, perceiving an uncommon drought and a noisome clamminess in my mouth, and using things to allay my thirst, but in vain, it was suggested to me that when Jesus Christ cried out 'I thirst', His sufferings were near over. Upon this I threw myself upon the bed and cried out, I thirst, I thirst .... When I said those words, 'I thirst, I thirst', my soul was in an agony; I thirsted for God's salvation and a sense of divine love. I thirsted for a clear discovery of my pardon through Jesus Christ, and the seal of the Spirit. I was at the same time enabled to look up to and act faith upon the glorious Lord Jesus as dying for sinners, and felt the blessed effects of it. Soon after, I perceived my load to go off; a spirit of mourning was taken from me, and I knew what it was truly to rejoice in the Lord. At first after this I could not avoid singing psalms wherever I was.

This was in the Spring of 1735. The Evangelical Revival had not quite begun, but its foremost public instrument had been prepared.

2. Dawn of the English Revival: Whitefield's preaching

Whitefield was ordained as an Anglican deacon in June 1736, at the age of twenty-one. His bishop, Martin Benson (1689–1752) of Gloucester, told him he was two years younger than he should have been for ordination, but Benson was so impressed by Whitefield's piety that he set aside the rule. One week later, Whitefield preached his first sermon in the Church of St Mary de Crypt in his home city of Gloucester. It was reported to Bishop Benson that his preaching had driven fifteen people mad, but Benson took no adverse action; in fact, he frankly asserted that he hoped the 'mad' folk would not forget their madness before the following Sunday! Clearly Whitefield's outspoken, emotional style, and 'ye must be born again' message, had shaken a sleepy congregation wide awake, although evidently not everyone appreciated being awakened. Whitefield's pulpit manner was distinctly and unusually theatrical: he would cry out, stamp his feet, weep, 'act out' biblical characters and events, and invent his own conversations with different figures from the scriptural narrative. His voice was loud and penetrating – no one could fail to hear or fall asleep when Whitefield was 'performing'.

George Whitefield

Whitefield then went to London, to a temporary position at Tower Chapel, preaching in many of London's Anglican churches on weekdays and Sundays. His dramatic pulpit oratory and prevalent theme of the new birth made waves of sensation, and for a time he was the talk of London. Admirers hailed him as a second Wycliffe, the Morning Star of a new English Reformation. Unfortunately, this adulation had a swelling effect on Whitefield's head, making him a ferocious critic of anyone who dared to question his style or methods. He later confessed this to a brother minister: 'Success, I fear, elated my mind. I did not behave to you, and other ministers of Christ, with that humility which became me.'

It may also be worth observing that most modern students of Whitefield are probably accustomed to visualizing the later, somewhat corpulent preacher, but in this earliest phase of his ministry Whitefield cut a very different figure. As one contemporary wrote:

> He looked almost angelical, a young slim tender youth. He looked as if he was clothed with authority from the great God. A sweet solemnity sat upon his brow.

He also had a pronounced squint, for which critics often mocked him as 'Dr Squintum'. Others, however, regarded the squint as a mysterious token of divine favour – he had one eye fixed on heaven, it was said, and the other on hell.

The slim, angelical, and squint-eyed Whitefield's bold experiment in revival preaching in England was soon interrupted, as he left for America (not yet an independent or united country), travelling to the newly established city of Savannah in the southern Colony of Georgia. Here he remained for a year (1737–38). He was following in the footsteps of his friend John Wesley, who had been working as an Anglican 'missionary' in Savannah for almost two years (preaching to his fellow Anglicans, founding one of America's first Sunday schools, trying to make Christian contact with native peoples).

On a spiritually troubled and exhausted Wesley's departure back to England (see below), Whitefield stepped into his place, becoming priest in charge of Savannah's Christchurch parish. Here he conceived it as integral to his life's work to build an orphanage – Bethesda, as it would be called when set up in 1740. Georgia's humid and subtropical climate, and various diseases unknown in Britain, had orphaned many colonist children.

Others had been forsaken by their parents, who had arrived in Georgia from debtors' prison to work off their debts, but then fled to freedom and a new life in northern colonies where their identities were unknown – abandoning their children in Georgia. Whitefield felt an overwhelming constraint to show practical Christian care for the orphans.

Returning to London in December 1738 to raise funds for his new orphanage project, Whitefield was ordained to the Anglican priesthood. Despite his ecclesiastical 'upgrade', however, he found that public opinion had now turned significantly against his style of preaching. Many of the Anglican clergy were professing themselves scandalised by his emotive proclamation of the necessity of the new birth – why should Anglican churchgoers need to be born again, when they had been baptised?

Although this hostility was by no means universal, the unexpected closure of many Anglican churches and pulpits to Whitefield inspired him to take what proved a momentous step – to engage in open-air preaching. He was driven to this, not simply by his experience of being barred from Anglican pulpits, but also by an increasing concern over the myriads who no longer attended any place of worship in 'Christian' England. Perhaps Whitefield could reach them outside the ineffective framework of the Anglican parish system? In consequence, on Wednesday February 21st 1739, Whitefield preached his first open-air sermon on Hanham Mount at Kingswood near Bristol, to a large body of miners (estimated at 2,000). Many of them stopped to hear the strange preacher, and the effect of Whitefield's captivating Gospel-oratory was stunning. He recorded it thus:

> Having no righteousness of their own to renounce, they were glad to hear of a Jesus who was a friend to publicans, and came not to call the righteous but sinners to repentance. The first discovery of their being affected was the sight of the white gutters made by their tears, which plentifully fell down their black cheeks as they came out of their coal-pits. Hundreds of them were soon brought under deep conviction which,

> as the event proved, happily ended in a sound and thorough conversion. The change was visible to all, though numbers chose to impute it to anything, rather than the finger of God.

On the following Friday, Whitefield repeated the experiment, this time drawing an audience of between four and five thousand. On Sunday, he reckoned that 10,000 came to hear him:

> I hastened to Kingswood. There were about 10,000 people to hear me. The trees and hedges were full. All was hush when I began; the sun shone bright and God enabled me to preach for an hour with great power, and so loudly that all, I was told, could hear me. The fire is kindled in this country and I know all the devils in hell shall not be able to quench it.

The success of Whitefield's open-air venture at Kingswood set the pattern for the rest of his life. He would be a travelling preacher, who often used open-air settings for proclaiming throughout Britain, to its unconverted multitudes, the old Reformation Gospel of a free justification and new birth in Christ, experienced immediately in the event and gift of faith rather than moral works or church rituals. He would use the same open-air, itinerant method to communicate the same message in America.

3. Dawn of the English Revival: John Wesley's spiritual journey

Although Whitefield was the most eloquent and impactful preacher of the new Evangelical movement, it was his friend and fellow Holy Club member, John Wesley, who left the deepest mark in public historical consciousness.[9] To this day, most people who know something of England's Evangelical Revival associate it more with the name of Wesley than Whitefield. We shall consider the reasons for this a little later.

Wesley's journey to Evangelical faith was rather different from that of Whitefield. He had from childhood been a serious

9. For the already existing friendship between Wesley and Whitefield through the Holy Club, see Part 2, section 1.

John Wesley

High Church Anglican. However, Wesley seemed to sense that something significant was absent from his piety. It first came home to him experientially during his voyage to Savannah, Georgia, in January 1735. The ship was caught in a violent storm, and Wesley was stricken with a stomach-churning fear of death. At one point, a massive wave swamped the ship, and sea water flooded into the cabins. The English passengers were crying out in panic – but a group of German Moravians on the ship simply sang hymns, apparently calm and joyful. Wesley was staggered. He recorded his impressions of the Moravians in his journal:

> Of their humility they had given a continual proof, by performing those servile offices for the other passengers, which none of the English would undertake; for which they desired, and would receive no pay, saying, 'it was good for their proud hearts,' and 'their loving Saviour had done more for them.' And every day had given them occasion of showing a meekness which no injury could move. If they were pushed, struck, or thrown down, they rose again and went away; but no complaint was found in their mouth. There was now an opportunity of trying whether they were delivered from the spirit of fear, as well as from that of pride, anger, and revenge. In the midst of the Psalm wherewith their service began, the sea broke over, split the main-sail in pieces, covered the ship and poured in between the decks, as if the great deep had already swallowed us up. A terrible screaming began among the English. The Germans calmly sung on. I asked one of them afterwards; 'Were you not afraid?' He answered, 'I thank God, no.' I asked: 'But were not your women and children afraid?' He

> replied mildly: 'No, our women and children are not afraid to die.'

Haunted by the experience, Wesley – once he was in Georgia – struck up a friendship with Moravian Bishop August Gottlieb Spangenberg (1704–92), who was conducting missionary work among native Americans and black slaves. Spangenberg counselled Wesley on spiritual matters: the new birth, assurance of personal salvation. Wesley was fascinated but disturbed, increasingly convinced that he lacked true saving faith. Despite this, he devoted himself to his preaching, pastoral, and missionary work in Savannah. When, however, he returned from Georgia to England in 1738, he famously wrote in his journal on February 1st:

> It is now two years and almost four months since I left my native country in order to teach the Georgian Indians [native Americans] the nature of Christianity – but what have I learned myself in the meantime? Why (what I the last of all suspected), that I, who went to America to convert others, was never myself converted to God ... This, then, have I learned in the ends of the earth: that I am fallen short of the glory of God, that my whole heart is altogether corrupt and abominable, and, consequently, my whole life (seeing that it cannot be that an evil tree should bring forth good fruit) is alienated from the life of God. I am a child of wrath, an heir of Hell. My own works, my own sufferings and my own righteousness are so far from making any atonement for the least of my sins, which are more in number than the hairs of my head. The best of them need atonement or they cannot abide His righteous judgment. Having the sentence of death in my heart, and having nothing in or of myself to plead, I have no hope but that of being justified freely through the redemption that is in Jesus.
>
> If it were said that I have faith (for many such things have I heard from many miserable comforters), I answer, so have the devils a sort of faith, but still they are strangers to the covenant of promise. The faith I want is a sure trust and confidence in God; that through the merits of Christ my sins are forgiven and I am reconciled to the favour of God. I want

> that faith which enables everyone who has it to cry out, 'I live, yet not I, but Christ liveth in me: and the life which I now live in the flesh, I live by the faith of the Son of God, who loved me and gave Himself for me' (Gal. 2:20).[10]

In England, Wesley was once again drawn to the Moravians, forming a friendship with Peter Boehler (1712–75) of Frankfurt, another Moravian missionary, ordained by the great Moravian leader Nicolaus von Zinzendorf.[11] Boehler was preparing for work in America, where he would establish many Moravian settlements in the religiously tolerant Colony of Pennsylvania. Wesley and Boehler conversed in depth on the true nature of saving faith in Christ. Boehler convinced Wesley that scripture taught justification by faith, with faith as a lively confidence in God's mercy for Jesus' sake; and to Wesley's rejoinder that such faith might have been limited to apostolic times, Boehler pointed to actual examples of the same faith in his and Wesley's day. All Wesley could now do was admit that such faith was not yet his.

Although Wesley's absence of personal assurance had now pushed him to the brink of abandoning the Anglican ministry, Boehler advised him to press on, with the suggestion, 'Preach faith until you have it.' This encouraged a downcast Wesley to persevere in his pastoral calling. He took Boehler's advice quite literally, preaching to others the Gospel of salvation through faith alone in Christ alone, despite lacking any sense that he had any such faith himself. He was astonished when one prisoner to whom he ministered underwent an immediate and profound conversion in response to Wesley's message.

---

10. Wesley's return to England was motivated by serious personal and pastoral problems in Savannah. He had been engaged (at least according to his own understanding of the situation) to a lady named Sophie Hopkey, but would not set any date for their marriage. At length, she broke off the relationship and married another man, William Williamson. When Sophie next appeared in Wesley's church, he excommunicated her. Sophie's husband then initiated legal proceedings to prosecute Wesley for defaming his wife's character. The judge's wife was Sophie's aunt. At this point, Wesley chose to leave America.

11. See Chapter 5, Part 2 for a detailed account of Zinzendorf.

At length, the decisive moment for Wesley came at a Moravian-led 'religious society'. This was a society for the mutual edification of its members, a highly significant form of Moravian religious life which would be massively adopted by English Evangelicals. The society met in a Moravian chapel in London's Aldersgate Street, on May 24th 1738. Wesley recorded in his journal:

> In the evening I went very unwillingly to a society in Aldersgate Street, where one was reading Luther's preface to the Epistle to the Romans. About a quarter before nine, while he was describing the change which God works in the heart through faith in Christ, I felt my heart strangely warmed. I felt I did trust in Christ, Christ alone for salvation, and an assurance was given me that He had taken away my sins, even mine, and saved me from the law of sin and death.

By a remarkable coincidence or providence, John's younger brother Charles had experienced conversion three days before – as an immediate fruit of which he penned the hymn *Where shall my wondering soul begin?* John straightaway told Charles of his own conversion. In his journal Charles wrote: 'Towards ten, my brother was brought in triumph by a troop of our friends, and declared, "I believe." We sang the hymn [*Where shall my wondering soul begin?*] with great joy, and parted with prayer.'

Wesley's account of his 'heart-warming' conversion at the Aldersgate Street meeting is the most celebrated conversion-story in the English language. The perhaps surprisingly key influence of Martin Luther on Wesley's conversion pointed forward to a fruitful connection between Methodism (as Wesley's English form of Evangelicalism would come to be called) and Lutheranism, with future Methodist academics making acclaimed studies of Luther's theology – notably Philip S. Watson's *Let God be God! An Interpretation of the Theology of Martin Luther* (1947), Gordon Rupp's *Luther's Progress to the Diet of Worms* (1951) and *The Righteousness of God: Luther Studies* (1953), and Arthur Skevington

Wood's *Captive to the Word: Martin Luther, Doctor of Sacred Scripture* (1969). Wesley himself remained a lifelong admirer of Luther and his theology of justification by faith, but came to think that Luther and the Lutheran tradition had been disastrously deficient in appreciating the grace of sanctification.

For a time, the Wesleys were happy to be part of the Moravian religious society that met in London's Fetter Lane. In June 1740, however, Wesley and the Moravians decisively parted ways over differing understandings of the nature of saving faith: the Moravian view was that such faith involved immediate and perfect assurance of salvation, which Wesley disputed. They also disagreed over whether those lacking this assurance should be discouraged from participating in the means of grace (the Moravians thought they should, whereas Wesley held that the means of grace were intended precisely to build up the desired assurance). Whitefield also parted company with the Moravians over his increasingly vigorous advocacy of Calvinism.

The exalted religious atmosphere of the early Revival is well attested in John Wesley's journal. For example, his entry for January 1st 1739 reads:

> Mr. Hall, Kinchin, Ingham, Whitefield, Hatchins, and my brother Charles, were present at our love-feast in Fetter Lane,[12] with about sixty of our brethren. About three in the morning, as we were continuing constant in prayer, the power of God came mightily upon us, in so much that many cried out for exceeding joy, and many fell to the ground. As soon as we were recovered a little from that awe and amazement at the presence of His Majesty, we broke out with one voice, 'We praise Thee, O God; we acknowledge Thee to be the Lord.'[13]

---

12. The Moravians had reintroduced the ancient Christian practice of the love-feast. See Chapter 5, Part 2, section 4, under the heading **Social religion**.
13. The first line of the traditional English translation of the *Te Deum*, the most illustrious of Latin patristic hymns.

The sense of the presence of God seems to have been remarkable for the participants in the Revival. Although it was probably more intense in the period 1738–42, when the Revival was at its most impactful, it by no means dissipated, and helped carry preachers and Evangelical converts through sometimes brutal experiences of persecution.[14]

One year after his 'Aldersgate experience' of May 1738, Wesley took the crucial step of following Whitefield into open-air preaching. This was at Whitefield's invitation; he was returning to Georgia again, and wished Wesley to carry on the evangelistic work Whitefield had pioneered in and around Bristol. So it was that on April 2nd 1739, having overcome his doubts about the open-air method, Wesley preached his first open-air sermon at St Philip's Marsh, near Bristol.

> In the evening I reached Bristol, and met Mr Whitefield there. I could scarcely reconcile myself at first to this strange way of preaching in the fields, of which he set me an example on Sunday: having been all my life (till very lately) so tenacious of every point relating to decency and order, that I should have thought the saving of souls almost a sin, if it had not been done in church.

Wesley proved as effective an open-air preacher to mass audiences as Whitefield, although their styles were different: Wesley was less emotional and theatrical than Whitefield, more narrowly focused on delivering a straightforward doctrinal message. But his delivery was powerful, and multitudes were soon professing conversion under his ministry. Wesley thereupon continued his path of following Whitefield's trailblazing example, becoming a travelling preacher, throughout England and further afield, who everywhere exploited the open-air meeting as a chief instrument for reaching the ungodly or totally unchurched masses. Remarkably, perhaps, Wesley never enjoyed open-air preaching ('field-preaching', as he called it), but submitted to it as a God-given means of reaching greater numbers. As he commented in 1759:

---

14. For the persecution of Methodists, see Part 9.

> I preached to twice the people we should have had at the house [church]. What marvel the devil does not love field-preaching! Neither do I: I love a commodious room, a soft cushion, a handsome pulpit. But where is my zeal, if I do not trample all these under foot in order to save one more soul?

In Whitefield and Wesley, the Evangelical Revival now had its two 'star' preachers: undoubtedly two of the most successful publicists for the Protestant Gospel the English-speaking world has ever known. Both were Anglicans, and both would live, minister, and die as Anglicans. Soon there was a small, dedicated army of Evangelical preachers in the Church of England (see below), walking in the way pioneered by Whitefield and Wesley. Many of these would function in the setting of a settled parish ministry, and despite evangelising outside their parish boundaries, none had the nationwide itinerancy of Whitefield or Wesley. Still, their spiritual message was that of Whitefield and Wesley, and their proclamation of the message as forthright, zealous, and transformative, albeit in a less widespread sphere. Anglicanism was thus the birthplace of the Revival, and for a generation would be its main arena of activity. It was not until the latter part of the 18th Century that English Dissent would begin to be as deeply affected as the Anglican Church by the Evangelical movement.[15]

15. See Part 6 for the Revival and Dissent.

3
Revival disrupted: the Calvinist-Arminian controversy

The 'golden' years of the English Evangelical Revival were roughly 1738–42, in the sense that these four or five years saw the most immediate and numerically fruitful effects of the preaching of Whitefield and Wesley (and others associated with them). This does not mean that the Revival thereafter dwindled away, only that it made its most intensive and extensive impact in that period. Certainly, however, it did not peter out; it flowed on richly for decades. But in early 1741 it would face one of its severest challenges: the disruption of its own unity in the Calvinist-Arminian controversy.

1. Origins of the controversy

Whitefield left England in August 1739 to further his orphanage project in Georgia. By then, thousands had professed conversion under his preaching; he entrusted them to the spiritual care of Wesley. Back in England in March 1741, however, Whitefield found to his shock that many of 'his' converts now shunned him. This startling turnabout was the result of Wesley's decision, in Whitefield's absence, to advocate very publicly for an Arminian understanding of grace, and a doctrine of the possibility of sinless perfection prior to the believer's death and glorification. Wesley was very successful, winning over large numbers to his Arminianism. These were the men and women who now cold-shouldered Whitefield as a known Calvinist.

Whitefield does not seem to have been a convinced or articulate Calvinist at the beginning of his converted life in 1735. However, he grew in his appreciation for the theology of Calvinism, a process nurtured by his reading of Puritan literature. By 1737, he was clearly a Calvinist. His commitment to Calvinism was then further deepened in 1740 by his close contact in America with Calvinists like Gilbert Tennent of New Brunswick in New Jersey and Jonathan Edwards of Northampton, Massachusetts.[1] Whitefield's widening acquaintance with historic Reformed theology fostered his assurance that he had not misread the Bible: 'This is my comfort, the doctrines I have taught are the doctrines of Scripture, the doctrines of our own and of other Reformed Churches.'

Wesley, by contrast, remained within the High Church Arminian tradition of his Anglican childhood. His father Samuel, Anglican rector of Epworth, had been a High Church Arminian, having abandoned the Calvinism of his youth within English Dissent. We also know that Samuel Wesley's best-loved commentator on scripture was the great Dutch Arminian, Hugo Grotius (1583–1645). Samuel's own theology anticipated major themes in his son's teaching, such as John's doctrine of prevenient grace (see below). Samuel had a number of published works to his credit, including a discourse on Holy Communion and a poetic life of Christ; in several of these, he denounced the Calvinist doctrine of election. Samuel's wife Susannah was equally anti-Calvinist, writing in a letter to John in 1725 (when he was twenty-two):

> The Doctrine of Predestination, as maintained by rigid Calvinists, is very shocking, and ought utterly to be abhorred; because it charges the most holy God with being the Author of Sin.

John evidently treasured this letter, printing it in the first issue of his publishing venture, *The Arminian Magazine*. He was also acquainted with some of the writings of Arminius himself, from at least 1731.

---

1. For Tennent see Chapter 4, Part 2, section 2, and for Edwards section 3.

From his upbringing and studies, then, John Wesley absorbed a lifelong understanding of Arminian theology as far superior to Calvinism in safeguarding the genuineness of God's love for all, and the practical necessity of striving to 'enter in at the strait gate', and then remaining on the narrow way through living faith made manifest in sanctification. Calvinism, for Wesley, threatened these fundamental truths.

Perceiving Whitefield's increasing zeal for Calvinism, therefore, as a menace to the spiritual purity and flourishing of the Evangelical movement, Wesley had already, even before Whitefield's departure to America in August 1739, preached a strongly Arminian sermon entitled *Free Grace* in March, and had it published two weeks later, the first of eleven printed editions – Wesley clearly regarded the sermon as an Arminian 'manifesto' of permanent worth. In this sermon Wesley made the (to Calvinists) notorious assertion that the God of Calvinism was worse than the devil:

> You represent God as worse than the devil; more false, more cruel, more unjust. But you say you will prove it by Scripture. Hold! What will you prove by Scripture? That God is worse than the devil? It cannot be. Whatever that Scripture proves, it never can prove this; whatever its true meaning be, this cannot be its true meaning.

One might think this was outspoken enough; but with Whitefield's partially restraining influence removed through his transatlantic trip, Wesley became far more pugnacious and polemical in his Arminianism. Among other things, he published a new hymnbook for the Revival movement in July 1740 which contained hymns asserting universal redemption and the possibility of sinless perfection on earth. Reports of Wesley's anti-Calvinist militancy at length prompted Whitefield to reply from America in December 1740, defending Calvinist beliefs and criticising the hymnbook and the *Free Grace* sermon:

> Dear, dear Sir, O be not offended! For Christ's sake be not rash! Give yourself to reading. Study the covenant of grace. Down with your carnal reasoning. Be a little child; and then,

> instead of pawning your salvation, as you have done in a late hymn book (if the doctrine of universal redemption be not true) – instead of talking of sinless perfection, as you have done in the preface to that hymn book, and making man's salvation to depend on his own free will, as you have in this sermon – you will compose a hymn in praise of sovereign distinguishing love. You will caution believers against striving to work a perfection out of their own hearts, and print another sermon the reverse of this, and entitle it 'Free Grace Indeed.' Free, not because free to all; but free, because God may withhold or give it to whom and when He pleases.
>
> Till you do this, I must doubt whether or not you know yourself. In the meanwhile, I cannot but blame you for censuring the clergy of our church for not keeping to their articles, when you yourself by your principles, positively deny the 9th, 10th and 17th [the more Calvinist statements in the Anglican Church's 39 Articles of Religion].
>
> Dear Sir, these things ought not so to be. God knows my heart, as I told you before, so I declare again, nothing but a single regard to the honour of Christ has forced this letter from me. I love and honour you for His sake; and when I come to judgment, will thank you before men and angels, for what you have, under God, done for my soul.
>
> There, I am persuaded, I shall see dear Mr. Wesley convinced of election and everlasting love. And it often fills me with pleasure to think how I shall behold you casting your crown down at the feet of the Lamb, and as it were filled with a holy blushing for opposing the divine sovereignty in the manner you have done.

Undaunted by this rebuke, in a public meeting in February 1741 Wesley tore up Whitefield's published letter, exhorting everyone else who had a copy to do the same. He claimed he did this because it was a private letter published without Whitefield's consent; but the symbolic gesture of ripping it up in public may have had a different emotional impact on others, convincing them that Wesley was doctrinally at war with Whitefield – a basically true perception. To compound matters, Wesley also now had his offending Arminian *Free Grace* sermon/manifesto republished in America.

2. The Evangelical Arminianism of John and Charles Wesley

John Wesley's Arminian theology was rooted, not in rationalism (i.e., the view that human nature retains significant inherent goodness despite the fall of Adam), but in his perception of the universal significance of Christ's redemptive work for a human race hopelessly fallen and lost in Adam. We can summarize Wesley's form of Arminianism as follows:

- Free-will is a supernatural gift of grace, flowing through the saving work of Christ and granted to all human beings. This gift offsets the total depravity inherited from Adam, so that all now have the grace-given ability to respond to the Holy Spirit. In Wesleyan terminology this was 'prevenient grace'. (The word 'prevenient' stems from the Latin *praevenire*, to come before.) Confusingly, Calvinists have also used the term 'prevenient grace', but in Calvinism it refers to an *efficacious* grace that positively awakens, illuminates, and regenerates the sinner. In Wesley's theology, prevenient grace bestows the *ability* to cooperate with the Spirit – and thus, ultimately, the possibility of faith – but it does not make it certain that the sinner will choose to cooperate.
- Conditional election: God chooses people for eternal salvation on the basis of His foreknowledge of how they will use their grace-given gift of free-will to respond to the Gospel.
- Universal atonement: Christ died in the place of all, with the intention of saving all, thus expressing His equal love for all.
- The possibility of the believer's total and final fall from grace – no assurance of ultimate salvation is possible.

Wesley's younger brother Charles was as adamant in Arminian conviction as John (Charles spoke in his journal of the 'poison of Calvin'), and he lent the full force of his personality, position, and talents to spreading Arminianism and combating Calvinism. The most brilliant hymnwriter of the Revival, Charles gave a vibrant expression to his anti-Calvinist belligerency in a series of hymns written for the express purpose of refuting, indeed mocking, Calvinist distinctives – his *Hymns on God's Everlasting Love* (1741). A specimen from this collection shows the aggressive, no-holds-barred character of the Wesleys' Arminianism and anti-Calvinism. Charles Wesley represented Calvinists thus:

> To limit Thee they dare,
> Blaspheme Thee to Thy face,
> Deny their fellow-worms a share
> In Thy redeeming grace:
> All for their own they take,
> Thy righteousness engross;
> Of none effect to most they make
> The merits of Thy cross.
>
> Sinners, abhor the fiend:
> His *other* Gospel hear –
> 'The God of truth did not intend
> The thing His words declare!
> He offers grace to all
> Which most cannot embrace,
> Mocked with an ineffectual call
> And insufficient grace.
>
> 'The righteous God consigned
> Them over to their doom,
> And sent the Saviour of mankind
> To damn them from the womb:
> To damn for falling short
> Of what they could not do,
> For not believing the report
> Of that which was not true.
>
> 'The God of love *passed by*
> The most of those that fell,
> Ordained poor reprobates to die,
> And forced them into hell.'
> 'He did not do the deed,'
> (Some have more mildly raved),
> 'He did not *damn* them – but decreed
> They never should be saved.

'He did not them bereave
Of life, or stop their breath;
His grace He only would not give,
And starved their souls to death.'
Satanic sophistry!
But still, all-gracious God,
They charge the sinner's death on Thee,
Who bought'st him with Thy blood.

At the same time, as Whitefield's December 1740 letter shows, John Wesley was also developing pronounced views on 'Christian perfection' that served to put him even more at odds with traditional Calvinism. We find these perfectionist views set out most fully in his later 1767 classic treatise, *A Plain Account of Christian Perfection*. He also called sinless perfection 'entire sanctification', 'perfect love', and 'the second blessing'. According to Wesley, this blessing, attainment, or experience delivered the believer from all voluntary sin, though not from weaknesses and temptations. Sin he famously defined as 'a voluntary transgression of a known law which it is in our power to obey' (not a Calvinist definition). The blessing of Christian perfection, Wesley argued, was received by faith, and given instantly. It could be received at any moment, and lost again. These views were contrary to the Augustinian/Reformed (and Lutheran) belief that the regenerate remained locked in daily conflict with 'indwelling sin' throughout their earthly pilgrimage, and that sinless perfection would be experienced only in heaven.

3. Effects of the controversy

Wesley's ardent advocacy of Arminianism, and Whitefield's equally zealous Calvinism, split the entire English Evangelical movement in half from Whitefield's homecoming to England in March 1741. Whitefield's return gave Calvinists a formidable figurehead in their opposition to Wesley's teaching, and Whitefield lost no time in preaching forthrightly on the doctrines of election and particular redemption (on one notable occasion, we are told, while Charles Wesley sat beside him grinding his teeth in furious frustration). John Wesley by now had begun organising 'his' converts into Moravian-type religious societies for mutual edification, known as the 'United Societies', leavened by Wesley's Arminian teaching; independent of these, the expansion occurred of alternative 'Calvinistic Methodist' Societies where, as the name indicates, Calvinism was the theological orthodoxy. Whitefield assumed leadership of the Calvinistic Methodist Societies.

This division of the Evangelical religious societies on Calvinist-Arminian lines was the visible fracturing of the Revival. Howell Harris, one of the foremost Revival figures in Wales,[2] endeavoured in the later 1740s to reconcile these now divergent, even antagonistic, forms of Evangelical life, but without success. Harris found that Calvinists were utterly unwilling to accept Wesley in any leadership role, while Arminians were unprepared to grant any leadership role to Whitefield. Indeed, Harris lost credibility by his fruitless attempts to unite them, and this was one reason why he had to withdraw from public involvement in the Evangelical movement, retiring to his Welsh home at Trevecca.[3]

The Calvinist and Arminian Evangelicals, therefore, went their different ways, and the Revival henceforth was a deeply divided movement. As far as possible, this parting of the ways was based on a mutual agreement to disagree as agreeably as they could, although in practice the disagreement at times was very disagreeable; one visitor to a Calvinist meeting in London was informed that Wesley had told people, 'If you wish to be damned, go there, but if you wish to be saved, stay with me.' The visitor disbelieved this as malicious gossip, but the existence of such gossip nonetheless illustrates the gulf in sentiment now dividing many Calvinists and Arminians. There were still some connections between them; the Wesleyan United Societies, for example, welcomed Whitefield as a 'guest preacher', and there were other examples of 'sharing' preachers. Wesley and

2. For Harris, see Part 8, section 2.

3. It was not the only reason for Harris' withdrawal – see the account in Part 8, section 2.

Whitefield also made a sort of pact of peace that neither would erect chapels in a locality where the other had a functioning religious society.

Still, the breach in the movement was made, and from 1741 onward the Revival in England flowed in two essentially separate streams, Calvinist and Arminian, each with their own leadership, religious societies, literature, interpretation of church history, and standards of doctrine and piety. Neither Whitefield nor Wesley was happy with this division; each looked back to the Springtime days of the Revival, when preachers and converts were at one, as a kind of lost Eden. Whitefield spoke wistfully of the early years as a now vanished 'heaven on earth', when all Evangelicals had been 'like little children' in a single spiritual family. The two great preachers also blamed each other for destroying this paradise. When in 1765 Wesley composed his brief account of the Revival, his *Short History of Methodism*, he clearly expressed the view that it was Whitefield and Calvinists who had broken the unity of the early movement by their truculent and intolerant Calvinism:

> They [the Revival leaders and converts] were hitherto perfectly regular in all things, and zealously attached to the Church of England. Meantime, they began to be convinced, that 'by grace we are saved through faith;' that justification by faith was the doctrine of the Church, as well as of the Bible. As soon as they believed, they spake; salvation by faith being now their standing topic. Indeed this implied three things: (1.) That men are all, by nature, 'dead in sin,' and, consequently, 'children of wrath.' (2.) That they are 'justified by faith alone.' (3.) That faith produces inward and outward holiness: And these points they insisted on day and night. In a short time they became popular Preachers. The congregations were large wherever they preached. The former name was then revived; and all these gentlemen, with their followers, were entitled Methodists. In March, 1741, Mr. Whitefield, being returned to England, entirely separated from Mr. Wesley and his friends, because he [Wesley] did not hold the decrees [the Calvinist belief in God's unconditional and eternal purposes of grace focused on the salvation of the elect]. Here was the

> first breach, which warm men persuaded Mr. Whitefield to make merely for a difference of opinion. Those, indeed, who believed universal redemption had no desire at all to separate; but those who held particular redemption would not hear of any accommodation, being determined to have no fellowship with men that 'were in so dangerous errors.' So there were now two sorts of Methodists, so called; those for particular, and those for general, redemption [Calvinists and Arminians – 'particular redemption' expressing the Calvinist belief in the 'particularity' of God's grace in election and the extent of the atonement, 'general redemption' expressing the Arminian belief in the universality of the atonement and its gift of prevenient grace to all].

On the other hand, Whitefield laid the burden of disunity at Wesley's door, pointing his finger at Wesley's anti-Calvinist *Free Grace* sermon of March 1739 as the beginning of all the troubles. Whoever was to blame, if indeed the 'blame' analysis is a correct or helpful model, English Evangelicalism has certainly been marked ever since, doctrinally and practically, by the Calvinist-Arminian divide that split asunder the river of Revival in the 18th Century.

4
Evangelical Calvinism in England

The widespread flowering of English Calvinistic Methodist Societies in the wake of Whitefield's preaching did not mean that Whitefield or the Societies had separated from the Church of England. The Societies were perfectly capable of functioning as voluntary associations while those belonging to them remained committed Anglicans in church membership. It was never Whitefield's intention to draw converts away from the Church of his ordination. Even when Whitefield's adherents in the Calvinist wing of the Revival built a preaching centre for him (a 'tabernacle', as he called it) in 1741 in London's Moorfields district, this was not intended as an act of schism against the Anglican Church. After all, Whitefield himself – the Tabernacle preacher – was and continued to be a loyal Anglican priest.

One chief effect of Whitefield's ministry, therefore, was to infuse a strong dose of Evangelical Calvinism into the established English Church. Other ordained men, touched by or caught up into the Revival, began proclaiming the new Evangelical Calvinism from Anglican pulpits in the context of the Anglican parish ministry. In their own geographically more limited way, these ministries had their decided effect alongside Whitefield's evangelism in promoting Evangelical Calvinism within the established Church, both through preaching and literary productivity. (Many of the Anglican Calvinists had a significant itinerant ministry, but not of Whitefield's nationwide reach.) It will be useful, then, to consider the most noteworthy of the Anglican Evangelical Calvinists and their impact.[1]

1. John Cennick (1718–55)

A descendant of a Moravian refugee, Cennick was born in Reading, Berkshire, and had a strict religious upbringing within the Anglican Church, although inwardly he hated it. However, at the age of nine, he was deeply impressed by the dying testimony of an aunt, who met her earthly end with a triumphant faith in Christ. The impression made on a young Cennick was unforgettable. Even so, he developed into a godless young man, whose chief delights were card games, dancing, and the theatre. These pleasures grew cold for Cennick when he turned seventeen, as his mind became burdened with a sense of sin, driving him to a state of spiritual despair that endured for two years. He described his experience thus:

> All this while I had no power over sin, nor the least strength to resist temptations, being carnal, and sold under sin, I committed it continually, though not in the eyes of the world. My chief sins were pride, murmuring against God, blasphemy, disobedience, and evil concupiscence; sometimes I strove against them, but finding myself always conquered, I concluded there was no help. Then was I weary of life, and often prayed that God would hide me in the grave.

Cennick was at last delivered in 1737 when he heard Psalm 34 being read during a church service:

> When I had entered the church, and fallen on my knees, I began murmuring (as I did often) because my cross seemed more heavy than ever was laid on anyone beside; and how untroubled all the children of God passed to Heaven, and how full of terror I must go down to Hell! and I was as if the sword of the Lord was dividing asunder my joints, and marrow: my soul and spirit; till near the end of the Psalms, when these words were read, 'Great are the troubles of the

1. I have arranged these accounts roughly in order of the date of the conversion of the men concerned.

> righteous, but the Lord delivereth him out of them all! And he that putteth his trust in God shall not be destitute': I had just room to think, who can be more destitute than me? when I was overwhelmed with joy, I believed there was mercy. My heart danced for joy, and my dying soul revived! I heard the voice of Jesus saying, I am thy salvation. I no more groaned under the weight of sin. The fear of hell was taken away, and being sensible [conscious] that Christ loved me, and died for me, I rejoiced in God, my Saviour.

Towards the end of 1738, Cennick discovered the published journal of George Whitefield, which impacted him deeply, so much so that he pled with God that he might come to know Whitefield personally. Hearing about a Methodist in Oxford University named Kinchin, Cennick journeyed there to find him, and found not only Kinchin but Whitefield and the Wesley brothers. In this way Cennick was initiated into the inner circle of Methodist leaders, soon joining their religious Society that met in the Fetter Lane Church in London in May 1739. John Wesley formed a sufficiently high opinion of Cennick to appoint him the following month as teacher in a school at the original Revival centre of Kingswood, Bristol, for the children of its miners. There, almost by accident, Cennick was thrust into open-air preaching, when the expected preacher one day did not turn up and the assembled listeners asked him to preach instead. This (it has been suggested) means he was the first Wesleyan lay preacher.

Cennick was present when the first strange physical reactions to John Wesley's preaching began to occur, in Kingswood and Bristol: the unnatural swelling of necks and tongues, profuse sweating, foaming at the mouth, and epileptic-style fits. Wesley thought these were supernatural signs from God, but Cennick attributed them to the devil:

> I often doubted if it was not of the enemy when I saw it, and disputed with Mr. Wesley for calling it the work of God ... And frequently, when none were agitated in the meetings, he [Wesley] prayed, Lord, where are Thy tokens and signs, etc., and I don't remember ever to have seen it otherwise than that

> on his so praying several men were seized and screamed out. I can't be persuaded but that, though there might be some who affected this, there was somewhat supernatural ... On Monday night I was preaching at the school on the forgiveness of sins when numbers cried out with a loud and bitter cry. Indeed, it seemed that the devil and the powers of darkness were come among us.

As the Calvinist-Arminian controversy grew, Cennick took the Calvinist side; this brought about his expulsion from the Wesley-dominated Kingswood Methodist Society in 1741. Cennick thereupon joined with Whitefield in London, where he was given pastoral responsibility for Whitefield's Tabernacle at Moorfields. In Wiltshire, he carried out a preaching tour that produced multitudes of converts and an extensive association of Calvinistic Methodist Societies. As a result, he was nicknamed 'the apostle of Wiltshire'.

However, Cennick at length became disillusioned with the Calvinistic Methodist Societies, troubled as they were by controversies over antinomianism. In his distress, Cennick found a refuge of peace among the Moravians – the church of his ancestors – who (he felt) avoided both the perfectionism of Wesley, and the potential for antinomianism among Calvinists. He went to Germany and met the Moravian leader Nicolaus von Zinzendorf, at that time banished from his community in Herrnhut and living in Marienborn Castle in Wetteravia; he also visited the Moravian community at Herrnhaag, a few miles from the castle. Overwhelmingly impressed by the piety of the Moravians, Cennick formally joined the Moravian Church in early 1746 (he was ordained to the Moravian diaconate in 1749).

After becoming a Moravian, in the summer of 1746 Cennick went to Ireland, which became the field of his evangelistic labours for the next nine years till his death in 1755. His Irish preaching met with widespread success, attracting large crowds; the rich fruit of this activity was the formation of around two hundred Moravian Societies in Ireland's northern counties. However, when Cennick stood at the peak of his labours and success, his mental and physical health broke down. Now seriously depressed, he abandoned the work in Ireland, and returned to London, arriving both exhausted and feverish. In this condition he died in the Moravian Fetter Lane church, at the youthful age of thirty-six, in July 1755, thus fulfilling one of his own poems:

> Now, Lord, at peace with Thee and all below,
> Let me depart, and to Thy Kingdom go.

Cennick was one of the significant hymnwriters of the Revival. Among his published collections of hymns were *Sacred Hymns, for the Children of God in the Days of Their Pilgrimage* (1741); *Sacred Hymns for the Use of Religious Societies* (1743); *A Collection of Sacred Hymns* (1749); and *Hymns to the Honour of Jesus Christ, Composed for Such Little Children as Desire to Be Saved* (1754). Cennick was the author of the original version of the popular hymn *Lo He comes with clouds descending*, revised by Charles Wesley. Three at least of Cennick's (unrevised) hymns have attained lasting acceptance: *Brethren, let us join to bless*, *A good High Priest is come*, and *Children of the heavenly King*. His grace before meals also retains a certain popularity:

> Be present at our table, Lord,
> Be here and everywhere adored;
> These mercies bless, and grant that we
> May feast in Paradise with Thee.

2. James Hervey (1713–58)

Hervey was one of the original Holy Club members in Oxford University. A native of Hardingstone, near Northampton, after his Oxford studies he held various ministerial positions in the Church of England. Ordained in 1737, he was curate at Dummer (in Hampshire), and chaplain at Stoke Abbey and curate at Bideford (both in Devon). Finally, from 1743 onward he pastored the parish of Weston Favell (near Northampton), initially as curate to his father, then as rector of the church himself from 1752. It was in 1741, while he was curate at Bideford, that Hervey finally and fully embraced Evangelical religion, a conversion to which he testified in two sermons known as his 'Recantation Sermons'. He described his conversion in a letter to George Whitefield:

> You are pleased to ask how the Holy Ghost convinced me of self-righteousness, and drove me out of my false rest. Indeed, sir, I cannot tell. The light was not instantaneous; it did not flash upon my soul, but arose like the dawning of the day. A little book by Jenks, upon 'Submission to the Righteousness of God,' was made serviceable to me. Your journals, dear sir, and sermons, especially that sweet sermon on the text, 'What think ye of Christ?' were a means of bringing me to the knowledge of the truth. Another piece has been also like precious eye-salve to my dim and clouded understanding – I mean Marshall's 'Gospel Mystery of Sanctification.' These, blessed be He who is a light to them that sit in darkness, have in some degree convinced me of my former errors. I now begin to see I have been labouring in the fire, and wearying myself for very vanity, while I have attempted to establish my own righteousness. I trusted I knew not what, while I trusted in some imaginary good deeds of my own ... As for my own beggarly performances, wretched righteousnesses, gracious Emmanuel! I am ashamed, I am grieved that I should thrust them into the plan of Thy divine, Thy inconceivably precious obedience! My schemes are altered. I now desire to work in my blessed Master's service, not *for* life, but *from* life and salvation.

Hervey became a close friend both of Whitefield and the Countess of Huntingdon,[2] decidedly adopting Calvinism, and strongly opposing Wesley's Arminianism and perfectionism. This was despite his having been personally very close to Wesley during their Oxford days.

One of the most erudite of the Evangelicals, Hervey exercised his largest and most lasting influence through his writings, which proved extremely popular. His two volumes of *Meditations and Contemplations* were phenomenally successful; first published in 1748, they went through fourteen editions in as many years, and reached their twenty-fifth edition in 1791. In

2. See section 11 for the Countess of Huntingdon.

this work, Hervey combined a reverential love of nature (there were sections entitled *Night, The Starry Heavens, Reflections on a Flower Garden, A Winter Piece, A Descant on Creation*) with an appreciation for what was then cutting-edge scientific investigation into nature. These were harnessed in the service of worshiping the God of nature and science: not the Supreme Being of Deism, but the Triune God of Christianity. The first entry in the work, *Meditations among the Tombs,* was particularly beloved – a prolonged contemplation of death and its meaning, giving special attention to 'premature' death (the young also die) and to the joy of reunion in heaven.

Alongside the *Meditations and Contemplations,* Hervey's three theological volumes of *Theron and Aspasio: or a Series of Dialogues and Letters upon the Most Important and Interesting Subjects* (1753) were also well-received in general, although some felt they pushed a Law-Gospel distinction to a potentially antinomian extreme. Doctrinally speaking, Hervey's literary output in essence was a repristinating of Puritanism for an 18th Century audience. He said of the Puritans:

> The Puritans, one and all of them, glory in the righteousness of their great Mediator; they extol His imputed righteousness in almost every page, and pour contempt on all other works compared with their Lord's. For my part I know no set of writers in the world so remarkable for this doctrine and diction. It quite distinguishes them from the generality of our modern treatises.

After his death, a volume of Hervey's letters was published in 1760 which further solidified his good public reputation.

Hervey was a strong influence on the great Romantic poet and artist William Blake (1757–1827), who admired Hervey's writings intensely. Blake made various references and allusions to Hervey in his own writings and his paintings.

3. William Grimshaw (1708–63)

A native of Brindle, near Preston, and educated at Cambridge University, Grimshaw had already been an ordained Anglican clergyman for ten years prior to his Evangelical conversion in 1741. His awakening came (like Whitefield's) through his reading; two Puritan works, John Owen's treatise on *The Doctrine of Justification by Faith,* and Thomas Brooks' *Precious Remedies Against Satan's Devices,* made a profound impact on him. He told a friend that after his conversion, 'if God had drawn up his Bible to heaven, and sent him down another, it could not have been newer to him.' Shaken by the thought that for ten years he had been a religious ignoramus dressed in clerical garb, Grimshaw devoted the rest of his life to proclaiming Christ – the Christ testified in the Gospel as understood by Evangelical Calvinism.

In his pulpit manner, Grimshaw was as intense and emotional as Whitefield, and his speaking style as plain and down-to-earth. This preaching ministry he carried out in the Anglican parish of Haworth in Yorkshire from May 1742, where his evangelism wrought a deep and widespread spiritual and moral renewal in Haworth itself and the nearby villages. When Grimshaw began his ministry in Haworth, only a dozen people attended Holy Communion in his church; as his ministry drew to a close, he estimated that 1,200 now flocked from the neighbouring communities to sit at the Lord's table during the Summer season.

Like Whitefield and Wesley, Grimshaw adopted the open-air itinerant method of evangelism; he travelled on horseback throughout an extensive area with Haworth as its epicentre, preaching both in the open air and in barns and chapels. Another Evangelical Calvinist, William Romaine (see below), spoke of Grimshaw as 'the most indefatigable preacher that ever there was in England'. From 1748, his itinerant evangelism included a large chunk of northern English territory, a preaching 'circuit' known as the Great Haworth Round, made up of the Furness district of Lancashire, Westmorland, and Cumberland. Converts were formed into Methodist Societies, and Grimshaw had overall supervision of them.

Grimshaw described the effect of his preaching thus:

> Souls were affected by the Word, brought to see their lost estate by nature, and to experience peace through faith in the blood of Jesus. My church began to be crowded, insomuch

> that many were obliged to stand out of doors. Here, as in many places, it was amazing to see and hear what weeping, roaring, and agony, many people were seized with, at the apprehension of their sinful state and wrath of God. After a season I joined people, such as were truly seeking, or had found the Lord, in society, for meetings and exercises. These meetings are held once a week, about two hours, and are called classes, consisting of about ten or twelve members each. We have much of the Lord's presence among them, and greatly in consequence must such meetings conduce to Christian edification.

Remarkably Grimshaw was able to cooperate with John Wesley in the running of the northern Methodist Societies, a relatively rare example of close and prolonged collaboration between a Calvinist and Arminian. It has been theorised that this was facilitated by the theologically moderate character of Grimshaw's Calvinism: perhaps too by his well-attested 'spiritual ecumenism', his sense of brotherhood among all the regenerate. He maintained strong links with Whitefield as well as with Wesley, inviting both to preach for him. We are informed that around six thousand people would gather in the Haworth cemetery to hear the two 'star preachers' of the Revival. Grimshaw also opened his pulpit to other Calvinists and Arminians: William Romaine and Henry Venn among Calvinists, Charles Wesley and John Nelson among Arminians.

Despite Grimshaw's thorough commitment to the Anglican Church, some of those converted through his preaching became Dissenters. By his own reckoning, at least five Dissenting congregations were formed as a result of his evangelism. He has even been nicknamed 'the father of Yorkshire Dissent'.

4. William Romaine (1714–95)

Romaine was the grandson of a Huguenot (French Calvinist) who fled with his family to England in 1681 from persecution in Catholic France, settling in Hartlepool. Although raised in a Huguenot home, this does not seem to have affected Romaine's spiritual outlook until much later. He studied at Oxford

University, where he attained scholarly distinction, especially in the Hebrew language; strikingly, he was a student in Oxford at the same time as Whitefield, the Wesley brothers, and the Holy Club, but had no association with them. In 1738, he was ordained into the Anglican priesthood, becoming a curate in Banstead (Surrey) and Horton (Middlesex). In 1741 he was appointed chaplain to Daniel Lambert, London's Lord Mayor; living now in London, Romaine worked on a new edition of a Hebrew dictionary and concordance until 1745.

As far as we can make out, 1745 was perhaps also the year when the ancestral French Calvinism of Romaine became a living reality for him. He left a poignant record of this event, referring to himself in the third person:

> He was a very vain, proud man, who knew almost everything but himself, and therefore was very fond of himself. He met with many disappointments to his pride, which only made him prouder, till the Lord was pleased to let him see the plague of his own heart. He tried every method that can be tried to find peace, but found none. In his despair of all things else, he betook himself to Jesus and was most kindly received.

Thereafter, for almost twenty years Romaine preached the Evangelical Calvinist Gospel in London and elsewhere, in various spheres of activity, and with evident success, yet without having his own parish. One arena of preaching was the chapels erected by the Countess of Huntingdon in Sussex on the English south coast.[3] Another was the London church of St Dunstan-in-the-West, not far from Fleet Street, where he held the position of 'lecturer' (essentially a preacher without pastoral or sacramental functions); Romaine preached regularly in St Dunstan from 1749 until his death some forty-five years later. A further field of opportunity was as a guest preacher in the London church of St George's, Hanover Square. From 1756, he was also the morning preacher in the church of St Olave's in Southwark. Romaine's preaching style had an unusual other-worldly quality; according to contemporary testimony, 'It was

3. See section 11.

as though he had been in heaven, and came back to earth to tell us what was doing there.'

Despite the strong impact made on Londoners by his 'heavenly' preaching, Romaine did not receive a parish appointment in the city until 1768, in the church of St Anne's, Blackfriars, recommended to the post by the Countess of Huntingdon. For the next twelve years Romaine was the only Anglican parish minister in London with Evangelical convictions (in 1780 his solitude was finally alleviated by the appointment of John Newton to St Mary's, Woolnoth – see section 8 for Newton).

Romaine's most abiding bequest to the wider Church was his treatise *The Life, Walk, and Triumph of Faith,* generally recognised as a classic of Evangelical Calvinist spirituality. It was originally published in three volumes: *The Life of Faith* (1763), *The Walk of Faith* (1771), and *The Triumph of Faith* (1795). The treatise sets out the main themes of Evangelical Calvinism – faith as trust in the righteousness and substitutionary atoning sacrifice of Christ as the sole way of acceptance with God, and its fruit in lifelong sanctification, issuing at last in the glorification even of the weakest believer. John Wesley denounced the treatise as antinomian, but this is almost certainly because it strongly opposed Wesley's perfectionism. It probably did not much help that Romaine was also militantly anti-Arminian.

By the time of his death, it was said of Romaine that as a preacher, he was second only to George Whitefield in popularity among Evangelical Calvinists.

5. Samuel Walker of Truro (1714–61)

Generally known as 'Walker of Truro', he has been described as the purest example of Anglican Evangelicalism, in that his Evangelical faith never stepped beyond the boundaries of what his Church deemed acceptable conduct (for example, he never evangelised outside his own parish). Born at Exeter in Devon, he studied at Oxford University and was ordained in 1737, becoming curate at Doddidcombe Leigh (not far from Exeter), then at Lanlivery in Cornwall, and then moving in 1746 to the parish for which he is remembered, Truro (also in Cornwall).

Up until this point, Walker had no Evangelical convictions. However, a great change came over him in Truro. He was to say of the earlier part of his clerical life:

> The week before my ordination I spent with the other candidates – as dissolute, I fear, as myself – in a very light and unbecoming manner; dining, supping, drinking, and laughing together, when, God knows, we should all have been on our knees, and warning each other to fear for our souls in the view of what we were about to put our hands to. I cannot but attribute the many careless, ungodly years I spent in pleasure after that time to this profane introduction; and, believe me, the review shocks me. While I write, I tremble in the recollection of the wounds I then gave Jesus.

In Truro, however, Walker came under the influence of George Conon, Evangelical master of Truro's Grammar School, whose friendship, holy character, and conversation on the topic of salvation and faith, were instrumental in Walker's conversion. Not only his person but his sermons were transformed: Walker now preached on the new birth, justification by faith, and the necessity of a sanctified life as the fruit of faith. His new style of preaching proved magnetically attractive, and people began to flock to his church. Over the next fifteen years until his death in 1761, Walker's preaching and pastoral ministry wrought a community-wide transformation in Truro.

An ingredient in this transformation was Walker's establishing small groups among converts who met regularly for mutual edification. These groups were also bound by a strict moral rule of personal behaviour. This practice endeared Walker to the Wesleys, who utilised a similar method among their converts (see Part 5); consequently, the Wesleys often corresponded with Walker about the best way of organising new believers. Walker, however, disapproved of the lay preaching that so strongly characterised Wesleyan Methodism, believing its influence on the overall movement to be harmful.

Walker wrote a number of treatises, essentially published sermons: *The Christian: a Course of eleven practical Sermons; Fifty-two Sermons on the Baptismal Covenant, the Creed, the Ten*

Commandments, and other important Subjects of Practical Religion; Practical Christianity illustrated in Nine Tracts; The Covenant of Grace, in Nine Sermons; The Refiner, or God's Method of Purifying his People. These were written in plain, flowing English, and modern readers still find them very accessible.[4]

6. John Berridge (1716–93)

C. H. Spurgeon once awarded Berridge the trophy for being the most eccentric preacher who ever lived. His eccentricities, however, were part and parcel of a personality given over to the service of the Gospel of Evangelical Calvinism, and his itinerant preaching had a widespread and transforming impact.

Berridge was born in Kingston on Soar in Nottinghamshire, a prosperous farmer's son; after studying at Cambridge University, he was ordained an Anglican deacon in 1744, then priest in 1745. Between 1750 and 1755, he served as curate in the parish of Stapleford, near Cambridge. His intentions were worthy; he preached seriously on the necessity of holiness. Yet he saw no fruit from his preaching, eventually resigning from Stapleford in despair. However, he was moved to try again, taking up a new post as vicar of Everton in Bedfordshire, in July 1755. The same pattern of failure met him: energetic preaching on holiness, but no effect on his hearers who remained as apathetic and worldly as ever.

After two years of this dismal performance, Berridge began to conclude that there was something wrong with the message he was preaching, since no matter how sincerely and earnestly he proclaimed it, it awakened no interest and touched no lives. He tells us that he was meditating on a certain verse of the Bible (we are unsure which verse) in Christmas 1757, when he heard a voice from heaven speak to him, saying, 'Cease from thine own works; only believe!' This quasi-mystical experience proved life-changing. Berridge became instantly convinced of the truth of justification by faith alone. Holiness, he now perceived, was

4. As far as I can ascertain from his writings, Walker was the mildest of Calvinists, which may have facilitated his positive relationship with the Wesleys.

the consequence of faith, and declaring Christ as the object of faith must be the preacher's overriding task.

The result of Berridge's conversion was remarkable. The new message that now fell from his lips in the pulpit was magnetically captivating to his listeners, and soon (he recorded) people began gathering from far and wide in great numbers to hear him. Berridge said in a letter to a friend:

> I preached up sanctification by the works of the law very earnestly for six years in Stapleford, and never brought one soul to Christ. I did the same at Everton for two years, without any success at all. But as soon as I preached Jesus Christ, and faith in His blood, then believers were added to the Church continually; then people flocked from all parts to hear the glorious sound of the Gospel; some coming six miles, others eight, and others ten. And what is the reason why my ministry was not blessed, when I preached up salvation partly by faith and partly by works? It is because this doctrine is not of God, and because He will prosper no ministers but such as preach salvation in His own appointed way; namely, by faith in Jesus Christ.

Encouraged, by 1759 Berridge had begun a successful ministry of itinerant evangelism, much of it in the open air, taking in the counties of Bedfordshire, Cambridge, Essex, Hertfordshire, and Huntingdonshire. He became friendly with Whitefield, sometimes preaching for him in the Tabernacle Church in London's Tottenham Court Road. This connection with Whitefield illustrates Berridge's adherence to the Calvinist wing of the Revival.

Berridge's reputation for eccentricity rests chiefly on his peculiar, often humorous style of speaking. He was aware of his mannerisms: 'Odd things break from me as abruptly as croaking from a raven.' Friends advised him to discipline his preaching style, and critics accused him of irreverent buffoonery. However, he was never able to rid himself of his 'quaint' way of speaking, nor did it hinder the converting power of the Gospel he preached. His most famous utterance in offbeat, humorous vein came not in a sermon, but a letter to the Countess of

Huntingdon, in which Berridge gave his negative judgment on the marriage of preachers, referring to the unhappy marriages of George Whitefield and John Wesley:

> Before I parted with honest George [Whitefield], I cautioned him much against petticoat snares. He has burnt his wings already. Sure he will not imitate a foolish gnat, and hover again about the candle? If he should fall into a sleeping-lap, like Samson, he will soon need a flannel night-cap, and a rusty chain to fix him down, like a chained Bible to the reading-desk. No trap so mischievous to the field-preacher as wedlock; and it is laid for him at every hedge corner. Matrimony has quite maimed poor Charles [Wesley], and might have spoiled John [Wesley] and George, if a wise Master had not graciously sent them a brace of ferrets. Dear George has now got his liberty again; and he will escape well if he is not caught by another tenter-hook. Eight or nine years ago, having been grievously tormented with house-keeping, I truly had thought of looking out for a Jezebel myself. But it seemed highly needful to ask advice of the Lord. So, kneeling down on my knees before a table, with a Bible between my hands, I besought the Lord to give me a direction.

The desired direction came as Berridge opened his Bible 'at random' and alighted on Jeremiah 16:2: 'Thou shalt not take thee a wife, nor have sons nor daughters in this place.'[5]

---

5. John Wesley's miserable marriage to Molly Vazeille in 1751 is well-known. Molly became consumed with jealousy over John's frequent correspondence with Methodist women as their spiritual adviser, and even subjected him at times to physical abuse. On the other side, John was so often absent from home on preaching tours that he could not be reckoned much of a companion. Eventually Molly walked out on him in 1771, never to return. John noted tersely in his diary: 'I did not forsake her; I did not dismiss her; I will not recall her.' Berridge's severe verdict on Whitefield's marriage seems far less merited. Whitefield married the widow Elizabeth James in 1741. George's endless itinerant preaching, and Elizabeth's increasing ill-health, meant that there was effectively little real companionship between the two; Elizabeth eventually remained 'at home' in London while George travelled the length and breadth of Britain and America. She died in 1768. However, I am not aware that they endured the long, poisonous conflict that so undermined Wesley's marriage.

7. Henry Venn (1725–97)

Henry Venn was born into an Anglican clerical family, third son of Richard Venn, the vicar of St Antholin's, London. He studied at Cambridge University from 1742 to 1749; at the end of this time, Venn underwent a quiet religious awakening that led him to become a devout disciple of the mystical Non-juror, William Law. He held several curacies, notably at Clapham from 1754 to 1759. It was during his time at Clapham that he abandoned William Law as a spiritual guide, in favour of the Evangelical Calvinist message of justification by grace alone through faith in Christ alone. There is reason to believe that, among other influences, it was the religious counsel of Selina, Countess of Huntingdon, that helped bring Venn decisively to Evangelical faith. The letter the Countess wrote him some time in 1756–57 may have been especially impactful:

> O my friend, we can make no atonement to a violated law; we have no inward holiness of our own; the Lord Jesus Christ is the Lord our righteousness. Cling not to such beggarly elements, such filthy rags, mere cobwebs of Pharisaical pride; but look to Him who hath wrought out a perfect righteousness for His people. You find it a hard task to come naked and miserable to Christ; to come divested of every recommendation but that of abject wretchedness and misery, and receive from the outstretched hand of our Immanuel the riches of redeeming grace. But if you come at all you must come thus; and, like the dying thief, the cry of your heart must be, 'Lord, remember me.' There must be no conditions; Christ and Christ alone must be the only mediator between God and sinful men; no miserable performance can be placed between the sinner and the Saviour. And now, my dear friend, no longer let false doctrine disgrace your pulpit. Preach Christ crucified as the only foundation of the sinner's hope. Preach Him as the Author and Finisher as well as the sole Object of faith, that faith which is the gift of God. Exhort Christless sinners to fly to the City of Refuge; to look to Him who is exalted as Prince and Saviour, to give repentance and the remission of sins.

From then onward, the religious sentiments expressed in this letter by the Countess would constitute Venn's Gospel.

In 1759, Venn was appointed vicar of the large Yorkshire parish of Huddersfield, a town dominated by the manufacturing industry. It was the twelve years he spent here for which he is most remembered. His Gospel preaching flowered into a captivating fullness of power, attracting multitudes of hearers and making myriads of converts. Nor did Venn limit himself to preaching from his pulpit; he became an itinerant open-air evangelist, proclaiming the Evangelical Calvinist message in many of the surrounding villages, hamlets, and regions (between eight and ten times a week). He also frequently preached by invitation in other parts of England for Lady Huntingdon, Whitefield, Grimshaw, and others. Venn's son recorded the following:

> As soon as he began to preach at Huddersfield, the church became crowded to such an extent that many were not able to procure admission. Numbers became deeply impressed with concern about their immortal souls; persons flocked from the distant hamlets, inquiring what they must do to be saved. He found them in general utterly ignorant of their state by nature, and of the redemption that is in Christ Jesus ... His whole soul was engaged in preaching; and as at this time he only used short notes in the pulpit, ample room was left to indulge the feelings of compassion, tenderness, and love, with which his heart overflowed towards his people. In the week he statedly visited the different hamlets in his extensive parish; and collecting some of the inhabitants at a private house, he addressed them with a kindness and earnestness which moved every heart.

We know from primary sources that Venn was a highly emotional preacher, like thunder in proclaiming the stern demands and penalties of God's Law, but melting into sunny countenance and tears in setting forth Christ and pleading with sinners to embrace Him. His listeners likewise were often in tears of terror and joy.

Historians frequently comment that when Venn's twelve years of ministry in Huddersfield came to an end, the whole town and its environs had been spiritually and morally transformed, in so striking a manner that few comparisons can be named (perhaps the ministry of Richard Baxter in Kidderminster the previous century).[6]

Venn left Huddersfield in 1771, shattered in health and inwardly broken by his wife's death, and went to the small rural parish of Yelling in Huntingdonshire, where he remained for the rest of his life and ministry. He left behind him a significant literary monument, the treatise *The Compleat [complete] Duty of Man,* a systematic exposition of Christian doctrine and practice, popular in its day. His letters, published after his death, also commanded a high degree of admiration for their spiritual wisdom.

8. John Newton (1725–1807)

Newton was born in Wapping, London, the son of a captain in the merchant navy. After his mother's early death, he began voyaging (from the age of eleven) with his father on his sea journeys. Things took an unexpected turn, however, after his father's retirement in 1742: the following year an eighteen-year-old Newton was 'impressed' against his will into the Royal Navy.[7] Naval life on board the HMS Harwich proved harsh, and Newton considered suicide after being brutally flogged. However, he endured, and later joined the slave-trading ship Pegasus, which transported slaves from West Africa to plantations in the Caribbean and the Colonies in North America. Further trials came when, in 1745, his shipmates abandoned him in West Africa to the slave-trader Amos Clowe, who was married to a princess of the Sherbro tribe, in the territory now called Sierra Leone. Newton became her slave, suffering worse abuse than the princess' other slaves, to whom she made him a servant.

---

6. See Volume 4, Chapter 3, Part 6, section 4, for Baxter and Kidderminster.
7. The practice of 'impressing' people against their wills into the armed services (navy and army) was common at that time in Britain. Public opinion was opposed to impressment, but it was deemed legal in repeated court cases, on the grounds that the practice was essential to the maintenance of the British armed forces. Impressment was finally legally abolished in 1815, at the conclusion of the Napoleonic Wars.

Newton's afflictions finally ended in 1748, when he was found by a ship's captain whom Newton's father had asked to search for his lost son. Free at last, he now voyaged back to England on the merchant ship Greyhound. During this voyage Newton's life took another unexpected turn: the Greyhound, struck by a storm, almost sank, and in terror Newton cried out to God. He ever afterwards celebrated this event each year as the birthday of his new spiritually awakened life. Back in England, he married his childhood sweetheart Mary Catlett in 1750.

Perhaps shockingly to enlightened sensibilities, the awakened Newton continued to act as a slave-trader; he was the ship's captain on board three slave-trading voyages between Africa and the Caribbean from 1750 to 1754.[8] After suffering a stroke, he left naval service in 1754, became a tax officer in the port of Liverpool, and in his spare time intensively studied religious topics, including the biblical languages. Sensing a call to pulpit ministry, in 1757 Newton sought ordination in the Anglican Church, although it was only in 1764 that he finally secured a parish as the curate of Olney in Buckinghamshire[9]. His preaching here over the next sixteen years attracted vast crowds of listeners. In 1767, William Cowper (see next section) moved to Olney, and the two men commenced their hugely creative and impactful hymn-writing

---

8. Newton later said he was not 'fully converted' until some years later. He also wrote about the slave trade: 'Disagreeable I had long found it; but I think I should have quitted it sooner, had I considered it, as I now do, to be unlawful and wrong. But I never had a scruple upon this head, at the time; nor was such a thought once suggested to me, by any friend. What I did, I did ignorantly; considering it as the line of life which Divine Providence had allotted to me, and having no concern, in point of conscience, but to treat the Slaves, while under my care, with as much humanity, as a regard to my own safety would admit ... The Slave Trade was always unjustifiable; but inattention and interest prevented, for a time, the evil from being perceived.'
9. One reason for the seven year delay in ordination was Newton's conscientious scruples about a few aspects of the Anglican Prayer Book which he insisted on raising when interviewed for ordination. In the 18th Century, it was not deemed acceptable for Anglicans to doubt the doctrinal and liturgical purity of the Prayer Book. The patronage of the Evangelical nobleman, Lord Dartmouth, eventually secured Newton's ordination and presentation to Olney.

partnership, embodied in the *Olney Hymns* (1779). Among Newton's more famous hymns of abiding popularity were:

Amazing grace
And dost Thou say ask what thou wilt?
Approach, my soul, the Mercy Seat
Come, my soul, thy suit prepare
Day of Judgment! Day of Wonders!
Glorious things of thee are spoken
How sweet the name of Jesus sounds
I asked the Lord that I might grow
In evil long I took delight
Let us love and sing and wonder
One there is, above all others
Though troubles assail and dangers affright
What think ye of Christ? is the test

Newton also cared pastorally for the mentally fragile and depressive Cowper.

In 1780, Newton moved from Olney to the Anglican parish of St Mary's Woolnoth in London, which made him only the second Evangelical Anglican minister in the city (William Romaine had been stationed there, labouring alone, since 1768). It was here in 1785 that Newton met William Wilberforce (1759–1833), a young Evangelical MP who seriously questioned whether politics was his true calling. Newton's advice was instrumental in persuading Wilberforce to continue as an MP, a position he exploited to help spearhead the British campaign to abolish the African slave trade. In 1787, Newton joined Wilberforce and others in founding the Anti-Slavery Society, Britain's foremost campaigning body against the slave trade. The next year, 1788, he finally spoke out in public against the slave trade in a short but rhetorically powerful treatise, *Thoughts upon the Slave Trade*, in which he grieved over his own part in the inhuman trans-Atlantic traffic, 'a business at which my heart now shudders'. Sending a copy to every British MP, he described in harrowingly vivid language his own experiences on slave-trading ships. Although the British parliament abolished the African slave *trade* in 1807, nine months before Newton's death, the existing *institution* of slavery continued to exist within the British Empire for another long generation, only being finally abolished well into the 19th Century, in 1833.[10]

Newton published in 1780 an influential collection of letters of spiritual counsel, *Cardiphonia, or the Utterance of the Heart,* which demonstrated his rare genius in this genre. He was also well-known for his sanctified wit. He once commented that on going to preach in Warwick, he was much comforted by God's word to Paul in Corinth, 'Do not be afraid, but speak, and do not hold your peace, for I have much people in this city' – until his disappointing experience impressed on him that Newton was not Paul, and Warwick was not Corinth!

9. William Cowper (1731–1800)

Cowper (pronounced Cooper)[11] was the only layman among the leading Evangelical Calvinists of the Revival. He was born in 1731 at Great Berkhampstead in Hertfordshire, son of the local Anglican minister. After his years at school, he trained to be a lawyer, although he spent more time joking and socialising than studying law. However, there was a debilitating strain of unnatural anxiety in Cowper's mind, and the darkness began closing around him in 1763, when he had not long turned thirty. His cousin, a man of influence, appointed him a clerk to the House of Lords. But Cowper suffered a total psychological collapse the day prior to his examination for the post. Rather than go through with the exam, he tried to commit suicide. He was saved by the fact that the cord with which he hanged himself broke just as the last drops of life were ebbing from his body.

Thereafter, Cowper sank deeper and deeper into a dejection which at last overwhelmed him totally. In his mental misery, he became convinced that he was on the way to hell in the hereafter,

10. A precisely similar situation obtained in America. The American government prohibited the slave trade in 1808, but the institution of slavery remained until 1865.

11. Contemporary testimony exists proving that Cowper pronounced his name 'Cooper'.

and that nothing could save him. His brother John once found him lying on the floor screaming. 'Brother,' William cried, 'think of eternity; think what it is to be damned!' Eventually Cowper's family committed him to a private lunatic asylum in St Albans, run by a kindly and sympathetic man by the name of Dr Cotton.

It was here that Cowper experienced a life-transforming conversion. In his lucid moments, Cowper would read the Bible. One morning, walking in the asylum garden, he found a Bible on a bench, and read in John's Gospel the account of Jesus raising Lazarus from the dead. It touched him deeply. Could Jesus perhaps raise Cowper out of his living death? Cowper tells the story:

> Having risen with somewhat of a more cheerful feeling, I repaired to my room where breakfast waited for me. While I sat at table, I found the cloud of horror which so long had hung over me was every moment passing away. I flung myself into a chair near the window, and seeing a Bible there, ventured once more to apply to it for comfort and instruction. The first verse I saw was the 25th verse of Romans 3: 'Whom God hath set forth to be a propitiation through faith in His blood, to declare his righteousness by the forgiveness of the sins that are passed, through the patience of God.'
>
> Immediately I received strength to believe it, and the full beams of the Sun of righteousness shone upon me. I saw the sufficiency of the atonement Christ had made, my pardon sealed in His blood, and all the fullness and completeness of His justification. In a moment I believed and received the Gospel ... Unless the Almighty arms had been under me, I think I should have died of gratitude and joy. My eyes filled up with tears, and I could only look up to heaven in silent fear, overwhelmed with love and wonder.

Cowper recovered sufficiently to resume life in the outside world, but was always mentally fragile (he was to make a second attempt to kill himself), and had to be looked after, notably by the Unwin family in their home, and by John Newton pastorally.

Cowper's enduring impact on church life came through his many admired contributions to the Olney Hymns; among other items he wrote:

A glory gilds the sacred page
God moves in a mysterious way
God of my life, to Thee I call
Heal us, Emmanuel, hear our prayer
Hark my soul, it is the Lord
Jesus, where'er Thy people meet
My song shall bless the Lord of all
O for a closer walk with God
Sometimes a light surprises the Christian while he sings
The Spirit breathes upon the Word
There is a fountain filled with blood
'Tis my happiness below not to live without the Cross
What various hindrances we meet

These are still sung today by a far wider audience than Cowper ever dreamt of.

Cowper also wrote non-hymnic poetry which scholars have considered the dawn of a new era in British literary history. He blazed a poetic trail that led to the glories of the Romantic movement, exemplified in such luminaries as William Blake (a particular admirer of Cowper), Lord Byron, Samuel Taylor Coleridge, John Keats, Percy Bysshe Shelley, and William Wordsworth. Cowper's masterpiece, hugely popular in his own day, has been reckoned to be *The Task* (1784), which is permeated by a love of nature as seen through Christian eyes. Cowper's 'rural romanticism' is summed up in these lines:

God made the country, and man made the town.
What wonder then that health and virtue, gifts
That can alone make sweet the bitter draught
That life holds out to all, should most abound
And least be threaten'd in the fields and groves?

The Task was a strong influence on Coleridge and Wordsworth. After Cowper's death his collected letters were issued as a book, praised by William Blake as 'certainly the very best letters that ever were published'.

10. Augustus Toplady (1740–78)

Born in Farnham, Surrey, the son of an officer in the Royal Marines, although Major Toplady died soon after his son's birth, Toplady was raised by his mother. They moved to Ireland, where Toplady studied at Dublin University from 1755. In his first year there, aged fifteen, he was converted while hearing a lay Wesleyan Methodist preacher named Morris. Some years later Toplady famously recorded:

> Strange that I, who had so long sat under the means of grace in England, should be brought nigh to God in an obscure part of Ireland, amidst a handful of God's people met together in a barn, and under the ministry of one who could hardly spell his name! Surely it was the Lord's doing, and is marvellous! The excellency of such power must be of God, and cannot be of man. The regenerating Spirit breathes not only on whom, but likewise when, where, and as He listeth.

Toplady spent the first few years of his Evangelical life as a fervent Wesleyan Arminian; but his mind, always hungry for knowledge, received a theologically transforming shock when he read the Puritan Thomas Manton's sermons on the 17th chapter of John's Gospel, given to him by an elderly Calvinist. Thereafter Toplady was a thoroughly convinced Calvinist.

In 1762 Toplady was ordained an Anglican deacon in the diocese of Bath and Wells, becoming curate of the church at Blagdon in Somerset. After his ordination to the priesthood in 1764, he at length became vicar of the churches of the two Devonshire villages of Harpford and Venn Ottery in 1766, moving to Broad Hembury (also in Devon) in 1768. Here he remained for the next seven years until illness brought about his relocation to London in 1775, where he preached regularly at the Huguenot (French Calvinist) chapel in Orange Street, until his death from tuberculosis in 1778 at the young age of thirty-seven.

Toplady's most distinctive contributions to Evangelical Calvinism were his hymn-writing and his theological works. He penned probably the greatest hymn of the Revival, *Rock of ages*, whose fame would far transcend its Calvinist origins (it was first published in full in the Calvinist *Gospel Magazine* in March 1776). It has been called the world's most popular hymn. Other Toplady hymns that have earned enduring acceptance include:

A debtor to mercy alone
A sovereign protector I have
Compared with Christ, in all beside
From whence this fear and unbelief
Happiness, thou lovely name
How vast the benefits divine
Your harps, ye trembling saints

Theologically, Toplady was the most erudite and outspoken defender of Reformed doctrine within the Revival's Calvinist wing. His masterwork in this vein was his weighty tome, *The Historic Proof of the Doctrinal Calvinism of the Church of England* (1774). He also translated into English the treatise by Italian Reformer Jerome Zanchius (1516–90), *Confession of the Christian Religion*, which Toplady re-titled *The Doctrine of Absolute Predestination Stated and Asserted* (1769). The Zanchius translation ignited a fierce literary controversy with John Wesley, who attacked the treatise and mocked its theology. In this dispute, Toplady certainly did not pull his punches; at one point he described Wesley's chief London congregation, the Foundery, thus:

> Its chief ingredients are: An equal portion of gross Heathenism, Pelagianism, Mahometism, Popery, Manichaeism, Ranterism, and Antinomianism; culled, dried and pulverized, *secundum artem* [according to his – Wesley's – accepted practice]; and, above all, mingled with as much palpable Atheism as you can possibly scrape together from every quarter.

Modern students will probably feel that this controversy was neither Wesley's nor Toplady's finest hour.

Toplady engaged in philosophy as well as theology, advocating a form of determinism in his *The Scheme of Christian and Philosophical Necessity Asserted* (1775).[12] He was also an

12. Determinism is the philosophical position that every event is predetermined by a natural cause, so that nothing can happen other

early champion of animal rights, as seen in his public lecture *Whether unnecessary cruelty to the brute creation is not criminal?*

11. Selina Hastings, Countess of Huntingdon (1707–91)

Although George Whitefield's hope (substantially realised) was to be an instrument of awakening and upbuilding for his own 'Mother Church', one development that occurred produced unexpected consequences in this regard. It grew out of the conversion of a member of the English aristocracy, Selina Hastings (1707–91), the Countess of Huntingdon. Born into the wealthy Shirley family, at Astwell Castle in Northamptonshire, the young Selina was already having soul-stirring experiences at the age of nine: she was out playing with her sisters one afternoon, when they stumbled across a funeral procession winding its way from a little village, heading for a cemetery on a hill. A tiny coffin was being carried by four men. Selina and her sisters tried to find out who had died, and found it was a nine-year-old girl. The thought of children dying had never occurred to Selina before. The discovery that children died when they were *her* age impressed her deeply.

At the age of twenty-one, Selina married Theophilus Hastings, the Earl of Huntingdon, a quiet and retiring man eleven years her senior. It was a happy marriage. In her new home, Selina – now Lady Hastings – devoted herself to looking after everyone who worked on the Huntingdon estate. She also spent time, energy, and money on a huge scale caring for the poor in the surrounding area, earning the nickname 'Lady Bountiful'. She was a devout Churchgoer, worshipping in her local Anglican church. For all this, however, Lady Hastings had no spiritual peace.

---

than what *does* happen. Calvinism has often been confused with determinism, but they are distinct. In Reformed theology, everything that happens is rendered certain by God's decree, but is not necessarily predetermined by natural causes. Therefore while some Calvinists have been determinists, others have not. The great 19th Century Scottish Reformed theologian, William Cunningham, distinguished carefully between Calvinism and determinism in his essay *Calvinism and the Doctrine of Philosophical Necessity*.

In 1738, at the age of thirty-one, while lying in bed seriously ill, the Countess was visited by her sister-in-law Lady Margaret Hastings, who had just herself experienced an Evangelical conversion in the early days of the Revival. Margaret told her sick relative about her conversion, and the spiritual joy in Christ that now filled her heart. The Countess was deeply moved, and as she read the Bible with fresh eyes, underwent a similar conversion. Thereafter Lady Hastings joined the Fetter Lane Moravian religious society in 1739, at a point when the Moravians had not yet parted company with John Wesley and George Whitefield. She attached herself, however, to the Revival in the form it took at the hands of Wesley and Whitefield, putting herself and her wealth at the movement's disposal. John Henry Newman in the 19th Century would pay this tribute to the Evangelical noblewoman:

> She was the representative, in an evil day, of the rich becoming poor for Christ; of delicate women putting off their soft attire and wrapping themselves in sackcloth for the kingdom of heaven's sake. She devoted herself, her means, her time, her thoughts to the cause of Christ. She did not spend her money on herself; she did not allow the homage paid to her rank to remain with herself; she passed these on, and offered them up to Him from Whom her gifts came. She acted as one who considered this life a pilgrimage, not a home – like some holy nun who had neither hopes nor fears of anything but what was divine and unseen.[13]

In the Calvinist-Arminian breach between Whitefield and Wesley in 1741, Hastings sided with Whitefield, who became personal chaplain to the Countess. To facilitate the exposure of her own social class to the Evangelical Gospel, Hastings often held aristocratic dinner parties, at which Whitefield gave an evangelistic talk after the meal.

---

13. Newman was not an Evangelical, so that his tribute may be seen as weighty and remarkable. He is famous, firstly, as the leader of the Oxford Movement in the Church of England from 1833 to 1845, which aimed at promoting what we would call Anglo-Catholicism, and latterly as a Roman Catholic theologian of great distinction.

In order to alleviate the problem of Whitefield's being barred from many Anglican pulpits, Hastings used her wealth to build meeting houses or chapels in which Whitefield could preach and people gather to hear him. Eventually over two hundred of these chapels were constructed, either fully or partly funded by Hastings; there were noteworthy Huntingdon chapels in Brighton, Bath, Tunbridge Wells, Worcester, Basingstoke, and Spa Fields (in London). Hastings appointed sympathetic Anglican ministers to be in charge of the chapels, requiring that the Anglican Prayer Book alone be used as the form of worship. When challenged by hostile anti-Revival Anglicans, Hastings' response was that as a member of the aristocracy, she had the legal right to appoint as many chaplains as she wished, and that the chapel ministers were her chaplains.

For a time this strategy succeeded, and the Huntingdon chapels remained within the Anglican system. At length, however, determined opposition secured a court ruling in 1779 that the chapels were in violation of Anglican Church law. At that point, Hastings was compelled to have the chapels registered as a Dissenting or Nonconformist denomination outside the Anglican Church – the 'Countess of Huntingdon's Connexion',[14] an Evangelical Calvinist body whose history continues to the present day. Whitefield by then was gone from the scene (he died in 1770), but the forced secession of the Evangelical Calvinist Huntingdon chapels from the Church of England was the first serious mass-separation from Anglicanism occasioned by the Revival. That it took place within Whitefield's wing of the Revival is often forgotten.

12. Some other Calvinist hymnwriters of the Revival: Philip Doddridge (1702–51), Joseph Hart (1712–68), and Anne Steele (1717–78).

The three Calvinist hymnwriters in this section were all Dissenters who bucked the trend of orthodox Dissent's disdain for the Revival. Philip Doddridge (1702–51) was the

14. An alternate spelling of 'connection'.

Congregationalist minister of a church in Northampton from 1729, whose published sermons were prized in the international Reformed community for their combination of doctrine and piety. Equally if not more important, from 1723 Doddridge was the head of a Dissenting Academy, which changed its location several times – it is best known as the Daventry Academy. Here Doddridge gave the sons of Dissenters as good an education as they could have received at the Anglican strongholds of Oxford and Cambridge, and trained a future generation of Dissenting ministers. Unlike most Dissenters, Doddridge welcomed the Evangelical Revival in the 1730s, becoming a good friend of George Whitefield who preached in Doddridge's church in 1743 (some other Dissenters rebuked Doddridge for this unseemly exercise in Evangelical ecumenism – an Anglican in a Dissenting pulpit!).

Doddridge wrote many hymns, some of which have stood the test of time and are still sung today:

And will the Judge descend?
Grace! 'Tis a charming sound
Hark the glad sound, the Saviour comes
My God! And is Thy table spread?
My gracious Lord, I own Thy right
O God of Bethel, by whose hand
O happy day that fixed my choice

Doddridge's fame also partly rests on his devotional classic, *The Rise and Progress of Religion in the Soul* (1745), to which the great anti-slavery campaigner William Wilberforce attributed the dawn of his own spiritual life.[15] Not so well-remembered today is his authorship of a biography of the Scottish Christian military hero, Colonel James Gardiner, who died at the battle of Prestonpans in 1745, fighting the Jacobite insurgency. In a previous day this biography was something of a religious classic.[16]

15. For Wilberforce, see Part 4, section 8, and Part 10. C.H.Spurgeon was also to be an admirer of *The Rise and Progress of Religion in the Soul.*

16. See the Primary Historical Sources section in Chapter 3.

Joseph Hart (1712–68) was raised in a Calvinist Congregationalist family in London, acknowledging that his parents instilled sound doctrine into him; but it had no transforming effect on his heart and life, until – after a long course of theological and spiritual wanderings – he came deeply under the influence of George Whitefield and his preaching at the Moorfields Tabernacle in the 1750s. Humbled by a crushing consciousness of sin, Hart experienced conversion at the Moravian Chapel in Fetter Lane in 1757 through a sermon on Revelation 3:10.[17] He wrote of this experience:

> I was hardly got home when I felt myself melting away into a strange softness of affection, which made me fling myself on my knees before God. My horrors were immediately dispelled, and such light and comfort flowed into my heart as no words can paint. The Lord, by His Spirit of love, came not in a visionary manner into my brain, but with such divine power and energy into my soul, that I was lost in blissful amazement. Tears ran in streams from my eyes. I threw my soul willingly into my Saviour's hands; lay weeping at His feet, wholly resigned to His will, and only begging that I might, if He was graciously pleased to permit it, be of some service to His church and people.

Two years later, Hart became the minister at London's Congregationalist Jewin Street Chapel. But his true vocation lay in his prolific hymn writing. Until quite recently, many hymnbooks – certainly Reformed ones – contained a sizeable body of Hart's worship songs. He published his own hymnbook in 1759, made up of his compositions (known in a previous day simply as 'Hart's Hymns'); phenomenally popular, it had reached its twenty-third edition by 1823. Although Hart has largely gone out of general favour as a hymnwriter now, some of his hymns are still widely sung:

---

17. 'Because thou hast kept the word of My patience, therefore I will deliver thee from the hour of trial, which will come upon the whole world, to try them that dwell upon the earth.'

A Man there is, a real Man
Come, Holy Spirit, come
Come, ye sinners, poor and needy
Great High Priest, we view Thee stooping
No prophet or dreamer of dreams

The last of these concludes with the oft-sung verse, *How good is the God we adore*, although Hart's original actually said *This God is the God we adore*.

Anne Steele (1717–78) of Broughton in Hampshire was the daughter of a Calvinistic Baptist preacher, William Steele. Her personal life is devoid of much interest; writers like to point out that the Calvinistic Baptist minister and poet, Benjamin Beddome (1717–95) of Gloucestershire, proposed to her, but she turned him down. Although by no means anti-social, Steele remained a somewhat retiring figure (partly owing to ill-health). Her historic importance lies in the large body of hymns and religious poetry she produced, marking her as the first great woman hymnwriter in the English language. Her first collection of hymns and poems was published in 1757; another volume followed in 1760. She wrote under the pseudonym 'Theodosia'. For a generation or more, Steele's hymns were the most widely used of any Baptist author among Baptists, and the most widely printed of any woman hymnwriter in British and American hymnbooks. Her deep, poetic love of nature within a framework of belief in the Trinitarian Creator reminds the 18th Century student of William Cowper.[18]

As with Joseph Hart, there has been a steep decline in popularity today, but a few of Steele's hymns are still sung:

Come ye that love the Saviour's name
Father of Mercies, in Thy Word
Father, whate'er of earthly bliss
The Saviour calls – let every ear

Although Steele wrote in the era when Hyper-Calvinism was fast spreading over the English Calvinistic Baptist churches, her

18. For Cowper see this Chapter, Part 4, section 9.

hymns and poems exhibit a fairly robust belief in the free offer of the Gospel.[19] Her personal connections with the Revival are not overwhelmingly strong, unlike Doddridge and Hart, but Steele's link with Benjamin Beddome is interesting, since he was one of the few Calvinistic Baptists well-disposed to the Revival. Later on, Caleb Evans (1737–91), a Welsh Baptist influenced by the Revival, championed Steele's hymns, including sixty-two of them in a 1769 Baptist hymnbook, and writing a preface to a 1780 printing of Steele's poetry.

19. See the example cited in Primary Historical Sources.

5
English Evangelical Arminianism

1. John Wesley's organisational genius

One of the key differences between George Whitefield and John Wesley was their respective roles within the Calvinist and Arminian Methodist Societies. Whitefield soon relinquished any organisational role in the English Calvinist Societies, preferring instead to focus his energies on the twin concerns of itinerant evangelism in Britain and America, and nurturing his Bethesda orphanage in Georgia. Initially Whitefield handed over organisation of the English Calvinistic Methodist Societies to John Cennick; when Cennick joined the Moravians in 1745, Howell Harris stepped into his place, until his own retirement from public affairs in 1749. Thereafter, the Calvinistic Methodist Societies of England lacked centralised leadership, operating in a rather fragmented way. A good many of them ended up becoming independent, self-governing Congregational churches.

By contrast, the United Methodist Societies (Arminians) remained always a cohesive movement under the formidable managerial genius of John Wesley. This gave them a spiritual direction and unity absent from their Calvinist counterparts. Wesley was fully as much an organiser as a preacher, and he held robust views about the need for converts to belong to communities that would sustain and shape their new-found faith. He was therefore committed to both creating and maintaining a strong functional network of local Methodist

Societies. At the same time, Wesley made sure that his Societies worked within the structures of the Church of England – his allegiance to Anglicanism was not in doubt.

Wesley's Societies, based on a Moravian model, had a threefold structure: the Society proper, the class meeting, and the band. The Society was the largest body of the three, embracing all converts in a locality. Its chief purpose was collective worship and doctrinal instruction from the Bible, carried out mainly on Sunday evenings (although the Society met at other times too). From 1742, Wesley introduced the class meeting into his Societies. This was a smaller body of between 10 and 12 people, drawn from a mixture of backgrounds (age, social occupation, length of time a person had been a convert). It was open to the converted and to the awakened seeker after salvation. It met every week with a view to promoting the spiritual life of members. This function was fulfilled through each member – starting with the class leader – giving an account of how they were doing spiritually. These testimonies encouraged openness and honesty about the state of a person's faith, and also trained people in expressing their life-experiences. There was an agreed set of spiritual rules for the guidance of conduct, drawn up by Wesley in 1743, and class members were interviewed regularly to see whether they were abiding by these rules; those who were not risked expulsion from the class.

The third level of Methodist social activity was the band. Unlike the Society proper or the class meeting, the band was open only to the converted and was made up of people from the same background – the same age, sex, marital status. Otherwise they operated in a similar way to the class meeting, with prayer, testimonies, confession of faults, discussion of spiritual experience.

The way that Wesley welded converts together into a tightly-knit nationwide organisation through Societies, class meetings, and bands, laid the groundwork – after Wesley's death in 1791 – for his United Methodist Societies to become the Methodist Church, breaking away from the Church of England in 1795 as a separate denomination.

It was Wesleyan Methodism's powerful organisational unity and ethos that ultimately gave John Wesley a higher profile in the English national consciousness than George Whitefield had. If Whitefield was remembered, it was simply as a preacher (an eccentric one, in much popular perception), whereas Wesley has been remembered as the founder of a united religious movement that became one of England's foremost Churches. Modern scholarship has done something to rehabilitate the memory and impact of Whitefield, but it remains the case that it is Wesley's name that is stubbornly attached, for most people, to the Evangelical Revival in England.

In addition to the Societies, Wesley's brand of Evangelicalism was also devoted to the training of lay preachers. The origin of the Wesleyan lay preachers can be traced to Wesley's preaching centre, the Foundery, in Moorfields, London, which Wesley used from November 1739 as a chapel as his breach with Moravianism increased (it became final in June 1740[1]). Since Wesley was often preaching in other parts of the country, in 1740 he placed the Foundery in the care of one of his converts, Thomas Maxfield (d.1784) of Bristol, who himself began preaching to the Foundery congregation.[2] Wesley however disapproved of lay preaching, and was on the verge of rebuking Maxfield, when Wesley's mother Susanna intervened, convincing her son that Maxfield, if suitably gifted, might have as much calling to preach as Wesley had. After listening to Maxfield preaching, Wesley's doubts were quenched, and with Wesley's blessing Maxfield became one of the pioneer lay preachers of the Evangelical Arminian wing of the Revival. Others followed.

A few of the lay preachers were women. Wesley's objections to 'female preaching' were overcome in the same way that his problems with any lay person preaching were resolved – the manifest reality of effectual gifting. 'God owns [acknowledges] women in the conversion of sinners, and who am I that I should withstand God?' By 1786, certainly, Wesley was quite

---

1. See Part 2, section 3.
2. For a fuller account of Maxfield see section 7 below.

outspoken on the essential equality of women with men. In his sermon that year *On Visiting the Sick*, he said:

> 'There is neither male nor female in Christ Jesus.' Indeed it has long passed for a maxim with many, that 'women are only to be seen, not heard.' And accordingly many of them are brought up in such a manner as if they were only designed for agreeable playthings! But is this doing honour to the sex or is it a real kindness to them? No; it is the deepest unkindness; it is horrid cruelty; it is mere Turkish barbarity. And I know not how any woman of sense and spirit can submit to it. Let all you that have it in your power assert the right which the God of nature has given you. Yield not to that vile bondage any longer. You, as well as men, are rational creatures.

One of the most outstanding of the women lay preachers was Mary Bosanquet (1739–1815), a woman of wealth, in whose house 'The Cedars' at Leytonstone, north-east London, Methodist meetings were held every night in the early 1760s. Mostly these were led by a layman supplied by Wesley, but on Thursday evenings Bosanquet and her assistant Sarah Crosby (1729–1804) held their own meeting, which soon attracted large numbers. This practice continued when Bosanquet and Crosby moved to Cross Hall in Morley, Yorkshire, in 1768. In 1771, Bosanquet wrote to Wesley seeking his permission to continue her preaching, arguing that women should be permitted to preach if they had an 'extraordinary call' from God to do so; Wesley wrote back, giving his consent. Bosanquet's assistant Sarah Crosby also became a recognised lay preacher after Wesley's 1771 letter, carrying out an itinerant ministry (latterly based in Leeds) that covered an area of around a thousand miles, according to her own testimony. Crosby proved a popular preacher, frequently speaking to crowds numbered in the hundreds. Other authorised Wesleyan women preachers included Anne Cutler, Grace Murray, Elizabeth Ritchie, Hester Rogers, and Sarah Taft.

Beginning in 1744, Wesley held annual national conferences of his lay preachers (all approved by himself), to give them a sense of brotherhood and to supply regular spiritual and theological input into their shared mission. To expedite their activities, Wesley divided up England and Wales into a number of 'circuits' for evangelism. These circuits were localised geographical groupings of Societies and preaching stations; Wesley had overall charge of the circuits, while each individual circuit was run by an 'Assistant' (to Wesley), later given the name 'Superintendent'. This infused the evangelistic endeavour of Evangelical Arminianism with a far more systematic and organised method than anything enjoyed by Evangelical Calvinism.

Wesley's instructions to his lay preachers included firm directions on how to (and how not to) conduct services of worship. He absolutely forbade preachers from shouting during their sermons: 'scream no more, at the peril of your soul.' The message of a sermon was often backed up with a personal testimony given by a convert. It is of likely interest to modern students to know that Wesley severely restricted hymn-singing to no more than two hymns per service, warning preachers he would cast them out of Methodism if they disobeyed him on this point. As he wrote to a pair of rebellious preachers:

> If you do not choose to obey me, you need not: I will let you go when you please, and send other preachers in your place. If you choose to stay with me, never sing more than twice, once before and once after Sermon.

The hymns were sung without any instrumental accompaniment.

2. Literary organs of Arminian unity

Wesley also employed multiple literary means to instruct, edify, and unify the United Methodist Societies. We can note the following:

(i) *The Christian Library*. This was a set of fifty volumes of spiritual literature, edited by Wesley and first published between 1749 and 1755, aimed at providing what Wesley believed was the best in historic Christian writing, chiefly for the education of his preachers, but also more generally for the upbuilding of converts. Most of the literature was taken from the 17th Century;

indeed, many of the volumes were Puritan works, albeit carefully purged of any trace of the Calvinist understanding of election and limited atonement. Among the Puritans (or those influenced by Puritan spirituality) included in the series were Isaac Ambrose, Richard Baxter, Robert Bolton, John Bunyan, Stephen Charnock, Jonathan Edwards, John Eliot, John Flavel, Thomas Goodwin, Philip Henry, John Howe, Thomas Manton, John Owen, John Preston, Samuel Rutherford, and Richard Sibbes. This meant that Wesleyan Methodists had the basis for a solid grounding in Puritan heart-spirituality (without the uncongenial doctrine of predestination).

The series was, however, more wide-ranging than Puritan spirituality alone. Other Protestant writers included historian John Foxe (lengthy extracts from his *Book of Martyrs*), Bishop Joseph Hall, Archbishop Robert Leighton, Bishop Edward Reynolds, Henry Scougal, Jeremy Taylor, the Cambridge Platonists (Henry More, Nathanael Culverwell, John Smith, Ralph Cudworth), and Lutherans Johann Arndt ('grandfather' of German Pietism) and August Hermann Francke. The early church fathers were represented by some of the apostolic fathers (Clement of Rome, Ignatius of Antioch, Polycarp of Smyrna), and by the renowned 4th Century desert father Macarius the Great of Egypt (c.300–91), a Pietist favourite, as well as treatises on the early Church by notable Anglican scholars Anthony Horneck and William Cave. Roman Catholic spirituality – such as most Protestants were willing to accept (it was not peculiar to Wesley) – included edited versions of Juan d'Avila, Antoinette Bourignon, Archbishop Fenelon, the Quietist Miguel de Molinos, and the Jansenist Blaise Pascal.[3]

Wesley also included biographical material on 'heroes of the faith'. Many of these were found in his version of Foxe's *Book of*

3. For Juan d'Avila (John of Avila), see Volume 3, Chapter 8, section 6. For Molinos, see Volume 4, Chapter 7, Part 2, section 1. For Archbishop Fenelon, see Volume 4, Chapter 7, Part 2, section 3. For Pascal, see Volume 4, Chapter 6, Part 4, section 9. Antoinette Bourignon (1616–80) was a French Catholic mystic who for a time attracted a significant following.

Martyrs. Foxe aside, among Wesley's Reformation heroes were Philip Melanchthon, Peter Martyr Vermigli, and (perhaps surprisingly) John Calvin, and from the post-Reformation era Robert Bruce, John Donne, John Eliot, Thomas Goodwin, Philip Henry, George Herbert, Richard Hooker, John Howe, John Owen, John Preston, and Richard Sibbes.

(ii) During a period of prolonged illness in 1754, Wesley wrote his own commentary on the New Testament, published in 1755 as *Explanatory Notes on the New Testament*. This became a quasi-authoritative exposition of scripture for Wesleyan Methodists (see next point on the 'model deed'). Five editions of the *Explanatory Notes* were published in Wesley's lifetime. A work of scholarship, it proposed a multitude of alternative translations to the King James Version; interestingly, many of these alternatives were incorporated into the Revised Version of 1881. Wesley's translation by itself, without the notes, was published in 1790. His concern as a translator was to modernise what he considered outdated language in the King James Version. The commentary was based on four existing New Testament commentaries: German Pietist Johann Albrecht Bengel's *Gnomon Novi Testamenti* (1742), Philip Doddridge's *Family Expositor* (six volumes 1739–56), John Guyse's *An Exposition of the New Testament in the form of a paraphrase* (three volumes 1739–52), and John Heylyn's *Theological Lectures* (1749). These were blended with Wesley's own exegesis to produce an enduring monument to Wesley's understanding of Christianity as enshrined in its founding documents.

(iii) A collection of some of Wesley's sermons, usually called his *Forty-Four Sermons*, also became a virtual doctrinal standard for Wesleyan Methodism. These were first mentioned as such in the 'model deed' of 1763, a legal trust deed for Methodist places of worship (chapels) constructed outside the official Anglican parish system. The model deed stated that such chapels must be used for the teaching of those doctrines contained in Wesley's *Explanatory Notes on the New Testament* and his 'four volumes of sermons'. At that juncture, the four volumes (1746) had forty-three sermons, but a forty-fourth was later added to the third volume. The *Forty-Four Sermons* are a mixture of doctrinal and practical instruction. Some of the titles illustrate the content: Justification by Faith, Original Sin, The Witness of the Spirit, The New Birth, The Marks of the New Birth, The Law Established through Faith, Satan's Devices, Christian Perfection, A Caution against Bigotry, The Use of Money, and thirteen discourses on the Sermon on the Mount.

(iv) *The Arminian Magazine*. In 1778, Wesley began editing and publishing a monthly religious magazine. Its full title, *The Arminian Magazine: Consisting of Extracts and Original Treatises on Universal Redemption*, exhibited its unflinching doctrinal standpoint (after Wesley's death in 1791, the title was eventually changed – from 1798 – to *The Methodist Magazine*). In part, *The Arminian Magazine* was Wesley's response to the militant Calvinism of *The Spiritual Magazine* and *The Gospel Magazine*, both of which critiqued Arminianism. The first issue of *The Arminian Magazine* set out Wesley's anti-Calvinist standpoint with an outspoken plainness, asserting that the rival Calvinist magazines were 'intended to show, that God is not loving to every man; that His mercy is not over all His works; and, consequently that Christ did not die for all, but for one in ten, for the elect only'.

Against such perceived Calvinist narrowness, Wesley declared that his new magazine would vindicate the truth that 'God willeth all men to be saved', and that it would do this, not only through biblical exegesis, but also by printing 'an extract from the life of some holy man' and 'accounts and letters containing the experience of pious persons, the greatest part of whom are still alive'. *The Arminian Magazine* thus became a treasury of the recorded religious experiences of Evangelical Arminians, not only Methodist preachers but ordinary folk both male and female. The appeal to experience was important for Wesley in corroborating the Arminian reading of scripture, in that Wesleyan converts experienced God as universal love, moving them to love all and desire the salvation of all.

(v) *The Methodist Hymnbook.* We have already noted Wesley's editing and publishing of hymnbooks – his 1740 collection of hymns was one reason for his breach with Whitefield, since the book contained hymns teaching universal redemption and sinless perfection. There were several different hymnbooks produced by the Wesley brothers that went through a number of editions, achieving widespread use among Evangelical Arminians: *Hymns and Sacred Poems* (first edition 1739), *Hymns and Spiritual Songs* (1753), *Select Hymns with Tunes Annext* (1761). But by far the most influential was the 1780 *A Collection of Hymns for the Use of the People Called Methodists.* The author of most of the hymns in these various collections was Charles Wesley. Since the Methodist Hymnbooks contained many hymns teaching the distinctives of Wesleyan theology and experience, they became a vehicle for spreading and sustaining those beliefs in the Arminian wing of the Revival.

3. Arminian success story

Wesley's organisational genius, in the forms outlined above, forged his version of Methodism into one of the greatest success stories in English religious history. By the time of Wesley's death in 1791, his Societies had a listed 71,688 members and 294 preachers in Britain, and 43,265 members and 198 preachers in America. The statistics speak for themselves, especially given the relatively small population of England in the 18th Century, and the intensely committed nature of Society membership – these figures do not represent a merely nominal Methodism.[4]

Our account of the Evangelical Arminian wing of the English Revival would be very incomplete without taking notice of Wesley's co-workers. Wesley was so dominating a figure, almost all these co-workers have fallen into obscurity, with the exception of John's brother Charles. Nonetheless, they were men of stature in their own day, whose impact was instrumental in shaping the success-story of Wesleyan Methodism.

---

4. At the close of the 18th Century, the English population was roughly ten million.

4. Charles Wesley (1707–88)

Younger brother of John and one of the original Holy Club members in Oxford University, Charles was ordained into the Anglican ministry in 1735, and went with John to Georgia, where he became the chaplain to the garrison at Fort Frederica in March 1736. However, a mere six months later he returned to England, physically ill and spiritually unsettled. Charles' High Church piety – like John's, completely lacking in any assurance of personal salvation – had been impacted (again, like John's) by the religious example of the German Moravians on the voyage to Georgia, and their serene confidence in the face of death. Back in England, the Moravian influence in Charles' spiritual pilgrimage was renewed through friendship with Peter Boehler of Frankfurt (see Part Two, section 3 and the account of John's conversion) and the London-based Moravian John Bray, in whose house in London's Little Britain district Charles lodged. In Bray's house, Charles was fully exposed to Moravian-style Evangelical life and piety, which affected him profoundly. On May 21st 1738, still in Bray's house, Charles himself experienced an enduring Evangelical conversion. In its own way, Charles' account of his conversion (in his journal) is at least as memorable as that of his brother three days later in the Aldersgate Street chapel:

> Sun., May 21st, 1738. I waked in hope and expectation of His coming. At nine my brother and some friends came, and sang a hymn to the Holy Ghost. My comfort and hope were hereby increased. In about half-an-hour they went: I betook myself to prayer; the substance as follows:
>
> 'Oh Jesus, Thou hast said, "I will come unto you"; Thou hast said, "I will send the Comforter unto you"; Thou hast said, "My Father and I will come unto you, and make our abode with you." Thou art God who canst not lie; I wholly rely upon Thy most true promise: accomplish it in Thy time and manner.' Having said this, I was composing myself to sleep, in quietness and peace, when I heard one come in (Mrs. Musgrave, I thought, by the voice) and say, 'In the name of Jesus of Nazareth, arise, and believe, and thou shalt be healed

of all thy infirmities.' I wondered how it should enter into her head to speak in that manner. The words struck me to the heart. I sighed, and said within myself, 'O that Christ would but speak thus to me!' I lay musing and trembling ...

I sent for Mr. Bray, and asked him whether I believed. He answered, I ought not to doubt of it: it was Christ spoke to me [in the words 'In the name of Jesus of Nazareth, arise, and believe.'] He knew it; and willed us to pray together: 'But first,' said he, 'I will read what I have casually opened upon: "Blessed is the man whose unrighteousness is forgiven, and whose sin is covered: blessed is the man to whom the Lord imputeth no sin, and in whose spirit is no guile."' Still I felt a violent opposition and reluctance to believe; yet still the Spirit of God strove with my own and the evil spirit, till by degrees He chased away the darkness of my unbelief. I found myself convinced, I knew not how, nor when; and immediately fell to intercession ...

I rose and looked into the Scripture. The words that first presented were, 'And now, Lord, what is my hope? Truly my hope is even in Thee.' I then cast down my eye, and met, 'He hath put a new song in my mouth, even a thanksgiving unto our God. Many shall see it, and fear, and shall put their trust in the Lord.' Afterwards I opened upon Isaiah xl. 1: 'Comfort ye, comfort ye, my people, saith your God: speak ye comfortably to Jerusalem, and cry unto her, that her warfare is accomplished, that her iniquity is pardoned; for she hath received of the Lord's hand double for all her sin.'

I now found myself at peace with God, and rejoiced in hope of loving Christ. My temper for the rest of the day was, mistrust of my own great, but before unknown, weakness. I saw that by faith I stood; by the continual support of faith, which kept me from falling, though of myself I am ever sinking into sin. I went to bed still sensible [aware] of my own weakness, (I humbly hope to be more and more so,) yet confident of Christ's protection.

Mon., May 22nd. Under His protection I waked next morning, and rejoiced in reading the 107th Psalm, so nobly describing what God had done for my soul. I fell asleep again, and waked out of a dream that I was fighting with two devils; had one under my feet; the other faced me some time, but

> faded, and sunk, and vanished away, upon my telling him I belonged to Christ.

Charles tried to capture the glory of his experience in a hymn – probably *Where shall my wondering soul begin?* In his journal he says:

> At nine, I began a hymn upon my conversion, but I was persuaded to break off for fear of pride. Mr. Bray coming, encouraged me to proceed in spite of Satan. I prayed Christ to stand by me, and finished the hymn. Upon my afterwards showing it to Mr. Bray, the devil threw in a fiery dart, suggesting that it was wrong, and I had displeased God. My heart sunk within me; when, casting my eye upon a Prayer book, I met with an answer for him. 'Why boastest thou thyself, thou tyrant, that thou canst do mischief?' Upon this, I clearly discerned it was a device of the enemy to keep back glory from God. And it is most usual with him to preach humility, when speaking will endanger his kingdom, or do honour to Christ. Least of all would he have us tell what things God has done for our souls, so tenderly does he guard us from pride. But God has showed me, He can defend me from it, while speaking for Him. In His name therefore, and through His strength, I will perform my vows unto the Lord, of not hiding His righteousness within my heart, if it should ever please Him to plant it there.

The hymn may be said to be the birth of Methodist hymnody, and in that respect is worth setting down.

> Where shall my wondering soul begin?
> How shall I all to heaven aspire?
> A slave redeemed from death and sin,
> A brand plucked from eternal fire,
> How shall I equal triumphs raise
> Or sing my great Deliverer's praise?
>
> O how shall I the goodness tell,
> Father, which Thou to me hast showed?
> That I, a child of wrath and hell,
> I should be called a child of God!
> Should know, should feel my sins forgiven,
> Blest with this antepast [foretaste] of heaven!

And shall I slight my Father's love,
Or basely fear His gifts to own?
Unmindful of His favours prove,
Shall I, the hallowed cross to shun,
Refuse His righteousness to impart
By hiding it within my heart?

No! though the ancient dragon rage
And call forth all his host to war,
Though earth's self-righteous sons engage,
Them and their god alike I dare:
Jesus, the sinner's friend, proclaim –
Jesus, to sinners still the same.

Outcasts of men, to you I call,
Harlots, and publicans, and thieves;
He spreads His arms to embrace you all,
Sinners alone His grace receive.
No need of Him the righteous have;
He came the lost to seek and save.

Come, O my guilty brethren, come,
Groaning beneath your load of sin;
His bleeding heart shall make you room,
His open side shall take you in.
He calls you now, invites you home:
Come, O my guilty brethren, come.

For you the purple current flowed
In pardon from His wounded side,
Languished for you the eternal God,
For you the Prince of Glory died.
Believe, and all your sin's forgiven,
Only believe – and yours is heaven.

After his conversion, Charles followed John's example of nationwide itinerant evangelism for many years. His itinerancy diminished after his marriage to Sarah (known as Sally) Gwynne of Garth, Breconshire (Wales) in 1749; the couple settled in Bristol, at length acquiring a property in the Marylebone district of London in 1771. Charles' last itinerant mission was in 1756. His turn away from evangelistic itinerancy meant that he focused on preaching in local Methodist chapels and ministering to existing Societies. He and Sally had eight children; three survived into adulthood, of whom two – Charles (1757–1834) and Samuel (1766–1837) – would be publicly recognised for their musical talent.

Records of Charles' preaching indicate that he was often regarded as a better preacher than his brother. However, he had a tendency to preach at inordinate length; once, after preaching for two hours, he was launching into his third hour, but it proved too much for his congregation – they booed and hissed him out of the pulpit. He was strongly opposed to disruptive demonstrations of emotion by listeners, and was rumoured always to have a bucket of water ready to throw over anyone he felt was disturbing the sermon.

Although the Wesley brothers were of one mind on most matters, Charles became seriously troubled when John began behaving as though he had episcopal powers (so Charles perceived it). This issue came to the fore in 1784, when John laid hands on Thomas Coke (1747–1814) – even though Coke had already been episcopally ordained as a priest in the Church of England in 1772. Wesley now ordained Coke as superintendent (effectively bishop) of American Methodists, thus paving the way for the establishment of the American Methodist Episcopal Church. Charles mocked John's bishop-like actions in a satirical poem:

> So easily are Bishops made
> By man's or woman's whim?
> *Wesley* his hands on Coke hath laid,
> But who laid hands on *him?*

Charles feared that such actions on John's part would lead eventually to the separation of Wesleyan Methodists from the Anglican Church (as they did separate from it in 1795). When Coke himself ordained Francis Asbury (1745–1816) as American superintendent (he later took the actual title bishop), Charles was even more scathing:

A Roman emperor, 'tis said,
His favourite horse a consul made;
But Coke brings greater things to pass –
He makes a bishop of an ass.[5]

Charles' richest legacy to Methodism – indeed to Protestantism globally – was the large body of hymns he wrote. Together with the hymns of Isaac Watts, Wesley's compositions became the most widely sung of any English hymnwriter, across all denominations. Among his hymns were:

And can it be that I should gain
Arise, my soul, arise
Christ the Lord is risen today
Christ, whose glory fills the skies
Come, O Thou Traveller unknown
Come Thou long-expected Jesus
Depth of mercy! Can it be
Hark, the glad sound! The Saviour comes
Hark! The herald-angels sing
Jesu, lover of my soul
Jesus! The name high over all
Let earth and heaven agree
Let earth and heaven combine
Lo! He comes with clouds descending
(originally by John Cennick, heavily revised by Wesley)
Love divine, all loves excelling
O for a heart to praise my God
O for a thousand tongues to sing
O Thou who camest from above
Soldiers of Christ arise
Thou hidden Source of calm repose

Wesley's hymns have done more to nourish Evangelical spirituality for the past three hundred years than any other single element to emerge from the Revival.

---

5. 'Ass' referring to Asbury. The Roman Emperor was Caligula (A.D. 37–41). For more about Coke, Asbury, and the formation of the American Methodist Episcopal Church, see Chapter 4, Part 2, section 6.

5. John Nelson (1707–74)

Nelson was born in Birstall, Yorkshire. From his childhood he had known something of the Bible; his father would read it out loud every night in family worship. One evening Mr Nelson senior read out Revelation chapter 20, with its description of the day of judgment, where everyone who has ever lived stands before the throne of God, and is judged according to how they have lived on earth. Everyone whose name is not found written in the Book of Life is cast into the lake of fire. This terrified a young John Nelson. He never forgot it. Even though he grew up to be a godless young man (a travelling stonemason by trade), he could never get out of his mind that graphic picture of final judgment, and of the ungodly and unbelieving being cast into hell. 'I shed many tears in private,' he wrote in his journal, 'yet when I returned to my companions, I wiped my face and went back again to my folly. But O! the hell that I found in my mind when I was alone!'

On Sunday June 17th in 1739, Nelson was in London, when John Wesley preached one of his early open-air sermons at Moorfields to a crowd of 10,000. Among Wesley's hearers was Nelson. As he listened to Wesley, Nelson found the light of the Evangelical Gospel pouring into his mind. Nelson recorded in his journal:

> I was like a wandering bird, cast out of the nest, till Mr. John Wesley came to preach his first sermon in Moorfields. O that was a blessed morning to my soul! As soon as he got upon the stand, he stroked back his hair, and turned his face towards where I stood, and I thought fixed his eyes upon me. His countenance struck such an awful dread upon me, before I heard him speak, that it made my heart beat like the pendulum of a clock; and, when he did speak, I thought his whole discourse was aimed at me. When he had done, I said, 'This man can tell the secrets of my heart: [but] he hath not left me there; for he hath showed the remedy, even the blood of Jesus.' Then was my soul filled with consolation, through hope that God for Christ's sake would save me; neither did I doubt in such a manner any more, till within twenty-four hours of the time when the Lord wrought a pardon on my heart.

Having thus been converted through Wesley's preaching, Nelson then travelled about the north of England, preaching to others the same Gospel of Evangelical Arminianism through which he had found peace and new life. Sometimes Nelson accompanied Wesley on preaching trips, far beyond his native Yorkshire (to Cornwall and the Scilly Isles); but more often he journeyed on his own. His evangelistic labours in York, Sheffield, Leeds, and Manchester were instrumental in establishing in those cities flourishing Wesleyan religious societies. John Wesley held Nelson in high esteem; he reported in 1751 that 'the societies of Yorkshire, chiefly under the care of John Nelson, [are] all alive, strong and vigorous of soul.' Indeed, some have reckoned Nelson almost Wesley's equal as an impact-making preacher. His forthright evangelism aroused much hostility among the unconverted, who at one point (in 1744) conspired to have him 'impressed' into the army against his will; however, the Countess of Huntingdon – a Calvinist who never practised a cold-shoulder bigotry against Arminians – secured Nelson's liberation.[6] On another occasion, when preaching in Manchester, Nelson was struck by a stone thrown by an angry heckler; blood gushing down his face from the wound, Nelson kept on preaching.

Nelson's journal was published several times, in various revised and expanded forms, and has become one of the most important primary source documents of early Methodist experience. It testifies, among other things, both to the persecution faced by early Methodists and their sense of spiritual exaltation. In Bradford once to preach, Nelson was arrested by hostile magistrates and locked away in a filthy dungeon. Yet he said in his journal, 'My soul was so filled with the love of God that it was a paradise to me. I wished my enemies were as happy in their houses as I was in their dungeon.'

6. John Fletcher of Madeley (1729–85)

Born at Nyon in the Swiss canton of Vaud, not far from Geneva, Fletcher (or De la Flechiere, as his Swiss name was) at

6. See footnote 7, page 144, for the practice of impressing people into the armed services.

first chose a military career. His life, though, took a different course when he visited England in 1750, spent eighteen months learning English, and in 1752 became tutor to the children of the Hill family in Shropshire. Up until now, Fletcher had been a sincere but nominal Protestant; however, he was very deeply disturbed by a dream about the day of judgment. Soon after, travelling to London with the Hill family (Thomas Hill was an MP and needed to attend parliament), Fletcher met an elderly lady 'who talked so sweetly of Jesus Christ that I knew not how the time passed away.' Noticing Fletcher's new interest in religion, Susanna Hill (wife of Thomas) remarked that he would surely soon become a Methodist. His curiosity sparked, Fletcher sought out this body of people unknown to him, and joined a Wesleyan Methodist Society. He found the help he needed in John Wesley's published journal:

> I found relief in Mr. Wesley's Journal, where I learned that we should not build on what we feel, but that we should go to Christ with all our sins and all our hardness of heart. On January 21st I began to write a confession of my sins, misery, and helplessness, together with a resolution to seek Christ even unto death, but, my business calling me away, I had no heart to go on with it. In the evening I read the Scriptures, and found a sort of pleasure in seeing a picture of my wickedness so exactly drawn in the third chapter of the Epistle to the Romans, and that of my condition in the seventh; and now I felt some hope that God would finish in me the work He had begun ...
>
> In the evening I read some of the experiences of God's children, and found my case agreed with theirs, and suited the sermon I had heard on Justifying Faith. I called on the Lord for perseverance and an increase of faith, for still I felt some fear lest this should be all delusion. Having continued my supplication till near one in the morning, I then opened my Bible and fell on these words, 'Cast thy burden on the Lord, and He shall sustain thee; He will never suffer the righteous to be moved.' Filled with joy, I fell on my knees to beg of God that I might always cast my burden upon Him. I took up my Bible again, and fell on these words, 'I will be

> with thee; I will not fail thee, neither forsake thee; fear not, neither be dismayed.' My hope was now greatly increased, and I thought I saw myself conqueror over sin, hell, and all manner of affliction.
>
> With this beautiful promise I shut my Bible, and as I shut it, I cast my eye on the words, 'Whatsoever ye shall ask in My name I will do it.' So, having asked perseverance and grace to serve God till death, I went cheerfully to take my rest.

Encouraged by John Wesley, Fletcher entered the Anglican ministry in 1757, ordained in that year as deacon and priest. After three years of itinerant preaching, sometimes for Wesley, sometimes for the Countess of Huntingdon, at other times independently, he was at length in 1760 appointed to the large industrial parish of Madeley in Shropshire, a town dominated by coalmining and ironworks. Here Fletcher toiled as an energetic and eloquent evangelist for sixteen years, among a people he described as 'heathen', until his health collapsed in 1776. After a five-year absence, he had sufficiently recovered to resume his labours in Madeley in 1781. Fletcher was married that same year, late in life, to the lay woman preacher Mary Bosanquet.[7] He died in Madeley of typhus fever in 1785.

Fletcher was a notable theological and spiritual writer. Of his eight collected volumes, four are devoted to an Arminian polemic against Calvinism, the best-known of which was his *Checks to Antinomianism* (1771). Apart from John Wesley, Evangelical Arminianism never had a more zealous advocate than Fletcher of Madeley. He not only defended an Arminian view of free-will, but also a Wesleyan understanding of Christian perfection. Politically he was an outspoken opponent of the American Colonies in their quarrel with Britain. Such writings obviously have a limited appeal. Fletcher's non-polemical writings, however, have been judged on all sides to be of noble quality: his *Defence of Experimental Religion, A Rational Vindication of the Catholic Faith* (a defence of Trinitarian doctrine), *Portrait of St. Paul,* and *Pastoral Epistles* (to his congregation in Madeley).

7. See section 1 for Mary Bosanquet.

From 1768 to 1771, Fletcher was the principal of the Countess of Huntingdon's pastoral training college at Trevecca – a striking instance of Evangelical ecumenism, given the strong Calvinism of the Countess and the fervent Arminianism of Fletcher. However, Fletcher found he was unable to sustain his work at Trevecca consistently with his parish responsibilities in Madeley, relinquishing the principalship after only three years.

Fletcher's most enduring legacy was his living example of a Christian man. John Wesley's verdict was echoed by many:

> I was intimately acquainted with Mr. Fletcher for thirty years. I conversed with him morning, noon, and night, without the least reserve, during a journey of many hundred miles; and in all that time I never heard him speak an improper word, or do an improper action. To conclude, within fourscore years I have known many excellent men, holy in heart and life; but one equal to him I have not known, one so uniformly devoted to God. So unblameable a man, in every respect, I have not found, either in Europe or America, nor do I expect to find another such on this side eternity.

7. Thomas Maxfield (d. 1784)

Maxfield's place and time of birth are uncertain. We do know, however, that in May 1739 he underwent a vivid conversion experience under John Wesley's preaching in Bristol. Wesley had a positive opinion of Maxfield, making him his lay assistant. Within two years, Wesley left Maxfield in charge of the Foundery chapel, Wesleyan Methodism's chief centre in London, instructing Maxfield to lead in prayer and give people spiritual counsel. Soon, however, without Wesley's approval, Maxfield began preaching. At this point Wesley did not approve of lay preaching, and was disposed to listen to complaints from some Foundery worshipers against Maxfield. Wesley's mind was changed, however, by a combination of his mother Susanna's advice and hearing Maxfield preach with power. Maxfield thus became the first recognised Wesleyan lay preacher.

Like other Evangelical preachers, Maxfield's open-air sermons often provoked popular opposition; as a result, he was forcibly 'impressed' by a hostile mob into the navy in 1745 during an evangelistic mission in Cornwall.[8] After the captain of the ship to which Maxfield was taken would not accept him, he was then conscripted into the army, where he served for several years. Maxfield was eventually released back into civilian life through Wesley's lobbying on his behalf. At Wesley's request, the Bishop of Derry, William Barnard, then ordained Maxfield into the Anglican ministry. Maxfield worked alongside Wesley for the next decade.

However, divisions began to appear when Maxfield fell under the influence of George Bell, a Foundery member who in 1761 affirmed he had experienced the blessing of sinless perfection, together with a gift of performing miracles and predictive prophecy. Wesley tried to reason with Maxfield, but proved reluctant to take a hard line. This allowed a new quasi-charismatic millennialism to take root, and in early 1763 roughly a fifth of the Foundery members (two hundred people) broke away, under the leadership of Maxfield and Bell, as an independent movement. However, Bell's prediction that the second coming would occur on February 28th 1763 (a prediction endorsed by Maxfield) caused sufficient disruptive conduct for Bell's arrest by London magistrates – he was accused of fostering public disorder.

Maxfield survived this debacle to be elected preacher by a new independent (non-Wesleyan) Methodist Society in Snowsfields, south London, around April 1763, moving a few years later to Moorfields where a large congregation established a chapel for him. Ironically, by 1770 Maxfield had surrendered his belief in sinless perfection. In 1772 he endeavoured to reunite with the Wesleyan mainstream, but Wesley kept him at a distance. Perhaps Wesley's continued antagonism fuelled a public attack on him made by Maxfield in 1778, when Maxfield published a pamphlet charging Wesley with deliberately alienating the hearts of English Methodists from Whitefield, during one of the latter's sojourns in America. Wesley responded with a

8. See footnote 7, page 144.

counter-pamphlet. When Maxfield died in March 1784, no official reconciliation with Wesley had been effected, although there had been a softening of personal feeling on both sides.

Maxfield's life illustrates aspects within Wesleyan Methodism sometimes underplayed by historians – claims to charismatic-style gifts, apocalyptic millennialism, internal schism, and broken relationships.

8. Some other Wesleyan hymnwriters: John Bakewell (1721–1819) and Thomas Olivers (1725–99)

John Bakewell (1721–1819) is famous for the popular hymn *Hail Thou once despised Jesus*, the original shorter version of which is traditionally attributed to him. He was also a noted Wesleyan evangelist. A native of Brailsford in Derbyshire, Bakewell experienced a spiritual awakening at the age of eighteen while he was reading the Scottish Evangelical doctrinal and devotional classic, *Human Nature in its Fourfold State*, by the illustrious 'Marrowman' Thomas Boston.[9] He began evangelising shortly thereafter in 1744, the year of the first Wesleyan Methodist preachers' conference, and served thereafter as one of John Wesley's local Methodist preachers for some seventy years. Buried in the Wesleyan cemetery by Wesley's chapel in London, the epitaph on Bakewell's gravestone says, 'Sacred to the memory of John Bakewell, who departed this life March 18, 1819, age 98. He adorned the doctrine of God, our Saviour, and preached His glorious Gospel about seventy years.'

Thomas Olivers (1725–99) is famous as the author of the hymn *The God of Abraham praise*, allegedly written in John Bakewell's house in Westminster; Olivers' other hymns, however, have generally fallen into disuse. He was, in any case, known as a preacher and Arminian controversialist rather than a hymnwriter in his own day. Olivers was Welsh, from Tregynon on Montgomeryshire. His parents died while he was young; they

9. For Thomas Boston, see Chapter 3, Part 2, section 5. For the Marrow controversy, see Chapter 3, Part 1, section 2.

left a substantial sum of money earmarked for his physical and intellectual care. Even so, he entered manhood without much of an education, becoming a wayfaring shoemaker of no fixed abode. Olivers' life was transformed when his meanderings took him to Bristol and he heard George Whitefield preach. Joining a local Methodist Society in Bradford, he was soon a full-time itinerant preacher under the direction of John Wesley, a calling he fulfilled for twenty-two years; his evangelistic labours stretched from Cornwall at England's south-western extremity to Dundee in Scotland. He was also known as a full-blooded anti-Calvinist writer; among his works in this vein were his *A Letter to the Rev. Mr. Toplady* (1771),[10] and his *A Full Refutation of the Doctrine of Unconditional Perseverance* (1790).

In 1775 Wesley put Olivers in charge of the Wesleyan Methodist printing press; this, however, finally ended in a less than glorious fashion in 1789, when Wesley sacked him for alleged gross incompetence. Retiring from active service, Olivers died in Lewisham, south London, ten years later. Like Bakewell, he was buried with honour in the Wesleyan cemetery by Wesley's London chapel.

---

10. Toplady the Anglican Calvinist, who was one of Wesley's chief literary opponents. See Part 4, section 10.

6
The Evangelical Revival and English Dissent

1. Dissenters shun the Revival

If there was division within the Revival between Calvinists and Arminians, there was also division between the Revival and orthodox Dissent (not anti-Trinitarian Dissent, which was not in any case interested in revivals). By and large, with some exceptions, the world of orthodox Dissent remained relatively untouched by the Revival in the movement's first generation. Indeed, many orthodox Dissenters were suspicious of the Revival and deliberately held aloof from it. This can be graphically illustrated in the life and ministry of Congregationalist minister Isaac Watts.[1] Watts had been holding high the torch of Puritan-Evangelical religion in London, through all the dark and barren years of the period from 1702, when Watts was ordained, to the dawn of the revival in 1736, when Whitefield first preached with such remarkable impact in London's Anglican churches. Surely Watts would welcome this new spiritual awakening?

Perhaps strangely to modern sensibilities, Watts was very ambivalent about the Revival. On the one hand, he entertained friendly relations with Jonathan Edwards, the foremost American figure in the Revival; Watts read to his congregation Edwards' 1737 treatise *A Faithful Narrative of the Surprising*

1. For Watts, see the concluding remarks in Part 1, section 3, and Part 7 on Evangelical hymnody.

Work of God in the Conversion of Many Hundreds of Souls in Northampton which described the local revival in Edwards' congregation in 1734. Watts also oversaw an English printing of the work. However, Watts' relations with George Whitefield, the English Revival's pre-eminent preacher, were seriously conflicted.

Whitefield knew all about the famous Dr Watts, the great Dissenting preacher and poet, and visited him in 1739, perhaps hoping for Watts' blessing. Watts, however, proved somewhat stand-offish. Although he was glad to see the Gospel being preached with such power by a young Whitefield (who at that point was only twenty-five), Watts felt there were things in Whitefield's attitudes and behaviour that were indefensible, actually bringing the Gospel into disrepute. Partly this was because Whitefield, in these early days of his preaching, claimed a direct divine inspiration and guidance that Watts felt was unbalanced and fanatical – Jonathan Edwards would help cure Whitefield of this in 1740.[2] Further, Whitefield was too emotional and melodramatic in his preaching for Watts, and far too prone to condemn from the pulpit anyone who did not agree with him. Watts told Whitefield so quite bluntly:

> I said many things to warn him of the danger of delusion, and to guard him against the irregularities and imprudences which youth and zeal might lead him into, and told him so plainly, that though I believed him very sincere and desirous to do good to souls, yet I was not convinced of any extraordinary call he had to some parts of his conduct.

This reserve on the part of Watts towards Whitefield soon hardened into a definite coolness. In 1742, we find Watts complaining that Whitefield had 'a narrow zeal for the Church of England as a party' which was making Whitefield unwelcome among Dissenters in general. Watts' observation here was substantially correct, and later admirers of the Revival have often forgotten the strict, even prejudiced Anglicanism of the original Revival preachers. While it would be pleasant for the

---

2. See Chapter 4, Part 2, section 3.

romanticists of revival, therefore, to think that Isaac Watts, the paragon of orthodox Dissent and torch-bearer of Protestant faith in England's hour of darkness, rejoiced to see the great renewal of Christianity under Whitefield and the Wesleys, the truth is that Watts had very mixed feelings about it, and his relationship with Whitefield in particular fizzled out into coldness.

Watts' attitude turned out to be typical, overall, of orthodox Dissenters toward the Revival in its birth and infancy. There were some exceptions. As we have seen, Philip Doddridge (1702–51), Watts' fellow Congregationalist minister, himself no mean preacher, was warmly disposed to the Revival, while the Anglican Revival preacher Augustus Toplady had a huge esteem for John Gill (1697–71), the learned Calvinistic Baptist theologian. But on the whole, the great majority of orthodox Dissenters found Anglican Revival preachers too emotional, too disorderly, and just too Anglican for their tastes. Even though some Dissenting ministers were committed to promoting a vital Biblical and Reformation spirituality in their churches, therefore, most of them would not embrace the Revival as an ally in this objective.

It was not until the 1770s that streams of new life began to gush forth widely among English Dissenters. As case studies, let us consider the Particular (Calvinistic) Baptists and the General (Arminian) Baptists.

2. Renewal among Particular Baptists: The life and work of Andrew Fuller (1754–1815)

Most of England's Particular Baptists not only stood aloof from the Evangelical Revival; they almost prided themselves on doing so. The chief reason was precisely the Anglican context of the Revival. Particular Baptists were so preoccupied with the correct form of church government (especially its baptistic nature), they could not bring themselves to believe that anything good could come out of the Church of England, which they routinely denounced as a false Church. There was thus a principled disdain for the Revival and all its works. 'It is unlawful for any to attend the meetings of the Methodists, or to join in any worship which is contrary to the doctrines and ordinances of our Lord Jesus': so reads a 1754 resolution passed in a Particular Baptist church in Norwich. By 'the doctrines and ordinances of our Lord Jesus' was meant Particular Baptist church life.

Consequently, while the rivers of revival were fertilising the Anglican Church far and wide, it is not entirely surprising that the Particular Baptist churches were shrivelling away, both spiritually and numerically. Their spiritual decline was partly evident in their widespread acceptance of 'Hyper-Calvinism', the theological view that in Gospel proclamation, preachers ought not to give indiscriminate invitations to sinners to trust in Christ for salvation. This restriction was grounded in the belief that since Christ had died only for the elect, it followed that elect sinners alone had any right or calling to trust Him as Saviour. This type of preaching threw its hearers back into themselves, seeking after potential signs that they were or might be among the elect, which alone would entitle them to come to Christ for salvation. This often created a cold, even paralysing sense of distance between the soul and the Saviour. Alongside this withering Hyper-Calvinism, contemporary testimony also suggests that the Particular Baptist churches were in a sorry state of piety. As one of their pastors put it in 1785:

> Few seem to aim, pray, and strive after eminent love to God and one other. Many appear to be contented if they can but remember the time when they had such love in exercise; and then, tacking to it the *notion* of perseverance without the *thing*, they go on and on, satisfied, it seems, if they do but make shift just to get to heaven at last, without much caring how.[3]

The causes behind the numerical decline among Particular Baptists during this period (they lost around a third of their churches) are perhaps complex, but their theological and spiritual decline probably had some connection with it.

---

3. Andrew Fuller in his discourse *Causes of Declension in Religion, and Means of Revival.*

The outstanding figure whose influence was key in helping revive the theological and spiritual health of Particular Baptists was Andrew Fuller (1754–1815). Born at Wicken, in Cambridgeshire, he belonged to a Christian farming family, who worshiped in a Particular Baptist church in Soham; its pastor, John Eve, was a Hyper-Calvinist. Under Eve's preaching, with its absence of invitations to trust Christ for salvation, a young Fuller suffered greatly; he became increasingly aware of his alienation from God as a sinner, but did not know how to find reconciliation with God. He tried to find help in the writings of John Bunyan (*Pilgrim's Progress* and *Grace Abounding*), reading them attentively and weeping profusely. But not even Bunyan could help him. Eventually, a fifteen-year-old Fuller resolved, in a kind of holy desperation, to trust Christ for himself, in spite of his pastor's restrictive Hyper-Calvinism. He tells us about his attitude at the time:

> I was not then aware that any poor sinner had a warrant to believe in Christ for the salvation of his soul, but supposed there must be some qualification to entitle him to do it. Yet I was aware that I had no qualifications. On a review of my resolution at that time, it seems to resemble that of Esther who went into the king's presence, contrary to law, and at the hazard of her life. Like her, I seemed reduced to extremities, impelled by dire necessity to run all hazards, even though I should perish in the attempt. Yet it was not altogether from a dread of wrath that I fled to this refuge, for I well remember that I found something attracting in the Saviour. I must – I will – yes, I will trust my soul – my sinful, lost soul in His hands. If I perish, I perish! However it was, I determined to cast myself upon Christ, thinking peradventure He would save my soul.[4]

This experience proved formative for Fuller's life and theology, and when he was called into the pastorate (in his own Soham church in 1775, moving to Kettering in Northamptonshire in 1782), he devoted a large part of his energy among Particular

4. From Andrew Fuller's *Memoirs*.

Baptists to vindicating the unconditional freeness of the Gospel – its unfettered invitation to all sinners without exception (regardless of their election, or any knowledge of their election) to trust immediately in Christ for salvation. His classic treatise on this topic was *The Gospel Worthy of All Acceptation* (1785). Fuller emphasised the exegetical case for the 'free offer of the Gospel', arguing for its biblical truth on a passage-by-passage basis; without denying the particular design of the atonement, he also stressed its universal relevance, that Christ had done everything necessary for the salvation of all, which laid the foundation for any and every sinner to trust Him for a reconciled relationship with God. Fuller's preaching, writing, and personal influence were instrumental in liberating Particular Baptists from the chilly reign of Hyper-Calvinism, propelling them instead into a new era of theological vitality, committed evangelism, and overseas mission.

The missionary aspect of Fuller's theology found concrete expression in 1792, in the establishment at Kettering of the Baptist Missionary Society (the Baptists being Particular Baptists). Its first missionary was William Carey (1761–1834), pastor of Harvey Lane Baptist Church in Leicester. Carey was deeply impacted by Fuller's *Gospel Worthy of All Acceptation*, and by the published accounts of the unevangelised world by British naval explorer James Cook (1728–79), who made three voyages, between 1768 and 1779, in the Pacific Ocean and to Australia. Carey joined his literary pro-evangelistic voice to Fuller's in a 1792 treatise, *An Enquiry into the Obligations of Christians to use Means for the Conversion of the Heathens*. Perhaps the chief burden of this work was the thesis that the Great Commission of Matthew 28:18-20 was binding on the Church in all ages.[5]

With India chosen as the field of missionary labour, Carey sailed from England with his pregnant wife Dorothy in 1793, landing in Calcutta in November, and settling ultimately

---

5. Carey was trying to overthrow a widespread Protestant interpretation of the Great Commission that restricted it to the age of the apostles.

in the city of Serampore (in West Bengal). The Baptist Missionary Society sent others to help Carey – the most well-known being Joshua Marshman (1768–1837) and William Ward (1769–1823); but Carey remains (rightly) etched into the Baptist imagination as the great pioneer. Andrew Fuller was Carey's strongest and lifelong supporter in England. Famously, comparing the new missionary enterprise to going down into a coalmine, Carey said to Fuller, 'I will go down if you will hold the rope.' From this Fuller derived the nickname 'the rope-holder'.[6]

In addition to Fuller's successful campaign against Hyper-Calvinism and his intimate involvement in the Baptist Missionary Society, he wrote voluminously and acutely on a rich variety of theological subjects, such as the Deist controversy, anti-Trinitarianism (defending the Trinity against Unitarianism), the nature of true religion as including the affections as well as the mind, the self-evidencing light of the Gospel as the basis of faith,[7] and many other topics. Given the quality and extent of his writings, it would be no exaggeration to esteem Fuller as the greatest theologian England produced in the 18th Century.[8]

---

6. Much more could be said, of course, about Carey and the Baptist Missionary Society; but they were simply following a missionary trail blazed by Pietists and Moravians in the early part of the 18th Century. See Chapter 5, Part Two, for the Moravians. I forbear, therefore, from giving any more detailed account of the Baptist Missionary Society: it was replicating among Calvinistic Baptists a work already widely undertaken, and described in detail in this volume, by Pietists and Moravians.

7. All one needs to be able to believe the Gospel is the light of the Gospel itself. It has self-authenticating power. Fuller sets this out in his *The Gospel Its Own Witness* (1799–1800).

8. Fuller's only serious rival for this title was another Particular Baptist, the erudite John Gill (1697–1771), whose Bible commentary and systematic theology (his *Body of Divinity*) are still valued today. However, Gill's theology had a Hyper-Calvinist streak, and his literary style is ponderous. It is nonetheless striking that Gill and Fuller – two Particular Baptists – should stand out as 18th Century England's pre-eminent theologians.

3. The Life and work of Anne Dutton (1692–1765)

In this treatment of English Particular Baptists, attention should also be given to Anne Dutton (1692–1765). The Countess of Huntingdon was the most famous female publicist of the English Revival in its Calvinist branch, but she did not stand alone. Anne Dutton was doubly significant for holding Particular (Calvinist) Baptist convictions, when very few English Particular Baptists were – as yet – interested in revivals, and for being a noted theological author at a time when the discipline of theology was almost wholly restricted to men.

Dutton (or Williams, as she was born) was from Northampton, the daughter of pious Congregationalist parents. However, she was baptised as a believer in a Baptist church in her native city, where she began worshiping in her teens. Her first husband[9] died in 1720 after only five years of marriage; a few years later she married Benjamin Dutton, who had trained for the preaching ministry, and at length – in 1731 – became pastor of the Particular Baptist church at Great Gransden in Huntingdonshire. The church flourished under his preaching. Benjamin however died in 1747, during a return voyage from America when the ship sank.

After Benjamin's death, his widow became increasingly known as an author. Her spiritual sympathies placed her in the Revival camp, and she corresponded with many of the Revival's leading figures – Whitefield, Wesley, Philip Doddridge, the Countess of Huntingdon, Howell Harris in Wales. Her letters were highly valued as expressions of warm and wise Evangelical spirituality; a century after her death, some of Dutton's letters were published in a volume entitled *Selections from Letters on Spiritual Subjects*.

Dutton did not limit her literary ministry to writing letters. A notable theological author, Dutton penned treatises on the Lord's Supper (the most intimate communion we can have with Christ in any ordinance, she claimed) and Christian perfection

9. His name is known to us only as Mr Cattell.

(the Wesleyan distinctive, which she opposed). She authored some sixty hymns. Whitefield was a friend of Dutton's and an admiring promoter of her writings, helping to get them published. It has been reckoned that Dutton produced around fifty publications – theological treatises, poetry, hymns.[10]

One of Dutton's most striking pieces was a defence of her own freedom as a woman to write on theology. Dutton argued that she was not violating Paul's well-known prohibition on women teaching (in 1 Timothy 2), because she was exercising no *authority* – no one was under any obligation to read her treatises, nor were they to be read out as authoritative teaching to a gathered congregation. Like Priscilla correcting and instructing Apollos privately (Acts 18:26), Dutton was simply offering her views as a biblically literate Christian to anyone who wished to read them in private.

4. Renewal among General Baptists: Daniel Taylor (1738–1816) and the New Connexion

When the Evangelical Revival began in England, the General (or Arminian) Baptists had undergone a serious drift into anti-Trinitarianism ('rational Dissent' as it was known), little interested in a revival whose theology and spirituality were intensely Trinitarian. Their restoration to the Trinitarian faith of their origins came about through the labours of a Methodist, Daniel Taylor (1738–1816).

Taylor was born at Sourmilk Hall in Yorkshire, the son of a coalminer. Touched by the creative impulses of the Evangelical Revival in its Arminian form, Taylor and his father both became Wesleyan Methodists (Taylor did this in 1761). To the end of his life, Taylor remained steeped in Wesley's brand of Arminian revivalism. However, he became swiftly disenchanted with Wesley's style of leadership – Taylor felt Wesley was too dictatorial. He also ceased believing in infant baptism after studying the treatise *The History of Infant Baptism* by Anglican

10. To my knowledge, none of her hymns are generally sung today, which is why I have not classed her principally as a Calvinist hymnwriter.

theologian William Wall (1647–1728); the treatise, of course, defended the infant baptist practice of the Anglican Church, but had the opposite of its intended effect on Taylor, who felt its arguments were weak.

Consequently he was baptised as a believer in February 1763, and was then ordained some months later as a General Baptist minister, pastoring a group of General Baptists at Hebden Bridge, in West Yorkshire's Upper Calder valley.

Itinerating among other General Baptists, Taylor gained an increasing sense of how far this body of Dissenters had drifted into anti-Trinitarianism, and how disillusioned its Evangelical minority was. He forged a particular relationship with a body of Evangelical General Baptist congregations in Leicestershire, Nottinghamshire, and Derbyshire, with their geographical centre in the Leicester village of Barton-in-the-Beans (which gave them the nickname 'the Barton Society'). The first of these churches had originated in 1745, at which point it called itself simply an Independent church; but in the 1750s, it embraced General Baptist principles. By 1760, the church had become five churches, in Barton, Kegworth, Kirby Woodhouse, Loughborough, and Melbourne. Taylor helped to unify these churches under a common Evangelical Trinitarian and Arminian banner.

The upshot of Taylor's activities was that in June 1770, in Whitechapel (London), Taylor oversaw the organising of Evangelical General Baptists into a new religious body, the 'New Connexion of General Baptists'. Under Taylor's inspiration the New Connexion flourished; a year after Taylor died in 1816, the New Connexion could boast seventy congregations. This growth was partly due to Taylor's own vigorous and extensive evangelism in northern England, notably in Halifax. In that light, the New Connexion has correctly been termed 'a child of the Evangelical Revival'.

Taylor occupied several pastorates, and in 1798 became the first theology teacher of the newly established General Baptist Evangelical Academy, located at Mile End, in the East End of London (near Charing Cross). Taylor also wrote prolifically.

His publications included a defence of believers' baptism, *A Compendious View of Christian Baptism* (1772); a hymnbook, *Hymns and Spiritual Songs* (1772); a systematic theology, *The Principal Parts of the Christian Religion* (eight volumes, 1802); and he was for a few years the editor of the Evangelical General Baptist periodical, *The General Baptist Magazine*, whose name was changed in 1802 to *The General Baptist Repository*.

7
The Evangelical Revival and the birth of English hymnody

When the Reformation came to England in the 16th Century, it followed a Reformed or Calvinist rather than a Lutheran pattern. One of the things that distinguished the Reformed from the Lutherans was their attitude to public worship. From the very beginning, Lutherans were ardent singers of hymns, Martin Luther himself writing some great and enduring specimens, such as *A safe stronghold our God is still, Christ Jesus lay in death's strong bands,* and *Come Holy Spirit, God and Lord.* The Reformed, however, took a different line. By and large, the Reformed view was that the songs of the Bible, rather than humanly composed hymns, ought to be the material for public worship. We should note three things about this, however, since the historic Reformed view is often misunderstood.

First, by the songs of the Bible, Calvin and those of his mind did not mean exclusively the Psalms. They had the highest regard for the Psalms, but they did not rule out the possibility of using other biblical songs. So, for example, in Calvin's order of worship in Strasbourg, the *Nunc Dimittis* was always sung at the close of the Lord's Supper. The *Nunc Dimittis* is the song of Simeon found in Luke 2:29ff, 'Lord, now lettest Thou Thy servant depart in peace, according to Thy word: for mine eyes have seen Thy salvation,' etc.

Second, the Reformed wing of the Reformation did not necessarily restrict itself to those passages of the Bible which could be described as songs or materials of praise. Calvin again put together orders of worship in which the worshipers sang the Ten Commandments, which are not normally seen as songs or materials of praise.

Third, the Reformed did not even strictly adhere to the Bible alone; it was not uncommon for a Reformed congregation to sing the Apostles' Creed. The Creed, of course, is not actually in the Bible, although it is a summary of biblical theology. In Reformed Scotland, prior to the time of the Covenanters, Presbyterians would always end every psalm by singing the *Gloria Patri* – 'Glory be to the Father, and to the Son, and to the Holy Spirit, as it was in the beginning, is now, and ever shall be, world without end, Amen.'

The basic pattern of Reformed worship, then, was to sing passages from the Bible, mainly but not exclusively the Psalms, with a few other things like the Apostles' Creed and the *Gloria Patri*. But newly composed hymns were avoided. The Creed and the *Gloria Patri* managed to scrape in probably because they were not newly composed – they carried the aura of ancient tradition, dating back to the early Church fathers.

This, then, was the situation that the dawning 18th Century faced. English Protestant worship was Reformed, not Lutheran. It was dominated by the Psalms, which were available in a number of different translations – the Sternhold and Hopkins psalter, the Tate and Brady psalter, the Francis Rous psalter, and the John Patrick psalter. (In Puritan America there was the Bay Psalm Book.) It was Francis Rous's version that was adapted and adopted by the Church of Scotland in 1650, so becoming the Scottish metrical psalter. In early 18th Century England, however, it was the Sternhold and Hopkins psalter, not the Rous psalter, that was the most popular.

More than any other single person, it was Isaac Watts, the famous and admired Congregationalist preacher of London, who was responsible for converting the English to hymn-singing. This does not mean that he was either the first or the only advocate of English Protestant hymn-singing, even though he was the most influential. In fact, the movement towards hymn-singing had begun some decades before Watts, in the latter half of the 17th Century. The Particular or Calvinistic Baptists played a prominent role in this. John Bunyan, for example, was in favour of hymn-singing. He did not manage to persuade everyone in his Bedford congregation, so in order to keep everyone together and avoid a split in the church, they adopted a practice of mutual forbearance; those in the congregation who did not approve of hymn-singing would simply remain silent. Benjamin Keach (1640–1704) was, after Bunyan, the most significant English Calvinistic Baptist of the 17th Century, and Keach was fervently committed to hymn-singing. Unfortunately he did not avoid a split when he introduced it into his Southwark congregation. Passions could obviously run high over this matter.

Among Presbyterians, Richard Baxter (1615–91) and Matthew Henry (1662–1714) advocated the singing of hymns; among Anglicans, John (1623–87) and Henry Playford (1657–1709) published collections of hymns, and in 1703, royal authority was given to a supplement to the Tate and Brady psalter which contained sixteen hymns. However, no great inroads had been made into the general practice of most English Protestant congregations by these pioneers of hymn-singing. They had struck the first blow; but it was Isaac Watts who would carry everything before him, transforming the trickle into a flood.

When Watts wrote and published his hymns, he was acting from a principled theological conviction that the Christian voice of sung praise was improperly restricted and impoverished, if believers sang passages taken only from the very words of the Bible. Watts was particularly unhappy with the way that the Old Testament psalms dominated English Protestant worship, to the exclusion of almost everything else. He argued that it was theologically and spiritually unsuitable for New Testament worshipers to quarantine their songs of worship within the narrow confines of the lyrics of the Old Covenant. No doubt, Watts acknowledged, the songs of the Old Covenant, treasured up in the Psalter, were divinely inspired; yet this did not alter the fact that they were specifically Old Covenant songs, their expressions of worship embodied in the types, shadows, and symbols of the pre-Christian era. By contrast, now that Christ and the fullness of salvation had come, the people of God (Watts maintained) enjoyed gracious rivers of new light, new experience, new life, and new joy, that were foreign to Israel under the yoke of the Law of Moses.

> Why should I now address God my Saviour in a song with burnt sacrifices of fatlings and with the fat of rams? Why should I pray to be sprinkled with hyssop, or recur to the blood of bullocks and goats? Why should I bind my sacrifices to the horns of an altar, or sing the praises of God to high-sounding cymbals, when the Gospel has shown me a nobler atonement for sin, and appointed a purer and more spiritual worship? ... What need is there that I should wrap up the shining honours of my Redeemer in the dark and shadowy language of a religion that is now for ever abolished, especially when Christians are so vehemently warned in the Epistles of St Paul against a Judaising spirit in their worship as well as doctrine?

Here, then, was the compelling motivation for Watts' outspoken advocacy of hymns: to articulate the plenitude and richness of New Testament light and life – to sing the songs of the New Jerusalem, not merely those of the Old. Others had already used these arguments, encouraging the singing of hymns; we recollect Bunyan, Keach, Baxter, Matthew Henry, and the Playford brothers. The difference was that Isaac Watts produced a hymnbook of outstanding literary excellence. It was published in 1707, with the title *Hymns and Spiritual Songs*. A second revised edition came out in 1709. Thereafter Watts sold the copyright, and the hymn-collection was removed from his control. By the year of Watts' death in 1748, there had been sixteen editions of his hymns. Paradoxically, his hymns proved to be most popular among the preachers and people of the Evangelical Revival in the Anglican Church – paradoxical when we remember Watts' rather cool and ambivalent response to the Revival. However, it was indisputably the Anglican Evangelicals who embraced the hymns of Watts and thrust them into the liturgical limelight, where they have remained ever since. Among Watts' most celebrated hymns are:

Alas! And did my Saviour bleed?
Are we the soldiers of the cross?
Before Jehovah's aweful throne
Come dearest Lord, descend and dwell
Come let us join our cheerful songs
Come, we that love the Lord, and let our joys be known
From all that dwell below the skies let the Creator's praise arise
I'm not ashamed to own my Lord
Give to our God immortal praise
How pleased and blessed was I to hear the people cry
I'll praise my Maker with my breath
I sing the almighty power of God
Jesus shall reign where'er the sun
Join all the glorious names of wisdom, love and power
Joy to the world, the Lord is come!
Long as I live I'll bless Thy name
Our God, our help in ages past
Sweet is the work, my God, my King
There is a land of pure delight
This is the day the Lord hath made
We give immortal praise to God the Father's love
When I survey the wondrous cross

When John Wesley produced his *Collection of Psalms and Hymns* in 1737, over a third of them were by Watts. When George Whitefield produced his *Hymns for Social Worship* in 1753, most of the hymns were by Watts. The unguessed multitudes who found newness of life in the Evangelical Revival found in the hymns of Watts a perfect vehicle to give a voice to their converted and sanctified feelings.

We have already taken note of other hymnwriters of the Revival – John and Charles Wesley,[11] John Cennick, William

11. John's contributions were by way of translating German Pietist hymns into English.

Cowper, John Newton, Augustus Toplady, Joseph Hart, Anne Steele. They trod the path opened up by Watts. Since many of their hymns possessed commonly recognised literary and theological virtues, they helped to cement hymn-singing in the affection and practice of all those in the English-speaking world who were concerned for Evangelical faith and piety.

8
The Evangelical Revival in Wales

The Evangelical Revivals in England and Wales were not isolated from each other; they permeated each other, sometimes involving the same figures, notably George Whitefield and Howell Harris. Like England, the form in which Wales experienced its share of the Revival was within a moribund Anglican Church. The conditions prevailing in the Anglican Church in Wales did not differ significantly from those in England (see Part 1). In the present writer's opinion, the Welsh branch of the wider British Evangelical Revival abounds in some of the most fascinating and spiritually effective preachers and movements of 18th Century awakening to be found in the whole vast terrain (Britain, America, Germany) affected by revival-led renewal of Churches and communities. It is a pardonable exaggeration, but one might almost say that in the 18th Century Revival, Wales stepped forward onto the global spiritual scene, glowing with a vitality unsurpassed in any other land.

1. Morning Star of the Welsh Revival: Griffith Jones (1683–1761)

Before the Evangelical Revival had a nationwide impact across Wales, there had already been a more localised revival under the Welsh Anglican preacher Griffith Jones (1683–1761), minister of the parish church of Llandilo-Abercowyn from 1711, and rector of Llanddowror from 1716. For this reason, Jones is often nicknamed the 'Morning Star' of the Welsh Revival.

Born in 1683, probably at Penboyr, in Pembrokeshire, to pious parents, Jones sensed from his early years that his destiny lay in the Anglican ministry. After his education, he was ordained in 1708 by the Bishop of St David's, soon being appointed curate at Laugharne in Carmarthen; in 1711, he became the parish minister at Llandilo-Abercowyn, moving to Llanddowror in 1716. His 'upgrading' to full parish minister seems to have been in recognition of his popularity as a preacher when a curate at Laugharne. This was not, however, a popularity based on pleasing rhetoric, but on his captivating presentation of the Protestant understanding of the Gospel of salvation. This continued at Llandilo-Abercowyn and Llanddowror, where so many flocked to hear his sermons, he often preached in the church graveyard to accommodate the crowd. He also began preaching in other parishes in the locality. For a whole year, Jones seriously considered becoming a missionary to India under the auspices of the Society for the Promotion of Christian Knowledge, but he concluded after anguished reflection that Wales was as much a mission field as India.

A contemporary, Lady Frances Hastings, wrote this account of Jones' preaching:

> When Mr Griffith Jones preached in a large field ... there was an extraordinary manifestation of the grace and power of God over the assembled multitude, so that many were deeply convinced of their misery and guilt, and cried aloud in the most awful manner. When the sermon was ended, Lady Huntingdon inquired of many of those who had been so affected, the cause of their loud bitter cries. Most of them replied that they were so powerfully and deeply convinced of their sinfulness and awful condition in the sight of God, that they were afraid that He would never have mercy on them. The people in general through the whole assembly seemed greatly bowed down and humbled before the Lord, and many said they should never forget the time that God was so gracious unto them.[1]

1. This is from a later period (1748) after the Evangelical Revival was well under way, but there is no reason to think that Jones' pre-Revival preaching was of a different character.

Jones did not have the nationwide impact that the Evangelical preachers of the next generation were to have, and today he is usually remembered, not so much for his preaching, as for his mighty labours in educational work. This work, however, had a profoundly spiritual aspect at its heart. Deeply disturbed by the ignorance and illiteracy of many churchgoers, in 1730 Jones began establishing 'Circulating Schools' to remedy the defect. Funded by donations, these schools were set up for three monthly periods in a particular parish, before moving to another. By 1738, there were there were thirty-seven such Circulating Schools in Wales, teaching both young and old. By 1748, they were operating in every Welsh county except Flintshire. It has been estimated that some 150,000 people were educated in the Circulating Schools (a very significant proportion of the Welsh population, which at that time was 450,000). Jones also set up a seminary in Llanddowror to train teachers for the schools; here he employed many Nonconformists or Dissenters as tutors, claiming he could not find enough suitable people among his fellow Anglicans. This, however, did not mean that Jones had in any way drawn back from his personal allegiance to the Church of his ordination.

Jones described the religious character of the Circulating Schools thus:

> The masters are instructed, hired, and charged to devote all their time, and with all possible diligence, not only to teach the poor to read, but to instruct them daily (at least twice every day) in the principles and duties of religion from the [Anglican] Church Catechism, by the assistance of such explanations of it as they and the scholars are provided with, which they are not only to repeat out of book, but also to give the sense thereof in their own words, with a Psalm and prayer night and morning after catechising ... The poor people desire and thirst for the knowledge of God, and flock in great numbers to these schools in several places, when they can hardly get bread enough to satisfy their hunger, and were never oppressed with so much poverty before in this country in the memory of man.

Jones encountered much opposition to his educational work, especially from the Anglican hierarchy – he was often hauled before ecclesiastical tribunals and rebuked for his allegedly unchurchly activities, and his ungodly association with Dissenters. However, Jones was so ardent an Anglican in his personal convictions, it proved impossible to make the charges stick.

When the Evangelical Revival began to flourish in Wales in the later 1730s, Jones at first welcomed it, acting as a spiritual guide to the young Revival preachers Howell Harris and Daniel Rowland (see below). However, he distanced himself from the Revival in the following decade, partly (it has been argued) because he was anxious about the reputation of his Circulating School movement if he became too publicly identified with the Revival, which in Wales, as everywhere else, was divisive.

2. The life and work of Howell Harris (1714–73)

Howell Harris was probably the most colourful figure of the Welsh Revival,[2] certainly its most controversial, and its first great preacher. Born the youngest son of a farmer or carpenter (accounts vary) in 1714 at Trevecca in Brecknockshire, in the south-east of Wales, not a great deal is known of Harris' early life. His emergence as a figure of religious significance came when he experienced conversion at the age of twenty-one, after hearing a very pointed sermon in his parish church at Talgarth on the importance of the Lord's Supper. Harris was thrown into an intense period of self-questioning concerning his own fitness to receive the sacrament. This culminated in his decision to take part in communion on Easter Sunday in May 1735 – an event accompanied by a profound sense of being a vessel of God's mercy in and through Jesus Christ.

> I was convinced by the Holy Ghost that Christ died for me, and that all my sins were laid on Him. I was now acquitted at the bar of justice, and in my conscience. This evidenced itself

---

2. And indeed the English Revival, since he spent a good deal of time preaching in England.

> to be true faith by the peace, joy, watchfulness, hatred to sin, and fear of offending God that followed it.

This was followed on June 18th that year by another transformative spiritual experience, a 'baptism of fire' which Harris underwent while reading and praying in the tower of the church at Llangasty (where he worked as a schoolteacher). Harris described his spiritual baptism thus:

> Suddenly I felt my heart melting within me like wax before a fire, and love to God for my Saviour. I felt also not only love and peace, but a longing to die and to be with Christ. Then there came a cry into my soul within that I had never known before – Abba, Father! I could do nothing but call God my Father. I knew that I was His child, and He loved me and was listening to me. My mind was satisfied and I cried out, 'Now I am satisfied! Give me strength and I will follow Thee through water and fire.'

Harris' conversion and baptism of fire led swiftly to evangelism, which took the shape of his reading out passages from edifying literature to other people of his parish in their homes. This then developed into the practice of directly preaching to them. As various people professed faith under his ministry, which rapidly spilled out beyond his parish, Harris began forming them into small groups for mutual edification; there were some fifty of these groups scattered across the south of Wales by 1736. Harris also read the leading American Evangelical Jonathan Edwards' *Faithful Narrative of the Surprising Work of God in the Conversion of Many Hundred Souls in Northampton*, describing the local revival in Northampton, Massachusetts, in 1734–35; the account impacted Harris profoundly.[3]

Harris' isolated evangelistic activity came to an end when, in 1737, he encountered the Anglican Evangelical curate Daniel Rowland, who in the Welsh village of Llangeitho was preaching the same core message as Harris to his congregation, with equal spiritual effect (see the next section for Rowland's life story). The

---

3. See Chapter 4, Part 2, section 3 for Edwards and the Northampton awakening.

two preachers joined forces, and their partnership of mutual encouragement and united activities lent a whole new force to the growing Welsh awakening. Unlike Rowland, Harris was not – and never would be – ordained in the Anglican Church. His various attempts at being accepted for ordination all failed, owing to the antipathy of the Welsh Anglican hierarchy to Harris' fiery, freestyle evangelism.[4] This, however, did nothing to dampen Harris' enthusiastic attachment to the Anglican Church, of which he declared 'that our Church is a pure Church, [and] that I could undertake to prove what it holds. I stay not in it because I was brought up in it, but because I see it according to God's Word.'

It was not long before other preachers were involved in the Welsh Revival, notably William Williams (see section 4) and Howell Davies (see section 5), the former of whom experienced Evangelical conversion under Harris' preaching. This of course spread the impact of the movement ever wider. Meanwhile the same waves of Evangelical Revival were now sweeping through England, and the Welsh and English Revivals became linked when Harris and George Whitefield met and became close friends. Whitefield had heard reports of Harris' preaching, and wrote to him in 1738. Harris responded warmly, and in early 1739 Whitefield arrived in Wales, where he preached in Cardiff, and then for the first time met Harris in the flesh. He recorded the event:

> After I came from the seat [the judge's seat at Cardiff Town Hall, from which Whitefield had been preaching to a crowd of a hundred] I was much refreshed with the sight of my dear brother Howell Harris, whom though I knew not in person, I have long since loved in the bowels of Jesus Christ, and have often felt my soul drawn out in prayer in his behalf. A burning and shining light has he been in those parts, a barrier against profaneness and immorality, and an indefatigable promoter of the true Gospel of Jesus Christ. About three or four years God has inclined him to go about doing good. He is now

4. Daniel Rowland was already ordained prior to becoming Evangelical.

> about twenty-five years of age. Twice he has applied (being every way qualified) for Holy Orders, but was refused, under a false pretence that he was not of age, though he was then twenty-two years and six months. About a month ago he offered himself again, but was put off. Upon this, he was, and is still resolved to go on in his work; and indefatigable zeal has he shown in his Master's service. For these three years (as he told me from his own mouth) he has discoursed almost twice every day for three or four hours together, not authoritatively, as a minister, but as a private person, exhorting his Christian brethren ....
>
> He has been made the subject of numbers of [hostile] sermons, has been threatened with public prosecutions, and had constables sent to apprehend him. But God has blessed him with inflexible courage – instantaneous strength has been communicated to him from above, and he still continues to go on from conquering to conquer. He is a most catholic spirit, loves all who love our Lord Jesus Christ, and therefore he is styled by bigots a Dissenter. He is contemned [scorned] by all who are lovers of pleasure more than lovers of God; but God has greatly blessed his pious endeavours. Many call and own him as their spiritual father, and, I believe, would lay down their lives for his sake. He discourses generally in a field, but at other times in a house, from a wall, a table, or anything else. He has established nearly thirty Societies in South Wales, and still his sphere of action is enlarged daily. He is full of faith, and the Holy Ghost.

At this point, Harris and Daniel Rowland felt the need to secure harmony and cooperation between the Gospel preachers of Wales, whether Anglican or Dissenter. To this end, Harris organised a gathering of ministers and lay teachers in August 1740 at Defynnog. However, Anglicans and Dissenters fell out over the vexed issue of denominational loyalty (one must never underestimate the severe frictions between Anglican and Dissenter in the 18th Century, when Dissenters routinely condemned the Anglican Church as false, and Anglicans often denounced Dissenters as schismatics). The two parties also differed over the emotive style of Anglican revival preaching, exemplified in Harris and Rowland, and in the strong responses such preaching generated in hearers (crying out, swooning, etc.), to which Dissenters objected as disorderly and unseemly. Unity was not achieved, therefore, and Welsh Anglicans and Dissenters had to part ways.

A greater measure of success crowned a fresh endeavour towards cooperation among those affected by the Revival in February 1741, at Llandovery in Carmarthenshire. Something like thirty Welsh Evangelical leaders met here, and drew up a set of rules for the Evangelical 'religious societies' that had sprung up in the wake of the preaching of Harris and Rowland. These rules bound Welsh Methodism to the Anglican Church, much as John Wesley had done in England, acknowledging the doctrinal soundness of the Anglican liturgy and the Thirty-Nine Articles of the Prayer Book.[5] Welsh Methodists, it was decided, should attend their local Anglican parish, meet in their Societies every two months, exercise an intimate brotherly and sisterly care over each other (including examination of each other's moral and spiritual lives, with rebuke where necessary), and consecrate one day each month to corporate prayer and fasting. These rules established the framework and ethos for Welsh Methodism in the succeeding generations.

The Societies also functioned within the overall context of an umbrella 'Association'. The first meeting of the 'Association of the Calvinistic Methodists in Wales' took place in January 1743 at Watford, near Caerphilly in south Wales (not the famous English Watford!). Among those who attended were Harris, Rowland, Whitefield, John Cennick,[6] and William Williams.

Meanwhile, George Whitefield had been so impressed by Harris, he resolved on introducing him at first hand to the English Revival. The Welsh preacher agreed, and once he was in London with Whitefield, Harris felt so burdened for the English work, and so bound in fellowship with his English Evangelical friends, that he spent roughly equal amounts of

---

5. The Thirty-Nine Articles are Anglicanism's official confession of faith.

6. See Part 4, section 1.

time over the 1740s in England and Wales. He often preached in Whitefield's London Tabernacle. In the division between the Calvinist and Arminian wings of the English Revival in 1741, Harris adhered to Calvinism; both Daniel Rowland and Whitefield were instrumental in helping cement his attachment to a Calvinist understanding of the disputed issues. When the religious Societies in England that embraced Calvinism became separate from Wesley's United (Arminian) Societies, Harris welded the English Calvinist Societies together with the Welsh societies (of which there now roughly seventy), creating an Anglo-Welsh Calvinistic Methodism. Whitefield was the overall supervisor of this movement, with Harris deputising for him in Wales. From 1745, Harris was also in charge of the English Societies – Whitefield was too busy preaching throughout Britain and the American Colonies.

It was, however, at this juncture that Harris began to lose his credibility as a Revival leader. He tried unsuccessfully to act as a peacemaker between the Calvinist and Arminian Societies, which merely ended in his alienating both sides. In his preaching, he began speaking in a perplexing way about the Trinity, as if it were the whole Godhead that had suffered and died on the cross, rather than God the Son in His incarnate humanity in obedience to His heavenly Father. Nor would Harris allow anyone to correct him; his attitude became increasingly abrasive and dictatorial.

The final straw for most Evangelical Calvinists came in 1749, when Harris took up with a woman other than his wife Anne, namely, 'Madam' Sidney Griffith, estranged spouse of a member of the Welsh gentry. Harris claimed she was a prophetess, insisting that others publicly acknowledge her. An alarmed Whitefield intervened, and in January 1750 removed Harris from all connection with the London Tabernacle. A few months later in Wales, Harris was also disowned by Daniel Rowland and Willliam Williams; most of the Welsh Calvinistic Methodists sided with Rowland and Williams. Harris thereupon withdrew from public involvement in the Revival, retreating into his home at Trevecca, accompanied by a faithful minority. His aberrant conduct over this period has been attributed to extreme physical and mental exhaustion, and the effects of a severe head-wound received from a heckler while he was preaching.[7]

Harris began to return to a more sober frame of mind after the death of Madam Sidney in 1752. The rift between the preacher and his wife was healed, and he now devoted himself to forming and nurturing at Trevecca the same type of spiritual community enjoyed by the Moravians at Herrnhut in Saxony.[8] The Trevecca community housed roughly a hundred people, who were put to work in a bakery, a printing press, orchards, and other places of employment, all under the close oversight of Harris as a sort of spiritual father. Their collective devotional life was ordered by a strict 'rule' (again, much like the Moravians at Herrnhut): a kind of Protestant monasticism without the vows of celibacy.

When the Seven Years' War (1756–63) broke out – an international conflict, in which the British Empire and Prussia fought an alliance comprising France, Spain, Sweden, Russia,[9] and most of the German states other than Prussia – Harris became a Captain Lieutenant in his local militia, after securing permission to preach to them. He actively recruited men for Britain's war effort. This included five men from the Trevecca community, who became part of Britain's 58th Regiment stationed at Hereford, the cathedral city of the English county of Herefordshire, lying along the eastern borders of the Welsh county of Powys (where Trevecca was located). In the War, Harris felt himself to be fighting for Protestant Britain against Catholic France, whose troops were at any moment expected to invade British soil.[10] The 58th Regiment was ultimately

7. It has been theorised that Harris suffered brain damage from this head-wound.

8. For Moravian community life at Herrnhut, see Chapter 5, Part 2, section 4, under the heading **Social religion**.

9. Russia changed sides in 1762, becoming an ally of Britain and Prussia.

10. The Seven Years' War ended as a very significant victory for Britain and Prussia.

disbanded in 1762, the year prior to the War's conclusion, at which point Harris exchanged his military life to be again an evangelistic soldier of Christ.

1762 witnessed a fresh and powerful wave of revival in Wales, with Daniel Rowland's village of Llangeitho at its heart. Harris once more preached alongside his old friends, Rowland and William Williams, but did not resume a position of leadership – a younger generation of Welsh lay preachers no longer looked to him for inspiration or guidance. He was, however, a key figure in 1768 in the creation, on his land at Trevecca, of a pastoral training college for equipping Evangelical preachers. The college was a venture in Calvinist-Arminian ecumenism: the leading Calvinists, George Whitefield and Lady Hastings of Huntingdon,[11] were closely involved, together with Harris, while from 1768 to 1771 the leading Evangelical Arminian, John Fletcher of Madeley, was head of the college.[12]

Harris died in July 1773, after a year of ill health. His funeral at Talgarth attracted many thousands of mourners. The Harris of latter years may seem a faint copy of the earlier dynamic, effectual preacher and brilliant organiser of converts into Societies; but no one questions the central role he played in the Evangelical Revival both in Wales and England. The large body of diaries he wrote are a major source for the religious history of the period.

3. Daniel Rowland (1713–90)

Along with Howell Harris, Daniel Rowland was the Welsh Revival's greatest preacher.[13] He was born in 1711 (or 1713 – accounts differ) in Nantcwnlle to the Anglican rector of Llangeitho. After his education was complete, the Bishop of St David's ordained him in 1734, the same year that he married

---

11. See Part 4, section 11, for the Countess of Huntingdon. She provided the finance for the Trevecca training college.
12. See Part 5, section 6, for Fletcher of Madeley.
13. Comparisons are odious. Many would say Rowland was greater, but the judgment simply plunges us into the complex question of what constitutes greatness.

Eleanor Davies of Caer-llugest, about whom we know little. He then became the curate of Llangeitho and Nantcwnlle. His brother John was also ordained, but at this point neither man had any experiential knowledge of religion – their father (by now dead) had not bequeathed this legacy to his sons. However, during the winter of 1734–35, Daniel heard Griffith Jones[14] preach to a crowd in a churchyard, perhaps at Llanddewibrefi; it seems that Jones observed some peculiar unsettledness in Rowland, pointed at him, and declared, 'Oh for a word to reach your heart, young man!' Rowland listened intently to the rest of the sermon, and it proved the beginning of a new spiritual life, mentored by Jones.

Soon ordained priest, Rowland's own preaching now became dynamic and riveting, but at this early stage was very lop-sided, thundering out the terrors of the law and hell without any expression of grace – so much so, people labelled him 'the angry clergyman'. He was corrected, however, by a brotherly Dissenting minister, the Presbyterian Philip Pugh (1679–1760), minister at Cllgwyn, who counselled him:

> Preach the Gospel to the people, dear Sir, and apply the Balm of Gilead, the blood of Christ, to their spiritual wounds, and show the necessity of faith in the crucified Saviour. If you go on preaching the law in this manner, you will kill half the people in the country, for you thunder out the curses of the law, and preach in such a terrific manner, that no one can stand before you.

Rowland accepted the fraternal rebuke, and his preaching was transformed; he now began proclaiming the love and mercy of God, expressed in the free gift of salvation in Christ from all the miseries of a broken law and its consequences. As a result, his hearers began to experience the assurance of salvation. As Rowland's friend William Williams (see next section) commented:

> After preaching for some years the stormy law and wounding very many, his tone changed; he proclaimed full, complete,

14. See section 1.

> perfect salvation through the Messiah's death on Calvary. Henceforth the power of his sweet doctrines nurtured faith by revealing the Mediator, God and Man, as the foundation of free salvation; the One who freely redeemed by His precious blood; and all the treasures of heaven for a poor believer.

Rowland also now took it upon himself to imitate Griffith Jones in preaching outside the boundaries of his own parish without permission (technically against Anglican church law). But men like Jones and Rowland felt driven by a higher law, that of the Gospel and its burning relevance to all sinners. People began flocking to Rowland's itinerant open-air preaching, which generally took place on weekdays – he was usually back in Llangeitho preaching in his own church on Sundays. He experienced his share of violent opposition during his preaching. For example, he was overwhelmed by such a continuous shower of stones and other objects at Llanilar, he had no option but to flee from the raging mob.

On one of the occasions when he was itinerating, preaching at Defynnog in 1737, Rowland met Howell Harris. The two men bonded instantly and formed a sort of preaching duo, with Rowland letting Harris preach from his pulpit in Llangeitho despite the latter's lay status. Harris recorded his exuberant estimate of Rowland as a preacher:

> He had vast power to call all to Christ. Never did I hear such calling, such earnest striving to call all to Christ (many cried out!), showing that God's love is eternal and unchangeable. Blessed be God for the amazing gifts and power given to dear brother Rowland. Surely there is no such ministry in Wales. I never heard of the like.

In his biography of Rowland, J. C. Ryle, the great Victorian Evangelical Bishop of Liverpool, gave this colourful but accurate description:

> The effect of Rowlands' ministry from this time forward to his life's end was something so vast and prodigious, that it almost takes away one's breath to hear of it. We see unhappily so very little of spiritual influences in the

> present day, the operations of the Holy Ghost appear confined within such narrow limits and to reach so few persons, that the harvests reaped at Llangeitho a hundred years ago sound almost incredible. But the evidence of the results of his preaching is so abundant and incontestable, that there is no room left for doubt. One universal testimony is borne to the fact that Rowlands was made a blessing to hundreds of souls. People used to flock to hear him preach from every part of the Principality [Wales], and to think nothing of travelling fifty or sixty miles for the purpose. On sacrament Sundays it was no uncommon thing for him to have 1,500, or 2,000, or even 2,500 communicants! The people on these occasions would go together in companies, like the Jews going up to the temple feast in Jerusalem, and would return home afterwards singing hymns and psalms on their journey, caring nothing for fatigue.[15]

George Whitefield's contemporary verdict bears out Ryle's words:

> The power of God at the sacrament, under the ministry of Mr Rowland, was enough to make a person's heart burn within him. At seven in the morning I have seen, perhaps, ten thousand from different parts, in the midst of the sermon, crying 'glory', 'praise', ready to leap for joy.

Whitefield's account shows some of the 'unseemly' responses to the preaching of Rowland (and Harris) in the Welsh Revival to which Welsh Dissenters objected.

Rowland's sermons began to be published – there were collections in 1739, 1762, 1772, and 1779. A number of these sermons were translated into English: see an example in the Primary Historical Sources section from a sermon on Romans 8:28. Rowland also turned his hand to hymn writing, and some of his hymns were included in early Welsh Evangelical hymnbooks in 1740 and 1742. He translated into Welsh some of the English-language classics of piety, such as John Bunyan's *Holy War* in 1744, and Thomas Boston's *The Crook in the Lot:*

---

15. Ryle calls him 'Rowlands', an alternate spelling.

or the Sovereignty and Wisdom of God in the Afflictions of Men, Displayed in 1769.[16]

Unfortunately, as we have seen in our account of Harris' life, he and Rowland drifted painfully apart in the latter half of the 1740s. This rift culminated in Rowland's disowning of Harris in 1750, after the latter had taken 'Madam' Sidney Griffith as his partner, declaring her a prophetess and demanding that others acknowledge her. The future of Welsh Methodism passed out of Harris' hands into those of Rowland and William Williams of Pantycelyn, whom the great bulk of the Evangelicals of Wales followed.

In the 1740s, Rowland increasingly found himself barred from Anglican churches and pulpits by hostile clergy, including churches where he had once been welcome. The most famous or notorious instance of such exclusion came on the heels of a fresh outpouring of revival in 1762, often reckoned to be even deeper and more powerful than the Springtime awakening of the 1730s. Rowland's church at Llangeitho was at the centre of the new movement. But in 1763, the Bishop of St David's revoked Rowland's license to preach, and appointed a new curate for Llangeitho, effectively sacking Rowland. A relative of one who was present when Rowland was dismissed from his own church has left this account:

> My uncle was at Llangeitho church that very morning. A stranger came forward and served Mr. Rowlands with a notice from the Bishop, at the very time when he was stepping into the pulpit. Mr. Rowlands read it, and told the people that the letter which he had just received was from the Bishop, revoking his license. Mr. Rowlands then said, 'We must obey the higher powers. Let me beg you will go out quietly, and then we shall conclude the service of the morning by the church gate.' And so they walked out, weeping and crying. My uncle thought there was not a dry eye in the church at the moment. Mr. Rowlands accordingly preached outside the church with extraordinary effect.[17]

16. For John Bunyan, see Volume 4, Part 1, section 6. For Thomas Boston, see this volume, Chapter 3, Part 1, section 2, and Part 2, section 5.

17. Again we see the alternate spelling 'Rowlands'.

Committed Anglican though he was, Rowland now had to behave like a Dissenter, conducting worship in a house. But the loss was the Anglican Church's, since virtually the entire congregation at Llangeitho adhered to Rowland, leaving the parish church almost deserted. A chapel was soon constructed for Rowland and his congregation at Gwynfil, not far from Llangeitho.

Rowland's last years were relatively free from harassment, and he continued his preaching with as much evident energy as ever before, to great crowds. One of Rowland's children wrote this narrative of his death:

> My father made the following observations in his sermons two Sundays before his departure. He said, 'I am almost leaving, and am on the point of being taken from you. I am not tired of work, but in it. I have some presentiment that my heavenly Father will soon release me from my labours, and bring me to my everlasting rest. But I hope that He will continue His gracious presence with you after I am gone.' He told us, conversing on his departure after worship the last Sunday, that he should like to die in a quiet, serene manner, and hoped that he should not be disturbed by our sighs and crying. He added, 'I have no more to state, by way of acceptance with God, than I have always stated: I die as a poor sinner, depending fully and entirely on the merits of a crucified Saviour for my acceptance with God.' In his last hours he often used the expression, in Latin, which Wesley used on his deathbed, 'God is with us'; and finally departed in great peace.

4. William Williams Pantecelyn (1717–91)[18]

William Williams has become known as the great hymnwriter of the Welsh Revival, indeed the great Welsh hymnwriter of any age. In his own day, he was at least equally known as an outstanding Evangelical preacher alongside Howell Harris and Daniel Rowland.

---

18. Or Williams Pantycelyn, or William Williams of Pantycelyn.

Surprisingly little was written about Wiliams, by himself or others, during his lifetime, but we can glean the following. He was born in 1717, a native of Llanfair-ar-y-bryn in Carmarthenshire. The family moved to Pantycelyn, not far away, in the 1740s, the new location giving Williams his 'nickname'. He was raised a Congregationalist (his father John was an elder in the Congregationalist church at Cefnarthen), and educated in the Dissenting Academy at Llwynllwyd close to Talgarth – Dissenting academies, as noted previously in this Chapter, often providing an education equal to anything Anglicans could obtain at Oxford or Cambridge. Williams' original purpose had been to specialise in medicine, but his life was radically diverted into a new course when, in 1737, he experienced conversion through the preaching of Howell Harris in the churchyard at Talgarth (where Harris' home parish was situated). 'I was caught by a summons from on high' was how he expressed it. In a funeral poem for Harris he wrote:

> Behold! the place I saw you first
> (The sight I never shall forget):
> Afront the church's doors you stood,
> On level path your feet were set.
> A solemn awe shone from your soul;
> One summons you had come to give:
> 'Delay not! Hear your God now call!
> O flee the judgment! Flee and live!'

Despite his Congregationalist upbringing, the converted Williams decided to follow his mentor Harris into the Anglican ministry; in 1740, the Bishop of St David's ordained him as a deacon, although Williams rose no higher – his Revival activities prejudiced the Anglican hierarchy against him, and his later application to be 'upgraded' from diaconate to priesthood was refused.

Williams became curate in the linked churches at Llanwrtyd, Llanfihangel Abergwesyn, and Llanddewi Abergwesyn. Some of his own parishioners officially complained about his conduct in June 1742, seeking to muzzle him (he was charged with no fewer than nineteen misdemeanours before the Archdeacon's Court). Undeterred, Williams – at the urging of George Whitefield – pursued a course of itinerant Evangelical preaching throughout Wales. By all accounts, his preaching was marked by a profound impact on his hearers; although remembered today as a hymnwriter, Williams in his own day was scarcely inferior to Howell Harris and Daniel Rowland as an effective Welsh Gospel orator. Many professed conversion through his evangelism, and – in keeping with the Methodist ideal – Williams organised converts into societies for ongoing mutual edification. In April 1743, he stepped down from his curacy to become Daniel Rowland's assistant at Llangeitho, which became his base of operations for continued lifelong itinerancy.

Williams underwent his own share of the violent persecution so often dealt out to Methodist preachers. On one striking occasion, he was preaching at Bala in an inn, when a crowd led by the local squire turned up, resolved on attacking him. Williams fled, changing his clothes to conceal his identity. However he was then inwardly stricken by Jesus' warning that He would be ashamed at the Last Day of all who denied Him before men. Williams thereupon put his own clothes back on, and returned to face the hostile crowd – who attacked him, forcing him again to flee.

It soon became apparent that the Welsh Revival had found in Williams, not only a preacher of unusual power, but its supreme poet. Most of his hymns were written in Welsh, and only a relatively small selection has been translated into English. This however includes the English version of *Arglwydd, arwain trwy'r anialwch* (O Lord, lead through the wilderness), translated as *Guide me, O Thou great Jehovah,* which has earned and retained widespread popularity across the English-speaking world. Williams published five Welsh hymn collections, beginning with *Aleluia* in 1744, and two English collections. The publication in 1762 of the collection *Caniadau y rhai sydd ar y môr o wydr* ('the songs of those on the crystal sea') was instrumental in helping stir a new movement of awakening centred in Llangeitho – frequently regarded as the single most pure and powerful manifestation of revival in Wales in the 18th Century, where preaching and song blended in an overwhelming spiritual and emotional harmony.

We must not limit Williams' literary activity and influence to his hymn writing. He wrote non-hymnic poetry – *Golwg ar deyrnas Crist* ('A View of Christ's Kingdom', 1756), and *Bywyd a marwolaeth Theomemphus* ('The Life and Death of Theomemphus', 1764), epics that express Williams' Evangelical Calvinist theology and spirituality. His theological prose included *Pantheologia, Neu Hanes Holl Grefyddau'r Byd* ('Pantheologia, or a History of All the World's Religions', published in several volumes between 1762 and 1779), which revealed Williams' breadth and depth of learning, and the more practical *Drws y society profiad* ('A Gateway to the Experience Meeting', 1777), a guidebook for the conduct of Welsh Methodist religious societies.

Taking Williams' literary works collectively, they had a highly significant effect on the future development of the Welsh language, their impact reaching far into the 20th Century. In the sphere of sacred poetry Williams remains unrivalled in Welsh to this day, the Isaac Watts and Charles Wesley combined of Welsh hymnody.

5. Howell Davies (1717–70)

Howell Davies was probably born in Monmouthshire, probably around 1717. We know almost nothing of his youth. He first comes to the historian's attention as a student in a school run by Griffith Jones, the Morning Star of the Welsh Revival (see section 1) – he was Jones' favourite pupil. It seems he was converted under Jones' preaching or teaching, although in a quiet, unspectacular manner.[19] Encouraged by Jones, Davies entered the Anglican ministry, ordained as deacon by the Bishop of St David's, and becoming curate at Llys-y-frân in Pembrokeshire in the Spring of 1740. His forthright Evangelical preaching alienated the congregation, however, and he left after eight

19. Others think he was converted through the preaching of Howell Harris.

months, an apparent failure. Nonetheless, in August 1740 he was ordained a priest, working as assistant to Jones at Llanddowror and Llandeilo Abercywyn. From here he began itinerating throughout Pembrokeshire; his open-air evangelism now met with phenomenal success, gaining him the nickname 'the apostle of Pembrokeshire'. The records (such as Howell Harris' journals) state that Davies' preaching was marked by tremendous emotional force, especially the attractive sweetness of his proclamation of God's saving love in Christ, which so moved his hearers that many fainted away. According to the testimony of the first generation of Welsh Revival converts, Davies was equal to Harris and Daniel Rowland in preaching power and the popular esteem in which he was held.

In 1748 Davies established a headquarters for his work in a building at Haverfordwest; here the religious society he had formed in the locality gathered for worship. Davies named it the Tabernacle, after George Whitefield's Tabernacle in London, where Davies (a good friend of Whitefield's) often preached. Davies was ably assisted in the Haverfordwest Tabernacle by John Sparks, who however sided with Howell Harris when the split came between Harris on one side, and Rowland and William Williams on the other – whereas Davies stood with Rowland and Williams.

Another important centre of Davies' work was a chapel constructed in 1754 at Woodstock; Whitefield preached the dedication sermon for the chapel in 1755. Davies innovated daringly at the Woodstock chapel by conducting both baptisms and the Lord's Supper there, in a building that was neither officially Anglican (unconsecrated by a bishop) nor registered in law as a Dissenting chapel. This innovation pointed forward to the time when Welsh Calvinistic Methodism would break with the Anglican Church in 1811 by beginning to ordain its own ministers. However, Davies retained a residual love for the Anglican liturgy, which he used during communion services, albeit interspersing edifying comments of his own.

Davies' ministry was not restricted to Wales. He often preached in England, notably in London, Bath, Brighton, and

Bristol, frequently in the Countess of Huntingdon's chapels. Uniquely among the front rank of Welsh Revival preachers, Davies escaped serious persecution, partly through significant family connections, partly through his close relationship with Griffith Jones who – having distanced himself from the Revival to guarantee the establishment's blessing on his Circulating Schools – exerted himself to protect Davies.[20]

Davies married twice. His first wife was Catherine Poyer, who belonged to a family distinguished for its royalism during the English Civil War; she and Davies married in 1744, but Catherine soon died in childbirth. Davies then married Luce Philips of Prendergast; their daughter Margaret married Nathaniel, son of Daniel Rowland.

Davies, who had never enjoyed robust health, died relatively young, aged fifty-three, in 1770. Although his renown has been eclipsed by that of Harris, Rowland, and Williams, it is clear that in his own day, he was not regarded as their inferior in spiritual gifts or the deep and widespread impact of his preaching.

---

20. See section 1 for the Circulating Schools.

9
Persecution of Methodists

Methodist open-air preachers – whether Calvinist or Arminian – were the frequent objects of persecution. Most of the time, this stemmed not from hostile magistrates but hostile mobs. These mobs, however, were quite often incited by hostile Anglican clergy, who inflamed popular feeling against the Methodist preachers by accusing them of being Jesuit agents or Jacobites,[1] tapping into the ugly anti-Catholicism of the British psyche. Sometimes the fury of the mob was not even directed at preachers but simply at people known to be Evangelicals.

John Cennick, the Evangelical Calvinist, published a narrative of an anti-Methodist riot in the city of Exeter in 1745, *An Account of a Late Riot at Exeter.*[2] The riot lasted for several days. Cennick describes how he and his helpers were daily assaulted by a vicious mob; the women were abused as 'Cennicking whores' and 'Whitefieldite bitches'. Evangelicals of both sexes were beaten, stripped, thrown into filthy gutters, and dragged in mud. Cennick relates the first day of the violence:

> At this time Mr. Kent was pushed about, till they sprained his leg. Mr. William Gale was tumbled in the dirt. Mrs. Rebecca Barret was twice thrown down, and was ready to have been torn in pieces, but that some other women rescued her from the persecutors' hands. Mrs. Lydia Sherry had her hat taken away, and received a violent blow on her shoulder. Mrs. Mary

1. See Chapter 3, Part 4 for the Jacobites.
2. For Cennick, see Part 4, section 1.

> Paramore was struck on the breast by one of the men, who cursed her, called her 'Cennicking whore', and having brought her out to the rest, they pushed her from side to side of the street in the dirt, and tore off some of her clothes, and then struck her over the face, and bid her go along. Mary Naron was also sadly thrust about, and frighted, but in the midst of all her trouble, our Saviour revealed Himself to her with those Words, I am thy Strength, and from that time she endured boldly. Mr Thomas Knight had a terrible blow on the left side of his head by a stone: and many others were struck, and dirtied, but not much hurt.

The 1745 Exeter riot was on a large scale, and lasted an unusually long time, but the mob violence it exhibited was typical in nature of the hostility that had to be endured by many Evangelical preachers and their helpers, from the beginning of the Revival and for decades afterward.

Methodism was not without its actual martyrs. The first to die for his faith was William Seward (1702–40) of Badsey in the Vale of Evesham, an affluent businessman and philanthropist, friend of Charles Wesley, George Whitefield, and Howell Harris. He had experienced conversion in 1738 through the preaching of Charles Wesley:

> I cannot sufficiently praise God for bringing me out of darkness into His marvellous light ... This is a faith I never felt, before Mr Charles Wesley expounded it to me. I cannot but always honour him as an instrument in God's hand for showing me the true way of salvation by Jesus Christ.

Seward was an active financial supporter of Methodist leaders (especially George Whitefield) and their endeavours from the outbreak of the English Revival in 1738, although it was only in 1740 that he began open-air preaching as a lay evangelist. He encountered fierce mob hostility in south Wales, where he and Howell Harris were violently assaulted by angry crowds in Newport , Caerleon, Usk, and Monmouth. The mob bombarded them with dirt, dung, eggs, dead animals, and stones. Seward lost the sight in his right eye after a mob showered him with stones at Caerleon:

> The noise drowned our voices till at length I was struck with a stone, brickbat or some other hard substance upon my right eye which caused so much anguish that I was forced to go away to the Inn and put an end to my discourse. It was given to me to pray all the way for the poor people and especially for the person who struck me. Brother Harris continued to discourse for some time after, and the other brethren declared their testimony against them.

In October 1740, at Hay-on-Wye, in Brecknockshire, Wales, a mob once again stoned Seward, and this time he received so serious a head wound that he died a few days later. His martyrdom sent shockwaves through the Evangelical community, whose leaders mourned his loss. Howell Harris recorded in his journal: 'Heard that my dear brother Seward has gone to heaven. Recollecting brother Seward's work and simplicity and especially his being buffeted with me with dung, it was more than I could bear, my heart is almost broken.' John Wesley said, 'the surprising news of poor Mr Seward's death was confirmed. Surely God will maintain His own cause. Righteous art Thou, O Lord.' Charles Wesley wrote: 'I was exceedingly shocked with the news of Mr Seward's death; but he is taken from evil, rescued out of the hands of wicked men.'

Sometimes the persecution was less brutal, more masked by the forms of law, but still damaging. In Oxford University – ironically the birthplace of Methodism – six students were cast out of St Edmund Hall (one of the University Colleges) in 1768, for the deplorable crime of 'holding Methodistical tenets, and taking upon them to pray, read, and expound the Scriptures, and sing hymns, in private homes'. The expulsion took place after the six transgressors were tried before a tribunal made up of the University Vice-Chancellor and the Heads of the Oxford Colleges.[3] At the town of St Just in Cornwall, the converted scoundrel Edward Greenfield was forcibly separated by law from his wife and family, so unbearable had his new-found

3. Apparently one of the worst crimes an Oxford student could commit was to read the Bible, pray, and sing hymns in a private home. *O tempora, O mores.*

Methodist sobriety of life become. John Wesley recorded the incident:

> We rode to St. Just. I preached at seven to the largest congregation I have seen since my coming. At the meeting of the earnest, loving society, all our hearts were in a flame: And again at five in the morning, while I explained, 'There is no condemnation to them which are in Christ Jesus.' When the preaching was ended, the Constable apprehended Edward Greenfield (by a warrant from Dr. Borlase), a tinner, in the forty-sixth year of his age, having a wife and seven children. Three years ago he was eminent for cursing, swearing, drunkenness, and all manner of wickedness; but those old things had been for some time passed away, and he was then remarkable for a quite contrary behaviour. I asked a little gentleman at St. Just, what objection there was to Edward Greenfield: He said, 'Why, the man is well enough in other things; but his impudence the gentlemen cannot bear. Why, Sir, he says, he knows his sins are forgiven!' – And for this cause he is adjudged to banishment or death!

This whole side of the Evangelical Revival has often been forgotten, in the mistaken assumption that the age of religious persecution ended in the 17th Century, and that the Age of Enlightenment could surely not witness such barbarities. The evidence, however, is clear and abundant. To be an Evangelical in 18th Century England and Wales was not necessarily a safe option.[4]

4. Compare the fierce persecution of American Separate Congregationalists and Baptists in Puritan New England and Virginia (see Chapter 4, Part 2, sections 3–5), and of Lutherans in Catholic Germany (see Chapter 5, Part 6).

10
Consequences of the Evangelical Revival in England and Wales

It used to be said that the Evangelical Revival saved England from experiencing its own version of a French Revolution, by persuading the lower classes to value holiness and heavenly-mindedness, rather than a violent overthrow of the existing order to create a socio-political heaven on earth. This notion has, however, been rejected by many historians on the grounds that there is insufficient evidence for revolutionary aspirations among the English lower classes. Besides, the French Revolution was not driven by the French lower classes, but by its middle classes or *bourgeoisie,* whose educational standards enabled them to grasp and appreciate the political ideals of the Enlightenment in such writers as Jean-Jacques Rousseau (while the lower classes toiled in illiterate ignorance). England's middle classes, by contrast, were not driven by anti-establishment revolutionary commitment.

Still, the Revival certainly impacted England and Wales in various important ways. The conversion of many to a doctrinally Trinitarian faith, which emphasised and bore fruit in a sanctified life, can hardly be denied. The previous narrative has demonstrated this. Allied to this, the Revival birthed a new style of evangelism, characterised by what we might call its systematic aggressiveness. The parish system – expecting people to attend their local church and be Christianised by its ministrations – was no longer seen as equal to the needs of 18th Century

England and Wales. The lion of unbelief had to be bearded in its den, by open-air preaching to the often unchurched multitudes, in an era that cherished public oratory, lacking the distractions of an electronic media. This aggressive assault on unbelief was systematised by John Wesley, as he divided up England and Wales into 'preaching circuits', training and supplying a host of preachers for these circuits. Preaching itself acquired a new urgency, as preachers became more outspoken and emotional than ever before in their proclamation of the faith, pleading with listeners to respond personally. When Evangelicals preached, religious nominalism was not allowed to hide under the guise of true faith.

To give a voice to the new feelings of the converted, the English and Welsh languages produced a whole new hymnody. We have already considered these hymns and their writers in preceding parts of this Chapter. But it may be as well to remark that in the judgment of many, this 18th Century hymnody marked the golden age of English and Welsh hymn-writing. There seemed to be an unusual outpouring of the spirit of lyricism, manifest in the enduring liturgical poetry of Isaac Watts, Charles Wesley, John Newton, William Cowper, Augustus Toplady, William Williams, and others. It is hard to argue that this outpouring and its fruits have ever been surpassed.

Allied to the lyrical harvest was a renaissance of Protestant literature, especially the literature of piety. John Wesley, James Hervey, William Romaine, John Newton, William Cowper, Augustus Toplady, Walker of Truro, Fletcher of Madeley, and others, wrote for the edification of believers, and some of their works have proved enduring. Older works, notably those of the Puritans, were reprinted, albeit purged of their objectionable Calvinism when it was Wesley who reprinted them. Religious magazines – *The Spiritual Magazine, The Gospel Magazine, The Arminian Magazine, The General Baptist Magazine* – helped to stimulate and sustain the beliefs and piety of converts. 1799 saw the creation of the Religious Tract Society, which printed and circulated a great amount of Christian reading material (much of it far longer than the word 'tract' might conjure up in our minds). In 1804, the British Foreign and Bible Society was established to distribute the Bible as widely as possible, both in Britain and other lands.

The Revival also flowered forth, perhaps inevitably, in the formation of new denominations. Evangelical Arminian Baptists formed a new religious body, the New Connexion of General Baptists, in 1770. The chapels erected by Selina Hastings, the Countess of Huntingdon, left their Anglican cradle to become a Dissenting Church, the Countess of Huntingdon's Connection, in 1779. Wesley's United Societies of Methodists severed their ties with the Anglican Church in 1795, four years after Wesley's death, to become another Dissenting body, the (English) Methodist Church. Wales saw the birth of the Calvinistic Methodist Church in 1811, when Welsh Methodists broke from the Anglican Church by beginning to ordain their own ministers. The Revival thus added richly to the religious pluriformity of English and Welsh society.

Missionary enterprise sprouted rather naturally from the Revival. The historian must be careful here; it was not as if there had been no English or Protestant missionary work before the quickening impulses of the Revival. The Society for Promoting Christian Knowledge, an Anglican organisation founded in 1698, had been helping to finance the Danish Pietist mission in Tranquebar, India, since the 1720s, on the understanding that the mission work would be extended into adjacent British territory. In keeping with this agreement, the Danish missionaries began using the Anglican Book of Common Prayer in worship, and their converts were baptized as Anglicans rather than Lutherans.[1] A good deal of Lutheran and Moravian missionary work had been going on before the Revival-inspired English missions were launched.[2]

Even so, the Anglo-Welsh Revival did inspire a new wave of missionary endeavour. In 1786, the Wesleyan Methodist

---

1. See Volume 4, Chapter 1, Part 5, for the Danish missionaries in India.
2. For the Moravian missions, see Chapter 5, Part 2, section 4, under the heading ***The impetus to missionary work.***

Conference sanctioned the plan of Thomas Coke to carry the Gospel to the West Indies; Coke made several missionary voyages there, in 1786, 1788–89, 1790, and 1792–93. The Particular Baptists formed the Baptist Missionary Society in 1792, under whose auspices William Carey went to India in 1793.[3] The London Missionary Society, an interdenominational body, was established in 1795; its most famous early missionary was the Scottish Congregationalist Robert Moffat (1795–1883), who worked in South Africa from 1816 till 1870. In 1799, the Church Missionary Society (originally named the Society for Missions to Africa and the East) was founded by Evangelical Anglicans; its first missionaries – two Lutherans from Württemberg, reflecting the old Anglican-Lutheran alliance in India – worked in West Africa from 1804. No one could doubt, if they had previously done so, that Evangelicals were committed to global mission.

The Evangelical Revival also gave rise to a new concern for improving the human condition – here on earth, that is. Rather than shunning the earthly wellbeing of men, women, and children, as somehow inconsistent with Christian heavenly-mindedness, Evangelicals pursued with passion the betterment of the human condition in society, as the necessary outflow of love for one's neighbour, itself a primary fruit of saving faith in the Gospel. Two areas in which Evangelicals strove for this betterment of humanity were educational and social reform.

In order to bring the blessings of literacy and mental improvement to the disadvantaged, Evangelicals pioneered the Sunday School. Perhaps the first trailblazer was the Methodist Hannah Ball (1734–92), a friend of John Wesley's who often gave her testimony of her experience of God's grace at meetings where Wesley preached, and wrote reports to him of her judgment on the abilities of Wesleyan lay preachers. Ball, a reasonably affluent lady, opened a Sunday School in her town, High Wycombe in Buckinghamshire, in 1769. Working children were instructed in reading and writing on Mondays,

3. See Chapter 6, section 2.

and in Christian truths on Sunday mornings just before the Sunday morning worship in the local Anglican church. Ball's sister Ann continued the school after Hannah's death.[4]

Although several others dispute with Ball the potential title to first founder of a Sunday School, it was clearly the Anglican layman Robert Raikes (1736–1811) who popularised the movement. Raikes grew up in the atmosphere of the Evangelical Revival in Gloucester; Whitefield and the Wesleys were frequent guests in his parents' home. As an adult, Raikes owned and ran a local newspaper, the *Gloucester Journal* (inherited from his father). When he became enthused by the idea of Sunday Schools, he utilised the *Journal* to publicise the work. Raikes' School was set up in 1780 to improve the desperate condition of Gloucester's disorderly slum children. His School was designed to teach the children literacy, with the Bible as the textbook of choice, enabling them to enter adulthood with better life-skills and a foundation of Christian knowledge. It is credibly recounted that within three years of the School's founding, an observable reformation of behaviour had spread through the Gloucester slum children, greatly reducing their previous half-criminal unruliness. Raikes' genius at promoting the enterprise through his newspaper led to a rapid mushrooming of Sunday Schools across the English Evangelical world. As early as 1785, a national body – the Sunday School Society – was established to bring a countrywide coordination to the movement.

Evangelical commitment to social reform included the reformation of Britain's prison system. The key campaigner was John Howard (1726–90), a Londoner raised in a strongly Dissenting and Calvinist household who inherited a considerable fortune from his father. He was quite an eccentric by the standards of his day – a vegetarian and total abstainer from alcohol. In 1773, he became High Sheriff of Bedfordshire,

---

4. It is recorded that at Hannah's funeral in her parish church, an unsympathetic Anglican minister commented that if an Arminian entered heaven, the angels would stop singing – whereupon Ann Ball gathered her Sunday school children, walked out in protest, and never entered the church again.

in which capacity he visited the local county prison, and was appalled by the inhumane and unhygienic conditions endured by its inmates. This spurred him to investigate prison conditions across Britain, resulting in his treatise *The State of the Prisons*, published in 1777, which gave meticulous descriptions of the prisons he had visited. Among his recommendations for enhancing the quality of prison life were an improvement in the diet of prisoners, a clean water supply, the provision of privacy (prisoners should not have to share a cell), instruction in the Bible, strict legal control over who could work within prisons, and regular prison inspection by an outside body. His basic philosophy was that once people were in prison, the aim should be to prevent them from reoffending, by giving them every opportunity to become better citizens (the betterment measured by a biblical standard).

Howard devoted the rest of his life to prison reform, appearing before parliament to give evidence, and encouraged by John Wesley, who knew Howard and pronounced him 'one of the greatest men in Europe'. Wesley himself frequently preached in prisons, and knew as well as Howard what foul places they were; the Methodist leader declared that London's Newgate Prison was the nearest thing to hell on earth. Howard for his part drew moral strength from Wesley's teaching and example, especially a sermon entitled *Whatsoever thy hand findeth to do, do it with thy might*. In the 19th Century, the continuing campaign for prison reform formed itself into the Howard Association, which in turn was renamed the Howard League for Penal Reform.

Of course, another facet of social reform was the campaign to abolish the African slave trade, which we have already considered in the cameo of John Newton in Part 4. Many Evangelicals were involved in this campaign – Newton, William Wilberforce,[5] Granville Sharp (1735–1813), Henry Venn,[6] Hannah More (1745–1833), Charles Simeon (1759–1836),

5. See Part 4, section 8.

6. See Part 4, section 7.

Henry Thornton (1760–1815), and Zachary Macaulay (1768–1838), among others. John Wesley was outspokenly anti-slavery, as expressed in his 1774 treatise *Thoughts upon Slavery*, one of the most eloquent and emotive assaults on the slave trade and the institution of black slavery ever written.[7] The Evangelical Calvinist poet William Cowper added his voice. However, fairness and accuracy compel the recognition that not all the anti-slavery campaigners were Evangelicals. Some belonged to Anglicanism's High Church wing, such as one of the foremost campaigners, Bishop Beilby Porteous (1731–1809), successively Bishop of Chester and London. Others were Quakers, or had Quaker connections, such as Thomas Clarkson (1760–1846) and Thomas Fowell Buxton (1786–1845). Others still were Unitarians, notably William Smith (1756–1835).

At grass roots level, the Methodist religious societies provided food and clothing for the destitute, acting as a kind of church version of the welfare state before the latter had any substantive existence in Britain. These efforts became more coordinated as Strangers' Friend Societies. In 1785, the Wesleyan Methodist John Gardner, who was part of the Foundery (Wesley's London chapel), pioneered such a welfare project in which members of the Foundery donated sums of money each week, creating a fund that was then distributed to the London poor (or at least, those poor people who, it was judged, would not waste the money on drink or gambling). In 1786, Bristol Methodists imitated the project, with the proviso that the fund should be used specifically for 'poor, sick, friendless strangers' in the city. The idea caught on among Methodists, and similar projects were soon established in other great urban centres, such as Birmingham, Hull, Leeds, Liverpool, Manchester, Sheffield, and Dublin. The social conscience for which British Dissenters (or Nonconformists) were to be famed in the Victorian era was being created.

---

7. See the extract from this treatise in the **Primary Historical Sources** section of Chapter 4, included there because of Wesley's attack on American slavery.

PRIMARY SOURCE MATERIAL

George Whitefield: Justification by Christ's righteousness

How the Lord is to be man's righteousness, comes next to be considered. And that is, in one word, by Imputation. For it pleased God, after He had made all things by the word of His power, to create man after His own image. And so infinite was the condescension of the high and lofty One, who inhabiteth eternity, that, although He might have insisted on the everlasting obedience of him and his posterity; yet He was pleased to oblige Himself, by a covenant or agreement made with His own creatures, upon condition of an unsinning obedience, to give them immortality and eternal life. For when it is said, 'The day thou eatest thereof, thou shalt surely die;' we may fairly infer, so long as he continued obedient, and did not eat thereof, he should surely live.

The 3rd of Genesis gives us a full, but mournful account, how our first parents broke this covenant, and thereby stood in need of a better righteousness than their own, in order to procure their future acceptance with God. For what must they do? They were as much under a covenant of works as ever. And though, after their disobedience, they were without strength; yet they were obliged not only to do, but continue to do all things, and that too in the most perfect manner, which the Lord had required of them: and not only so, but to make satisfaction to God's infinitely offended justice, for the breach they had already been guilty of.

Here then opens the amazing scene of Divine Philanthropy; I mean, God's love to man. For behold, what man could not do,

Jesus Christ, the son of His Father's love, undertakes to do for him. And that God might be just in justifying the ungodly, though 'He was in the form of God, and therefore thought it no robbery to be equal with God; yet He took upon Him the form of a servant,' even human nature. In that nature He obeyed, and thereby fulfilled the whole moral law in our stead; and also died a painful death upon the cross, and thereby became a curse for, or instead of, those whom the Father had given to Him. As God, He satisfied, at the same time that He obeyed and suffered as man; and, being God and man in one person, He wrought out a full, perfect, and sufficient righteousness for all to whom it was to be imputed.

Here then we see the meaning of the word righteousness. It implies the active as well as passive obedience of the Lord Jesus Christ. We generally, when talking of the merits of Christ, only mention the latter, – His death; whereas, the former, – His life and active obedience, is equally necessary. Christ is not such a Saviour as becomes [befits] us, unless we join both together. Christ not only died, but lived, not only suffered, but obeyed for, or instead of, poor sinners. And both these jointly make up that complete righteousness, which is to be imputed to us, as the disobedience of our first parents was made ours by imputation. In this sense, and no other, are we to understand that parallel which the apostle Paul draws, in the 5th of the Romans, between the first and second Adam. This is what he elsewhere terms, 'our being made the righteousness of God in Him.' This is the sense wherein the Prophet would have us to understand the words of the text; therefore, Jer. 33:16, 'She (i.e. the church itself) shall be called, (having this righteousness imputed to her) The Lord our righteousness.' A passage, I think, worthy of the profoundest meditation of all the sons and daughters of Abraham.

George Whitefield
Sermon *The Lord Our Righteousness*

George Whitefield: Defence of itinerant preaching

For supposing the practice of itinerant preaching was primarily occasioned by the low talents of many incumbents in the more *early* days of the Reformation, does it therefore follow, that there can be no other just cause assigned for itinerant preaching now? What if the generality of the present many incumbents depart from the good old doctrines that were preached in the more early days of the Reformation, and notwithstanding their liberal education, make no other use of their learning but to explain away the Articles and Homilies [of the Church of England] to which they have subscribed in the grammatical and literal sense? Is it not necessary in order to keep up the doctrines, and thereby the real dignity of the Church, that either the clergy thus degenerated, should be obliged to read the Homilies as formerly, and to preach consistently therewith, or that those who do hold the doctrines of the Reformation, should go about from place to place, and from county to county, nay from pole to pole, if their sphere of action extended so far, to direct poor souls that are everywhere ready to perish for lack of knowledge, into the right way which leadeth unto life?

That this is the case between the established clergy and these itinerant preachers will appear presently; and how then can this author charge them with making it their *principal* employ, wherever they go, to instill into the people a few *favourite tenets of their own*? Has the author followed them wherever they have preached, that he asserts this so confidently concerning them? Is it not to be wished that he had at least taken care to have been better informed? For then he would have saved himself from the guilt of a notorious slander. For is it not evident to all that hear them, that the favourite tenets the itinerant preachers make it their *principal* employ to instill into people's minds wherever they go, are the great doctrines of the Reformation, Homilies and Articles of the Church? Such as man's bringing into the world with him *a Corruption which renders him liable to God's Wrath and eternal Damnation – That the Condition of Man after the Fall of* Adam, *is such that he cannot turn and prepare himself, by his own natural Strength and good Works to Faith and calling upon God – That we are accounted righteous before God, only for the Merit of our Lord and Saviour Jesus Christ by Faith, and not for our own Works or Deservings – That they are to be accursed, that presume to say, that every Man shall be saved by the Law or*

Sect which he professeth, so that he be diligent to frame his Life according to that Law, and the Light of Nature.[1]

These, my Lords, are some of the favourite tenets of these itinerant preachers – their others are like unto them. Can these, my Lords, be properly called their *own*? Or ought it not to be the *principal* employ of every true minister wherever he goes, to instill such tenets, and that too with the utmost diligence and zeal into the people's minds? Does not a great part of Christianity depend on them? And are not all pretensions to a true Christian life, without a belief of these tenets, vain and ineffectual? And may I not take the freedom of acquainting your Lordships, that if all the Right Reverend the Bishops did their duty, (especially my Lord of *London,* whose diocese is of such a vast extent), they would all of them long since have commenced itinerant preachers too?

George Whitefield

An answer to the first and second part of an anonymous pamphlet, entitled, Observations upon the conduct and behaviour of a certain sect usually distinguished by the name of Methodists. In two letters to the Right Reverend the Bishop of London, and the other the Right Reverend the Bishops concerned in the publication thereof.

John Wesley: Free grace

1. How freely does God love the world! While we were yet sinners, 'Christ died for the ungodly.' While we were 'dead in our sin,' God 'spared not His own Son, but delivered Him up for us all.' And how freely with Him does He 'give us all things!' Verily, FREE GRACE is all in all!

2. The grace or love of God, whence cometh our salvation, is FREE IN ALL, and FREE FOR ALL.

3. First. It is free in all to whom it is given. It does not depend on any power or merit in man; no, not in any degree, neither in whole, nor in part. It does not in anywise depend either on the good works or righteousness of the receiver; not on anything he has done, or anything he is. It does not depend on his endeavours. It does not depend on his good tempers,

1. Quotes from the Anglican Thirty Nine Articles.

or good desires, or good purposes and intentions; for all these flow from the free grace of God; they are the streams only, not the fountain. They are the fruits of free grace, and not the root. They are not the cause, but the effects of it. Whatsoever good is in man, or is done by man, God is the author and doer of it. Thus is His grace free in all; that is, no way depending on any power or merit in man, but on God alone, who freely gave us His own Son, and 'with Him freely giveth us all things' …

20. And as this doctrine [the Calvinist view of election] manifestly and directly tends to overthrow the whole Christian Revelation, so it does the same thing, by plain consequence, in making that Revelation contradict itself. For it is grounded on such an interpretation of some texts (more or fewer it matters not) as flatly contradicts all the other texts, and indeed the whole scope and tenor of Scripture. For instance: The assertors of this doctrine interpret that text of Scripture, 'Jacob have I loved, but Esau have I hated,' as implying that God in a literal sense hated Esau, and all the reprobated, from eternity. Now, what can possibly be a more flat contradiction than this, not only to the whole scope and tenor of Scripture, but also to all those particular texts which expressly declare, 'God is love.'

Again: They infer from that text, 'I will have mercy on whom I will have mercy,' (Rom. 9:15) that God is love only to some men, viz., the elect, and that He hath mercy for those only; flatly contrary to which is the whole tenor of Scripture, as is that express declaration in particular, 'The Lord is loving unto every man; and His mercy is over all His works.' (Ps. 145:9.)

Again: They infer from that and the like texts, 'It is not of him that willeth, nor of him that runneth, but of God that showeth mercy:' that He showeth mercy only to those to whom He had respect from all eternity. Nay, but who replieth against God now? You now contradict the whole oracles of God, which declare throughout, 'God is no respecter of persons:' (Acts 10:34), 'There is no respect of persons with Him.' (Rom. 2:11.)

Again: from that text, 'The children being not yet born, neither having done any good or evil, that the purpose of God according to election might stand, not of works, but of Him that calleth'; it was said unto her, unto Rebecca, 'The elder shall serve the younger;' you infer, that our being predestinated, or elect, no way depends on the foreknowledge of God. Flatly contrary to this are all the scriptures; and those in particular, 'Elect according to the foreknowledge of God;' (1 Pet. 1:2) 'Whom He did foreknow, He also did predestinate.' (Rom. 8:29)

21. And 'the same Lord over all is rich' in mercy 'to all that call upon Him:' (Rom. 10:12) But you say, 'No; He is such only to those for whom Christ died. And those are not all, but only a few, whom God hath chosen out of the world; for He died not for all, but only for those who were "chosen in Him before the foundation of the world."' (Eph. 1:4.)

Flatly contrary to your interpretation of these scriptures, also, is the whole tenor of the New Testament; as are in particular those texts: – 'Destroy not him with thy meat, for whom Christ died,' (Rom. 14:15) – a clear proof that Christ died, not only for those that are saved, but also for them that perish: He is 'the Saviour of the world;' (John 4:42;) He is 'the Lamb of God that taketh away the sins of the world;' (John 1:29;) 'He is the propitiation, not for our sins only, but also for the sins of the whole world;' (1 John 2:2;) 'He,' the living God, 'is the Savior of all men;' (1 Tim. 4:10;) 'He gave Himself a ransom for all;' (1 Tim. 2:6;) 'He tasted death for every man.' (Heb. 2:9.)

22. If you ask, 'Why then are not all men saved' the whole law and the testimony answer, First, Not because of any decree of God; not because it is His pleasure they should die; for, 'As I live, saith the Lord God, I have no pleasure in the death of him that dieth.' (Ezek. 18:23, 32.) Whatever be the cause of their perishing, it cannot be His will, if the oracles of God are true; for they declare, 'He is not willing that any should perish, but that all should come to repentance;' (2 Pet. 3:9;) 'He willeth that all men should be saved.' And they, Secondly, declare what is the cause why all men are not saved, namely, that they will not be saved: So our Lord expressly, 'Ye will not come unto Me that ye may have life.' (John 5:40.) 'The power of the Lord is present to heal' them, but they will not be healed. 'They reject the counsel,'

the merciful counsel, 'of God against themselves,' as did their stiff-necked forefathers. And therefore are they without excuse; because God would save them, but they will not be saved: This is the condemnation, 'How often would I have gathered you together, and ye would not!' (Matt. 23:37.)

John Wesley
Sermon on Free Grace

John Wesley: Rules for the first Methodist society meetings

This evening our little society began, which afterwards met in Fetter Lane. Our fundamental rules were as follow:

In obedience to the command of God by St James, and by the advice of Peter Bohler, it is agreed by us,

1. That we will meet together once a week to 'confess our faults one to another, and pray for one another, that we may be healed.'
2. That the persons so meeting be divided into several bands, or little companies, none of them consisting of fewer than five or more than ten persons.
3. That every one in order speak as freely, plainly, and concisely as he can, the real state of his heart, with his several temptations and deliverances, since the last time of meeting.
4. That all the bands have a conference at eight every Wednesday evening, begun and ended with singing and prayer.
5. That any who desire to be admitted into the society will be asked, 'What are your reasons for desiring this? Will you be entirely open; using no kind of reserve? Have you any objection to any of our orders?' (which may then be read).
6. That when any new member is proposed, every one present speak clearly and freely whatever objection he has to him.

7. That those against whom no reasonable objection appears be, in order for their trial, formed into one or more distinct bands, and some person agreed on to assist them.
8. That after two months' trial, if no objection then appear, they may be admitted into the society.
9. That every fourth Saturday be observed as a day of general intercession.
10. That on the Sunday seven-night following be a general love-feast, from seven till ten in the evening.
11. That no particular member be allowed to act in anything contrary to any order of the society; and that if any persons, after being thrice admonished, do not conform thereto, they be not any longer esteemed as members.

John Wesley
Journal, May 1st 1738

Strange phenomena: John Wesley encounters, and opposes as Satanic, a spirit of hysterical laughter

I was a little surprised at some, who were buffeted of Satan in an unusual manner, by such a spirit of laughter as they could in no wise resist, though it was pain and grief unto them. I could scarce have believed the account they gave me, had I not known the same thing ten or eleven years ago. Part of Sunday my brother and I then used to spend in walking in the meadows and singing psalms. But one day, just as we were beginning to sing, he burst out into a loud laughter. I asked him; if he was distracted; and began to be very angry, and presently after to laugh as loud as he. Nor could we possibly refrain, though we were ready to tear ourselves in pieces, but we were forced to go home without singing another line ...

In the evening, such a spirit of laughter was among us, that many were much offended. But the attention of all was fixed on poor LS, whom we all knew to be no dissembler. One so violently and variously torn of the evil one did I never see before.

Sometimes she laughed till almost strangled; then broke out into cursing and blaspheming; then stamped and struggled with incredible strength, so that four or five could scarce hold her: Then cried out, 'O eternity, eternity! O that I had no soul! O that I had never been born!' At last she faintly called on Christ to help her. And the violence of her pangs ceased. Most of our brethren and sisters were now fully convinced that those who were under this strange temptation could not help it. Only EB and Anne H. were of another mind; being still sure, anyone might help laughing if she would. This they declared to many on Thursday; but on Friday, 23, God suffered Satan to teach them better. Both of them were suddenly seized in the same manner as the rest, and laughed whether they would or no, almost without ceasing. Thus they continued for two days, a spectacle to all; and were then, upon prayer made for them, delivered in a moment.

John Wesley

***Journal*, May 9th and 21st 1740**

Persecuted and delivered: Wesley and a mob at Falmouth

Thursday, 4th July. I rode to Falmouth. About three in the afternoon I went to see a gentlewoman who had been long indisposed. Almost as soon as I sat down, the house was beset on all sides by an innumerable multitude of people. A louder or more confused noise could hardly be at the taking of a city by storm. At first Mrs. B. and her daughter endeavoured to quiet them. But it was labour lost. They might as well have attempted to still the raging of the sea. They were soon glad to shift for themselves and leave Kitty [a young woman who had accompanied Wesley] and me to do as well as we could. The rabble roared with all their throats, 'Bring out the Canorum! Where is the Canorum?' (an unmeaning word which the Cornish generally use instead of Methodist). No answer being given, they quickly forced open the outer door and filled the passage. Only a wainscot partition was between us, which was not likely to stand long. I immediately took down a large looking glass which hung against it, supposing the whole side would fall in at once. When they began their work with abundance of bitter imprecations, poor Kitty was utterly astonished and cried out, 'O sir, what must we do?' I said, 'We must pray.' Indeed at that time, to all appearance, our lives were not worth an hour's purchase. She asked, 'But, sir, is it not better for you to hide yourself? to get into the closet?' I answered, 'No. It is best for me to stand just where I am.'

Among those without were the crews of some privateers which were lately come into harbour. Some of these, being angry at the slowness of the rest, thrust them away and, coming up all together, set their shoulders to the inner door and cried out, 'Avast, lads, avast!' Away went all the hinges at once, and the door fell back into the room. I stepped forward at once into the midst of them and said, 'Here I am. Which of you has anything to say to me? To which of you have I done any wrong? To you? Or you? Or you?' I continued speaking till I came, bareheaded as I was (for I purposely left my hat that they might all see my face) into the middle of the street and then raising my voice said, 'Neighbours, countrymen! Do you desire to hear me speak?' They cried vehemently, 'Yes, yes. He shall speak. He shall. Nobody shall hinder him.' But having nothing to stand on and no advantage of ground, I could be heard by few only.

However, I spoke without intermission and, as far as the sound reached, the people were still; till one or two of their captains turned about and swore that not a man should touch me. Mr. Thomas, a clergyman, then came up and asked, 'Are you not ashamed to use a stranger thus?' He was soon seconded by two or three gentlemen of the town and one of the aldermen; with whom I walked down the town, speaking all the time, till I came to Mrs. Maddern's house. The gentlemen proposed sending for my horse to the door and desired me to step in and rest the meantime. But, on second thought, they judged it not advisable to let me go out among the people again: so they chose to send my horse before me to Penryn and to send me thither by water, the sea running close by the back door of the house in which we were.

I never saw before, no, not at Walsall itself, the hand of God so plainly shown as here. There I had many companions who were willing to die with me: here, not a friend but one simple girl, who likewise was hurried away from me in an instant as soon as ever she came out of Mrs. B.'s door. There I received some blows, lost part of my clothes, and was covered over with dirt: here, although the hands of perhaps some hundreds of people were lifted up to strike or throw, yet they were one and all stopped in the midway; so that not a man touched me with one of his fingers, neither was anything thrown from first to last; so that I had not even a speck of dirt on my clothes. Who can deny that God heareth prayer, or that He hath all power in heaven and earth?

John Wesley
Journal, July 4th 1745

James Hervey: Christ obedient in our place

Aspasio: In order to accomplish our redemption, the Son of God submitted Himself to the authority of the law, and became obedient to its precepts. But this was His own spontaneous act, the matter of His free choice; to which He lay under no manner of obligation, till He engaged to be our Surety. 'Being in the form of God,' He was Lord of the law; and no more subject to its commands than obnoxious to its curse. Nevertheless, 'He took upon Him the form of a servant, and was made under the law.' Wherefore? That He might obtain everlasting life and glory for Himself? No; but that He might 'redeem those who were under the law,' Gal. iv . 5. From which it appears, that both His engagement and His obedience were not for Himself, but for His people. Therefore the prophet cries out, with holy exultation, 'To us a Child is born; to us a Son is given!' His incarnate state and human nature, together with all that He did and suffered in both, were for us; those assumed on our account, these referred to our advantage. Let us consider this, and be amazed, and be charmed. The great universal Lord vouchsafes to pay universal obedience: what condescension was here! He vouchsafes to pay it, for us men, and for our redemption: what goodness was this!

Theron: Before we indulge the devotional strain, we should take care that our devotion is founded on rational principles; otherwise it may prove, like the flash of a sky-rocket, transient and momentary

Aspasio: For this, I think, there is a solid foundation in reason, as well as Scripture. As soon as the man Christ Jesus was united to the second person of the Trinity, He must have, by virtue of that union, an unquestionable right to everlasting life and glory; therefore He could be under no necessity of obeying, in order to procure either honour or happiness for Himself. But all that He performed in conformity to the preceptive part of the law, He performed under the character of a public person, in the place and for the benefit of His spiritual seed, that they might be interested in it, and justified by it.

Theron: Be it so: the believer is interested in Christ's righteousness. Pray, is he interested in all, or only in part? If in all, then every believer is equally righteous, and equally to be rewarded; which is contrary to an allowed maxim, that there will be different allotments of happiness in the heavenly world. If in part only, how will you ascertain the degree – what proportion belongs to this person, and what to the other? Either way, your scheme is inextricably embarrassed.

Aspasio: The reply to my Theron's inquiry is easy; and the embarrassment he mentions is but imaginary. Every true believer is interested in all Christ's righteousness – in the whole merit of His spotless nature, of His perfect obedience, and expiatory death. Less than the whole would be unavailable; whereas the whole renders us completely justified. You are a great admirer of anatomy, Theron, and must undoubtedly remember the very peculiar structure of the ear. Other parts of the body are progressive in their growth: their bulk is proportioned to the infantile or manly age. But the organs of hearing, I have been informed, are precisely of the same size in the feeble infant and the confirmed adult.

Justification likewise, being absolutely necessary to a state of acceptance with God, is in every stage of the Christian course, and even in the first dawn of sincere faith, complete. With regard to the existence of the privilege, there is no difference in the babes, the young men, the fathers in Christ. The perception, the assurance, the comfortable enjoyment of the mercy, may increase; but the mercy itself is incapable of augmentation. The various advances in sanctification account for the various degrees of future glory; and not account for them only, but render them entirely reasonable, and, according to our apprehension of things, unavoidable. As to settling the proportion, we may safely leave that to the supreme Arbitrator. He 'who meteth out the heavens with a span, and setteth a compass upon the face of the deep,' cannot be at a loss to adjust this particular.

James Hervey
***Theron and Aspasio: or a Series of Dialogues and Letters upon the Most Important and Interesting Subjects,* Dialogue V**

William Romaine: The believer's blessedness

After the believer is thus grounded and established in the knowledge of his union with Christ, it behooves him then to inquire, what God has given him a right to in consequence of this union; and the Scripture will inform him, that, in the covenant of grace, it has pleased the Father, that all fullness should dwell in His Son, as the head for the use of His members. He has it to supply all their need. They cannot possibly lack anything, but it is treasured up for them in His infinite fullness – there they may have it, grace upon grace, every moment as their occasions require; and they have it in no other way, and by no other hand than faith, trusting the word of promise, and relying upon Christ's faithfulness and power to fulfill it; as it is written, 'The just shall live by his faith,' Habakkuk 2.4.

Having received justification to life by faith in the righteousness of Christ, he depends on Christ to keep him alive, and makes use of Christ's fullness for all the needs of that spiritual life which He has given; he trusts Him for them all, and lives upon Him by faith for the continual receiving of them all, and according to his faith so it is done unto him. Let this be well weighed and considered, that the justified person lives and performs every act of spiritual life by faith. This is a very important lesson, and therefore it is taught in Scripture as plainly as words can speak. Everything is promised to, and is received, by faith. Thus it is said, 'You are all the children of God by faith in Christ Jesus; and if children, then heirs, according to the promise, heirs of God, and joint-heirs with Christ, who of God is made unto us wisdom, righteousness, and holiness' – made for their use wisdom to teach them, righteousness to justify them, and holiness to sanctify them. Yes, He has all things in His fullness for their use, as the free grant speaks, 1 Corinthians 3:21, etc. 'All things are yours, whether Paul, or Apollos, or Cephas, or the world, or life, or death, or things present, or things to come; all are yours, and you are Christ's, and Christ is God's!'

William Romaine
The Life, Walk, and Triumph of Faith

Walker of Truro: Christ's righteousness, not ours

The question is not about your sinfulness, but Christ's righteousness. Has Christ done His part in the covenant of grace? Has He been obedient unto death, and thereby has He vindicated God's government, and satisfied His justice? Why, then, believer, God, in justice to Christ, doth justify you. So the words of Scripture run all along. 'The Lamb of God that taketh away the sins of the world; He is able to save them to the uttermost, who come to God by Him; the blood of Jesus Christ His Son, cleanses them from all sin.' Now, therefore, what mean you that you are crying, 'I have been so provoking a sinner'? Why, it matters not what your sins have been; the question is about Christ's righteousness, not yours. St. Paul had been a provoking sinner; you will seldom hear of a worse; he had been a blasphemer, a persecutor, injurious, yet he obtained mercy. Ay, but St. Paul was not such a poor unprofitable creature afterwards as you are; you can never do anything as you ought, your heart is corrupt and deceitful, you are so dead sometimes and heartless. I tell you, believer, it is much if there be a saint in heaven who had not some such complaint to make while he was upon earth; it is Christ's righteousness that is accepted, not yours; and your unprofitableness cannot destroy His merit, I suppose. Nay, but perhaps you are fallen into some foul sin, and, therefore, you are without hope. Still, I say, 'If any man sin, we have an Advocate with the Father, Jesus Christ the righteous, and He is the propitiation for our sins.' As long as He sits there, as long as God's righteousness stands, the way is open for you.

Samuel Walker
***Nine Sermons on the Covenant of Grace*, Sermon III**

Augustus Toplady: The comfort of being in God's hands

How sweet must the following considerations be to a distressed believer! There most certainly exists an almighty, all-wise and infinitely gracious God. He has given me in times past, and is giving me at present (if I had but eyes to see it), many and signal intimations of His love to me, both in a way of providence and grace. This love of His is immutable; He never repents of it nor withdraws it. Whatever comes to pass in time is the result of His will from everlasting, consequently. My afflictions were a part of His original plan, and are all ordered in number, weight and measure, the very hairs of my head are (every one) counted by Him, nor can a single hair fall to the ground but in consequence of His determination.

Hence, my distresses are not the result of chance, accident or a fortuitous combination of circumstances, but the providential accomplishment of God's purpose, and designed to answer some wise and gracious ends, nor shall my affliction continue a moment longer than God sees meet. He who brought me to it has promised to support me under it and to carry me through it. All shall, most assuredly, work together for His glory and my good, therefore 'The cup which my heavenly Father hath given me to drink, shall I not drink it?' Yes, I will, in the strength He imparts, even rejoice in tribulation; and using the means of possible redress, which He hath or may hereafter put into my hands, I will commit myself and the event to Him, whose purpose cannot be overthrown, whose plan cannot be disconcerted, and who, whether I am resigned or not, will still go on to work all things after the counsel of His own will.

Above all, when the suffering Christian takes his election into the account, and knows that he was by an eternal and immutable act of God appointed to obtain salvation through our Lord Jesus Christ; that, of course, he hath a city prepared for him above, a building of God, a house not made with hands, but eternal in the heavens; and that the heaviest sufferings of the present life are not worthy to be compared with the glory which shall be revealed in the saints, what adversity can possibly befall us which the assured hope of blessings like these will not infinitely overbalance?

> A comfort so divine,
> May trials well endure.[2]

Augustus Toplady
The Doctrine of Absolute Predestination

William Cowper: The theology of the Cross

Hear the just law – the judgment of the skies!
He that hates truth shall be the dupe of lies:
And he that will be cheated to the last,
Delusions strong as Hell shall bind him fast.
But if the wanderer his mistake discern,
Judge his own ways and sigh for a return,
Bewildered once, must he bewail his loss
For ever and for ever? No – the cross!
There, and there only (though the deist rave,
And atheist, if earth bear so base a slave),
There, and there only, is the power to save.
There no delusive hope invites despair;
No mockery meets you, no deception there.
The spells and charms, that blinded you before,
All vanish there, and fascinate no more.
I am no preacher, let this hint suffice:
The cross once seen is death to every vice;

---

2. A quotation from Isaac Watts' hymn, *Behold the amazing gift of love.*

Else He that hung there, suffered all His pain,
Bled, groaned, and agonised, and died in vain.

William Cowper
***The Progress of Error*, lines 606–24**

William Cowper: The black slave's lament

Forced from home and all its pleasures
  Afric's coast I left forlorn,[3]
To increase a stranger's treasures
  O'er the raging billows borne.
Men from England bought and sold me,
  Paid my price in paltry gold;
But, though slave they have enrolled me,
  Minds are never to be sold.
Still in thought as free as ever,
  What are England's rights, I ask,
Me from my delights to sever,
  Me to torture, me to task?
Fleecy locks and black complexion
  Cannot forfeit nature's claim;
Skins may differ, but affection
  Dwells in white and black the same.

William Cowper
The Negro's Complaint

John Newton: How not to preach

Beware of *affecting the orator*. I do not advise you to pay no regard to a just and proper elocution; it deserves your attention, and many a good sermon loses much of the effect it might otherwise produce, by an awkward and uncouth delivery. But let your elocution be natural. Despise the little arts by which men of little minds endeavour to set themselves off; they will blast your success, and expose you to contempt. The grand principle of Gospel oratory, is simplicity. Affectation is displeasing in all people – but in none is it so highly disgusting as in a preacher.

---

3. Afric is a poetic name for Africa.

A studied attitude, a measured motion, a close attention to cadences and pauses, a mimicry of theatrical action, may be passable in the recital of a school lecture – but is hateful in the pulpit. Men never do, never can, speak thus, when they speak from the emotion of their hearts.

How is it possible then for a man who professes to speak for God, who addresses himself to immortal souls, who discourses upon the most important subjects, the love of Christ, the joys of heaven, or the terrors of the Lord; how is it possible for this man to find time or disposition for such pompous trifling, if he really understands and believes what he says? The truly pious will weep for his ill-timed vanity. And if any seem pleased, it is chiefly because this manner of preaching seldom disturbs the conscience, for it cannot be expected that God will vouchsafe the testimony of His Spirit, even to His own truths, when the poor worm who delivers them, is visibly more solicitous for the character of an eloquent speaker, than for the success of his message.

Sometimes *vociferation* [shouting] seems to be considered as a mark of powerful preaching. But I believe a sermon that is loud and noisy from beginning to end, seldom produces much good effect. Here again, my friend, if you are happily possessed of simplicity, it will be a good guide. It will help you to adjust your voice to the size of the place or congregation, and then to the variations of your subject. When the explanation of the text and the application of the sermon are both in the same boisterous tone, I am led to consider it rather as a proof of the lack of power, than otherwise. It seems impossible for a preacher to be equally affected in every part of his discourse, and therefore, if he appears to be so, his exertion, in some parts at least, must be constrained and artificial, and this thought will often bring a suspicion upon the whole. Especially if his voice is as vehement in prayer as in preaching.

We doubt not, but if he were with the King of England, that a certain composure and modesty of air, would indicate that he considered whom he was speaking to, and those who speak to God, would certainly give tokens of a reverence and awe upon their spirits, if they really felt it; very loud speaking is far from being a token of such a frame. At the best, very loud preaching is the effect of a bad habit; and though it may be practiced by good men and good preachers, I am persuaded it is neither sign nor cause of the Word being received with power by the hearers. People are seldom, if ever, stunned into the love of the truth.

There is another strain of preaching, which, though it wears the garb of zeal, is seldom a proof of any power but the power of self. I mean *angry and scolding preaching*. The Gospel is a benevolent scheme, and whoever speaks in the power of it, will assuredly speak in love. In the most faithful rebukes of sin, in the most solemn declarations of God's displeasure against it, a preacher may give evidence of a disposition of good-will and compassion to sinners, and assuredly will, if he speaks under the influence of the power of truth. If we can indulge invective and bitterness in the pulpit, we are but gratifying our own evil tempers, under the pretence of a concern for the cause of God and truth.

A preacher of this character, instead of resembling a priest bearing in his censer hallowed fire taken from God's altar, may be compared to the madman described in the Proverbs, who scatters at random firebrands and arrows and death, and says, *Am not I in sport?* Such people may applaud their own faithfulness and courage, and think it a great attainment that they can so easily and constantly set their congregation at defiance; but they must not expect to be useful, so long as it remains a truth, that the wrath of man works not the righteousness of God.

John Newton

A letter to a young minister, on preaching the Gospel with the power and demonstration of the Spirit

Joseph Hart: This God is the God we adore

No prophet, nor dreamer of dreams,
No master of plausible speech,
To live like an angel who seems,
Or like an apostle to preach;
No tempter, without or within,
No spirit, though ever so bright,
That comes crying out against sin,
And looks like an angel of light;

Though reason, though fitness he urge,
Or plead with the words of a friend,
Or wonders of argument forge,
Or deep revelations pretend,
Should meet with a moment's regard
But rather be boldly withstood,
If anything, easy or hard,
He teach, save the Lamb and His blood.

Remember, O Christian, with heed,
When sunk under sentence of death,
How first thou from bondage wast freed;
Say, was it by works, or by faith?
On Christ thy affections then fixed,
What conjugal truth didst thou vow!
With Him was there anything mixed?
Then what wouldst thou mix with Him now?

If close to the Lord thou wouldst cleave,
Depend on His promise alone;
His righteousness wouldst thou receive,
Then learn to renounce all thy own.
The faith of a Christian indeed
Is more than mere notion or whim;
United to Jesus, his Head,
He draws life and virtue from Him.

Deceived by the father of lies,
Blind guides cry, 'Lo here!' and 'Lo there!'
By these our Redeemer us tries,
And warns us of such to beware.
Poor comfort to mourners they give,
Who set us to labour in vain;
And strive, with a 'Do this and live'
To drive us to Egypt again.

But what says our Shepherd divine?
For His blessèd word we should keep;
'This flock has My Father made Mine,
I lay down My life for My sheep.
'Tis life everlasting I give,
My blood was the price that it cost;
Not one that on Me shall believe,
Shall ever be finally lost.'

This God is the God we adore,
Our faithful, unchangeable Friend,
Whose love is as large as His power,
And neither knows measure nor end;
'Tis Jesus, the First and the Last,
Whose Spirit shall guide us safe home;
We'll praise Him for all that is past,
And trust Him for all that's to come.

Anne Dutton: The sweetness and beauty of Christ

If you smelt any fragrancy on us, it was Christ's sweetness cast upon us that delighted your spiritual sense. And if unction from the Holy One, a drop of that Holy Oil cast upon a creature, be so fragrant, what must the immeasurable fulness of the Lord's Anointed, the Christ of God, be! For God giveth not the Spirit by measure unto Him. Oh the transcendent fragrancy of our Beloved! The smell of His garments delights the saints, both in the upper and lower worlds.

There are little sparks of beauty and excellency scattered up and down in the creatures, especially among the saints, the excellent of the earth, as new creatures: but all beauties, in their flaming glories, are summed up, and radiantly shine in the Person of Christ, as God-Man! There is in Christ, not only the beauty of the whole creation, but even uncreated beauty itself. What's all the beauty of the creatures, of men and angels in both worlds, if compared to His, in whom the fulness of the Godhead dwelleth bodily! None in the Heavens can be compared unto the LORD, none among the Sons of the Mighty can be likened unto the LORD: the LORD, the Mediator. No, the Heavens praise Him as God's WONDER! Psal. lxxxix 5, 6. The glorious hosts of saints and angels above, under the surprising and increasing displays of His Glory, eternally adore that uncreated beauty and brightness which shines forth in our exalted Jesus!

The crowned saints cast down their crowns before His throne, and shrink to nothing, as it were, in themselves, before the displays of His infinite majesty, love, and grace! Rev. iv.10. The whole host of seraphims, angels, and archangels, veil their faces, and cover their feet, as unworthy to stand in His Presence, or to look on the refulgent brightness of His unsearchable glory, as the train of divine perfections fills the temple of His glorified human nature! Isa. vi. 1,2. And as for the saints below, when favoured with the least glimpse of His glory, He is the chiefest of ten thousand in their esteem, and altogether lovely! They have none in Heaven but Him, nor upon the Earth that they desire besides Him, or in comparison with Him. Song v. 10, 16. Psa. lxxiii. 25. Oh how happy, are those souls who have an interest in this great Lord Jesus! and are blest with the transforming Shine of His inconceivable glory!

Oh, what folly are we guilty of, when we forsake this *Fountain of living waters*, and *hew out to ourselves broken cisterns that can hold no water!* Jer. ii. 13. When we forsake the infinite fulness of Christ, and seek contentment in creatures, and creature-excellencies! *The way of life is above to the wise:* Prov. xv. 24. The way of faith, by which life is possessed and enjoyed, is to live out of ourselves, upon the Christ of God, in all His infinite fulness and fitness to save sinners, from the depths of misery, to the height of glory.

Anne Dutton
***Letters on Spiritual Subjects*, Letter VI**

Anne Steele: The urgent invitation of the Gospel

Ye thoughtless young, who vain and gay
In flowery paths of ruin stray,
Think where you are: the way you go
Leads down to everlasting woe!

Think! Endless life or endless death
Hangs trembling on a moment's breath.
This moment's yours; the next may bear
Your souls to darkness and despair.

Fly from the world's deluding wiles
While time is yours, and Mercy smiles!
From sin and all its fatal charms,
Fly to the Saviour's open arms!

'Tis now with kind inviting voice
He courts you to immortal joys;
O hear that winning voice! Improve[4]
The boundless blessings of His love!

Ere long, that voice with dreadful sound
Shall with expressless terrors wound
The guilty souls who dare despise
His grace, nor life nor glory prize.

Say, can your now relentless heart
Sustain the dreadful word 'Depart'?
'Depart, accursed, down to hell,
Where endless fire and torture dwell.'

Reflect, and tremble at the view!
The downward path no more pursue!
Fly for your lives, to safety fly!
O wretched souls, why will you die?

Now is the time, th'accepted day;
O seize the blessing while you may!
Receive with joy the boundless grace,
And Christ and Happiness embrace!

Anne Steele
To the Young and Thoughtless

4. Improve = make good use of.

Andrew Fuller: Everyone's duty to trust Christ for salvation

John xii. 36, 'While ye have the light; believe in the light, that ye may be the children of light.' The persons to whom this passage was addressed were unbelievers, such as 'though Jesus had done so many miracles among them, yet believed not on Him' (ver. 37); and it appears that they continued unbelievers, for they are represented as given over to judicial blindness and hardness of heart, ver. 40. The light which they were exhorted to believe in appears to be Himself as revealed in the Gospel: for thus He speaks in the context, 'I am come a light into the world, that whosoever believeth in Me should not abide in darkness.' And that the believing which Christ required of them was such as, had it been complied with, would have issued in their salvation, is manifest from its being added, 'that ye may be the children of light:' an appellation never bestowed on any but true believers.

John vi. 29, 'This is the work of God, that ye believe on Him whom He hath sent.' These words contain an answer to a question. The persons who asked it were men who 'followed Christ for loaves,' who 'believed not,' and who after this 'walked no more with Him,' ver. 26. 36. 66. Christ had been rebuking them for their mercenary principles in thus following Him about, and charging them, saying, 'Labour not for the meat that perisheth, but for that which endureth unto everlasting life,' ver. 27. They replied by asking, 'What shall we do, that we might work the works of God?' which was saying in effect, 'We have been very zealous for Thee in following Thee hither and thither: yet Thou dost not allow that we please God: Thou directest us to labour for that which endureth unto everlasting life. What wouldest Thou have us to do? what can we do? what must we do, in order to please God?' To this question our Lord answers, 'This is the work of God, that ye believe on Him whom He hath sent;' which, if it be a proper answer, is the same as saying, This is the first and greatest of all duties, and without it no other duty can be acceptable ...

John v. 23, 'The Father hath committed all judgment unto the Son, that all men should honour the Son, even as they honour the Father. He that honoureth not the Son honoureth not the Father which hath sent Him.' That men are obliged to honour the Father, by a holy hearty love to Him, and adoration of Him under every character by which He has manifested Himself, will be allowed by all except the grossest Antinomians: and if it be the will of the Father that all men should honour the Son, even as they honour the Father, nothing less can be required of them than a holy, hearty love to Him and adoration of Him [Christ] under every character by which He has manifested Himself. But such a regard to Christ necessarily supposes faith in Him: for it is impossible to honour Him, while we reject Him in all or any of His offices, and neglect His great salvation. To honour an infallible teacher is to place an implicit and unbounded confidence in all He says: to honour an advocate is to commit our cause to Him: to honour a physician is to trust our lives in His hands: and to honour a king is to bow to His sceptre, and cheerfully obey His laws. These are characters under which Christ has manifested Himself. To treat Him in this manner is to honour Him, and to treat Him otherwise is to dishonour Him.

The Scriptures both of the Old and New Testament abound with exhortations to hear the Word of God, to hearken to His counsel, to wait on Him, to seek His favour, &c., all which imply saving faith. 'Hearken unto Me, O ye children: for blessed are they that keep My ways. Hear instruction, and be wise, and refuse it not. Blessed is the man that heareth Me, watching daily at My gates, waiting at the posts of My doors. For whoso findeth Me findeth life, and shall obtain favour of the Lord. But he that sinneth against Me wrongeth his own soul. All they that hate Me love death. How long, ye simple ones, will ye love simplicity? and the scorners delight in their scorning, and fools hate knowledge? Turn you at My reproof: behold, I will pour out My Spirit unto you, I will make known My words unto you.' – 'Hear, ye deaf, and look, ye blind, that ye may see. Hearken diligently unto Me. Incline your ear, and come unto Me: hear, and your soul shall live.' – 'Seek ye the Lord while He may be found, call ye upon Him while He is near.' – 'This is My beloved Son: hear Him.' – 'And it shall come to pass that every soul which will not hear that Prophet shall be destroyed from among the people.' – 'Labour not for the meat that perisheth, but for that which endureth unto everlasting life.'

Andrew Fuller
The Gospel Worthy of All Acceptation, Part Two: Arguments to Prove that Faith in Christ is the Duty of All Men who Hear, or have Opportunity to hear, the Gospel

Daniel Rowland: All things work together for good

Observe what he says. Make thou no exception, when he makes none. All! Remember he excepts nothing. Be thou confirmed in thy faith; give glory to God, and resolve, with Job, 'Though He slay me, yet will I trust in Him.' The Almighty may seem for a season to be your enemy, in order that He may become your eternal friend. Oh! Believers, after all your tribulation and anguish, you must conclude with David, 'It is good for me that I have been afflicted, that I might learn Thy statutes.' Under all your disquietudes you must exclaim, 'O the depth of the riches both of the wisdom and knowledge of God! How unsearchable are His judgments, and His ways past finding out!' His glory is seen when He works by means; it is more seen when He works without means; it is seen, above all when He works contrary to means. It was a great work to open the eyes of the blind; it was a greater still to do it by applying clay and spittle, things more likely, some think, to take away sight than to restore. He sent a horror of great darkness on Abraham; when He was preparing to give him the best light. He touched the hollow of Jacob's thigh, and lamed him, when He was going to bless him. He smote Paul with blindness, when He was intending to open the eyes of his mind. He refused the request of the woman of Canaan for a while, but afterwards she obtained her desire. See, therefore, that all the paths of the Lord are mercy, and that all things work together for good to them that love Him.

Even affliction is very useful and profitable to the godly. The prodigal son had no thought of returning to his father's house till he had been humbled by adversity. Hagar was haughty under Abraham's roof, and despised her mistress; but in the wilderness she was meek and lowly. Jonah sleeps on board ship, but in the whale's belly he watches and prays. Manasseh lived as a libertine at Jerusalem, and committed the most enormous crimes; but when he was bound in chains in the prison at Babylon his heart was turned to seek the Lord his God. Bodily pain and disease have been instrumental in rousing many to seek Christ, when those who were in high health have given themselves no concern about Him. The ground, which is not rent and torn with the plough, bears nothing but thistles and thorns. The vines will run wild, in process of time, if they be not pruned and trimmed. So would our wild hearts be overrun with filthy, poisonous weeds, if the true Vinedresser did not often check their growth by crosses and sanctified troubles. 'It is good for a man that he bear the yoke in his youth.' Our Saviour says, 'Every branch that beareth fruit, My Father purgeth, that it may bring forth more fruit.' There can be no gold or silver finely wrought without being first purified with fire, and no elegant houses built with stones till the hammers have squared and smoothed them. So we can neither become vessels of honour in the house of our Father till we are melted in the furnace of affliction, nor lively stones in the walls of new Jerusalem till the hand of the Lord has beaten off our proud excrescences and tumours with His own hammers.

He does not say that all things will, but do, work together for good. The work is on the wheel, and every movement of the wheel is for your benefit. Not only the angels who encamp around you, or the saints who continually pray for you, but even your enemies, the old dragon and his angels, are engaged in this matter. It is true; this is not their design. No! They think they are carrying on their own work of destroying you, as it is said of the Assyrian whom the Lord sent to punish a hypocritical nation, 'Howbeit, he meaneth not so'; yet it was God's work that he was carrying on, though he did not intend to do so. All the events that take place in the world carry on the same work – the glory of the Father and the salvation of His children. Every illness and infirmity that may seize you, every loss you may meet with, every reproach you may endure, every shame that may colour your faces, every sorrow in your hearts, every agony and pain in your flesh, every aching in your bones, are for your good. Every change in your condition – your fine weather and your rough weather, your sunny weather and your cloudy weather, your ebbing and your flowing, your liberty and your imprisonment, all turn out for good. Oh, Christians, see what a harvest of blessings ripens from this text! The Lord is at work; all creation is at work; men and angels, friends and foes, all are busy, working together for good. Oh, dear Lord Jesus, what hast Thou seen in us that Thou shouldst order things so wondrously for us, and make all things – all things to work together for our good?

Daniel Rowland
Sermon on Romans 8:28

William Williams' most famous hymn

Guide me, O Thou great Jehovah,
Pilgrim through this barren land.
I am weak, but Thou art mighty;
Hold me with Thy powerful hand.
Bread of Heaven, Bread of Heaven,
Feed me till I want no more;
Feed me till I want no more.

Open now the crystal fountain,
Whence the healing stream doth flow;
Let the fire and cloudy pillar
Lead me all my journey through.
Strong deliverer, strong deliverer,
Be Thou still my strength and shield;
Be Thou still my strength and shield.

Lord, I trust Thy mighty power,
Wondrous are Thy works of old;
Thou deliverest Thine from thralldom,
Who for naught themselves had sold:
Thou didst conquer, Thou didst conquer,
Sin, and Satan and the grave,
Sin, and Satan and the grave.

When I tread the verge of Jordan,
Bid my anxious fears subside;
Death of deaths, and hell's destruction,
Land me safe on Canaan's side.
Songs of praises, songs of praises,
I will ever give to Thee;
I will ever give to Thee.

Musing on my habitation,
Musing on my heavenly home,
Fills my soul with holy longings:
Come, my Jesus, quickly come;
Vanity is all I see;
Lord, I long to be with Thee!
Lord, I long to be with Thee!

By William Williams Pantecelyn,
translated from the Welsh in 1771 by Peter Williams

Chapter 3

Scotland in the Era of the Evangelical Revival

1
The Background of the Evangelical Revival in Scotland

1. Political, constitutional, and legal background: The Union of 1707

As Scotland entered the 18th Century, a number of important changes in its secular and ecclesiastical situation occurred. In particular, at the dawn of the new century, the year 1707 saw the momentous Union of Parliaments.[1] The Scottish parliament voted itself out of existence on January 16th 1707, and a new united Anglo-Scottish Parliament sitting in Westminster was established. This meant that the Scottish people would no longer have their own parliament, but instead have representatives within the Westminster Parliament. This Union of Parliaments created a remarkable situation in Europe: a single great nation-state under a single legislative body, with two different religions and Churches – Presbyterian in the north, Anglican in the south: historically antagonistic to each other in matters of church government, yet both fully recognised in the nation-state's constitution, and equally established by the law of the land.

---

1. The monarchies had already been united in 1603, when Queen Elizabeth I of England, having no children, left her kingdom to King James VI of Scotland, who thus became King James I of England-and-Scotland. However, the countries had separate parliaments until 1707, apart from a brief Anglo-Scottish parliament under the Protectorate of Oliver Cromwell (Cromwell's reign as Lord Protector lasted from 1653 to 1658).

There were significant religious factors in the 1707 Union of Parliaments which awakened some grave heart-searchings in Scotland:

(1) There was a generalised anxiety about the official Anglican faith of English society. Anglicanism was Episcopalian – governed by diocesan bishops appointed by the crown. What effect would this have, in a united parliament, on Presbyterian Scotland, which had decisively rejected Episcopalianism in the 1690 revolution?[2] Episcopalians were a small, marginalised minority in Scotland; in England, they were the reigning faith, embodied in an Anglican monarchy whose king (or queen) was the supreme governor of the English Church. And England was by far the more powerful of the two nations, in terms of population and military and economic resources.

(2) Scottish MPs now sitting in Westminster came under a legal obligation to take holy communion according to the Anglican form, before being allowed to take their seats in the united parliament. Was this not an insult to Scottish Presbyterian faith and piety?

(3) The supreme court of appeal for Scotland would no longer be the Court of Session in Edinburgh, but the House of Lords in Westminster, with its twenty-six Anglican bishops sitting and having authority as 'lords spiritual'. Could this be counter-productive in securing the interests of Presbyterian Scotland?

(4) Some conservative ministers of the Scottish Church opposed the Union as a betrayal of the Solemn League and Covenant of 1643 – one of the key documents of the Civil War period, uniting the English parliamentarians with the Scottish Covenanters in a joint struggle against the monarchy of King Charles I. The Solemn League and Covenant had committed England and Scotland to establish a single Presbyterian Church,

---

2. The revolution which, in Scotland, had toppled the Roman Catholic James VII (James II of England) from the throne, replacing him with the Dutch Calvinist, William of Orange. The equivalent event in England was the 1689 'Glorious Revolution'. The English were slighter quicker than the Scots to weary of King James and remove him from the throne.

faith, and worship, for the English and Scottish peoples.[3] Some of the strongest opponents of the Union of Parliaments within the Scottish Church turned out to be its most fervent Calvinists. Their Reformed, Covenanting opposition to the Union found lively expression in a treatise by James Webster (1659–1720), minister of Edinburgh's Tolbooth Church, entitled *Lawful Prejudices against an Incorporating Union with England* (1707). Webster was a noted theological and spiritual writer, whose works included *Sacramental Sermons and Discourses at the Lord's Table* and *The Covenants of Redemption and Grace Displayed.* The Scottish Reformed hostility of Webster and others to the Union of Parliaments was, ironically, counterpointed by the huge enthusiasm for the Union among English Reformed Dissenters, including English Presbyterians. This, however, merely served to exacerbate the suspicions of men like Webster, who saw English Reformed Dissent as tainted with the error of 'Baxterianism' (the views of Richard Baxter, the 17th Century English Presbyterian, regarded by many stricter Calvinists as unsound on the doctrines of the atonement and justification).[4]

To try to take the sting out of some of these Scottish qualms, some concessions were made to Scottish feeling in the Treaty of Union. Included in the Treaty was an Act recognising and securing the Presbyterian character of the Church of Scotland. The British monarch would now have to swear to uphold and preserve the rights and privileges of the Scottish national Church as established in Scottish law (i.e., the Reformed and Presbyterian Church of Scotland); all professors and principals in Scottish universities, and all teachers in the national school system, would have to subscribe to the Westminster Confession of Faith, and attend Presbyterian worship in their parish church. In these ways the Treaty sought to reassure Presbyterian Scots that their faith was not being compromised by the Union of Parliaments. In the 1730s, a new parliamentary Act was passed

3. For the Solemn League and Covenant, see Volume 4, Chapter 3, Part 5, section 6.

4. For Richard Baxter see Volume 4, Chapter 3, Part 6, section 4.

'forgiving' those Scottish MPs who did not or would not take holy communion according to the Anglican form. (This was a muddled, some might say typically English, way of maintaining in theory the legal obligation to receive Anglican communion as a precondition of sitting in the Anglo-Scottish parliament, while in practice evacuating that obligation of its force where Scottish MPs were concerned.)

However, in spite of these concessions to Scottish Presbyterian feeling, in 1712 the new united Anglo-Scottish parliament passed an Act which was to unleash storms of disruptive controversy on Scotland's Church life for the next one hundred and fifty years. This was an Act restoring the practice of unrestricted patronage, which had been abolished in the 1690 revolution settlement. The 1690 Act had granted the right to *nominate* parish ministers to the 'heritors' (the landowning gentry) and the elders of a parish. To counterbalance this, the congregation itself was also granted the legal right to *accept* or *veto* any nominee. However, the new Tory government elected in 1710 was determined to restore the unchecked power of the landowners in Scottish Church life, and carried this purpose through in its 1712 Act, without any consultation with the Scottish Church. At a stroke, local Scottish congregations lost the legal right to have final say on who their minister should be. That right now belonged exclusively to landowners (either local gentry or the crown itself).

The General Assembly of May 1712 expressed outrage, protesting robustly against the obnoxious Act, and instructing the Commission of Assembly to do everything possible to have the Act expunged from the statute books.[5] This instruction remained a standing order to every Commission of Assembly, every year until 1784. But it was all in vain. The controversial Act remained in legal force, and was to provoke almost unbounded strife in the subsequent religious history of Scotland.

---

5. The Commission of Assembly is a body made up of one tenth of the members of any given General Assembly, able in some circumstances to act in the Assembly's name.

2. Religious and theological background: The Marrow Controversy and First Secession

On the eve of the Scottish Evangelical Revival, the Church of Scotland underwent a convulsive theological controversy that has become a classic in Scottish Church history – the Marrow controversy. It was sparked off by events in the presbytery of Auchterarder in Perthshire. The Auchterarder presbytery added some of its own terms of subscription for candidates to be licensed as preachers or ordained to ministry; these additional terms were known as the Auchterarder Creed. One of the terms in the Creed to which candidates had to subscribe stated: 'I believe that it is not sound and orthodox to teach that we must forsake sin in order to our coming to Christ and instating us in covenant with God.' The presbytery's intention was to safeguard against any idea that God's grace is conditional – that a person must fulfil certain conditions before he is entitled to come to Christ for salvation. In the Evangelical theology that prevailed in the Auchterarder presbytery, a sinner did not forsake sin in order to come to Christ; he came to Christ as a sinner, and his very union with Christ empowered him to forsake sin as the first-fruit of faith and conversion. However, a disgruntled divinity student, William Craig, complained about the Auchterarder Creed to the General Assembly of 1717, and the Assembly condemned the offending proposition in the Creed.

In the context of this dispute, Thomas Boston (1676–1732), minister of Ettrick near Selkirk, one of Scotland's most creative Reformed theologians with a rare gift for popular communication, recommended to a friend a book called *The Marrow of Modern Divinity* as the clearest statement of the contested question. As a result, the *Marrow* was reprinted in 1718 with a preface by James Hogg (1658–1734), the prominent minister of Carnock.[6] The *Marrow* had first been published in 1645 by an English Presbyterian, Edward Fisher (dates

6. Not to be confused with James Hogg (1770–1835), 19th Century Scottish poet and novelist.

uncertain: flourished around 1627–55).[7] Boston and Hogg thought that the *Marrow* upheld the theology of unconditional grace that lay behind the Auchterarder Creed. Admirers of the *Marrow* came to be called 'Marrowmen'.[8]

It is difficult to sum up the whole theology of the *Marrow* concisely and accurately, but two points stand out which were to become matters of heated controversy. First, the *Marrow* – while not denying that God had a particular intention in the death of Christ (the actual salvation of the elect) – emphasised that there was also a proper universality in the atonement. Using language from Scottish law, the Marrow argued that God had made 'a deed of gift and grant' of Christ crucified to all mankind. An analogy used in Marrow theology was that a wealthy patron might pay for a physician to be appointed to a regiment in the army, with guaranteed right of access to the physician for every soldier in the regiment (even if only some soldiers availed themselves of this access). Likewise, God had appointed Christ to the whole human race as its spiritual physician, with every sinner having a graciously guaranteed right of access to Christ for salvation (although only some made actual use of that right, in the divine mystery of election). Therefore, while in Gospel proclamation it might not be technically correct to tell unbelievers 'Christ died for you' (died in order actually to save you), it was correct to tell them 'Christ is dead for you' (His death is available to you).[9]

Second, the *Marrow* argued that faith precedes repentance. This should not really have been controversial, since others (notably Calvin) in the Reformed tradition had held this[10],

7. Fisher is normally regarded as the author of the *Marrow*, but without total certainty.

8. Or Marrow Brethren.

9. The phrase 'Christ is dead for you' was taken from the great English Puritan, John Preston (1587–1628).

10. See Calvin's *Institutes* Book 3, Chapter 2, which is devoted to proving that faith precedes repentance. This view holds that apart from faith, only 'legal repentance' is possible – repentance based on the Law, which is only external in character and non-saving. Faith, however, enables

but it became controversial for the Scottish opponents of the *Marrow*. The *Marrow* taught that repentance – turning from sin to holiness as a way of life – could not take place *prior* to faith, because such a turning could occur only *as a result* of union with Christ through faith. Jesus Christ saved from the power of sin as well as the guilt of sin. Therefore, in order to be delivered from sin's power, and undergo true repentance, one must first be united with Christ as Saviour; and the mode or instrument of this union was God-given faith. Critics of the *Marrow* saw this as a form of 'cheap grace', as if a sinner could become a Christian without repentance. This, however, was really a misperception (or caricature) of *Marrow* teaching. The *Marrow* was simply endeavouring to rule out the view that a sinner must first repent before he is entitled to believe, which for the Marrowmen was a legalistic conception of 'conditional grace', alien to the Gospel.

The *Marrow* was attacked fiercely by James Hadow (1667–1747), principal of St Mary's College (part of St Andrews University). Hadow criticised the *Marrow* for various perceived errors – its view of God's universal gift of Christ as a Saviour for the human race, its teaching that the belief 'Christ died for me' was woven into the exercise of saving faith, its insistence that Christ must be offered to all sinners without exception. On this last point, Hadow argued that Christ died only for the elect, so He should be offered only to the elect – in practice, to sinners who showed signs of being elect through their consciousness of their sin.[11]

After two years of pamphlet warfare, the 1720 General Assembly finally condemned the *Marrow*, forbade all Church of Scotland ministers from recommending the book to their people, and indeed demanded that they admonish their congregations *against* reading it. The Marrowmen were incensed. In 1721, twelve ministers (including Boston, Hogg, and the

---

'evangelical repentance', a repentance flowing from the Gospel and an apprehension of its grace, which alone is saving in character.

11. The similarities with Hyper-Calvinism will be evident.

brothers Ralph and Ebenezer Erskine) presented a petition to the Assembly, bluntly complaining that in condemning the *Marrow*, the Assembly had both misrepresented its teaching and in fact condemned the very Gospel itself. The 1722 Assembly, however, confirmed the 1720 decision, and officially rebuked the Marrowmen. Some found themselves facing accusations of theological deviancy in the Church courts. They continued, even so, to protest against the Assembly's decision, and openly to teach the doctrines of the *Marrow* by pulpit and pen. In 1726, Boston defiantly issued another edition of the *Marrow* with extensive notes by himself – these notes have come to be regarded as a theological masterpiece.[12]

The Marrow controversy ceased to be a purely theological affair when its teachings flowed out into the 'First Secession', a breakaway body from the Church of Scotland.[13] The First Secession was steeped in Marrow theology. This breakaway movement was prompted by a vacancy in the parish of Kinross in 1726. The congregation wanted to call the Marrowman Ebenezer Erskine (1680–1754) as their minister. He, however, went to Stirling in 1731. In 1732, the landowner-patron of Kinross appointed Robert Stark as the new parish minister, against the wishes of the congregation. Since the local presbytery (of Dunfermline) refused to ordain Stark, the Commission of Assembly appointed a 'riding committee' to ordain him (a committee of ministers from outside the presbytery, sent in to carry out an unpopular ordination by the authority of General Assembly). The Dunfermline presbytery, however, animated by a spirit of Evangelical mutiny, refused to accept the ordained Stark as a member of presbytery. The Assembly peremptorily ordered them to accept him in 1732 and 1733, but the presbytery persistently refused.

This and similar situations persuaded the Assembly to take more comprehensive action aimed at quelling the Evangelical

12. Most Evangelical Calvinists would now see the Marrowmen as having been substantially in the right in this controversy.

13. A Second Secession took place in 1761: see Part 3.

insubordination of some presbyteries toward the patronage laws. Already the previous year (1731) the Assembly had sent an overture to presbyteries in which the right to call a minister, in cases where presbytery had responsibility, was stated more emphatically to belong to the heritors and elders, with the rights of the congregation being marginalised if not utterly denied. The 1732 Assembly found that thirty-one presbyteries had opposed this overture, eighteen approved, and eighteen expressed no opinion. Despite this widespread opposition, the Assembly passed the overture as an Act.

An incensed Ebenezer Erskine led a resistance movement, both in the Assembly and outside, to what he and others saw as an act of unconstitutional tyranny. The 1733 Assembly censured Erskine for his outspoken language in opposing the Act. He and three other Evangelical ministers – Alexander Moncrieff (1695–1761) of Abernethy, James Fisher (1697–1775) of Kinclaven, and William Wilson (1690–1741) of Perth's West Church – tabled a protest (a process in Scottish Presbyterian church procedure, which allowed disagreement to be officially expressed). The Assembly, in no mood to compromise, ordered the four protesters to withdraw their protest and to express humble contrition for having protested at all. They refused, and as a punishment were deposed from their parishes (although retaining their ministerial rank). On December 5th 1733, the four deposed ministers met together at Gairney Bridge in Kinross, and formed what they called the 'Associate Presbytery', although in popular language they were known as the Seceders.

The General Assembly made some conciliatory moves toward the Seceders over the next few years, including repealing the obnoxious Act of 1732, but the Secession ministers would not return to the Church of Scotland; they felt it was by now too steeped in error and beyond any realistic hope of genuine overall reformation. By 1738, four more ministers had joined the Associate Presbytery, including Ebenezer's brother Ralph Erskine (1685–1752) of Dunfermline. On their own authority, they now began acting as though they were a Church, licensing men to preach. In 1740, the General Assembly deposed them all from the ministry: the breach was final.

So was born Scotland's First Secession Church. It speedily prospered. By 1742, there were twenty congregations with regular ministers, plus some vacant congregations. Also significant, in 1742 the Associate Presbytery passed an 'Act Concerning the Doctrine of Grace', in which it vindicated Marrow theology. This demonstrates how the passions generated by the Marrow controversy had spilled over into the Secession. The Seceders were committed to Marrow theology, which lived on vibrantly in their churches. By 1745, the new Church had grown sufficiently to form itself into three presbyteries under the name of the Associate Synod.[14]

The unity of the First Secession Church, however, did not last. It was badly split by a controversy over the Burgess Oath of 1744. This was an oath taken by citizens of Edinburgh, Glasgow, and Perth, which contained the clause, 'I profess and allow with my heart the true religion presently professed within this realm and authorised by the laws thereof'. The controversy was over whether this referred to Protestantism in general (in which case a Seceder could take the oath) or to the Church of Scotland in particular (in which case a Seceder could not take the oath without seeming to approve of the Church of Scotland as embodying the true religion, rather than being a corrupt body). The issue was also important because the numerical strength of the Associate Synod was concentrated precisely in Edinburgh, Glasgow, and Perth.

After much debate, the Synod broke apart in 1747 into two rival bodies, each claiming to be the true Associate Synod. Those opposed to the Burgess Oath, the 'Anti-Burghers', called themselves the General Associate Synod; those who refused to make condemnation of the Oath into a test of orthodoxy, the 'Burghers', continued to call themselves the Associate

14. This is not to suggest that Marrow theology had no supporters within the Church of Scotland: it certainly did, among Evangelicals. But Marrowmen among Church of Scotland Evangelicals did not prioritise Marrow theology to the extent of splitting with the national Church.

Synod. The most famous of the Seceders, Ralph and Ebenezer Erskine, were Burghers. Despite the split, both branches of the First Secession continued to grow, not only in Scotland, but in Ireland, America, and Canada.

3. Religious and theological background: Moderatism

As the 18th Century dawned, there came a distinct loss of Reformed faith in the Church of Scotland, comparable to the severe decline of Evangelical faith in England prior to the preaching of Whitefield and Wesley. This loss of traditional faith helped form the backdrop to Scotland's experience of revival in the 1740s. The new century witnessed a novel, dominant ethos coming to the fore in the Scottish Church, an outlook known as Moderatism. There has been much discussion about the origins of both the word and the religious vision it embodied. We can, with some certainty, sum up the movement under three aspects:

(1) *Moderates had no enthusiasm for the Reformed theology of their Church's Westminster Confession.* To a greater or lesser degree, Moderate clergy were decisively influenced by the thought of the Enlightenment rather than by classical Reformed thinking. They tended to soft-pedal, or even blithely ignore, the Westminster Confession's teaching about man's total depravity, divine election, substitutionary atonement, and justification by faith, in favour of a more rationalist outlook, emphasising the human will's natural capacity for virtue. Morality they looked upon more as an expression of the natural inclinations of the human mind, rather than obedience to the revealed will of the triune God. An amusing anecdote illustrates the difference between Moderate and Evangelical teaching in this respect. William Robertson (1721–93), a leading Moderate, preached a sermon one Sunday morning in Old Greyfriars Church, Edinburgh, in which he sang the praises of virtue, declaring that if virtue were to appear in visible form, all men would love and adore her. In the afternoon, his ministerial colleague, John Erskine (1721–1803), an Evangelical Calvinist, preached another sermon, in which he declared that virtue had indeed

appeared in visible form in the person of Jesus Christ – and so far from loving and adoring Him, men had crucified Him!

A clear symptom of budding Moderate attitudes occurred quite early on in the 18th Century, when in 1714 John Simson (1668–1740), Professor of Divinity in Glasgow University, was accused of teaching Socinianism and Arminianism. His case came to the General Assembly of 1716, and was discussed at length; the 1717 Assembly at length found Simson guilty of teaching unnecessary private opinions (e.g., that the moon might be inhabited), and of tending 'to attribute too much to natural reason and the power of corrupt nature'. But the Assembly let him off with a warning; no disciplinary action was taken. Nine years later in 1726, Simson was up before the Assembly again, this time accused of Socinianism and Arianism. It was alleged he had said, 'the proposition "Christ is the supreme God" is to be taken with a grain of salt'. The Assembly permanently suspended Simson from his duties, but on full salary, and no further action was taken (he was neither deposed from the ministry nor excommunicated).

The generosity shown to Simson scandalised Evangelical ministers, especially the illustrious Thomas Boston, who in the General Assembly of 1728 – alone and unsupported – protested against the Assembly's leniency, declaring that the honour of Christ required Simson's deposition. Simson, however, was shielded from all further consequences by family connections and the support of the Glasgow divinity faculty; he continued drawing his salary until his death in 1740.

(2) *Moderates cultivated a new style of preaching* – ethical, rational, polished. This was a revolt against 17th Century Scottish preaching, which had often based itself on a single text and perhaps derived from it the entire scheme of redemption. The most distinguished of the Moderate preachers was Hugh Blair (1718–1800), who ministered in various churches; his longest period was at St Giles High Church, Edinburgh, from 1758 to 1800. He was also Professor of Rhetoric at Edinburgh University. Blair's sermons, published in five volumes (1777 onwards), were hugely popular as literature; by 1794, the first

volume had reached its nineteenth edition. They won the praise of England's famous Dr Samuel Johnson, who called them 'golden sermons'. Blair paid the closest attention to language and style, spending the whole week writing his Sunday homily. The sermons were practical, lucid, reasonable – one critic described them as virtually an eloquent statement of the obvious. Evangelicals denounced this style of sermonising as 'moonlight preaching' – mere cold morality, without the life-giving warmth of the Sun of Righteousness. Sometimes Moderates went too far, provoking even non-Evangelicals to censure them; the great sceptical Scottish philosopher, David Hume (1711–76), accused a leading Moderate, Alexander Carlyle (1722–1805), minister of Inveresk, of 'preaching Cicero from the pulpit'.[15]

(3) *Moderates embraced and encouraged a less intense attitude to life and religion.* They were notably more open-minded toward diversity in outlook and lifestyle than Scottish Protestantism had conventionally been. For example, in 1755–56, the General Assembly had the opportunity to prosecute arch-sceptic David Hume, one of the great philosophers of the Enlightenment, for heresy – Hume was still nominally a Church member. Evangelicals tried to seize the occasion to censure Hume for his philosophical scepticism, but Moderates protected him, exalting freedom of opinion as a positive virtue. Moderates also violated traditional Evangelical cultural restrictions, especially in relation to the theatre. In 1756, the play *Douglas* by the Moderate minister John Home (1722–1808) was staged in Edinburgh. There was an Evangelical uproar against Moderate clergy who were present in the theatre to watch the play; Alexander Carlyle of Inveresk, who had caused a commotion by going to the theatre garbed in his clerical dress, was prosecuted in the church courts for licentiousness. The General Assembly, however, at length let Carlyle off with a mere caution. It was Carlyle's attitude that would prove victorious in the long run.

15. Cicero (106–43 B.C.) was the Roman Pagan philosopher and moralist who lived in the dying years of the Roman Republic, before it became the Roman Empire.

When the streams of thought that went into the making of Moderatism coalesced into a distinctive outlook in the Church of Scotland in the 1730s, Moderatism's first leader was Patrick Cuming (1695–1776), minister of Edinburgh's Old Kirk and Professor of Church History at Edinburgh University. However, the most celebrated Moderate leader, from the 1760s, was William Robertson (1721–93). Robertson was the son of the minister of Borthwick; he followed his father into the Church of Scotland ministry, ordained in 1744 as minister of Gladsmuir, East Lothian. He then moved to Edinburgh in 1758, as minister of Lady Yester's Church, and then from 1761 was minister of Old Greyfriars. In 1762, he became Principal of Edinburgh University, a position he held at the same time as his parish ministry. In his own day, Robertson was a distinguished and famous historian, compared with England's renowned Edward Gibbon.[16] In the Church, Robertson was eloquent and highly effective in the Church's courts and committees, dominating them by his unrivalled political skill.

The Moderate contribution to Church affairs can be assessed by Robertson's attitude to three outstanding problems:

(1) *Moderates upheld patronage.* By contrast, Evangelicals (sometimes called the Popular Party in this respect) continued to look upon patronage as a serious blemish in the life of the national Church, desiring its abolition. It was the patronage issue that caused the two great 18th Century secessions from the Church of Scotland in 1733 (the First Secession) and 1761 (the Relief Church – see Part 3). Evangelicals advocated the right of a congregation to choose its own minister, regardless of a patron's will. In taking this stance, Evangelicals probably always embodied majority opinion among the ministers and congregations of the Scottish Church. The pro-patronage Moderates, however, were much better organised, able to hold sway over the Church's courts and committees. Robertson argued that the Church must accept patronage because it was the law of the land, and Christians must obey the law. He

16. Author of *Decline and Fall of the Roman Empire.*

was not blind to the defects of patronage; Robertson wanted the existing system to function as efficiently as possible. Nonetheless, he argued that popular opposition to a patron's choice of minister should be ignored. Such opposition often stemmed, he suggested, from a minority of hot-headed dissidents. What about the alleged right of the congregation to elect its own pastor? Robertson believed this was of little significance. The only proper objection, he maintained, against a patron's nominee was demonstrable immoral character. Those who would not submit to these conditions, Robertson maintained, had only one option: to secede from the national Church. The ideal Church of Scotland minister, for Robertson, was a man of intellect and social grace, able to command respect from the ruling classes and associate with them on equal terms.

(2) *The relationship between the national Church's General Assembly and its presbyteries.* Robertson believed in the complete subjection of all the Church's lesser courts to its General Assembly as the all-powerful supreme court. As we have seen, during the first part of the 18th Century there was serious friction between presbyteries and the Assembly, revolving around patronage. Some presbyteries would refuse to accept a patron's nominee if the congregation rejected him. This generated the unpopular system of 'riding committees' (committees of a synod or of the Assembly) being sent out to act in place of a local presbytery and induct the unwanted nominee to a parish. The evidence suggests that in the period 1740–1752, more than fifty ministers were inducted to their parish charges by riding committees, when presbyteries refused to do so.

Robertson was resolved to break the independent spirit of presbyteries. This he triumphantly accomplished in 1752 in the famous or infamous Inverkeithing case. Rather than send in a riding committee to induct the unpopular nominee to Inverkeithing parish church, Robertson convinced the Assembly that it ought to discipline the presbytery of Dunfermline for its refusal to accept the patron's choice. This in turn led to presbytery member Thomas Gillespie, minister of Carnock, being deposed from the Church of Scotland ministry for his forthright opposition to the patron's nominee, and thus at length to the Second Secession from the national Church and the founding of the Relief Church (see Part 3 for more about the Relief Church). Robertson's strategy led to the absolute subordination of all the national Church's lesser courts to the overruling and centralised authority of the General Assembly. Presbyteries henceforth were no longer free to defy the patronage laws without being penalised by the Assembly, and perhaps their ministers being deposed. The General Assembly, under Moderate control, used its augmented power to apply the patronage laws unsparingly.

(3) *Schism and dissent.* By the 1760s, so many congregations were breaking away from the national Church to join either the First or Second Secession Churches, that a thoroughly unnerved General Assembly began conjecturing the unthinkable – perhaps it should throw its weight behind the abolition of the patronage laws in order to bring an end to the seemingly endless drip-drip of congregational secessions. A great debate on this was consequently held in 1766. Robertson stood forth as the champion of patronage in this debate. To make his point, he argued rather paradoxically that schism and secession could be of benefit to the Church and the nation. Human nature being what it is, Robertson contended, it was unavoidable that there would always be disagreements and divisions in matters of religion; the wise churchman must candidly accept this fact. 'The beauty of the garden lies in the diversity of the flower beds.' He went to the lengths of paying handsome tribute to the men of the First Secession as 'honourable and devout men' who had shown striking virtue in their loyalty to the Hanoverian monarchy during the Jacobite Rising of 1745.[17] Perhaps not so openly or zealously admitted by Robertson, he also smiled on secession because it got rid of the Evangelical troublemakers from the national Church, thus leaving it more docile to control by the Moderates.

17. See Part 4 for the Jacobite Risings.

2
The Evangelical Revival

1. Origins of the Revival in Scotland

Before the Evangelical Revival in Scotland flowed out in a nationwide way, there was a more localised Highland revival in 1739 centred on the parish church of Nigg in Easter Ross. The Evangelical parish minister, John Balfour, presided over prayer meetings each week that were attended by unusually large numbers of people, gathered under a sense of the presence of God. Lay preaching was undertaken at these meetings by 'The Men' (see Part 6, section 2 for The Men). This more local manifestation of Scottish revival is often forgotten, eclipsed by the glory of what took place two years later under the preaching of George Whitefield and those who cooperated with him. An account of the Nigg revival was given by John Gillies (see section 5 for Gillies):

> The revival of religion in the parish of Nigg, East Ross, has been upon the advance since the year 1730, though for most part in a gradual slow way, and with several stops and intermissions. As to new awakenings, the most considerable concern appeared in 1739 ; then several persons awakened (and who had never done it before) applied to the minister about their spiritual interest, each day in the week, for one week, Saturday not excepted ... The work of grace upon convinced souls here, appears to be in its rise, progress and issue, in the same scriptural way, and the same in kind and substance, as in these other parts, from which narratives have come to hand. Very few, not one in forty, who have been awakened, have fallen off from a religious profession,

> or given open scandal to it. The general meeting for prayer and spiritual conference, which sometime consisted only of the members of session, and a few others, became at length so numerous, that about three years ago, it was necessary to divide it into two, each of which is since considerably increased. Besides these general meetings, which convene in two places of the parish, at a proper distance, each, every third Monday respectively, and in which the minister always presides, there are ten societies which meet in several places of the parish every Saturday for prayer, and other religious exercises. Care is taken that in each of these societies, one or more of the elders, or some Christians of distinguished experience, be always present; and nothing as yet appears about them, but what has a tendency to promote the most valuable ends and interests of religion.

Despite this awakening in Nigg and the surrounding areas, it would be a distortion of history to deny that the Evangelical Revival in Scotland, in its largest dimensions, was mediated – at least initially – through the ministry of George Whitefield. Through his instrumentality, the great religious movement that began in England and Wales in the mid-to-late 1730s rapidly penetrated north into Scotland too. In England, as we have seen, the Evangelical Revival is usually linked in popular consciousness with John Wesley and his brand of Methodism. Wesley, however, made comparatively little impact on Scotland, owing to his Arminian theology: the traditional Scottish 'Evangelical' theology was far too solidly Reformed to give much credence to any kind of Arminianism.[1]

However, the first and greatest of the English open-air evangelists, George Whitefield, was a Calvinist, a fact which formed

1. I use 'Evangelical' here to denote the salvation-oriented theology that flowed from the Scottish Reformation, convinced as it was of the depth and seriousness of human sin, salvation objectively accomplished in the person and work of Jesus Christ as God incarnate, crucified and risen, and made manifest in human lives in justification by faith and regeneration. This type of theology and its connected piety already existed in Scotland, a fruit of the Reformation and the Scottish theologians who remained true to its spirit.

a natural bond between himself and Scottish Evangelicals. Having become so well-known in England and North America, Whitefield was invited in 1741 to preach in Scotland by Ralph Erskine of the Seceders (the Associate Presbytery).[2] Whitefield gladly accepted the invitation; he already knew of Erskine, referring to him as 'a field preacher of the Scots Church, a noble soldier of the Lord Jesus Christ,' and had been reading some of Erskine's writings with much appreciation.[3] John Wesley, by contrast, had a dim view of the Seceders, simply because they were Presbyterians – Wesley was always more deeply attached to Anglicanism and its distinctives than Whitefield ever was. The Seceders, for their part, had been in friendly communication with Whitefield since 1739.

The English Calvinist preacher, then, came willingly to Scotland, arriving on July 29th 1741.[4] Things went well, at first. The people of the Secession welcomed Whitefield warmly, and his preaching among them proved highly acceptable. It seemed that the premier evangelist of England had brought the fire of revival to Scotland. Ralph Erskine recorded:

> He preached in my meeting-house this afternoon. The Lord is evidently with him.

However, Whitefield's relationship with the Seceders swiftly degenerated. They urged him to condemn Episcopacy (the form of government in Whitefield's own Church of England, in which he had been ordained) as unbiblical, and to accept Presbyterianism as the proper form of Church government authorised by scripture. Whitefield refused, pleading instead for an attitude of mutual forbearance and toleration. The Seceders also wanted Whitefield to preach for them alone, claiming that 'We are the Lord's people in Scotland.' Whitefield's response was

---

2. See Part 1, section 2, for the First Secession and the Associate Synod.
3. See under Primary Historical Sources at the end of the Chapter for an extract from Ralph Erskine's *Gospel Sonnets*.
4. It may be worth reflecting that Whitefield's conversion was mediated through a work of Scottish piety, Henry Scougal's *The Life of God in the Soul of Man* (1677). Scougal was a Scottish Episcopalian.

that those who were *not* the Lord's people in Scotland needed his ministry even more! As Whitefield recorded the incident:

> I asked, why only [preach] for them? Mr Ralph Erskine said, 'They were the Lord's people'. I asked them then whether there were no other Lord's people but themselves? And, supposing all others were the devil's people, they certainly had more need to be preached to; and therefore I was more and more determined to go out into the highways and hedges.

In consequence the Seceders disowned Whitefield and began denouncing the Revival, of which Whitefield was an instrument, as a hysterical delusion. Whitefield commented on the breach:

> I retired; I wept; I prayed; and after preaching in the fields, sat down and dined with them, and then took a final leave. At table a gentlewoman said she had heard that I had told some people that 'the Associate Presbytery' were building a Babel. I said, 'Madam, it is quite true; and I believe the Babel will soon fall down about their ears.' But enough of this. Lord, what is man? what the best of men? but men at the best!

2. Whitefield and the Church of Scotland

Cast out by the Seceders, Whitefield now found his true home among the Evangelical ministers of the Church of Scotland. Preaching at first in the open air, his sermons and their spiritual impact drew the admiration of a number of Church of Scotland Evangelicals, who embraced him and his preaching warmly. Many of these men sympathised with the Seceders theologically, even spoke out on their behalf against their harsh treatment by the Church of Scotland, but saw no need themselves to leave the national Church in pursuit of Evangelical principles.

After taking his leave of the Seceders, Whitefield preached in the open air in Edinburgh. On August 8th he recorded:

> On Sunday evening (last) I preached in a field near the Orphan House [in Edinburgh] to upwards of fifteen thousand people; and on Monday, Friday, and Saturday evenings to near as many. On Tuesday I preached in the Canongate Church; on Wednesday and Thursday at Dunfermline; and on Friday morning at Queensferry. Everywhere the auditories

> [audiences] were large and very attentive. Great power accompanied the Word. Many have been brought under conviction.

A week later he recorded, again in Edinburgh:

> Every morning I have a levée [assembly] of wounded souls. At seven in the morning we have a lecture in the fields, attended not only by the common people, but persons of great rank. I have reason to think several of the latter sort are coming to Jesus. Little children are also much wrought upon. Congregations consist of many thousands. I preach twice daily, and expound in private houses at night, and am employed in speaking to souls under distress great part of the day.

This first of Whitefield's evangelistic visits to Scotland lasted for thirteen weeks, and the excerpt from his journal cited above characterised the entire visit, which included Edinburgh, Glasgow, Paisley, Stirling, and Aberdeen, increasingly in Church of Scotland pulpits or churchyards. One of his Church of Scotland supporters, John Willison (1680–1750), minister of Dundee South Church, wrote after Whitefield's first visit was over:

> I look upon this youth[5] as raised up by God for special service, for promoting true Christianity in the world, and for reviving it where it is decayed. I see the man to be all of a piece: his life and conversation to be a transcript of his sermons. He is singularly fitted to do the work of an evangelist; and I have been long of opinion that it would be for the advantage of the world were this still to be a standing office in the Church. I have myself been witness to the Holy Ghost falling upon him and his hearers oftener than once; not in a miraculous, though in an observable manner. Many here are blessing God for sending him to this country, though Satan has raged so much against it. Though he is ordained a minister of the Church of England, he has always conformed to us both in doctrine and worship, and lies open to conform to us in other points. God, by owning him so wonderfully, is pleased to give

5. Whitefield was only twenty-six years old.

> a rebuke to our intemperate bigotry and party zeal, and to tell us that neither circumcision nor uncircumcision availeth anything, but the new creature.

Notable among Whitefield's Church of Scotland supporters were the ministers John Erskine (1721–1803) and Alexander Webster (1707–84) of Edinburgh, John Gillies (1712–96) of Glasgow, William McCulloch (1691–1771) of Cambuslang, James Robe (1688–1753) of Kilsyth, John Willison (1680–1750) of Dundee, and James Ogilvie (1695–1776) of Aberdeen. Some of these were noted authors of Christian literature. John Gillies wrote a pioneering history of revivals, his *Historical Collections Relating to Remarkable Periods of the Success of the Gospel* (two volumes, 1754), and the first ever biography of Whitefield, *Memoirs of the Life of the Rev.G.Whitefield* (1772). James Robe wrote an eyewitness account of the powerful revival in Cambuslang and Kilsyth, *Narrative of the Extraordinary Work of the Spirit of God at Kilsyth* (1742) – see the next section for this local revival. John Willison produced an abundance of edifying works: *A Sacramental Catechism* (1720), *A Treatise concerning the Sanctifying of the Lord's Day* (1722), *The Mother's Catechism* (1731), *The Afflicted Man's Companion* (1737), *A Sacramental Directory: or, A Treatise concerning the Sanctification of a Communion Sabbath* (1741), and *The Balm of Gilead* (1742).

John Erskine of Edinburgh, although not so notable as a writer, emerged as the leader within the Church of Scotland of an Evangelical party revitalised by the Revival. His preaching, writing, activities in the Church courts, and personal influence among the Scottish upper classes, helped to promote Evangelicalism in the Church of Scotland. His contemporary, Sir Henry Moncrieff Wellwood, described Erskine thus:

> In his character were concentrated extensive learning; fervent piety; purity of doctrine; energy of sentiment; enlarged benevolence, uniformly animated by an ardent zeal for the glory of his Master and the salvation of men.[6]

---

6. Sir Henry Moncrieff Wellwood (1750–1827) succeeded Erskine as leader of the Evangelical party in the national Church.

Erskine became sufficiently celebrated as an Edinburgh preacher to find a place in the novel *Guy Mannering* by Scotland's greatest Romantic novelist Sir Walter Scott, who in his sympathetic pen-portrait said that Erskine combined 'much learning, metaphysical acuteness, and energy of argument'.[7] A multi-faceted individual, Erskine was an early supporter of overseas mission, an opponent of British war with the American Colonies, an enemy of the slave trade, and a critic of the French Revolution. His support for mission was memorably expressed in the 1796 General Assembly, when a delegate to the Assembly had poured cold water on the missionary movement, arguing that the primary concern should be to civilise, not to evangelise, 'heathens'. Erskine stood up and famously said, 'Moderator, rax me [reach me] that Bible!' He then proceeded to expound scripture to the effect that it knew no imperative to civilise unbelievers before they could be evangelised.

3. The Cambuslang Revival and its aftermath

The single most famous episode of the Scottish Revival took place at Cambuslang and Kilsyth, near Glasgow, often simply called the Cambuslang Revival (or Cambuslang Work). Spurred on by Whitefield's example, the minister of the Cambuslang parish church, William McCulloch, began holding preaching services every night in 1742, assisted by ministerial colleagues. These meetings occurred in the open air. The place where the meetings were held is described thus:

> The place chosen was peculiarly well adapted for the purpose. It is a green brae on the east side of a deep ravine near the church, scooped out by nature in the form of an amphitheatre. At present it is sprinkled over with broom, furze, and sloe-bushes, and two aged thorns in twin-embrace are seen growing side by side near the borders of the meandering rivulet which murmurs below.

Many of McCulloch's listeners came under deep conviction of sin, sometimes accompanied by physical manifestations –

7. This is in ch. 37 of *Guy Mannering* (1815), the second of Sir Walter Scott's Waverley novels.

trembling, swooning, etc. Great crowds were soon attracted from all quarters as news of the local revival spread. It reached its pinnacle when Whitefield himself, during his second visit to Scotland, preached at Cambuslang. His journal for June 19th 1742 says:

> At mid-day I came to Cambuslang, and preached at two to a vast body of people; again at six and again at nine at night. Such commotions, surely, were never heard of, especially at eleven o'clock at night. For an hour and a half there was much weeping, and so many falling into such deep distress, expressed in various ways, as cannot be described. The people seemed to be slain in scores. Their agonies and cries were exceedingly affecting. Mr M'Culloch preached, after I had done, till past one in the morning; and then could not persuade the people to depart. In the fields all night might be heard the voices of prayer and of praise. The Lord is indeed much with me.

The local revival became even more intense at the communion season in July. Whitefield again recorded:

> July 15, 1742. Last Friday night I came to Cambuslang to assist at the blessed sacrament. On Saturday I preached to above twenty thousand people. On the Sabbath scarce ever was such a sight seen in Scotland. Two tents were set up, and the holy sacrament was administered in the fields. When I began to serve a table the people crowded so upon me that I was obliged to desist, and go to preach in one of the tents, whilst the ministers served the rest of the tables. There was preaching all day by one or another; and, in the evening, when the sacrament was over, at the request of the ministers, I preached to the whole congregation of upwards of twenty thousand persons. I preached about an hour and a half. It was a time much to be remembered. On Monday morning I preached again to near as many. I never before saw such a universal stir. The motion fled, as swift as lightning, from one end of the auditory to the other. Thousands were bathed in tears – some wringing their hands, others almost swooning, and others crying out and mourning over a pierced Saviour. In the afternoon the concern was again very great. Much prayer

> had been previously put up to the Lord. All night, in different companies, persons were praying to God and praising Him. The children of God came from all quarters. It was like the Passover in Josiah's time.

Identical scenes took place in August, when even greater numbers gathered – some thirty thousand. The revival spread from Cambuslang to the adjacent parish of Kilsyth, where James Robe was the minister. He wrote:

> The countenances of [some] quite changed. There was an observable serenity, a brightness, and openness, so that it was the observation of some concerning them, that they had got new faces.

The Seceders denounced the revival as a deception, but Robe vindicated it in his *Narrative of the Extraordinary Work of the Spirit of God at Kilsyth* (1742).[8] Meanwhile similar revivals broke out across Scotland. One historian lists Glasgow, Edinburgh, Cumbernauld, St Ninians, Gargunnock, Calder, Campsie, Baldernock, Auchterarder, Muthill, Dundee, Crieff, Monzievaird, Nigg, Rosskeen, Nairn, Rosemarkie, Irvine, Coldingham, Easter Logie, Alness, Cromarty, Golspie, Kirkmichael, Avoch, and Rogart as experiencing revival.

Whitefield's third visit to Scotland in 1748 occasioned some controversy within the Church of Scotland, as some ministers (perhaps taking their cue from the narrowness of the Seceders) tried to have resolutions passed to prohibit Whitefield from

8. Robe's treatise was attacked by the leading Secession minister James Fisher of Glasgow, in his *Review of the Preface to a Narrative of the Extraordinary Work at Kilsyth* (1743). Ralph Erskine also went into print against the revival with his *Faith No Fancy* in 1745. This was a sad end to the initially positive Secession-Whitefield relationship. The Secession Church even appointed a day of humiliation and fasting on August 4th 1742, in order to lament the 'sin' of other Presbyterians in aiding and abetting the abominable Whitefield in his delusive revival work. If we inquire what was so abominable about Whitefield, the Secession's answer was simply that he was an Anglican. Apparently the Holy Spirit did not work through Anglicans. Whitefield wrote: 'To what lengths may prejudice carry even good men! From giving way to the first risings of bigotry and a party spirit, good Lord deliver us!'

preaching in Church of Scotland parishes. These resolutions were defeated, and provoked some outspoken and eloquent defences of Whitefield from a number of Church of Scotland Evangelicals. Alexander Webster of Edinburgh's Tolbooth Church said:

> I shall conclude by observing that the grave opposition made to this divine work [the Revival] by several good men through misinformation or mistaken zeal, and the slippery precipice on which they now stand, may teach us that it is indeed a dangerous thing to censure without inquiry. It may serve likewise as a solemn warning against a party spirit which so far blinds the eyes. It also gives a nobler opportunity for the exercise of our Christian sympathy towards these our erring brethren, and should make us long for a removal to the land of visions above, where are no wranglings, no strivings about matters of faith, and where, the whole scheme of present government being removed, we shall no more see as through a glass, but face to face, where perfect light will lay a foundation for perfect harmony and love. It is with peculiar pleasure that I often think how my good friend Ebenezer [Erskine – the famous Seceder, brother of Ralph] shall then enter into the everlasting mansions with many glorified saints, whom the Associate Presbytery [the Seceders] have now given over as the work of Satan. May they soon see their mistake, and may we yet altogether be happily united in the bonds of peace and truth.

Altogether Whitefield made fourteen evangelistic visits to Scotland. Apart from the multitudes of professed conversions, the chief long-term effect of the Calvinist wing of the Scottish Evangelical Revival, of which Whitefield was the main voice, was to infuse new spiritual life and energy into the Evangelicals within the national Church. This laid the foundations for the new, revitalised Church of Scotland Evangelical party that was led by John Erskine, then Sir Henry Moncrieff Wellwood, then Andrew Thomson, and finally the great Thomas Chalmers in the early 19th Century. This Evangelical party in the national Church was, in the Victorian era, to overthrow the Moderate ascendancy in the Church, and to find its ultimate issue in the last and greatest of the anti-patronage secessions in the Disruption of 1843 and the creation of the numerically enormous Free Church of Scotland. Without the Evangelical Revival in the 18th Century, these subsequent events would have been unthinkable.

4. John Wesley in Scotland

It was ten years after Whitefield's first visit to Scotland in 1741 that John Wesley finally set foot on Scottish soil in order to preach. He came at the invitation of Captain Gallatin, an English army officer stationed in Musselburgh, near Edinburgh. Wesley arrived in Musselburgh on April 24th 1751, together with one of his lay preachers. He went in the teeth of strong discouragement from Whitefield, who told him:

> You have no business there, for your principles are so well known that if you spoke like an angel, none would hear you.

By Wesley's principles, Whitefield meant his Arminianism and perfectionism. Whitefield's warning may have had an impact on Wesley; he resolved that in Scotland he would never attack Calvinism in his preaching, but limit his preaching to setting forth the essential Gospel of salvation by faith. As Wesley himself put it:

> From the first hour that I entered the kingdom [Scotland], it was a sacred rule with me never to preach on any controverted point – at least, not in a controversial way.

He extended this rule to his lay preachers in Scotland, rebuking one of them as 'lost to all common sense' when, in 1770, he preached against the doctrine of perseverance.

Wesley made twenty-two visits to Scotland, and was usually given a positive reception, preaching both in Presbyterian and Episcopal churches (at a time when Anglican pulpits in England were closed to him). John Gillies of Glasgow was his strongest supporter among Church of Scotland ministers. Scotland's ruling classes were well-disposed, and in 1772 Wesley was given the freedom of the city in Perth and Arbroath.[9] Wesley's journal records that the ordinary masses of Scottish people received him more warmly than their English counterparts did:

> O what a difference there is between North [Scotland] and South [England] Britain! Everyone here [in Scotland] at least loves to hear the Word of God and none takes it into his head to speak one uncivil word to any for endeavouring to save their souls.

In a striking contrast to Wesley's rough experience in England, he encountered violence only once in Scotland, when in 1768 in Aberdeen, a few of his 'listeners' were disruptive and threw potatoes at him.

Yet in spite of this friendly reception, Wesley did not succeed in winning many disciples in Scotland for his brand of Methodism. He complained in his journal during his 1784 Scottish visit:

> I am amazed at this people. Use the most cutting words, and apply them in the most pointed way, still they hear but feel no more than the seats they sit upon.

By 1767, there were only 468 Methodists in Scotland, and 1,079 by the time of Wesley's death in 1791. Adam Clarke, who was responsible for the practical administration of Scottish Methodist missions in the Shetland Islands, noted that Wesleyan Methodism had put down no deep roots in Scotland except in Edinburgh and Glasgow. Wesley did not begin ordaining preachers for Scotland until 1785 (thirty-four years after his first visit): these were John Pawson, Thomas Hanby, and Joseph Taylor. In 1788, a Scot named Alexander Mather (1733–1800) was ordained by Wesley as one of the first superintendents for the wider British movement. Mather, from Brechin, had been an itinerant Methodist preacher since 1757, notable for his courage and endurance amid much violent opposition in England.

---

9. The freedom of the city was a sort of honorary recognition by a city of an individual's special value.

Wesley's failure to win many committed followers in Scotland was probably owing, in significant measure, to open antagonism from influential Scottish Calvinists toward his Arminianism and perfectionism. Perhaps the most notable example of this antagonism was a treatise by John Erskine, leader of the Church of Scotland Evangelicals: *Mr Wesley's Principles Detected* (1765). Erskine was very ready to acknowledge Wesley's genuine piety and Christian sincerity, but expressed grave concern about Wesley's Arminianism and views on sinless perfection, taught by Wesley in England even if he remained silent about them in Scotland. Erskine also republished the English Evangelical Calvinist James Hervey's anti-Arminian work, *Eleven Letters to Mr John Wesley* (1765).[10]

Wesley's Scottish work was also undermined when, in 1771, the leading Scottish Evangelical laywoman, Lady Glenorchy (see below), came down decisively against Wesley, refusing henceforth to allow any Wesleyan preachers to occupy the pulpit of her new chapel in Edinburgh. (Other such chapels were subsequently built, in Scotland and England, and Wesleyan preachers were barred from these too.) Lady Glenorchy's influence was strong enough to counteract Wesley's Scottish work quite significantly.

Several other factors have been suggested to explain the relatively small success of Wesley's work in Scotland (contrasted with England): his apparent unwillingness to establish a locally settled rather than itinerant form of ministry, his direction of the Scottish work from England (as if Scotland were merely a province of English Methodism), and the comparatively high standard of religious education enjoyed by Scottish people, which inclined them to hear Wesley's preaching more as judges than humble learners.

5. Other leading Scottish Evangelicals

Thomas Boston (1676–1732). Boston died shortly before the Evangelical Revival, but his writings would nourish the children

---

10. For James Hervey, see Chapter 2, Part 4, section 2.

of the Revival to an unparalleled degree, an influence enduring (albeit in attenuated form) even to the present day. Born at Duns, educated at Edinburgh University, Boston was ordained to the Church of Scotland ministry in 1699, serving the parish of Simprin, near Coldstream, until he moved in 1707 to Ettrick, near Selkirk. His ministry at Ettrick transformed the spiritual life of the parish for generations to come. Boston took part in all the great controversies of his time, notably the Marrow controversy, in which he was one of the most zealous supporters of the *Marrow* and its theology; his 1726 edition of the *Marrow*, with a large body of accompanying notes by himself, is often regarded as the best edition of the *Marrow* owing to the theological richness of Boston's comments.

Thomas Boston

In addition to his notes on the *Marrow*, Boston wrote several other religious classics. His *Memoirs* is a spiritual autobiography of the highest order (first edited and published by Boston's grandson in 1776). More important for Scottish religion was his *Human Nature in its Fourfold State* (1720), a phenomenally successful popular presentation of Reformed theology. The four 'states' are human nature in innocence, in sin, in grace, and in glory. The *Fourfold State* was reprinted some hundred times, translated into many languages, and for a century or more it had an influence on grass-roots Scottish piety second only to the Bible – the Scottish equivalent of Bunyan's *Pilgrim's Progress* in England.

A prolific author, Boston's collected writings fill twelve volumes. Some of the treatises in these volumes are significant works in the history of Scottish Reformed theology, such as *A View of the Covenant of Works, A View of the Covenant of Grace,*

A Complete Body of Divinity (based on the Westminster Shorter Catechism), and *Sermons on Communion Occasions*. Boston's covenant (or federal) theology was unusual for its time in rejecting the normal threefold scheme of covenants: the *pactum salutis* (covenant of peace) in eternity between the Trinitarian persons, the covenant of works in Adam, and the covenant of grace in Jesus Christ. Boston preferred to collapse the *pactum salutis* and the covenant of grace into a single covenant, in which Christ is the only agent, acting as the Second Adam, and in which faith is not a condition for entering into the covenant, but rather a free and gracious promise and gift to the new humanity.

John Gillies (1712–96). Gillies was born at Careston, in Angus, and after theological training became the minister of the Church of Scotland's College Church in Glasgow in 1742, a position he held until his death. His preaching and teaching ministry involved three sermons each Sunday and mid-week lectures. Among Gillies' treasured writings were his *Exhortations to the South Parish of Glasgow* (two volumes, 1750–51), *A Catechism upon the Suffering of the Redeemer* (1763), and *Devotional Exercises on the New Testament* (1769). He was outstanding among Scottish Evangelicals for his warm support of George Whitefield and John Wesley, both of whom preached from Gillies' pulpit.

Gillies' concern for revival led him to investigate the history of unusual outpourings of the Holy Spirit in the life of the Church, which he published in two volumes in 1754 as *Historical Collections Relating to Remarkable Periods of the Success of the Gospel*. This was a trailblazing historical study of revivals, and its publication contributed hugely to an interest in, and hunger for, revival among English-speaking Evangelicals. As previously noted in section 3, Gillies also wrote the first ever biography of George Whitefield in 1772, drawing upon his close friendship with the Anglican evangelist.

Lady Glenorchy (1741–86). Willielma Maxwell was born into wealth and privilege, the daughter of William Maxwell of Preston. In 1761, aged twenty, she married Viscount Glenorchy, the oldest son of one of Scotland's greatest landowners, the Earl of Breadalbane. A grave illness in 1765 precipitated a religious conversion, when during her recovery Lady Glenorchy was ministered to by the sister of Anglican Evangelical preacher Rowland Hill (1744–1833). When her husband died in 1771, she then gave over the rest of her life to helping spread the Evangelical Gospel. In this, Glenorchy often relied on the advice of her English Evangelical friend, the Countess of Huntingdon.[11]

In fact, Glenorchy had already started down this path in 1770, when she used her wealth to construct a chapel in Edinburgh. The chapel's pulpit was made available to Evangelical preachers of all persuasions – Presbyterians, Episcopalians, and Wesleyan Methodists. However, in 1771, Glenorchy came to hold Calvinist views in a far stronger way, as a result of which she closed the chapel's pulpit to Wesleyan Methodists. Henceforth she championed Evangelical Calvinism, especially within the Church of Scotland. In 1773, she refurbished a chapel in Strathfillan (Perthshire), with a grant of money to support both a settled minister and two evangelists. In 1774, she financed a new Edinburgh chapel; this chapel, for several generations, proved a stronghold in the Scottish capital for Evangelical Calvinism within the national Church.

In addition to her chapel-building work, Lady Glenorchy sponsored many evangelistic meetings in her Edinburgh home; these meetings were open to people from every social class, not merely the aristocracy. She also employed a number of Evangelical chaplains, of whom some became staunch Evangelical ministers in the national Church.

Lady Glenorchy has been called the most impactful Scottish woman of her day in matters of religion. Her legacy lived on far beyond her death in 1786, since she bequeathed a large slice of her wealth to the support of her chapels in Scotland and England,[12] a fund devoted to educating young men for the

---

11. For the Countess of Huntingdon, see Chapter 2, Part 4, section 11.

12. Lady Glenorchy built English chapels in Bristol, Carlisle, Exmouth, Matlock, and Workington.

preaching ministry, and the Scottish Society for the Promotion of Christian Knowledge.[13]

Lady Maxwell (1742–1810) of Pollok. Darcy Brisbane was born in Brisbane, Largs (Ayrshire), educated in Edinburgh, and then lived in London with her aunt, the Marchioness of Lothian. Married in 1760 to Sir Walter Maxwell, baronet of Pollok, she was deeply impacted by his early death soon after the marriage in 1762, their young child dying around the same time. Lady Maxwell interpreted these events as a providential call from God to remain single: 'I see God requires my whole heart, and He shall have it!' Maxwell thereafter lived in Edinburgh, worshiping in St Cuthbert's Church (Church of Scotland). In 1764 she began attending Methodist meetings, joined a Methodist Society, and came into direct personal contact with John Wesley, whom she admired intensely. Maxwell and Wesley commenced a regular correspondence, and she became one of his most committed supporters in Scotland. In particular, Maxwell championed Wesley's Arminian view of grace. This placed serious strains on her friendship with Scotland's other prominent female Evangelical, Lady Glenorchy (see above), who was a firm Calvinist. Maxwell also accepted Wesley's teaching on sinless perfection, claiming in 1787 to have experienced this herself.

Maxwell used her wealth to support a wide variety of philanthropic and evangelistic causes. She is especially remembered for erecting and funding a charity school in Edinburgh, personally overseeing its financial management and daily functioning. When the Sunday School movement was in its infancy, she took it under her wing and established two Sunday Schools in Scotland and one in London.[14]

Lady Maxwell's journal has become a treasured record of Methodist religious experience, documenting her rich communion with God. Some have classed her as a mystic; among

13. See Part 6 for more about the Scottish Society for the Promotion of Christian Knowledge.

14. See Chapter 2, Part 10, for Sunday Schools.

her convictions was a belief that she could distinguish in feeling between the three persons of the Trinity, each person having (as it were) His own unique experiential 'flavour'. She also claimed to be so close to heaven's reality that she could sense its inhabitants (the glorified saints).

3
The Second Secession

We have already looked at the First Secession of 1733, when some ministers and congregations of the Church of Scotland broke away from the parent body to form the Associate Presbytery (later renamed the Associate Synod). Although the Seceders were influenced by Marrow theology, the primary cause of their secession was Scotland's patronage laws, whereby a local landowner (or the crown) could force a minister on a congregation without the congregation's consent. In 1761, a Second Secession took place. It was again precipitated by the patronage laws.

Thomas Gillespie (1708–74) was the Evangelical minister of Carnock parish church, a keen supporter of the Evangelical Revival in Scotland. In 1752, the General Assembly ordered the presbytery of Dunfermline (within which Gillespie's Carnock parish was situated) to induct to Inverkeithing parish church the nominee of its patron, despite the congregation's protests – it did not want the man as their minister. Six presbytery members refused to obey the Assembly's instruction to induct the unpopular nominee, among them Gillespie. The Assembly decided to make an example of Gillespie (picking on him for his unusually outspoken opposition to the patron's unwanted nominee), deposing him from the ministry. This, however, backfired; Gillespie's great popularity as an Evangelical preacher meant that many left the Church of Scotland with him, and a large new independent congregation was formed in nearby Dunfermline, with Gillespie as minister.

This by itself would not have led to the formation of a Second Secession Church, but other events began to unfold. Thomas Boston Junior (1713–67), son of the illustrious Marrowman Thomas Boston of Ettrick, received a call to the parish church of Jedburgh in 1755. However, the crown refused to present Boston, and forced on the congregation a different candidate, an unpopular choice – so unpopular that only five people in the entire parish could be found to support his call! So the congregation broke away from the Church of Scotland, built its own independent meeting house, and called Boston to be their minister; he was inducted in 1757.

The final factor in the origin of the Second Secession was when the Church of Scotland congregation of Colinsburgh, in Fife, seceded in 1760 over the obnoxious patronage laws, and called an English Nonconformist, Thomas Colier of Westmoreland, as its minister.

These three individual secessions dovetailed to create the Second Secession Church. In October 1761, Gillespie, Boston, and Colier, and their three congregations, formed themselves at Colinsburgh into a presbytery 'for the relief of Christians oppressed in their Christian privileges'. They adopted the title 'Presbytery of Relief' – popularly known as the Relief Church. The basic 'relief' desired by the Second Secession was the freedom for congregations to choose their own ministers. They shared this ideal with the First Secession.

There was, however, a serious difference. Unlike the First Secession, the Relief Church rejected the binding obligation of the 17th Century covenants[1] and their imposition as terms of fellowship. The Relief Church embraced the principle of 'free communion', classically expressed by Thomas Gillespie: 'I hold communion with all that visibly hold the Head [Christ], and with such only.' This empowered Relief ministers to share worship-services and pulpits with orthodox ministers of other Churches, and to admit all orthodox believers of whatever

1. The 1638 National Covenant and the 1643 Solemn League and Covenant.

Church to the Lord's Supper. With supreme irony, this catholicity of outlook put the Relief Church at odds with the Churches of the First Secession (the Associate Synod and the General Associate Synod) which denounced the Relief Church for 'latitudinarian, unscriptural terms of communion'.

Another feature of the Second Secession that set it apart from the First was that most of the Relief Church's ministers embraced 'Voluntary' views of Church-state relations (that the state should not establish and endow any denomination) – an ideal they shared with English Nonconformists, but contrary to the Scottish Presbyterian tradition which believed that the Church should be established in law and endowed by the state. Also remarkably for a Presbyterian body, the presbyteries and synods of the Relief acted more as consultative meetings than as legislative courts, thus giving maximum liberty of thought and conduct to individual ministers and congregations.

The Relief Church prospered. By 1776, it had grown so successfully, through more congregations leaving the Church of Scotland to join the Second Secession, that the new denomination had three presbyteries, meeting jointly as the Relief Synod. Nor was numerical growth on home soil its only concern. It was the first Scottish Presbyterian Church to endorse the cause of overseas mission, when in 1796 the Synod passed a resolution giving strong support to such missions, exhorting its members to 'unite their exertions with any society that may be formed to promote such a good and great design'.

Not only regarding overseas mission, but in various other ways too, the Relief Church was 'ahead of its time' in the stances it adopted. For example, it took an early committed stand against the slave trade. In 1788 it petitioned the two branches of the First Secession (the Associate Synod and the General Associate Synod) to join it in combating 'the inhuman system of the slave trade'. A Relief Church minister and evangelist, Niel[2] Douglas (1750–1823), authored one of the most widely read British polemics against the slave trade, his *The African Slave Trade* (1792).

2. This is the correct spelling.

Another area of progressive thinking in the Relief Church was its espousal of congregational hymn-singing, at a time when other Scottish Presbyterians were wedded to exclusive psalm-singing. James Stewart, minister of the Relief congregation in Anderton, introduced a selection of one hundred and eighty hymns into his worship-services. Two other ministers followed his example, Patrick Hutchison of Paisley and James Dun of Glasgow. The Relief Synod of 1794 gave its backing to this development, recommending Stewart's hymnbook, and officially attaching a preface vindicating the use of hymns as well as psalms in Christian worship. The new hymnbook was dominated by the compositions of Isaac Watts, with other hymns by English Congregationalist Philip Doddridge and Evangelical Anglican John Newton. The hymnbook was fairly rapidly adopted by the generality of Relief congregations.

As previously noted in Part 1, the actions of the Church of Scotland General Assembly in deposing Thomas Gillespie in 1752 (precipitating the formation of the Relief Church) proved decisive in breaking the spirit of Church of Scotland presbyteries, rendering them pliant and subordinate to the Assembly. This brought about a more centralised and streamlined form of Church government in the national Church; but it also meant that when future disputed settlements of ministers occurred (through the patronage laws), a frustrated congregation could much more swiftly opt to leave the national Church and join one of the existing Secession Churches. By 1766, it has been estimated that the various Secession Churches – the Covenanters,[3] the Associate Synod, the General Associate Synod, and the Relief Church – had between them one hundred and twenty places of worship in Scotland, and one hundred thousand worshippers. Scotland was now more religiously pluralistic than at any time in its history.

3. The small body that had not returned to the newly Presbyterian national Church of the 1690 revolution settlement.

4
The Jacobite Risings of 1715 and 1745

A fog of romanticism surrounds the Scottish Jacobite risings of 1715 and 1745. The reality was perhaps less romantic, but it had strong religious dimensions, and to that extent it holds a significant place in Scotland's religious history. The term itself – Jacobitism – describes continued loyalty to Britain's dethroned Stuart dynasty.[1] The Roman Catholic James II of England (James VII of Scotland) had been cast out in the revolutionary events of 1688–90, replaced by the Dutch Calvinist William of Orange. After William's death in 1702, the Anglo-Scottish throne fell to Britain's last Stuart monarch, the Protestant Queen Anne (1702–14), daughter of James VII (but untainted by her father's Roman Catholicism). Anne's death, however, spelled the end of the Stuart dynasty, and she was succeeded by the first of the Hanoverian monarchs, George I (see below). The new dynasty, however, was not well received in the Scottish Highlands, where devotion to the Stuart cause retained much strength. Consequently, there brewed in Scotland a number of Jacobite plots and rebellions against the Hanoverian monarchy; the most momentous of these broke out in positive bids for the throne in 1715 and 1745.

1. Jacobite derives from the Latin for James, Jacobus, referring to James VII of Scotland (James II of England), deposed in the Glorious Revolution of 1688–89 for his Roman Catholicism and absolutism (trying to run the country without parliament).

1. The 1715 Rising

The 1715 Jacobite Rising was provoked by the death of Queen Anne, the last Stuart monarch, in August 1714. Prior to this, in 1701 the English parliament had enacted a law of royal succession, with two provisions: (i) Anne, the Protestant daughter of the deposed Roman Catholic James VII, should follow William of Orange as monarch, but (ii) after Anne's own death, if she died childless, the throne should then pass to the German princess Sophia of Hanover (or Brunswick-Lüneburg – Hanover was its capital). Sophia was the Protestant granddaughter of James I of England (James VI of Scotland). This English law of succession was aimed at preventing the Roman Catholic bloodline of James VII from regaining the throne – to ensure a Protestant monarchy and thus a Protestant constitution for Britain.[2]

When Queen Anne died without children in 1714, therefore, the throne legally passed to Sophia's son, the Protestant Duke George of Hanover (who thus became King George I of Britain). George was strongly supported by the Whig party, the more radically Protestant of Britain's two political parties of Whig and Tory. The Whigs then won a huge historic victory in the general election of 1715. Ominously, though, there was a yawning gulf of opinion separating England from significant parts of Scotland, especially the Scottish Highlands. For instance, when George of Hanover was proclaimed king in Inverness in 1715, the official cries of 'God save the king!' were drowned out by cries of 'God damn them and their king!'

This element of Scottish unfriendliness toward the new Hanoverian dynasty was partly because the house of Hanover had gained Scotland's throne by virtue of an *English* law – the law of succession enacted by the English parliament in 1701. Some Scots felt that this violated Scotland's 1690 Revolution settlement, when the Scottish parliament had offered Scotland's crown to William of Orange, but had specifically retained

2. Fear of Roman Catholicism was far more intense in the English than the Scottish national psyche.

for itself the power thereafter to determine the Scottish royal succession.[3] On top of this, since William of Orange and the cause of Presbyterianism had won out as a single package in Scotland in 1689–90, Scottish Episcopalians (strongly opposed to Presbyterianism) were much inclined to support the previous Stuart dynasty which, although Roman Catholic, had allowed a Protestant Episcopalian Church to function as Scotland's national Church, with bishops appointed by the crown. There was therefore in Scotland, on the death of Queen Anne, a combination of Scottish nationalism and Episcopalian faith which put a significant body of Scots in the Jacobite camp. In August and September 1715, the new Hanoverian regime dismissed nearly one fifth of all Scottish justices of the peace[4] because of presumed Jacobite sympathies. Large numbers of Scottish justices of the peace were also thrown out of office *after* the 1715 Rising – manifestly the first clear-out had been unsuccessful.

The political mastermind behind the 1715 Jacobite Rising was John Erskine, the Earl of Mar (1675–1732). Mar had been removed from all political office in 1714 by the new Hanoverian monarch George I, who suspected his loyalty. Mar's nickname was 'Bobbing John', owing to his 'bobbing about' from one political side to the other, Whig and Tory. However, when the new Whig-Hanoverian regime came to power in 1714, Mar was at that time on the Tory side, and suffered the fate of many Tories in being dismissed from office. The following year, he journeyed to France, and there swore his allegiance to the Roman Catholic court-in-exile of the Jacobite claimant to the British throne, James Edward Stuart (1688–1766), son of the deposed James VII (who had died in 1701). Returning to Scotland, Mar then raised the Jacobite banner of revolt at Braemar on September 6th 1715, declaring James Edward

---

3. Nothing could now be done about this by the Scottish parliament because it had ceased to exist under the 1707 Union of Parliaments. There was now only a relatively small number of Scottish MPs sitting in the united (and overwhelmingly English) parliament of Westminster.
4. Magistrates of lower courts – judicial officers charged with upholding the law and 'keeping the peace'.

Stuart as true king of Scotland. Supporting Mar in this Jacobite rebellion were the nobility and gentry of Scotland's north-eastern Lowlands and the Grampian Highlands, inspired either by political Jacobitism, or Episcopalian religion, or indeed by both. Mar also succeeded in convincing the clan chiefs of the central Highlands to join the insurgency.

At first, the 1715 Rising swept everything before it. Perth, Aberdeen, and Inverness were all captured by Jacobite forces. There was hardly a breath of resistance: to the contrary, definite enthusiasm for the Jacobites blazed forth in the Lowlands of the Scottish north-east. However, military catastrophe came crashing down on the Jacobite army at the battle of Sherrifmuir on November 13th, where a small Hanoverian army of 1,000 commanded by the Earl of Argyll forced a stalemate on a much bigger Jacobite army of 4,000 under the Earl of Mar. The psychological blow thus dealt against the Rising proved irreversible. By the time the Jacobite would-be king, James Stuart, set foot in Scotland in December, the Jacobite cause was already lost, and James had to flee within weeks. The Earl of Mar also fled into exile, living out the rest of his days in France, a death sentence for treason hanging over his head in Britain.

The failed Rising's outcome for Scottish Episcopalians was ruinous. They were from that moment looked upon as actual or potential traitors by the Hanoverian regime, and restrictive new laws were now strongly enforced against them. For example, in 1719 the British parliament enacted a law prohibiting any clergyman from leading worship in any Scottish Episcopal church or meeting-place, if nine or more people were in attendance, and if the clergyman did not pray for the Hanoverian monarch George I as the lawful king of Britain. Some Episcopalian clergy submitted, but most did not. Ironically, therefore, while Episcopalianism in the shape of the Anglican Church was the established religion in England, it became a virtually outlawed sect in Scotland.[5]

5. It was not until 1792 that the bishops of the Scottish Episcopal Church at last accepted the legitimacy of the Hanoverian regime.

2. The 1745 Rising

The 1745 Jacobite Rising, from a religious standpoint, differed from the 1715 Rising in having a Roman Catholic rather than Episcopalian inspiration. Its geographical base was the Roman Catholic Highlands, where (as yet) Protestantism had made comparatively little impact. Moreover, the 1745 Rising was led in person by a Roman Catholic prince, Charles James Stuart (1720–88), young son of the Jacobite claimant to the British throne, James Edward Stuart.[6] The French government had promised to back the Rising, a promise which helped launch it, although in fact very little French support materialised. With hardly any military supplies, but buoyed up by a vibrant belief in his cause, Charles landed on the isle of Eriskay, and then journeyed to Moidart on Scotland's north-west coast. He raised the Jacobite standard of rebellion at Glenfinnan on 19th August. By sheer personal charisma, Charles succeeded in attracting a legion of Highland followers.

It is not, however, the case that all Highlanders threw in their lot with Charles' Jacobite crusade, not even those who were staunchly Roman Catholic. Many of the Highland clan chiefs judged that his enterprise was futile and doomed to failure, and consequently refused to yield any positive cooperation. Even so, Charles recruited enough backing to gather a Highland army of just over a thousand, with which he proceeded to march on Edinburgh, where he resoundingly defeated a government army of 2,000 at the battle of Prestonpans on 21st September 1745. One of the slain on the government side was the devout Protestant hero, Colonel James Gardiner (1688–1745), whose influential life-story was written up by the great English Congregationalist preacher Philip Doddridge (1702–51).

Having made himself master of Edinburgh, the dashing and charismatic Charles was welcomed with considerable warmth in the city. One of the most striking things he did while in the Scottish capital was to annul the 1707 Union of Parliaments, thus restoring Scotland's independence. He also declared a

6. The prince became known popularly as Bonnie Prince Charlie.

policy of religious freedom – he would not seek forcibly to re-Catholicise his Scottish Protestant subjects. Some historians have argued that if Charles had been willing to rest content with this, he might have been able to control an independent Jacobite Scotland without serious risk. Fatefully, however, Charles was resolved upon conquering England as well as Scotland. This was despite the opposition of all but one of the Highland clan chiefs to any English adventure. Obedient to its prince, however, on November 8th the Jacobite army marched into England, where some English Catholics joined them. Still, there was no significant active support forthcoming from the English population, not even from those with Jacobite sympathies.[7]

Charles' forces managed to reach Derby – a mere three days' march from London – but by then, the Highlanders had lost all heart for their invasion of what to them was an alien land, pleading with Charles to take them back to Scotland. Their concern was reinforced by two government armies closing in upon them, from north and south. On 5th December the retreat to Scotland began. Once back on Scottish soil, Charles and his advisors decided that meeting the government forces on the battlefield was their best choice for securing a Jacobite Scotland. On 16th April 1746 the two armies met at Culloden, near Inverness, where government forces of 9,000 under William, Duke of Cumberland (youngest son of King George II), crushed the Jacobite army of 6,000, by superior tactics and firepower. Charles himself succeeded in escaping back to France. With the prince's flight, Jacobitism was effectively now a lost cause in Britain.

The 1745 Rising should not be seen as a conflict between Scotland and England. There was serious opposition to the Jacobites in Scotland, especially from the Presbyterian clergy, both the Church of Scotland and the Seceders. One of the leading ministers of the Secession, Ebenezer Erskine, personally raised a volunteer force to defend the Protestant Hanoverian

7. It has been estimated than maybe up to a third of Tory MPs had Jacobite leanings.

government against the Catholic Jacobite insurgency. Hostility to the Jacobites also stemmed from the Scottish legal establishment, and many of the large southern towns and cities where Protestantism reigned supreme. For this reason, some historians have chosen to describe the conflict as a Scottish civil war, between a backward-looking agricultural Highland society and a progressive capitalist Lowland economy. This seems too simplistic, but the Jacobite and Hanoverian causes in Scotland did represent a clash of cultures.

The victorious Hanoverian government was hardly generous in victory. Its response after the 1745 Rising was far more ruthless than it had been after the 1715 Rising. All Jacobites who were found bearing arms were either killed on the spot, or else transported across the Atlantic to become slaves in the Caribbean plantations, even if they were simply handing over their weapons to surrender. Regions and communities that had actively supported the Rising were placed under the heel of a harsh military terrorism. Entire villages were destroyed. The houses of Jacobite Highland chiefs were torched. In many places, this government terror brought about the total collapse of law and order. Jacobite landed estates were systematically seized from their one-time owners; the wearing of tartan (regarded as a Highland Jacobite symbol) and the owning of bagpipes (considered to be the music of rebellion) were outlawed. Meanwhile, the government built many new forts in the Highlands, and thousands of miles of new military roads, which were methodically patrolled by government troops. For a generation, the Highlands became, in effect, a land under grim military occupation by the regiments of the Hanoverian monarchy.

5
The Highlands become Protestant and Presbyterian

In the Revolution Settlement of 1690, the national Scottish Church had ceased to be Episcopalian and become decisively Presbyterian. This was welcomed in the Scottish Lowlands, where Presbyterianism had already become the popular religion. By contrast, Presbyterianism experienced huge challenges in trying to put down roots in the Highlands. Episcopalianism there kept a comparatively strong hold on the faith of many, and the old pre-1690 Episcopalian clergy, although now evicted from their parish churches, were often able to ignite local opinion against the new Presbyterian parish ministers as wolfish intruders into the sheepfold.

The religious quarrel was also explosively intermeshed with politics: as we have seen, there was substantial ongoing loyalty to the dethroned House of Stuart in the Highlands. The leaders of the Highland Jacobite cause, in the aftermath of 1690, were almost all Episcopalian in faith. This blend of Episcopacy in religion and Jacobitism in politics proved itself a dynamic enemy to Presbyterianism. The potency of this opposition may be illustrated by local examples. In 1716, the Presbyterian minister of Gairloch fled from his parish, terrified that his parishioners might murder him; they had repeatedly attacked and looted his manse, burned his crops, and stolen his cattle. In Killearnan, likewise, hostile parishioners torched the manse of the new Presbyterian minister, threatening to kill him.

1. The work of the Society in Scotland for Propagating Christian Knowledge

For several generations, the Highlands remained by and large a barren wasteland for Presbyterianism. In a remarkable turnabout, however, the latter part of the 18th Century (and on into the early 19th) witnessed the effective spread of Presbyterianism into the Highlands. The seeds of this rich Presbyterian flourishing had been sown earlier. In particular, the Society in Scotland for Propagating Christian Knowledge (the SSPCK) laboured energetically to stimulate Protestant faith at a grass-roots level in the Highlands. The SSPCK was founded by royal charter in 1708. It acted as the trailblazer for the Presbyterian transformation of the Highlands, by setting up schools to teach Protestantism to the young. Its endeavours were at first cramped by an imprudent policy decision to carry out this teaching in English, rather than the Gaelic of the Highlands; the hope was to bring about the Anglicising of Highland culture as well as its conversion to Protestantism. The English language policy was, however, eventually reversed. By 1792, the SSPCK was operating one hundred and forty-nine schools in the Highlands, although the bulk of these were situated in the southern part of the region, with a particular cluster in the Moray and Easter Ross area.

With its new pro-Gaelic policy, the SSPCK now began vigorously promoting Christian literature in Gaelic. One of the finest fruits of this policy was a new Gaelic New Testament. A chief driving force behind the Gaelic translation was the poet Dugald Buchanan (1716–68), of Kinlochrannoch in Perthshire. Buchanan's people had been Jacobites, suffering dreadfully for their part in the 1745 Rising; Buchanan himself had not taken arms for the Jacobite cause, but he grieved deeply for the afflictions of his kinsfolk. Nonetheless, he believed that the best balm for their wounds was not political revenge, but conversion to the true Gospel of the Reformation. Together with the Presbyterian minister James Stuart (1701–89) of Killin, Buchanan translated the New Testament into Gaelic; it was published by the SSPCK in 1767. (In 1801, the SSPCK published the complete Bible in Gaelic.) Buchanan also authored a body of Gaelic Protestant hymns which proved popular in the Highlands, helping to earn him the nickname 'the Scottish Cowper'.[1]

Another way in which Presbyterianism began to blaze a trail into the Highlands was through the Church of Scotland General Assembly's appointment of itinerant preachers and lay catechists specifically for the Highlands. Not many itinerant preachers were actually sent forth (only ten by 1764), but the lay catechists were a more impactful influence: between 1725 and 1728, around seventy began working in the Highlands. Historians have acknowledged these lay catechists as the 'shock troops' of Presbyterian penetration into the Highlands.

2. The Men

Yet another force contributing to the growth of Protestantism in the Highlands was a lay movement called simply 'The Men' (in Gaelic, *Na Daoine*). The Men seem to have originated back in the Covenanting era, when some parishes in the northern Highlands, notably in Easter Ross, came to have ministers marked by Covenanter sympathies. For example, one of the 'founding fathers' of The Men was the craftsman John Munro of Kiltearn (Evanton), whose spiritual mentor Thomas Hog had been the Presbyterian minister of Kiltearn, cast out in 1663 by the Restoration regime of King Charles II. Hog, it seems, had begun a prayer meeting in his parish, and this proved to be the wellspring of the 'Fellowship Meeting' that became so characteristic of The Men. In the Fellowship Meeting those who were concerned over the state of their souls were counselled, and the Meeting's lay leaders – The Men – even took it on themselves to determine who should be admitted to communion at the Lord's Table.

The connection with holy communion was underscored by the development of the Question Meeting. This was a public

1. After William Cowper, the great poet and hymnwriter of the English Evangelical Revival. See Chapter 2, Part 4, section 9.

meeting (unlike the private Fellowship Meeting) which took place on the Friday before the weekend communion during the communion season. At the Question Meeting, the minister would address a question set by one of The Men relating to spiritual life, and The Men would themselves 'speak to the question'. This exercise became a powerful means of fostering Highland Presbyterian spirituality, especially in setting spiritual standards which were used as criteria for distinguishing between real committed Christians and the merely nominal.

By 1790, The Men were thoroughly established in northern Highland parishes. They were a potent force among the laity in opposing Moderatism. In parishes where there was no Evangelical ministry, they acted as lay evangelists, with notable success. Between the 1790s and 1870s, The Men also led a Separatist movement within the established Church, which stopped short of actual secession. Where they deemed a parish minister to be corrupt, the Separatists (led by The Men) withdrew from his pastoral ministrations, yet still regarded themselves as members of the established Church, receiving holy communion from its ministers.

3. Lachlan Mackenzie of Lochcarron and John Macdonald of Ferintosh

The part played by Christian preaching in the growth of Presbyterianism in the Highlands owed much to Lachlan Mackenzie (1754–1819) and John MacDonald (1779–1849). Mackenzie was the minister of Lochcarron parish church, whose status in Highland Presbyterianism has become legendary. A fervent preacher under whose ministry many professed faith, he was also something of a mystic and prophet. He foretold the death of a number of those who opposed his preaching, and in each case they were dead within a week! He was also a fierce adversary of the Moderates, preaching with a voice of thunder against the patronage laws which imposed unwanted ministers on congregations against the congregation's will.

John Macdonald, sometimes known by his nickname 'the apostle of the North', or even 'the Whitefield of the Scottish

Highlands and islands', was the Church of Scotland minister at Ferintosh from 1813. From 1816 onward, he not only preached to his own congregation, but also went on evangelistic tours throughout the Highlands and islands of Scotland, especially although not exclusively in Highland Perthshire. These tours could be long-lasting, perhaps up to six months. Macdonald's evangelistic preaching, often during communion seasons, attracted almost unbelievably huge audiences: during one communion season in Ferintosh, some ten thousand gathered to hear him in the open air. He also wrote a significant body of Gaelic hymns.

As Evangelicalism began to permeate the Highlands, some prominent landowners were themselves converted, and used the patronage laws to promote the Evangelical cause in the Church of Scotland, by appointing Evangelical ministers. This move wrong-footed the Moderates, who could hardly condemn the use of the law they themselves so strongly upheld. One example was Mrs Stewart Mackenzie of Seaforth. She owned vast tracts of territory on the Island of Lewis, utilising her patronage rights to appoint Evangelical ministers to vacant parishes on her land.

4. Gaelic schools

Mackenzie and Macdonald are proof of the way that the Evangelical Revival was beginning to penetrate and transform the religious culture of the Highlands. Another factor was the formation of Gaelic schools under the patronage of the Edinburgh Society for the Support of Gaelic Schools. This society was founded in 1811, taking over the enterprise already promoted by the SSPCK in furthering Gaelic education in the Highlands. By 1828, the Edinburgh Society had established no fewer than eighty-five Gaelic schools. The Evangelical aspect of this work stated clearly in the Society's constitution: its 'sole object [was] to teach the inhabitants of the Highlands and Islands to read the Sacred Scriptures in their native tongue'. The schools were particularly abundant in the Hebrides and the north. In order to eliminate any tension with the Church's parish ministers, the Society prohibited its teachers from preaching. But they were allowed to read the Scriptures in public on Sundays.

However, serious friction emerged in parishes where the minister was a Moderate, and therefore did not preach Evangelical doctrine. Some of the Gaelic schoolteachers were so unsettled by the absence of Gospel preaching in Moderate parishes, they began mingling their own Evangelical comments with the text of the Scripture passage they were reading to their pupils. One example of this was John Macleod, Gaelic schoolteacher in Barvas on the Isle of Lewis. Macleod's parish minister, William Macrae, was a Moderate, which provoked Macleod into making Evangelical comments in his Bible readings. His comments soon developed into full-blown expositions, little short of sermons, to compensate for what Macleod perceived as the spiritual sterility of Macrae's preaching. Indeed, Macleod's school preaching became so popular that folk were soon flocking to his Sunday meetings. Macrae contested his unauthorised ministry, and the Society for the Support of Gaelic Schools at length sacked Macleod for transgressing the Society's rules. By then, however, it was too late: Macleod had such a widespread following, the people themselves erected a new house and new school for him, employing him both as a schoolteacher and Bible preacher at their own cost.

5. The Haldane brothers

Another factor in the spread of Protestantism in the Highlands was the evangelistic work of Robert (1764–1842) and James (1768–1851) Haldane, wealthy brothers and lay members of the Church of Scotland. After both undergoing profound conversion experiences, the Haldanes decided to dedicate their money and energy to missionary work. Frustrated in their attempt to establish an overseas mission work in India, they turned their attention to home mission. In July 1797, James Haldane undertook his first great evangelistic tour of northern Scotland, travelling as far as Westray on Orkney. The tour ended in November. James published an account of the tour in 1798. His preaching attracted great crowds. Listeners were summoned by handbells or drums; meetings were held in Relief churches, town halls, marketplaces, churchyards, hospitals, and barns.

The outcome in January 1798 was the Haldanes' founding of the Society for Propagating the Gospel at Home. The Society, characterised by both a staunch Reformed theology and a strong commitment to evangelism, trained and sent out itinerant evangelists, catechists, and schoolteachers. For ten years Robert Haldane trained the evangelists in a seminary; classes lasted two years, and were held in Edinburgh, Glasgow, Dundee, Elgin, and Grantown. Gaelic speakers were enlisted for the evangelisation of the Highlands. Preaching centres – 'tabernacles' – were also established where the visiting evangelists preached. There were tabernacles erected in Glasgow, Dundee, Perth, Thurso, Elgin, Wick, Dunkeld, and Dumfries.

James and Robert Haldane eventually left the Church of Scotland and became first Congregationalists, then Baptists, and to that extent ceased to promote Presbyterianism in the Highlands; nevertheless, the evangelistic movement they spearheaded was a significant aspect in the transition of the Highlands to a more general Evangelical Protestantism. Despite their ultimately becoming Baptists, the Haldane brothers retained the admiration of Evangelical Presbyterians, although not of Moderates who despised the Haldanes and – at the General Assembly of 1799 – issued a Pastoral Admonition against unqualified preachers. This was aimed against the Haldanes; the Assembly decreed it must be read out from every Church of Scotland pulpit in the land.

6. Conclusion

As a result of all the above factors, by the middle of the 19th Century the Scottish Highlands had been remarkably transformed from a region predominantly Roman Catholic and Episcopalian, to one now predominantly Protestant and Presbyterian. This paved the way for the triumph of the Free Church in this region, when most of the Church of Scotland's Evangelical ministers seceded in 1843 to form a new denomination founded on Reformed principles. The Free Church became virtually *the* expression of Protestant Church life in the Highlands.

6
Scottish 'common sense' philosophy

18th Century Scotland gave rise to a new school of philosophy, variously called Common Sense Philosophy, Scottish Realism, and Scottish Common Sense Realism. Its significance lay in its wider adoption, in the Kantian era, as a response to sceptical tendencies in philosophy, especially scepticism about the reality of the external world revealed to the senses.[1] Kant of course provided one such response, but many conservatively minded Protestants, not ready to embrace Kant's 'Copernican revolution', preferred the Scottish alternative. Two thinkers were paramount in the development of Common Sense Realism – Francis Hutcheson and Thomas Reid.

1. Francis Hutcheson (1694–1746)

Born in Ireland, son of the Presbyterian minister of Armagh, Hutcheson was from 1729 onwards professor of moral philosophy at Glasgow University. He also taught apologetics, utilising the 'evidences of Christianity' approach that was so popular in the 18th Century: one proved that Christianity was true by appealing to various historical and philosophical arguments. In the hope of making his teaching as accessible as he could, Hutcheson abandoned Latin as the language of lecturing, and taught in English – the first tutor at Glasgow to do so. Students testified to the potency of Hutcheson's eloquence.

---

1. For the life and thought of Immanuel Kant, see Chapter 1, Part 3.

Hutcheson proved highly influential as a philosopher, often acclaimed as 'the father of the Scottish Enlightenment'. His chief work was *A System of Moral Philosophy, An Inquiry into the Original of our Ideas of Beauty and Virtue* (1725). He claimed that his philosophical method was to investigate human nature empirically, in order to discover 'what is Man', and thereby to discern 'for what purposes nature has formed us'. From this foundation, he went on to work out a theology of God as Creator and His moral purposes for His human creatures. His most impactful contribution to moral philosophy was his argument that humankind possesses a 'moral sense' analogous to the physical senses. Through this moral sense, humans immediately perceive the loveliness of virtue and are moved to embrace and follow it. Hutcheson, however, differentiated this intuitive moral sense from the final moral standard that justifies moral action – the standard is the promotion of human wellbeing in general.

Hutcheson's philosophical career did not run smooth. In 1738 he was brought before the presbytery of Glasgow, charged with teaching the error that the pursuit of human happiness was the ultimate standard of morality (rather than the glory of the triune God), and that human beings could have a true knowledge of good and evil without any knowledge of God. Of these charges he was acquitted.

Hutcheson's philosophy sowed the seeds of the more fully developed Common Sense Realism of Thomas Reid (see below). Hutcheson was highly regarded by Moderates; prominent Moderate minister Alexander Carlyle of Inveresk said of Hutcheson, and of his colleague William Leechman (1706–85) who taught theology at Glasgow:

> A new school was formed in the western provinces of Scotland where the clergy till that period were narrow and bigoted ... Though neither of those professors taught any heresy, yet they opened and enlarged the minds of the students, which soon gave them a turn for free enquiry, the result of which was candour and liberality of sentiment.

2. Thomas Reid (1710–96)

Born at Strachan, in Aberdeenshire, Reid became Professor of Moral Philosophy at Glasgow University in 1764, after some years in the Church of Scotland ministry (in the parish church of New Machar). Reid's philosophy was in large measure a response to Scotland's radically sceptical thinker David Hume (1711–76). In this, Reid was much like Immanuel Kant, who also fashioned his philosophy as a response to Hume's scepticism.

However, Reid articulated a response very unlike Kant's. Building on foundations laid by Hutcheson, Reid argued that the ordinary 'common sense' beliefs of human beings – that there was an external world populated by other persons, the scientific laws of cause and effect, etc. – were inescapable intuitions shared by all human minds. It was impossible, Reid maintained, for human beings to live, to function practically and humanly, as if there were no external world, or as if I were the only person who existed, and so forth. Humans presupposed common sense beliefs in their rational activities: for instance, in seeking to convince others that my philosophical convictions are true, I presuppose that those other people actually exist, and have minds capable of receiving and assessing my arguments. Refusal to accept this, Reid stated, was absolutely absurd:

> If there are certain principles, as I think there are, which the constitution of our nature leads us to believe, and which we are under a necessity to take for granted in the common concerns of life, without being able to give a reason for them; these are what we call the principles of common sense; and what is manifestly contrary to them, is what we call absurd.

Moreover, what humans knew (according to Reid) was not just the internal sensations and ideas of their own minds, as in John Locke's influential philosophical system, but the external realities which gave rise to these sensations and ideas. The mind did not interact with its own ideas about external realities, but directly experienced those realities. Human thought and language, Reid argued, both presupposed this, and it was artificial and unnatural to deny it.

Reid's philosophy was hugely influential both on Scottish philosophers and clergy. While it found its most enthusiastic welcome among Moderates, many Evangelicals also adopted Common Sense Realism, perhaps persuaded by the argument that it was the view assumed in Scripture. Nor was Scotland alone in its acceptance of Reid's philosophy; it proved popular in America too, where leading American Evangelicals endorsed it. For example, at Princeton Seminary in New Jersey, the foremost Reformed theological school in 19th Century America, its greatest theologian Charles Hodge (1797–1878) incorporated Common Sense Realism into his famous and influential *Systematic Theology* (1872–73). In its opening chapter, Hodge compared theology to 'the inductive method' in science, arguing that both (theology and science) are grounded on fundamental Common Sense presuppositions: (i) the reliability of our physical senses; (ii) the reliability of the mind's basic functions; (iii) the reliability of truths rooted in the very constitution of human nature, rather than gathered from ongoing experience. He illustrated each of these Common Sense assumptions with material taken straight from the writings of Reid.

PRIMARY SOURCE MATERIAL

The Marrow of Modern Divinity: The sinner's warrant to trust in Christ for salvation

I beseech you consider, that God the Father, as He is in His Son Jesus Christ, moved with nothing but with His free love to mankind lost, hath made a deed of gift and grant unto them all, that whosoever of them all shall believe in this His Son, shall not perish, but have eternal life. And hence it was, that Jesus Christ Himself said unto His disciples, (Mark 16:15), 'Go and preach the Gospel to every creature under heaven': that is, Go and tell every man without exception, that here is good news for him; Christ is dead for him; and if he will take Him, and accept of His righteousness, he shall have Him. Therefore, says a godly writer, 'Forasmuch as the holy Scripture speaketh to all in general, none of us ought to distrust himself, but believe that it doth belong particularly to himself.'

And to the end, that this point, wherein lies and consists the whole mystery of our holy faith, may be understood the better, let us put the case, that some good and holy king should cause a proclamation to be made through his whole kingdom, by the sound of a trumpet, that all rebels and banished men shall safely return home to their houses: because that, at the suit and desert of some dear friend of theirs, it has pleased the king to pardon them; certainly, none of these rebels ought to doubt, but that he shall obtain true pardon for his rebellion; and so return home, and live under the shadow of that gracious king. Even so, our good King, the Lord of heaven and earth, has, for the obedience and desert of our good brother Jesus Christ, pardoned all our sins,[1] and made a proclamation throughout the whole world, that every one of us may safely return to God in Jesus Christ: wherefore I beseech you make no doubt of it, but 'draw near with a true heart in full assurance of faith,' (Heb. 10:22) …

'Go,' says Christ, 'and preach the Gospel to every creature under heaven,' that is, Go tell every man without exception, whatsoever his sins be, whatsoever his rebellions be, go and tell him these glad tidings, that if he will come in, I will accept of him, his sins shall be forgiven him, and he shall be saved; if he will come in and take Me, and receive Me, I will be his loving husband, and he shall be Mine own dear spouse. Let me, therefore, say unto you, in the words of the apostle, 'Now, then, I as an ambassador for Christ, as though God did beseech you by me, I pray you, in Christ's stead, be ye reconciled unto God; for He hath made Him to be sin for you, who knew no sin, that ye might be made the righteousness of God in Him,' (2 Cor. 5:20,21) …

Sweetly, says Luther, 'Because the nature of God was otherwise higher than that we are able to attain unto it, therefore hath He humbled Himself for us, and taken our nature upon Him, and so put Himself into Christ. Here He looketh for us, here He will receive us; and he that seeketh Him here shall find Him.' – 'This,' says God the Father, 'is My beloved Son, in whom I am well pleased,' (Matt. 3:17); whereupon the same Luther says in another place, 'We must not think and persuade ourselves that this voice came from heaven for Christ's own sake, but for our sakes, even as Christ Himself says, (John 12:30), "This voice came not because of me, but for your sakes." The truth is, Christ had no need that it should be said unto Him, "This is My beloved Son," He knew that from all eternity, and that He should still so remain, though these words had not been spoken from heaven; therefore, by these words, God the Father,

---

1. The *Marrow* is using the secular/political analogy whereby a king issues a general pardon to an entire body of transgressors (e.g. rebels), but where that pardon only becomes *effective* to an individual transgressor upon his personal submission to it. It is not teaching that everyone is effectually and personally pardoned apart from faith's submission to Christ.

in Christ His Son, cheers the hearts of poor sinners, and greatly delights them with singular comfort and heavenly sweetness, assuring them, that whosoever is married unto Christ, and so in Him by faith, he is as acceptable to God the Father as Christ Himself; according to that of the apostle, "He hath made us acceptable in His Beloved," (Eph. 1:6). Wherefore, if you would be acceptable to God, and be made His dear child, then by faith cleave unto His beloved Son Christ, and hang about His neck, yea, and creep into His bosom; and so shall the love and favour of God be as deeply insinuated into you as it is into Christ Himself; and so shall God the Father, together with His beloved Son, wholly possess you, and be possessed of you; and so God, and Christ, and you, shall become one entire thing, according to Christ's prayer, "that they may be one in Us, as Thou and I are one," (John 17:21).'

The Marrow of Modern Divinity,
Part 1, Chapter 2, section 3

Thomas Boston: The mystical union between Christ and the Church

1. It is a spiritual union. Man and wife by their marriage-union become one flesh; Christ and true believers by this union become one spirit, 1 Corinthians 6:17. As one soul and spirit actuates both the head and the members in the natural body, so the one Spirit of Christ dwells in Christ and the Christian. 'If any man have not the Spirit of Christ, he is none of His,' Romans 8:9. Corporal union is made by contact; so the stones in a building are united. This is a union of another nature. Were it possible we could eat the flesh, and drink the blood of Christ, in a corporal and carnal manner, it would profit nothing, John 6:63. It was not Mary's bearing Him in her womb, but her believing on Him, that made her a saint, Luke 11:27,28 ...

2. It is a real union. Such is our weakness in our present state, so much are we immersed in sin, that we are prone to form in our fancy an image of everything proposed to us; and as to whatsoever is denied to us, we are apt to suspect it to be but a

fiction, or what has no reality. But nothing is more real than what is spiritual, as approaching nearest to the nature of Him who is the fountain of all reality, namely God Himself. We do not see with our eyes the union that is betwixt our own soul and body; neither can we represent it to ourselves truly by imagination, as we do sensible [sensory] things; yet the reality of it is not to be doubted. Faith is no fancy, but the substance of things hoped for, Hebrews 11:1. Neither is the union thereby made betwixt Christ and believers imaginary, but most real, for we are members of His body, of His flesh and of His bones, Ephesians 5:30.

3. It is a most close and intimate union. Believers, regenerate persons, who fiduciously credit Him [trustingly believe Him] have put on Christ, Galatians 3:27. If that be not enough, He is in them, John 17:23, formed in them as the child in the mother's belly, Galatians 4:19. He is the foundation, 1 Corinthians 3:11, they are the lively stones built upon Him, 1 Peter 2:5. He is the head and they the body, Ephesians 1:22,23. Nay, He liveth in them as their very souls in their bodies, Galatians 2:20. And what is more than all this, they are one in the Father and the Son, as the Father is in Christ and Christ in the Father, John 17:21, 'that they all may be one as Thou, Father, art in Me and I in them, they also may be one in Us' ...

Lastly, it is a mysterious union. The Gospel is a doctrine of mysteries. It discovers to us the substantial union of the three persons in one Godhead, 1 John 5:7 'These three are one'; the hypostatical union of the divine and human natures in the person of the Lord Jesus Christ, 1 Timothy 3:16 'God was manifest in the flesh.' And the mystical union betwixt Christ and believers is a great mystery also, Ephesians 5:32. O what mysteries are here! The Head in heaven, the members on earth, yet really united! Christ in the believer, living in him, walking in him, and the believer dwelling in God, putting on the Lord Jesus, eating His flesh and drinking His blood! This makes the saints a mystery to the world, yea a mystery to themselves

Thomas Boston

Human Nature in its Fourfold State: The State of Grace – Mystical union.

Ralph Erskine: Faith not feelings

FAITH has for its foundation broad
A stable rock on which I stand,
The truth and faithfulness of God:
All other grounds are sinking sand.

My frames and feelings ebb and flow;
And when my faith depends on them,
It fleets and staggers to and fro,
And dies amidst the dying frame.

That faith is surely most unstayed,
Its staggering can't be counted strange
That builds its hope of lasting aid
On things that every moment change.

But could my faith lay all its load
On Jesus' everlasting name,
Upon the righteousness of God,
And divine truth that's still the same;

Could I believe what God has spoke,
Rely on His unchanging love,
And cease to grasp at fleeting smoke,
No changes would my mountain move.

But when, how soon, the frame's away,
And comfortable feelings fail;
So soon my faith falls in decay,
And unbelieving doubts prevail.

The smallest trials may evince
My faith unfit to stand the shock,
That more depends on fleeting sense,
Than on the fixed eternal Rock.

The safest ark when floods arise,
Is stable truth that changes not;
How weak's my faith, that more relies
On feeble sense's floating boat?

For when the fleeting frame is gone,
I strait my state in question call;
I drop and sink in deeps anon,
As if my frame were all in all.

But though I miss the pleasing gale,
And heav'n withdraw the charming glance;
Unless JEHOVAH'S oath can fail,
My faith may keep its countenance.

The frame of nature shall decay.
Time-changes break her rusty chains;
Yea, heav'n and earth shall pass away;
But faith's foundation firm remains.

Heaven's promises so fixedly stand,
Engraved with an immortal pen,
In great IMMANUEL'S mighty hand,
All hell's attempts to raze are vain.

Did faith with none but truth advise,
My steady soul would move no more,
Than stable hills when tempests rise,
Or solid rocks when billows roar.

But when my faith the counsel hears
Of present sense and reason blind,
My wavering spirit then appears
A feather tossed with every wind.

I would, when dying comforts fly,
As much as when they present were,
Upon my Living Joy rely:
Help, Lord, for here I daily err!

Ralph Erskine
***From Gospel Sonnets*, ch.4, section 6**

The revival in Cambuslang and Kilsyth

Among the particular good fruits already appearing, both in Cambuslang and elsewhere, the following instances seem very encouraging: a visible reformation of the lives of persons who were formerly notorious sinners; particularly, the laying aside of cursing and swearing and drinking to excess, among those who were addicted to these practices; remorse for acts of injustice, and for violation of relative duties, confessed to the persons wronged, joined with new endeavours after a conscientious discharge of such duties; restitution, which has more than once been distinctly and particularly inculcated in public since this work began; forgiving of injuries; all desirable evidences of fervent love to one another, to all men, and even to those who speak evil of them; and among those people both in Cambuslang and other parishes, more affectionate expressions of regard than ever to their own ministers, and to the ordinances dispensed by them; the keeping up divine worship in families where it was neglected very often by some and entirely by others; the erecting of new societies for prayer, both of old and young, partly within the parish, where no less than twelve such societies are newly begun, and partly elsewhere, among persons who have been awakened on this occasion; and together with all these things, ardent love to the Holy Scriptures, vehement thirsting after the public ordinances, earnest desires to get private instructions in their duty from ministers and others, with commendable docility and tractableness in receiving such instructions.

This thirst after knowledge is particularly remarkable in those who were more ignorant; several who cannot read, and some of them old persons, being so desirous to be better acquainted with the word of God that they are resolved to learn to read, and some of the younger sort actually putting themselves to school. I would further add, that these good impressions have been made on persons of very different characters and ages; on some of the most abandoned as well as the more sober; on young as well as old: on the illiterate as well as the more knowing; on persons of a slower as well as those of a quicker and more sprightly genius ; and, which seems to deserve special attention, on persons who were addicted to scoffing at sacred things, and at this work in particular at the beginning of it …

I leave it to you to judge how far such facts make it evident that this work is from God, when to use the words of a pious divine treating of a subject of the same nature: 'He that was formerly a drunkard lives a sober life, when a vain, light, and wanton person becomes grave and sedate, when the blasphemer becomes a praiser of God, when carnal joy is turned into heaviness, and that professedly on account of their souls' condition; when the ignorant are filled with knowledge of divine things, and the tongue that was dumb in the things of God speaks the language of Canaan, when secure sinners have been roused with a witness about the state of their souls, Luke, xi , 21 , 22, those who were ignorant can speak skilfully about religious things, and even the graceless are increased in knowledge, swearers drop their oaths and speak reverently of God: vain persons who minded no religion, but frequented taverns and frolics, passing their time in filthiness, foolish talking and jesting, or singing paltry songs, do now frequent Christian societies (for prayer), seek Christian conversation and talk of soul-concerns, and choose to express their mirth in psalms and hymns and spiritual songs : they who were too sprightly to be devout, and esteemed it an unmanly thing to shed tears for their souls' state, have mourned as for an only son, and seemed to be in bitterness as for a first-born, Zech. xii, 10. And persons who came to mock at the lamentations of others have been convinced, and by free grace proselyted to such ways as they formerly despised.

James Robe

Narrative of the Extraordinary Work of the Spirit of God at Kilsyth

The conversion of Colonel James Gardiner

[Colonel James Gardiner was held in high esteem among Protestants in the 18th Century as a great Christian hero. After a conversion of unusually dramatic quality in 1719, the Scottish soldier lived as a pre-eminently devout Protestant Christian. His death at the hands of Bonnie Prince Charlie's army at Prestonpans on September 21st 1745 made him effectively a Protestant martyr in the eyes of many, and his memory was celebrated and made widely known through a biography by the illustrious Congregationalist preacher of the Evangelical Revival, Philip Doddridge. Colonel Gardiner was so famous in the 19th Century that Sir Walter Scott, Scotland's foremost Romantic writer, featured Gardiner as a character in his popular 1814 novel *Waverley*. The novel has Jacobite sentiments, but Gardiner is presented sympathetically as a good man and a true believer.]

He [Gardiner] went into his chamber to kill the tedious hour, perhaps with some amusing book, or in some other way. But it very accidentally happened that he took up a religious book which his good mother or aunt had, without his knowledge, slipped into his portmanteau. It was called, if I remember the title exactly, *The Christian Soldier, or Heaven taken by Storm*, and was written by Mr. Thomas Watson. Guessing by the title of it that he should find some phrases of his own profession spiritualized in a manner which he thought might afford him some diversion, he resolved to dip into it; but he took no serious notice of anything he read in it; and yet, while this book was in his hand, an impression was made upon his mind, (perhaps God only knows how,) which drew after it a train of the most important and happy consequences.

There is indeed a possibility, that while he was sitting in this solitude, and reading in this careless and profane manner, he might suddenly fall asleep, and only dream of what he apprehended he saw. But nothing can be more certain than that, when he gave me this relation, he judged himself to have been as broad awake during the whole time as he ever was in any part of his life; and he mentioned it to me several times afterwards as what undoubtedly passed, not only in his imagination, but before his eyes.

He thought he saw an unusual blaze of light fall on the book while he was reading, which he at first imagined might happen by some accident in the candle. But, lifting up his eyes, he apprehended, to his extreme amazement, that there was before him, as it were suspended in the air, a visible representation of the Lord Jesus Christ upon the cross, surrounded on all sides with a glory; and was impressed as if a voice, or something equivalent to a voice, had come to him to this effect (for he was not confident as to the very words): 'Oh, sinner! did I suffer this for thee, and are these the returns?' But whether this were an audible voice, or only a strong impression on his mind equally striking, he did not seem very confident, though, to the best of my remembrance, he rather judged it to be the former. Struck with so amazing a phenomenon as this, there remained hardly any life in him, so that he sunk down in the armchair in which he sat, and continued, he knew not exactly how long, insensible (which was one circumstance that made me several times take the liberty to suggest that he might possibly be all this while asleep), but however that were, he quickly after opened his eyes, and saw nothing more than usual.

It may easily be supposed he was in no condition to make any observations upon the time in which he had remained in an insensible state, nor did he, throughout all the remainder of the night, once recollect that criminal and detestable assignation which had before engrossed all his thoughts. He rose in a tumult of passions not to be conceived, and walked to and fro in his chamber till he was ready to drop down in unutterable astonishment and agony of heart, appearing to himself the vilest monster in the creation of God, who had all his lifetime been crucifying Christ afresh by his sins, and now saw, as he assuredly believed, by a miraculous vision, the horror of what he had done. With this was connected such a view of both the majesty and goodness of God, as caused him to loathe and abhor himself, and to repent as in dust and ashes.

He immediately gave judgment against himself, that he was most justly worthy of eternal damnation, he was astonished that he had not been immediately struck dead in the midst of his wickedness, and (which I think deserves particular remark) though he assuredly believed that he should ere long be in hell, and settled it as a point with himself for several months that the wisdom and justice of God did almost necessarily require that such an enormous sinner should be made an example of everlasting vengeance, and a spectacle as such both to angels and men, so that he hardly durst presume to pray for pardon;

yet what he then suffered was not so much from the fear of hell, though he concluded it would soon be his portion, as from a sense of that horrible ingratitude he had shown to the God of his life, and to that blessed Redeemer who had been in so affecting a manner set forth as crucified before him.

In this view it may naturally be supposed that he passed the remainder of the night waking, and he could get but little rest in several that followed. His mind was continually taken up in reflecting on the divine purity and goodness; the grace which had been proposed to him in the gospel, and which he had rejected; the singular advantages he had enjoyed and abused; and the many favours of providence which he had received, particularly in rescuing him from so many imminent dangers of death, which he now saw must have been attended with such dreadful and hopeless destruction. The privileges of his education, which he had so much despised, now lay with an almost insupportable weight on his mind; and the folly of that career of sinful pleasure which he had so many years been running with desperate eagerness and unworthy delight, now filled him with indignation against himself, and against the great deceiver, by whom (to use his own phrase) he had been 'so wretchedly and scandalously befooled.' This he used often to express in the strongest terms, which I shall not repeat so particularly, as I cannot recollect some of them.

But on the whole it is certain that, by what passed before he left his chamber the next day, the whole frame and disposition of his soul was new-modelled and changed; so that he became, and continued to the last day of his exemplary and truly Christian life, the very reverse of what he had been before.

Philip Doddridge
The Life of Colonel James Gardiner

Lady Maxwell of Pollok: Methodist piety

O, who is a God like unto our God? Since I wrote last, I have experienced much of the divine goodness – much indescribably sweet nearness to and sinking into Jehovah: holy fellowship with the Father and the Son, which sinks self into nothing. My God is ever with me: O how condescending [humble and self-effacing]; I can neither express nor explain it, but it is well known to my friend. With all this, I am kept little and poor in my own eyes; experience many stripping seasons and springtides of painful temptations from the powers of darkness. I believe these enlarge my receptive powers; for frequently, soon after, there is such an influx of Deity, such glorious displays of future glory, as fill with wonder, and love, and silent adoration.

I find the truth of these words, 'Israel shall dwell alone.' I meet with few that understand my language; and if they did, I often find that words cannot convey an adequate idea of the work and ways of the Lord, in these inner and higher walks of the Christian life. And yet I seem so far short of what the Lord often shows me is my privilege, in point of enjoyment and conformity to the divine image, that I feel ashamed; and grieve because my progress is so small. Help me to get forward. I sometimes think that the abstract of my life is a continual passing through the veil of outward things, and gasping to live more fully in God. I am kept in perpetual pursuit of higher attainments, that I may be capacitated to bring more glory to God, as well as to enjoy Him more. How clearly is the grand prize set before me! Almost every morning my soul is fired and filled with a holy ambition, for the full possession of every purchased and promised blessing; but still I do not attain: restless, resigned, I wait for it. I long now to find words sufficiently plain to convince you how poor, how unworthy, how unfruitful I am. The Lord knows it, and I feel it; yet cannot properly describe it; but beg you will do me the justice to believe it.

I still feel much on account of public affairs; what adds to my sufferings is the most piercing convictions of the astonishing longsuffering patience and goodness of the Lord. This penetrates my inmost soul, makes me blush and be ashamed to intreat for our guilty land. I so feel the weight of the iniquity of us all: and have such views of His consummate wisdom, and boundless love, that I am silent before Him; and sink into His will. Yet, again, when I take a view of the distress of my fellow countrymen; what we are exposed to, what variegated misery, etc., I again open my mouth, and plead much. Prayer is poured forth in public, and private, and secret; great the exertions for the spread of the Gospel at home and abroad; and the Lord is greatly reviving His work in some parts of England. These things lead me to think He will not make an utter end of us; but chastise us in a measure.

Lady Maxwell of Pollok

Letter quoted in *The Life of Darcy, Lady Maxwell, of Pollock*[2] by John Lancaster (published for the Methodist Episcopal Church, 1848)

Niel Douglas: The inhuman horrors of the African slave trade

The Societies, lately instituted for effecting the Abolition of the African Slave Trade, are justly entitled to the thanks of the Christian world, for their humane and benevolent attempts to promote an object so desirable and important. Every real friend of the human race will cordially wish success to their laudable endeavours, in a cause so worthy of Britons, and of Christians. It is good and praiseworthy to be zealously affected in a good thing. They have been directed to the most effectual method of gaining the sentiments of the Public on the subject, and exciting a just detestation of such detestable traffic; provided the stated Teachers of religion, to whom they more immediately address themselves, would so far lay the matter to heart, as to comply with their instructions and request.

That humane and benevolent religion, whose public ministers they profess themselves to be, powerfully recommends and explicitly demands their most vigorous efforts to promote, so far as in them lies, the happiness of their fellow men; and, acting in character, they will not decline to employ them for that purpose. Jesus the Son of God came to save men's lives, and to proclaim liberty to captives, and is it not honourable to concur with Him in so glorious a work? Too many however, in opposition to His benign example, and express precepts, while they mind their

2. Pollock is an alternate spelling of Pollok.

own things, feel not the general claims of philanthropy, or love to the human kind, where they themselves are not immediately affected; and, in this respect, it sometimes happens, that they who should be first to set the laudable example, are among the last to follow it, tho' it ought not to be so ...

Ye who possess the sensibilities of a humane heart, imagine to yourselves such a scene. Perhaps hundreds at a time, of all sexes, ages, and relations, are driven like cattle for the space of two or three hundred miles, or more (for so far up the country do they often go on these occasions) till they reach the coast, where they are confined, and, so soon as may be, sold and put on board the Slave ships, without paying the least regard to their bitter cries and lamentations! Ah, the dearest relatives torn from each other's arms, in all probability never more to meet! Such the mercy of their captors and new masters, that even children are separated from their Parents, except the sucking infants, who are permitted, for obvious reasons, to accompany the mother. What a moving scene! Parents and Children, Husbands and Wives, Brothers and Sisters, not only forced from their native country, but denied in their exile and captivity the small consolation of mingling their sighs and tears in mutual condolence and commiseration! Such a scene must exceed the powers of language to express, or of the human mind to conceive, where not felt or seen.

Some of the native kings keep a number of war-canoes always in readiness for these piratical expeditions, some of which have six or eight swivels, a three or four pounder lashed on their bows, and are generally furnished with a complement of men. These return, in the course of between ten days and three weeks, with as many prisoners as they can procure, one of the evidence[3] heard, once to the amount of twelve hundred; when notice is sent to the Captains of the Slave vessels, who have them equally divided among them. For these barbarous expeditions the European traders furnish arms, and ammunition, and

3. One of the compilers of the evidence presented to the House of Commons.

sometimes in person take an active part in the depredations which accompany them. They are so frequent, and so desolating to the country, that burnt and deserted towns and villages are everywhere to be seen.

Thus, the Slave Trade is the occasion of kings making war, in the manner above described, on their own subjects, as well as on those of neighbouring princes. Tho' the ignorance in which they are bred may partly excuse this in them, can we once suppose God will hold those innocent who instigate them to these and the like cruel practices? Verily their day of retribution is fast coming, when God will distribute to such sorrows in His anger, if speedy and deep repentance prevent not.

Niel Douglas

The African Slave Trade: or a short view of the evidence, relative to that subject, produced before the House of Commons

Francis Hutcheson: The sovereignty of conscience

This nobler sense which nature has designed to be the guide of life deserves the most careful consideration, since it is plainly the judge of the whole of life, of all the various powers, affections and designs, and naturally assumes a jurisdiction over them; pronouncing that most important sentence, that in the virtues themselves, and in a careful study of what is beautiful and honourable in manners, consists our true dignity, and natural excellence, and supreme happiness. Those who cultivate and improve this sense find that it can strengthen them to bear the greatest external evils, and voluntarily to forfeit external advantages, in adhering to their duty toward their friends, their country, or the general interest of all: and that in so doing alone it is that they can throughly [thoroughly] approve themselves and their conduct. It likewise punishes with severe remorse and secret lashes such as disobey this natural government constituted in the soul, or omitted through any fear, or any prospect of secular advantages, the Duties which it requires.

That this Divine Sense or Conscience naturally approving these more extensive affections should be the governing power in man, appears both immediately from its own nature, as we immediately feel that it naturally assumes a right of judging, approving or condemning all the various motions of the soul; as also from this that every good man applauds himself, approves entirely his own temper, and is then best pleased with himself when he restrains not only the lower sensual appetites, but even the more sublime ones of a selfish kind, or the more narrow and contracted affections of love toward kindred, or friends, or even his country, when they interfere with the more extensive interests of mankind, and the common prosperity of all. Our inward conscience of right and wrong not only prefers the most diffusive goodness to all other affections of soul, whether of a selfish kind, or of narrower endearment: but also abundantly compensates all losses incurred, all pleasures sacrificed , or expenses sustained on account of virtue, by a more joyful consciousness of our real goodness, and merited glory; since all these losses sustained increase the moral dignity and beauty of virtuous offices, and recommend them the more to our inward sense: which is a circumstance peculiar to this case, nor is the like found in any other sense, when it conquers another of less power than its own.

And further, whoever acts other ways cannot throughly approve himself if he examines well the inward sense of his soul: when we judge of the characters and conduct of others, we find the same sentiments of them: nay, this subordination of all to the most extensive interests is what we demand from them; nor do we ever fail in this case to condemn any contrary conduct; as in our judgments about others we are under no bias from our private passions and interests. And therefore altho' every event, disposition, or action incident to men may in a certain sense be called natural; yet such conduct alone as is approved by this diviner faculty, which is plainly destined to command the rest, can be properly called agreeable or suited to our nature .

Francis Hutcheson

A Short Introduction to Moral Philosophy,

Book 1, section XII

Hugh Blair: Moderate preaching at its most eloquent

Our times are altogether *in His hand.* Let us take notice, that they are not in the hands either of our enemies, or of our friends. It is not in the power of man to shorten or to prolong our life, more or less than God has decreed. Enemies may employ craft or violence in their attacks; friends may employ skill and vigilance for the preservation of our health and safety; but both the one and the other can have effect only as far as God permits. They work in subserviency to His purpose. By Him they are held in invisible bonds. To the exertions of all human agents He says, *Hitherto shalt thou come, and no further.*

We are to observe next, that *our times are in the hand of God,* not only as an almighty Disposer, but as a merciful Guardian and Father. We are by no means to imagine, that from race to race, and from year to year, God sports with the lives of succeeding generations of men, or, in the mere wantonness of arbitrary power, brings them forth, and sends them away. No; if we have any confidence in what either the light of nature suggests to all men, or what the revelation of the Gospel has confirmed to Christians, we have full ground to believe, that the administration of human affairs is conducted with infinite wisdom and goodness.

The counsels of the Almighty are indeed too deep for our limited understandings to trace. *His path* may often, as to as, be *in the sea, and His footsteps in the mighty waters;* while, nevertheless, *all His paths are mercy and truth.* He who, from the benignity of His nature, erected this world for the abode of men; He who furnished it so richly for our accommodation, and stored it with so much beauty for our entertainment; He who since first we entered into life, hath followed us with such a variety of mercies, surely can have no pleasure in our disappointment and distress. *He knows our frame; He remembers we are dust;* and looks to frail man, we are assured, with *such pity as a father beareth to his children.* To Him we may safely commit ourselves, and all our concerns; as to one who is best qualified, both to direct the incidents proper to happen to us in this world, and to judge of the time when it is fit for us to be removed from it.

Even that ignorance of our future destiny in life, of which we sometimes complain, is a single proof of His goodness. He hides from us the view of futurity, because the view would be dangerous and overpowering. It would either dispirit us with visions of terror, or intoxicate us by the disclosure of success. The veil which covers from our sight the events of this and of succeeding years, is a veil woven by the hand of mercy. Our *times are in His hand;* and we have reason to be glad that in His hand they are kept, shut out from our view. Submit to His pleasure as an almighty Ruler we must, because we cannot resist Him. Equal reason there is for trusting in Him as a Guardian, under whose disposal we are sat.

Such is the import of the text, that *our times are in the hand of God.* Our times are unknown to us, and not under our own direction. They are in the hands of God as a Governor and Ruler; in the hands of God as a Guardian and Father. These separate views of the text require, on our part, separate improvements.

Seeing our times are not in our own hand, seeing futurity is unknown to us, let us, first, check the vain curiosity of penetrating into what is to come. Conjecture about futurity we often must; but upon all conjectures of what this year is to produce, let us lay a proper restraint. Let us wait till God shall bring forward events in their proper course, without wishing to discover what He has concealed; lest, if the discovery were granted, we should see many things, which we would wish not to have seen.

Hugh Blair

Sermon on Our Lives being in the Hand of God

Chapter 4

The Great Awakening in America

Introduction

The 'Great Awakening' is the name historians give to North America's share in the religious phenomenon which, in a British context, is known as the 'Evangelical Revival'. Modern historians have opened up the question of whether the Awakening was an authentically America-wide movement, or perhaps more a linked series of localised revivals. Those who take the second view often speak of 'the Great Awakenings' (plural). Even if the American experience ought to be understood as more of a linked set of local awakenings, however, those links seem quite strong. To that extent, we may still think it meaningful to speak of a more country-wide 'Great Awakening', while at the same time conceding that there were significant regional variations in the character and impact of the broader movement. As a linked movement in American popular consciousness at the time, the focus of the Awakening – as we shall see – was George Whitefield, the premier English evangelist. Whitefield made seven trips to America, where he stayed for extended periods and preached the Evangelical Calvinist Gospel with huge impact.

Students should also note that a second widespread revival took place in America, known as the Second Great Awakening. This began around 1795, and continued until sometime between 1810 and 1840 (different historians reckon its duration differently). Because of this, the Great Awakening we are about to consider is often called the First Great Awakening.

It may be necessary to remind ourselves that what today is the United States of America, at this juncture in its history, was not yet an independent or united nation. The American War of Independence against Britain was not to commence until 1775,[1]

1. Although America's Revolutionary War against Britain began in 1775, the famous American Declaration of Independence came the following year in 1776.

by which time the original Awakening was long over in most parts of America,[2] and its foremost instrument, Whitefield, had worn himself out and been in his grave for five years. The arena of the Great Awakening, therefore, was a cluster of politically separate American Colonies, established by (largely) British migrants from the early 17th Century onwards. Prior to the War of Independence, their only political connection with each other was a common allegiance to the British crown. The Thirteen Colonies, with their dates of founding in chronological order, were Virginia (1606), New York (1626), Massachusetts (1630), Maryland (1633), Rhode Island (1636), Connecticut (1636), New Hampshire (1638), Delaware (1638), North Carolina (1653), South Carolina (1663), New Jersey (1664), Pennsylvania (1682), and Georgia (1732).[3] The famous settlement of Plymouth created by the Pilgrim Fathers in 1620 had been absorbed into the Colony of Massachusetts.

Together with South America, North America was often called the 'New World' by Europeans from the 16th Century onward. There was an excited sense of discovery – a whole new continent, previously unknown – and of its possibilities in terms of colonisation and mineral exploitation. Some (not many, admittedly) even saw the New World as a new field of Gospel labour, as Europeans encountered Native Americans.[4]

---

2. Methodism in the Southern Colonies would be an exception: the Awakening was still running its course there when rudely interrupted by the War of Independence. See Part 2, section 5.

3. The British were not the only settlers and colonists in North America. There were also French, Dutch, Swedish, Russian, Spanish, and others. However, by the time of the Great Awakening, the Thirteen Colonies controlled the entire Eastern coast of North America, from Maine (then part of Massachusetts) in the upper North to Georgia in the deep South. And these Thirteen Colonies were all politically part of the British Empire.

4. Or America's First People or First Nation, although the latter term is often limited to the original inhabitants of what is now Canada (but it excludes the Inuit). They were originally called 'Indians' because when Christopher Columbus landed in America in 1492, he mistakenly believed he had arrived at the Indies (South Asia). The term 'Red Indians' or 'redskins' derived (probably) from the perceived red colour of the skin of the 'Indians'.

1
Religious background of the Awakening

What was the 'religious map' of America on the eve of the Awakening? Perhaps our minds go immediately to New England, where the heirs of the English Puritans had famously settled in significant numbers.[1] The term 'New England' embraces the Colonies of the north-eastern coast of America – Massachusetts, Rhode Island, Connecticut, and New Hampshire. Later, after America had gained its independence from Britain in the Revolutionary War of 1775–83, the territories of Vermont and Maine also became organised and recognised New England states (Vermont in 1791, Maine in 1820).

The New England Puritans were almost all Congregationalists. They were at first known for the fiery warmth and zeal of their Puritan-Congregational faith, for which they had fled their native England in order to find religious freedom from Anglican persecution. However, most of them were not (unfortunately) equally distinguished for their willingness to tolerate any type of Christianity but their own; as someone wittily but acidly commented, they left Old England and went to New England to secure the liberty to worship God according to their own consciences, and the power to deny the same to everyone

1. Strictly speaking, according to contemporary English definition, the New England Congregationalists were Separatists rather than Puritans. But I defer to common usage. Certainly the New England Colonists were steeped in the godly literature of English Puritanism.

else.[2] The New England Congregationalists' record of violent religious intolerance against Baptists and Quakers does not make happy reading. The exception was the Colony of Rhode Island, whose pioneer Roger Williams (1603–83) was disgusted by the intolerance of other Puritans, and helped to found Rhode Island (smallest of the New England Colonies) as a haven of religious toleration. Williams' book *The Bloody Tenent of Persecution for Cause of Conscience* (1644) was one of the classic treatises arguing for religious liberty.[3]

In the latter part of the 17th Century, New England's Congregationalists began to show signs of drift from their one-time zeal for pure religion as they understood it. Many of the children did not or could not attest to the same experience of grace and conversion as their parents. This threatened the entire ecclesiastical and social order of communities that had based their whole collective life on Congregational Puritanism. It was in response to this unsettling development that, in 1662, there was inaugurated among many of the Congregationalists of Massachusetts and Connecticut the famous 'Halfway Covenant' scheme. This religious scheme related to those who had been baptised as infants in a Congregational church, but who had (as yet) made no profession of personal faith. Such people were not church members, and therefore did not take part in the Lord's Supper, but they wanted to have their own children baptised. This baptism was permitted under the Halfway scheme. It helped to maintain a semblance of corporate Congregationalist life in the New England Colonies, in spite of the children no longer having undergone the transformation of life in Christ their parents had known.

The Halfway Covenant was not at first adopted by all the Congregational churches, a good number of which considered it unbiblical. Its popularity, however, increased as the 17th Century drew to a close, by which time (for example) most of the Massachusetts churches had accepted the scheme. Its result

---

2. Also said of the 17th Century Scottish Covenanters.

3. 'Tenent' is a 17th Century form of 'tenet' (belief, conviction).

was the growth of a large body of New England Congregational churchgoers who were regarded as Christians in terms of their moral conduct, but were not church members, lacking any testimony to any personal experience of grace.

The Halfway Covenant was then modified further under the influential ministry of Solomon Stoddard (1643–1729), Congregational pastor in Northampton, Massachusetts, from 1672 – 'Pope Stoddard' as his critics called him. Stoddard adapted the Halfway Covenant in an even more inclusive direction, so that those who had not professed conversion or faith could, nonetheless, participate in the Lord's Supper, on condition that they were leading morally upright lives. In Stoddard's view, the sacrament of the Lord's Supper became a 'converting ordinance' – that is, designed to *produce* religious conversion, rather than a confirming and nourishing ordinance for those who were already in the faith. This may at first have helped maintain the solidarity of Congregational church order within a society founded on Congregational principles, but it sowed the seeds of disruptive division once the Great Awakening began to take hold on the Congregationalists of Massachusetts under the preaching of Jonathan Edwards and George Whitefield (see below).

Outside of Puritan New England, Anglicanism was often the dominant faith. The Church of England was the established Church in the Colonies of the South – Virginia, North Carolina, South Carolina, and Georgia – and in the borderline state of Maryland. Parts of New York in the North were also strongly Anglican. Anglicanism in the New World did not significantly differ from its English mother-Church in doctrine, piety, and practice.[4]

British and Irish Presbyterians were present in some force in the Colonies of Maryland, New York, and New Jersey. Their Dutch equivalents, the Dutch Reformed Church, an ethnically based Church of Dutch settlers, also had a significant presence

4. See Chapter 2, Part 1, section 1 for the condition of the Anglican Church in England in the decades leading up to the Evangelical Revival.

in New York and New Jersey. We shall see how the Great Awakening brought division to these religious communities.

The Colony of Pennsylvania was unusual. Outside of New England and its Puritan heritage, and thus unconnected with its one tolerant Colony of Rhode Island, Pennsylvania allowed religious liberty to all who believed in one God. Founded by the Quaker theologian and millionaire, William Penn (1644–1718), this Northern Colony followed the broad-minded and non-coercive religious attitudes of its Quaker founder. It therefore extended the arms of liberty and toleration to Quakers, Mennonites, Baptists, British and Irish Presbyterians, German and Dutch Reformed, Anglicans, Roman Catholics, and Jews, thereby forming a richly diverse religious life. This made Pennsylvania unlike other Colonies (save little Rhode Island) in refusing to make a single established Church the arbiter of citizenship.

Historians have noted that in the closing decades of the 17th Century, and on into the early 18th, many American pastors expressed grave and growing concern about the spiritual state of their congregations, and of society at large, whether in Puritan New England or elsewhere. There was a sense that the European settlers in the New World were less focused on spiritual realities than their forefathers had been, more preoccupied with their worldly wellbeing. Perhaps not quite knowing what to do about this, preachers had a tendency to deliver sermons of scolding rebuke, which did little or nothing to reverse the unspiritual trend. In addition to this, the impact of Enlightenment thinking was beginning to make itself felt (at least among the educated), with its potential for scepticism about the inherited religious worldview of the medieval and Reformation eras.[5] These tendencies prepared the way for many traditionally religious people in the churches to extend a hearty welcome to the Awakening when it came, as a remedy for widespread unbelief – although, as we shall see, others proved doubtful or antagonistic to the movement.

---

5. See the whole of Chapter 1.

2
The Great Awakening

In looking at the Great Awakening, we shall consider its course and impact on a case-by-case scenario, examining the different religious and/or regional communities that were affected by the movement. We begin with its earliest potential manifestation, among the Dutch Reformed settlers of the Northern Colony of New Jersey.

1. The Dutch Reformed

The ministry of Dutch Reformed minister Theodorus Frelinghuysen (1691–1748) in the 1720s is seen by some historians as a manifestation of genuine religious revival in the Dutch Reformed Church in America, and as a precursor to the greater revival or revivals to come in the 1730s. Certainly some of the mighty preachers of the Great Awakening, such as George Whitefield, Gilbert Tennent, and Jonathan Edwards, appealed to Frelinghuysen's example as a blessed forerunner of their own activities. Other historians, however, have denied that Frelinghuysen presided over a true revival, subjecting the claim to rigorous and unfavourable scrutiny.

What seems clear is that Frelinghuysen, who held a collective pastorate over four Dutch Reformed churches in New Jersey from 1720, conducted his ministry in some respects like an 'Awakener' (as American revival preachers in this period are known). Steeped in the writings of the English Puritans, as many Dutch Reformed were,[1] Frelinghuysen expressed an outspoken anxiety about

1. The so-called 'Second Dutch Reformation', roughly in the mid-17th Century, was deeply influenced by English Puritanism.

what he felt was the mere external formalism of many Dutch Reformed, and the way that Dutch Reformed religion had become, for them, merely a badge of their ethnic identity. His drive toward a more sincere Christianity led him to restrict (or try to restrict) admission to the Lord's Supper only to those who showed signs in their lives of an authentic faith and piety.

This precipitated bitter division in America's Dutch Reformed community, as parties formed for and against Frelinghuysen and his reform measures. Both sides appealed to their 'mother' authority, the Dutch Reformed 'Classis' in Amsterdam (in the Netherlands).[2] The controversy continued until 1734, when reconciliation was finally achieved between the two warring parties. This controversy became entangled with another, the desire of Frelinghuysen and his followers for greater autonomy for the American Dutch Reformed, rather than being treated as a mere province of the Dutch homeland in the Netherlands. They believed that more autonomy would favour their own reforming stance, whereas rule from the Netherlands would tend to perpetuate the stiff formalism and 'ethnic identity' stance of their opponents. The reform party eventually won this struggle in 1747, when the Dutch homeland granted a significant level of ecclesiastical autonomy to the New World settlers, allowing them to form their own Classis. The conservative faction in America, however, opposed this development, refusing to acquiesce in the new Classis, which they saw as tainted by a reformism they disliked; this resulted in more decades of internal strife, which was not finally quenched until 1771–72.

Historians argue over whether Frelinghuysen was an Awakener, but what cannot be disputed is that significant numbers of conversions took place under his preaching, and that his spiritual impact on Gilbert Tennent, the Presbyterian Awakener, was immense.

2. The Presbyterians

The Awakening within the American Presbyterian Church (of Anglo-Scottish origin) centred around the Tennent family,

---

2. Classis is the Dutch Reformed equivalent of presbytery.

headed by the father William Tennent (1673–1746). Although William and his sons were Presbyterian ministers of like Evangelical mind, it was William's oldest son Gilbert Tennent (1703–64) who emerged as the family's foremost preacher. Gilbert was born and raised in Ireland; his father William then took the family across the Atlantic to reside in Philadelphia, chief city in the Colony of Pennsylvania. Gilbert graduated from Yale College in 1725, and the following year was called to the city of New Brunswick (in the Colony of New Jersey), tasked with setting up a new Presbyterian congregation. It was here that Tennent was profoundly affected by the life and ministry of the Dutch Reformed preacher Theodorus Frelinghuysen (see previous section), who was also stationed in New Jersey. As a result of Frelinghuysen's influence, the young Tennent began increasingly emphasising, in his own preaching, the futility of a faith that was nothing more than head-knowledge, the importance of conviction of sin, and the sole sufficiency of Christ as Saviour of sinners. One of his friends wrote of Tennent's ministry at this time:

> In his manners, at first view, he seemed distant and reserved; yet, upon nearer acquaintance, he was ever found affable, condescending [humble], and communicative. And what greatly endeared his conversation was an openness and undisguised honesty, at the greatest remove from artifice and dissimulation, which were the abhorrence of his soul.

Tennent's ministry became marked by genuine revival in the early 1730s: the first indisputable green shoots of the Great Awakening, as Tennent's preaching matured into a more stable and balanced type of Evangelical Calvinism, which began to impact deeply on his hearers. Meanwhile a similar revival was underway in the nearby New Jersey township of Freehold, through the preaching of Gilbert's younger brother John. From there, the movement started to spread to other Presbyterian preachers and churches.

The Awakening mediated through the Tennents became distressingly entangled with a controversy over the extent to which

Presbyterian ministers should subscribe to the Westminster Confession. Presbyterians of Scottish and Irish descent tended toward a very strict 'jot-and-tittle' view of confessional subscription. Those of English Puritan background, however, were less concerned with strict confessional orthodoxy, and more with authentic personal piety; they took the view that only a broad agreement with the system of doctrine contained in the Confession was necessary, rather than perfect submission to its every minutest statement. The Tennents, despite their Irish background, sided with the less strict party in this controversy.

A degree of peace had been reached in 1729 with the Adopting Act, which allowed ministers to state whether they had problems with aspects of the Confession, and remitted to local presbyteries and to Synod[3] the power to adjudicate on such scruples: a candidate could be accepted if his scruples were judged to be about 'articles not essential and necessary in doctrine, worship, or government'. In 1736, however, after the Awakening had begun, this peace unravelled in a spectacular fashion. The strict subscriptionist group found itself that year in the ascendant in Synod, and they used their voting power to alter the Adopting Act, in order to require jot-and-tittle subscription to the whole Confession. This move was in fact aimed at Gilbert Tennent and other Presbyterian Awakeners, one of whose fundamental concerns was to warn against the idea that saving faith could be identified with rigid doctrinal orthodoxy. Strict subscriptionists therefore now reacted against what they perceived as the Awakening's ungodly liberalism by doubling down on the most absolute requirements for confessional orthodoxy, as being far more important than what they regarded as overly emotional revivals. The following year, they also tried to hamstring the work of the Awakeners by demanding that no minister preach to a congregation other than his own without permission of presbytery (this was aimed against the itinerant ministries of the Awakeners).

3. At this time the Synod was the supreme church court among American Presbyterians; the first General Assembly was not constituted until 1789.

Another aspect of the conflict had to do with ministerial training. The Awakeners had their own seminary, the Log College in Neshaminy, just outside Philadelphia, run by William Tennent. Anti-Awakeners fastened much blame on the Log College for producing revivalist preachers who disregarded proper Presbyterian church order in their passion for itinerant proclamation of the Gospel (e.g., preaching in vacant churches outside their own presbyteries). In 1738, the Synod – controlled by the anti-Awakeners – passed a resolution requiring all ministerial candidates to receive theological education at a European college or at the respected American colleges of Harvard or Yale. William Tennent and the Log College ignored this resolution and carried on training their own ministers. The New Brunswick presbytery, dominated by Awakeners, continued to ordain men trained at the Log College.

All the above factors meant that it looked as though a deadly civil war was brewing within American Presbyterianism. The Awakeners were being called the 'New Side', and their opponents the 'Old Side', in this conflict.

It was at this crucial juncture that George Whitefield arrived for the second time in America. His first visit had been to Georgia in the South in 1737–38. This time, in November 1739, he preached in the North, the territory of the Presbyterian Awakeners – in Philadelphia, where his sermons created the same electrifying sensation they had been producing in England. This swiftly led to many invitations by the Awakeners to Whitefield to preach in their Presbyterian churches – or rather, generally to preach outside the churches in the open air, in order to accommodate the many thousands of listeners. Whitefield, ever the Anglican Evangelical ecumenist, was happy to comply and cooperate with Presbyterians, and the river of the Awakening flowed on abundantly. Surviving accounts from this time attest to Whitefield's piercing power. When he preached in Middletown, Connecticut in 1740, a farmer named Nathan Cole heard him and recorded his impression:

> When I saw Mr Whitefield come upon the scaffold he looked almost angelical; a young, slim, slender youth before some

> thousands of people with a bold undaunted countenance, and my hearing how God was with him everywhere as he came along, it solemnized my mind; and put me into a trembling fear before he began to preach; for he looked as if he was clothed with authority from the great God; and a sweet solemnity sat upon his brow. And my hearing him preach gave me a heart wound; by God's blessing my old foundation was broken up, and I saw that my righteousness would not save me; then I was convinced of the doctrine of election; and went right to quarrelling with God about it, because that all I could do would not save me, and He had decreed from eternity who should be saved and who not.

Cole experienced a life-transforming conversion soon after this.

A strong relationship was forged between Whitefield and the Tennents, which had the effect of cementing more deeply Whitefield's already existing attachment to Calvinism. The Presbyterian Awakeners in turn received a great boost to their morale from the effect of Whitefield's preaching. After Whitefield's departure to preach in other areas, Gilbert Tennent felt confident to preach a sermon at Nottingham (Pennsylvania) early in 1740, published as *The Dangers of an Unconverted Ministry*. It was a scathing piece of rhetoric, in which Tennent gave no quarter to opponents of the Awakening. He advised those who were troubled by the unconverted state of their ministers to leave their ministry and churches, and worship elsewhere. This deeply embittered Tennent's anti-Awakening antagonists – he was clearly giving advice subversive of the Presbyterian system.

Whitefield arrived back in Philadelphia in April 1740, where he preached with overwhelming effect to crowds of up to eight thousand nearly every day for a whole month. This intense period has been described as one of American Christianity's most astonishing and transformative moments, the very heart and soul of the entire Great Awakening. Again, Whitefield's ministry had a galvanizing effect on the Presbyterian Awakeners; emboldened beyond measure by the English evangelist and his overpowering preaching, they became more sharply divided against their Old Side opponents than ever. The acrimonious conflict now took on a church court dimension, with the pro-Awakening New Side advocating the right of presbyteries to manage their own internal affairs (which favoured the Awakeners), and the anti-Awakening Old Side insisting that presbyteries must submit absolutely to the overriding centralised authority of Synod (which favoured the anti-Awakeners, who could use the authority of Synod to quell the local activities of the Awakeners).

The quarrel between the New Side and the Old Side came to a poisonous head in May 1741, when the Presbyterian Synod expelled the entire presbytery of New Brunswick from the Church for its New Side loyalties. Observing these events, the Anglican missionary Robert Jenney, stationed in Philadelphia, wrote to his senders in London, 'The Presbyterians are almost broken to pieces.' The New York presbytery (which was New Side) made attempts at reconciliation between New Brunswick and the Synod. These however failed, and in 1745 the ejected New Siders of New Brunswick amalgamated with the presbytery of New York to form a new, separate Synod, the Synod of New York, which was resoundingly New Side. The American Presbyterian Church was thus split asunder into two, divided by the Awakening.[4]

The newly formed New Side Synod of New York went on to express official approval of the Awakening, loosening the terms of confessional subscription for its ministers by returning to the Adopting Act of 1729. The New Side Synod prospered richly. In 1745 it had twenty-two ministers; by 1758 it had seventy-three. It also established a number of colleges or academies, the most famous being the College of New Jersey, founded in 1747, which in 1752 settled permanently at Princeton. This was the origin of Princeton Seminary, which was to become America's most celebrated Reformed seminary: cradled in the Great Awakening, committed to a generous understanding of the Reformed faith

4. Anyone who thinks that revival brings peace and unity to the church should have his head examined.

in all matters theological, and equally determined to provide the finest possible education at the cutting edge of 18th Century knowledge – a synthesis of the best of the Enlightenment with the best of experiential Calvinism. The first president of the New Jersey College was Jonathan Dickinson (1688–1747), an Awakener who, in 1745, had been elected the first moderator of the newly formed New Side Synod of New York. Dickinson was well-known as a literary defender of the Reformed faith against its critics. His *Familiar Letters to a Gentleman, upon a Variety of Seasonable and Important Subjects in Religion* was popular, going through several editions.

By contrast with this impressive record of New Side growth, the anti-Awakening Old Side declined. It had twenty-seven ministers in 1745, but only twenty-two by 1758.

Nonetheless, Old and New Sides finally reunited in 1758, after years of separate church existence. The original fierce passions generated by controversy over the Awakening had by then subsided, and Gilbert Tennent in particular took a conciliatory stance. Still, the reunion was essentially on New Side terms. The reunited Church followed the less strict New Side position in its stance on confessional subscription, and accepted the basic authenticity and blessing of the Awakening as 'a gracious work of God', albeit issuing sober and measured cautions about counterfeit revival.

3. New England Congregationalists

The first true signs of the Great Awakening in New England came in 1734–35 in Northampton, Massachusetts, under the ministry of Jonathan Edwards (1703–58). Edwards was born at East Windsor in Connecticut, son of the Congregationalist pastor Timothy Edwards. An obvious intellectual prodigy from his youth, Edwards Junior studied theology at Yale College, and then had a short period as a Presbyterian supply preacher in New York city. Then he became a tutor at Yale in 1724, until finally coming to occupy the position for which history remembers him in 1727 – the associate pastor with his

Jonathan Edwards

grandfather Solomon Stoddard[5] at the Congregationalist Church of Northampton in the Colony of Massachusetts (Edwards was the son of Stoddard's daughter). When Stoddard died two years later, Edwards became the congregation's sole pastor.

In the period 1734–35, Northampton experienced a powerful local revival, described in rich and gripping detail in Edwards' highly influential *Faithful Narrative of the Surprising Work of God in the Conversion of Many Hundred Souls in Northampton* (1737) – the first of his writings to receive a wide circulation. It was avidly studied by British Evangelicals: Isaac Watts, John Wesley, James Robe.[6] The revival in Northampton was so community-wide in its impact, it resulted in three hundred of the town's young men and women being received into church membership in a six-month period. The movement spread from Northampton across the Connecticut River valley. Edwards gives this account in his *Faithful Narrative*:

> A great and earnest concern about the great things of religion and the eternal world, became universal in all parts of the town, and among persons of all degrees, and all ages. The noise amongst the dry bones waxed louder and louder; all other talk but about spiritual and eternal things, was soon thrown by; all the conversation, in all companies and upon all occasions, was upon these things only, unless so much as was necessary for people carrying on their ordinary secular business. Other discourse than of the things of religion would scarcely be tolerated in any company. The minds of people

5. For Stoddard, see Part 1.
6. For Watts and Wesley, see Chapter 2, and for Robe see Chapter 3.

were wonderfully taken off from the world, it was treated amongst us as a thing of very little consequence ...

But although people did not ordinarily neglect their worldly business, yet religion was with all sorts the great concern, and the world was a thing only by the bye. The only thing in their view was to get the kingdom of heaven, and everyone appeared pressing into it. The engagedness of their hearts in this great concern could not be hid, it appeared in their very countenances. It then was a dreadful thing amongst us to lie out of Christ, in danger every day of dropping into hell; and what persons' minds were intent upon, was to escape for their lives, and to fly from wrath to come. All would eagerly lay hold of opportunities for their souls, and were wont very often to meet together in private houses, for religious purposes: and such meetings when appointed were greatly thronged ...

This work of God, as it was carried on, and the number of true saints multiplied, soon made a glorious alteration in the town: so that in the spring and summer following, 1735, the town seemed to be full of the presence of God: it never was so full of love, nor of joy, and yet so full of distress, as it was then. There were remarkable tokens of God's presence in almost every house. It was a time of joy in families on account of salvation being brought to them; parents rejoicing over their children as new born, and husbands over their wives, and wives over their husbands. The doings of God were then seen in His sanctuary, God's day was a delight, and His tabernacles were amiable. Our public assemblies were then beautiful: the congregation was alive in God's service, every one earnestly intent on the public worship, every hearer eager to drink in the words of the minister as they came from his mouth; the assembly in general were, from time to time, in tears while the word was preached; some weeping with sorrow and distress, others with joy and love, others with pity and concern for the souls of their neighbours.

The Northampton revival died down, but beginning in September 1740, there was an even deeper movement of Awakening. This was precipitated by George Whitefield's preaching in Boston, Massachusetts, and the surrounding area, which was followed by Whitefield's preaching tour through Connecticut. Multitudes professed conversion, and many new congregations were formed. Whitefield wrote in his journal of his preaching in Boston:

> O how the Word did run! It rejoiced my heart to see such numbers greatly affected, so that some of them, I believe, could scarcely refrain from crying out, that the place was no other than a Bethel and the gate of heaven. Many wept exceedingly, and cried out under the Word, like persons that were hungering and thirsting after righteousness. The Spirit of the Lord was upon them all.

At the personal level, Whitefield's New England tour meant that a strong friendship developed between Whitefield and Edwards, which had the effect of giving a more sober, more rational, less impulsive texture to Whitefield's piety.

If Whitefield was the dominating preacher of the Awakening, Edwards became its dominating theologian. Indeed, if any person can lay claim to be America's greatest theologian of all time, in terms of intellectual power and influence, it would almost certainly be Edwards. Perhaps his true theological masterpieces were those works in which he stood forth as a pastoral and experiential theologian, seeking to investigate and discern the nature of authentic spiritual experience, and to expose its counterfeits. His outstanding works in this genre were his *Distinguishing Marks of a Work of the Spirit of God* (1741), *Thoughts Concerning the Present Revival in New England* (1743), and *Treatise Concerning Religious Affections* (1746).

Edwards sought to map out a 'golden mean' between a dry and dead orthodoxy on the one hand, and an unbalanced and delusive emotionalism on the other. The latter, he thought, would always be found in revivals, giving people of dead orthodoxy the perfect excuse to denounce all revivals as ungodly hysteria from beginning to end. Edwards, however, was convinced that scripture gave guidelines for spiritual leaders to be able to distinguish between the genuine wheat of the Holy Spirit, and the spurious chaff of the human spirit (or Satan), in any apparent work of divine grace. His recourse to scripture as the ultimate touchstone of true and false experience marks Edwards as pre-eminently Protestant in this area of his theology.

In the realm of 'dogmatic' theology, Edwards' profoundest works were probably his *A Careful and Strict Inquiry into the Modern Prevailing Notions of the Freedom of the Will* (1754), and *The Great Christian Doctrine of Original Sin Defended* (1758). In these treatises, he explored and vindicated a basically Augustinian/Reformed understanding of sin and salvation. Much of Edwards' thinking was developed in response to the English Arminian theologian Daniel Whitby (1638–1726), who perceived huge problems in affirming both divine foreknowledge of all future events and the genuine freedom of moral agents – how could they be free if their choices were infallibly foreknown by God? (In other words, divine foreknowledge meant that they could not really choose otherwise than they were divinely and eternally foreknown to choose.) Faced with this dilemma, Whitby argued that it was better to deny God's foreknowledge than man's freedom. Edwards countered these lines of thinking, arguing that man could have true freedom as long as he was free to act in harmony with his own strongest motive. This position was actually a kind of 'determinism' (all human choices are inevitably determined by the strongest motive); it dovetailed neatly with Edwards' Reformed convictions about God's absolute foreknowledge and sovereign control over human choices and actions. Yet despite this determinism, it remained true for Edwards that we possess significant freedom, if we are free to act on our own strongest motive without external coercion.[7]

---

7. This view of human freedom is known as compatibilism. It should be noted that not all Calvinists have been compatibilists. For example, the profound Scottish Calvinist of the 19th Century, John Duncan, rejected Edwards' view because (he argued) it could not apply to Adam before the Fall. If Adam sinned because his strongest motive was to disobey, then his heart was already sinful; but God created Adam innocent. Where then did his 'strongest motive' to disobey come from? The great 19th Century Southern Presbyterian theologian John L. Girardeau made similar criticisms of Edwards. I am not arbitrating on this controversy among Calvinists, merely noting its historical existence.

Edwards also offered a wide-ranging biblical defence of God's foreknowledge, citing a multitude of texts, and arguing that God's transcendence over time meant that He 'saw' future events in the same way that He saw past ones. The truth and certainty of both past and future were thus guaranteed in the divine mind.[8]

Edwards also provided an exposition and defence of the leading points of Reformed soteriology against Arminianism – what we know today as the 'five points of Calvinism'. Human nature was in a bondage to sin irremediable by human power; the sovereign, transforming work of the Spirit of Christ alone liberated from this bondage; those who were liberated had been eternally chosen by God for this blessedness; the atoning work of Christ was aimed at saving these chosen people; and once they were set free by His Spirit, they could never lose their salvation.

Edwards' influential biography of David Brainerd cannot be omitted from an account of his writings. Brainerd (1718–47), a native of Hadam, Connecticut, had been expelled from Yale College for his outspoken advocacy of the Awakening (which went down badly with his tutors, especially when he remarked that one of them 'had no more grace than a chair'). Having ruined his reputation among New England's Congregationalists, Brainerd came to the attention of the pro-Awakening New Side Presbyterians of New York, and – financially supported by the Scottish Society for the Promotion of Christian Knowledge – was commissioned in 1742 as a missionary to Native Americans, at Nassau in New York, the Delaware River in Pennsylvania, and Crossweekung in New Jersey. Serious illness compelled Brainerd's retirement in 1746, and he died of tuberculosis in Jonathan Edwards' house in 1747. Edwards was so impressed by the young man's spiritual-mindedness, he set aside all his other literary projects to write Brainerd's biography. Published in 1749, it was entitled *An Account of the Life of the Late Reverend Mr. David Brainerd*; it included an edited version of Brainerd's

8. This is not far from the position outlined by the ancient philosopher-theologian Boethius (480–524) in his *Consolation of Philosophy*. For Boethius, see Volume 1, Chapter 11, section 1.

journal.[9] The biography almost immediately became a best seller, and has never been out of print, inspiring untold numbers to emulate Brainerd's piety and evangelistic commitment.

To an unusual degree, Edwards' theology was governed by the concept of God's beauty or loveliness. He presented this beauty as God's chief distinguishing attribute (the 'beauty of holiness'), argued that it was made known supremely in Christ, and wove it deeply into his apologetics – the Christian was enabled by the Spirit to see the unique and all-surpassing beauty of the Gospel of Jesus Christ, which was enough to convince him or her of the Gospel's divine origin and truth. All positive relationships with God were rooted and grounded in perception of His beauty:

> It is unreasonable to think otherwise, than that the first foundation of a true love to God, is that whereby He is in Himself lovely, or worthy to be loved, or the supreme loveliness of His nature. This is certainly what makes Him chiefly amiable. What chiefly makes a man, or any creature lovely, is his excellency; and so what chiefly renders God lovely, and must undoubtedly be the chief ground of true love, is His excellency. God's nature, or the Divinity, is infinitely excellent; yea it is infinite beauty, brightness, and glory itself. But how can that be true love of this excellent and lovely nature, which is not built on the foundation of its true loveliness? How can that be true love of beauty and brightness which is not for beauty and brightness' sake?[10]

---

9. At the end of his short life Brainerd had suffered from serious depression; he wrote about this in his journal, but some of these references were removed as too unedifying for the Christian reading public.

10. The centrality of beauty in Edwards' theology and philosophy seems (arguably) to be derived from Enlightenment thought, perhaps especially the philosophical writings of the great Scoto-Irish Enlightenment philosopher Francis Hutcheson, who wrote and reflected much on beauty, and with whose writings Edwards was definitely acquainted. (See Chapter 3, Part 6, section 1 for Hutcheson.) Edwards applied the concept of beauty to his understanding of the Trinity. Since beauty (or excellence, one of Edwards' synonyms for beauty) involved harmony, agreement, and consent, but there could be no harmony, agreement, or consent where only a single isolated entity existed, it followed that God's beauty required Him to be plural. As

Edwards has had a bad press among many, owing to his most famous (or infamous) sermon, *Sinners in the Hands of an Angry God*, being taken as typical of his output (sometimes being the sole writing by Edwards reprinted in collections of 18th Century American literature). The sermon was preached at Enfield, Connecticut, in 1741, during the height of the Awakening. But it was by no means typical; Edwards devoted immeasurably more time to preaching and writing about the beauty of Christ and His perfections than about God's wrath, and the theme of divine anger is not very prominent in his theological writings overall. It is therefore unfair to regard this one sermon as summing up the theology and spirituality of Edwards. If we must consider a specific divine quality as characterising Edwards, he was the Theologian of Beauty, not the Theologian of Wrath.

Despite Edwards' vast stature as the theologian of the Great Awakening, his personal popularity in his own congregation, and the popularity of his preaching, diminished. At length in 1750, he was dismissed from the pastorate. The chief cause was Edwards' attempt to reform the inclusive Halfway Covenant scheme adopted under Solomon Stoddard, whereby those without a credible profession of faith were admitted to the Lord's Supper, so long as they lived morally upright lives. Edwards' thinking had, since the early 1740s, been moving toward the view that a credible profession was a biblical necessity for partaking in the Supper. He finally outlined these

---

Edwards puts it: 'we have shown that one alone cannot be excellent, inasmuch as, in such case, there can be no consent. Therefore, if God is excellent, there must be a plurality in God; otherwise, there can be no consent in Him.' (*Works of Edwards*, vol.13, p.284). Here we encounter Edwards the speculative philosophical theologian. It was this strain of philosophical, metaphysical speculation in Edwards that has led some Reformed theologians to be suspicious of the value of his theology taken as a whole. The great English Evangelical Calvinist John Newton was critical of Edwards on this account: 'Mr. Edwards was an excellent man, but some of his writings are too metaphysical, and particularly that book [*The Freedom of the Will*]. If I understand it, I think it rather establishes fatalism and necessity than Calvinism in the sober sense. I could object likewise to his book on *Original Sin*, though there are many excellent things in it.'

views in his 1749 treatise, *An Humble Inquiry into the Rules of the Word of God Concerning the Qualifications Requisite to a Compleat Standing and Full Communion*. However, the majority of his congregation disagreed, so that Edwards found himself voted out of office. This event among others forced Edwards to reconsider the depth and value of the Awakening.

Edwards now went as a missionary to the frontier settlement of Stockbridge in Massachusetts, preaching both to white settlers and the Native Americans of the Housatonic valley – he preached to the Native Americans through an interpreter. It was at Stockbridge that Edwards wrote his masterworks on original sin and the freedom of the will. In January 1758, he was appointed President of New Jersey College at Princeton (which is why he is often called 'President Edwards'). His presidency, however, was short-lived. There was an outbreak of smallpox in the Princeton area in 1757–58, and Edwards gladly agreed to accept what was then the medical precaution against the disease, a method known as variolation (an early form of inoculation). As a man of the Enlightenment and its science, Edwards was strongly in favour of inoculations. He was duly inoculated on 23rd February 1758.

Unfortunately, the science of inoculation was then in its infancy, and those who underwent variolation against smallpox had a 2–3 per cent chance of dying. Edwards, never in robust health, died on 22nd March as a consequence of complications arising from the inoculation. He left behind a large family (three sons and eight daughters), and his wife Sarah Edwards (1710–58) whose deep spiritual-mindedness had left an awe-inspiring impression both on Edwards himself and on George Whitefield – 'overwhelmed in the light and joy of the love of God', according to Edwards. Sarah survived her husband only by a period of six months.[11]

---

11. Sarah Edwards' depth of spirituality has led to her being classed as a 'mystic' in Wikipedia at the time of writing. 'Mystic', however, is a slippery term, and the present writer prefers to regard her as a woman of profound Christian virtue and heavenly-mindedness. See under Primary Historical Sources for Edwards' account of his wife's faith

One of Edwards' sons, Jonathan Edwards Junior (1745–1801), himself became a distinguished and influential New England theologian. Edwards Junior and those in New England who, like him, took their theological bearings from his father, are generally known as Edwardseans, and their form of Calvinism as 'the New Divinity' (or simply 'New England Theology'). Their foremost theologian was Samuel Hopkins (1721–1803), pastor of the Congregational church in Newport, Rhode Island, from 1770 to his death in 1803, and Jonathan Edwards' literary executor; Hopkins was so impactful that those in his line of thought have been christened 'Hopkinsians'. Although broadly Reformed, the Edwardseans (and/or Hopkinsians) struggled with some aspects of the Reformed heritage, notably in their understanding of original sin. In place of the traditional Reformed doctrine of Adam's federal headship of humankind, the Edwardseans preferred the theory of 'sovereign constitution'. This was particularly developed by Hopkins, who taught that God had sovereignly ordained that 'all mankind should sin as Adam had done, and fully consent to his transgression.' Rather than any real relationship of union between Adam and humanity as the ground of the universality of original sin, Hopkins' view simply resolved everything into God's sheer sovereignty. Although Edwardseans liked to call their view 'consistent Calvinism', the great majority of Calvinists have not followed them.

Hopkins, however, was also one of the first American theologians unequivocally to condemn black slavery, in his 1776 treatise *A Dialogue Concerning the Slavery of the Africans; shewing it to be the duty and interest of the American states to emancipate all their African slaves.* He addressed the treatise to all thirteen Colonies as they were in the throes of freeing themselves from the British yoke, rebuking his fellow white Americans for their 'strong prejudices' against people of colour, who were 'by nature and by right, on a level with our brethren and children'.

---

and piety.

Jonathan Edwards' concern in his writings to distinguish true from false spirituality was imperative in the setting of the Awakening, which was brought into disrepute by some of its practitioners. One notable example was James Davenport (1716–57), Congregational minister of Long Island, at the eastern edge of the Colony of New York. Davenport's itinerant evangelism was a source of pain to both supporters and opponents of the Awakening, as he delivered incoherent extemporary sermons that strayed into ranting, and made bizarre claims, e.g., that he could tell who was saved and who was lost simply by looking at them. He ended up in prison, declared mentally unsound by the courts. Later Davenport publicly recanted his unbalanced conduct, in his *Retractions,* but it was too late – the harm had been done. Partly in consequence of the conduct of extremists like Davenport, New England Congregationalists became as divided over the Awakening as the Northern Presbyterians were. Rather than 'New Side' versus 'Old Side', the party names in New England were 'New Light' (Awakeners) and 'Old Light' (anti-Awakeners).

The Old Light anti-Awakeners of New England found their most persuasive spokesman in Charles Chauncy (1705–87), minister of First Church, Boston, in whom Enlightenment rationalism was fast superseding Evangelical faith. In 1743 Chauncy published his *Seasonable Thoughts on the State of Religion in New England,* a searing indictment of the revival as little more than emotionalism, hysteria, mindless mysticism, and antinomianism. He also attached the damaging label of Quakerism – as if the Awakening had bypassed the written Word of God in favour of inner impulses (the 'light within' beloved of Quaker theology). The general criticism of the Awakening and its excesses had become so powerful by 1744 that Whitefield himself found many of the New England pulpits closed to him. He was even officially rebuked by the divinity faculties at Harvard and Yale Colleges. By then, the original blazing fires of the New England Awakening had generally waned.

As a result of the Great Awakening in New England, some New Light Congregationalists adopted a stance that created ecclesiastical division and the birth of a new religious body, the Separate Congregationalists, particularly after 1745. They were marked by their view that only the regenerate should be accepted as church members, and by their opposition to state-sponsored religious taxes to support the ministry of the established Congregational Church. This opposition to religious taxes brought them severe persecution; their property was seized, and some individuals were imprisoned. The Separate Congregationalists, however, never crystallised into a genuine, coherent denomination; some returned to the established Church, won over by the New Light ministries of some of the pastors. Many more, however, abandoned Congregationalism altogether and became Baptists.

4. Northern Baptists

The Awakening had a profound impact on the Northern Baptists, especially through the Philadelphia Baptist Association. This was a Calvinist body that dominated American Baptist life in the North during the Great Awakening period. It was founded in 1707, originally including only five congregations, otherwise isolated, who covenanted together in order to 'execute designs of common good.' The original founding churches were in Pennsylvania, New Jersey, and Delaware. In 1742, at the height of the Awakening, the Association adopted a revised version of the 1689 Baptist Confession as its own confession of faith. Known as the Philadelphia Confession, it was to wield great influence over Calvinistic Baptist church life in America.[12] In the 1740s and 50s, the Awakening revitalised the congregations of the Association, to the extent that it sent out evangelists to spread the Awakening as far south as North and South Carolina. In the South, the Northern-backed Baptist churches adopted

12. The revisions included a new statement on the singing of psalms, hymns, and spiritual songs as a divine ordinance of New Testament worship (chapter 23) and an affirmation that the laying on of hands was necessary to the right performance of baptism (chapter 31).

the name Regular Baptists to distinguish themselves from the Separate Baptists (see the next section on the Awakening in the South).

The rapid numerical growth of the Association led to a clearer definition of the relationship between local churches and the Association: the autonomy of the local church was endorsed, but the Association was also deemed to have the right and duty to offer general declarations of what was Scriptural in church life. Congregations that rejected the Association's declarations could be disfellowshipped from the Association.

In Congregationalist-dominated New England, Baptists also prospered as a result of the radicalising effect the Awakening had on the Congregational churches. Prior to the Awakening, most of the Baptist churches in New England had been Arminian, and they opposed the Awakening owing to its Calvinist character. The growth, however, of Separate Congregationalist churches (see previous section) led to significant numbers of these ultimately abandoning their Congregationalist commitment to infant baptism, and becoming Separate Baptist churches. The Separate Baptist movement brought new strength to the Calvinistic Baptist cause; most of the Separate Baptists aligned themselves with the few existing Calvinistic Baptist churches of New England. Ultimately a new Calvinistic Baptist Association for New England was formed in 1767, modelled on the existing Association in Philadelphia.[13] This is often called the Warren Association, after the location of the church of James Manning (1738–91), the guiding hand behind the enterprise. A graduate of Princeton, Manning was also the first president of the new Calvinistic Baptist academy, Rhode Island College (later Brown University), founded in 1764. Rhode Island, with its distinctive tradition of religious toleration, was the ideal New England home for the first American Baptist centre of learning and training.

One of the most important Calvinistic Baptist figures to emerge from the Separate Baptist tendency in New England

---

13. There had been a short-lived Separate Baptist Association in New England in the 1750s, but it had not endured.

was Isaac Backus (1724–1806). Born at Yantic, now part of Norwich in Connecticut, he was converted in 1741 as the Great Awakening blazed through New England. Like others, Backus' experience of salvation convinced him that the traditional New England Congregational system was compromised through state funding and the Halfway Covenant, resulting in his becoming a Separate Congregationalist. He began preaching in 1746. His refusal to pay the church tax almost landed him in prison:

> This morning I was seized by the officer, who threatened to carry me to prison for the precinct-rate [church tax]; but, glory to God, He gave me a sweet calmness and serenity of soul, so that I was able not to fear the officer, or treat him with any bitterness. I told him that they were going on in an unscriptural way to support the Gospel, and therefore I could do nothing to countenance them in such a way. He told me that if I would not pay him he would immediately carry me to jail; but just as he was about to drag me away, there came in a man, who called him out and paid him the money, so that he was forced to let me go.

Other Separatists were not so fortunate, and were imprisoned. Such experiences helped strengthen Backus in his view that church and state should be separate. Again, like many Separate Congregationalists, Backus eventually embraced Baptist views (in 1751), becoming the pastor of a Baptist church in Middleboro, Massachusetts, continuing in this ministry for the rest of his long life. As well as his local pastoral duties, Backus journeyed widely on preaching tours across the whole of New England. His preaching powers were of a high magnitude, and mini-revivals broke out through his evangelism. He wrote to his mother in 1762:

> People generally not only flock to hear preaching, but they have also set up neighborhood meetings for prayer, exhortation, etc ... I wrote to you some time ago of the work at Fresh Meadows, and that two or three were hopefully converted among us in July. I have now the comfort of saying that the work prevails and increases among us still. A young woman

> was brought out of darkness into marvellous light at a meeting on the 3rd. This had a great influence upon others, and many are now under concern. Yea, in truth, the fields appear to me to be white unto the harvest. I daily look upon myself as a vile creature, yet the worth of souls and the great concerns of the kingdom of Christ, have, I think, engaged my mind as fully as ever in my life, to labor in his vineyard. Oh, these are golden moments, and woe to those who trifle them away.

Backus was not a polished preacher, but what he lacked in literary polish he made up for in the eloquence of the heart. As an early biographer attested:

> They [his hearers] saw that he was speaking from the heart; they felt that he was bearing witness for God; they perceived the impulses of a divine life in the simplicity, solemnity and fervor of his appeals; they recognized the ambassador of a king when he repeated the words of his master. This was the secret of his usefulness in the pulpit.

Despite some doubts at first, Backus fully supported cooperation between Baptist churches, and was involved in the forming of the Warren Association in 1767; he also became a trustee of the new Baptist Rhode Island College, helping to defuse Baptist prejudices against university-level education. He wrote a three-volume history of Baptists in New England, a treasury of historical information; among other things it chronicles the harsh persecution of Baptists by the Congregationalist civil authorities.

Backus became one of America's most active and zealous campaigners for religious liberty and the separation of church and state. The Warren Association had a special committee dedicated to helping New England Baptists persecuted for refusal to pay the church tax; Backus headed the committee. His most famous treatises on the topic were his *A Seasonable Plea for Liberty of Conscience, against some late oppressive proceedings* (1770), and *Appeal to the Public for Religious Liberty, Against the Oppressions of the Present Day* (1773). When the Revolutionary War of Independence came in 1775, Backus was an ardent advocate of independence from Britain, and when independence was gained, outspokenly supported the church-state separation clause in the new American constitution. Perhaps no other American figure so completely combined the causes of revival, Calvinist theology, Baptist ecclesiology, religious liberty, and American independence, as Backus.

5. The Southern Colonies

The Awakening in the Southern Colonies – Virginia, North and South Carolina, and Georgia[14] – had a distinctive character:

(i) The way was not paved as it had been in the North by the Evangelical Calvinist ministries of figures like the Tennents and Edwards.

(ii) The Awakening in the South was more prolonged, more diffuse, less concentrated into the 1739–42 time-frame. It continued on into the period of the War of Independence (1775–83).

(iii) Different denominations in the South experienced high points of revival at different times.

Whitefield preached in the Southern Colonies to great effect. The established Anglican Church – Whitefield's Church – was, however, less than hearty in its approval, except perhaps in Savannah, Georgia, where Whitefield's orphanage was located (Whitefield seems to have been regarded in Savannah as a 'local boy' who had achieved stardom). Generally, though, Whitefield's refusal to limit his preaching to the 'sacred interior' of Anglican church buildings, and his obvious willingness to preach for non-Anglicans, cooled the enthusiasm of most Southern Anglicans toward him. In South Carolina, the delegate of the Bishop of London, Alexander Garden (1685–1756), tried to use his authority to suppress Whitefield's scandalous non-Anglican activities, but failed. The overall lack of warmth among Southern Anglicans for Whitefield's awakening work meant

14. Other territories later to be famous as Southern States – Texas, Florida, Alabama, Mississippi, Louisiana, Tennessee, and others - had not yet been formed at the time of the Great Awakening.

that the Anglican Church in the South suffered numerical loss, as those awakened by his preaching went into more sympathetic religious groupings.

Unappreciated in his own Church, Whitefield continued to visit and preach with power in America, where at length he died on September 30th 1770, aged fifty-five, in the Presbyterian manse at Newburyport in Massachusetts, where he was buried. Back in England, his old friend John Wesley preached a noble funeral sermon for him, the Calvinist-Arminian controversy forgotten:

> What an honour it pleased God to put upon His faithful servant, by allowing him to declare His everlasting Gospel in so many various countries, to such numbers of people, and with so great an effect on so many of their precious souls! Have we read or heard of any person since the Apostles, who testified the Gospel of the grace of God through so widely extended a space, through so large a part of the habitable world? Have we read or heard of any person who called so many thousands, so many myriads, of sinners to repentance? Above all, have we read or heard of any who has been a blessed instrument in His hand of bringing so many sinners from darkness to light, and from the power of Satan unto God?

Whitefield's preaching in America's Northern Colonies aroused sympathetic notice in the South early on, and a number of interested laypeople in Hanover, Virginia, met in homes to read Whitefield's sermons and Martin Luther's Bible commentaries. This led to unexpected numerical growth, so that meeting houses had to be built to accommodate the numbers of affected people. They were hauled before Virginia's civil authorities, who looked upon their religious concerns about conversion as shameful in an Anglican Colony; but the awakened layfolk secured toleration by claiming to be Lutherans![15] In 1743, they were shepherded out of the Church of England altogether into Presbyterianism by William Robinson (d. 1746), a graduate of the Log College and missionary of the pro-Awakening New

15. There was legal provision for the toleration of Lutherans.

Brunswick presbytery. Robinson, a one-time Quaker, had experienced a remarkable conversion through meditating on the starry heavens:

> He was riding at a late hour, one evening, when the moon and the stars shone with unusual brightness, and when everything around him was calculated to excite reflection. While he was meditating upon the beauty and grandeur of the scene which the firmament presented, and was saying to himself, 'How transcendently glorious must be the Author of all this beauty and grandeur,' the thought struck him with the suddenness and force of lightning: 'But what do I know of this God? Have I ever sought His favor or made Him my friend?' This happy impression, which proved, by its permanence and effects, to have come from the best of all sources, never left him until he took refuge in Christ as the hope and life of his soul.

We have a contemporary account of Robinson's first preaching to the awakened Anglican layfolk of Hanover:

> On the 6th day of July, 1743, Mr. Robinson preached his first sermon to us, from Luke 13:3, and continued with us, preaching four days successively. The congregation was large the first day, and vastly increased the three following. It is hard for the liveliest imagination to form an image of the condition of the assembly on these glorious days of the Son of Man. Such of us as had been hungering for the Word before were lost in an agreeable surprise and astonishment, and some could not refrain from declaring their transport. We were overwhelmed with the thoughts of the unexpected goodness of God in allowing us to hear the Gospel preached in a manner that surpassed our hopes. Many that came through curiosity were pricked to the heart, and but few in the numerous assemblies on these four days appeared unaffected. They returned alarmed with apprehensions of their dangerous condition, convinced of their former entire ignorance of religion, and anxiously inquiring what they should do to be saved. And there is reason to believe there was as much good done by those four sermons as by all the sermons preached in these parts before or since.

Under such revival preaching, the first body of gathered Presbyterian worshipers was formed in Virginia, made up of awakened Anglicans no longer welcome in their mother Church.

Another Northern Presbyterian Awakener, Samuel Davies (1723–61), author of the famous hymn *Great God of Wonders,* also laboured in Virginia. Davies, another graduate of the Log College, was one of the most vivid and compelling preachers of the Awakening. His sermons combined a strong literary structure with very direct and searching calls to personal faith and repentance. W. B. Sprague (1795–1876), author of what would be the classic *Lectures on the Revival of Religion* (1832), said of Davies that 'he spoke with a glowing zeal and an eloquence more impressive and effective than had [until] then ever graced the American pulpit'. Another witness, eulogising Davies after his death, said:

> Whenever he ascended the sacred desk, he seemed to have not only the attention, but all the various passions of his auditory entirely at command. And as his personal appearance was noble and venerable, yet benevolent and mild, so he could speak with the most commanding authority, or melting tenderness, according to the variation of his subject. With what majesty and grandeur, with what energy and striking solemnity, with what powerful and almost irresistible eloquence, would he illustrate the truths and inculcate the duties of Christianity! *Mount Sinai* seemed to thunder from his lips, when he denounced the curses of the law, and sounded the dreadful alarm to guilty sinners. The solemn scenes of the last judgment seemed to rise in view, when he arraigned, tried, and convicted, self-deceivers and hypocrites. And how did the *balm of Gilead* distill from his lips, when he exhibited a bleeding Savior to sinful man, as a remedy for the wounded heart and guilty conscience! In a word, whatever subject he undertook, persuasive eloquence dwelt upon his tongue; and his audience was all attention. He spoke as on the borders of eternity, and as viewing the glories and terrors of an unseen world, and conveyed the most grand and affecting

> ideas of these important realities; realities which he then firmly believed, and which he now sees in the clearest light.[16]

By 1755, largely under Davies' influence, six Virginian Presbyterian congregations had been established, forming themselves into the presbytery of Hanover (the first ever Southern presbytery). Davies was also instrumental in forcing the hostile Anglican establishment in Virginia to concede that England's 1689 Toleration Act applied in the Colony. He has thereby earned an honoured place in the history of American religious and civil liberty.

Davies was also very effective as an evangelist among black slaves in Virginia. Although he was not in principle antagonistic to the institution of black slavery, Davies was fiercely insistent that slaves must be taught to read in order that they might encounter the Scriptures for themselves. In Davies' mind, education and conversion belonged together. Possibly over a hundred slaves professed faith under Davies' preaching. He then integrated them into the worship of the Presbyterian Church – whites and blacks worshiping together in the same congregations. This integrationist approach, however, did not long endure; from the 1750s onward, a movement grew (promoted by whites) to establish separate churches for blacks.[17]

Davies' life and career drew to an end while he was President of the College of New Jersey from 1759 to 1761, also pastoring the Presbyterian congregation in the locality. His relatively early death aged thirty-seven was owing to tuberculosis.

The Baptist cause in the South prospered chiefly through the work of two New Englanders, Shubal Stearns (1707–71) and Daniel Marshall (1706–84). Stearns was a native of Boston, Massachusetts, who experienced conversion under the preaching of George Whitefield, and in 1746 became a Separate

16. The great American statesman and political orator, Patrick Henry (1736–99), one of America's 'Founding Fathers', often as a youngster heard Davies preach, and used to recite his sermons aloud. Henry claimed Davies was the most inspiring public speaker he had ever heard.

17. See Part 4 for a brief excursus on black slavery.

Congregationalist pastor.[18] His contact with New England Baptists, however, won him over to the Baptist standpoint, and he was baptised as a believer in 1751. In 1754, Stearns and his congregation moved south to Hampshire in Virginia, and in 1755 they established the Sandy Creek Separate Baptist Church in Piedmont, North Carolina. The other Baptist pioneer, Daniel Marshall, was born in Windsor, Connecticut, and like Stearns was also converted through Whitefield's preaching in around 1745. He became a Separate Congregationalist, preached for several years as a lay evangelist in the Colonies of New York and Pennsylvania, and (after his first wife's death) married Stearns' sister Martha. Inspired by Jonathan Edwards' biography of David Brainerd, in 1750 the Marshalls became missionaries to the Native Americans of the Delaware valley, until the outbreak of a war involving the British, French, and Native Americans forced them to relocate. They joined up with Shubal Stearns in Virginia, preached in and around the Shenandoah valley, and at length became part of the Sandy Creek Separate Baptist Church in North Carolina.

The Sandy Creek Church became a base of operations for wide-ranging evangelistic activities by Stearns and Marshall in North Carolina, South Carolina, and Virginia. Around the time of Stearns' death in 1771, Marshall extended the evangelistic church-planting into Georgia. Another Baptist, Morgan Edwards, has left an impression of Stearns' charismatic preaching:

> Mr. Stearns was a man of small stature, but of good natural parts, and sound judgment. Of learning he had but a little share, yet was pretty well acquainted with books. His voice was musical and strong, which he managed in such a manner as, one while, to make soft impressions on the heart, and fetch tears from the eyes in a mechanical [automatic] way, and anon to shake the very nerves, and throw the animal system into

18. The Separate Congregationalists broke away from the traditional Congregationalist Church of New England through their radical insistence on a regenerate church membership and their refusal to pay state taxes in support of the traditional Congregational Church. See section 3.

> tumults and perturbations. All the Separate Baptists copied after him in tones of voice and actions of body; and some few exceeded him. His character was indisputably good as a man, a Christian, and a preacher. In his eyes was something very penetrating – there seemed to be a meaning in every glance.

Under the preaching of Stearns and Marshall, many professed faith – enough to worry the Anglican authorities of the Southern Colonies, who subjected the evangelists and their converts to severe, sometimes violent harassment. For example, in 1771 this was the experience of Baptists who were trying to start a church in Tidewater, Virginia:

> The [Anglican] Parson of the Parish [accompanied by the local sheriff] would keep running the end of his horsewhip in [the Baptist pastor Jack Waller's] mouth, laying his whip across the hymn book, etc. When done singing [Waller] proceeded to prayer. In it he was violently jerked off the stage; they caught him by the back part of his neck, beat his head against the ground, sometimes up and sometimes down, they carried him through the gate, where a gentleman [the sheriff] gave him twenty lashes with his horsewhip.

Such ugly scenes of violent intolerance against Baptists in Virginia helped to convince a horrified Virginia statesman James Madison (1751–1836), one of America's 'Founding Fathers' in the Revolutionary War of Independence (1775–83), that religious liberty must be a foundational principle of the American Republic.[19]

In spite of the opposition and persecution, the Baptist movement spearheaded by Stearns and Marshall grew rapidly. Morgan Edwards attested:

> In seventeen years, [Sandy Creek] has spread its branches westward as far as the great river Mississippi; southward as far as Georgia; eastward to the sea and Chesapeake Bay; and northward to the waters of the Potomac; it, in seventeen years, is become mother, grandmother, and great grandmother to

19. Madison became the fourth President of the United States from 1809–17.

> forty-two churches, from which sprang one hundred and twenty-five ministers.

There was, however, tension and friction between the Stearns' and Marshall's Separate Baptists and the older Calvinistic Baptists. The latter had also grown numerically in the South as a result of the Awakening and missionary work stemming from the Philadelphia Baptist Association in the North. In the Southern Colonies, the older Calvinistic Baptists took the name 'Regular Baptists' in 1765. The differences between Regulars and Separates arose from a certain mistrust on the part of the Northern-sponsored Regulars that the Separate Baptist movement was too given to overly emotional revivals, and lacked proper structure and discipline as a movement, with each congregation doing what was right in its own eyes. These tensions between Separate and Regular Baptists were at length resolved in 1787. Both Separates and Regulars united theologically around a common allegiance to the Philadelphia Confession, and the Separates came around to an acceptance of the benefits of congregational association.

6. Methodists

Methodism – spiritual revitalisation within the Church of England – came late to America. The first Methodist Societies appeared as a result of immigration in Maryland and New York in the 1760s. These Societies, however, following the English example, functioned strictly within the boundaries of the Anglican Church, as a leaven of renewal. From 1771, Francis Asbury (1745–1816) – sent out by Wesley – took on the role of directing and re-energising Methodism in America. Asbury was born in Birmingham, England, and experienced conversion through a Methodist meeting in Wednesbury at the age of sixteen, soon after which he became one of Wesley's itinerant preachers, active in Bedfordshire, Essex, and Wiltshire. In 1771 he volunteered for American service, an offer Wesley accepted, perceiving unusual gifts in the relatively young preacher (he was twenty-six).

Asbury's great task in the American Colonies, as Asbury saw it, was to make itinerant preaching central to the movement, something that had been forgotten in the Colonies when he arrived. Beginning in Philadelphia and New York, Asbury's preaching journeys took him around an increasingly wide area, until the coming of the Revolutionary War of Independence put a temporary end to his activities. A contemporary described him thus:

> Five feet nine in height, he was erect in person and of very commanding appearance. His features were rugged but his countenance was intelligent. His eyes were of a bluish cast, and so keen that it seemed as if he could look right through a person. He seemed born to sway others.

Asbury was living and working in Maryland when the War of Independence broke out in 1775. This event put American Methodists in a supremely awkward position. John Wesley, just a few months after fighting began, strongly condemned the Colonies' bid for independence – which provoked a virulent reaction in America, with Wesley being publicly denounced as 'a wolf in sheep's clothing, a madman, a chaplain in ordinary to the furies, a cunning fox, a Jesuit in disguise, and a Jacobite traitor.'[20]

Asbury did not go quite so far as Wesley in condemning the pro-independence War, but declared he would remain neutral in the conflict, in order to avoid politicising Methodism, urging other Methodists to follow his example. Unfortunately this strategy proved unworkable in Maryland, since the Colony's government – strongly pro-independence – imposed an oath of loyalty to the new independent American government on all its citizens. Refusing to take the oath, Asbury had to flee to the Colony of Delaware (where no oath of loyalty was required). The Methodists of Maryland who likewise refused the oath were persecuted as pro-British 'traitors' to the American cause. In other words, by proclaiming Methodist neutrality, Asbury

20. A Jacobite traitor, i.e. supporting a foreign government (Britain) as in another context the Jacobites had done in Britain itself. See Chapter 3, Part 4.

had in effect given Methodism a pro-British, anti-independence flavour wherever he had influence. He had to sit out the conflict in hiding (in Kent County, Delaware) before he could resume his active ministry.[21]

Asbury worked mainly in the North and in the border state of Maryland.[22] In the South, Methodism first took off through the ministry of Devereux Jarratt (1733–1801), Anglican rector of the parish of Bath in Virginia from 1763, who had been spiritually quickened under the preaching of the Presbyterian Awakeners in the 1750s. His future theological loyalties, however, were to a very diluted form of Calvinism (accepting, for example, universal atonement, and expressing scepticism about the role played by predestination in orthodox Calvinism) which enabled him to cooperate closely with Wesleyan Arminians. Jarratt, who had met with both Wesley and Whitefield while he was in England to be episcopally ordained, began preaching with such effect in Virginia as rector of Bath in the 1760s that huge crowds were soon attending his ministry. This compelled him to adopt an open-air form of preaching. A contemporary left this pen-portrait of Jarratt:

> He was blest with a most retentive memory, a sound judgment, and a power of voice which few possess, over which

---

21. Not all Anglicans in the English homeland were enemies of the American Colonies. The great Anglo-Irish MP Edmund Burke (1729–97), the 'father of modern conservatism' (although he was a Whig, not a Tory), was a devout Anglican and sympathetic to the Colonies. When in November 1775, King George III called for a religious fast to be observed in the Church to support British troops in their war against the Colonies, Burke's response was robust: 'In this situation, Sir, shocking to say, are we called upon by another proclamation, to go to the altar of the Almighty, with war and vengeance in our hearts, instead of the peace of our blessed Saviour. He said "my peace I give you;" but we are, on this fast, to have war only in our hearts and mouths; war against our brethren. Till our churches are purified from this abominable service, I shall consider them not as the temples of the Almighty, but the synagogues of Satan.'
22. Maryland is customarily described as a border state between the North and the South. Its general character, however, certainly in the 18th and 19th centuries, was rather more Southern than Northern.

> he had entire command. In the reading desk and in the pulpit he was in his element. All that sat under his ministry can bear witness to his zeal and affection in dispensing the word of life. He was raised up by Divine Providence and rendered a fit instrument to sound the Gospel trumpet, which during a long life he continued to do with the utmost fidelity and diligence. His aim was not to amuse for the moment, but to convince his hearers of the necessity of experimental and practical religion.

When Methodist lay preacher Robert Williams began preaching in Virginia in the 1770s, Jarratt joined forces with him. Williams was a fiery Irish Methodist in John Wesley's circle; Wesley had been reluctant to make too much use of him in Britain because of Williams' seemingly unconquerable habit of denouncing Anglican clergy (Wesley thought this counter-productive[23]). However, Williams at length convinced Wesley to send him as an evangelist to America, where his preaching proved highly effective in New York and Maryland. He then moved down into Virginia, where he and Jarratt combined their efforts as Anglican-Wesleyan Awakeners. Jarratt became unsettled by some of the physical and emotional effects that manifested themselves under his and Williams' brand of revival preaching, but found a safe guide to discern the true from the false in the practical treatises of Jonathan Edwards, despite disagreeing with Edwards' strong Calvinism.

In 1773 the first Methodist Conference in America took place; it appointed four lay preachers to work in Virginia. In 1774, Wesley set up a preaching circuit in Virginia. Flowing from this, the period 1775–76 saw a widespread Methodist

---

23. Wesley said of Williams' preaching in the Black Mountain area of Ireland, overlooking Belfast: 'There was a general love to the Gospel here (until simple [foolish] Robert Williams preached against the clergy). It is strange everyone does not see, 1.The sinfulness of railing at the clergy; if they are blind leaders of the blind, let them alone. 2. The foolishness of it. It can never do good, and has frequently done much harm.'

revival, in which the preaching of George Shadford (1739–1816), a favourite of John Wesley's, was especially impactful; this propelled the membership of the Methodist Societies in Virginia from some three hundred people in 1774, to 2,500 a mere two years later. The Methodist revival spread to North Carolina with similar results. These Southern Methodist awakenings deeply affected many people of colour, who (we are told) often crowded into the evangelistic meetings. The coming of the Revolutionary War of Independence, however, put an end to this Methodist awakening. Many Southern Methodists had a crisis of conscience over the War; they had been pro-independence until Wesley had almost immediately come out so strongly against it. However, not all Southern Methodists chose to heed Wesley's counsel. Devereux Jarratt, for example, was strongly in favour of American independence, and urged his fellow Virginians that they should 'go patch upon patch[24] rather than suffer their just rights to be infringed' by Britain.

In spite of the loss to Methodism of some pro-British loyalists in both North and South, the movement (once the War was over in 1783) was shown to have weathered the storm, and it continued its existence and activities within the now independent Colonies. Francis Asbury came out of hiding and resumed his leadership of the movement. Indeed, he was instrumental in leading the great bulk of American Methodists to secede from their Anglican parent body in 1784, becoming the Methodist Episcopal Church. The newly won independence of the Colonies made it problematic for American Methodists to remain 'loyal' to the Church of England (whose supreme governor was the very king, George III, whose rule the Colonies had thrown off), especially for Methodists who had supported American independence and been reviled by Anglicans for having done so.[25] Wesley, however, pragmatically bowed to the

24. Never buy new clothes but keep patching up the old ones.

25. Most of the Anglican clergy in the Colonies had left America and returned to England when the War of Independence broke out – they felt their duty lay with the English crown. American Methodists felt abandoned, and that sense of abandonment by 'English' clergy was a

need for American Methodists to become a separate body in the new circumstances created by independence. Still, he valued the Anglican Book of Common Prayer, and provided a new revised form of the Book for American Methodists, in which he adapted it in what he felt was a more fully Protestant direction. To that extent, liturgical continuity was maintained between Anglicanism and the Methodist Episcopal Church.

On the other hand, when Francis Asbury in 1787 took upon himself Episcopal status among American Methodists (which gave the new American Methodist Church its authentically Episcopalian character), Wesley strongly disapproved. He had never styled himself the Bishop of English Methodism, and saw no reason for Asbury's assumption of the venerable title. Charles Wesley, however, thought John was to blame for having approved the title 'superintendent' for Thomas Coke (1747–1814), Asbury's colleague in leading American Methodism, and for setting Coke apart to that office by the laying on of hands (as if Wesley were himself a bishop with powers of ordination). It was Coke who then ordained Asbury as his fellow superintendent over American Methodism in 1784. But Coke soon left the American Methodist Church for other fields of labour, leaving the Church in Asbury's hands – and Asbury insisted on the name and rank of bishop.

---

pivotal factor in the birth of the new American Methodist Episcopal Church.

3
Results of the Great Awakening

1. Changed lives

The most obvious result of the Great Awakening across the American Colonies was a legacy of changed lives. Jonathan Edwards emphasised this in his classic 1737 treatise, *Faithful Narrative of the Surprising Work of God in the Conversion of Many Hundred Souls in Northampton*:

> It was very wonderful to see how persons' affections were sometimes moved – when God did as it were suddenly open their eyes, and let into their minds a sense of the greatness of His grace, the fullness of Christ, and His readiness to save – after having been broken with apprehensions of divine wrath, and sunk into an abyss, under a sense of guilt which they were ready to think was beyond the mercy of God. Their joyful surprise has caused their hearts as it were to leap, so that they have been ready to break forth into laughter, tears often at the same time issuing like a flood, and intermingling a loud weeping. Sometimes they have not been able to forbear crying out with a loud voice, expressing their great admiration. In some, even the view of the glory of God's sovereignty, in the exercises of His grace, has surprised the soul with such sweetness, as to produce the same effects. I remember an instance of one, who, reading something concerning God's sovereign way of saving sinners, as being self-moved – having no regard to men's own righteousness as the motive of His grace, but as magnifying Himself and abasing man, or to that purpose – felt such a sudden rapture of joy and delight in the consideration of it: and yet then he suspected himself to be

> in a Christless condition, and had been long in great distress for fear that God would not have mercy on him.

Edwards gave several individual examples of the transformation wrought in individuals, their personal awakening out of spiritual deadness (a deadness perhaps encased within religious orthodoxy) to the knowledge and love of God in Christ. One such individual example was the young Northampton woman Abigail Hutchinson:

> At the last time, on Wednesday morning, while in the enjoyment of a spiritual view of Christ's glory and fullness, her soul was filled with distress for Christless persons, to consider what a miserable condition they were in. She felt a strong inclination immediately to go forth to warn sinners; and proposed it the next day to her brother to assist her in going from house to house; but her brother restrained her, by telling her of the unsuitableness of such a method.
>
> She told one of her sisters that day, that she loved all mankind, but especially the people of God. Her sister asked her why she loved all mankind. She replied, Because God has made them. After this, there happened to come into the shop where she was at work, three persons who were thought to have been lately converted: her seeing of them, as they stepped in one after another, so affected her, and so drew forth her love to them, that it overcame her, and she almost fainted. When they began to talk of the things of religion, it was more than she could bear; they were obliged to cease on that account. It was a very frequent thing with her to be overcome with the flow of affection to them whom she thought godly, in conversation with them, and sometimes only at the sight of them.
>
> She had many extraordinary discoveries of the glory of God and Christ; sometimes, in some particular attributes, and sometimes in many. She gave an account, that once, as those four words passed through her mind, wisdom, justice, goodness, and truth, her soul was filled with a sense of the glory of each of these divine attributes, but especially the last. Truth, said she, sunk the deepest! And, therefore, as these words passed, this was repeated, truth, truth! Her mind was so swallowed up with a sense of the glory of God's truth and

> other perfections, that she said, it seemed as though her life was going, and that she saw it was easy with God to take away her life by discoveries of Himself.

Such accounts could be multiplied almost indefinitely. This is not to say that the majority of Colonists experienced such a personal transformation, but simply that one of the observed characteristics of the Awakening was a sudden intensification of the number of conversions and their spiritual depth compared to 'normal' periods in church life.

2. Regional effects

In New England, the Awakening brought about a renewal of Congregational church life, and the unprecedented growth of Baptist churches (largely Calvinistic in theology). It has been estimated that around one hundred and fifty new Congregational churches were founded. As for Baptist churches, there were only twenty-five in the whole of New England in 1740, as the Awakening began to take hold; by 1804, there were three hundred and twelve. Then, as we have seen, there were also the Separate Congregational churches who broke away from the traditional New England system of a state-sponsored Church funded by a general tax on all citizens. These developments, however, although multiplying churches, had the effect of destroying the social sense of Puritan unity that New England had previously enjoyed. One modern historian of American religious history[1] argues that four distinct parties emerged in a once cohesive New England as a consequence of the Awakening:

(i) There were those who, in the wake of revival, separated from the established Congregational state-churches in the Colonies – the Separate Congregationalists and Baptists.

(ii) There were 'awakened' Congregationalists like Jonathan Edwards, who remained within the traditional system, but were willing to sacrifice the church's influence over

1. Mark Noll, in recent times the foremost Evangelical interpreter of American religious history.

the general population in order to purify the church of merely nominal members.

(iii) There were the 'Old Calvinists', who approved of the spiritual effects of the Awakening but wanted to maintain the old New England structures of a unified Christian society.

(iv) There were the principled opponents of the Awakening, typified in Congregationalist minister Charles Chauncy: influenced by Enlightenment ideals of rationalism, and hostile to revival for its perceived emotionalism. These men drifted off into Unitarianism.

In the Northern Colonies outside of New England (the 'Middle Colonies'), there was significant numerical growth of Presbyterians and Dutch Reformed. But there was schism too: both denominations broke apart in the 1740s into pro-Awakening and anti-Awakening wings. However, reconciliations were effected over the next two decades. When the broken Churches were finally reunited, the synthesis of old and new resulted in the retention of a strong Presbyterian and Dutch Reformed consciousness of their European churchly traditions, but also a less official and conventional, more democratic perception of church life. Ultimately, the Awakening in the Middle Colonies had a more unifying religious effect than in New England.

In the Southern Colonies, the chief outcome of the Awakening was the phenomenal growth of Baptists (see Part 2, section 5). No longer would Anglicanism be the exclusive or overwhelmingly dominant form of Protestantism. As an outcome of Baptist growth in the South and in New England, Baptists had become – by the time the Revolutionary War of Independence came in 1775 – the third largest Christian group in America, outstripped only by Congregationalists and Presbyterians.

3. General effects of the Awakening on America and American Protestantism

There can be little doubt that the Great Awakening had a significant overall impact on the character of Protestantism in the Colonies, and even more widely on the American consciousness. It strengthened the popular, democratic impulse within American Protestantism. This was bound up with the fact that intimately associated with the Awakening were vast, socially indiscriminate audiences in the open air, the deliberate use of what we would call the news media to promote the Awakening (adverts, personal accounts, printed and published sermons), a frequently off-the-cuff style of preaching designed to appeal directly to the heart (rather than the previous norm of the carefully prepared and read sermon), and a willingness to break with traditional denominations in pursuit of 'awakened' ideals.

It has been argued, with some plausibility, that the Awakening introduced a new spiritual flavour into American Protestantism, somewhat akin to German Pietism. Historian Mark Noll describes this as a shift from *English Puritanism* to *American Evangelicalism*. If we ask what the differences were, we should preface any answer by stating that they were subtle and nuanced, not an overnight transformation into some totally novel religion. With this proviso, it has been suggested that the following differences can be perceived. On the one hand, English Puritans certainly sought a vital spirituality, but they pursued it within the boundaries of a highly educated ministry, a firm reverence for the historical creeds and confessions of the Church, and an attitude of deference to the inherited Reformation tradition of how the biblical message and its textual basis should be understood. On the other hand, the emerging spirit of American Evangelicalism was more welcoming of strong and overt religious emotion as a norm, moulded and channelled by the wisdom of spiritual leaders chosen by the converted themselves, by private study of Scripture, and by deeply individual and personal experience-grounded conviction which, if provoked, was more than ready to defy establishments quite openly, forming new churches and denominations. A historically informed consciousness will discern that these are differences of emphasis rather than a sheer contrast between different religions. Even so, many historians judge that it is crucial to notice the fresh accent birthed in the American Awakening.

On a wider platform, the Awakening helped to stimulate a national consciousness among the Colonies as 'America' in distinction from Europe. The Awakening has been called America's first national event. George Whitefield and his preaching and its outcomes were being discussed loudly in every Colony. Ministers throughout the Colonies corresponded seriously with one another, taking up both pro- Awakening and anti-Awakening stances. The general indifference or antagonism of the Anglican Church in the Colonies toward the Awakening fostered suspicion of the English establishment among the Awakeners and the awakened, who were tempted to look upon 'English religion' as something unsympathetic to American concerns. This, it has been argued, was a factor helping to lay the groundwork for the American Revolution of 1775.

4
A word about slavery

In relatively recent times, there has been huge and even vitriolic controversy over the involvement of some of the American Awakeners in the institution of black slavery. George Whitefield, Jonathan Edwards, Samuel Davies, Devereux Jarratt, and other mighty evangelists and spiritual leaders, were slave-owners.[1] Does this in some way invalidate their status as "heroes of the faith"? Should we topple their statues and erase their names from the roll-call of Evangelical fame?

It should be recognised that this is not a historical but a moral controversy. The *facts*, largely, are not in dispute. Whitefield, Edwards, Davies, Jarratt, and others, were indeed slave-owners. The quarrel, rather, is over *values*. Sometimes the values of a

1. To give a concrete example, George Whitefield had black slaves working at his Bethesda orphanage in Georgia. On his death, his last will and testament bequeathed the orphanage to the Countess of Huntingdon; the legacy included fifty slaves. Whitefield was also instrumental in convincing the Colony of Georgia to legalise slavery. It had been outlawed in Georgia in 1735, but Whitefield helped persuade the Colony to change its mind, and in 1751 legal permission was given for black slaves to live in the Colony. Whitefield had come to believe that slaves were economically necessary to the upkeep of his orphanage with its four thousand acres of land. (It cost too much to employ non-slave labour.) It will of course not assuage anti-slavery sentiment, but it may be worth noting that Whitefield was also outspoken in arguing for humane treatment of slaves. By way of contrast, John Wesley became a strong opponent of the institution of black slavery, especially the slave trade, from the early 1770s onward. See the extract from his *Thoughts Upon Slavery* (1774) below.

previous age in church history – or of some people living in that age – are found to be unacceptable in the present age, and sometimes an honest reading of Scripture will show that those previous ages were in the wrong. This in turn leads to scepticism about the spiritual worth of those who held such abandoned values, now deemed offensive, even though those men were once regarded as among the luminaries of the faith.

Since this is not a historical controversy over facts, but a moral controversy over values, there is a sense in which the church historian, as a historian, has little to say about it. We record the facts. Our *moral* task, however, is to record *all* the facts, even those which may set our heroes in a bad light, as is the fate of the slave-owning Awakeners. They truly are set in a bad light. Yet it ought to be acknowledged that this is no new story. In previous volumes in this series, we have seen analogous incongruities. We recollect the fiercely and distastefully partisan personality of Cyril of Alexandria, a flawed saint and yet one of the most brilliant theologians of the patristic era; the enthusiastic endorsement of the wretched and bloody Crusades by Bernard of Clairvaux, one of the most spiritually-minded men of the Middle Ages; the death penalty (death by drowning) inflicted on Anabaptists in Zwingli's Zurich, with the noble Zwingli's tragic approval; the savage persecution of English Nonconformists by the Anglican authorities, especially under the repressive Clarendon Code in the period 1662–88; and other such moral anomalies.

Three things may be pointed out. First, there is no point in denying the failures of our ancestors. Glossing over sin is never appropriate. The present writer regards the slave-trade and the institution of black slavery as morally and theologically indefensible. The anti-slavery protests of John Wesley and Samuel Hopkins, recorded below, represent a purer insight. Second, no Christian or body of Christians in any age is ever promised or guaranteed an error-free moral consciousness, especially when certain errors are rife in their society. To think that such freedom is promised or guaranteed would be a species of sinless perfectionism. Third, it is humbling to reflect that future generations (if the Lord tarries) may discern serious moral errors in us, to which we ourselves are quite blind. C. S. Lewis was aware of this possibility, and once commented of his own generation that the future would probably discover in them moral aberrations in totally unexpected areas – areas in which President Roosevelt (regarded as a paragon of right moral sentiment) and Adolf Hitler shared a common mind.[2] Perhaps this humility about ourselves is the best lesson we can take away from the unsettling moral blind spots of our spiritual heroes in other times.

2. This observation is found in Lewis' essay *On the Reading of Old Books.*

PRIMARY HISTORICAL SOURCES

John Wesley's funeral sermon on George Whitefield

We are, in the second place, to take some view of his character. A little sketch of this was soon after published in the Boston Gazette; an extract of which is subjoined:

> 'Little can be said of him but what every friend to vital Christianity who has sat under his ministry will attest. In his public labors he has, for many years, astonished the world with his eloquence and devotion. With what divine pathos did he persuade the impenitent sinner to embrace the practice of piety and virtue! Filled with the spirit of grace, he spoke from the heart, and, with a fervency of zeal perhaps unequalled since the day of the Apostles, adorned the truths he delivered with the most graceful charms of rhetoric and oratory. From the pulpit he was unrivalled in the command of an ever-crowded auditory. Nor was he less agreeable and instructive in his private conversation; happy in a remarkable ease of address, willing to communicate, studious to edify. May the rising generation catch a spark of that flame which shone, with such distinguished luster, in the spirit and practice of this faithful servant of the most high God!'

2. A more particular, and equally just, character of him has appeared in one of the English papers. It may not be disagreeable to you to add the substance of this likewise:

> 'The character of this truly pious person must be deeply impressed on the heart of every friend to vital religion. In spite of a tender and delicate constitution, he continued

to the last day of his life, preaching with a frequency and fervour that seemed to exceed the natural strength of the most robust. Being called to the exercise of his function at an age when most young men are only beginning to qualify themselves for it, he had not time to make a very considerable progress in the learned languages. But this defect was amply supplied by a lively and fertile genius, by fervent zeal, and by a forcible and most persuasive delivery. And though in the pulpit he often found it needful by "the terrors of the Lord" to "persuade men", he had nothing gloomy in his nature; being singularly cheerful, as well as charitable and tender-hearted. He was as ready to relieve the bodily as the spiritual necessities of those that applied to him. It ought also to be observed, that he constantly enforced upon his audience every moral duty; particularly industry in their several callings, and obedience to their superiors. He endeavoured, by the most extraordinary efforts of preaching, in different places, and even in the open fields, to rouse the lower class of people from the last degree of inattention and ignorance to a sense of religion. For this, and his other labours, the name of GEORGE WHITEFIELD will long be remembered with esteem and veneration.'

3. That both these accounts are just and impartial, will readily be allowed; that is, as far as they go. But they go little farther than the outside of his character. They show you the preacher, but not the man, the Christian, the saint of God. May I be permitted to add a little on this head, from a personal knowledge of near forty years. Indeed, I am thoroughly sensible how difficult it is to speak on so delicate a subject; what prudence is required to avoid both extremes, to say neither too little nor too much! Nay, I know it is impossible to speak at all, to say either less or more, without incurring from some the former, from others the latter censure. Some will seriously think that too little is said; and others, that it is too much. But without attending to this, I will speak just what I know, before Him to whom we are all to give an account.

4. Mention has already been made of his unparalleled zeal, his indefatigable activity, his tender-heartedness to the

afflicted, and charitableness toward the poor. But should we not likewise mention his deep gratitude to all whom God had used as instruments of good to him – of whom he did not cease to speak in the most respectful manner, even to his dying day. Should we not mention, that he had a heart susceptible of the most generous and the most tender friendship? I have frequently thought that this, of all others, was the distinguishing part of his character. How few have we known of so kind a temper, of such large and flowing affections! Was it not principally by this, that the hearts of others were so strangely drawn and knit to him? Can anything but love beget love? This shone in his very countenance, and continually breathed in all his words, whether in public or private. Was it not this, which, quick and penetrating as lightning, flew from heart to heart which gave that life to his sermons, his conversations, his letters? Ye are witnesses!

5. But away with the vile misconstruction of men of corrupt minds, who know of no love but what is earthly and sensual! Be it remembered, at the same time, that he was endued with the most nice and unblemished modesty. His office called him to converse very frequently and largely with women as well as men; and those of every age and condition. But his whole behaviour towards them was a practical comment on that advice of St. Paul to Timothy: 'Entreat the elder women as mothers, the younger as sisters, with all purity.'

6. Meantime, how suitable to the friendliness of his spirit was the frankness and openness of his conversation! – although it was as far removed from rudeness on the one hand, as from guile and disguise on the other. Was not this frankness at once a fruit and a proof of his courage and intrepidity? Armed with these, he feared not the faces of men, but 'used great plainness of speech' to persons of every rank and condition, high and low, rich and poor; endeavouring only 'by manifestation of the truth to commend himself to every man's conscience in the sight of God.'

John Wesley
Funeral Sermon for George Whitefield

John Wesley: Against black slavery

May I speak plainly to you? I must. Love constrains me: Love to *you*, as well as to those you are concerned with.

Is there a GOD? you know there is. Is He a just GOD? Then there must be a state of retribution: A state wherein the just GOD will reward every man according to his works. Then what reward will He render to *you*? O think betimes! Before you drop into eternity! Think now, *He shall have judgment without mercy, that shewed no mercy.*

Are you *a man?* Then you should have a *human* heart. But have you indeed? What is your heart made of? Is there no such principle as compassion there? Do you never *feel* another's pain? Have you no sympathy? No sense of human woe? No pity for the miserable? When you saw the flowing eyes, the heaving breasts, the bleeding sides and tortured limbs of your fellow-creatures, was you a stone, or a brute? Did you look upon them with the eyes of a tiger? When you squeezed the agonizing creatures down in the ship, or when you threw their poor mangled remains into the sea, had you no relenting? Did not one tear drop from your eye, one sigh escape from your breast? Do you feel no relenting *now*? If you do not, you must go on, till the measure of your iniquities is full. Then will the great GOD deal with *you*, as you have dealt with *them*, and require all their blood at your hands. And at that day it shall be more tolerable for *Sodom* and *Gomorrah* than for you! But if your heart does relent, though in a small degree, know it is a call from the GOD of love. And today, if you hear His voice, harden not your heart. – Today resolve, GOD being your helper, to escape for your life. – Regard not money! All that a man hath will he give for his life? Whatever you lose, lose not your soul: nothing can countervail that loss. Immediately quit the horrid trade: At all events, be an honest man.

This equally concerns every merchant, who is engaged in the slave-trade. It is you that induce the *African* villain, to sell his countrymen; and in order thereto, to steal, rob, murder men, women and children without number: By enabling the *English* villain to pay him for so doing; whom you overpay for his execrable labour. It is *your* money, that is the spring of all, that impowers him to go on: So that whatever he or the *African* does in this matter, it is all *your* act and deed. And is your conscience quite reconciled to this? Does it never reproach you at all? Has gold entirely blinded your eyes, and stupefied your heart? Can you see, can you *feel* no harm therein? Is it doing as you would be done to? Make the case your own. 'Master,' (said a slave at *Liverpool* to the merchant that owned him), 'what if some of my countrymen were to come here, and take away my mistress, and master *Tommy*, and master *Billy*, and carry them into our country, and make them slaves, how would you like it?' His answer was worthy of a man: 'I will never buy a slave more while I live.' O let his resolution be yours! Have no more any part in this detestable business. Instantly leave it to those unfeeling wretches, 'Who laugh at human nature and compassion!' Be *you* a man! Not a wolf, a devourer of the human species! Be merciful, that you may obtain mercy!

And this equally concerns every gentleman that has an estate in our *American* plantations: Yea all slave-holders of whatever rank and degree; seeing *men-buyers* are exactly on a level with *men-stealers*. Indeed you say, 'I pay honestly for my goods: and I am not concerned to know how they are come by.' Nay, but you are: You are deeply concerned, to know they are honestly come by. Otherwise you are partaker with a thief, and are not a jot honester than him. But you know, they are not honestly come by: You know they are procured by means, nothing near so innocent as picking of pockets, house-breaking, or robbery upon the highway. You know they are procured by a deliberate series of more complicated villainy, of fraud, robbery and murder than was ever practiced either by *Mahometans* or *Pagans*: in particular by murders, of all kinds; by the blood of the innocent poured upon the ground like water.

Now it is *your* money that pays the merchant, and thro' him the captain, and the *African* butchers. *You* therefore are guilty, yea, principally guilty, of all these frauds, robberies and murders. You are the spring that puts all the rest in motion: they would not stir a step without *you*: – Therefore the blood of all these wretches, who die before their time, whether in their country, or elsewhere lies upon *your* head. *The blood of thy brother,* (for, whether thou wilt believe it or no, such he is in the sight of Him that made him) *crieth against thee from the earth,* from the ship, and from the waters. O, whatever it costs, put a stop to its cry before it be too late. Instantly, at any price, were it the half of your goods, deliver thyself from blood-guiltiness! Thy hands, thy bed, thy furniture, thy house, thy lands are at present stained with blood. Surely it is enough; accumulate no more guilt; spill no more blood of the innocent! Do not hire another to shed blood: Do not pay him for doing it! Whether you are a Christian or no, shew yourself a man; be not more savage than a lion or a bear!

Perhaps you will say, 'I do not *buy* any negroes: I only *use* those left me by my father.' – So far is well; but is it enough to satisfy your own conscience? Had your father, have *you,* has any man living, a right to use another as a slave? It cannot be, even setting revelation aside. It cannot be, that either war, or contract, can give any man such a property in another as he has in sheep and oxen. Much less is it possible, that any child of man, should ever be *born a slave.* Liberty is the right of every human creature, as soon as he breathes the vital air. And no human law can deprive him of that right, which he derives from the law of nature.

If therefore you have any regard to justice, (to say nothing of mercy, nor of the revealed law of GOD) render unto all their due. Give liberty to whom liberty is due, that is to every child of man, to every partaker of human nature. Let none serve you but by his own act and deed, by his own voluntary choice.--Away with all whips, all chains, all compulsion! Be gentle towards men. And see that you invariably do unto everyone, as you would he should do unto *you.*

O Thou GOD of love, thou who art loving to every man, and whose mercy is over all Thy works: Thou who art the Father of the spirits of all flesh, and who art rich in mercy unto all: Thou who hast mingled of one blood, all the nations upon earth: Have compassion upon these outcasts of men, who are trodden down as dung upon the earth! Arise and help these that have no helper, whose blood is spilt upon the ground like water! Are not these also the work of Thine own hands, the purchase of Thy Son's blood? Stir them up to cry unto Thee in the land of their captivity; and let their complaint come up before Thee; let it enter into Thy ears! Make even those that lead them away captive to pity them, and turn their captivity as the rivers in the south. O burst Thou all their chains in sunder; more especially the chains of their sins: Thou, Saviour of all, make them free, that they may be free indeed!

John Wesley
Thoughts upon Slavery

Gilbert Tennent: The Danger of an Unconverted Ministry

The ministry of natural men is uncomfortable to gracious souls. The enmity that is put between the seed of the woman and the seed of the serpent will, now and then, be creating jars. And no wonder; for as it was of old, so it is now: 'He that was born after the flesh, persecuteth him that was born after the Spirit.' This enmity is not one grain less in unconverted ministers than in others; though it is possible it may be better polished with wit and rhetoric, and gilded with the specious names of zeal, fidelity, peace, good order, and unity. Natural men, not having true love to Christ or the souls of their fellow creatures, find their discourses are cold and sapless, and, as it were, freeze between their lips. And not being sent of God, they lack the divine authority with which the faithful ambassadors of Christ are clothed, who herein resemble their blessed Master of whom it is said, 'He taught as one having authority, and not as the scribes' (Matt. 7:29).

And Pharisee-teachers, having no experience of a special work of the Holy Ghost upon their own souls, are therefore neither inclined to nor fitted for discoursing frequently, clearly, and pathetically upon such important subjects. The application of their discourses is either short or indistinct and general. They do not distinguish the precious from the vile, and divide not to every man his portion, according to the apostolic direction to Timothy. No! They carelessly offer a common mess to their people, and leave it to them to divide it among themselves as they see fit. This is, indeed, their general practice, which is bad enough; but sometimes they do worse by misapplying the Word through ignorance or anger. They often strengthen the hands of the wicked by promising him life. They comfort people before they convince them, sow before they plow, and are busy in raising a fabric before they lay a foundation. These foolish builders do but strengthen men's carnal security by their soft, selfish, cowardly discourses. They do not have the courage or honesty to thrust the nail of terror into sleeping souls. Nay, sometimes they strive with all their might to fasten terror into the hearts of the righteous, and so to make those sad whom God would not have made sad!

And this happens when pious people begin to suspect their hypocrisy, for which they have good reason, I may add that, inasmuch as Pharisee-teachers seek after righteousness, as it were, by the works of the law themselves, they therefore do not distinguish as they ought between Law and Gospel in their discourses to others. They keep driving, driving, to duty, duty, under this notion that it will recommend natural men to the favor of God, or entitle them to the promises of grace and salvation. And thus those blind guides fix a deluded world upon the false foundation of their own righteousness, and so exclude them from the dear Redeemer. All the doings of unconverted men not proceeding from the principles of faith, love, and a new nature, nor being directed to the divine glory as their highest end, but flowing from, and tending to, self as their principle and end, are, doubtless, damnably wicked in their manner of performance, and deserve the wrath and curse of a sin-avenging God.

Neither can any other encouragement be justly given them but that, in the way of duty, there is a peradventure or probability of obtaining mercy. And natural men, lacking the experience of those spiritual difficulties which pious souls are exposed to in this vale of tears, do not know how to speak a word to the weary in season. Their prayers are also cold; little child-like love to God or pity to poor perishing souls runs through their veins. Their conversation has nothing of the savor of Christ, neither is it perfumed with the spices of heaven. They seem to make as little distinction in their practice as preaching. They love those unbelievers that are kind to them better than many Christians, and choose them for companions, contrary to Psalm 15:4, Psalm 119:115 and Galatians 6:10. Poor Christians are stunted and starved who are put to feed on such bare pastures, on such 'dry nurses,' as Rev. Mr. (Arthur) Hildersham justly calls them. It's only when the wise virgins sleep that they can bear with those dead dogs who can't bark; but when the Lord revives His people, they can't but abhor them. O! It is ready to break their very hearts with grief, to see how lukewarm those Pharisee-teachers are in their public discourses, while sinners are sinking into damnation in multitudes.

Gilbert Tennent
The Danger of an Unconverted Ministry

Jonathan Edwards' conversion

I began to have a new kind of apprehensions and ideas of Christ, and the work of redemption, and the glorious way of salvation by Him. I had an inward, sweet sense of these things, that at times came into my heart; and my soul was led away in pleasant views and contemplations of them. And my mind was greatly engaged, to spend my time in reading and meditating on Christ; and the beauty and excellency of His person, and the lovely way of salvation, by free grace in Him. I found no books so delightful to me, as those that treated of these subjects. Those words, Cant. 2:1, used to be abundantly with me: 'I am the rose of Sharon, the lily of the valleys.' The words seemed to me, sweetly to represent, the loveliness and beauty of Jesus Christ. And the whole Book of Canticles used to be pleasant to me; and I used to be much in reading it, about that time. And found, from time to time, an inward sweetness, that used, as it were, to carry me away in my contemplations; in what I know not how to express otherwise, than by a calm, sweet abstraction of soul from all the concerns of this world; and a kind of vision, or fixed ideas and imaginations, of being alone in the mountains, or some solitary wilderness, far from all mankind, sweetly conversing with Christ, and wrapped and swallowed up in God. The sense I had of divine things, would often of a sudden as it were, kindle up a sweet burning in my heart; an ardor of my soul, that I know not how to express.

Not long after I first began to experience these things, I gave an account to my father, of some things that had passed in my mind. I was pretty much affected by the discourse we had together. And when the discourse was ended, I walked abroad alone, in a solitary place in my father's pasture, for contemplation. And as I was walking there, and looked up on the sky and clouds; there came into my mind, a sweet sense of the glorious majesty and grace of God, that I know not how to express. I seemed to see them both in a sweet conjunction: majesty and meekness joined together: it was a sweet, and gentle, and holy majesty; and also a majestic meekness; an awful sweetness; a high, and great, and holy gentleness ...

It is affecting to me to think, how ignorant I was, when I was a young Christian, of the bottomless, infinite depths of wickedness, pride, hypocrisy and deceit left in my heart.

I have vastly a greater sense, of my universal, exceeding dependence on God's grace and strength, and mere good pleasure, of late, than I used formerly to have; and have experienced more of an abhorrence of my own righteousness. The thought of any comfort or joy, arising in me, on any consideration, or reflection on my own amiableness, or any of my performances or experiences, or any goodness of heart or life, is nauseous and detestable to me. And yet I am greatly afflicted with a proud and self-righteous spirit; much more sensibly, than I used to be formerly. I see that serpent rising and putting forth its head, continually, everywhere, all around me.

Though it seems to me, that in some respects I was a far better Christian, for two or three years after my first conversion, than I am now; and lived in a more constant delight and pleasure: yet of late years, I have had a more full and constant sense of the absolute sovereignty of God, and a delight in that sovereignty; and have had more of a sense of the glory of Christ, as a mediator, as revealed in the Gospel.

Jonathan Edwards
Personal Narrative (c.1740)

Jonathan Edwards: The affections in religion

That religion which God requires, and will accept, does not consist in weak, dull, and lifeless wishes, raising us but a little above a state of indifference: God, in His word, greatly insists upon it, that we be good in earnest, 'fervent in spirit,' and our hearts vigorously engaged in religion: Rom. 12:11, 'Be ye fervent in spirit, serving the Lord.' Deut. 10:12, 'And now, Israel, what doth the Lord thy God require of thee, but to fear the Lord thy God, to walk in all His ways, and to love Him, and to serve the Lord thy God with all thy heart, and with all thy soul?' and chap. 6:4, 6, 'Hear, O Israel, the Lord our God is one Lord: And thou shalt love the Lord thy God with all thy heart, and with all thy might.' It is such a fervent vigorous engagedness of the heart in religion, that is the fruit of a real circumcision of the heart, or true regeneration, and that has the promises of life; Deut. 30:6, 'And the Lord thy God will circumcise thine heart, and the heart of thy seed, to love the Lord thy God with all thy heart, and with all thy soul, that thou mayest live.'

If we be not in good earnest in religion, and our wills and inclinations be not strongly exercised, we are nothing. The things of religion are so great, that there can be no suitableness in the exercises of our hearts, to their nature and importance, unless they be lively and powerful. In nothing is vigor in the actings of our inclinations so requisite, as in religion; and in nothing is lukewarmness so odious. True religion is evermore a powerful thing; and the power of it appears, in the first place in the inward exercises of it in the heart, where is the principal and original seat of it. Hence true religion is called the power of godliness, in distinction from the external appearances of it, that are the form of it, 2 Tim. 3:5: 'Having a form of godliness, but denying the power of it.' The Spirit of God, in those that have sound and solid religion, is a spirit of powerful holy affection; and therefore, God is said 'to have given the Spirit of power, and of love, and of a sound mind,' 2 Tim. 1:7. And such, when they receive the Spirit of God, in His sanctifying and saving influences, are said to be 'baptized with the Holy Ghost, and with fire;' by reason of the power and fervor of those exercises the Spirit of God excites in their hearts, whereby their hearts, when grace is in exercise, may be said to 'burn within them;' as is said of the disciples, Luke 24:32.

The business of religion is from time to time compared to those exercises, wherein men are wont to have their hearts and strength greatly exercised and engaged, such as running, wrestling or agonizing for a great prize or crown, and fighting with strong enemies that seek our lives, and warring as those, that by violence take a city or kingdom. And though true grace has various degrees, and there are some that are but babes in Christ, in whom the exercise of the inclination and will, towards divine and heavenly things, is comparatively weak; yet everyone that has the power of godliness in his heart, has his inclinations and heart exercised towards God and divine things, with such strength and vigor that these holy exercises do prevail in him above all carnal or natural affections, and are effectual to overcome them: for every true disciple of Christ 'loves Him above father or mother, wife and children, brethren and sisters, houses and lands: yea, than his own life.' From hence it follows, that wherever true religion is, there are vigorous exercises of the inclination and will towards divine objects: but by what was said before, the vigorous, lively, and sensible [felt] exercises of the will, are no other than the affections of the soul.

Jonathan Edwards
Treatise Concerning Religious Affections, Part 1

Jonathan Edwards: God's foreknowledge

First, I am to prove, that God has an absolute and certain Foreknowledge of the free actions of moral Agents. One would think it wholly needless to enter on such an argument with any that profess themselves Christians: but so it is; God's certain

Foreknowledge of the free acts of moral Agents, is denied by some that pretend to believe the Scriptures to be the Word of God; and especially of late. I therefore shall consider the evidence of such a prescience in the Most High, as fully as the designed limits of this essay will admit; – supposing myself herein to have to do with such as own the truth of the Bible.

Arg. I. My first argument shall be taken from God's prediction of such events. Here I would, in the first place, lay down these two things as axioms. 1. If God does not foreknow, He cannot foretell such events; that is, He cannot peremptorily and certainly foretell them. If God has no more than an uncertain guess concerning events of this kind, then He can declare no more than an uncertain guess. Positively to foretell, is to profess to foreknow, or declare positive Foreknowledge. If God does not certainly foreknow the future Volitions of moral Agents, then neither can He certainly foreknow those events which are dependent on these Volitions. The existence of the one depending on the existence of the other, the knowledge of the existence of the one depends on the knowledge of the existence of the other; and the one cannot be more certain than the other.

Therefore, how many, how great, and how extensive soever the consequences of the Volitions of moral Agents may be; though they should extend to an alteration of the state of things through the universe, and should be continued in a series of successive events to all eternity, and should in the progress of things branch forth into an infinite number of series, each of them going on in an endless chain of events; God must be as ignorant of all these consequences, as He is of the Volition whence they first take their rise: and the whole state of things depending on them, how important, extensive, and vast soever, must be hid from Him. These positions being such as, I suppose, none will deny, I now proceed to observe the following things.

1. Men's moral conduct and qualities, their virtues and vices, their wickedness and good practice, things rewardable and punishable, have often been foretold by God. – Pharaoh's moral conduct, in refusing to obey God's command, in letting His people go, was foretold. God says to Moses, Exod. iii. 19.

'I am sure that the king of Egypt will not let you go.' Here God professes not only to guess at, but to know Pharaoh's future disobedience. In chap. vii. 4. God says, 'but Pharaoh shall not hearken unto you; that I may lay mine hand upon Egypt,' &c. And chap. ix. 30. Moses says to Pharaoh, 'as for thee, and thy servants, I know that ye will not fear the Lord.' See also chap. xi. 9.

The moral conduct of Josiah, by name, in his zealously exerting himself to oppose idolatry, in particular acts, was foretold above three hundred years before he was born, and the prophecy sealed by a miracle, and renewed and confirmed by the words of a second prophet, as what surely would not fail, (1 Kings xiii. 1 – 6, 32.) This prophecy was also in effect a prediction of the moral conduct of the people, in upholding their schismatical and idolatrous worship until that time, and the idolatry of those priests of the high places, which it is foretold Josiah should offer upon that altar of Bethel. Micah foretold the foolish and sinful conduct of Ahab, in refusing to hearken to the word of the Lord by him, and choosing rather to hearken to the false prophets, in going to Ramoth Gilead to his ruin, (1 Kings xxii. 20 – 22.)

The moral conduct of Hazael was foretold, in that cruelty he should be guilty of; on which Hazael says, 'what, is thy servant a dog, that he should do this thing!' The prophet speaks of the event as what he knew, and not what he conjectured, 2 Kings viii. 12. 'I know the evil that thou wilt do unto the children of Israel: Thou wilt dash their children, and rip up their women with child.' The moral conduct of Cyrus is foretold, long before he had a being, in his mercy to God's people, and regard to the true God, in turning the captivity of the Jews, and promoting the building of the temple, (Isa. xliv. 28. and xlv. 13. compare 2 Chron. xxxvi. 22, 23. and Ezra i. 1 – 4.)

How many instances of the moral conduct of the kings of the north and south, particular instances of the wicked behaviour of the kings of Syria and Egypt, are foretold in the 11th chapter of Daniel! Their corruption, violence, robbery, treachery, and lies. And particularly, how much is foretold of the horrid wickedness of Antiochus Epiphanes, called there 'a vile person,' instead of Epiphones, or illustrious! In that chapter, and also in chap. viii. ver. 9, 14, 23, to the end, are foretold his flattery, deceit, and lies, his having 'his heart set to do mischief,' and set 'against the holy covenant,' his 'destroying and treading under foot the holy people,' in a marvellous manner, his 'having indignation against the holy covenant, setting his heart against it, and conspiring against it,' his 'polluting the sanctuary of strength, treading it under foot, taking away the daily sacrifice, and placing the abomination that maketh desolate;' his great pride, 'magnifying himself against God, and uttering marvellous blasphemies against Him,' until God in indignation should destroy him.

Withal, the moral conduct of the Jews, on occasion of his persecution, is predicted. It is foretold, that 'he should corrupt many by flatteries,' (chap. xi. 32 – 35.) But that others should behave with a glorious constancy and fortitude, in opposition to him, (ver. 32.) And that some good men should fall and repent, (ver. 35,) Christ foretold Peter's sin, in denying his Lord, with its circumstances, in a peremptory manner. And so, that great sin of Judas, in betraying his master, and its dreadful and eternal punishment in hell, was foretold in the like positive manner, Matt. xxvi. 21 – 25, and parallel places in the other Evangelists.

Jonathan Edwards
***The Freedom of the Will*, section 11**

Sarah Edwards: Jonathan Edwards' first impressions

They say there is a young lady in [New Haven, Connecticut] who is be loved of that Great Being, who made and rules the world, and that there are certain seasons in which this Great Being, in some way or other invisible, comes to her and fills her mind with exceeding sweet delight, and that she hardly cares for anything, except to meditate on Him – that she expects after a while to be received up where He is, to be raised up out of the world and caught up into heaven; being assured that He loves her too well to let her remain at a distance from Him always.

There she is to dwell with Him, and to be ravished with His love and delight forever. Therefore, if you present all the world before her, with the richest of its treasures, she disregards it and cares not for it, and is unmindful of any pain or affliction. She has a strange sweetness in her mind, and singular purity in her affections; is most just and conscientious in all her conduct; and you could not persuade her to do anything wrong or sinful, if you would give her all the world, lest she should offend this Great Being. She is of a wonderful sweetness, calmness, and universal benevolence of mind; especially after this Great God has manifested Himself to her mind. She will sometimes go about from place to place, singing sweetly; and seems to be always full of joy and pleasure; and no one knows for what. She loves to be alone, walking in the fields and groves, and seems to have someone invisible always conversing with her.

Jonathan Edwards
Writing in 1723 (when Sarah Pierrepont, as she then was, was aged thirteen)

Preaching to Native Americans

Friday, Oct. 5. We arrived at Susquehannah river, at a place called Opeholhoupung: found there twelve Indian houses: after I had saluted the king in a friendly manner, I told him my business, and that my desire was to teach them Christianity. After some consultation, the Indians gathered, and I preached to them. And when I had done, I asked if they would hear me again. They replied, that they would consider of it; and soon after sent me word, that they would immediately attend, if I would preach: which I did, with freedom, both times. When I asked them again, whether they would hear me further, they replied, they would the next day. I was exceeding sensible of the impossibility of doing anything for the poor heathen without special assistance from above: and my soul seemed to rest on God, and leave it to Him to do as He pleased in that which I saw was His own cause: and indeed, through divine goodness, I had felt something of this frame most of the time while I was traveling thither, and in some measure before I set out.

'Saturday, Oct. 6. Rose early and besought the Lord for help in my great work. Near noon preached again to the Indians; and in the afternoon visited them from house to house, and invited them to come and hear me again the next day, and put off their hunting design, which they were just entering upon, till Monday. "This night," I trust, "the Lord stood by me," to encourage and strengthen my soul: I spent more than an hour in secret retirement; was enabled to "pour out my heart before God," for the increase of grace in my soul, for ministerial endowments, for success among the poor Indians, for God's ministers and people, for distant dear friends, &c. Blessed be God!'

David Brainerd

***Life and Diary of David Brainerd*, edited by Jonathan Edwards**

The Philadelphia Confession: The additions to the 1689 Baptist Confession

Chapter 23

Of Singing of Psalms & etc.

We believe that singing the praises of God, is a holy ordinance of Christ, and not a part of natural religion, or a moral duty only; but that it is brought under divine institution, it being enjoined on the churches of Christ to sing psalms, hymns, and spiritual songs; and that the whole church in their public assemblies (as well as private Christians) ought to sing God's praises according to the best light they have received. Moreover, it was practised in the great representative church by our Lord Jesus Christ with His disciples, after He had instituted and celebrated the sacred ordinance of His holy supper, as a commemorative token of redeeming love.

Chapter 31

Of the Laying On Of Hands

We believe that laying on of hands, with prayer, upon baptised believers, as such, is an ordinance of Christ, and ought to be submitted unto by all such persons that are admitted to partake of the Lord's Supper, and that the end of this ordinance is not for the extraordinary gifts of the Spirit, but for a farther reception of the Holy Spirit of promise, or for the addition of the graces of the Spirit, and the influences thereof; to confirm, strengthen, and comfort them in Christ Jesus, it being ratified and established by the extraordinary gifts of the Spirit in the primitive times, to abide in the church as meeting together on the first day of the week was, that being the day of worship, or Christian sabbath, under the Gospel, and as preaching the word was, and as baptism was, and prayer was, and singing psalms, etc. was, so this laying on of hands was, for as the whole Gospel was confirmed by signs and wonders, and divers miracles and gifts of the Holy Ghost in general, so was every ordinance in like manner confirmed in particular.

Samuel Davies on Repentance

Let me then, in the first place, publish the royal edict of the King of Heaven in this assembly: *God commandeth all men to repent*; He commands you in various ways; commands you with the motions of His Spirit, striving with you, and by the voice of your own consciences, which is the voice of God! commands you by His providence, which tends to lead you to repentance, and especially by His Gospel, which He has sent to you for this end. He now commands you by my mouth; for while I speak what His word authorises, it does not lose its efficacy, nor cease to be His word by passing through my lips. Remember, He commands you, He lays His authority upon you, to repent. You are not left to your discretion in the case. Dare you reject the known, express command of the divine Majesty? Should a voice now break from the excellent glory, directed to each of you by name, saying, *Repent! repent!* would it not startle you? would it not shock you, to set yourselves in opposition to so express and immediate a command of the God that made you?

Well, His command to you in the Gospel is as real, as authoritative and binding, as an immediate voice from heaven. And dare you disobey it? Dare you go home this day with this additional guilt upon you, of disobeying a known command of the supreme Lord of heaven and earth? Dare you provoke Him to jealousy? Are you stronger than He? Can you harden yourselves against Him, and yet prosper? I again proclaim it aloud in your hearing. The King of kings, my Master, has issued out His royal mandate, requiring you, by these presents,[1] to repent, upon pain of everlasting damnation. This day it is proclaimed in your ears, therefore, this day repent. If you refuse to repent, let this conviction follow you home, and perpetually haunt you, that you have this day, when you were met together under pretence of worshipping God, knowingly disobeyed the great Gospel-command. And to the great God you must answer for your disobedience.

In the next place, my text tells you, He commands all men to repent: all men, of all ranks and characters. This command, therefore, is binding upon you all. The great God cries to you all, *Repent!* Repent, young and old, rich and poor, white and black, free and bond: – Repent, ye young sinners, now, while your hearts are soft and tender, and your passions easily moved, and you are not hardened by a long course of habitual sinning: – Repent, ye grey-headed veteran sinners, now at last repent, when the load of sins, heaped up for so many years, lies so heavy upon you, and you are walking every moment on the slippery brink of eternity: – Repent, ye rich men; ye are not above this command: – Repent, ye poor; ye are not beneath it: – Repent, ye poor slaves; your colour, or low state in life, cannot free you from this command: – Repent, ye masters, for your sins against your Master, who is in heaven. In short, God commandeth all men, kings and subjects, the highest and the lowest, and all the intermediate ranks, to repent.

To render the call still more pointed and universal, it is added, *He commandeth all men everywhere, to repent*. Everywhere, in city and country, in palaces and cottages; in Europe, Asia, Africa and America, wherever the trumpet of the Gospel sounds the alarm to repent; in Virginia, in this very spot, where we now stand. Here the command of God finds you out, and calls you

1. These present words.

to repent. Repentance is not a local duty, but it extends as far as human nature, as far as the utmost boundaries of this guilty world. Wherever there are sinners under a dispensation of grace, there this command reaches. It reaches to the busy merchant in his store, to the laborious planter in the field, and to the tradesman in his shop; to the sailor tossing on the waves, and to the inhabitant of solid ground; to the man of learning in his study, and to the illiterate peasant; to the judge upon the bench, as well as to the criminal in the dungeon; to the man of sobriety, to the unthinking rake, and to the brutish debauchee; to the minister in the pulpit, and to the people in their pews; to the dissenter in the meeting-house, and to the conformist in church; to husbands and wives; to parents and children; to masters and servants; to all the sons of men, whatever they are, wherever they dwell, whatever they are doing; to all these the command reaches. And do you not find yourselves included in it? If you are men, if you dwell anywhere upon this guilty globe, you are included; for let me tell you once more, God commandeth all men, everywhere, to repent.

Nor are you allowed to delay your compliance. Repentance is your present duty: For *now He commandeth all men everywhere to repent*: Now, when the times of ignorance are over, and the Gospel sheds heavenly day among you: Now, when He will no longer wink, or connive at your impenitence, but takes strict notice of it with just indignation: Now, while the day of grace lasts, and there is place left for repentance: Now, before you are hardened through the deceitfulness of sin, and while His Spirit is striving with you: Now, while His judgments are in the earth, and your country is surrounded with the terrors of war:[2] Now, while He is publishing His command to a guilty country to repent, by the horrid sound of trumpets and cannon: Now, while you have time, which may be taken from you the next year, the next week, or perhaps, the very next moment: Now, while you enjoy health

2. The French and Indian War of 1754–63, in which the Colonies and the British (and some Native Americans) victoriously fought the French (and some other Native Americans). It resulted in a massive loss of French American territory to the British.

of body, and the exercise of your reason; and your attention is not tied down to pain and agony: Now, and not tomorrow; not upon a sickbed; not in a dying hour: Now is the time, in which God commands you to repent: He does not allow you one hour's delay; and what right have you to allow it to yourselves?

Therefore, now, this moment, let us all repent; all, without exception. Why should there not be one assembly of true penitents upon our guilty globe? And, O! why should it not be this? Why should not repentance be as universal as sin? And, since we are all sinners, O! why should we not all be humble penitents? Repent you must, either in time or eternity, upon earth, or in hell. You cannot possibly avoid it. The question is not, Shall I repent? for that is beyond a doubt. But the question is, 'Shall I repent now, when it may reform and save me? or shall I put it off to the eternal world, when my repentance will be my punishment, and can answer no end but to torment me?'[3] And is this a hard question! Does not common sense determine it in favour of the present time? Therefore, let the duty be as extensively observed as it is commanded: Let all men everywhere repent. Blessed God! pour out upon us a spirit of grace and supplication, that there may be a great mourning among us, that each of us may mourn apart, and our wives apart; that we may *mourn, as one that mourneth for an only son; and be in bitterness, as one that is in bitterness for a firstborn.* Zech. xii. 10. Grant this, for Jesus's sake! Amen.

Samuel Davies

The Nature and Necessity of True Repentance

Isaac Backus: Religious liberty

In all civil governments some are appointed to judge for others, and have power to compel others to submit to their judgment: but our Lord has most plainly forbidden us, either

3. The traditional Augustinian view that the torments of hell include 'a sterile repentance', a remorse for sin without any change of heart to the love of God. This was seen as a spiritual and eternal counterpart to the tears of Esau: 'For you know that afterward, when Esau desired to inherit the blessing, he was rejected; he found no place for repentance, even though he sought it earnestly with tears' (Heb. 12:17).

to assume or submit to any such thing in religion (Matt. 23:1-9, Luke 22:25-27). He declares, that the cause of His coming in to the world, was to bear witness unto the truth; and says He, Every one that is of the truth heareth My voice. This is the nature of His Kingdom, which He says, Is not of this world: and gives that as the reason why His servants should not fight, or defend Him with the sword (John 18:36-37). And it appears to us that the true difference and exact limits between ecclesiastical and civil government is this, That the church is armed with light and truth, to pull down the strong holds of iniquity, and to gain souls to Christ, and into His church, to be governed by His rules therein; and again to exclude such from their communion, who will not be so governed; while the state is armed with the sword to guard the peace, and the civil rights of all persons and societies, and to punish those who violate the same.

And where these two kinds of government, and the weapons which belong to them, are well distinguished, and improved according to the true nature and end of their institution, the effects are happy, and they do not at all interfere with each other: but where they have been confounded together, no tongue nor pen can fully describe the mischiefs that have ensued of which the Holy Ghost gave early and plain warnings. He gave notice to the church, that the main of those antichristian confusions and abominations, would be drawn by philosophy and deceit, from the hand-writing of ordinances that Christ has blotted out. And to avoid the same, directs the saints to walk in Christ Jesus as they received Him, rooted and built up in Him, and established in the faith as they have been taught; viewing that they are complete in Him, which is the HEAD over ALL PRINCIPALITY and POWER. Therefore he charges them not to be beguiled into a voluntary humility, by such fleshly minds as do not hold this Head, but would subject them to ordinances after the doctrines and commandments of men (Col. 2).

Now 'tis well known that this glorious Head made no use of secular force in the first setting up of the Gospel church, when it might seem to be peculiarly needful if ever; and it is also very evident, that ever since men came into the way of using force in such affairs, their main arguments to support it have been drawn from the old Jewish constitution and ordinances.

Isaac Backus
Appeal to the Public for Religious Liberty, Against the Oppressions of the Present Day

Samuel Hopkins: The barbarous nature of black slavery

This trade has been carried on for a century and more, and for many years past, above an hundred thousand have been brought off the coast in a year, so that many, many millions have been torn from their native country, their acquaintance, relations and friends, and most of them put into a state of slavery, both themselves, and their children for ever, if they shall have any posterity, much worse than death. When numbers of these wretched creatures are collected by the savages, they are brought into the public market to be sold, all naked as they were born. The more than savage slave-merchant views them, and sends his surgeon, more particularly to examine them, as to the soundness of their limbs, their age, etc. All that are passed as fit for sale, are branded with a hot iron in some part of their body, with the buyer's mark; and then confined, crowded together in some close hold, till a convenient time to put them on board a ship. When they are brought on board, all are immediately put in irons, except some of the women perhaps, and the small children, where they are so crowded together in that hot climate, that commonly a considerable number die on their passage to the West-Indies, occasioned partly by their confinement, partly by the grief and vexation of their minds, from the treatment they receive, and the situation in which they find themselves. And a number commonly die after they arrive at the West-Indies, in seasoning to the climate; so that, commonly, not above seventy in an hundred survive their transportation; by which means about thirty thousand are murdered every year by this slave-trade, which amounts to three millions in a century.

When they are brought to the West-Indies, they are again exposed to market, as if they were so many beasts, and sold to the highest bidder; where again they are separated according to the humour of the traders, without any regard to their friendships or relations, of husbands and wives, parents and children, brothers and sisters, &c. being torn from each other, without the least regard to anything of this kind, and sent to different places, without any prospect of seeing each other again. They are then put under a task master, by the purchasing planter, who appoints them their work, and rules over them with rigour and cruelty, following them with his cruel whip, or appointing one to do it, if possible, more cruel than himself. The infirm and feeble, the females, and even those who are pregnant, or have infants to take care of, must do their task in the field equally with the rest; or if they fall behind, may be sure to feel the lash of their unmerciful driver.

Their allowance of food at the same time is very coarse and scant, and must be cooked by themselves, if cooked at all, when they want to be asleep. And often they have no food but what they procure for themselves, by working on the sabbath; for that is the only time they have to themselves. And to make any complaint, or petition for relief, will expose them to some severe punishment, if not a cruel death. The least real or supposable crimes in them, are punished in the most cruel manner. And they have no relief; there being no appeal from their master's sentence and will, who commonly are more like savage beasts, than rational, human creatures. And to petition for liberty, though in the most humble and modest terms, is as much as their lives are worth; as few escape the most cruel death, who presume to hint anything of this kind to their masters: It being a maxim with those more than cruel tyrants, that the only way to keep them under, and prevent their thinking of the sweets of liberty, is to punish the least intimation of it in the severest manner, as the most intolerable affront and insult on their masters. Their labour is so hard, and their diet so scant and poor, and they are treated in all respects with such oppression and cruelty, that they do not increase by propagation in the islands, but constantly decrease, so that every planter must every year purchase five at least to every hundred he has on his plantation, in order to keep his number from diminishing.

But it is in vain to attempt a full description of the oppression and cruel treatment these poor creatures receive constantly at the hands of their imperious, unmerciful, worse than Egyptian task-masters. Words cannot utter it. Volumes might be written, and not give a detail of a thousandth part of the shockingly cruel things they have suffered, and are constantly suffering. Nor can they possibly be conceived of by anyone, who has not been an eyewitness. And how little a part does he see! They who are witnesses to any part of this horrid scene of barbarous oppression, cannot but feel the truth and propriety of Solomon's words: 'So I returned, and considered all the oppressions that are done under the sun: and behold the tears of the oppressed, and they had no comforter; and on the side of the oppressors there was power; but they had no comforter. Wherefore I praised the dead, which are already dead, more than the living which are yet alive.' Solomon never saw any oppression like this, unless he looked forward to this very instance, in the spirit of prophesy.

Samuel Hopkins

A Dialogue Concerning the Slavery of the Africans; shewing it to be the duty and interest of the American states to emancipate all their African slaves

A slave reflects on the death of George Whitefield

Hail, happy saint, on thine immortal throne,
Possest of glory, life, and bliss unknown;
We hear no more the music of thy tongue,
Thy wonted auditories cease to throng.
Thy sermons in unequalled accents flowed,
And every bosom with devotion glowed;
Thou didst in strains of eloquence refined
Inflame the heart, and captivate the mind.
Unhappy we the setting sun deplore,
So glorious once, but ah! it shines no more.

Behold the prophet in his towering flight!
He leaves the earth for heaven's unmeasured height,
And worlds unknown receive him from our sight.
There Whitefield wings with rapid course his way,
And sails to Zion through vast seas of day.
Thy prayers, great saint, and thine incessant cries
Have pierced the bosom of thy native skies.
Thou moon hast seen, and all the stars of light,
How he has wrestled with his God by night.
He prayed that grace in every heart might dwell,
He longed to see America excell;
He charged its youth that every grace divine
Should with full lustre in their conduct shine;
That Saviour, which his soul did first receive,
The greatest gift that even a God can give,
He freely offered to the numerous throng,
That on his lips with listening pleasure hung.

'Take Him, ye wretched, for your only good,
'Take Him ye starving sinners, for your food;
'Ye thirsty, come to this life-giving stream,
'Ye preachers, take Him for your joyful theme;
'Take Him, my dear Americans, he said,
'Be your complaints on His kind bosom laid:
'Take Him, ye Africans, He longs for you,
'Impartial Saviour is His title due:
'Washed in the fountain of redeeming blood,
'You shall be sons, and kings, and priests to God.'

Great Countess,[4] we Americans revere
Thy name, and mingle in thy grief sincere;
New England deeply feels, the Orphans mourn,
Their more than father will no more return.
But, though arrested by the hand of death,
Whitefield no more exerts his labouring breath,

---

4. The Countess of Huntingdon. See Chapter 2, Part 4, section 11.

Yet let us view him in th'eternal skies,
Let every heart to this bright vision rise;
While the tomb safe retains its sacred trust,
Till life divine re-animates his dust.[5]

---

5. The poem is by Phillis Wheatley (1753–84), the first Afro-American writer of published poetry. She was born in West Africa, captured as a slave at the age of seven or eight, transported to the American Colonies, and sold to the Wheatley family of Boston, Massachusetts. They at length set her free in 1774 after the Countess of Huntingdon had secured publication for her book of poems. Phillis wrote in a way that showed the desperate, tragic entanglement of slavery and Christianity:

    'Twas mercy brought me from my Pagan land,
    Taught my benighted soul to understand
    That there's a God, that there's a Saviour too:
    Once I redemption neither sought nor knew.
    Some view our sable race with scornful eye,
    'Their colour is a diabolic dye.'
    Remember, Christians! Negroes – black as Cain –
    May be refined, and join th'angelic train.

Chapter 5

Germany and the Lutheran Faith

1
Background

Lutheranism is often the forgotten story of the Protestant faith among English-speaking Evangelicals of Reformed or Wesleyan heritage. This is a great pity, even a serious defect, since Lutherans are (so to speak) one of the two historic wings of the 16th Century Reformation; or, changing the metaphor, Lutheranism is one of the two lungs of the Reformation, and it can be argued that those in the Reformed tradition are, in a certain sense, breathing with only one lung if they ignorantly or pridefully neglect their Lutheran brethren. Lutherans have always had their own rich and fascinating history, and (not infrequently) it offers surprising and fruitful connections with the Anglo-Saxon Protestant narrative. In this Chapter, we shall – as in the previous two volumes in this series – continue to explore the Lutheran branch of the Reformation, convinced of its intrinsic value and significant overflow into a wider Christian setting. We shall take Germany as a supremely convenient representative of the Lutheran world: the home and heartland of the Lutheran faith.

It is perhaps tedious to remind the reader that Germany, prior to the latter part of the 19th Century and the empire-building of Otto von Bismarck, was not a politically unified nation under a single government; it was a patchwork quilt of many smaller states and cities, whose only unity lay in their shared Germanic language and culture. Nevertheless, since we are so accustomed to thinking of the different European 'nationalities' as having concrete manifestations in a 'nation-state', the reminder may still be timely. Neither Germany nor Italy would be unified nation-states until the second half of the 19th Century.

The German-speaking lands of the 18th Century were predominantly Lutheran in faith. Lutheranism had sunk deep into the mind and heart of the great majority of German-speakers, and if they had a 'national' hero, it was Martin Luther. There was, however, a strong Roman Catholic minority in Germany's 'deep south', concentrated in the territories of Austria and Bavaria.[1] And we must not discount the presence of the Reformed Churches in some parts of Germany; Calvinism had finally been guaranteed legal toleration by the Peace of Westphalia (1648) which had ended the carnage of the Thirty Years War (1618–48), fought out by many of the European powers on German soil. The Reformed faith had a particular stronghold in the state of Prussia, which in our period was the militarily most powerful state in Germany; the ruling princely house of Prussia, the Hohenzollerns, were Reformed in religion, and provided shelter and support to Calvinists within their traditionally Lutheran lands.[2]

In the 16th Century, Germany had enjoyed sixty years of religious stability through the Peace of Augsburg (1555), which at length broke down in 1618, giving birth to the Thirty Years War. This earlier period of stability had enshrined the principle *cuius regio, eius religio* – whose region, his religion (the religion of a territory is determined by the religion of its ruler). This

1. Although Austria would not become part of the unified German nation-state in the 19th Century, it was – prior to this, at least – considered part of the wider Germanic world. The great question in the 19th Century was whether Catholic Austria or Protestant Prussia would lead a unified Germany. Prussia won that contest, and Austria was consequently left out of the new German nation-state.

2. The Hohenzollerns had embraced Calvinism under Prince John Sigismund (1608–19). This ensured that although the majority of Prussians remained Lutheran, the Reformed Church enjoyed princely protection and patronage, enabling Calvinism to enjoy a safe existence in Prussia.

principle, however, had been modified by the 1648 Peace of Westphalia. The ruling authority in each German territory could now change religion without having the right to impose that religion on their subjects.

One of the most striking examples of this changed relationship between ruler and people is found in the Protestant Rhenish Palatinate, where from 1697 – owing to French military intervention – Roman Catholic princes held power, with the Jesuits as their instrument for propagating Catholicism among their people. Yet in spite of the invincible grip of princely Catholicism and the Jesuit order, the majority of the inhabitants of the Palatinate remained stubbornly Protestant (either Lutheran or Reformed). It has been estimated that the Protestant population of the Palatinate never fell below two-thirds. Ironically, it would be French military intervention again that changed this, breaking the power of the Jesuits, when the Palatinate fell under the imperial sway of Napoleon Bonaparte in the French Revolutionary wars of the early 19th Century. Another vivid example of this mismatched relationship between ruler and people was the significant Lutheran territory of Württemberg, which had Roman Catholic princes from 1733–97, but a devout Lutheran Church where Pietism flourished.[3]

The Lutheran view of church government was very flexible, even pragmatic. Based on early 16th Century models, the ultimate authority in local church life was vested in the magistrate (prince, noble, or city council). This made for great diversity in how the church was administered from one Lutheran territory to another. In some territories, the Lutheran authorities were happy to have their churches run by various forms of ecclesiastical government – e.g., superintendents (Lutheran bishops) or church courts – as long as the civil ruler's final authority was acknowledged. In other territories, the churches enjoyed hardly any kind of ecclesiastical government alongside or under the power of the civil ruler, and the accusation of

---

3. See below, Part 4, and the life of Bengel, for the Pietism of Württemberg.

Calvinism was likely to be levelled against anyone who said that church courts were a good idea.[4] For most Lutherans, all was well so long as the Gospel (as understood by Lutheran theology) was being preached from the pulpits, and the sacraments (again, as understood by Lutheranism) were being administered.

Lutheran ministers were often appointed by lay patrons – frequently landowners – and they sometimes imposed scandalous terms on would-be candidates (e.g., marrying his precursor's widow or his patron's mistress). However, as the 18th Century advanced, such scandals became fewer, and the public esteem in which the Lutheran ministry was held increased. Serious professional preparation for the ministry was demanded, including theological study at the Lutheran universities, the leading centres of Protestant intellectual life in Europe. After their academic study, many Lutheran students temporarily became private tutors, since a church appointment was not always immediately available. Once a qualified student had become a minister in a congregation, his life was often divided between pastoral duties and acting as an agent for his local government. In the latter capacity, he collected useful statistics, imparted what his ruler deemed to be suitable morality (especially patriotism), officiated as judge in some of the lesser courts, and even acted as a recruiting officer for the local militia.

However, despite what may seem a less than edifying picture of Lutheran church life, many Lutheran ministers succeeded in being intellectually more-than-competent and religiously estimable men – Spener, Francke, Zinzendorf, Rothe, Bengel, Oetinger, and Muhlenberg were among these, to whom not just Lutherans but the whole wider Church is indebted.[5]

---

4. One of the distinctives of Calvinism or the Reformed faith was its belief in the church's institutional independence of the state.

5. For Spener and Francke, see Volume 4, Part 1, Section 4. Zinzendorf, Rothe, Bengel, Oetinger, and Muhlenberg are covered in what follows.

2

The Moravian movement

The greatest contribution of 18th Century Lutheranism to global Christianity, at least in terms of influence, was its intimate (if conflicted) involvement in the Moravian movement. We may justly consider Moravianism the seedbed of the Evangelical Revival in the English-speaking world. This is partly because Moravianism's own intense revival – the 'Moravian Pentecost' – preceded and heralded Britain's Evangelical Revival and America's Great Awakening by a full decade, and partly because the Moravian revival went on to have a direct and far-reaching effect on its English counterpart. In some ways, it would even be fair to characterise John Wesley as an 'English Moravian'. At key points in his life, Wesley was decisively affected by Moravianism in its revival phase; in particular, as we have seen, Wesley's conversion in 1738 occurred at a Moravian religious society. Thereafter he deliberately incorporated key aspects of Moravian piety and practice into his branch of Methodism.[1] Given the international impact of Moravianism, then, it seems appropriate to begin our detailed treatment of Lutheranism in this period with an account of the Moravian movement nurtured in its bosom, with its multi-faceted nature and fruits.

1. Wesley's contact with Moravianism has previously been considered in Chapter 2, Part 2, section 3.

1. The pivotal figure: Nicolaus Ludwig von Zinzendorf (1700–1760)

The central figure in the Moravian movement was the German Lutheran aristocrat, Nicolaus Ludwig von Zinzendorf (1700–1760). Zinzendorf was born in the city of Dresden in Saxony on May 26th 1700. He was the son of a nobleman, Georg Ludwig, a counsellor in the court of the Prince of Saxony. We remind ourselves yet again that Germany at that time had not been unified as a nation; it was a many-coloured patchwork of hundreds of smaller states. Among these, Saxony was one of the larger and stronger. Zinzendorf's mother was Charlotte Justine von Gersdorf (1675–1763). However, Zinzendorf's father died in the sixth week of the youngster's life, and when he was four years old, his mother remarried. Charlotte's new husband was a high-ranking officer in the army of Prussia, the most powerful German state, and Charlotte went to live in the Prussian capital, Berlin. She left the young Zinzendorf in the care of his maternal grandmother, Henrietta Catherine, the Baroness von Gersdorf (1648–1726), whose lands lay in Saxony's Upper Lusatia region.

This upbringing was to be a critical factor in Zinzendorf's spiritual development. His grandmother, the Baroness, was closely connected to the leaders of the German Pietist movement, Philipp Jacob Spener (1635–1705) and August Hermann Francke (1663–1727). Pietism, we recollect, was a widespread movement for spiritual revitalisation within the Lutheran Churches of the 17th and 18th centuries, cradled in (but not confined to) Germany.[2] Through his Pietist grandmother, the young Zinzendorf would be a vessel, as it were, into whom the spiritual influences of Pietism would be poured forth in abundance. When Zinzendorf was baptised as a Lutheran infant, his godfather was none other than Spener himself.

This Lutheran Pietist background provides the key to understanding most of Zinzendorf's adult life. Zinzendorf himself described his early spiritual experience like this:

---

2. For Pietism, see Volume 4, Chapter 1, Part 4.

Nicolaus Ludwig von Zinzendorf

> During the time I stayed with my revered grandmother, two things took place that determined my whole future. When I was six years old, my tutor, Herr Christian Ludwig Edeling, having served our family for three years, departed and said his farewell to me. In this farewell, he said a few words to me concerning the Saviour and His excellences, and the sense in which I belonged to Him and to Him alone. These words made so profound and vital an impression on me that I wept over and again, firmly resolving that I would live only for Him who had laid down His life for me. My much-loved Aunt Henrietta tried to keep me in this state of mind by frequently speaking loving words concerning the Gospel. I opened my whole heart to her, and we spread my situation prayerfully before the Lord .... I gladly told her everything about myself, both the bad and the good. My free and honest fellowship with her was such a great blessing to me that I shall always remember it. This confidential exchange of thought and feeling inspired all my efforts, in later years, to form 'bands' or 'societies' in which believers might confer with one another for mutual edification.

From 1710–16, young Zinzendorf received a Pietist education in the famous Halle Pietist Foundation established by August Francke. However, he then moved to Lutheranism's old historic headquarters at Wittenberg University, where he studied law from 1717–19. In Wittenberg, he came up against Lutheran Orthodoxy and its principled hostility to Pietism. Wittenberg indeed was the great power-centre of strict, orthodox, confessional Lutheranism at this period. We would not be much exaggerating to say that there was a virtual state of war between Wittenberg and Halle – between orthodox Lutherans and Pietists. The soured relations between the two were made almost comically manifest, when the theologians of Wittenberg University let it be known that they had unearthed no fewer than 284 heresies in the teachings of the Pietists!

If we ask the reasons for this hostility, we may say that orthodox Lutherans, with their traditional focus on the doctrine of justification by the imputed righteousness of Christ, were highly suspicious of the subjective emphasis of Pietism, with its focus on Christian life and sanctification. Certainly the orthodox Lutherans pronounced harshly against the moral standards that were held to be normative in Pietism. Pietists practised an ethically rigorous and austere lifestyle, holding (for example) that the theatre, dancing, and games of chance were intrinsically sinful. Orthodox Lutherans, by contrast, argued that such matters were 'things indifferent', or *adiaphora* to use the technical term. Hence the quarrel was known as the 'adiaphoristic controversy'. Zinzendorf sided firmly with the strict Pietist outlook, to which he was faithful throughout his life and ministry.

During the time he studied at Wittenberg University, Zinzendorf endeavoured to promote Pietism with fiery zeal among his fellow students. To this end, he started up a group called 'The Order of the Grain of Mustard Seed.' Those belonging to the Order promised fidelity to Christ's teaching, and moral conduct befitting such fidelity, which included devoting their energies to pursuing the salvation of both Jews and people of other religions. Each member of the Order wore a ring that had engraved upon it the Pauline saying, 'No one lives to himself' (Romans 14:7).

After Wittenberg, from 1719–20 Zinzendorf followed the not uncommon practice, among the young men of the more affluent classes, of seeking to broaden his knowledge and experience by travelling across Europe. In the course of his travels, for the first time he had immediate encounters with both Calvinism and Roman Catholicism. This was a landmark event for Zinzendorf; it convinced him that sincere lovers of Christ could be found in both the Reformed Churches and in

Rome, vilified though these Churches were by strict Lutherans. In consequence, Zinzendorf became one of the early pioneers of a sort of 'spiritual ecumenism': he experimented with grand theoretical schemes of reunion between all Christians, whether Protestant, Roman Catholic, or Eastern Orthodox.

However, by far the most dramatic milestone-experience of Zinzendorf's life came to him when he was making his way through the city of Dusseldorf in Electoral Palatine (west Germany, not far from the borders with the Netherlands). Here there was a famous art gallery, established by the Prince-Elector Johann Wilhelm II (1690–1716). Zinzendorf visited the art gallery where he saw a picture of Christ crowned with thorns, over which was written, 'All this I have done for you; what have you done for Me?'[3] The words overwhelmed Zinzendorf; he never lost the vivid and graphic impression they made on his soul. 'From this time,' he said, 'I had but one passion, and that was Christ, only He.'

At the age of twenty-one, in the year 1721, Zinzendorf returned to his native Saxony. He took up a career in the Saxon civil service. Significantly (see below) he purchased a tract of land in Berthelsdorf, south-eastern Saxony. In 1722, he married another Pietist, Erdmuthe Dorothea von Reuss-Ebersdorf (1700–1756).

Erdmuthe was born at Ebersdorf, in the state of Thuringia (eastern-central Germany), the daughter of Count Henry X of Reuss-Ebersdorf. Raised in an aristocratic household that was saturated in Pietism, Erdmuthe was brought in close touch with Jacob Spener, the father of Pietism, and from her early childhood (we are told) loved God according to the mode of Pietist spirituality. Her mother, Countess Erdmuthe Benigna of Solms-Laubach, also trained Erdmuthe in the more down-to-earth skills of looking after the financial affairs of the household.

When Zinzendorf's life first overlapped with that of the Von Reuss family, he was enchanted by Erdmuthe's older sister, Benigna. Her deeply religious nature and joyous delight in Christ were exhilarating to Zinzendorf. However, he also had

3. This was the painting *Ecce Homo* by Domenico Fetti or Feti (1589–1623).

many prolonged conversations with Erdmuthe about spiritual things, which attracted Zinzendorf to what he called her 'fine character'. They married on September 7th, 1722.

One of Zinzendorf's later biographers, Catherine Winkworth (1827–78), described the man and his wife at this time:

> He was a remarkably handsome man, tall, and exactly of what is termed aristocratic bearing and manners; he was also a ready speaker, with a clear ringing voice, and graceful and imposing action. In private he was energetic and impetuous, but obliging in trifles, and full of vivacity and humour. Fortunately for him he had found a wife who entered heart and soul into all his plans, who travelled with him wherever he went, and managed his [financial] affairs and the details of daily arrangements with a skill and prudence which he did not himself possess in such matters.

2. Zinzendorf, Herrnhut, and the Moravians

A key event in Zinzendorf's life came in the year of his marriage, 1722.[4] That year, he invited a group of persecuted Hussites from the region of Moravia to settle on his land in Berthelsdorf. The proper 'denominational' name of these immigrants was the *Unitas Fratrum* – which we could translate *Unity of the Brethren* or *United Brotherhood*. More popularly, they are often known as the Bohemian Brethren. As Hussites, they were followers of the great 15th Century Bohemian Reformer and martyr John Huss, often and rightly hailed as a forerunner of the Reformation.[5] Hussites, early on in their history, founded churches in Moravia, a territory directly to the east of Bohemia; it had been permanently united with its larger Bohemian neighbour since 1490, under the Bohemian monarchy. (Moravia now constitutes the eastern part of the present-day Czech Republic.) Persecution by Roman Catholic authorities led to Moravian

4. No doubt his marriage was also a key event for him personally, but I mean an event that was to have global repercussions.

5. For John Huss and the Hussites, see Volume Two, Chapter 10, section 5. For the fortunes of the Hussites in the Reformation era, see Volume Three, Chapter 6, section 6. For the Hussites and their persecution by Roman Catholics in the 17th Century, see Volume Four, Chapter 1, Part 3.

Hussite emigration in the 16th and (especially) 17th Century, into Hungary, Poland, Saxony, Holland, and England. In 1722, a group of ten Moravian Hussites emigrated to Berthelsdorf at the invitation of Zinzendorf. This proved to be the first stream of a significant Moravian influx into Berthelsdorf over the next ten years. Within a mere three years, by 1725, Berthelsdorf already had a community of ninety Moravian settlers.

The Moravian refugees, however, were not the only body with distinctive religious convictions to settle in Berthelsdorf. The others were mostly Lutheran, sharing Zinzendorf's faith; but there were also some Calvinists, and some Anabaptists, seeking refuge in Zinzendorf's land from religious persecution elsewhere. This was made possible by Zinzendorf's previously noted 'ecumenism' and religious tolerance. The Moravian community in Berthelsdorf gave itself the name 'Herrnhut' (meaning 'The Lord's Watch', 'Protected by the Lord').

Despite the religious diversity of its inhabitants, Berthelsdorf had one church where they were expected to worship on Sundays, a Lutheran church. Zinzendorf was at this point still a thoroughly conforming member of the established Lutheran Church in Saxony, and envisaged that those who lived on his land would also conform outwardly to Saxony's Church order on the Christian day of worship. On May 19th 1722, Zinzendorf invited the Lutheran Johann Andreas Rothe (1688–1758) to become minister of the Berthelsdorf church, after being impressed by one of Rothe's sermons which he heard in nearby Großhennersdorf, the home town of Zinzendorf's beloved grandmother. Rothe took up his new position on August 30th. (Rothe was a qualified preacher but was not formally ordained to the Lutheran ministry until 1724.) Zinzendorf's plan to incorporate the Moravians into Berthelsdorf's Lutheran church was partly motivated by a hope that the warmth and vitality of Moravian piety would act as an effective spiritual leaven among the Lutheran worshippers. Berthelsdorf's new minister, Rothe, is now largely known for his authorship of some thirty-five hymns, in particular for the classic *Now I have found the ground wherein sure my soul's anchor may remain*, translated into English by John Wesley.

In 1724, Christian David (c.1690–1751), and the brothers Melchior (1702–29) and David Nitschmann (1698–1772), came in a fresh body of Moravian settlers to Berthelsdorf. They had experienced religious revival in Moravia, suffering severe persecution by its Roman Catholic political establishment. This new group carried the fire of revival with them to Herrnhut. They also brought a vigorous resolve that the Moravians should establish their own distinctive church community, based on the old, traditional Hussite model of the United Brethren. This at first triggered an acute falling-out with the Lutheran pastor Rothe, who perceived the new Moravian immigrants as divisive sectarians bent on overthrowing the good Lutheran church order of Berthelsdorf.

With this Lutheran-Moravian rupture, Zinzendorf now became progressively more concerned about, and committed to, the life and affairs of the Berthelsdorf settlers. The outcome was that he began to lose interest in his civil service job at the Saxon court. Although Zinzendorf's original ideal had been to absorb Moravianism and its good qualities into Berthelsdorf's Lutheran church, revitalising the whole congregation, this now dwindled in his mind. The more Zinzendorf came to have first-hand knowledge of the Moravians and their unique ways of 'doing church', the more he came to believe they had something precious he had not found in his own Lutheran tradition – namely, that Moravianism had a stronger and healthier grasp of the reality of Christian community life than Lutherans did.

The final upshot was that in 1727, Zinzendorf stepped down from his position at the Saxon court, in order to give himself single-mindedly to the spiritual concerns of Berthelsdorf in general, and the Moravian immigrant community at Herrnhut in particular. He was first and foremost overflowing with 'catholic' desire to bring peace and unity amid the unedifying clash between Moravians and Lutherans over church life. (By now, the adult population of Berthelsdorf had reached about three hundred, roughly half of whom were Moravians.)

In fact, Zinzendorf scored a resounding success in ending the Moravian-Lutheran controversy that very year. This took the shape of a mutual agreement that the Moravians could manage their own internal community affairs at Herrnhut along Moravian lines, as long as they attended the worship at the Berthelsdorf church on Sundays. This would empower the Moravian immigrants to develop their own collective spiritual life at Herrnhut, while still continuing formally to exist within Saxony's Lutheran Church. The Moravians thus became a sort of officially recognised church-within-a-church. To solemnise and validate this pact of religious peace, Zinzendorf and Rothe drafted a covenant called the 'Statutes of the Congregation', to which both parties, Lutherans and Moravians, unanimously gave their consent at a public meeting on May 12th 1727.

At Herrnhut, the Moravian immigrants now constructed their own distinctive religious community under the leadership of twelve elders, four of whom were then chosen by lot to be the senior presiding elders. The Moravians asked Zinzendorf himself to act as the overall superintendent of the new community – which demonstrates how far he now identified his spirituality with Moravianism rather than his cradle Lutheranism.

3. The Moravian Pentecost

Two months after Zinzendorf and Rothe had restored peace and unity to Berthelsdorf through the Statutes of the Congregation, an intense spiritual awakening and revival took place among the Moravians (to judge by contemporary witnesses). The human instrument was a public prayer offered at Herrnhut by Zinzendorf , on July 16th 1727, when 'he poured out his soul in a heart-touching prayer, delivered with gushing tears; this prayer made an extraordinary impact, and it was the origin of the activities of the life-giving and dynamic Spirit of God that followed thereafter' (this is a quotation from *The Memorial Days of the Renewed Church of the Brethren*, a set of documents published by the Moravian Church in 1821 that presents a full account of the revival and its aftermath).

On July 22nd, ten Moravians met to engage in hymn-singing and prayer; once again, extraordinary experiences were manifest, which they emphatically interpreted as an unusually powerful outpouring of the Holy Spirit on their gathering. On August 5th, Zinzendorf and twelve others assembled for a prayer-meeting that lasted a whole night. The following midnight, a larger prayer meeting took place; the meeting was overwhelmed by astonishingly deep and vibrant religious feelings, especially sorrow for sin and rejoicing in salvation. Over the next few days, according to accounts written at the time, 'a truly distinctive and overwhelming power of God was experienced at the evening meetings for hymn-singing.'

On August 10th, Berthelsdorf's Lutheran pastor Rothe presided at the Herrnhut meeting. We are told:

> he experienced an overwhelming, wondrous, and almighty power of the Lord, and together with him the whole gathered congregation sunk to the ground in an ecstasy of feeling. This state of mind endured until midnight, as they took part in prayer, singing, weeping, and supplication.

Now that Rothe had personally experienced and accepted the awakening, the religious divide between Lutheran and Moravian was decisively removed in Berthelsdorf. This union of once-divided brethren was sealed on August 13th at a communion service held in Berthelsdorf, among the gathered Moravians and Lutherans:

> Journeying to Berthelsdorf, groups of two or more could be seen, here and there, of people who were holding heart-conversation with each other; all those who had been alienated from each other now lovingly embraced, entering into a mutual covenant of friendship and love. At the Berthelsdorf church, the worship-service began with the hymn *Unbind me, O my God, from all my bonds and fetters.* While the hymn was sung, a very wicked man, who was there as an observer, was overwhelmed with a sense of repentance. Mr. Rothe then spoke a really apostolic blessing upon two sisters who were undergoing confirmation,[6] and the congregation added its own Amen in zealous agreement. The earnest self-consecration of these sisters to the Lord their God could not be looked upon without stirring up the most heartfelt feeling.

---

6. Confirmation = the traditional rite in paedobaptist Churches, in which those baptised as infants now consciously take upon themselves the duties and privileges of church membership.

> Immediately after this, the whole assembly fell to the ground in the Lord's presence. All of them were melted together in tears, and began to sing the hymn *My soul before Thee prostrate lies*. It was hardly possible to know whether they were weeping or singing – both were mingled together.

Zinzendorf himself named this communion service as the Moravian 'Pentecost'. We have his own account of the event:

> All of us at the same time received a sense of the closeness of Christ. The Saviour allowed the Spirit to come upon us – that Spirit of whom we had not previously had any experience or knowledge. Prior to this, *we* had been the leaders and workers. Now the Holy Spirit Himself took complete charge of everything and everyone.

The Moravian Pentecost gathered into its embrace the children of Herrnhut as well; many of them now professed conversion to Christ. On August 18th, contemporary testimony tells us that the Moravian children were filled with 'a universal fire of love towards our Saviour'.

The Moravian Pentecost, at least a decade before John Wesley and George Whitefield proclaimed a similar life-changing message in Britain, brought about an enduring transformation of the spiritual life of Berthelsdorf's Moravian community. As Zinzendorf wrote:

> A deep hunger for the Word of God took control of us, so that we felt ourselves compelled to have three worship-services every day, at 5 AM, 7:30 AM, and 9 PM. Everyone's supreme desire was that the Holy Spirit would have complete mastery. Self-love, self-will, and all disobedience to God, vanished away, and an overpowering flood of grace swept all of us out into the vast ocean of God's love.

4. Effects of the Moravian Pentecost

Let us now consider the far-reaching consequences of the Moravian Pentecost of 1727. Students of history may profitably do this under four broad headings.

1 – Worship

The Moravian Pentecost produced a flood of brilliant new hymns, many of which have become a prized part of the Evangelical heritage. As previously noted, Zinzendorf himself was a hymnwriter; he is reckoned to have written some two thousand hymns in German. English translations based on Zinzendorf's hymns include:

> *Jesus Thy blood and righteousness*
> *I thirst, Thou wounded Lamb of God*
> *Christ will gather in His own*
> *Eternal depth of love divine*
> *Christian hearts, in love united*[7]
> *Jesus, still lead on, till our rest be won,* and
> *Thou to whose all-searching sight.*

Most of these were translated into English by John Wesley. Other Moravian hymnwriters included Zinzendorf's son, Christian Renatus (1727–52); August Gottlieb Spangenberg (1704–92), the first biographer of Zinzendorf, consecrated as a Moravian Bishop in 1744, and missionary among native Americans and black people in the 'New World'; Henrietta Louise von Hayn (1724–82), a teacher at Herrnhut from 1751 to 1766, and thereafter a carer for the community's female invalids; John de Watteville (dates unknown), head of the Moravian community at Marienborn in Saxony-Anhalt, to whom is credited the invention of the Christingle;[8] Christian Frederick Hassé (1771–1831), more well-known as a composer of church music; and English Moravian John Cennick (Cennick wrote the original version of *Lo He comes with clouds descending,*

---

7. Older translation, *Flock of Jesus, be united.*

8. Christingle derives from the German *Christkindl* ('little Christ-child'). Essentially it involves lighting and holding a candle representing Christ as the light of the world. In modern times the candle is generally embedded in an orange, into which also are placed four cocktail sticks with sweets or dried fruits attached. Normally a Christingle service is held at Christmas but perhaps at several other points, too, in the 'Christian year'. It has spread from its native Germany to many other parts of the world and to denominations other than Moravian/Lutheran.

revised by Charles Wesley; his best-known unrevised hymns are *Brethren, Let Us Join to Bless,* and *Children of the Heavenly King*). Zinzendorf edited five hymnbooks between 1725 and 1735.

The distinctive mark of the Moravian hymns is that they tend to be both Christ-centred and experiential. They had a huge impact on the hymnwriting of John and Charles Wesley. One classic example of a Zinzendorf hymn (translated into English by John Wesley) is his *O Thou to whose all-searching sight*:

> O Thou to whose all-searching sight
> The darkness shineth as the light,
> Search, prove my heart; it pants for Thee;
> O burst these bonds, and set it free!
>
> Wash out its stains, refine its dross,
> Nail my affections to the cross;
> Hallow each thought; let all within
> Be clean, as Thou, my Lord, art clean!
>
> If in this darksome wild I stray,
> Be Thou my light, be Thou my way;
> No foes, no violence I fear,
> No fraud, while Thou, my God, art near.
>
> When rising floods my soul o'erflow,
> When sinks my heart in waves of woe,
> Jesu, Thy timely aid impart,
> And raise my head, and cheer my heart.
>
> Saviour, where'er Thy steps I see,
> Dauntless, untired, I follow Thee!
> O let Thy hand support me still,
> And lead me to Thy holy hill!
>
> If rough and thorny be the way,
> My strength proportion to my day;
> Till toil, and grief, and pain shall cease,
> Where all is calm, and joy, and peace.

Perhaps under this heading of 'worship', we can also note the intercessory prayer meetings that sprung up as an immediate flowering of the Moravian Pentecost. A document of that time describes the prayer meetings thus:

At that time, our minds were deeply concerned with pondering how very necessary it was that the Congregation in its current condition of infancy, and having Satan as her enemy, who never sleeps by day or by night, should be kept safe from his crafty deceptions, and be under an unceasing and holy protection. We therefore decided to awaken the fire of a free and voluntary sacrifice of intercession in our community, which would not cease to burn by day or by night. However, we were careful not to limit or obstruct the effectual working of the Lord Himself concerning prayer, and were content simply to put the subject before the brothers for their attention.

On August 23rd fourteen of the brothers offered themselves for this work. Two days later, the suggested plan had matured sufficiently that a specific rule could be adopted, according to which the brothers and sisters, in their respective places of gathering, were minutely and sincerely to lay before our Saviour the suffering and situation of all who were known to them, whether belonging to the Congregation or not. On August 26th twenty-four brothers and an equal number of sisters assembled, and covenanted together to pray from one midnight to the next; for that purpose, they divided up the twenty-four hours of night and day among themselves by lot. On August 27th this new rule was put into practice.

This number of intercessors rapidly grew, and increased to seventy-seven; even the converted children began a similar plan among themselves. Everyone conscientiously observed the hour of prayer that had been assigned to him. Still, because it was a principle at Herrnhut that nothing of a compulsory nature should be found there, the decision was taken that if anyone was unable to spend the entire hour in prayer (either because of deficiency of spirit, or official matters impeding him), he could instead sing spiritual songs and hymns of praise to the Lord; in this way, he could bring to Him, for himself and his fellow community members, the sacrifice of thanksgiving or an offering of prayer and supplication.

The intercessors had met on a weekly basis, and at these meetings they were given the details of what they should consider special topics for prayer and remembrance before the Lord. The news received from friends near or distant,

> whether joyful or sad; the particular situation of one or another nation, of various churches or individuals: these were shared with the intercessors, to stir them up to ardent praise and thanksgiving, or to sincere supplication and prayer.

It is said that these round-the-clock intercessions continued unbroken for something like a hundred years.

2 – *Social religion*

The conviction took ever deeper possession of Zinzendorf's mind and heart that an authentic New Testament church could not be a mere loosely connected set of individuals who happened to meet on Sundays. It must be a bonded-together community, a genuine spiritual family. 'There can be no Christianity without community.' Not that Zinzendorf originated this outlook; it was already held and practised by the Moravians themselves as part of their own traditional ideals, as we have already seen. However, in the aftermath of the Moravian Pentecost, it developed more fully in Herrnhut into a radical experiment in Christian community life.

The Moravians at Herrnhut were organised into small groups known as 'bands'. Each band was made up of between eight and ten people (of the same sex). The band elected its own leader; all the band leaders gathered each week with Zinzendorf to confer with each other. The purpose and function of the band was to provide an intimate social framework for the cultivation and growth of personal faith, as band members helped and encouraged one another spiritually, praying for each other. In fashioning the structure of the bands, Zinzendorf was at least partly reacting against an individualistic view of faith as something essentially private. For him, Christian faith was an inter-personal reality; it had a necessary horizontal dimension (between believers) as well as a vertical one (between the believer and God). As noted in Chapter 2, these were the origin of the bands in Wesleyan Methodism. Townsend, Workman, and Eayrs, in their classic *New History of Methodism*, pointed out regarding the Moravians' influence on John Wesley that when he visited Herrnhut in August 1738, he encountered group gatherings for mutual edification (including bands and class meetings), open air preaching, lay preaching, itinerant preaching, and Christian orphanages. He would also have witnessed the *agape* or love feast: a Moravian reinvigoration of an early church practice that had faded away after the 6th Century.[9] Many such features of Moravian religious life were to be adopted by early Methodism, including itinerant lay preaching, class meetings, and love feasts. Wesley indeed was so impressed by Herrnhut that he wrote:

> I would gladly have spent my life here; but my Master calling me to labour in another part of His vineyard, on Monday, 14 [of August], I was constrained to take my leave of this happy place; Martin Dober, and a few others of the brethren, walking with us about an hour. O when shall this Christianity cover the earth, as the 'waters cover the sea?'

Later on, Zinzendorf significantly modified and adapted the band system, re-structuring the bands into what were called *choirs*. Members of these choirs were divided into groups for Little Boys, Little Girls, Older Boys, Older Girls, Single Brothers, Single Sisters, Married Brothers, Married Sisters, Widowers, and Widows. Worship-services for each of the choirs underscored specific aspects of Jesus' life, which it was thought best suited the makeup of each choir. Children learned about Jesus as a child. Single Brothers focused their attention on Jesus as a single man. In the Sisters' and Older Girls' Choirs, emphasis was placed on Jesus as spiritual husband, and the Virgin Mary as the one through whom the Son of God became Man.

The choirs made sure their members had a place to live (within the wider structure of an overall community house), along with food, clothing, and suitable employment. The choirs also took responsibility for childcare and schooling, which operated according to Zinzendorf's own educational theories. Some of

---

9. For the *agape* or love feast of the early church, see Volume One, Chapter 3, section 2, under the heading Church Worship.

the choirs virtually embraced a social type of communism: the needs of each member were catered for, in return for his or her labour. 'From each according to their ability, to each according to their need': the classic ideal of the original 19th Century Marxists was made real by 18th Century Moravians.[10]

The community ideals practised at Herrnhut have been variously assessed. Some visitors thought them artificial and unnatural; others, however, praised their practical effectiveness in providing social and spiritual care to their members. As we have already noted, aspects of these Moravian community ideals found their way into British Methodism via John Wesley.

3 – *Religious experience and theology*

The impact made by the Moravian Pentecost on the Moravians themselves was profound. It created a new spiritual atmosphere of joy and peace, a dynamic sense of the sheer reality of spiritual things. This in turn led to an even deeper appreciation of the subjective side of religion, already encouraged by Pietism. Perhaps nowhere have a 'felt Christ', and a conscious experience of the Holy Spirit, been more cherished and lived out than among the Church of the Moravians. Revived Moravianism, at its best, presented a model of 'living orthodoxy' where the beauty as well as the truth of Christian faith was made manifest. We can see this experiential faith expressed lyrically in Moravian hymnology. Evangelicals have generally sympathised with the warmth and vitality of Moravian piety, perceiving it as a standing rebuke to the cold, dull, formal, even unsanctified orthodoxy that has too often afflicted the Reformed and Lutheran Churches.

Yet a note of caution has also been sounded about Moravian revival piety. It led to a somewhat anti-intellectual ethos, a suspicion of theology *per se*. As Zinzendorf stated in his treatise *Thoughts for the Learned yet Good-Willed Students of Truth*:

---

10. Zinzendorf was, however, no socialist or communist in his view of how the civil community or state should be organised. In order to gain the widest possible support from governments, his 'earthly' politics remained conservative.

> Religion is a subject we must be capable of grasping through experience alone, without the use of any concepts. Were this not the case, a person who was born deaf or blind, or a mentally defective person, or a child, would not be able to enjoy the religion necessary for salvation. The first [the deaf] would not be able to hear the truth, the second [the mentally defective] would lack the intellectual capacity to think about and understand religious matters, and the third [the child] would lack the capacity to grasp concepts, organise them, and test them. Less important issues hang in the balance in *concepts* of truth than in the truth of *experience*; mistakes in theology are not as bad as mistakes in methods. Reason undermines experience.

Zinzendorf's distrust of reason meant that he rejected the very concept of a systematic theology. 'The moment truth becomes a system, one no longer possesses truth.' This in turn led him to a radical 'Christ-concentration' in his theology. The very Person of Jesus Christ, not human reason, was for him the organising principle of theology. He saw all knowledge of God as mediated through the Son, and the Son Himself as known in the immediate experience of faith, which transcended mere reason. Moravian evangelists, therefore, were not to trouble themselves, in their missionary preaching and teaching, with trying first of all to prove that God existed; they were directly to preach Jesus Christ, trusting that the Holy Spirit would make the true God known in and through Him.

Zinzendorf's 'Christ-concentration' may not, in and of itself, be thought very objectionable. It may even be judged fruitful. Still, it must be said that the intensity of the Moravian experience of Christ in revival led Moravians to place unusual stress on the place and significance of feelings in the Christian life, immediate assurance of salvation as a sign of true conversion, and among some, the possibility of sinless perfection (although Zinzendorf himself rejected this). This birthed a sense of intimacy with God that gave rise to ways of speaking about Him which most have judged to be sentimental and unsuitable. The Trinity, for example, was addressed as Papa (God the Father), Little Lamb or 'Lambkin' (Christ), and Mama (the Holy Spirit). In the late 1740s, there developed an intense obsession with the blood and wounds of Jesus, sometimes frankly erotic in the language and symbolism it employed.

The most painful and embarrassing excesses in this regard took place, not at Herrnhut, but at Herrnhaag, the Moravian community in the German state of Hesse, near Frankfurt, which was led by Zinzendorf's son, Christian Renatus. Zinzendorf had the highest admiration for his son, trusting that he would step into Zinzendorf's place as the new leader of the Moravian movement, and at first he would not hear of any criticisms; but several of Zinzendorf's co-workers at length succeeded in persuading him to acknowledge how serious were the spiritual aberrations at Herrnhaag. As a result, Zinzendorf, who had journeyed to England, compelled Christian Renatus to join him there, and to relinquish religious oversight of the Herrnhaag community. Under his father's close care, the young son (he was twenty-two) found his way back to a more sober and acceptable state of mind. In the wake of the Herrnhaag debacle, the Moravian communities in general stepped back from the emotional extravagances that had been running rampant; the period when they had embraced them became known in their history as the Time of Testing (or Sifting).

We can hardly leave the matter without noting that Moravianism's subjective emphasis was to have a strange (if perhaps understandable) offshoot at the close of the 18th Century, in the life and work of the epoch-making German theologian, Friedrich Schleiermacher (1768–1834), the oft-named 'father of Liberal Protestantism'. Schleiermacher was reared as a Moravian Pietist. In his theology, he would take the Moravian Christ-concentration, and stress on personal experience and religious feeling, designating it as the key to a radical reinterpretation of Christian doctrine. For Schleiermacher, Jesus Christ was not God incarnate as classically understood; Jesus was rather the one human being who had experienced God to the full – the only perfectly 'God-conscious' Man – who now imparted the definitive richness of His experience to others, through the medium of the community He founded (the Church). The experientialism of Moravian Pietism thus unwittingly provided the seedbed of Liberal Protestantism.[11]

4 – *The impetus to missionary work*

The Moravian Pentecost of 1727 led to a new depth of concern to bring the Christian faith to unevangelised peoples; this concern overflowed in a remarkable way into missionary enterprise. The Moravians of Herrnhut were among the first Protestant missionaries to work outside of Europe. They were not absolutely the first, but they were probably the most zealous, and arguably the most impressive in their spiritual integrity, their freedom from the baggage of European colonialism.

The spark that ignited this Moravian missionary fire came in 1731. Zinzendorf was visiting Denmark, and in Copenhagen he met two Inuit converts from Greenland who had been baptised by a Danish Pietist missionary. When he heard that the Greenland mission was in danger of being abandoned through lack of manpower, Zinzendorf decided that the community at Herrnhut must step into the breach. So began the great Moravian missionary adventure, which would penetrate far and wide across the globe. A rapid series of snapshots of the first five years alone yields the following:

- In 1732, David Nitschmann and Johann Leonhard Dober of Herrnhut went to St Thomas in the Virgin Islands to evangelise the negro slaves there.
- In 1733, Christian David headed a group of Moravian missionaries to Greenland, to carry on and supplement the work begun by the Danish Pietist mission.
- In 1734, the first Moravian missionaries went to North America.

11. A fuller account of Schleiermacher is reserved for the next volume in the series.

- In 1735, Moravians began work in Lapland and South America.
- In 1736, they arrived in South Africa.

By the time of Zinzendorf's death in 1760, it has been estimated that the Moravians had sent out at least 226 missionaries into sixteen different geographical regions. The Moravians had become arguably the most mission-minded Church in Christian history.[12]

The Moravian mission in Labrador in the 1770s is especially well-documented, and we can take it as a template for examining how the Moravian missionaries worked. Labrador is the north-eastern region of present-day Canada[13] along whose shores the Atlantic Ocean rolls, with Greenland away off in the north-east, and inhabited by the people group known as the Inuit.[14] The Moravians who were instrumental in establishing the Christian faith among the Labrador Inuit were Jens Haven (1724–96), Christian Larsen Drachardt (1711–78), and Christoph Brasen (1738–74). After some other Moravians had made contact with the Labrador Inuit in the 1750s, Haven renewed that contact in the 1760s.

Haven was the son of a Danish Lutheran farmer.[15] Born at Wurst in Jutland, his early religious experience reminds us

---

12. Baptists should reflect that this was a generation before William Carey, who therefore can hardly be truthfully considered the originator of modern Protestant missions.

13. Canada became recognisably something like modern Canada in the aftermath of the American War of Independence (1775–83), when the peace treaty that ended the war apportioned the 'Canadian' part of North America to Britain. Large numbers of American 'Loyalists' (those Americans who had fought for Britain in the War of Independence) then migrated into and settled in Canada. It may be worth reflecting that many Americans did fight for Britain in the War of Independence – it was not a simplistic, straightforward conflict between Americans and Britons. Prominent Britons also favoured **the** American Colonies, notably the 'father of British conservatism', the Anglo-Irish MP Edmund Burke (1729–97).

14. A previous generation knew them as Eskimos, a term now regarded as derogatory.

15. The national religion of Denmark, we recollect, was Lutheranism.

of Luther's: during a storm he was almost struck by a bolt of lightning, and on recovering, cried out to God to enable him to become a new person with a new God-devoted life. Attracted to the Moravians by what he heard about their piety, Haven was apprenticed to a Moravian carpenter in Copenhagen, the Danish capital. His apprenticeship over, Haven moved to the Moravian headquarters of Herrnhut, becoming a member of the community, where he lived and worked for ten years. He then became convinced that he should engage in the missionary work that had become so central to the Moravian vision; the Herrnhut community sent him to work among the Inuit of Greenland in 1758. He was commissioned by Zinzendorf, who told him, 'Go, my son, and learn the language of the Greenlanders: the Saviour will provide.' Haven went to Greenland, learned the language, and made fruitful contact with the Inuit in preparation for teaching them the Gospel. Native Inuit religion was a form of spiritism in which a high place was given to shamans[16] who mediated the power of spirits.

However, it is for his work among the Inuit of Labrador that Haven is remembered. He himself would gladly have remained among the Inuit of Greenland, but was directed to Labrador by a dream, in which he experienced the voice of God telling him, 'This is not your destination. You must make My Name known to the people of Labrador who have not yet heard of Me.' After some initial exploratory contacts in Labrador in the 1760s, which proved very positive, the full Labradorian mission began in 1771. In that year, Haven (now married to an English Moravian, Mary Butterworth) arrived in Labrador. He was accompanied by two other Moravian missionaries: the Danish deacon and physician Christoph Brasen (who actually led the mission), and Christian Larsen Drachardt, another Dane, raised by his uncle (a Lutheran pastor), who at first trained to be a Lutheran missionary, but then transferred his spiritual loyalties to the Moravians after coming into close touch with them in their Danish community of New Herrnhut.

---

16. Witch doctors, in older accounts.

Haven became the foremost missionary worker among the Labrador Inuit. Three mission stations were built – at Nain (1771), Okak (1776), and Hopedale (1782). Haven's evangelism at Okak proved very fruitful; by the time he moved on to Hopedale, he had baptised thirty-eight Inuit. Worn out by his labours, he and his wife returned to Herrnhut in 1784. On a human level, his success can be attributed to several factors: his knowledge of the native language (in which he preached), his refusal to reside in any Inuit territory unless they invited him, his refusal to carry weapons (seen by the Inuit as a token of his trust in them), and the strong focus of his message on the love and death of Christ. He became known among the Inuit as 'Jens Ingoak', Jens the Friend of the Inuit. The missionary seed he planted blossomed into a thriving Moravian Church, so that even today most of the inhabitants of the Labradorian north coast are Moravians.

5. Zinzendorf and further Moravian developments

After the Moravian Pentecost, the rest of Zinzendorf's life was far from uneventful. His intimate association with the Moravians brought him under dark storm-clouds of suspicion from the reigning Lutherans of Saxony. Was this wealthy nobleman not bringing his baptismal faith into disgrace by working so closely with these non-Lutheran 'sectarians' from Moravia? To try to quench the flame of Lutheran hostility, Zinzendorf had himself officially ordained into the Lutheran ministry in 1734, affirming his allegiance to the Lutheran Augsburg Confession. However, this move was ultimately unsuccessful. Two years later in 1736, the government of Saxony banished Zinzendorf. Religious intolerance was alive and well in 18th Century Europe.

Zinzendorf in exile was able to avoid financial destitution because of his private wealth. He at first settled in Prussia, where its King, Frederick William I (1713–40), despite initial doubts, became a fervent supporter after meeting the Count personally. Frederick William is reported to have said:

> The devil himself could not have told me more lies than I have been told about this Count. He is neither a heretic nor a disturber of the peace. His only sin is that he, a well-to-do Count, has devoted himself to the spread of the Gospel. I will not believe another word against him. I will do all I can to help him.

Zinzendorf was consecrated as a Bishop of the Moravian Church in 1737. This was part of a wider move within German Moravianism to restore the Episcopate to their Church order. The older Hussites had had Bishops, and the last surviving Bishops of historic Hussitism were now in Poland – Daniel Ernst Jablonski (1660–1741) and Christian Sitkovius (dates unknown). Jablonski was the grandson of John Amos Comenius (1592–1670), one of Moravianism's most original thinkers, whose writings had made a deep impression on Zinzendorf. The transition to Episcopalianism was prompted by Zinzendorf's desire to make Moravianism more acceptable to governments that acknowledged Episcopacy, especially England and its Colonies in America. As a result, David Nitschmann was first of all consecrated Bishop in 1735, prior to his sailing to England's American Colony of Georgia.[17] His consecration was then followed by Zinzendorf's in 1737.

Zinzendorf had some serious doubts about whether he could honestly be a faithful Lutheran if he became a Moravian Bishop. His doubts, however, were overcome by the advice of King Frederick William, who thought Zinzendorf's consecration as Bishop a good idea, and by discussions with England's then Archbishop of Canterbury, John Potter (1737–47), who was favourably disposed to Moravianism and convinced Zinzendorf that Moravians possessed genuine apostolic Episcopal succession. Zinzendorf's consecration seems to have helped his cause; he was able to establish a significant number of new Moravian settlements in other parts

17. Bishop Nitschmann sailed to America on the same ship as John Wesley, and was one of the Moravians whose serenity in the face of death, when a storm struck the ship, so deeply impressed Wesley. See Chapter 2, Part 2, section 3.

of Germany, and new Moravian congregations in the Dutch Republic and the Baltic states.

Zinzendorf also spent some years in England, where he paved the way for the creation of several Moravian churches there. He interacted with some of the leaders of the new movement of English Evangelical Revival, notably John Wesley and George Whitefield. These interactions were not always happy. Whitefield fell out with Zinzendorf over alleged mishandling of money by the Moravian Bishop. As for Wesley and Zinzendorf, they parted company in 1741, disagreeing vehemently over the doctrine of sanctification. The two men were far apart on this issue. Zinzendorf saw little place for any ongoing, detailed process of spiritual growth in a Christian's holiness; he regarded faith itself, and the assurance it brings, as making up the essential holiness of the justified believer. Apart from this faith, Zinzendorf insisted that the Christian remained, and knew himself to be, a wretched sinner throughout his earthly pilgrimage. Wesley, by contrast, was already exploring ideas of entire sanctification: an experiential holiness that would free the believer from all 'willing and witting sin'.[18]

With this rupture between Zinzendorf and both Whitefield and Wesley, the Moravian stream of revival in England flowed apart from the Calvinist and Arminian English Evangelical Revival. There was at least one prominent exception to this rule: the great Calvinistic evangelist John Cennick. He had sided with Whitefield against Wesley in the breach between the two leaders, and thereafter Cennick gravitated towards the Moravians, becoming a full member of their denomination. Cennick embodied the blending of the Moravian and English revivals.[19]

From 1741–43 Zinzendorf was in America, where he helped establish new Moravian churches in New York and Pennsylvania,

---

18. Strikingly, the conversation in which Zinzendorf and Wesley expressed their disagreement and parted ways with each other was conducted entirely in Latin – a sign of how theological culture in the 18th Century differed from today.
19. For more on John Cennick, see Chapter 2, Part 3, section 1.

and was one of the trailblazers of evangelism among Native Americans. In 1747, the Saxon government underwent a change of heart and lifted Zinzendorf's banishment, enabling him to return to Berthelsdorf after eleven years of exile. Two years later, the government even gave official recognition to the Moravians as a legally protected religious body in Saxony. Incidentally, so did the British Parliament that same year (1749).

The closing ten years of Zinzendorf's life were plagued with problems. The Moravian missionary programme incurred serious monetary debts. Zinzendorf's son, Christian Renatus, died young in 1752, dashing his father's hopes that he would take over the leadership of Herrnhut. His beloved wife Erdmuthe died in 1756. Zinzendorf remarried in 1757; his new spouse was Anna Nitschmann (1715–60), who had held a prominent place among the women of Herrnhut. Three years later Zinzendorf died, and was buried in the Herrnhut cemetery.

It is relatively easy to describe and assess Zinzendorf's work and impact as a church leader and vessel/instrument of religious revival. It is not so easy to do this in his capacity as a theologian. This is because Zinzendorf always tried to cut beneath theological divisions among Christians, to an underlying unity of heart-faith and experience. He came to regard all Protestant Churches as valid forms of the one Church of Jesus Christ, divided only by different apprehensions and expressions of a common truth – the truth of the Person of Jesus Christ. This outlook, as noted above, prevented him from even attempting to write a systematic theology. Nevertheless, Zinzendorf had at least one vote of appreciation from one of the Church's greatest systematic theologians: Karl Barth in the 20th Century praised Zinzendorf as 'perhaps the only genuine Christocentric of the modern age'.[20]

---

20. Barth also said in 1952, 'I have more and more become a "Zinzendorfian", in that only the one central figure in the New Testament [i.e. Jesus Christ] has come to occupy my thoughts.'

3
Lutheranism's Enlightenment genius: the life and work of Gottfried Wilhelm Leibniz (1646–1716)

If Lutheranism produced an intellectual genius whose thought intersected with the Enlightenment, that genius was the philosopher and theologian Gottfried Wilhelm Leibniz (1646–1716). In many ways, Leibniz stood in the current of Enlightenment thinking; in other ways, however, he represented a more conservative Christian outlook rooted in his cradle Lutheranism. The shadow (or sunshine) of his genius rested on the whole of 18th Century German philosophy and theology. Leibniz is perhaps even more respected among philosophers today than he was in his own time.

1. Life of Leibniz

Gottfried Wilhelm Leibniz was born in the city of Leipzig, in Saxony, on July 1st 1646. His father Friedrich taught moral philosophy at Leipzig University. In 1661, Leibniz went to the University to study law; during his legal studies, he also began reading the various treatises of great Enlightenment philosophers such as Descartes and Bacon. In 1667, he commenced a civil service career in the territory of the Prince-Archbishop of Mainz, Johann Philipp von Schönborn (1647–73), one of the seven 'electors' of the Holy Roman Empire.[1]

1. The seven electors had the power of choosing the successive Holy Roman Emperors – the Empire was an elective not a hereditary monarchy.

From 1672–76 Leibniz was in Paris on a diplomatic mission for the Prince-Archbishop of Mainz, aimed at distracting the French from military intervention in German affairs by persuading them to turn Eastward and invade and conquer Egypt. This mission was unsuccessful, although a hundred years later, during the French Revolution, Napoleon carried out an almost identical plan. In Paris, Leibniz mingled with many of the European intellectual elite of the day – France had become Europe's dominant cultural entity in the late 17th Century, and French the international language of culture, under the majestic and powerful monarchy of the 'Sun King', Louis XIV (1643–1715).[2] It was in Paris that Leibniz' interest in mathematics was quickened, leading to his ground-breaking formulation of 'calculus' in 1675.[3] There has been dispute about whether Leibniz or the English genius Sir Isaac Newton (1643–1726) was the first to originate calculus, and whether Leibniz stole Newton's ideas (as some accused him of doing); most scholars probably now accept that the two towering thinkers came to their conclusions independently, and at roughly the same time.

On his return to Germany in 1676, Leibniz relocated from Mainz to the city of Hanover, the residence of the Dukes of Brunswick-Lüneburg,[4] where he remained the rest of his life. Here he occupied several roles – court librarian, linguist, engineer, diplomat. As a diplomat, he pursued a grand vision of seeking to reunite Protestants (especially Lutherans) and Roman Catholics on the basis of agreed common beliefs (see below for more details), which makes Leibniz one of the early pioneers of ecumenism. He also wrote voluminously on matters of philosophy, including the crossroads between philosophy and theology, and on science, mathematics, linguistics, history, and politics.

---

2. For the life and reign of Louis XIV, see Volume 4, Chapter 6, Part 1, section 2.

3. Calculus is the mathematical study of rates of change. It has many practical applications, for example in physics, medicine, engineering, and economics.

4. The Duke of Brunswick-Lüneburg was another of the electors of the Holy Roman Empire.

Leibniz never married, and died aged seventy on November 14th 1716. His greatness as a thinker was vividly set forth by one of his intellectual opponents, the French atheist Denis Diderot:

> There has perhaps been no man who has read so much, studied so much, thought more deeply, and written more treatises than Leibniz. What he has written about the world, God, nature, and the soul possesses the most lofty eloquence. Had his ideas been expressed with the literary genius of Plato, then the philosopher of Leipzig would be no less great than the philosopher of Athens ... When I compare my talents with those of Leibniz, I am tempted to throw away my own books, and go and die quietly in some dark forgotten corner.[5]

2. Ideas of Leibniz: religion and theology

Leibniz remained a loyal Lutheran throughout his life (at least in his outward profession of faith), and was distressed by the anti-Christian turn taken by aspects of the leading philosophy of his day, especially under the impact of the Dutch-Jewish pantheist Baruch Spinoza.[6] He therefore responded by trying to give the essentials of orthodox Christianity a solid philosophical undergirding. Two areas in which he sought to achieve this lay in the realm of apologetics: the existence of God, and that branch of apologetics known as theodicy (vindicating the goodness of God – or as Puritan poet John Milton put it in *Paradise Lost*, 'justifying the ways of God to men'[7]).

Leibniz made a serious philosophical attempt to reinvigorate convincing rational proofs of the existence of God. He did this against the counter-claims of atheism, pantheism, and even Christian scepticism (the 17th Century's most brilliant Christian philosopher, Blaise Pascal, had been deeply sceptical about the usefulness of rational proofs for God[8]). Leibniz's most original contribution was his refurbishing of Anselm's 'ontological'

---

5. For Diderot, see Chapter 1, Part 2, section 7.
6. For Spinoza and his thought, see Chapter 1, Part 4, section 1. We recollect that pantheism identifies the universe with God.
7. For Milton, see Volume 4, Chapter 4, Part 1, section 6.
8. For Pascal, see Volume 4, Chapter 6, Part 4, section 9.

argument, which had been roundly and influentially rejected by Thomas Aquinas.[9] Anselm had argued that the very idea of God requires God's existence: God is 'that than which nothing greater can be conceived', and such an entity *must* exist in order to meet its definition. Descartes had sought to revive the ontological argument;[10] Leibniz took this revival further by restating the argument to include a proof that existence is itself a perfection (so that a perfect being must have existence to be perfect), and that 'necessary existence' belongs to the intrinsic essence of God (by virtue of His very nature, God cannot 'not exist').

Alongside his recasting of the ontological argument, Leibniz also reaffirmed the 'cosmological' argument, this time agreeing with Aquinas. This argument stated that since the universe is 'contingent' (might not have existed), its existence requires a cause – and this is God, who is not a contingent but necessary being, Himself uncaused. However, Leibniz restated the traditional argument thus: the 'principle of sufficient reason' requires that every *particular* existing thing in the universe must have a sufficient reason for its existence. This in turn requires that *all* such things together must have an *ultimate* reason for their collective existence, a reason lying beyond the universe. This ultimate reason is what we call God.

Leibniz's philosophically sophisticated arguments for God's reality gave a new lease on life to rational theistic proofs. These led to the 'Christian rationalism' of Leibniz's disciple, the philosopher Christian Wolff (1679–1754), and his widespread Wolffian school of philosophy, which had such influence in mid-18th Century Germany. However, Leibniz's arguments also provided a foil for the mighty intellect of Immanuel Kant, the supreme Enlightenment philosopher, who rejected all rational proofs of God. As we saw in the Chapter on the Enlightenment, Kant preferred to locate God (i.e., the Enlightenment deity, the Supreme Being) in the

---

9. For Anselm and the ontological argument, see Volume 2, Chapter 7, section 3.

10. See Chapter 1, Part 1, section 2.

category of a 'postulate' – a sort of hypothesis or theoretical assumption – needed to make sense of the moral law, but incapable of being proved.[11]

Concerning theodicy, Leibniz showed himself unusually sensitive to the critique of the Christian view of God that arose from the suffering of the world (a critique made by atheists and some Deists). Can the absolutely good and loving God of Christian revelation exist, consistently with the known and experienced suffering of life on earth? In response, Leibniz put forward his famous or infamous argument that this world, with all its suffering, is the 'best of all possible worlds'. His argument ran as follows. God, the world's Creator, is all-powerful, all-knowing, and perfectly good. This God sees, in His all-knowing mind, many possible worlds He has the power to create. But if our world is not the best of all possible worlds, one of the following positions must be true:

(i) God was unable to create a better world;

(ii) God was unable to foreknow how our world's history would unfold;

(iii) God did not desire the actual world to be the best world;

(iv) The world was not created by God but by some other being;

(v) There were no other possible worlds God had the power to create.

But all these positions, Leibniz argued, violated the fundamental truths that God, the world's Creator, is all-powerful, all-knowing, and perfectly good, and that He sees, in His all-knowing mind, many possible worlds He has the power to create. Necessary conclusion: this world – the actual created world – must be the best of all possible worlds.

When critics pointed to various aspects of the world which they found unworthy of an all-powerful, all-knowing, and perfectly good Creator, Leibniz responded with an argument

---

11. For Wolff and Kant, see Chapter 1, Part 3, sections 1 and 2.

classically expressed by the English Catholic poet, Alexander Pope (1688–1744), in his *Essay on Man*:

> All nature is but art, unknown to thee;
> All chance, direction which thou canst not see;
> All discord, harmony not understood;
> All partial evil, universal good:
> And, spite of pride, in erring reason's spite,
> One truth is clear: Whatever is, is right.

Leibniz's 'best of all possible worlds' argument entered into the very mainstream of Enlightenment thought in a way unintended by Leibniz, when the French Deist and literary genius Voltaire made it the central target of his hugely popular novel *Candide* (1759). The novel's character Professor Pangloss is a satire on Leibniz. Journeying across the world with his pupil Candide, and encountering many evils and disasters, Pangloss cheerfully explains them all away with his endless declaration that 'all is for the best in the best of all possible worlds'. Voltaire's treatment of Pangloss aims at exposing his Leibnizian optimism as shallow, glib, and unreal in the face of the world's actual suffering.[12]

Leibniz was also a pioneer ecumenist in seeking reconciliation between the varieties of Protestantism (chiefly Lutheran and Reformed), and between Protestants and Roman Catholics. We saw that Zinzendorf was committed to the same goal, but on a different foundation: for the Moravian leader, a common experience of salvation through Christ provided the basis, whereas for Leibniz the basis was reason. A rational theology, he thought, could (as it were) negotiate the differences between Lutheran, Calvinist, and Catholic, so that all could unite around the essential truths about God known to 'right reason'. Reason could show, Leibniz believed, that many of the differences between the three confessions were ultimately a matter of words, verbal formulations, not substantial truths. In pursuit of this vision, Leibniz engaged in serious discussions with a number of prominent Roman Catholic theologians, notably Bishop

12. For Voltaire and Candide, see Chapter 1, Part 2, section 3.

Jacque-Bénigne Bossuet of Meaux (1627–1704) – France's most celebrated preacher – and the brilliant French Jansenist leader, Antoine Arnauld (1612–94).[13] These discussions bore no final practical fruit, largely because the 'ecumenism' of the Roman Catholic dialogue partners resolved itself, ultimately, into a desire to convert Leibniz and all Protestants to the Church of Rome as possessing the fullness of truth. But the discussions did at least present the spectacle of some of Europe's foremost theologians seriously and honestly discoursing with each other about Christian reunion across their confessional divides. This would have been almost unthinkable a mere generation prior to Leibniz, when Europe was still convulsed with religious wars.

---

13. For Bossuet, see Volume 4, Chapter 6, Part 3, section 5. For Arnauld, see Volume 4, Chapter 6, Part 4, section 6.

4

Lutheran Bible commentator: the life and work of Johann Albrecht Bengel (1687–1752)

18th Century Lutheranism produced the age's most brilliant Bible commentator – Johann Albrecht Bengel (1687–1752), whose contributions to biblical scholarship and interpretation overflowed far beyond his native Germany and his Lutheran tradition. Bengel was, in effect, the first modern Evangelical Bible commentator. He occupied this position by virtue of his strong combination of devout believer who took the biblical message totally seriously as the recorded revelation of God's grace to sinful humanity, and cutting-edge scholar who came to terms with the reality of the imperfect process of the New Testament's textual transmission, with its competing manuscripts and variant readings.

A previous generation had tended to set these elements against each other. This tendency found a notorious expression in the fierce conflict, in 17th Century England, between leading Puritan theologian John Owen (1616–83) and Anglican Bishop and textual scholar Brian Walton (c.1600–1661). Walton had published, between 1653 and 1657, the *London Polyglot,* a critical edition of the Bible in nine languages; in the *Polyglot,* Walton had openly recorded and discussed the variant readings in the different biblical manuscripts. For this, Owen had attacked Walton, fearing that the integrity of Scripture would be unsettled by the Anglican scholar's exposure of its manuscript variations. In this conflict, it seemed that the cause of honest biblical scholarship lay with Walton, while the cause of profound theology and piety lay with Owen. Thomas Chalmers, the great 19th Century Scottish Presbyterian leader, was to say concerning this Walton-Owen conflict:

> The amalgamation of the two properties, thus arrayed in hostile conflict, would have just made up a perfect theologian. It would have been the wisdom of the letter in alliance with the wisdom of the Spirit – instead of which I know not what was the most revolting – the lordly insolence of the Prelate [Walton], or the outrageous violence of the Puritan.[1]

The amalgamation so much desired by Chalmers was achieved in Bengel in a way that set the whole course of future biblical scholarship among Evangelical believers.

1. The Life of Bengel

Bengel was born in Winnenden, in the south-western German state of Württemberg, on June 24th 1687. His father was a Lutheran preacher, but died when Bengel was only five or six years old; the orphan was subsequently cared for by David Wendel Spindler, a friend of his father. Spindler was a schoolteacher who had a passion for theology; his spiritual impulses were Pietist, which he took to the level of 'Radical Pietism'. Radical Pietists, in contrast to 'Church Pietists', had a separatist tendency, distancing themselves from the state-established Lutheran Churches, sometimes breaking with them completely. The mature Bengel would come to reject Radical Pietism; it is arguable that his rejection was a reaction against the example of his childhood mentor.[2]

Spindler became a tutor in Württemberg's Stuttgart high school in 1699, an institution with an unsurpassed reputation for excellence in the education of youth. (In 1710 Spindler was ultimately sacked from the Stuttgart school for his separatism

1. 'Prelate' is a generally disparaging term for a bishop.
2. For Radical Pietism, see Volume 4, Chapter 1, Part 4, section 4.

and his eschatological-millennial speculations.) Bengel studied at the Stuttgart school, before moving on in 1703 to Tübingen University, Württemberg's centre of advanced learning. It was here that Bengel first discovered the variant readings in different New Testament manuscripts. This initially unsettled his faith: how could the New Testament be the inspired Word of God if it had been transmitted through variant manuscript traditions? He overcame his doubts, however, by concluding that Scripture as the Word of God – like the Church as the body of Christ – became subject to human weakness through genuinely existing within the flux of earthly history, rather than floating above it. This weakness (he felt) did not negate the divine character of the Church as Christ's body, nor the saving power of Scripture as God's Word. The Saviour was still found in His Church, and His saving truth was still found in His Word, despite the unavoidably 'human character' of Church and Word. Besides, Bengel forcefully argued, the amount of textual variation in the different New Testament manuscripts was relatively minor, and did not affect the broad substantial basis of the New Testament's doctrinal teaching. His trust in the doctrinal integrity of the New Testament was vastly enlarged by lectures he attended at Halle, given by the renowned Pietist leader August Hermann Francke (1663–1727).

Bengel remained at Tübingen for ten years, first as student, then as tutor. The opposing influences of Pietism and Lutheran Orthodoxy flowed into him: the Pietist influence was Professor Andreas Adam Hochstetter (1668–1717); the Orthodox Lutheran influence was Professor Johann Wolfgang Jäger (1647–1720). From Hochstetter, Bengel continued to absorb Pietist ideals of Christian spirituality; from Jäger, he learned to appreciate the value of orthodox Lutheran theology and the traditions of Lutheran church life. His adherence to the Lutheran Church order of Württemberg would later place him in conflict with Zinzendorf and the Moravians, despite their shared Pietism; Bengel came to regard Zinzendorf's Moravianism as an unbalanced separatist movement. In addition to his academic life in Tübingen, Bengel was ordained to the ministry of Württemberg's Lutheran Church in 1706, preaching regularly to a congregation in Metzingen, some fourteen miles east of the university.

At the close of 1713, Bengel was appointed head of a new school at Denkendorf, north-east of Tübingen; the school's aim was to prepare young men for theological study at Tübingen University. Here, Bengel utilised what he believed were the best teaching methods found in Lutheran, Reformed, and Roman Catholic educational institutions, perhaps reflecting Pietism's readiness to look beyond its Lutheran origins. Shortly after settling in Denkendorf, he married Susan Regina Seeger, with whom he had six surviving children (another six died young). Bengel's goal as a tutor was not only to educate his students but to form their characters; he became so famous for his effective discipline of unruly students that other schools began sending their student troublemakers to Denkendorf to be 'sorted out' by Bengel. His chief subject area in his teaching was languages – Latin, Hebrew, Greek, Arabic and other Oriental languages were all cultivated. He also taught history, mathematics, and logic, and introduced into the curriculum geography and science (comparatively novel subjects at that time).

Bengel remained in this teaching post at Denkendorf until 1741, when he became the Lutheran Superintendent of the churches in the Herbrechtingen region of Württemberg. In 1749, he also became a member of the Lutheran consistory (governing Church body) in Stuttgart. As a consistory member, Bengel tried to bring an emphasis on a more concerted practice of congregational discipline, and the freedom of the Church from undue meddling by the state (in particular, he argued for a generous measure of religious toleration). He died in Stuttgart in 1752, aged sixty-five, after nine months of painful illness that left him bedridden.

2. Bengel as biblical scholar

Bengel's spiritual and intellectual passion was the Greek New Testament. At the Denkendorf school, he had his students join him in a two-year project of reading through the whole of the

Greek New Testament. As Bengel studied, he made extensive notes on the New Testament's textual variations, collecting over thirty different versions of the Greek text. He assembled these partly by appealing for international scholarly help; this resulted in Bengel's obtaining a large body of previously unknown New Testament manuscripts in Greek, Latin, Coptic, and Armenian. Bengel did not believe any of these was infallible or perfect; it was the task of the Christian scholar, he held, to sift through the various manuscripts and their readings, with a view to producing a text that most likely reflected the original reading.[3] The outcome was Bengel's 1734 critical edition of the Greek New Testament, a milestone in Western biblical scholarship. Despite disapproval from ultra-conservative scholars wedded to older versions of the Greek text, Bengel's new edition achieved widespread circulation. Zinzendorf, for instance, vigorously promoted it among Moravians, having the highest regard for Bengel as a Christian scholar.

Bengel also made a fresh translation of the Greek New Testament into German, which was published in 1753, just after Bengel's death. This was intended as a correction to Luther's translation, which Bengel did not think was sufficiently faithful to a strict understanding of the original Greek. Bengel's version never replaced Luther's in popular esteem, but was a useful tool for serious students.

Bengel's most famous, influential, and enduring work of New Testament scholarship was his *Gnomon* of 1742. The word *gnomon* means a pointer on a sundial. This work, which it took Bengel twenty years to finalise, consisted of a fresh translation of the Greek New Testament into Latin (still at that time the international language of scholarship), and an exegetical commentary on the text. His comments were brief: Bengel regarded exegetical brevity as a positive virtue, disliking the long, rambling comments favoured by other exegetes. He did not, however, limit his comments to interpreting the text in its

---

3. We should recollect that Bengel did not think the variations affected the greater portion of Scripture nor any of its doctrines.

original meaning; he included practical applications. In this he was seeking to fulfil his own celebrated maxim: 'Apply yourself wholly to the text; apply the text wholly to yourself.'

In the preface to the *Gnomon*, Bengel explained his methodology for dealing with textual variations, in twenty-seven rules. Most of these are reproduced at the close of this Chapter under Primary Historical Sources. This methodology has, in substance, become the accepted way among biblical scholars of dealing with textual variations.[4] It should be noted, however, that Bengel was very conservative in his own utilisation of these rules, for example in defending the 'Johannine Comma' (1 John 5:7) with its Trinitarian reference; no critical scholar today would argue for the authenticity of this verse.[5]

The *Gnomon* enjoyed huge success, setting the standard for all New Testament scholarship and exegesis for generations to come among German Protestants – or at least among the more religiously conservative (scholars more deeply impacted by the Enlightenment became progressively more detached from traditional exegesis: see the following section, **Chill Winds and Radical Response: Michaelis and Hamann**). Nor was the impact of the *Gnomon* restricted to Germany. In the English-speaking world, it found a zealous advocate in John Wesley, who hailed Bengel as 'a burning and a shining light, equally eminent in piety and in learning'.[6] Wesley translated the *Gnomon* into English, making extensive use of it in his 1754 *Explanatory Notes on the New Testament*, one of the key documents of Wesleyan Methodism.[7]

3. Bengel as end-times speculator

There was a strain of piety among 18th and 19th Century Evangelicals which lent itself to detailed speculation about the

---

4. Apart from those who accept the infallible perfection of a particular family of manuscripts (either the Byzantine Text of the Greek Church, or the 'Textus Receptus' of Reformation scholarship).

5. 'And there are three who bear witness in heaven, the Father, the Word [Greek *logos*], and the Holy Spirit; and these three are one.'

6. Wesley's Sermon 132, preached on April 21st 1777.

7. See Chapter 2, Part 5, section 2.

end-times, including the exact time of Christ's return. Bengel fell into this category. His study of the Bible, especially the book of Revelation, led him to believe that Christ's return and the millennium would begin in the year 1836. Nor was he shy about publishing this view. However, he added humbly, 'Should the year 1836 come to an end without any obvious change, there must be a basic error in my system; people would have the duty to work out where that error occurred.' In his own day, his date-setting had significant influence on Lutheran congregations that were open to Pietism; they pursued reform and renewal in order to ready themselves (or their children and grandchildren) to meet the soon-returning Lord.

Two German Pietists impacted by Bengel's end-time speculations were the theologian and philosopher Friedrich Christoph Oetinger (1702–82), and the writer of religious novels, Johann Heinrich Jung-Stilling (1740–1817). Oetinger, another Württemberg Pietist, was a Lutheran minister and later superintendent of the Lutheran churches in the region of Weinsberg, and later Herrenberg. A devotee both of Zinzendorf and Bengel, he accepted Bengel's predicted date of 1836 as ushering in the millennium; through Oetinger this millennial expectation gained a hold on others. Meanwhile, Oetinger devoted himself to combatting rationalism and furthering Pietism. In this regard, Oetinger looked for signs of a spiritual and supernatural order breaking into earthly reality (perhaps as forerunners of the millennium) – visions, heavenly dreams, visitations by angels and spirits. For a time, he was attracted to the visionary revelations of Swedish seer Emmanuel Swedenborg (1688–1772), founder of the New Jerusalem Church, translating some of Swedenborg's writings into German.[8] Oetinger's

---

8. Swedenborg and the New Jerusalem Church lie beyond the scope of detailed examination, since they belong more correctly in a history of cults and sects. They do, however, typify the kind of sectarian movement that became more common and prominent in the 19th Century, with a leader claiming extra-biblical divine guidance, perhaps visions, and a special heavenly mission to restore true Christianity out of the alleged apostasy of all its mainstream historical embodiments.

enthusiasm cooled, however, when Swedenborg's visions encountered almost universal mockery among Germany's educated classes.[9] Even so, this did not dampen Oetinger's resolve to see the physical world as being permeated by the spiritual world, rather than being (as in general Enlightenment science) a materialistic system of mechanistic cause-and-effect. Oetinger's Pietist campaign against rationalistic science shows how easily such a concern could shade off into magical and quasi-occult beliefs and practices.[10]

Johann Heinrich Jung-Stilling, from the village of Grund in the north-western German territory of Westphalia, held a startling variety of vocations: schoolteacher, tailor, physician, lecturer on agriculture, technology, commerce, veterinary medicine, economics, and statistics. His theological influence flowed through his writings, especially his novels (which fell into the genre of 'religious romances'). The common thread uniting everything Jung-Stilling wrote was an advocacy of Pietism and critique of rationalism. Like Oetinger, he accepted Bengel's date-setting of 1836 as the last year of the world's history, and gave this currency by including it in his most well-known novel *Das Heimweh* (1794–7 – the word means homesickness, nostalgia). The novel had such an impact among Württemberg Pietists that it motivated some to emigrate to Solyma in the Caucasus, where Jung-Stilling said the heavenly kingdom would descend.[11]

---

9. Immanuel Kant rejected Swedenborg as an 'occult dreamer'.
10. As if today, in order to combat atheistic materialism, a Christian should embrace the New Age movement.
11. He seems to have started out looking upon Solyma as an aspect of his Christian fiction, but increasingly swung round to taking it seriously as a reality.

5
Chill Winds and Radical Response: Michaelis and Hamann

Most of Germany was Protestant, and most of German Protestantism was Lutheran (apart from a much smaller Reformed community). When the chill winds of Enlightenment rationalism began to blow in the German Churches, therefore, the largest arena for the new currents of thought was German Lutheranism.[1]

The conservative biblical scholarship of Bengel, with its continuing recognition of the divine inspiration and unique saving message of Scripture, did not ultimately command the allegiance of the German academic establishment. Instead, a far more critical and rationalistic attitude took root, shaped by the outlook of Baruch Spinoza, Richard Simon, Jean Leclerc, and Jean Astruc.[2] The biblical scholarship of German Lutheranism thus entered its Enlightenment rationalist period. One of the most significant of the German Lutheran rationalists was the distinguished biblical critic, Johann David Michaelis (1717–91), who provides a useful 'human face' to Lutheranism in its growing Enlightenment phase. The influence of Michaelis, however, radiated out far wider than his native Germany or the Lutheran Churches; in the following century, for example, his biblical-critical work would make a large impact on Reformed Scotland.

---

1. For the Enlightenment and its various forms and facets, see Chapter 1.
2. For these thinkers and their critical approach to Scripture, see Chapter 1, Part 4.

1. Life and Work of Johann David Michaelis (1717–91)

Michaelis was born in 1717 in the Pietist headquarters of Halle, son of Christian Benedikt Michaelis, a theologian and specialist in Middle Eastern studies. The younger Michaelis studied at Halle University, and in 1739–40 achieved the necessary qualifications to become a German university lecturer. At this stage, Michaelis' youthful mind still moved in the orbit of Pietism and conservative Lutheran theology; we can see this in a dissertation he wrote around this time, in which he championed the traditional view that the 'vowel points' in the Hebrew text of the Old Testament (the Masoretic text) belonged to the original form of the text, and were in fact divinely inspired.[3] However, he acquired at Halle a supreme love for history, which would soon become the lens through which he viewed everything theological and religious.

It seems to have been a trip to England in 1741–42 that shook Michaelis' mind free from the constraints of his Pietist beliefs, as he encountered English Deistic and rationalist views of the Bible. This allowed Michaelis to move in the direction of Enlightenment critical perceptions of religion. His budding rationalism was enhanced by his falling deeply under the intellectual spell of Dutch thinker Albert Schultens (1686–1750), the outstanding Arabic scholar of his day. Schultens argued that there was nothing special, privileged, or 'sacred' about Hebrew – it was simply one of several related Semitic languages, all equally human. The comparative study of Hebrew and Arabic, for Schultens, could shed much light on the language (and hence the religion) of the Old Testament. Schultens' influence reinforced Michaelis' determination to treat the Bible and its religion from a detached academic standpoint, as developing phenomena of human history, rather than divine incursions into that history through prophecy and miracle. The outcome of these transitions in Michaelis'

---

3. By modern standards, this is an ultra-conservative position now held by almost no one.

mind meant that he no longer felt at home in Pietist Halle. He therefore relocated in 1745 to Göttingen in Lower Saxony as a private tutor. The following year he was appointed Professor of Oriental Languages in Göttingen University, where he lived and worked for the rest of his life.

Michaelis' most influential work in the field of critical scholarship was an annotated translation of the Old Testament, published in thirteen volumes between 1769 and 1786, after which he turned his searching intellect to the New Testament with a two-volume annotated translation published in 1790. These volumes were landmarks in the emergence of a modern 'scientific' approach to criticism of the Church's sacred text, disconnected from the setting of the Church's traditional theological assumptions. Michaelis also wrote a rational-critical *Introduction to the New Testament* (first edition 1750, many later revised editions), which fairly soon found its way into English in four volumes, published between 1793 and 1801.

Michaelis' rationalistic theology was expressed in perhaps its most controversial form in his *Commentaries on the Laws of Moses* (1770–75). In this work, he argued that the Pentateuch – far from being a divinely given law or a divinely inspired text – was the earthly product of Moses' skilful human statesmanship. By means of the Pentateuch, the Jewish political leader set out to find a way of differentiating Israel from the surrounding Pagan-Gentile nations, thereby forming the Jews into a distinct, separate, and cohesive cultural entity. One might say that for Michaelis, the Pentateuch was all politics and no prophecy. In his *Compendium of Dogmatic Theology* (1760), Michaelis endeavoured (perhaps surprisingly) to synthesise old-style Lutheran theology with his progressive critical views of Scripture, in spite of his lacking any personal belief in the Church's traditional orthodoxy. The outcome, at least in the eyes of orthodox Lutherans, was a succession of unconvincing compromises.

The Enlightenment rationalism for which Michaelis was a foremost Lutheran spokesman spread far and wide into the academic halls of Lutheran learning. Other significant Lutheran advocates of this type of thinking included the hugely learned and influential Church historian, Johann Lorenz von Mosheim (1693–1755) of Helmstedt University, who approached the Church's history from a perspective that emphasised secular causation (rather than supernatural direction) and a critically 'objective' analysis of source material; Johann August Ernesti (1707–81) of Leipzig University, pioneer in New Testament hermeneutics, who argued that the New Testament documents must be studied in exactly the same way, with the exact same methods, as any and all other historical writings of the ancient world; Johann Salomo Semler (1725–91), Bible commentator and historian of doctrine, who managed to transform Pietist Halle itself into a centre of rationalism; and the slightly absurd Karl Friedrich Bahrdt (1741–92), archenemy of everything supernatural in Christianity, who between 1773 and 1775 produced his own 'improved' version of the New Testament, *God's Recent Revelations in Letters and Stories*.

As the 18th Century began to draw to its close, an Enlightenment rationalist approach to the Bible had come to reign supreme in the theological faculties of German universities. Consequently, English-speaking religious conservatives were soon using the term 'German Neology' to designate the perceived evils the Enlightenment had wrought within Protestant theology.[4] This, however, did not mean that all German Lutherans bought into a rationalist view of religion. Some simply fought a rear-guard action, seeking to stave off the advances of the Enlightenment by doubling down on traditional Lutheran preaching and catechising. This might have played well among rank-and-file Lutherans in insular conservative congregations; it did nothing to speak to the more educated

4. Neology strictly means 'new language', but conservative religious thinkers employed the word to mean 'new theology' – new in a bad sense, i.e., wrong and misleading innovations. It is hard to escape the conclusion that there was also a touch of nationalism and patriotism when British and American Evangelicals sneered at *German* Neology, as if to say, 'We will have none of that German nonsense on the fair shores of Britain/America.'

culture of the day. Unexpectedly, however, a far more creative and challenging response came from a maverick Lutheran thinker, hailed by some as arguably the greatest philosophical genius of the 18th Century – Johann Georg Hamann (1730–88).

2. Life and Work of Johann Georg Hamann (1730–88)

Hamann was born in the city of Königsberg in east Prussia (now Kaliningrad in Russia)[5], son of a barber who also practised surgery (a fairly common combination at that time).[6] His first academic pursuit was theology, which he studied at Königsberg University; but he never finished his studies, and ended up working for a company of merchants. They sent him to carry out business for them in England. Here he lived rather like the prodigal son in the parable, 'wasting his substance in riotous living' (Luke 15:13). But at length the money, and the friendship money can buy, ran out. Reduced to abject poverty, suffering from depression, in 1758 Hamann turned to the Bible, reading it through from beginning to end. In consequence he experienced a profound religious conversion. This convinced him that the Enlightenment offered a false light, and that true illumination – true enlightenment – flowed from Jesus Christ and the Holy Spirit. He contrasted the crisis of the Reformation era with the Enlightenment era thus: in place of a system of salvation by human works manifest in 'law' (late medieval Catholicism), there was now a system of salvation by human reason manifest in 'philosophy' (Enlightenment humanism). But neither could save. Christ alone saves.

Returning to Prussia, Hamann spent virtually the rest his life as a civil servant working in the tax office of the Prussian monarch Frederick the Great (1740–86). However, he spent his leisure time reading a myriad of religious and philosophical treatises in

5. We remind ourselves again that Germany was not a politically united land in the 18th Century, and that Prussia was one of its largest and most militarily powerful states.

6. The barber did everything from cutting hair to cutting off limbs. By contrast the trained physician at that period often shunned the bloody business of surgery.

many different languages (he was a highly talented linguist), and writing a series of brief but epoch-making works of his own, in which he made fundamental criticisms of major aspects of the entire Enlightenment project (see below). His new-found faith alienated many of his 'enlightened' friends, and indeed cost him his marriage with his beloved Katharina Berens, when her rationalist brother refused permission for the two to marry. After this disappointment, Hamann never married – at least not in the strict sense of the word; but he did live with a 'common law' wife, to whom he was completely faithful, and with whom he had several children to whom he was devoted. Among those who knew him closely, he could be revered as a modern living saint.

Hamann's thought, expressed in his writings, is not easy to grasp; he seems to have gone out of his way to *force* readers to think about what they were reading, a task which he believed was hindered by a dull insistence on clarity. As he put it, 'A writer who makes haste that he should be understood today or tomorrow, runs the risk of being misunderstood the day after tomorrow.' He therefore wrote under many strange pseudonyms (the Knight of the Rosy Cross, the Sibyl, Angry Prophet from the Brook Cherith, A Lover of Boredom, A Preacher in the Wilderness, Zacchaeus the Publican, A Northern Savage), none of whom necessarily represented Hamann's own convictions. He also indulged in an uproarious level of offbeat humour – one of his treatises claimed to be written by the letter H in defence of its usefulness to language. The reader must consequently work hard to discover what Hamann himself was actually, seriously saying.[7] However, if we focus on his critique of Enlightenment rationalism (the outlook often summed up in the works of his friend, the philosopher Immanuel Kant[8]), we can make the following observations.

---

7. Soren Kierkegaard in the 19th Century would call Hamann the greatest Christian humourist of all time. It may be noted that another problem in understanding Hamann is that he was so well acquainted with all previous literature, his endless direct and indirect references to it can be baffling to those of us who are not so well-read.

8. For Kant, see Chapter 1, Part 3.

Hamann voiced grave scepticism about the Enlightenment rationalist concept of reason itself. He regarded 'reason' as a cold abstraction. The fundamental reality was concrete 'reasoning', not abstract reason. And reasoning was done by 'reasoners' who were – perhaps quite unwittingly – controlled by various passions, commitments, and attitudes of heart-trust that preceded all exercises of reason. Not that Hamann was rejecting passion and commitment; he held them to be essential to the human mind and its relationship to reality. The so-called detachment and objectivity required by rationalism were both impossible and undesirable. Life itself was so constructed that passion and commitment were necessary to any true penetration into reality and thus any true understanding. Self-knowledge, Hamann argued, cannot be obtained by naked reason seeking to think in isolation (this was Hamann's retort to Descartes[9]); one can truly know oneself only in relation to one's neighbour and to God. Remove neighbour and God, and the human mind can have no genuine understanding of itself. What I truly am is defined by my actual living relation to my neighbour and to God my Creator, and involves love, not merely intellectual understanding.

Moreover, Hamann maintained that prior to any reasoning, there existed certain deep heart-commitments of trust, without which reasoning lacked any intelligible framework. Examples we might give of Hamann's meaning here are trust in the reality of the world, in the general reliability of the senses, in memory and the existence of the past. Such core 'trusts' cannot be justified by reason, but (Hamann argued) existed underneath and before all reasoning, supplying its material and its context. The activity of reason was 'married' to all these other forms of knowing, and no divorce made any sense. As a result, reasoning for Hamann was always the action, not of some ideal 'reason' abstracted from existing individuals, but the activity of a whole human person, with all his core trusts, his passions and commitments, and his interconnected relationship in the

9. For Descartes, see Chapter 1, Part 1, section 2.

world to his neighbour and to God. Hamann thereby sought to undermine what he believed was a shallow view of reason, in favour of deeper and more basic 'pre-rational' attitudes of the heart. (In this respect, although Hamann was not a Deist, he preferred Rousseau's intuitive 'Deism of the heart' to the more typical Enlightenment obsession with proving God by supposed rational argument.[10])

Another of Hamann's assaults on superficial rationalism was his insistence that human experience is finite and fragmentary, necessarily resulting in an inescapable imperfection of knowledge. Although there was a profound unity to life, the human mind could not perceive that unity in a simplistic, rationalistic way, misled by the false analogy that the mind is a perfectly seeing eye and reality a perfectly visible object. The truthful mind was driven, rather, to posit what Hamann called 'the principle of the union of opposites'. We can express the perceived nature of reality only by a series of apparent contradictions or paradoxes. Hamann explained his view thus, while discussing the ideas of Kant:

> Every day in ordinary life I experience this – that a person always has to contradict himself from two different viewpoints, which can never be harmonised. We cannot transform one of these viewpoints into the other, without doing the gravest violence to each of them. Our knowledge is thus made up of fragments.

For Hamann, the absence of apparent contradiction always led to, or was a symptom of, an unrealistic and abstract dogmatism that sacrificed reality to systematic (but false) unity. He certainly believed that reality *itself* was a unified whole, not an irrational chaos, but he rejected the human mind's capacity to *grasp* this unity through mere reason. One must instead proceed along the more honest and jagged pathway of antithesis and paradox.

Hamann's critique of rationalism is perhaps best laid out in his 1784 essay, written in response to Kant, *A Meta-Critique of the Purism of Reason*, and in a letter he wrote that year to

---

10. For Rousseau, see Chapter 1, Part 2, section 4.

Christian Jacob Krauss (1753–1807), accomplished linguist and student of Kant.[11]

Lastly, as one might have expected from a believing Lutheran, Hamann contested the Enlightenment conception of God – chiefly Deism, but with a particular concern for the kind of Deism found in the philosophy of Kant. He protested that Kant's God was nothing more than an intellectual concept derived from human reason. This was not the God encountered in the narrative of Christian Scripture: a living, dynamic God, active in the world, taking sovereign initiative in dealing with humanity, and transforming lives by His inbreaking, sanctifying presence in Jesus Christ. Those who knew the biblical God would not exchange Him for the remote and sterile Supreme Being of the Enlightenment. 'Knowing God' in Jesus Christ trumped 'knowing about the existence of a Deity' in Kantian philosophy. The first was true enlightenment that brought salvation; the second was a pseudo-enlightenment that left men in spiritual darkness.

Hamann's challenge to key concepts of Enlightenment rationalism helped to inspire a whole new generation to look beyond a detached intellectual idolatry of reason, and to revive the role played by the heart in human life and knowledge. It reminds us of a similar point made in the 17th Century by the great Jansenist philosopher Blaise Pascal: 'the heart has its reasons of which reason knows nothing.'[12] Among the future leaders of thought who regarded Hamann as a towering genius were the great linguistic theorist, poet, and theologian Johann Gottfried von Herder (1744–1803); Germany's supreme Romantic author (poet, novelist, playwright, literary critic) Johann Wolfgang von Goethe (1749–1832); the pre-

---

11. The *Meta-Critique of the Purism of Reason* remained unpublished in Hamann's lifetime. It finally came out in 1800, twelve years after Hamann's death.

12. For Pascal and Jansenism, see Volume Four, Chapter 6, Part 4, section 9. We can trace a line of anti-rationalist apologetics from Luther and Calvin, through Pascal, Hamann, and S. T. Coleridge, to Kierkegaard and Karl Barth.

eminent 19th Century German philosophers Friedrich Heinrich Jacobi (1743–1819), G. W. F. Hegel (1770–1831), and F. W. J. Schelling (1775–1854); and the profound Danish thinker Søren Kierkegaard (1813–55).

It was partially at least from the fountain of Hamann's anti-rationalist Lutheranism that there gushed the rich and fertilising streams of the *Sturm und Drang* ('Storm and Stress') movement in German music, painting, and literature in the late 18th Century, the subsequent glories of the Romantic movement in philosophy, poetry, music, and art, and Lutheran philosopher Kierkegaard's unsettling existentialism, all of which rebelled against rationalism. But Hamann's challenge also flowed into the religious life of Lutheranism itself, in the form of the *Erweckung* or Awakening, in the early 19th Century.[13] The Awakening motivated many Lutherans to turn away from rationalism, and rediscover the vitality of spiritual experience, together with the centrality of Bible reading (divine revelation, not human reason, is the ultimate authority), and the life of the Lutheran worshiping community and its liturgy.

13. Not to be confused with the Great Awakening in America.

6
Lutheranism in the New World

1. Beginnings

Lutheranism got off to a shaky start in North America in the mid-17th Century, largely through Swedish settlers, whose religious leadership was provided by several ministers who seemed to prefer the wine-bottle to the Bible. However, a new era began in 1697. Two Swedish ministers, Andreas Rudman (1668–1708) and Eric Bjork (dates unknown), were sent out by the Swedish Lutheran Church, to reinvigorate the Lutheran presence and witness in the New World. Rudman worked in Philadelphia, Bjork in Christina (now Wilmington), in the Delaware valley.[1] The work, regarded as taking place within the jurisdiction of the Lutheran Archbishop of Uppsala (the chief bishopric in Sweden), now flourished. On February 23rd 1704, Rudman was officially appointed Superintendent of all Swedish Lutherans in America by King Charles XII (1682–1718) of Sweden.

The imprint of Pietism was soon felt on American Lutheranism. In 1703, at the Swedish Lutheran church in Wicaco (now in southern Pennsylvania), Rudman ordained the young Justus Falckner (1672–1723), a student of German Pietist leader August Hermann Francke. Falckner had been trained at the Halle Pietist Foundation in Prussia, and was the first Lutheran

1. Philadelphia is in the state of Pennsylvania, Wilmington in the state of Delaware. These states were not yet organised as independent 'states' in the period of the Colonies.

minister to be ordained on American soil. The Pietist training and spirituality of Falckner were the first sign that the future shape of American Lutheranism would be moulded far more by Pietism than by Lutheran Orthodoxy. His ministry was geographically wide-ranging, taking in several congregations in Pennsylvania, New York, and New Jersey. Falckner's Pietism meant that he felt open to minister not only to Lutheran but also to Dutch Reformed congregations.[2] This, too, was pregnant with significance for America's Lutheran future (see below).

The number of Lutheran immigrants into North America became quite large by the middle of the 18th Century, from both Sweden and Germany. The attraction was partly material: America was portrayed as a new Canaan, flowing with milk and honey, where honest Lutherans could carve out decent lives for themselves and their children. Sometimes, however, Lutherans were crossing the Atlantic for religious reasons, fleeing from intolerance and persecution. For example, in the prosperous Austrian Catholic city of Salzburg, its ruling Prince-Archbishop decreed in 1731 (on October 31st, anniversary of the 95 Theses) that all his Lutheran subjects must forsake their Protestantism and conform to Roman Catholicism. Just over 20,000 Lutherans refused, and were forcibly evicted from Salzburg and its lands. Many fled to Prussia, whose Calvinist king, Frederick William I, welcomed them. But some fled to America, settling in Georgia.

The American Lutheran connection with Pietism was especially strong in the Colony of Pennsylvania, founded by the Quaker William Penn in 1681 on the principle of religious liberty. This meant (as we noted in Chapter 4) that religious believers of all stripes found a home in Pennsylvania: not only Penn's fellow Quakers, but also Anglicans, Presbyterians, Baptists, Roman Catholics, Jews, and Lutherans, all on an equal footing in the eyes of the law. Lutherans in Pennsylvania began looking to the Pietist Foundation in Halle for help and

---

2. Reflecting the pan-Protestant impulse that often pulsated within Pietism.

inspiration. As a result, twenty-four Pietist-trained Lutheran ministers were sent to America in 1742, the bulk of them to Pennsylvania. One of them was Henry Melchior Muhlenberg (see below). The Halle Foundation began publishing regular reports about the situation in the New World; these had a wide readership in Germany, and stimulated Pietist interest and support for American Lutherans. The American Lutheran gravitation toward Pietism was itself strengthened in consequence.

2. The life and work of Henry Melchior Muhlenberg (1711–87)

Muhlenberg has been called 'the church father (or patriarch) of American Lutheranism'. Prior to his arrival in the New World, the American Lutheran congregations – although flourishing in some ways – were disunited, subject to conflicting influences, and troubled by unauthorised preachers who sought to build a personal following. Muhlenberg was instrumental in changing all this.

Henry Melchior Muhlenberg was born in 1711 at Einbeck in the north German state of Hanover, ruled by the Dukes of Brunswick-Lüneburg (who enjoyed the privilege of being 'electors' of the Holy Roman Empire). He studied theology at the University of Göttingen in Lower Saxony. Here he was drawn into Pietist circles, and when his studies were finished in early 1738, he became a tutor in a Pietist orphanage in the Pietist 'headquarters' of Halle. Ordained to the Lutheran ministry in 1739, he accepted a call in 1741 from German Lutherans in Pennsylvania to relocate to America and serve them as a pastor. Muhlenberg arrived in the city of Philadelphia, chief city of Pennsylvania, in 1742. His ministry, however, was not locally confined; Lutheran churches in Pennsylvania, New York, and Maryland all came under his care. In this work, he devoted himself to ridding the churches of unauthorised preachers, and establishing the authority of properly trained, theologically educated ministers.

The key event in Muhlenberg's campaign was a synod of Lutheran ministers meeting in Philadelphia on August 26th

1748, convening at Muhlenberg's initiative; present were six ministers, and lay representatives from ten of the American Lutheran congregations of German origin (mostly located in Pennsylvania) – later meetings also involved American Lutherans of Swedish origin. The 1748 synod, and its successor synods, came to be known as the Ministerium. The first synod held a general discussion about the state of Lutheranism and its churches in North America, sanctioned a Lutheran liturgy for the churches (which Muhlenberg helped to draft), and ordained a new minister, Johann Nicholas Kurtz (1720–88), a Pietist from Halle. The bond with German Pietism was now fully forged; the Ministerium would take no major decisions without consulting Pietist leaders in Germany.

The Ministerium was a comparatively informal body at first, but in 1781 a formal constitution was adopted, along with the name 'the German Evangelical Lutheran Ministerium of North America'. The Pietism of Muhlenberg and the other members of the Ministerium was evident in their willingness to learn from the Reformed tradition as they had encountered it in America: they embraced the Dutch Reformed pattern of church government, with its four offices of pastor, presbyter, deacon, and teacher. This included the Reformed democratic element of congregations electing church officers. The end result of all this denomination-building, under Muhlenberg's presiding influence, was a form of Lutheranism in North America that was less European, less medieval and aristocratic, more adapted to the popular culture of the New World.

This native character of American Lutheranism was also evident in its worship-forms. Unlike most European Lutherans, American Lutherans generally had little religious adornment in their church buildings (stained glass windows, crucifixes, etc.). Their ministers wore ordinary black suits, not ecclesiastical gowns. Preaching, not ceremony – not even the Lord's Supper – held the supreme priority. The preaching was, however, allied to a strong system of catechising, and sermons were required to be faithful to the traditional Lutheran confessions of faith.

Despite the predominance of Pietism in American Lutheranism, there was some pushback from Lutheran Orthodoxy. The orthodox Lutherans condemned Pietists as not being true Lutherans at all, or (possibly worse) of being crypto-Moravians. Muhlenberg had to defend himself personally against such accusations. He stymied his orthodox opponents by proclaiming his unswerving adherence to the theology of the Lutheran confessions, and turning the accusation against his detractors, asserting somewhat tartly that their trouble was 'adhering to the unchanged Augsburg Confession with unchanged hearts'. Eventually, it was Muhlenberg's Pietism that won out, and Lutheranism in North America would be a Church leavened all through by Pietist influences.

PRIMARY SOURCE MATERIAL

Leibniz: Reason and piety

Virtue is reasonable and based on knowledge – when it is related to God, since He is the ultimate reason of everything. A person is unable to love God without knowing His perfections; this knowledge carries within itself the principles of genuine piety. The aim of religion should be to impress these principles on our souls. And yet in some puzzling way, people and teachers of religion have wandered far from this aim. Against the purpose of our divine Master, religious devotion has been shrunk down to rituals, and religious doctrine has been overburdened with verbal formulas. These rituals have, far too frequently, been badly designed to sustain the exercise of virtue; the verbal formulas have sometimes been devoid of clarity. Can you believe it? Some Christians have dreamt that they could be spiritual without loving their neighbour, and religious without loving God! Or else people have imagined they could love their neighbour without serving God, and could love God without any knowledge of Him. Many centuries have gone by without any widespread recognition of this deficiency. Indeed, there are still great signs that darkness reigns.

There are many people who speak much of godliness, of religious devotion, of religion (they may even be busy teaching these things!), who show themselves to lack knowledge of the divine perfections. They poorly understand the goodness and justice of the Lord of the universe; they imagine a God who does not deserve either to be imitated or to be loved. This has truly seemed to me to be treacherous in its outcome, since it is a serious matter to preserve from contamination the very wellspring of piety. The ancient errors of those who condemned the Deity, or who turned Him into a principle of evil, have been given new life in our own days, at least in some circles. People have asserted God's irresistible power, when they should have presented His supreme goodness; and they have presumed Him to possess a tyrannical power, when they should have understood His power as being governed by the most perfect wisdom. I have noticed that such views, which are well able to do harm, were based especially on confused ideas about freedom, necessity, and destiny.

Several times I have taken up my pen to give explanations on these vital issues. But now at last, I feel compelled to collect my thoughts on all these related questions, and to communicate them to the public. This is what I have endeavoured here in the essays I now offer, on the goodness of God, the freedom of Man, and the origin of evil.

Gottfried Wilhelm Leibniz
Essays in Theodicy (1710)

Zinzendorf: Christianity and religious denominations

It is an absolute rule of a true Christian's character that (rightly speaking) he is neither Lutheran nor Calvinist, neither of this nor that religious denomination – in fact, not even 'Christian'! What else can we say more clearly, more definitely? Which of the reformers – Huss, Luther, Wycliffe, or whoever – would be so arrogant as to hold that people are saved because they follow him? Paul even excludes Christ Himself from this party spirit: 'Not of Paul, nor Cephas, nor Apollos, nor Christ' (1 Cor. 1:12) ....

An honest Christian can say, 'I am on Calvin's side.' Another equally honest Christian can likewise say, 'My judgment puts me on Luther's side.' But this does not give either of them the slightest right or title to salvation. All it does is set them apart according to their respective insights, and demonstrate their honesty as believers. It also gives them the right not to be ignorantly and subjectively condemned by others in their conduct, their form of doctrine, their method of treating souls, and their external manner of worship. Everything has its own distinctive outward form, its outward shape; not everything looks the same. No individual has the exact same viewpoint as another; each person, by having his own particular viewpoint, is merely showing his individuality, in an innocent and inoffensive way ... It is an ill-mannered and mean-spirited attitude, when people from one religious denomination take positive delight in contradicting those from another denomination, and exhibit hostility to each other out of denominational rivalry ...

To this extent, I agree that it is good we should have a variety of religious denominations. In fact, unless a person has the deepest and most thoroughly examined reasons, I have no respect for someone who switches from one denomination to another. Nothing sounds more absurd to me than such a frivolous 'convert'. I can hardly force myself to have dealings with him, especially when he swaps one *Protestant* denomination for another, where each denomination acknowledges Scripture as the governing rule of its faith. Let such frivolity not prevail in matters of denomination! The existing diversities of denomination are important matters worthy of esteem, and are a manifestation of God's wisdom. Denominational distinctives should not stir up troubles.

However, all these differing denominational outlooks show their manmade origins, so that three hundred, five hundred, a thousand years ago, no one thought of matters in this way. It is of Christ alone that we can say, 'The same yesterday, today, and forever' (Heb. 13:8).

> His own Church stands as ever she has stood,
> And the Almighty Father is her God;
> Still she retains her first, her earliest dress,
> Jesus' own blood and Jesus' righteousness.[1]

Nicolaus von Zinzendorf

***On the Essential Character and Circumstances of the Life of a Christian*, from his *Nine Public Lectures on Important Subjects in Religion* (1746)**

---

1. Zinzendorf is contrasting religious denominations with the spiritual body of Christ that transcends denominations.

Zinzendorf: Self-righteousness excludes from the Kingdom

'He casts down the mighty from their thrones and raises up the lowly' (Luke 1: 52). All who are puffed-up, all who are self-important, all who are self-righteous, all who are holier-than-thou, all who seek their justification apart from the justification that is grounded upon Jesus' blood and His merits, who try to build up their holiness from reading books, undergoing experiences, and practising pious exercises, who devote their lives to such works, and are consequently revered by half the world – such are those who think they need no wedding garment. When the wedding garment is held out to them, when you speak to them about Christ's blood and righteousness, explaining that this is the jewelled garment of glory in which a person must stand in the presence of God, they look upon such things as fit only for children, mere trivialities, for as long as their minds are abiding in the world. Yet they could have experienced this differently; they really knew better; their education placed them far beyond such thoughts, or else they had gained deeper insights into the matter.

However, they depart from the world and appear before God's throne with the same self-important and blinded mind, without ever becoming spiritually sober. They are allowed into the wedding feast, but it only results in their rejection. The Master asks them why they have come and yet are not wearing the expected wedding garment. They do not know how to reply! How often they heard, 'You will be cast out first, before all the saints who lived sinfully. The Saviour's compassion, enjoyed by others, will not rest upon them; they will be ejected without respect.' All this this is part and parcel of being rejected.

That is the reason for their rejection. That is the meaning of the Saviour's words, 'Many are called, but few are chosen.' Those who are called always have a reason for not responding aright. One is called and fails to come, giving excuses. Another comes to the feast, but he does not come rightly; he comes with a puffed-up attitude, with airs and graces about himself. He would prefer to bring things with him, rather than submit to be given things.

If we must ever be rejected, what a blessing, what a good thing it would be for us, were this to take place here in the present world! Esau had great contempt for God's gifts. He fancied it would be a trivial matter to barter away his birthright. Later on, when he desired to regain it, he discovered there was no way he could accomplish this, although he wept tears in the attempt. The apostle says, 'Beware in case any among you is the sort of person who scorns common grace, the beggar's grace' (Heb. 12:15-16 paraphrased).

Esau's behaviour is not uncommon. Naaman virtually acted in the same way. He thought that a prophet ought to have all manner of special rituals in his hand, or engage in profound discussions. However – 'The prophet said, Go and wash yourself in the Jordan. My word, Naaman thought, if that is all there is to it, I could have done it better in my own country! But his servants responded, Dear father, had the prophet told you to do something remarkable, you would have taken it very seriously. How much more should you do so, when he says, Go and wash yourself, and you will be made clean. And he went and washed himself, and he was made clean' (2 Kings 5:13-14).

This is always the case, in harmony with the saying of the Saviour: 'The healthy do not need a physician, but the sick' (Matt. 9:12).

> All those who need nothing, receive nothing.
> All those who are not poor, will never become rich.
> All those who suffer no sorrow, will never be comforted.
> All those who are not sick, will never become healthy.
> All those who are not lost, will never be sought by the Lamb, still less found.
> All those who are not naked, all those who do not feel their nakedness and desire to be clothed, receive nothing.

This is sad but true. In this we find the entire mystery of the reality of rejection. It means that all puffed-up spirits who do not wish to bow the knee, who do not wish to flatten themselves in the dust, who lack poverty of spirit, who do not wish to be sick, who do not wish to take the same path that every other poor sinner and beggar takes on the journey to heaven – such people may perhaps be allowed into the wedding feast, but only for the purpose of being all the more publicly cast out again.

Nicolaus von Zinzendorf
Third Sermon **in Germantown, Pennsylvania, in 1742**

The Moravian revival

On July 22nd a number of the Brethren[2] freely covenanted together to gather often on the Hutberg,[3] to pour out their hearts in prayers and hymns, and to submit to each other in love, so that an idea proposed by one might be approved by all, if the idea rested on a right foundation. The first hymn they sang was *Our conversation is in heaven*. Consequently a great religious awakening took place. The names of these Brethren were Melchior Nitschman, George Schmidt, Melchior Zeisberger, David Tanneburger, Fredric Boehnisch, Leonard and Martin Dober, Frederic Kiihnel, Christian David, and Augustan Neisser. Their number was increased by others. That same day, Count von Zinzendorf embarked on his journey to Silesia, intending to visit Count Gersdorf at Hartmannsdorf. He was not deterred from this journey by information received the previous day, that the magistrates of Silesia had been ordered to arrest him if he entered that land. Before leaving Herrnhut, several Brethren promised that they would carefully oversee the grain of spiritual wheat that was now springing up from the ground, promoting its growth to the best of their ability. To this end, they pledged attentively and faithfully to continue the gatherings appointed for singing and prayer.

A short time later, they thought it better to change the singing meetings into meetings for mutual edification, at which not one person alone, but several people in turn, spoke on this or the other biblical passage, according to the experience and

---

2. That is, the United Brethren or Brethren of the Unity, the technical name of the Moravian Hussites.

3. The hilltop in Herrnhut where Moravians buried their dead.

faith enjoyed by each. Thus these gatherings became, strictly speaking, opportunities for those who met together to hold conversations with each other, in which they would relate and lay open the condition of their hearts. Baron Reichwein, who had been greatly moved by the awakening, insisted strongly that the principle of love was the supreme matter — the wellspring of authentic Christianity. In response, others urged that love must indeed prevail, but should take its proper place in that order pointed out by 2 Peter 1:7, where love follows godliness: trees must first be planted before they can bear the necessary fruit. There was, furthermore, one individual in the assembly who seemed resolved on every occasion to stir up discussions that would lead to controversies; but the young congregation was of a different sort of spirit, enabling it to meet the efforts of this individual with wisdom and meekness. In this way, the evil he had intended was frustrated and overcome.

When Melchior Nitschman, Christian David, and Martin Dober were conversing about the best way to regulate the public discussions, they adopted a method suggested by Christian David — to work through the entirety of the First Letter of Saint John, in order to preserve everyone in the proper path of love. When this was proposed to the assembled congregation, it made an immediate and profound impression on the minds of all. During the subsequent meditations on that Epistle, many were led to speak in a striking way about the sentiments and feelings of their hearts. This greatly increased the confidence and love already existing among the Brethren; suspicion, envy, and offence vanished away, replaced by a humble and heavenly spirit uniting the hearts of all. Eccentricity of opinion, discord, and resentment were wholly put aside. The spark of love grew more and more, becoming a flame that devoured straw and stubble, or gathered additional light and warmth by the excellent fuel poured upon it. Thus the fire kept on burning without interlude.

From *The Memorial Days of the Renewed Church of the Brethren* (1821)

Bengel: Rules for textual criticism

1. Thanks be to God, the overwhelmingly greater part of the Sacred Text is not burdened with any significant variation of reading.

2. This portion of the text contains the entire plan of salvation, and establishes every aspect of it by every test of truth.

3. Every variation in reading may and should be measured against this portion as a standard, and be judged by it.

4. The text of the New Testament, and its various readings, are found in manuscripts, and in books printed from manuscripts, in Greek, Latin, Graeco-Latin, Syriac, etc., Latinizing Greek, or in other languages, in the clear quotations of Irenaeus, etc., according as divine providence deals out its riches to each generation. We include all these under the title of 'codices', which sometimes has a comprehensive meaning.

5. These codices, however, have been spread and scattered through the churches of all times and countries. Yet when taken together, they approach so close to the original autographs that, despite the multitude of their variations, they give us the genuine text.

6. No mere speculation about how a text reads should ever be listened to. When a particular portion of the text is burdened with insoluble problems, the safest thing is to place it in brackets.

7. The entire body of codices taken together should form the normal standard, by which each taken separately should be judged.

8. The Greek codices are so ancient that their years surpass in number the textual variations themselves. They are not many of them, but the other textual witnesses are very numerous.

9. Versions in other languages, and quotations in the writings of the Fathers, where these differ from the Greek Manuscripts of the New Testament, have little authority. However, where the Greek Manuscripts of the New Testament differ from each other, those variations have the greatest authority with which the versions and the Fathers agree.

10. The text of the Latin Vulgate, where it is confirmed by the consent of the Latin Fathers, or even of other competent textual witnesses, merits the most weighty consideration, on account of its great antiquity.

11. The number of textual witnesses who support each particular reading of each passage should be carefully examined. In doing this, we should distinguish between those codices which contain only the Gospels, from those which contain the Acts and the Epistles, with or without the book of Revelation, or those which contain that book alone; those which are complete, from those which have been damaged and truncated; those which have been gathered together for the Stephanus edition, from those which have been gathered for the Complutensian Polyglot, or the Elzevirian, or any obscure edition; those which are known to have been carefully collected and organised, as for instance, the Alexandrine, from those which are not known to have been carefully collected and organised, or which are known to have been carelessly collected and organised, as for instance the Vatican Manuscript which, otherwise, would be almost without equal.

12. The greater number of specific textual witnesses are of greater value than those of fewer number. More importantly, witnesses that differ from each other in country, age, and language, are of greater value than those that are closely related to each other. Most important of all, ancient witnesses are of greater value than modern ones. Since the original autographs (written in Greek) can alone claim to be the wellspring of Scripture, the degree of authority possessed by codices drawn from primitive sources (Latin, Greek, etc.) depends on their proximity to that fountainhead.

13. A variation which does not tempt by its reading too easily, but shines with its own native dignity of truth, should always be preferred above those which may justly be reckoned to owe their origin to the carelessness (or insufficient care) of copyists.

14. A corrupted text is often given away by alliteration, parallelism, or the convenience of Church Lectionary, especially

at its beginning or ending. From the occurrence of the same words, we are led to suspect an omission; from too an ease of reading, we suspect a gloss. When a passage has a great variety of readings, the middle reading is the best.

15. There are, therefore, five main criteria, by which to settle a disputed text: the antiquity of the textual witnesses, the diversity of their geographical origin, their multitude, the apparent source of the corrupt reading, and the native colour of the genuine reading.

16. When these criteria all agree, no doubt can exist, save in the mind of a sceptic.

17. When, however, we find that some of these criteria favour one reading, and some favour another, the textual critic may be drawn sometimes in one direction, sometimes in another. Even if he makes a definite decision, others may be less ready to agree with him. When one man surpasses another in power of vision (whether physical or mental), discussion is pointless. In that case, one man cannot force his own conviction on another, nor destroy another's conviction – unless, indeed, the original autographic Scriptures ever come to light.

18. It is not the best kind of textual criticism, which reduces itself into the following shape: 'Erasmus, and the Stephanus brothers, and almost all the printers, have printed it in this way; therefore this reading must remain, even to the end of time, without the slightest variation. Witnesses from antiquity, as far as they confirm this reading, are to be granted; but as far as they call it in question, even with universal consent, they should be rejected.' We must speak the truth: this is a most hasty and unsatisfactory kind of textual criticism, utterly unworthy of men who have attained years of maturity. This type of textual criticism encourages an obstinate and naïve attachment to the 'received text', and a perverse and suspicious distrust of ancient documents.

Johann Albrecht Bengel

Introduction to the Gnomon of the New Testament **(1742)**

Friedrich Christoph Oetinger: True enlightenment

Behold the end-purpose of enlightenment: that all of us should see the glory of God that He outpoured in Christ. Without this vision, no genuine knowledge exists, no genuine harmony or spiritual community in anything. As Paul states, 'the God who commanded the light to shine in the darkness has given us the light of the knowledge of His glory in the face of Jesus Christ' (2 Cor.4:6). But unbelieving minds grow hard, unable to comprehend this. Why? Because the 'god of this world' (2 Cor.4:4) removes their desire to comprehend, by means of the power of this world, and sympathy with it, so that they cannot see the shining light of the Gospel in the face of Jesus Christ, which in itself is not difficult.

The world contains quite enough book-knowledge that lacks any desire for life, which means it never arrives at enlightenment. In fact, mere book-knowledge puts an end to enlightenment! Possessed by the spirit of mockery, it ends up with a warped wisdom in order to extinguish enlightenment, with reckless impudence joining the foolish virgin who vainly desires the Lord to open the doorway of life everlasting. This shows you how urgent it is that you should be instructed in true knowledge! This is why I set before you the way to enter into true enlightenment, through the holy words of the apostles, assuming you are sincerely open to the way God works and equips, giving true understanding of the multi-faceted nature of the holy teaching found in what has been handed down to us.

'Send forth Your light and Your truth, O Lord, that they might lead us to Your holy hill!' (Psalm 43:3) The light of Your face has given enlightenment to all who believe; we ask for Your grace, then, to lead us to this end …

Many people make great progress in natural knowledge who remain far off from true enlightenment. They do not understand what is well-pleasing to God, but imprison themselves within the created realm. Yet true enlightenment is no trivial matter – never think such a thing! It comes by God's grace. Through His holy Word, God makes known to the individual's inner being His subtle operations and interior workings.

Friedrich Christoph Oetinger
Sermon on Enlightenment

Selections from Johann Georg Hamann

Against Enlightenment philosophers who deny the ultimate foundations of knowledge

TO THE PEOPLE AT LARGE, OR NOBODY THE INFAMOUS

You have a name, and yet you have no obligation to prove your own existence; you call others to put their faith in your teachings, and yet you perform no sign that would make such faith possible; the world gives you honour, and yet you lack any concept or sense of honour. 'We know that no idol in the world has real existence' (1 Cor. 8:4). You are not even a true man, and yet you clearly have a human form, which false piety has deified. You have eyes and ears, which however neither see nor hear. You create an artificial eye and an artificial ear, which you plant in your devotees; but like them, it is blind and deaf. You want to know everything, and yet you learn nothing. You want to control everything, and yet you understand nothing. You are 'ever learning, and yet can never come to the knowledge of the truth' (2 Tim. 3:7).

Johann Georg Hamann
Works II p.59

On the sacredness of words

'He speaks and it is done!' (Ps. 33:9). 'And whatever the man named the animals, that is what they were named' (Gen. 2:19). In keeping with this example and illustration of 'definition', that is how it should be for every human word, and should remain so. Upon this likeness of 'image and superscription' (Matt. 22:20) as exemplified in our race (Gen. 1:27) and the

Guide of our youth (Jer. 3:4) — upon this natural law of using the word as the truest, noblest, and most powerful method for revealing and communicating our inner 'declaration of will' — upon this is based the lawfulness of all promises and covenants. This mighty fortress of the truth, although hidden, is superior to all Enlightenment schemes, manoeuvrings, sophistries, and quackery. The abuse of language and of its natural statements is the worst untruth. Whoever violates this first Law of Reason and its strictness becomes the most troublesome enemy of Man. He commits high treason against genuine uprightness and honesty, upon which our worth and happiness depend.

Johann Georg Hamann
Works III p.301

Neither rigid orthodoxy, nor irreligious free-thinking, will bring the life-giving Spirit

Neither the dogmatic beliefs and attitudes of the Pharisee-like 'orthodox', nor the fanciful frothiness of the Sadducee-like freethinkers, will bring about a renewed outpouring of the Spirit.

Johann Georg Hamann
Works II p.211

We are justified neither by good works nor by good doctrine

I know that I am a straying sheep, in doctrine and in life. However, my great comfort is that I belong to a Church [the Lutheran Church] that makes righteousness-before-God to consist as little in good works as in orthodox doctrine.

Johann Georg Hamann
Letter to J. G. Lindner, April 11th 1761

Chapter 6

Roman Catholicism in the Eighteenth Century

Introduction

In the first half of the 18th Century, if there was any single dominating theme in Roman Catholicism, it was the ongoing life-and-death struggle between Jansenism and the Jesuit order: a conflict whose heartland was France, but with wider repercussions across the rest of the Catholic world. This story we have already told in the previous volume of this series.[1] When we move into the second half of the 18th Century, it is easy to become swiftly fascinated by the impact of the French Revolution of 1789 on the Catholic Church in France and in the rest of Europe. There can be little doubt, indeed, that this was the outstanding narrative that followed after the Jansenist-Jesuit war of (roughly) 1640–1740. We enter a strange new Catholic world, in which the Jansenists had been thoroughly defeated and were no longer a serious presence in French Catholicism, the Jesuit order had been officially abolished and suppressed by Pope Clement XIV,[2] and French Catholics suddenly found their religion – once the lifeblood of France – outlawed, their priests guillotined, their churches forcibly transformed into Temples of Reason, and their government hell-bent (quite literally, it must have seemed to devout Catholics) on 'dechristianising' France at every level. Merely to write these sentences already invites the fascination that would rush us from the Jansenist-Jesuit conflict straight into the French Revolution.

We shall, however, seek to resist this temptation, at least for a few pages. There are things to be said about Catholicism

1. For the long-drawn-out battle between Jansenists and Jesuits, see Volume 4, Chapter 6, Part 4.

2. See Part One, section 5 for the abolition of the Jesuit order.

outside the framework of the Jansenist-Jesuit battleground, and prior to the outbreak of the French Revolution in the earth-shaking year 1789. Before we plunge ourselves into the almost apocalyptic events that gripped France (and most of Europe) from 1789 onward, let us pause to reflect on other persons, other events, other achievements within the world of 18th Century Catholicism. We have the Catholic Church's greatest moral theologian to meet; we have one of Catholicism's most famous and cherished treatises on the Christian life to examine; we have one of the most universally esteemed Popes, Benedict XIV, to consider; we have Junipero Serra to encounter, and his extensive missionary labours among the indigenous American peoples of California; and we have the perhaps unexpected and sudden downfall of the Jesuit order to throw its immense shadows on our imagination. To these matters, let us now direct our thoughts.

1
The pre-Revolutionary Church: Outstanding figures, achievements, and events

1. Alphonsus Liguori (1696–1775): patron saint of moral theologians

Alphonsus Liguori was arguably the outstanding Roman Catholic theological and spiritual writer in the 18th Century prior to the French Revolution. Born at Marianella in the Kingdom of Naples (southern Italy, before Italy was unified as a single nation-state), he belonged to an aristocratic family that had fallen on hard times. After studying at Naples University, he became a successful lawyer. However, after suffering an unexpected failure in a particular legal case in 1723, and experiencing a quasi-mystical call to a religious life (he heard God's voice commanding him, 'Forsake the world and surrender yourself to Me'), he tried to join the Oratorian movement founded by the celebrated Counter-Reformation saint, Philip Neri.[1] Liguori's father, however, forbade his twenty-seven-year-old son to make so radical a decision; a kind of bargain was struck between father and son, which allowed Liguori Junior to live at home while training for the priesthood, but not as a member of the Oratorian order. He was ordained in 1726.

The new priest proved highly popular as a plain-spoken preacher among the lower classes of Naples. He was also a

1. For Philip Neri, see Volume 3, Chapter 8, section 5, under **The Oratorians**.

talented composer of hymns, both lyrics and tunes, including what became a popular Italian Christmas carol, *From Starry Skies Descending.*[2] An enduring accomplishment dating from this time was Liguori's establishment of 'Evening Chapels' for young people: these were focal points for religious and social activity, in which the young themselves shared a major part of the organisation and leadership.

In 1749, Liguori spearheaded a new religious order, the Congregation of the Most Holy Redeemer, known more popularly as the Redemptorists. He conceived the mission of the new order as primarily preaching, especially among the socially disadvantaged, e.g., in city slums. The order flourished, with new congregations being set up in a number of Italian cities. By the end of the century, the movement had grown beyond Italy into various Germanic territories. The following century, it spread into Switzerland, Belgium, Holland, Spain, Portugal, and South America. As well as preaching and ministering among the poor, the Redemptorists during their founder's lifetime also played their part in what was then the ongoing turmoil of the Jansenist controversy, taking a strongly anti-Jansenist stance theologically and morally. Liguori was repelled by the stern Augustinian perception of human depravity that permeated Jansenist piety, preferring a more gentle and generous attitude to the failings of human nature.

In 1762, Liguori was (against his wishes) appointed Bishop of Sant'Agata dei Goti in Campania, north-east of Naples. Despite physical enfeeblement through advancing age, he turned out to be a zealous Episcopal reformer, devoting his energies to upgrading pastoral standards among the priests of his diocese. If he ever discovered a priest who sprinted his way through the mass, gabbling it out in under fifteen minutes, Liguori suspended the hasty priest from his duties. He reorganised and improved the local seminary. At length, almost prostrate with illnesses, he was allowed to lay aside the burden of the bishopric in 1775, spending the last dozen years of his life in the Redemptorist community at Pagani in Campania.

---

2. See Primary Historical Sources section.

Liguori's reputation as a theological and spiritual writer has suffered greatly among Protestants owing to his discourse *The Glories of Mary*, in which he expounded Roman Catholic Mariology with forthright eloquence, denouncing all 'heretics' who dared to disagree. Still, his range of writings was far wider than this contentious work. He wrote on the incarnation, the atonement, the Christian life, prayer, the eucharist, apologetics, historical theology, and other topics, as well as publishing collections of sermons. These have been translated into many languages, achieving global popularity among a Catholic readership.

However, Liguori's most admired work lay in the area of moral theology, in a 1748 treatise entitled simply *Moral Theology*. The original version of the treatise was expanded into a richer two-volume edition in 1753 and 1755. This was received with widespread acclaim, going through a further seven editions in Liguori's lifetime. In the pages of the treatise, he set forth a system for working out the best course of moral action known as 'equiprobabilism', which charted a middle path between what he perceived as the excessive rigorism and severity of the Jansenists and the undue laxity and flexibility of the Jesuits. *Moral Theology* is composed of seven books: (i) conscience and laws in general; (ii) faith, hope, and love; (iii) the Ten Commandments; (iv) priestly and monastic life, and the specific moral duties attaching to various secular callings – lawyers, doctors, merchants; (v) the philosophy of human action, and how actions acquire a sinful character; (vi) the sacraments; and (vii) the role of the Church in disciplining sinners.

Liguori's system of equiprobabilism dealt with a much disputed issue in Roman Catholic moral theology ('casuistry'), concerning the believer's freedom to follow a debated opinion on moral choice and action, if moral theologians deemed that opinion 'less probable' among the available options. Liguori argued that a believer should not follow a less probable option (thus rejecting the view held by many Jesuits), and was free of binding obligation to follow a specific option only if the available options were equally probable.

As a result of *Moral Theology*, Liguori was recognised as 'the prince of moral theologians', and (in 1950) Pope Pius XII pronounced him the patron saint of Catholic confessors and moralists.

2. Jean Pierre de Caussade (1675–1751) and *Abandonment to Divine Providence*

The most widely read and popular devotional treatise to emerge from Roman Catholicism in the 18th Century was the oft-reprinted classic *Abandonment to Divine Providence*. It has traditionally been attributed to the Jesuit Jean Pierre de Caussade (1675–1751), the spiritual director of a community of Visitandine nuns in Nancy, north-eastern France. The Visitandines were a 17th Century contemplative religious order (the Order of the Visitation of Holy Mary), founded by the famous Francis de Sales and his co-worker Jeanne Frances de Chantal.[3] Unfortunately very little is known of the life of Caussade. We know that in 1731–33 he came under severe suspicion of the Quietist heresy, the view that the believing soul is wholly passive in relation to God, such that not self-will alone, but all will, must be surrendered in God's presence. This view was officially condemned in 1687 by Pope Innocent XI, and those suspected of harbouring it (notoriously, Madame Guyon) were often subjected to stern discipline, even persecution, by the Catholic authorities.[4] Since Caussade fell victim to this suspicion, it has been conjectured that this was why he decided not to publish his treatise during his lifetime, afraid that it might draw fresh condemnation upon him, since some of the teachings and expressions of *Abandonment to Divine Providence* could be construed (or misconstrued) as endorsing a form of Quietism. The treatise may originally have been simply a collection of letters of spiritual counsel written by Caussade to Visitandine nuns.

Abandonment to Divine Providence was finally published from manuscript material in 1861 by the great French Jesuit

3. See Volume 4, Chapter 6, Part 3, section 3.

4. For Quietism and Madame Guyon, see Volume 4, Chapter 7, Part 2.

scholar Henri Ramière (1821–84). Since then, dozens of editions have been published, including translations into other languages, and the work has taken its place among the most cherished treasures of all Catholic literature of piety. In language of beauty it almost sings of the relationship between the human soul and God, as God deals with the soul through His all-pervading providential direction and care, seeking by all means to draw the soul into ever closer union with Himself in and through Jesus Christ. This loving will of God, the treatise says, approaches the soul through all the daily details of ordinary life, its mundane duties and its often trivial trials, all of which cease to be ordinary when seen in the light of providence. The believer's task and joy are to discover, and submit to, God's will in each and every moment, living *coram Deo* (before the face of God) in the present, where alone God is to be found and known – one must forsake the persistent and recurrent temptation to dwell on the past or live fantasy-like in the future (a more recent translation gave the treatise the revealing title *Sacrament of the Present Moment*).

The traditional attribution of the work to Pierre de Caussade has been questioned by significant modern scholarship. According to the revisionist view, the treatise was very likely not written by Caussade himself, but by one of his female disciples, who nonetheless based her discourse on Caussade's teachings. Since no one has been able to identify the authoress, she has been given the pseudonym 'Lady Abandonment'. If the revisionist view is correct, the *Abandonment to Divine Providence* stands as one of the profoundest of all devotional works by a Catholic female writer.

3. Pope Benedict XIV (1740–58)

Pope Benedict XIV earned the extraordinary distinction of being admired by non-Catholics at a time when Catholicism was under sustained attack by its enemies (the traditional foe, Protestantism, and the new Enlightenment foes, Deists and atheists). He was warmly regarded for his combination of deep scholarship, moral integrity, and attractive personality.

Benedict's birth name was Prospero Lorenzo Lambertini (born 1675), a native of the north Italian city of Bologna, at that time part of the papal states. He belonged to an aristocratic family; after studying both law and theology at the Collegio Clementino (a papal school in Rome), he entered on a varied ecclesiastical career. This included holding office within the Inquisition, where he penned an important treatise on the right procedures for canonisation of saints. Lambertini was eventually rewarded for his services to the Church when Pope Benedict XIII (1724–30) made him a Cardinal in 1726, although the appointment did not become public till 1728. Then in 1731, Pope Clement XII (1730–40) made him Archbishop of his native Bologna.[5] In 1740, upon the death of Clement XII, the Cardinals met to elect his successor. When the choice for pope came down to three Cardinals – Lambertini himself, Cardinal Gotti, and Cardinal Aldrovandi – Lambertini is reported to have remarked to the assembled Cardinals, 'If you want to elect a saint, choose Gotti. If you want to elect a politician, choose Aldrovandi. But if you want to elect an awkward simpleton, choose me.'[6] The Cardinals duly elected Lambertini as the new pope; he took the name Benedict XIV.

Benedict's reign was marked by a number of significant issues and achievements. He proved a great financial reformer, introducing a whole swathe of measures aimed at reducing the huge deficit of the papal administration. He was not entirely successful, but he did leave the papal economy in a better state than he found it. Meanwhile he distinguished himself by his devotion to literature and learning, securing for himself a justified reputation as one of the most scholarly popes. He established four new educational institutions

5. He had in fact been the Bishop of Theodosia since 1724, but this was a nominal appointment; his actual work was in the papal Curia (court), not the Episcopal diocese.

6. 'Awkward simpleton' is 'booby' in the account recorded by the English poet Thomas Gray who was in Italy at the time. The Italian word is literally somewhat obscene, so Gray chose to translate it more politely as booby!

in the city of Rome, for the closer study of ancient Roman history and culture, church history, canon law, and liturgy. He also appointed the illustrious Syrian Maronite[7] scholar, Joseph Assemani (1710–82) – one of the wonders of the age for erudition – to catalogue the treasure-trove of books and manuscripts held in the vast Vatican library. In Rome's Sapienza University, a stellar seat of academic learning founded by Pope Boniface VIII in 1303, Benedict created new professorships of chemistry and mathematics. All of this and other activities in the same vein brought unfeigned scholarly recognition to Benedict from the French Enlightenment philosopher Voltaire, normally anti-Catholic to a ferocious degree; Voltaire referred to the Pope as 'Lambertini, Rome's boast, the world's father, who teaches the world by his writings and honours it by his virtues'.[8]

Benedict's relations with the civil rulers of Europe were flexible, tactful, and marked by a spirit of well-intentioned compromise; he was always ready to make concessions, where these did not affect his essential spiritual authority as the successor of St Peter and Bishop of Rome. This meant that he was willing to concede a large amount of practical authority in Church affairs to national rulers in Catholic lands. His moderation extended to Protestant rulers too; in particular, he acknowledged the title 'King of Prussia' that had been taken by the Calvinist Hohenzollern princes of Brandenburg-Prussia in 1701. Since Prussia was militarily the mightiest state in Germany, Benedict's concessionary spirit meant that he secured a reasonable working relationship with this champion of the Protestant cause, rather than allow himself to be mired in futile quarrels over a mere title. He did this in the teeth of strong opposition from his own papal court.

---

7. Maronites were a body of Middle Eastern Christians who had originated in the 7th Century as heretical Monotheletes (or Monothelites), but abandoned their heresy in the 13th Century and submitted to the authority of the papacy whilst retaining their Eastern forms of worship. See Volume 1, Chapter 12, section 5.

8. For Voltaire, see Chapter 1, Part 2, section 3.

Benedict is also known for bringing a final end to the long-boiling controversy over Jesuit missionary practices in China and India. Jesuits had allowed their Chinese converts to retain the various rites (rituals) they had once practised as Confucians to venerate their ancestors, prior to their conversion to Christianity. The Jesuit argument was that these rites were essentially social, not spiritual, in nature. Dominican and Franciscan missionaries, however, disagreed strongly, arguing that these rites had a spiritual character inconsistent with Christian belief. The controversy was bitter, and in 1715, Pope Clement XI came down decisively against the Jesuit practice in China in the papal bull *Ex illa die*. Benedict confirmed Clement's decision in 1742 in the bull *Ex quo singulari*, which equally affected Jesuit practice in India, where the great Jesuit missionary Robert[9] de Nobili (1577–1656) had adapted himself radically to a Hindu Brahmin (high caste) way of life, including vegetarianism and the outward appearance (garb, shaven head) of a Hindu holy man, in order to win Brahmin converts. The anti-Jesuit decisions by Popes Clement and Benedict continue to provoke lively discussion among missiologists. Certainly their practical effect in China was to terminate Chinese mission, so outraged was Chinese Emperor Kangxi, who banished all Christian missionaries from China.[10]

As a personality, Benedict was well-known for his wit, vivacity, cheerfulness, and sometimes outrageous expressions that scandalised the more sensitive and polite in the papal court. He once summed up how he felt about the reality of his own authority in the cynical jest, 'The Pope orders, the Cardinals don't obey, and the people do whatever they like.' He could also be quite blunt when he believed the occasion required it. Famously, when arguing once with the French ambassador, Benedict finally lost all patience with the obstinate and

9. Robert is probably the more usual way of naming him in English, but as an Italian his actual name was Roberto.

10. For a fuller account see Volume 4, Chapter 7, Part 4, sections 2 and 3, where the main thrust of Catholic mission in the far East in the 18th Century is covered.

quarrelsome Frenchman, grabbed hold of him, thrust him down on the papal throne, and exclaimed, 'All right, then, you be Pope.' By the time of his death in 1758, Benedict had earned from British Prime Minister Robert Walpole an immortal expression of praise: 'loved by Papists, esteemed by Protestants, a priest without insolence or interest, a prince without favourites, a Pope without nepotism, an author without vanity, a man whom neither intellect nor power could corrupt.'

4. Junipero Serra (1713–84) and the Franciscan mission among the indigenous American people of California

Junipero Serra was born on the Spanish island of Mallorca. After his education at a local Franciscan school, he joined the Franciscan order in 1730. Ordained to the Catholic priesthood in 1737, he spent the next three years teaching philosophy, acquiring a reputation for outstanding academic talent. This enabled him to take up the Duns Scotus professorship in philosophy at the Lullian College on Majorca. It looked as if a distinguished intellectual career lay ahead of Serra; but his heart had been captivated by the vision of working as an overseas missionary in Spain's American territory.[11] When his parents expressed grief at the separation this would entail from their son, Serra wrote: 'My parents will come to know how delightful is the Lord's yoke. He will transform any bitterness they might now feel into abundant joy. This present time is not suitable for pondering or vexing oneself over life's events. Instead, this is the time for us to be harmonised completely with God's will. My parents should do their utmost to ready themselves for that blessed death that is the chief object of our concern above all other things in this world.' Receiving the approval of Spain's colonial office for his missionary project, Serra set sail with other Franciscans in 1749 for the Spanish colony of Veracruz on the coast of what is now Mexico. Serra then journeyed on foot

11. Serra went to the 'Viceroyalty of New Spain', Spanish-owned land on North America's west coast, also including present-day Mexico.

to Mexico City; during this journey, his foot became infected (possibly from a mosquito bite), resulting in a permanent limp.

After orientation training at the missionary College of San Fernando de Mexico, Serra and his friend Palou (with whom he had travelled from Spain) began their work in the Mexican Sierra Gorda, an expansive region characterised by seemingly never-ending hills and mountains. Here they found themselves in a tense situation, caught between the Spanish military as the guarantors of law and order, the native Pame people, and a body of anti-Spanish guerrilla units of insurgent Pames who had never submitted to the rule of Spain. Among the more docile Pames, Serra and Palou laboured to 'civilise' and Christianise them through intensely emotional and dramatic preaching, theatrical re-enactments of scenes from Jesus' final suffering and death, and teaching them crafts such as crop cultivation, animal husbandry, and weaving. At one juncture, turbulent hostility developed between Spanish military colonists and the native Pames over ownership of land. In this conflict, Serra and the Franciscans sided with the Pames. After much legal wrangling, the Spanish courts awarded victory to the Pames. Palou wrote an optimist account of the success of the Sierra Gorda mission: 'there did not remain even one solitary Pagan in that whole area; all those who live here were baptized by my revered Padre [Serra] and his co-workers, and became a civilised people, dwelling in towns under the sound of church bells.'

In 1758, Serra was back at the College of San Fernando de Mexico, where he functioned for the next nine years as an administrator, with supervisory missionary duties over five Catholic dioceses. An aspect of his work was as an officer of the Inquisition, seeking to stamp out what his Church saw as occult practices among native Americans. A whole new field of endeavour opened up for Serra in 1767, when King Carlos III of Spain legally and forcibly expelled all Jesuits from his American lands – see the next section for the widespread action against the Jesuit order taken by many European governments, and ultimately the papacy itself, over this period. Into the void left by the banishment of the Jesuits, the Franciscans stepped, with

Serra and Palou playing a leading role. In 1768, the Spanish inspector general of American Spanish territory ('New Spain') appointed Serra to spearhead a fresh missionary enterprise among the indigenous population of Upper California, with San Diego as the original mission headquarters, although Serra relocated to Monterey in 1770. His missionary leadership resulted in numerous other mission centres being established throughout Upper California over the next twelve years. It is hard, perhaps impossible, to reckon precisely the multitudes of indigenous people who embraced Catholic Christianity through Serra's mission.

Serra's approach to native converts was twofold. On the one hand, he strove to protect them against abuse on the part of the Spanish military and political authorities. On the other hand, controversially, he made them work hard to support the mission, which has led to accusations that he treated them as little better than slaves under his patriarchal overlordship, which including the infliction of corporal punishment (e.g., chaining and whipping) when he deemed them to have been disobedient. This latter aspect of Serra's work, in very recent times, has provoked a backlash against his name and memory among those who identify as indigenous people in the California area; statues of Serra have been vandalised and toppled, and his name removed from public spaces (e.g., street names). Others, however, including indigenous people of Catholic faith, have revered him as a true evangelist and a saint, and he was at last canonised (officially declared a saint) in 2015. He is, by devout Catholics, looked upon as the patron saint of California. His legacy stands as a prominent example of the troubling ambiguity with which people of the present regard the religious past.

5. Jean Nicolas Grou (1731–1803) and the suppression of the Jesuit order

Jean Grou was one of the figures who kept the Jesuit flame burning during the years of their official suppression as a religious order. This event – the suppression of the Jesuits in 1773 by order of Pope Clement XIV – was one of the most paradoxical of the 18th Century, certainly within Roman Catholicism. As described in detail in Volume 4 of this series, the Jesuit order had waged a long and relentless war against Jansenism within the French Catholic Church, from the inception of the Jansenist movement in 1640, until its final defeat as a widespread, popular, clerically led movement a hundred years later. Since France was, and was seen as, the very heartland of Catholicism in the 17th and 18th Centuries, this Jesuit Jansenist conflict was pregnant with significance for the entire Catholic Church.

The chief Jesuit point of antagonism to Jansenism was the latter's fervent espousal of a strongly Augustinian doctrine of God's sovereign, saving grace, which had won the Jansenists considerable admiration among Calvinists. The most celebrated Jansenist writer, Blaise Pascal (1623–62), has remained a firm favourite among conservative Protestant thinkers ever since, especially among Protestant apologists sceptical of the traditional 'theistic proofs' (trying to prove God's existence by rational arguments from the nature of the observable universe, something Pascal found essentially unattractive and unproductive). It might seem, therefore, in the after-effects of the long-fought Jesuit triumph over Jansenism, that the Jesuits would enter into a period of glory and honour, dominating their Church. Perhaps to the student's astonishment, even shock, the exact reverse took place.

In the very hour of the Jesuit victory over Jansenism, hostile forces in the European Catholic nations began to mobilise against the Jesuit order. The most fundamental reason for this hostility was the pervasive view among Catholic political establishments that the Jesuit order had become a movement dangerous to their authority, owing to its international character, its penetration into every level of Catholic society, and its (perceived) undue influence on Catholic people and government policies. Perhaps the Jesuit-inspired conquest and persecution of Jansenism – a movement that had once been so prominent in the Catholic heartland of France, supported by so many outstanding French Catholics – was itself a factor in convincing Catholic political rulers that the time had come to deal with the Jesuit 'menace' once and for all.

We shall not comb through the complex details of how the Catholic nations now took severe action against the Jesuit order, but some brief account should be offered. In a series of government clampdowns between 1759 and 1782, the Jesuit order was legally and forcibly suppressed in France, Spain, Portugal, Austria, Hungary, and indeed elsewhere. In France, the deadly blow supressing the order fell in 1764,[12] at the hands of King Louis XV (1715–74); Louis was egged on by the Jesuits' unpopular anti-Gallican sentiments, the vehement and influential anti-Jesuit crusading of the Paris parlement, and Louis' mistress Madame de Pompadour (an elegant, intelligent, and politically powerful figure, admired by Voltaire) who was a strong opponent of the Jesuit order. However, the most bitter pill for the Jesuits, the 'shock troops of the papacy' as they have been nicknamed, was when the papacy itself turned on them in 1773, and Pope Clement XIV abolished the Jesuit order in the papal bill *Dominus ac Redemptor*. It seems that Pope Clement probably agreed with the criticisms of the Jesuits made by their enemies, and he had good precedent for hostility in Pope Benedict XIV's recent official condemnation of Jesuit missionary policy in China and India (see section 3 above). However, Clement was also under pressure from the kings of France, Spain, and Portugal, who had already suppressed and expelled the order.

The papal abolition of the Jesuit order did not lead to its disappearance. Rather, it 'went underground', or indeed in places far away from Italy continued to function without papal approval, regarding the Pope's decision as incorrect and hoping for a better day to dawn.[13] One Jesuit who kept his order's

12. Jesuit colleges had already been suppressed in 1763.

13. Belief in papal infallibility is not normally extended to cover every action of a pope, but only his official definitions of Catholic doctrine. The suppression of the Jesuit order does not fall in this category. Protestants often have a hard time understanding what the Catholic belief in papal infallibility actually means and entails, and think it means that whatever any pope decides about anything must be infallible – a position far from the authentic Catholic view.

legacy alive was Jean Grou. Grou was a French Jesuit, a native of Calais; he joined the order very young in 1746, aged fifteen, after being educated at the Jesuit-run Lycée Louis-le-Grand in Paris, France's most prestigious secondary school. As a Jesuit scholar, Grou's first love seems to have been the ancient Greek philosopher Plato; he translated Plato's *Republic, Laws,* and other writings into French.

When King Louis XV suppressed the Jesuits in France in 1764, Grou fled to Lorraine on France's eastern frontier, which – after the War of the Polish Succession – had fallen into the hands of Poland's ex-king, Stanisław Leszczyński. When Leszczyński died, France annexed Lorraine in 1766, and expelled all Jesuits. Grou now fled to the religiously tolerant Protestant Dutch Republic (Holland). At length, however, he was able to return to France under the false identity of 'Leclaire', settling in Paris, where the city's Archbishop Beaumont treated him kindly. Now began his career as a significant religious author, in which he penned treatises on the spiritual life: *The Lesson Drawn from the Confessions of St Augustine, Marks of True Devotion, Spiritual Maxims Explained.* He also wrote a series of brief expositions of spiritual counsel for a female member of the French aristocracy, which were collected in nine slim volumes.

When the French Revolution broke out in 1789, Grou – on the advice of a Visitandine nun, who (rightly) perceived great danger to the Catholic religious orders in the Revolution – once again fled, this time to England. The expediency of his decision to flee Revolutionary France is shown in the fate of a French aristocratic female friend, with whom he had lodged a manuscript of his for safekeeping – a discourse he had been working on for fourteen years. This lady was soon arrested during the Revolution's infamous Reign of Terror (September 1793–July 1794), and the manuscript was destroyed. Grou's response was, 'Had God desired to receive any glory from this work, He would have kept it safe.'

In England, Grou became the chaplain of a long-established English Catholic family, the Welds, at Lulworth Castle in Dorset. He continued to write practical religious treatises:

Meditations in the Form of a Retreat upon the Love of God, The Gift of One's Self to God, The School of Christ, and *The Inner Life of Jesus and Mary.* After Grou's death in 1803, his Jesuit superiors discovered other treatises from his hand that were published later, generally on his consistent theme of living the Christian life. His writings have found new appreciative readers in the 20th and 21st Centuries. He certainly shines out as an example of how a Jesuit could continue to live and work during the period of his order's official suppression, producing spiritual treatises that have stood the test of time. The order may have been cast out into the wilderness, but its activity was ongoing.

2
The Catholic Church and the French Revolution

France, once the flourishing centre both of European culture and Catholic faith, had suffered severe religious decline in the 18th Century, as the more sceptical side of the Enlightenment had taken root, spreading its ideals among the French middle classes or *bourgeoisie*.[1] Deism and atheism now gained large numbers of followers, especially under the impact of Voltaire and Rousseau, the two most influential of the French-speaking Enlightenment philosophers, both strongly anti-Christian Deists.[2] Perhaps it was only a matter of time before the swelling forces of the French Enlightenment finally challenged France's traditional Catholic religion.

When that challenge came in the French Revolution of 1789, it shattered the long-established relationship between Church and state in France. Since that country was widely looked upon as the heartland of European Catholicism, this

1. France's cultural dominance of Europe was shown in the fact that the French language was regarded as the international language of civilisation, much as Latin had once been. Latin was however still used in most universities.
2. Deism, we recollect, was the purely reason-based belief in a Supreme Being. It denied all claims to special divine revelation, claiming to be a 'rational religion', and was the majority religious creed among those in the Enlightenment who rejected Christianity. The arch-philosophers of the Enlightenment – Voltaire, Rousseau, and Immanuel Kant – were all Deists. These men and their worldviews are all dealt with in Chapter 1.

event had far broader significance than for France alone. It reverberated across the whole of Europe, both signifying and foreshadowing the end of the traditional 'throne and altar' alliance that had dominated all of European culture and society since the conversion of the Roman emperors to Christianity in the 4th Century. Indeed, the French Revolution's dissolution of the throne-and-altar alliance did more than simply this: for quite soon, the Revolution became militantly anti-Christian at every level of society, driven by the radical Deism and atheism of the French Enlightenment. We have already looked more generally at the origins and course of the French Revolution in our treatment of the Enlightenment in Chapter One. We shall now study much more closely how it impacted on Roman Catholicism in France, and from there consider the wider effect on Catholicism across Europe, especially on the papacy itself.

1. The impact of the Revolution 1789–99

It did not seem a foregone conclusion that the French Revolution would turn against the Church. The Catholic clergy were one of France's Three Estates of the Realm – Nobility, Clergy, and Commons. When the Third Estate, the Commons (all who belonged neither to the Nobility nor Clergy), unilaterally voted to form themselves into a National Assembly in order to reform France, a decision ratified in the famous Tennis Court Oath of June 20th 1789, the majority of the Clergy sided with the Commons against the Nobility.

The initial cooperation between the Church and the middle-class revolutionaries of the Third Estate, however, soon broke down. This was because the National Assembly decided that it had the unrestricted authority to reform the Church itself: to remould the French Catholic Church into something more in harmony with Revolutionary ideals. In the Assembly's eyes, the nation-state was now the sovereign entity, within which the Church was nothing more than a department of state. All religious believers – whether Catholic, Protestant, or Jew – were required to be Citizens of France, first and foremost, with their religion taking a back seat. France was now no longer, officially, a Catholic nation, but a secular nation where citizenship and its rights were determined by the National Assembly without regard to any claims of traditional religion. This meant that traditional religion no longer enjoyed any necessary protection from the state, which now felt free to do as it wished toward religious institutions in the name of 'enlightened' humanity. The first sign of this totalitarian attitude on the part of the National Assembly was its legal prohibition of all future monastic vows in October 1789, and annulment of all existing monastic vows in February 1790. There was no place for monks in the new Revolutionary France.

Even so, at this juncture, the Assembly still recognised that the Catholic Church was a massive existing reality in French society; rather than seek to uproot it entirely, therefore, the Enlightenment revolutionaries who now held power decided to reshape the Church in keeping with the values of the new society they were creating. Many of them may have sincerely believed they were acting in the Church's own best interests. In July 1790, this policy resulted in the Assembly's imposition of a radical new structure on the French Catholic Church – the so-called 'Civil Constitution of the Clergy'. This simplified and streamlined the Church's organisation (many bishoprics were abolished,[3] with surviving Episcopal dioceses now corresponding territorially with districts of civil administration), and took governmental control of all Church property in the name of 'the people' and the national good. The Civil Constitution also introduced a thoroughgoing democracy into Church life, legally requiring that all Church officials (bishops, priests, etc.) must be democratically elected by all citizens in a parish – which meant that non-Catholics, even atheists, had a vote! It further abolished the authority of the papacy over the French Church's internal affairs, and demanded that all clergy take an oath of loyalty accepting these measures, on pain of being deposed from office.

The Civil Constitution put the French clergy in a very awkward position. Many of them did not want to appear

---

3. Fifty-one bishoprics were abolished, leaving eighty-five still functional.

disloyal to the Revolution, but they remembered enough of their faith to recoil from granting politicians this level of absolute authority over the Church. The Archbishop of Aix, Jean de Dieu-Raymond de Cucé de Boisgelin (1732–1804), expressed majority clerical opinion when he protested that the Church, despite its admitted need for reform, did not recognise the Assembly's right to enact this reform on its own autonomous authority. Consequently, the French clergy issued an appeal to the then Pope, Pius VI (1775–99), to make a decision on their behalf concerning whether or not they should swear the oath of loyalty to the Civil Constitution. Pope Pius was deeply unsympathetic to the ideals of the Revolution, but felt unsure of how best to secure the Church's interests in the new France; after much boggling, in March 1791 he finally condemned the Civil Constitution, sternly ordering all French clergy not to swear the oath.

As it happened, the National Assembly had pre-empted Pope Pius' decision in March by imposing the Constitution on the Church in November, compelling the clergy to make up their minds in advance of the Pope's decision. When the clergy voted in January, the outcome was that almost all the bishops refused to take the oath, and roughly half the lesser clergy (priests, etc.) likewise refused. The French Church thus found itself split asunder into two opposed factions, effectively two rival Churches. Across virtually the whole country, in cities, towns, and even villages, there now faced each other a Constitutional Church (the clergy who had sworn the oath, together with those of the laity who followed them), and a traditionalist Catholic Church (the clergy who had rejected the oath – Nonjurors, as they were called – together with those of the laity who followed them).[4] The National Assembly declared the Nonjuror clergy to be deposed from office, banning them from all public preaching, and appointed new Constitutional clergy to take over their parishes. This frequently resulted in

---

4. A nonjuror is simply one who does not swear an oath, from the Latin *iurare* (Anglicised as *jurare*), to swear.

serious unrest in those parishes that remained loyal to the deposed Nonjuror clergy, as anti-Revolutionary members of the Catholic laity expressed their anger at what was happening – mocking, rejecting, attacking, perhaps even killing the new state-sponsored Constitutional priests.

Things became very ugly for the Nonjuror clergy when the Holy Roman Emperor Leopold II (1790–92), brother of the French Queen Marie Antoinette, massed troops along the French border. Leopold's threatening action was a symptom of the total horror with which the established order in other European countries viewed France's increasingly radical, anti-monarchical Revolution. This German anti-Revolutionary posture prompted the French Legislative Assembly – the successor to the National Assembly – to declare war on Austria (seat of the Holy Roman Empire) in April 1792,[5] and to regard the Nonjuror clergy as potential allies of the Germans and traitors to France. Consequently, the Assembly enacted a harshly persecutory law against the Nonjurors in May 1792. According to this law, if twenty French citizens could be found who would denounce a Nonjuror to the authorities, that priest must be forcibly deported from France. As the law swung into effect, a staggeringly large number of French clergy were driven into exile (or went into hiding) – estimates put the number between thirty and forty thousand clergy who suffered this fate. Many of them fled to religiously tolerant Britain, which – although Protestant – sympathised with the plight of Christian clergymen upon whom a non-Christian state had declared war. This incidentally helped to spark a new attitude of leniency toward Catholics in the British Protestant establishment. Meanwhile the French Legislative Assembly decreed that any deported priest who dared to set foot again on French soil would be put to death.

With this head-on collision between the Revolutionary state and the Nonjuror clergy of France, it did not take long for popular passions to erupt against the clergy on the part of

5. Austria was part of the wider Germanic world and considered part of 'Germany' in a cultural sense, at a time when none of the Germanic lands had been unified into a German nation-state.

France's pro-Revolution masses. As a German army marched on Paris, the Paris mob went wild, storming the prisons (where enemies of the Revolution were held captive). The first casualties of mob fury were twenty Nonjuror priests scheduled for deportation – the mob killed them all. This was the first spark in an anti-Church massacre that raged in Paris from the 2nd to the 5th of September 1792. By the time the bloodshed was over, the mob had killed two hundred and twenty priests and three bishops.

We may wonder how things were faring, in the meantime, with the Constitutional clergy. At first, they maintained their good relations with the state. When French armies won a military victory against foreign anti-Revolution foes, they solemnly celebrated the event as good patriots. However, the relationship soon deteriorated. One important factor in bringing about this deterioration was the decision of the Legislative Assembly to abolish the French monarchy in September 1792, and to proclaim France a republic. Most of the Constitutional clergy were still conservative enough in sentiment to feel reverence for King Louis XVI, 'the Most Catholic King' (the traditional title of French monarchs). Matters were worsened beyond remedy when the Assembly then decided to put Louis XVI on trial in December 1792. He was found guilty of crimes against the nation, and publicly executed on January 21st 1793. All Europe shuddered; the Constitutional clergy felt in their bones that the Revolution was no longer their friend. They were correct. Running parallel with Louis' dethronement, trial, and execution, there began a concerted attempt to dislodge Christianity itself as France's national religion, replacing it with an Enlightenment-inspired 'cult of Reason', in which – if any God was acknowledged – it was the Supreme Being of Deism, who was most famously celebrated in the Festival of the Supreme Being on June 8th 1794, where arch-Revolutionary Maximilien Robespierre (1758–94) extolled the Deist God as the only divinity worthy of Enlightened Man's worship.[6]

---

6. For Robespierre, see Chapter 1, Part 6, section 2.

The ensuing 'dechristianisation' campaign that gathered pace across France has already been described in Chapter One. We may add some personal colour by describing two of the most fanatical anti-Christian zealots, Jacques-René Hébert (1757–94) and Joseph Fouché (1759–1820). Hébert, a disciple of Voltaire, ran a radical working-class newspaper, *Le Père Duchesne*, distinguished by its ferocious attacks on the aristocracy and the Church. At the forefront of the dechristianisation campaign, the newspaper advocated the suppression of all forms of Christianity, and their replacement by a Cult of Reason. Hébert presented Jesus as a militant working-class radical, rather than God incarnate. His prolonged assault on the French clergy was both bitter and obscene. Hébert's followers, the Hébertists, reached their zenith of public fame (or infamy) when they masterminded the Festival of Reason on November 10th 1793, which ended with the desecration of Notre Dame Cathedral, where they enthroned an actress on the altar as the Goddess of Reason. Hébert, however, quarrelled with Robespierre, who regarded Hébert as a wild-eyed extremist – he was guillotined in March 1794.

Fouché stood out as one of the most ardent members of the Revolution's radical Jacobin faction that held power during 'The Terror' (September 1793 – July 1794), the period of the Revolution's most savage suppression of real or imagined opponents.[7] Fouché was a key figure in inaugurating the dechristianisation campaign, in the Nièvre civil district in central France, where he plundered the churches of all their valuables and converted them into Temples of Reason. Catholic Clergy were forced either to resign or to marry (violating their vow of celibacy); on the new Temples of Reason, Fouché imposed secular ceremonies celebrating Man's Enlightened Reason in place of the Christian God. He erected a sign above the local cemetery proclaiming 'Death is an eternal sleep' in defiance of the Christian belief in human immortality. Fouché's

7. Jacobins were so named from their original meeting place in the Saint Jacques Monastery in Paris. The Latin for Jacques is Jacobus, hence Jacobin. Robespierre was their most famous member.

radically anti-Christian policies in Nièvre became a template for the wider dechristianisation campaign in the rest of France. He would tolerate no opposition to the Revolution, becoming notorious for his bloody suppression of anti-Revolutionary sentiment in the city of Lyons in late 1793 through to the Spring of 1794 – some one thousand eight hundred people were executed. All of this Fouché justified as necessary for the rebirth of Man as a Citizen of France's new Republic of Reason.

With the dechristianisation campaign raging, no Catholic was now safe, whether he had favoured the Nonjurors or the Constitutional Church. Following Fouché's lead, church buildings across France were forcibly transformed into Temples of Reason, or else closed down altogether. Priests of all types, whether Nonjuror or Constitutional, were now denounced as obstacles to the Revolution and its enlightened re-creation of humanity. It has been estimated that during the period of dechristianisation, which finally ended in 1799, something like six per cent of those condemned to death in France for anti-Revolutionary crimes were clergy. Exact figures are impossible to obtain, but scholars reckon that several thousand French priests and members of religious orders were sent to the guillotine in a few short years, simply for their Catholicism. Most of the martyrs were Constitutional clergy, who were easier to locate and arrest – the Nonjurors had already either fled or gone into hiding. The unpalatable truth stood revealed: the bargain with the state made by the Constitutional clergy had turned out to be a temporary reprieve from ideological persecution, not the dawn of a new age of harmony between Christianity and the Enlightenment.

In one region of France, the Vendée (the western French coastland), a civil war erupted between the Catholic faithful and their Revolutionary anti-Christian enemies. The Vendée was a unique area in which the local nobility enjoyed relatively good relations with their social inferiors, and a strong, traditional Catholic faith permeated the lives of multitudes. When in March 1793 the Legislative Assembly tried to conscript the Vendean populace into France's national army, by now an instrument of radical Revolutionary action, the Vendeans rebelled. Their revolt was in the name of their Catholic faith and – perhaps to a slightly lesser extent – allegiance to the now defunct French monarchy (the Vendean rebels became known as the Royal Catholic Army). This insurgency diverted a significant chunk of Revolutionary military resources to crushing the Vendeans, a long and bloody process that occupied Revolutionary troops between 1793 and 1799.

In this conflict, the Revolutionary forces behaved with extreme ruthlessness. They destroyed entire villages, burned down forests and crops, and deliberately massacred civilians, including women and children. One estimate puts the number of slaughtered civilians at somewhere between twenty thousand and fifty thousand in the period January-May 1794. The Vendean War has ever since lived in Catholic memory as one of the most brutal and shocking episodes of anti-Catholic violence carried out by a non-Christian government. Even after the last elements of the rebellion were finally put down in 1799, anti-Revolutionary sentiment continued to smoulder in the Vendée, breaking out in fresh uprisings in 1813, 1814, and 1815. The last of these rebellions played its part in the ultimate defeat of Napoleon; in order to quell the insurgency, he had to send an army of ten thousand – a body of soldiers he sorely needed at the battle of Waterloo.

The French Revolutionary armies spread the Revolution to the countries they invaded. The impact in Germany, Belgium, Spain, and Italy was profound: devout Roman Catholics became enemies of the Revolution, with its now fiercely anti-Catholic Deism and atheism. In Belgium, clergy were among the leaders of a violent resistance movement to the French armies of occupation. In Spain, it was the clergy and monks who fuelled the flame of national resistance to the French invaders. In Germany, a social revolution occurred: almost all the lands owned by Catholic Bishops and monasteries were confiscated. This led to the death of many monasteries, unable now to support themselves economically. The German Catholic Church never recovered its pre-Revolutionary position in German Catholic society.

In Italy, the situation was even more pointed. A French army led by the rising military star of the Revolution, Napoleon Bonaparte (see next section), fought the troops of the papal states in 1796, vanquishing them on the battlefield. One might say at that juncture that the French Revolution had literally made war on the papacy. The reigning Pope, Pius VI, capitulated and made peace, but it did not last very long. In December 1797, there was an anti-French riot in French-occupied Italy, which resulted in the death of the French military commander, Léonard Mathurin Duphot, who was killed by papal troops trying to restore order. The French Republic was incensed (Duphot was not only a high-ranking Revolutionary general but a popular poet); in retaliation a French army once again invaded, capturing Rome in February 1798, and declaring it henceforth to be no longer a papal city but a Roman Republic, patterned on the French Revolutionary model. Pope Pius refused to accept this, and was consequently arrested by French soldiers, and moved as a prisoner from one Italian city to another, until he arrived at length in Valence in France's Rhone valley in July 1798, where he was held captive, dying six weeks later. Meanwhile in Italy, local clergy often headed anti-French guerrilla units; one of the most famous Italian clerical guerrilla leaders was the Archpriest of Cottanello, in northern-central Italy, who led a resistance unit that numbered many thousands, and was fond of the verse from Psalm 144, 'Blessed be the Lord my Strength, who teaches my hands to war, and my fingers to fight'. It looked as though the ancient alliance between Church and state had not only been shattered, but that the French Revolutionary state and the Catholic Church across Europe were now locked in an open and bloody struggle to the death.

2. The Church and Napoleon Bonaparte 1799–1815

When Napoleon Bonaparte (1769–1821), the French Revolution's most brilliant and successful general, seized power over France in 1799, it transformed the religious situation in the land of the Revolution. Although raised a Catholic, Napoleon's

Napoleon Bonaparte

adult religion seems to have been some kind of undogmatic theism, not far different from Deism. However, he did not share the typical Deist hostility to Christianity. France's new ruler strongly recognised the social utility of religion in the life of a nation, and was not convinced that Deism could ever replace Catholicism. One of Napoleon's personal valets, Louis Étienne Saint-Denis, said of his master:

> Was the Emperor [Napoleon] a religious man according to the idea of religion held by genuine believers? I never saw any evidence of this. However, he was religious in the sense given to that word by philosophers. It is true that the Emperor attended mass and other religious rituals, and had listened to a number of sermons during the course of his life; but he did not think this was sufficient reason to ascribe great significance to religious devotions, or place much confidence in them. His mind ascended to a higher level, which meant that his belief differed from the general faith of churchgoers. Someone will respond, 'But he went to mass!' Indeed he did; yet what was his understanding of that ceremony? He stood up when he was supposed to stand up, and when everyone else sat down, he also sat down. He knelt when they knelt, and when the Bible was handed to him, he kissed it. During worship his outward demeanour was serious; his hat was clasped beneath his left arm (that is, if he did not place it on the seat in front of him), while his right hand was usually in his trouser pocket. However, he never showed any other sign of reverence according to the manner of genuine believers.

Napoleon brought an end to the dechristianisation campaign, although its worst excesses had already spent their force by the time he seized power. In order to unite France under his rule, he was determined to pursue, at the very least, a policy of religious toleration. Religious divisions fostered by government persecution he regarded as a threat to the unity of the France over which he now held sway (initially as 'First Consul', and from 1804 as Emperor). However, he went a step further than mere toleration. Realising that many of the religious assumptions of Catholicism were still ingrained in the hearts of most French people, Napoleon decided to give special recognition to Catholicism in his new constitution, which stated: "The government of the Republic recognises the Catholic, Apostolic, and Roman religion, as the religion of the great majority of the French people.' This was a long way from endorsing Catholicism as the only true religion, or even as the official state religion; but it restored a large measure of prestige to the Catholic Church in France.

This fresh acknowledgement of Catholicism in France was part and parcel of a Concordat between Napoleon and Pope Pius VII (1800–1823), signed in July 1801. The Concordat ended the bitter schism between the Constitutional and Nonjuror clergy, who were again united under papal leadership on terms both factions could accept. Besides, the fact that both Constitutional and Nonjuror priests had recently suffered violent persecution during the dechristianisation campaign had made them seem on the same side, against the Revolution's more fiercely anti-Christian aspects, which Napoleon had ended.

According to the terms of the 1801 Concordat, the existing Catholic bishops of France (the Constitutionalists and Nonjurors alike) had to resign their positions to Pope Pius; Napoleon then had the authority to nominate new bishops, but only the Pope could appoint them to office, and could also depose them; all Catholic clergy would be salaried by Napoleon's government; and the Catholic faith, while officially acknowledged as the religion of the French majority, would nonetheless function under the laws of the French Republic, including any restrictions deemed necessary for the maintenance of good order. This last provision was exploited by Napoleon in such a way as to consolidate his own power over the French Catholic Church, for example by decreeing that all Catholic seminaries in France must teach the old Gallican Articles of

1672, which asserted the French Church's independence of the papacy in all matters of internal organisation.[8]

Other ways in which Catholicism was kept in subjection to the Napoleonic state included the secularisation of marriage (it was now essentially a civil contract, controlled by the state); a secular system of public education; government approval being necessary for all religious catechisms, gatherings of clergy to transact church business, and the establishment of new seminaries; and the legal requirement that public prayers must be offered for the Republic as France's legitimate government – no prayers for the restoration of the monarchy! It was perhaps galling, too, for traditional Catholics that the ending of dechristianisation brought with it the legal toleration of Protestantism and Judaism in France, contrary to the old ideal of 'one king, one law, one faith' in which Catholicism had been the absolute religious basis of French national life. Protestants had been persecuted as severely as Catholics by the Jacobin Revolutionaries during the Revolution's most radical phase; now Napoleon extended the olive branch of toleration to both the devotees of Rome and the disciples of Calvin, hoping thereby to secure the support of both.[9]

Napoleon's motivation in giving official recognition to Catholicism, and in extending full civil rights to Protestants, had roots not only in a pragmatic desire to win support for his regime, but also in his deeper conviction of the usefulness of religion in providing coherence to human society. The great philosophers of the French Enlightenment, Voltaire and Rousseau, had taught this lesson, but had opposed Christianity, preferring some version of Deism. Napoleon, however, was highly sceptical that Deism could fulfil such a social role. His political instinct told him that Christianity was best suited to

---

8. Gallicanism was a long-held and widespread belief among French Catholics that their Church had a relative autonomy in relation to papal authority.

9. For the persecution of Protestants during the Revolution's dechristianisation campaign, see the Primary Historical Sources section, and the account given by G. de Felice.

playing this vital part in a well-organised society. He referred to this as the 'mystery of religion', and said:

> By 'mystery of religion' I do not speak of the mystery of the incarnation. That is not my concern, nor any other doctrine taught by the Church. Rather, I perceive in religion the entire mystery of human society. My belief is that the moral teachings and doctrines of the Gospel are the only basis for a flourishing society and genuine civilisation. What convinces the poor person to accept that my palace burns with ten chimneys while he is perishing with cold? Or that I have ten different costumes in my wardrobe while he goes naked? Or that my table is daily loaded with sufficient food to feed an entire family for a week? Religion gives him this conviction. It tells him that there is another life in which he will be my equal, in fact that he has more chance of blessedness than I have.

Napoleon's outlook on this point was far removed from what the great majority of his Revolutionary co-workers believed, most of whom could not progress beyond the contempt for Christianity espoused in the earlier phases of the Revolution. But Napoleon, with a seemingly invincible army at his back and devoted to him as their beloved general, overrode the anti-Christian attitudes of other Revolutionary leaders. As long as Napoleon held supreme power in France, there would be no return to the dechristianisation campaign. For this, both Catholics and the papacy, and French Protestants, could only be grateful.

Even so, the developing relationship between Napoleon and the papacy was a troubled one. The 1801 Concordat between Napoleon and Pope Pius VII was so obviously tainted by 'Erastianism' (state control of the Church, where the state itself made no pretensions to sincere Christian faith), it helped to strengthen in French Catholic minds the view that the papacy was the only serious guarantee of the French Church's integrity. The long-standing anti-papal Gallican traditions of French Catholicism were thus dealt a severe blow, and the Napoleonic state unwittingly encouraged a new appreciation for the papacy among France's devout Catholics.

Napoleon's coronation as Emperor proved rather double-edged from the Pope's point of view. On December 2nd 1804, in Notre Dame Cathedral in Paris, Napoleon had himself crowned Emperor of France, after a referendum in which the vast majority of French voters approved of this prospect. Napoleon's purpose was to lay a more solid basis for his regime by appealing to Catholic and royalist sentiment: France would again have an anointed kinglike ruler, crowned in an elaborate Catholic ceremony. Napoleon also wanted to found an enduring Napoleonic dynasty. Pope Pius VII was at the coronation, lending it the sanction of his presence. Pius even handed the imperial crown to Napoleon. To that extent, the papacy was acknowledged. But once the French ruler had received the crown from the Pope's hands, he then placed it on his own head. Napoleon thereby got the best of both worlds: by receiving the crown from the Pope, Napoleon obtained the blessing of the Catholic religion for his rule, whereas by placing the crown on his own head he was declaring that he did not actually owe his authority to the Pope, but to his own virtue and destiny and to the recent French referendum.

Not long after the coronation, Napoleon's relationship with Pope Pius deteriorated badly. From 1805, Napoleon's wars with other European powers (Britain, Prussia, Sweden, Russia) produced endless military and diplomatic tensions with Pius. In his political capacity as ruler of the papal states – the territory in central Italy controlled by the papacy – Pius by and large would not cooperate with Napoleon's war policies, preferring to maintain a neutral stance. Outraged at length beyond endurance, Napoleon sent his troops into the papal states, annexing them to his French empire in May 1809. Pius retaliated by excommunicating Napoleon in June. The excommunication of Napoleon both signified and strengthened the increasing hostility to his aspirations as world-ruler on the part of non-French Catholic Europe. There had been a certain horror among conservative, historically aware Catholics outside of France at Napoleon's virtual destruction of the Austria-based Holy Roman Empire, through his victory over imperial forces at the battle of Austerlitz in December 1805; in the wake of Austerlitz, a large slice of Holy Roman land had sheered off into a French-dominated 'Confederation of the Rhine'. The last of the Holy Roman Emperors, a humiliated Francis II, abdicated from the much-diminished imperial throne in August 1806, ending the thousand-year history of the Holy Roman Empire. Since the Empire had received its deathblow from Napoleon, the event gave him the appearance (in the eyes of Austrian Catholics, at least) of arch-enemy of traditional Catholic civilisation in Europe. His forcible annexation of the papal states only reinforced and widened this perception.

When Pope Pius excommunicated Napoleon, therefore, many Catholics welcomed Pius' uncompromising action. Napoleon responded to his excommunication by having his troops arrest Pius, who spent the following five years as Napoleon's prisoner, first in Savona (in French-controlled Genoa), then in Fontainebleau (thirty-five miles south-east of the centre of Paris). The circumstances of his imprisonment were demeaning: Pius was frequently kept in isolation, denied all contact with friends and advisors, spied on, and prevented from communicating with the world outside his prison. Pius struck back with the only weapon left to him under the terms of the 1801 Concordat: he refused to appoint fresh candidates to any vacant bishoprics.

Pius' five-year imprisonment at the hands of Napoleon produced an extraordinary change of attitude on the part of Europe's non-Catholic powers, whether the Protestants of Britain, Prussia, and Sweden, or the Orthodox of Russia. Since Napoleon was their enemy, they began to look on the captive Pope as their friend and ally. Pius' dignified bearing in captivity – conducting himself as though he were a devout monk, studying, praying, and persevering in his refusal to bend the knee to Napoleon – made him seem a martyr for Christian principle. This endeared him to the French Emperor's non-Catholic foes, who soon made it a central point of their war strategy, and their demands on Napoleon, to liberate Pius from his imprisonment. In the aftermath of the catastrophic failure of Napoleon's invasion of Russia in June-December 1812, the French Emperor's foes were able to invade a weakened France in 1814; this resulted in the liberation of Pope Pius, who re-entered Rome in triumph in the May of that year, to the rapturous applause and cheers of the Roman populace. This event marked the visible origin of the 'Ultramontanism' that would dominate the Catholic Church throughout the 19th Century – the viewpoint that idealised the papacy as the true and total principle of unity within the Church, to the detriment of all other potential sources of unity (especially Bishops and Church councils).[10]

One of the newly freed Pius' first acts was to restore the Jesuit order, suppressed by Pope Clement XIV in 1773. Pius had come to this decision during his captivity. The Jesuits were traditionally the most fervent upholders of papal authority, and (Pius believed) would be a strong ally in the struggle against French Revolutionary oppression of the Church, whether in the radical form of dechristianisation, or in the Napoleonic form of a secular dictator exploiting the Church for his own self-serving imperialism. The Jesuit restoration took place via the papal bull *Solicitudo omnium ecclesiarum* in August 1814. The existing leader of the order, Thaddeus Brzozowski, who was living at a safe distance from Rome in Russia, was legitimised. Ironically, Russia thereupon expelled the Jesuits from its borders, having sheltered them during their period of suppression![11]

3. The aftermath

Napoleon's final defeat at the battle of Waterloo on June 18th 1815 led to his permanent exile as a prisoner on the island of St Helena, a British possession in the South Atlantic Ocean. Here the once mighty Emperor lived out the last six years of his life under close British supervision. Napoleon became

---

10. Ultramontanism is from the Latin *ultra montes*, beyond the mountains. The mountains are the Alps, and the reference is to the papacy situated beyond the Alpine Mountains in Italy (in Rome), as the true seat of authority over all national Catholic Churches.

11. It was one thing for Orthodox Russia, traditionally anti-Catholic, to shelter an order that Rome had suppressed, It was another to support an order that Rome now favoured.

more formally Catholic on St Helena, cared for spiritually by a Catholic chaplain, Abbé Ange Paul Vignali, from whom he received the last rites.

The victorious anti-Napoleonic powers redrew the map of Europe at the Congress of Vienna, which ended in June 1815. Protestant Prussia, Catholic Austria, and Orthodox Russia enlarged their lands significantly. The aim was partly to simplify the territorial map of Europe, and partly to create a workable 'balance of powers' to help prevent future wars. However, another central purpose of the Congress was to set the clock back to a pre-Revolutionary time, seeking to efface the spirit and outcomes of the French Revolution. For France itself, this meant the restoration of the old Capetian or Bourbon monarchy in the person of King Louis XVIII (1815–24), the brother of Louis XVI who had been executed by the Revolutionaries in 1793.[12] This anti-Revolutionary purpose, however, failed in its endeavour. There was just too much continued enthusiasm for the ideals of the Revolution in France. French radicals succeeded in deposing Louis XVIII's successor, Charles X (1824–30), in 1830, which finally extinguished the old Bourbon monarchy. Charles was replaced by King Louis Philippe (1830–48), who began as a popular liberal ruler, 'the citizen king', but became increasingly conservative and unpopular as his reign went on.

Meanwhile in the rest of Europe, it soon became clear that many of the Revolution's values were smouldering with repressed life; that life erupted like a political volcano in 1848, when many capital cities of European nations were shaken by revolutions against the ultra-conservatism sponsored by the Congress of Vienna. In France, for instance, Revolutionary sentiment once again boiled over, leading to the abdication and flight of Louis Philippe. The Enlightenment political genie of Voltaire and Rousseau was not so easily re-bottled.

---

12. The King in between these two, Louis XVII (1793–95), was the young son of the executed Louis XVI. However, he was not recognised by the French government, which was then a Revolutionary republic, and he seems to have died young as a government prisoner (or possibly vanished, a ripe topic for speculation). Louis XVIII was his uncle.

PRIMARY HISTORICAL DOCUMENTS

From Starry Skies Descending: Alphonsus Liguori's Italian Christmas Carol

1. From starry skies descending, O heavenly King,
   Into a cold and frosty cave!
   O my heavenly Babe,
   I see You trembling there.
   O blessed God,
   This is the price You pay for loving me.

2. You are the world's Creator, Lord,
   Yet You appear without garment, without fire.
   Precious little chosen Babe,
   Your frightful poverty
   Fills me with increasing love for You,
   Because it was Your love for me that made You poor.

3. You leave the beauty and glory of the Father's bosom
   To suffer on a bed of straw.
   O sweet delight of my heart,
   To what lengths did love carry You?
   O my Jesus, why are You undergoing such suffering?
   Because of Your love for me.

4. But if You chose to suffer,
   Why do You now desire to shed tears? Why do You cry?
   O my Jesus, my Lord,
   I understand why!
   It is not suffering,
   But love that makes You weep.

5. You weep because You see my lack of gratitude.
   Such great love for me, yet I love You so little!
   O beloved of my heart,
   If once I was like this,
   Now I love You alone.
   Weep no more, precious One, for I love You, I love You.

6. Sleep, my Child. In the meantime,
   The heart does not sleep but ever wakes.
   O my Lamb of pure beauty,
   What do You think of? Tell me,
   O infinite Love! You reply:
   'My thought is that one day I shall die for you.'

7. My God, Your thoughts are of dying for me:
   Who else, then, can I love besides You?
   O Mary, my hope,
   If I have little love for your Jesus,
   Do not be angry.
   If I cannot love Him, love Him for me!

Alphonsus Liguori on Mary our Hope

MARY IS THE HOPE OF ALL.

The heretics of our time cannot bear it, that we should greet Mary as our hope. Hail, our hope, *spes nostra salve*! Heretics say that only God is our hope, and that anyone who puts his hope in a created being comes under God's curse. Mary, they declare, is a created being; and how can a created being be our hope? So say the heretics. In spite of them, the Church requires all its clergy and members of religious orders to uplift their voices every day, and – in the name of all believers – to call upon Mary by the delightful name of our hope, the hope of all: 'Hail, our hope!'

The angelic St Thomas[1] tells us that there are two ways in which we can we put our hope in someone: namely, as the chief cause of what is hoped for, and as the intermediate cause. If we hope to gain some gift from a king, we hope for this gift from

1. The traditional title of Thomas Aquinas is 'the Angelic Doctor' (where 'doctor' means 'teacher').

the king as the sovereign, and we hope for it from his servant or favourite as one who intercedes for us. Should the gift be bestowed, it comes principally from the king himself, but it also comes through the channel of his favourite. Thus, whoever seeks a gift, rightly refers to that intercessor as his hope.

The heavenly King, since His nature is infinite goodness, greatly wishes to bless us with His gifts. But on our side, trust is necessary. So in order to strengthen our trust, He has given His Mother to be our Mother too, and our advocate, and has equipped her with all power to help us. That is why He wants us to place in Mary all our hopes of salvation, and indeed of all blessings. Certainly (as Isaiah says) God's curse rests on those who put all their hope in created beings, but without relying upon God; this is what sinners do, who are ready to offend God in order to gain human friendship and favour. But those who put their hope in Mary as the Mother of God, mighty to gain graces for them and indeed eternal life, are blessed, and bring joy to God's heart. For He desires to see Mary honoured as the most noble of His creatures, since she loved and honoured Him on earth more than all humans and angels did.

This is why we properly refer to the Virgin as our hope: hoping, as Cardinal Bellarmine[2] puts it, to gain through her intercession what we would be unable to gain through our own prayers alone. We pray to Mary, St Anselm says, so that the exalted status of our intercessor will make good our own shortcomings. Therefore, St Anselm adds, praying to the Virgin with the aforementioned hope does not indicate any distrust in God's mercy, but a fear of our own unworthiness. This, then, is the reason that the Church gives to Mary those words of the Book of Ecclesiasticus, with which the writer greets her: 'Mother of holy hope'.[3] She is that Mother who kindles

---

2. Cardinal Bellarmine was the greatest theologian of the Catholic Counter-Reformation, highly esteemed by Protestants as a worthy opponent. See Volume 4, Chapter 6, Part 3, section 1.

3. 'I am the mother of fair love, and of fear, and of knowledge, and of holy hope,' Ecclesiasticus 24:18. These are the words of Wisdom personified as a woman, 'Lady Wisdom', and understood by Liguori as referring to Mary.

within us no empty hope of this life's wretched and short-lived blessings, but the holy hope of the vast and everlasting blessing of the happy life that is yet to come.

Alphonsus Liguori
***The Glories of Mary*, ch.3**

Abandonment to Divine Providence

Abandonment a Token of Predestination.

The condition of abandonment to God embraces within itself pure faith, hope, and love. Such abandonment is, in a manner, a combination of faith, hope, and love in one single act, uniting the soul to God and to His way of working. Thus united, these three qualities together make a single quality, in a single act, namely the heart's uplifting to God, and abandoning oneself to His working. But how can I explain this divine combination, this spiritual unity? How can I find a name to communicate a concept of the nature of this oneness, making this three-in-one unity understandable? I can explain it as follows. It is only by way of these three qualities that we can arrive at the possession and enjoyment of God and His will. The adorable God, seen by faith, is loved, and we hope for all things from Him. Any of these qualities can with equal truth be called purity of love, purity of hope, or purity of faith. True, the condition of which we are speaking is more often described by the last name, purity of faith. But it is does not exclude the other theological qualities of hope and love; rather, we understand them as subsisting and being practised in a hidden way in this condition of abandonment to God.

Nothing can be more secure than this condition, as far as it concerns the things of God; nothing can be more self-forgetful than the disposition of the heart abandoned to God. On God's side we have the absolute assurance of faith, and on the heart's side we have same assurance seasoned with fear and hope. O most desirable one-in-three unity of these holy qualities! Have faith, then, and hope, and love. Yet have these by a simple feeling which the God-given Holy Spirit will bring about in your soul. It is there, in the heart's centre, that the unction of

God's name is shed abroad by the Holy Spirit. Here is the word, the spiritual revelation, and a token of predestination with all its blessed outcomes. 'How good is God to Israel, even to those with a right heart' (Ps. 73:1).

This seal of the Holy Spirit, in souls set on fire with His love, is called pure love owing to the flowing river of joy that streams into every faculty, together with an abundance of confidence and illumination. However, in souls that are immersed in a bitter state, we call it pure faith, since the darkness and murkiness of night exist without betterment. Pure love sees, and feels, and believes. Pure faith, by contrast, believes without seeing or feeling. Behold the difference between these two conditions. But this difference is only a seeming difference, not a real one. The appearances are not like each other. In truth, as the condition of pure faith does not lack love, so the condition of pure love does not lack faith nor abandonment to God. We merely apply the terms according to which quality is uppermost.

The different nuances of these qualities, under the hand of the Holy Spirit, make up the multiplicity of all supernatural and exalted conditions. Since God can arrange them in a different order with endless diversity, no single soul fails to receive this invaluable seal in a manner that befits it. The difference is of no significance; the same faith, hope, and love dwell in all. Abandonment to God is the general way whereby to receive special qualities, in every form of the various divine seals upon the soul. All souls cannot claim the same, nor even a similar condition; but they can all be united with God, they can all be abandoned to His working, they can all receive the seal that is best suited to each, and in fact they can all live under God's reign, experiencing a share in His righteousness and all its blessings. In God's kingdom every soul can seek after a crown; whether it is a crown of love, or a crown of faith, it is still a crown, and still the kingdom of God.

True, this difference exists: one soul is in light, another in darkness. But what real difference does this make, if the soul belongs to God and follows His will? Our attention is not focused on knowing the name of this condition, its features, its distinctive excellence; no, we seek God alone and His working. *How* precisely God works should be a matter of no concern to the soul. Consequently, let us cease from preaching to souls about the condition of pure love, or perfect faith – the way of joy, or the way of the Cross. These cannot be bestowed on all to the same extent nor in the same way. Rather, let us preach abandonment to God in general, abandonment to His working. Let us preach this to all meek souls who fear God, making them all understand that this is how they will arrive at the particular condition that has, from all eternity, been chosen and destined for them through God's working. Let us not discourage, nor reject, nor chase off anyone from that most prominent perfection to which Jesus calls everyone, as He requires from them a submission to His heavenly Father's will, thus making them into members of His mystical body. Jesus is their Head only so far as their will is in harmony with His. Let us ever repeat to all souls that this delightful and compassionate Saviour's invitation does not demand anything very hard from them, nothing extraordinary. He does not ask for genius and resourcefulness. All Jesus wants is that they should have a good will, wishing to be united with Him, so that He can lead, guide, and befriend them in the measure in which they enjoy union with Him.

Pierre de Caussade
***Abandonment to Divine Providence*, Book 2, Chapter 1, section 3**

The Spiritual Maxims of Jean Grou

SEVENTEENTH MAXIM
Beware of self-love: it is the rival of God's love

'I will go in the strength of the Lord God; I will make mention of Thy righteousness only' (Ps. 71:16).

XVII. CONCERNING SELF-LOVE
The nature of self-love is best shown by this description (and nothing should make us hate it more): *the rival of God's love*. 'What we love shapes the way we behave,' says St Augustine. We can give the whole of our love to one alone of two objects:

to God or self. To put God above everything else, and refer everything to Him, is to be moved by charity or divine love; this makes us good and delightful in His sight, bestowing on our deeds a worth above what they merit, and perfecting us to the degree that this love is pure and simple. But to refer everything to self is to be drenched in self-love. This love is sinful and exaggerated, totally distasteful to God, ruining deeds that otherwise would be most holy, and making us increasingly depraved to the degree that it controls our hearts.

These two loves are totally opposed to each other; they are not just rivals but enemies, warring for control of the same heart. There can be no truce between them. They detest, strike at, and torment each other unto death. The perfect annihilation of self-love, either in this life or that which is to come, opens the gates of heaven for us, and guarantees our eternal happiness. The annihilation of the love of God, when we depart from this life, drags us down into hell, and is the essence of our everlasting sorrow.

The moment a Christian truly yields Himself to God and to His service, divine love takes ownership of his heart, erects its throne within, and immediately begins to expel self-love. But self-love tries to keep itself intact; if expelled from one region, it flees to another. Thus it retreats from stronghold to stronghold, until it takes refuge in the innermost reaches of the soul. This is its final haven, from which it is very hard to dislodge it. It employs every method to seek to wound and weaken its adversary, and to diminish (if it is unable to prevent) the triumph of God's love. It is always a menace, even when it is defeated; and frequently, when we think we have trampled it into the dust, it rises up more dangerous than ever. Such is the foe we must fight with the help of grace. It is an adversary born with us, and in a sense an aspect of our very selves. Increasing age, our passions, our habits, our ways of thinking, at times our better qualities and even virtues, all add to its strength and its grip upon us. We muddle it up with ourselves so that it looks impossible to free ourselves from it, and the idea of killing it seems to imply a threat to our very existence!

We have no power against a foe we love so much, which occupies so strong a position. Saddest of all, it robs us of our sight, taking away all possibility of even seeing its reality. It is only by the light of grace that we can perceive it. Grace unmasks its schemes, opens our eyes to see the blows it is about to strike, teaches us how to deflect them, and empowers us to strive against it. But if we give no attention to the light of grace, or indeed forfeit its radiance through our own sin, then we become totally helpless; not only are we unable to overcome self-love, we cannot even oppose it, since we cannot even see our adversary, and do not even believe it is truly an enemy! Our blindness is so total, it convinces us that self-love is a friend and a most beloved and devoted comrade. This ruinous blindness is the general malady of Christians, even of those who are more pious. It is all the more harmful because we do not discern or suspect that it is there, and it is extremely hard to persuade the mind of its reality and presence. On the whole, we are mostly in the same state as the Pharisees who, with respect to our Lord, were made blind by a conceited self-love, and yet imagined they were clear of sight. Jesus said to them: 'You claim "we see", and therefore your sin remains.' By your stubborn perversity, you are filling up the measure of the very sin you should detest.

We may take it for granted, without fear of contradiction, that we ourselves are blind concerning many things that relate to our growth in spiritual maturity, even perhaps our actual salvation. Therefore let us at all times pray to God that He would illuminate us, either immediately by His Spirit, or in an indirect way through the counsel of friends or the rebuke of foes. However the light might come to us, it is a blessing God has sent to us. We should embrace it and accept it with thanks, urge others to offer such light to us, and overlook nothing that might help us in gaining benefit through this light. This is a mental attitude we should pray for very seriously, but which most of our natural inclinations totally oppose. We need to be forearmed (not against flattery: I am presupposing that our spiritual directors and Christian friends will not give us that!) – but forearmed against deeds and words that convey esteem and deference! That is particularly necessary if our position, age, or character seem to demand such consideration. We should automatically assume the tact and generosity of our companions will overlook or excuse our faults, and that when they praise us, it is not for what we actually are, but for what we could be. When they find fault with us, our own hearts should admit it and judge that we are even worse than they say. When people praise us, we should silently belittle our right to the praise. In these ways we can guard ourselves carefully against ourselves, and against our most intimate foe, self-love.

Jean Grou
***Spiritual Maxims*, Maxim 17**

The suppression of the Jesuits: the papal bull *Dominus ac Redemptor* (1773)

When we look at the spirit and words of the apostolic [papal] decrees, we plainly understand that in the Society [of Jesus], virtually from its very origin, there sprang up seeds of discord and rivalry. This discord was found, not only among members of the Society, but also between the Society and the members of other religious orders, with the secular [parish] clergy,[4] with colleges and universities, with public academies of literature, and even with rulers in whose territory the Society had been welcomed. These quarrels and dissensions were aroused over the character and nature of the Jesuit vows, the time when people were received by profession in the Order, the power of ejecting members, the promotion of members into holy orders without an appropriate rank or taking final vows, a promotion that contravenes the decrees of the Council of Trent and of our forerunner Pope Pius V. Again, discord sprang up over the unlimited power held by the Society's Father-General, and other issues relating to how the Society was governed. There was argument about a number of doctrinal matters, about the Society's schools, and its immunities and privileges, which local

---

4. 'Secular' clergy are priests not belonging to a religious order – normally the ordinary parish priest.

church authorities, and others holding ecclesiastical or political power, maintained were detrimental to their authority and rights. Lastly, there was an abundance of very serious charges against Jesuits that brought about considerable disturbance of the peace and harmony of Christian society.

So it was that many protests were expressed against the Society. Some rulers supported these protests by their own authority and by detailed reports. The reports were sent to our forerunners, popes of recent memory, namely Paul IV, Pius V, and Sixtus V. Among the rulers, the late Philip II, Spain's Catholic king, required from our forerunner Pope Sixtus V that he should decree, and bind himself to undertake, an apostolic [papal] investigation of the Society. King Philip had his own substantial reasons for seeking this; furthermore, the Spanish Inquisition made loud allegations about the excessive privileges enjoyed by the Society, the way it was governed, and doubtful matters on which erudite and holy members of the Jesuits maintained strong positions. Philip made sure that all this was explained to Pope Sixtus V. Sixtus granted the demands of King Philip, which he perceived were warranted. He selected for the office of apostolic [papal] investigator a bishop whom everyone accepted on account of his wisdom, integrity, and scholarship. Again, Sixtus appointed a committee made up of various Cardinals in order to oversee this task with a close supervision. However, Sixtus V died prematurely. Consequently, this wholesome enterprise that he set in motion ground to a halt and produced no results …

These events did nothing to quell the outcry and accusations against the Society, so that highly distasteful quarrelling engulfed the world regarding the Society's teaching, which multitudes reported were inconsistent with sound faith and proper morality. Disputes sprouted both within and without the Society. An increasing number of allegations were brought against the Society for its extravagant greed after the riches of this world. As a result of all these commotions, a vast grief and trouble burdened the Apostolic Throne [the papacy], and also the measures taken by some rulers against the Society …

It brings great grief to our heart to see that the previously noted solutions, in addition to many ensuing ones, have proved impotent and ineffectual in removing and driving out such a multitude of disorders, allegations, and protests against the Society. Without any good outcome, others of our forerunners – Urban VIII, Clement IX, X, XI, and XII, Alexander VII and VIII, Innocent X, XI, XII, and XIII, and Benedict XIV – endeavoured to re-establish the supremely desired tranquillity of the Church. They set forth many wholesome edicts on how business should be conducted, and on the very serious discords and disputes that were so rife ...

After such a multitude of serious eruptions and storms, all good people hoped that the desired day would arise when harmony and peace would be restored. However, even more thorny and trying times engulfed the Throne of Peter during the reign of our forerunner Pope Clement XIII. Strident protests against the Society of Jesus became more frequent with every passing day. In fact, in some regions there arose extremely perilous agitations, commotions, conflicts, and scandals, that disturbed and deeply wounded the bond of Christian love. They set on fire the minds of believers with a party-spirited fanaticism, animosity, and hostility.

Circumstances were perceived as reaching the point of such disharmony and danger that our beloved children in Christ, the Kings of France, Spain, Portugal, and the Two Sicilies,[5] turned against the Society. They had been distinguished by a legacy of commitment and liberality toward the Society from their kingly precursors, and the Society had been greatly praised by virtually all of them. Now, however, these kings were compelled to dismiss and banish members of the Society from their kingdoms and provinces, and whatever land they owned. In their minds, this drastic action was the only cure for a multitude of evils, utterly necessary in order to retain Christian people within the embrace of Holy Mother Church,

5. The Kingdom of the Two Sicilies was made up of Sicily itself and southern Italy.

so that they would no longer oppose, incite, and strike out at each other. Still, these beloved sons in Christ understood that this remedy could not be guaranteed and well-suited for bringing reconciliation to the whole Christian world, unless the Society itself was totally abolished and utterly suppressed ...

Therefore, we pronounce as follows: all authority in both spiritual and temporal matters of the Jesuit Father-General, the Society's provincials, visitors, and any other superiors of the Society, is forever terminated and absolutely abolished. We reassign their jurisdiction and authority to the local church authorities. Below, we shall set out further details regarding the way, the persons, and the conditions of this reassignment. We further forbid with this mandate that anyone else should be received into the Society and take upon him the habit of a novice ... [There follow details of the complete abolition and suppression of the Jesuit order.]

Pope Clement XIV
Dominus ac Redemptor (1773)

The Civil Constitution of the Clergy (selections)

July 12, 1790

The National Assembly, after hearing the report of the church committee, has ordained and does ordain these articles of the constitution:

Heading I

ARTICLE I. Each civil department shall form a single Episcopal diocese, and each diocese must have the same size and the same boundaries as the civil department.

II. The seat of the bishoprics within the eighty-three civil departments of the realm shall be recognised as follows: the civil department of the Lower Seine at Rouen; the civil department of Calvados at Bayeux ... All other bishoprics in the realm's eighty-three civil departments, which are not named in the present article, are, and shall forever be, abolished. The realm shall be divided into ten archepiscopal districts, whose dioceses shall be located at Rouen, Rheims, Besancon, Rennes, Paris, Bourges, Bordeaux, Toulouse, Aix, and Lyons. These archbishoprics shall have the following names: that of Rouen shall be known as the Archbishopric of the Channel Coast...

IV. No French church or parish, and no French citizen, is allowed to acknowledge at any time, or for any reason at all, the authority of an ordinary bishop or archbishop whose diocese is under the authority of a foreign power, nor the authority of that person's representatives dwelling in France or elsewhere. But we say this without trying to diminish the unity of the faith, and the fellowship which shall be preserved with the visible head of the Church Catholic [the pope], as provided for in what follows.

XX. Apart from those named in the present constitution, all church titles and offices ... are from the day of this ruling terminated and abolished, and they shall never again be set up in any way.

Heading II

ARTICLE I. Starting from when this present ruling is published, there shall be only one way of choosing bishops and parish priests, namely by popular election.

II. All elections must be by ballot, and the outcome determined by the absolute majority of votes cast.

III. The election of bishops must be carried out according to the methods for the election of members of the civil departmental assembly, and by the electoral body of each civil department, as specified in the ruling of December 22nd 1789.

VII. In order to be eligible to be elected as bishop, a person must have at least fifteen years of service in the church ministry within that diocese, as a parish priest, serving minister, curate, superior, or director of its seminary.

XIX. The newly elected bishop is not allowed to apply to the pope for any kind of confirmation of his position, but shall simply write to him (as the visible head of the Church Catholic) to show the unity of faith and fellowship maintained with him.

XXI. Before the bishop is consecrated to his office, he must swear a solemn oath, in the presence of the civic officers, the people, and the clergy, carefully to watch over the faithful of his diocese who are entrusted to him, to be loyal to the nation, to the law, and to the king, and to uphold with all his might the constitution established by the National Assembly and endorsed by the king.[6]

XXV. The election of the parish priests must be carried out according to the methods, and by the electors, specified in the ruling of December 22nd 1789 for electing members of the administrative assembly of each civil district.

XI. Bishoprics and pastorates must be regarded as vacant until those elected to take charge of them have sworn the oath mentioned above.

Heading III

ARTICLE I. The ministers of religion shall be supported by the nation, since they carry out the primary and most important of social functions, and by necessity live at all times in the locality where they fulfil the duties to which the people's trust has called them.

II. Every bishop, priest, and serving cleric in a chapel other than the parish church shall be given suitable housing, with the proviso that he must make all necessary repairs. This shall not be to the detriment of those parishes in which the priest is currently paid a cash equivalent in place of housing. The civil departments shall, moreover, have jurisdiction over legal cases that arise arising in this area, brought to the courts by the parishes and the priests. Salaries shall be allocated to each cleric, as specified below.

III. The Bishop of Paris shall be paid fifty thousand livres; Bishops in cities that have a population of fifty thousand or more, shall be paid twenty thousand livres; while other Bishops shall be paid twelve thousand livres.

V. The salaries of parish priests shall be along these lines: in Paris, they shall be paid six thousand livres; in cities with a

---

6. This was before the abolition of the monarchy in September 1792.

population of fifty thousand or more, they shall be paid four thousand livres; in cities with a population of less than fifty thousand, but more than ten thousand, they shall be paid three thousand livres; in cities and towns where the population is less than ten thousand but more than three thousand, they shall be paid twenty-four hundred livres ...

VII. The salaries of the ministers of religion shall be paid to them at the beginning of every three-monthly period, by the treasurer of the civil district where they dwell.

Heading IV

ARTICLE I. The law that requires clerics to reside in the civil districts under their pastoral care shall be strictly obeyed. Everyone entrusted with a clerical office or function shall be bound by this requirement, without any distinctions or exceptions.

II. No bishop is allowed to be absent from his diocese for more than two consecutive weeks during the year, unless a genuine necessity demands it, and he has the permission of the local government of the civil department where his diocese is located.

III. Likewise, the parish priests and curates [assistants to the priests] are not allowed to be absent from the locality where they perform their duties longer than the period specified in the previous article, unless there are grave reasons; and even in those grave cases, the priests must secure the permission both of their bishop and of the local government of their civil district, while the curates must get permission from their parish priest.

VI. Bishops, parish priests, and curates are allowed, as active citizens, to be present at the primary and electoral civil assemblies of the nation; they may be chosen as electors, or as deputies to nation's legislative body, or as members of the general council of the civil communes or the administrative councils of the civil districts or departments where they reside.

The festival of the Supreme Being: Maximilien Robespierre on the new Deist religion of Revolutionary France

First Speech

By Maximilien Robespierre, the president of the National Convention: delivered to the people assembled together to celebrate the festival of the Supreme Being, Décadi 20 Prairial, the year 2 of the French Republic,[7] which is united and incapable of being divided.

The day has finally come, the day forever blessed, which the French people dedicate to the Supreme Being. The world He created has never presented a sight so worthy of His favour. He has looked upon tyranny, crime, and deception ruling the earth. But now, at this moment, He looks upon an entire nation fighting all mankind's oppressors, yet breaking off the progress of its heroic endeavours in order to uplift its thoughts and vows to the Great Being who bestowed this mission and the power to undertake it.

Is it not He whose imperishable hand wrote the death-sentence of tyrants in the human heart, by inscribing there the law of justice and equality? Is it not He who, from the moment when time began, ordained our Republic, and made it the first priority that freedom, honesty, and justice should prevail for all centuries and all peoples?

God did not create kings to consume and destroy mankind. He did not create priests to put a yoke upon us like contemptible beasts, chaining us to the chariot of kings – priests who set an example of corruption, self-centred haughtiness, treachery, greed, immorality, and lies. God created the universe to reveal His power. But He created human beings to give mutual help and love to one other, and to obtain happiness by following the pathway of virtue.

---

7. The French Republican calendar. The month Prairial corresponded to the second part of May and the first part of June. 20 Prairial is June 8th. The year 2 is 1794 (Year 1 of the Republican calendar began on September 22nd 1792, marking the abolition of the monarchy and proclamation of France as a republic).

It is God who has implanted remorse and fear in the heart of the conquering oppressor, but serenity and self-respect in the heart of the innocent man oppressed. It is He who compels the just man to despise the wicked, and the wicked to feel reverence toward the just man. It is He who embellished the beautiful face with modesty, which makes it even lovelier. It is He who makes a mother's heart tremble with tenderness and delight. It is He who drenches with joyful tears the eyes of a child held fast to its mother's breast. It is He who quells the most commanding emotions and tenderest feelings before the exalted love of one's country. It is He who clothed nature with beauties, treasures, and majesty. Everything that is good is either His work or is Himself. Evil flows from the morally corrupted man who oppresses his fellows or allows them to be oppressed.

The Author of nature binds together all mortal men in a vast web of love and happiness.

May the tyrants who dared to break this web go down to destruction! Republican Frenchmen, it is your responsibility to cleanse the land the tyrants have polluted, and to bring back the justice they have driven out. Freedom and virtue were born together from the breast of the Deity, and neither can endure among mortals without its twin.

Large-hearted people, do you wish to be victorious over your adversaries? Then be just in your manner of life, thereby giving to the Deity the only worship worthy of Him. O people, let us today dedicate ourselves, under the Deity's protection, to the just ecstasies of a stainless joy! Tomorrow we will once more take up the struggle against vices and tyrants; we will show the world a pattern of republican virtues. In so doing, we again honour the Deity.

Second Speech

By the president of the National Convention, delivered at a time when atheism, devoured in flames, has vanished, and in its place wisdom stands forth to be admired by the People.

It has disappeared away into nothingness, this monstrosity that the spirit of kingship spewed into France. May all the crimes and miseries of the world vanish along with it. Carrying weapons – either the blades of fanaticism or the venom of atheism – kings never fail to join forces to assassinate mankind. If they are no longer able to mar the face of the Deity by superstition, associating It with their evil deeds, they then endeavour to banish Him from the earth, so that they alone might reign with their evil.

O people, have no more fear of their irreverent plots! They can no longer wrench the world from the breast of its Maker than they can remove the shame from their own souls. O oppressed ones, raise up your crushed heads; you can still lift your eyes up to heaven without fear. O heroes of your native land, your large-hearted dedication to God is not a splendid folly. If the accomplices of tyranny can assassinate you, yet they have no power to destroy you completely. O humanity, whoever you might be, you are able to find high thoughts kindling within yourself; you can anchor your brief earthly life in God Himself and in immortality. Allow nature to take on once more its entire confidence, and wisdom its all-embracing empire! No one destroys the Supreme Being!

The great thing our foes wished to expel from the Republic was Wisdom. Wisdom alone solidifies the success of empires; Wisdom promises us the fruits of our courage. We must partner ourselves with Wisdom, then, in all our endeavours. Let us be grave and prudent in all our plans, like those who are ordering the welfare of the world. Let us be zealous and unyielding in our indignatio against confederated tyranny, unshaken in the midst of peril, persevering in our labour, fierce when fortune frowns, humble and cautious in success. Let us be large-hearted towards the good, merciful toward the miserable, relentless against the wicked, and just toward all. We must not rely on having an unmixed success or easy victories, or on what derives from the fortune or treachery of others. We should trust only in our determination and our virtue. These alone are the infallible sponsors of our independence. Trusting in these, let us shatter the unholy confederation of kings, more through the splendour of our character than by the strength of our weapons.

O French people, you are struggling against kings! Thus you are worthy of honouring the Deity. O Being of beings, O Author of nature, you are insulted when you are called upon by the befuddled slave, the debased accomplice of tyranny, the treacherous and merciless aristocrat. But the defenders of freedom can surrender themselves with confidence to your Fatherly heart. O Being of beings, we have no need to offer you unjust prayers! You know Your own creations, Your own handiwork; their needs are no more concealed from Your eyes than their most hidden thoughts. The hatred of treachery and tyranny rages as fire in our hearts, together with the love of justice and of our native land. It is for the cause of humanity that we shed our blood. Behold our prayer, and behold our sacrifices! This is the worship we give You.

Maximilien Robespierre
Festival of the Supreme Being, **Speeches One and Two**

The persecution of French Protestants (the Huguenots) during the French Revolution

On the 7th of November, 1793, Gobel, the Constitutional Bishop of Paris, abjured the Catholic faith at the bar of the Convention [the French Revolutionary Assembly], accompanied by some priests, who were well worthy to follow in his rear. He laid down the insignia of his office upon the table, declaring that there was no necessity for any other worship than that of liberty, equality, and morality. Certain members of the Assembly, Catholic and Protestant ecclesiastics, followed his example. The Bishop Gregory alone had the courage to ascend the tribune and disavow this apostasy.

The abjuration of Gobel was the signal for the invasion of the churches and the abolition of all religious worship. No one spoke any longer, according to the language of the period, but of invoking Reason, of listening to the voice of Nature, of lighting the lamp of Truth upon the altar, and of rendering mankind happy by stifling the monster of superstition. The temples [churches] of the Protestants, which had been opened only the day before, were closed like the churches of the Roman Catholics, and the pastors were compelled to abstain from their functions under pain of being held as suspected, and consequently liable to capital punishment. The delegate of the Convention in Gard and Lozère, published, on the 16th Prairial, in the year 2,[8] a decree commanding the priests and the pastors to withdraw, within the space of eight days, to a distance of twenty leagues from the communes where they had exercised their ministry. The Terrorist [supporter of 'the Terror', the period from September 1793 – July 1794] had invented nothing new; he merely copied or reproduced an ordinance dictated by the Jesuits in the reign of Louis XIV.

Some of the pastors perished by the Revolutionary axe; others were imprisoned, and among them the veteran of the desert, Paul Rabaut, who was led to the citadel of Nismes upon an ass, as his age and infirmities had deprived him of the strength to travel on foot. 'He had seen his eldest son die upon the scaffold, had wept over the proscription of two other children (Rabaut-Pomier and Rabaut-Dupuy), and he was in his turn incarcerated himself. We are witnesses of the resignation be displayed at this painful moment. Imperturbably calm with respect to his own fate, he showed anxiety only for his children and for his fellow-captives, whom he consoled and supported by his example.'

Protestantism counted as many victims in proportion to Catholicism, if not more, either pastors or laymen, in the days of 1793. The Dictionary of the Condemned indicates, for the department of Gard, where the Reformed did not constitute half of the whole population, forty-six Protestants, ninety-one Catholics, and one Jew. The members of the Revolutionary tribunal of Nismes were, with one exception, all Catholics. The French Reformation, to use the expression of M. Aignan, was never named in the mourning and terror of France, and it paid the tribute of blood twice over, first to the intolerance of Rome, next, to that of impiety.

G. de Felice

***History of the Protestants of France* (1853).**

---

8. Dates in the French Republican calendar. See footnote 7, page 556.

Concordat between Pope Pius VII and the French Government (headed by Napoleon he was First Consul from 1799 to 1804)

Signed on the 26th of Messidor in Year 9 of the French Republic (15th July 1801), and ratified on the 23rd of Fructidor (10th September 1801)[9]

The government of the Republic acknowledges the Catholic, Apostolic and Roman religion as the religion of the great majority of French citizens. His Holiness [the Pope] also acknowledges this religion as deriving, and now once more expecting, the greatest benefit and dignity from the legal establishment of Catholic worship in France, and from its being personally professed by the Consuls of the Republic.

Therefore, after this shared acknowledgement, both for the benefit of religion and for the preservation of France's internal tranquillity, they have come to an agreement on the following points:

Article 1
The Catholic, Apostolic, and Roman religion will enjoy free exercise in France. Its worship will be public, and subject to whatever police regulations the Government deems necessary to maintain public peace.

Article 2
The Holy Throne of Rome, in collaboration with the French government, will bring about a new set of boundaries for the French dioceses.

Article 3
His Holiness will declare to those who occupy French bishoprics that, in the interests of peace and unity, he assuredly expects them to make every kind of sacrifice, even if it means sacrificing their dioceses. Following on this exhortation, if the Bishops refuse to make the sacrifice required for the wellbeing of the

9. Once again we find the Revolutionary calendar, with its months of Messidor and Fructidor.

Church (not that His Holiness expects such a refusal), the new dioceses with their new boundaries will be governed by their new Bishops along the following lines:

Article 4

Within a period of three months after the bull of His Holiness has been published, the First Consul of the Republic will appoint Archbishops and Bishops for the newly defined dioceses. His Holiness will institute them in their office, according to canonical law, as it existed in the form that prevailed in France prior to the recent changes of government.

Article 5

Nominations of new Bishops when a diocese becomes vacant in the future, will be made by the First Consul; but the Bishop shall be invested by the Holy Throne of Rome, in keeping with the previous article.

Article 6

Before taking up their duties, Bishops must, at the hands of the First Consul himself, swear the oath of loyalty that was customary prior to the recent change of government, an oath that reads in the following way: 'I swear and promise in the presence of God, and on the Holy Scriptures, to give my obedience and allegiance to the government established by the Constitution of the French Republic. I also promise that I shall have no contacts or transactions, attend no gathering, and communicate with no group, whether within or without France, where any of these aforementioned things would be at odds with the public peace. If, in my diocese or anywhere else, I discover that something is being plotted to the harm of the State, I will inform the government.'

Article 7

Clerics below the rank of Bishop shall swear the same oath at the hands of the civil authorities selected by the government.

Article 8

At the conclusion of divine worship in all French Catholic churches, a prayer will be offered in the following words:

Domine, salvam fac Rempublicam [Lord, save the Republic!]
Domine, salvos fac Consules [Lord, save the Consuls!]

Article 9
The Bishops will set new boundaries for the parishes within their dioceses, but these shall be valid only after the government has given its consent.

Article 10
The Bishops shall nominate priests for their parishes. But their choice will be restricted to persons acceptable to the government.

Article 11
Bishops shall be allowed to have a chapter[10] in their cathedral and a seminary in their diocese, but the Government shall not be obligated to give these any financial support.

Article 12
All archepiscopal, cathedral, parish, and other churches owned by the Catholic Church and required for worship shall be put at the disposal of the Bishops.

Article 13
His Holiness, in order to secure peace and the blessed re-establishment of the Catholic faith, pronounces that neither he nor his papal successors shall in any way disturb those who have gained possession of possessions that were once owned by the Church, and that consequently the ownership of these possessions, and the various rights and revenues belonging to them, will stay forever in their hands, or in those of their legal heirs.

Article 14
The government shall guarantee a suitable degree of financial support for the Bishops and curates whose dioceses and parishes are included in the new definition of boundaries.

---

10. A cathedral chapter is a body of clerics who act as advisors to the Bishop in his cathedral church (the church in and over which he acts as pastor).

Article 15
The government will also ensure that French Catholics, if they so desire, shall be able to act for the material good of churches and religious foundations.

Article 16
His Holiness recognises that the First Consul of the French Republic enjoys the same rights and privileges that the previous government enjoyed.

Article 17
The parties to this Concordat agree that, if one of the successors of the current First Consul should not be a Catholic, the rights and privileges mentioned in the previous article, and the authority to nominate men to bishoprics, will be regulated with reference to such a successor by means of a new Concordat.

Settled in Paris, on the 26th of Messidor, in the Year 9 of the French Republic [15th July 1801].

The French Imperial Catechism of 1806: what French Catholic youngsters were taught about Napoleon

Question: What duties do Christians owe to those who rule over them, and more especially what duties do we owe to our Emperor Napoleon I?

Answer: Christians owe to the rulers who govern them, and more especially we owe to our Emperor Napoleon I, love, reverence, obedience, loyalty, military service, and paying the taxes imposed for the maintenance and defence of the empire and the Emperor's throne. We also owe it to him to offer ardent prayers for his safety, and for the spiritual and earthly welfare of the state.

Question: Why are we liable to all these duties to our Emperor?

Answer: Firstly, because God, who has formed empires and allocates them by His own will, has established him as our lord and made him the instrument of His power and

His image upon earth, by outpouring upon our Emperor blessings both in peace and war. To revere and give service to our Emperor is therefore to revere and give service to God Himself. Secondly, because our Lord Jesus Christ Himself, equally by what He taught and what He did, has instructed us in the duties we owe to our sovereign. When He was born, in that very event He obeyed the decree of Augustus Caesar; He paid the ordained tax; He commanded us to give to God whatever belongs to God, but also to give to Caesar whatever belongs to Caesar.

Question: Are there any special reasons that should move us to bind ourselves more thoroughly to our Emperor Napoleon I?

Answer: Yes. God has raised him up these troubling times to restore the public worship of the holy religion of our ancestors and to be its guardian; he has restored and maintained public order by his deep and energetic wisdom; he protects the state by his strong arm; he has become the Lord's Anointed through the consecration bestowed on him by the sovereign pontiff, the head of the Catholic Church.

Question: What should we think of those who fail in their duties to our Emperor?

Answer: According to the apostle Paul, such people are opposing the government ordained by God Himself and making themselves worthy of everlasting condemnation.

Chapter 7

The Eastern Orthodox world

Introduction

If Reformed people often forget the rich history of their Lutheran brethren, Western Christians often forget the equally rich history of Eastern Orthodoxy. That Eastern history continued no less rich in the 18th Century. It was an era marked both by a remarkable willingness on the part of many Orthodox to see whatever was good in Western Christianity (especially the Lutheran tradition), and adapt it to their own uses, and also by a concerted endeavour to mine the gold of their own spiritual traditions (notably hesychasm), which had been so forgotten in large sections of Orthodoxy that those who sought to recover those traditions were – ironically – accused of introducing heretical innovations.[1] 18th Century Orthodoxy also had its fair share of intellectual, literary, and spiritual giants; they included high-ranking ecclesiastics like Metropolitan Platon of Moscow, hugely popular devotional writers like Tikhon of Zadonsk, heroic retrievers of lost traditions like Paisius Velichkovsky, and the John Wesley of Eastern Orthodoxy, preacher extraordinaire Cosmas the Aetolian. All these and other significant figures we shall meet in what follows. After this, a Western reader may still have his problems with Eastern Orthodoxy in the 18th Century, but at least he or she will no longer be able to say it is colourless and devoid of interest.

1. The fate of many a knowledgeable teacher – accused of innovating, when all he is doing is reminding the ignorant of their own authentic history and traditions. I recollect the way Scottish theologian Hugh Ross Mackintosh described the typical reaction of British Evangelicals to a teaching perceived as incorrect. The reaction, said Mackintosh, went in three distinct stages: (i) We have never heard this before. (ii) This isn't in the Bible. (iii) It is what we believed all along.

1
Russian Orthodoxy: The school of Prokopovich

Up until the 1830s, the dominant school of theology within the Russian Orthodox Church was the one associated with Feofan Prokopovich (1681–1736). He was the favourite theologian of Russia's mighty westernising Tsar, Peter the Great, who (after being a child-tsar dominated by others) took the reins of government into his own hands from 1689 till his death in 1725. Peter brought Prokopovich to St Petersburg in 1716, in order to spearhead a campaign within the Russian Church against the influence of the disciples of theologian Peter Moghila (1596–1646), whose understanding of Orthodoxy had, in Peter's reckoning, tilted much too far in a Roman Catholic direction. Prokopovich, by contrast, was very anti-Roman Catholic, and more oriented towards Protestantism in the sense of utilising and exploiting Protestant writings against Rome as a supremely useful polemical armoury. His Protestant theologians of choice were the illustrious Lutheran divines, Martin Chemnitz (1522–86), Johann Gerhard (1582–1637), and Johannes Quenstedt (1617–88). In his deep study of Protestant literature, Prokopovich absorbed some outlooks normally identified with a Protestant theological perspective, such as an emphasis on justification by faith and the Protestant canon of the Old Testament (downscaling the Apocrypha to secondary status). Prokopovich, who was appointed Bishop of Pskov in 1718, and then Archbishop of Novgorod in 1724, succeeded in creating a strong school of thought that followed his theological methods, and acted as a widespread leaven within the body of Russian Orthodoxy for a hundred years.[1]

1. The life and work of Platon Levshin (1737–1812)

In Moscow, the Theological Academy (otherwise known as the Slavic-Greek-Latin Academy) – regarded as the headquarters of Russian education and culture – became thoroughly steeped in the approach of Prokopovich. The most towering Moscow theologian of this type was Platon Levshin (1737–1812), one of the most fascinating figures in Russian Orthodox life in the 18th Century, who was to become known to the English-speaking world through the translation of his systematic theology into English.

Levshin was a native of Chashnikovo, not far from Moscow, the son of a trained church psalm-singer. After his schooling in Moscow's Slavic-Greek-Latin Academy, he became a monk in 1758 at Russia's most distinguished and influential monastic community, the St Sergius Holy Trinity Monastery, some forty-five miles north-east of Moscow. Here he took the monastic name Platon, in accordance with the monastic tradition of seeing a monk as newly born and receiving a new name to signify this. 'Platon' is a Russian form of Plato, the pre-eminent philosopher of Pagan Greece – Levshin's birth name was Peter. Such was Platon's intellectual brilliance and learning, he was rapidly appointed the rector of the monastery's seminary. He also acquired a brilliant reputation as a preacher.

Platon's life took a turn into high court circles when the Tsarina Catherine the Great (1762–96), the German Empress of Russia, spotted him. Catherine, who had come to the throne after a coup against her estranged husband Tsar Peter III, became aware of Platon's talents when she heard him preach what she deemed an excellent sermon. She was also frankly impressed by his physical beauty – such a handsome monk! As a result, the Tsarina befriended Platon, and discovered his remarkable depth

---

1. For a much fuller account of Peter the Great and Prokopovich, see Volume 4, Chapter 8, Part 4, section 2.

and breadth of scholarship. A well-read lady, and a devotee of Enlightenment ideals who corresponded with the famous French Enlightenment philosophers Voltaire and Diderot,[2] Catherine was always bedazzled by erudition, and Platon's ample share captivated her. In 1763, therefore, the Tsarina made him tutor to her eight-year-old son Paul, the future Tsar. Platon now lived in the imperial palace, and Catherine liked to show him off to high-ranking visitors from other countries: the learned monk-sage who could speak German and French. She once requested that Platon give a guided tour of Moscow to King Joseph II of Austria, and afterwards, when Joseph was asked what he had enjoyed most about the tour, he replied, 'Platon!'

As tutor to the crown-prince Paul, Platon gave him a series of catechetical talks on basic Christian doctrine. These were published in 1765 as *Orthodox Teaching: or, A Short Compendium of Christian Theology*. It was a mini-systematic-theology of the Orthodox faith, arranged in three parts. Part One dealt with general revelation, creation, providence, the Fall, and the consequences of the Fall in sinful man's inability to obey God. Part Two dealt with God's salvific self-revelation in Christ, covering the topics of Scripture as God's Word, the Church as the divinely created and indestructible community of the Word, the content of the Church's proclamation (the Nicene Creed, expounded at some length), and the sacraments. Part Three dealt with the Christian life, set forth in terms of the Ten Commandments (understood from a Gospel standpoint) and the Lord's Prayer. The work was translated into English, German, Dutch, French, Greek, Armenian, and Georgian. It secured Platon's fame outside his own country as a learned Christian theologian, acceptable even to English, German, and Dutch Protestants for his non-polemical presentation of Orthodoxy, and his incorporation of justification by faith into Orthodox soteriology.[3]

---

2. For Voltaire, a Deist, see Chapter 1, Part 2, section 3. For Diderot, an atheist, see Chapter 1 Part 2, section 7.

3. I have an 1857 translation of this work under the title *The Orthodox Doctrine of the Apostolic Eastern Church*. I have argued elsewhere that

As a court preacher, Platon routinely gave homilies to Russian royalty, nobility, and the upper echelons of the civil service, using the opportunity to propagate his religious and moral ideals with his accustomed eloquence. One of his most striking sermons was delivered in 1795 on the Orthodox feast day of St Nikon the Penitent (26th November), in which Platon emphasised that the kind of spiritually fruitful life lived by the Saint was not a possibility for men alone, but for women too. There was no difference between male and female in the pursuit of Christian perfection and heavenly glory: God did not privilege one sex over the other. In other sermons, Platon carried forward this inclusive ideal to insist that social class made no difference to salvation and spiritual riches, and that deformity of body was wholly compatible with beauty of soul. This element in Platon's thought has been seen as a Christianising of Enlightenment values of human moral equality, or at least an exploitation of Enlightenment values to communicate timeless Christian truths.

At that point in Russian history, the Moscow patriarchate had been abolished (by Peter the Great) and replaced by the Holy Synod, a small body with a membership of a dozen, appointed and dismissed by the tsar (or tsarina).[4] The Synod governed Russian church affairs on a collective basis. Platon became a member of the Synod in 1766, thus cementing his place at the heart of Russian ecclesiastical life. In 1770 he was elevated to the episcopate as Archbishop of Tver in western Russia, where the Rivers Volga and Tvertsa meet. Then in 1775 he achieved a far higher dignity as Archbishop of Moscow – in the absence of a patriarch, Russian Orthodoxy's most high-status bishop. In this role he devoted himself to raising standards of clerical education, reforming Moscow Theological Academy's curriculum so that it now took in history, geography, mathematics, Old Testament Hebrew, and the living languages of other countries.

---

there is nothing in classical Orthodox sources of theology to rule out justification by faith.

4. The Moscow patriarchate was not restored until November 1917, after the Tsarist regime had fallen.

In 1787, the Tsarina Catherine 'upgraded' Platon from Archbishop to Metropolitan of Moscow.[5] This was not quite the token of pure favour it might seem; Catherine had by now cooled in her admiration for Platon, partly owing to protracted conflict between Platon himself and the Tsarina's father-confessor, Archpriest John Pamfilov, who for some reason had a near-pathological hatred of monks and bishops. It looked for a while as if Platon would have to leave Moscow on account of his feud with Pamfilov; but Platon's pupil Paul, Catherine's son, stepped in, and demanded that his mother make his revered tutor into Moscow's Metropolitan, in order to keep him in the city. Catherine acquiesced.

After Catherine's death, Metropolitan Platon crowned the next two Tsars, Paul (1797–1801) in 1797, and Alexander I (1801–25) in 1801. During the reign of Tsar Paul, there was for a time great harmony between the Tsar and his old tutor; Paul looked upon Platon as his true friend and spiritual guide. Unfortunately, disillusionment was once again to be Platon's lot, since in his latter days as Tsar, Paul began feeling an attraction toward Roman Catholicism. Before anything could come of this Romeward drift, Paul was assassinated in 1801 by a conspiracy among some of the leading Russian nobles, who vehemently objected to Paul's policies, such as diminishing their authority over their serfs.

Platon's not entirely happy experiences of being a court figure instilled into him some measure of disenchantment with the condition of the Church. He wrote:

> Everything appears to be deteriorating. The pitiful position of our clergy does not really surprise me, knowing that worldly principles begin to prevail. This is why all the corruption arises, since all power is entrusted to these worldly men. O good God, nothing comforts me anymore. I am crushed with the affairs of my situation. The strength of my soul and body withers away. I no longer look for anything more than dismissal and peace.

---

5. Suffice it to know that in Russian Orthodoxy a metropolitan is a grade above an archbishop. In Greek Orthodoxy, confusingly, the reverse is true.

Even so, Platon's literary activity had been flowing on richly. In 1766 he wrote his *Exhortation of the Orthodox Eastern Catholic Church of Christ to her former Children, now on the Road to Schism,* in which he entreated Russian religious dissenters (such as the Old Believers[6]) to be reconciled with the Orthodox Church. Alongside this, he also advocated generous and non-coercive treatment of such dissenters by the Russian authorities. This attitude he exemplified personally in allowing Old Believers to build their first places of worship in Moscow, and their own cemetery. In 1775 he produced a new Orthodox catechism for Russian priests to instruct the laity; in 1776 he published a catechism for children. In 1777, he issued the first comprehensive history of the Church in Russia to be written in Russian. Platon's collected writings stretched to as many as twenty volumes, published between 1779 and 1807; the bulk of the content was Platon's sermons.

This literary and other ecclesiastical work was carried out against a backdrop of constant ill health; from early in life, Platon had suffered severely from kidney stones, and was frequently prostrate with exhaustion. He often petitioned his superiors (latterly the tsars) to release him from his burdens, but they seem to have regarded him as irreplaceable.

Platon's last significant act as Metropolitan of Moscow was to ratify an agreement with the Old Believers that allowed them to return to the Orthodox Church while continuing to practise their distinctive forms of worship, although this permission was not taken up by huge numbers of Old Believers. It is also worth mentioning that Platon was helping in the preliminary stages of organising what became in the winter of 1812–13 (a few months after Platon's death) the Russian Bible Society. The Society was a branch or offshoot of the British and Foreign Bible Society, a Protestant organisation – but it had the backing of Tsar Alexander I, a pious king who was zealous to see the distribution of the Bible in Russian among his people.

---

6. For the Old Believer schism and its effects, see Volume 4, Chapter 8, Part 3.

The last glimpse we catch of Platon is of the aged Metropolitan fleeing Moscow, with so many others, in November 1812, before the advancing troops of Napoleon Bonaparte's French army of invasion.

Platon's theology was one of the most perfect embodiments of the school of Prokopovich. If one reads his treatise of systematic theology, *Orthodox Teaching: or, A Short Compendium of Christian Theology*, one discovers a system of doctrine that is essentially Orthodox (no traditional Orthodox doctrine is denied), yet is woven all through with perceptions absorbed from the Protestant sources favoured by Prokopovich, especially the 17th Century Lutheran divine Quenstedt. Orthodox distinctives are not stated polemically, but kept relatively low-key, although they are still plainly present – the Eastern view of the Trinity (rejecting the Western filioque clause[7]), the priesthood, the sacraments, veneration of icons, the role of inherited traditions in church life. Alongside this, we find a presentation of (for instance) the atoning work of Christ and its appropriation by faith that no Lutheran could fault. Christ died as a penal substitutionary sacrifice, whereby the triune God made His justice and mercy harmonious in saving sinners; Christ and His gift of salvation, notably justification, are on man's part received and enjoyed through the medium of faith in the Gospel, not the performance of moral works (although Platon was careful to stress that this was living faith which went on to bear moral and spiritual fruit in the believer, not the dead faith of mere head-knowledge).[8] There was little in the treatise to which a Protestant could take exception; Platon had produced a masterpiece of 'ecumenical theology'.

---

7. The clause 'and from the Son' (Latin *filioque*) inserted by the Western Church into the Nicene Creed's teaching on the Holy Spirit. The original wording of the Creed was simply that the Spirit proceeds 'from the Father'.

8. Levshin, however, does reject the Reformed view of predestination (or what he takes to be the Reformed view). He seems to offer a Christological understanding of predestination whereby it is Christ who is the true object of predestination – He was predestined to glory as the God-Man before the creation of the universe.

2. Other teachers of the school of Prokopovich

Platon Levshin was not alone in producing theology according to Prokopovich's methodology. Among the foremost figures in the movement fostered by Prokopovich – men who carried on his work after his death in 1736 – were a group of theologians all based in Kiev: Georgy Konisky (d. 1795), Arsenius Mogiliansky, Samuel Mislavsky (d. 1796), and Irenei Folkovsky (d. 1827). These all taught in Kiev's prestigious Theological Academy in Ukraine, then part of Poland-Lithuania.[9] They made direct use of the Lutheran systematic theologies of Johann Gerhard and Johannes Quenstedt, amongst others, synthesising what they felt were the best insights of Lutheran faith with Orthodox teaching.

Other important figures included Cyril Florinsky (d. 1744) and Gavril Petrov (d. 1801), both of whom taught in Moscow. Florinsky was a professor in the Moscow Theological Academy, who was later appointed Bishop of Tver. His principal work was his *Positive and Polemic Theology*, in which he situated Orthodoxy over against Roman Catholicism, Protestantism, and Enlightenment rationalism. Florinsky was not so enamoured of mining Protestant source material as Prokopovich; but he still helped open up the Moscow Academy to an anti-Roman Catholic reading of Orthodoxy, thereby probably disposing others to look more kindly on Protestant critiques of Rome and its theology (which did not necessarily differ substantially from Orthodox critiques, but could often be expounded with greater depth of learning and mastery of patristic history, a benefit of the Western Renaissance). A generation later, Gavril Petrov was rector of the Moscow Academy, and perpetuated the style of theology advocated by Prokopovich and Levshin in a more full-blooded way.

Bishop Theophylact Gorsky (d.1788), rector of the Kazan Theological Academy, was another practitioner of this type of theology; it found expression in his treatise *Dogmas of the Orthodox Eastern Church* (1784). Archbishop Sylvester

9. For more about Poland-Lithuania, see Part 4.

Lebedinsky (d.1808) of Astrakhan and the Caucasus also belonged to the Prokopovich school, earning a reputation as a sophisticated expositor and interpreter of Jesus' parables. Juvenaly Medvedsky (1767–1809) had an illustrious theological career, teaching at the Trinity Sergius Lavra,[10] the theological school at the Novgorod Bishop's House, and the Ladoga Theological School. His particular distinction was to write one of the first full-blown systematic theologies in Russian, in three volumes (1806), entitled *Christian Theology for those who Wish in Piety the Highest Success.*[11]

A follower of Prokopovich about whom we know rather more was Archbishop Methodius Smirnov (1761–1815), praised by Platon Levshin as possessing 'a keen and scholarly mind'. He held a wide variety of teaching and episcopal positions, including rector of the Lavra Trinity Seminary, rector and Theology Professor of Moscow Theological Academy, Bishop of Voronezh and Cherkassky, Bishop of Kolomna and Kashira, Bishop of Tula and Belevsky, and Archbishop of Pskov, Livonia, and Courland. In 1803 he was appointed a member of the Holy Synod. Smirnov's theological penchant was for biblical exposition; he produced the first translation of Paul's Epistle to the Romans into Russia's literary form of language. When Smirnov was rector of Moscow Theological Academy, the translation was read out, with comments offered, in 1792 at a public meeting. In 1794, Smirnov published a commentary on Romans that went through several editions. To promote the study of New Testament Greek, he wrote *Rules and Summary of the Simple Greek Language* (1783).

Prokopovich, then, had succeeded in blazing a trail for several generations of Russian Orthodox theologians, who trod his pathway of learning 'ecumenically' to read and draw upon Protestant (especially Lutheran) materials, in a strategic attempt to ward off undue Roman Catholic influence within

10. In Orthodoxy a lavra is a group of hermit's cells connected by a church, and sometimes by a place for common meals.

11. This was far lengthier and more detailed than Levshin's earlier treatise.

Orthodoxy. A Protestant will of course appreciate this. In the 20th Century, however, significant Orthodox thinkers reacted against both the Roman Catholic and Protestant influences that had flowed into their faith, seeking instead to move back beyond the Reformation controversies to patristic theology as providing the proper norm.

2
Tikhon of Zadonsk: Russian pietism

Tikhon of Zadonsk (1724–83), for many generations, was the most cherished spiritual writer among Russian Orthodox who were serious about their faith. His eloquence in the cause of practical, heartfelt piety earned him the nickname 'the Russian Chrysostom'. The famous Russian novelist, Fyodor Dostoevsky (1821–81), sympathetically portrayed Tikhon twice in his fiction, as Father Zosima in *The Brothers Karamazov*, and as Bishop Tikhon in *The Possessed*, a fact that demonstrates Tikhon's profound impact on the Russian mind and heart. He was not exactly of the school of Prokopovich, yet in a way Tikhon strongly resembled that movement in his drinking deep from Protestant, specifically Lutheran, literature. In Tikhon's case, however, it was not the Lutheran systematic theologians from whom he took inspiration, but the devotional writings of Lutheran Pietists.[1] In the approach of the Pietists to revitalising Lutheran spirituality, Tikhon discovered a creative wellspring perfectly adaptable (in his view) to the needs of Orthodoxy in his day. His reputation may perhaps have suffered to some degree

1. Some would argue for a far closer connection between Tikhon and the school of Prokopovich. I am simply pointing out a different emphasis, the latter focusing on systematic theology and associated branches of study, where Tikhon focused closely on the heart-awakening literature of piety. For Pietism, see Volume 4, Chapter 1, Part 4, and this volume, Chapter 5, Part 1.

Tikhon of Zadonsk

in modern times, owing to a trend among important Orthodox thinkers to distance themselves from any form of Orthodoxy influenced by Western sources; but this must not be allowed to obscure Tikhon's massive status in his own day, and for long afterward, as arguably the pre-eminent Russian Orthodox author of popular devotional literature. Nor has he been relegated to the ranks of the forgotten; Tikhon's works are still in print, and still nourishing Orthodox piety to the present time.

1. The life of Tikhon

Tikhon was born in Korotsko, in the area of western Russia dominated by the city of Novgorod. His birth name was Timothy Kirillov, and he was the son of a trained psalmodist or church singer, a very poor man who died when Tikhon was a child, of whom he had no memory. The almost destitute circumstances of Tikhon's bereaved mother and family meant that he grew up with an often empty stomach, undertaking physically gruelling labour alongside peasants to secure little more than a crust of bread each day.

Still, Tikhon survived, and in 1740, at the age of sixteen, his mother enrolled him in the seminary in Novgorod, after he had won a government grant through his top academic performance at school. The Novgorod seminary, like many others in the post-Reformation and Enlightenment era in Russia, had a certain Western orientation in scholarly matters; Tikhon, for example, studied the early church fathers in Latin translations. Among these he became well-acquainted with Augustine of Hippo. At this juncture, Augustine had not yet had any significant effect on Russian Orthodoxy; now, however, his writings (or some of them) began to make serious inroads into Russian affections. Augustine's Orthodox admirers, such as the young Tikhon, may not have taken on board his doctrinal teachings on divine sovereignty in election, but they warmed hugely to his God-centred spiritual-mindedness, especially his *Confessions*. Augustine was to be, within Orthodoxy, not the theological 'doctor of grace' as in the West, but the 'doctor of piety' for the heart.

Tikhon later spoke of his time at the seminary:

> I carried on my studies, funded by the government, but being without any personal wealth I still suffered great hardships. When I was given bread, I used to keep half; the other half I sold, using the money to buy a candle. Then I would seat myself on the stove and read a book. My fellow students, who had wealthy fathers and wasted their time in messing around, used to mock me. Holding a tattered shoe, they used to wave it at me, yelling 'We salute you!'

This was to be a recurring note in Tikhon's life – mockery by others.

Despite his ill treatment by his classmates, Tikhon prospered intellectually and spiritually in the seminary, and in 1754 was appointed as a tutor there, initially teaching Greek, and then moving to the subjects of philosophy and rhetoric. In 1758, he decided to embrace monastic life – it was at this point that he took the name Tikhon, the Russian form of Tychon, the 5th Century saint and Bishop of Amathus in Cyprus, often known as Tychon the Wonder-Worker. The following year, Tikhon left the Novgorod seminary and went to the Zheltikov Monastery in Tver, as its archimandrite.[2] However, he was soon relocated to be head of the Tver Seminary and of Tver's Otroch Monastery.

Tikhon's ecclesiastical 'career' continued to flourish. Next came his elevation to the rank of bishop, which took place in

---

2. Archimandrite derives from a Greek term meaning 'ruler of a sheepfold', and in the Orthodox world is applied to the leader of a significant monastery or a group of monasteries.

a bizarre manner. While he was celebrating the Easter liturgy in Tver Cathedral with his superior, Bishop Athanasius, the Bishop was at one point meant to say to him, 'Your holy dignity of archimandrite shall be remembered in heaven' – but instead of that, he said, 'Your holy dignity of *bishop* shall be remembered in heaven.' Realising his mistake, Athanasius grinned and swiftly added, 'May God grant you to become a bishop!' That very same day in St Petersburg, the Holy Synod was deliberating about whom to appoint a bishop to Keksgolma and Ladoga. Seven names were submitted. At the last moment, and against protests that he was too young, Tikhon's name was added. The eight names were then jumbled, and one was chosen 'randomly' by lot. This selection by lot took place three times, and every time Tikhon's name came up. Young or not, the Synod concluded, it was evidently the Lord's will to make Tikhon a bishop.

In 1761, therefore, Tikhon was duly appointed Bishop of Keksgolma and Ladoga (an assistant Bishop to the higher-ranking Bishop of Novgorod). Shortly thereafter, in 1763, he was transferred to the new and developing diocese of Voronezh as its sole Bishop. Voronezh was a border settlement; it looked out on vast unwooded grasslands, the home of Cossacks.[3] In Voronezh itself, Tikhon found himself in the midst of eight hundred thousand lawless townspeople, and eight hundred churches staffed by disorderly priests who each did what was right in his own eyes. Rising to the challenge, the new Bishop proved a dedicated and fervent reformer, preaching to the townsfolk, instructing and galvanising the clergy in their proper duties, and establishing a new seminary. His Christian zeal led him to stamp out a remnant of Paganism in the town, a fertility rite to the god Jarilo (a Slavic deity associated with springtime, vegetation, and harvest).

3. Cossacks (from the Russian *kazak*, free men, adventurers) were militarised self-governing communities of East Slavs, given relative autonomy by the Russian state, who occupied 'buffer zones' between the Russian Empire and other lands. They earned a fearsome international reputation as soldiers. When Napoleon Bonaparte invaded Russia, he dreaded the Cossacks more than any other contingent of the Russian army.

One aspect of Tikhon's endeavours to improve clerical standards in his diocese was to ensure that every priest and monk possessed a New Testament, which the Bishop urged them to read every day – Tikhon was always a devotee of Scripture. As he himself put it:

> Take delight in the Word of God, I mean the Scriptures that have been handed down to us by the prophets and apostles, even as you would take delight in God Himself. For God's Word is the very Word of God's own mouth. If you take delight in God, then for certain you will also take delight in the Word of God. For God's Word is God's epistle or letter to us, unworthy though we are, and is His superlative gift to us to bring us salvation. If you take delight in the Sender, then make sure you also take delight in the letter He has sent to you. For God's Word is given by God to me, to you, and to everyone, so that all who wish to be saved can receive salvation through it. You rejoice when an earthly king writes a letter to you; you read his letter with delight and joy. How much more should we read the Heavenly King's letter with delight and joy!

Even as an effective reformer-Bishop, however, Tikhon's heart was always attracted to withdrawing from the public arena, and living the monastic life in obscurity as a near-hermit. He said:

> If it were possible, I would lay aside my Episcopal rank, and even the monk's hood and cassock, and seclude myself in the most far-off monastery, giving myself to manual work, carrying water, chopping up wood, and sifting the flour to bake loaves.

He dreamt of the glories of the monasteries on Mount Athos in Greece, and was almost overwhelmed when some Greek Athonite monks visited him in Voronezh. At last, Tikhon suffered a shattering crisis of vocation, which manifested as a breakdown in health; he stepped down from his Episcopal position in 1767, and virtually fled to the Tolshevsk Monastery, some twenty-six miles from Voronezh. The swampy water at Tolshevsk, however, made him sick. Two years later, therefore, he relocated to the Monastery of the Theotokos in Zadonsk, near the River Don, situated about two hundred and forty miles south of Moscow. Here he remained for the rest of his life – hence 'Tikhon of Zadonsk'. He was often criticised for abandoning his role as Bishop, but in the Zadonsk Monastery Tikhon at last clearly found his true calling, as a spiritual counsellor (in Russian, a *starets*) to troubled individuals, and a writer of some of Russia's best-regarded literature of piety.

Tikhon tried to live as solitary an existence as he could at Zadonsk, living by himself in a monk's cell, and never (for instance) eating at the common table in the refectory[4] with the other monks. He shunned contact with most people, especially the prosperous classes and nobility, merely becoming irritable in their presence; he found them superficial and uninterested in spiritual things. One of his biographers[5] recorded:

> He used to take note of the members of the upper classes who were visiting the monastery as pilgrims: the ladies dressed up in flamboyant finery, parading around flirtatiously, their faces plastered with paint and powder. Seeing this, his Grace would say, 'Alas for these poverty-stricken, blind "Christians"! They decorate their perishing bodies, but hardly bother to adorn their souls. Their souls are as spiritually dark as the skin of a Moroccan Muslim who has no knowledge of God and no faith in Jesus Christ our Lord.' When some of these dolled-up ladies sought his blessing, if he had no personal acquaintance with them, he used to decline them admittance into his cell, claiming that he was unwell. At other times he would send them away, through me, to be blessed by the monastery's hieromonks.[6]

The only people Tikhon felt at home with were children, uneducated peasants, beggars, and lawbreakers who had been thrown into gaol (whom he would frequently visit). However,

---

4. The room set apart for common meals in a monastery.
5. Ivan Yefimov – see below.
6. Monks who had been ordained to the priesthood.

he had a few special friends among his fellow monks, notably an aged and illiterate peasant named Theophanes, with whom he almost always shared his meals, and Tikhon's devoted cell-attendants and biographers, Chebotarev and Ivan Yefimov. When he was out and about, taking fresh air or away to visit some needy individual, we are told that Tikhon often sang the psalms, knowing them all off by heart.

Tikhon's cell-attendant Yefimov emphasised, in his life of his master, that he often had supernatural experiences – visions of Christ, the Virgin Mary, and glorified saints, heavenly dreams, hearing the singing of angels and the trampling of demons, clairvoyance,[7] and accurately foretelling future events.[8] Others observed that his face was often bathed in tears, a token of the saint's uncommonly profound sense of his own sinful unworthiness (the 'grace of tears' was a highly prized spiritual gift in the Eastern tradition). When he was mocked for his plain unworldly lifestyle, as he frequently was, even by other monks, his close companions Yefimov and Chebotarev heard him respond with, 'It is the will of God that – on account of my sins – the brethren should laugh at me. But I do not follow the path of revenge. Forgiveness is better than revenge.'

Tikhon's personal faith had – for a Russian Orthodox believer – an extraordinarily intense focus on the sufferings of Christ, an emphasis more common in Western piety. Not only did he write about these sufferings with heartfelt emotion, he also surrounded himself with icons depicting the events that together made up the Redeemer's ordeal as He began to suffer in Gethsemane. It has been conjectured that these 'icons' might themselves have been Western in origin, and thus (technically) not true icons but simply pictures.[9] Yefimov recorded:

---

7. Knowing about current events from a distance.

8. Chebotarev by contrast does not focus on these at all in his biography. Among Tikhon's prophecies, he is said to have predicted the Russian triumph over Napoleon's army of invasion in 1812.

9. A religious picture cannot really count as an Orthodox icon if it originates from outside the Orthodox tradition and its distinctive methods of iconography.

In 1770, while he was writing *True Christianity*, he had this vision: he was meditating on the sufferings of Christ, God's Son. He had a strong delight and reverence for our Lord's agony, which he did not merely keep in his mind – almost all the events of the Passion were portrayed on pictures in his cell. As he sat on a couch in front of a picture depicting the Crucifixion, the Descent from the Cross, and the Burial of Jesus, he became lost in profound meditation, so that he was (if I may so put it) outside of himself. He then saw Christ coming down from Golgotha, leaving the Cross, and walking toward him, His tortured body swathed in bloody wounds. The vision made his heart overflow with joy, and yet at the same time it rent him asunder with pity. He fell at the feet of Christ to kiss them, and said, 'O my Saviour, have You indeed come to me?' He felt that he was actually at the very feet of the Saviour. From that moment onward, he meditated still more deeply on the Lord's suffering and, thereby, Man's redemption.

2. Tikhon and the literature of piety

The zenith of Tikhon's literary work in his cell was the composition of his six-volume masterpiece of Orthodox spirituality, *True Christianity* (1776). The title reflects the deep and abiding impact made on Tikhon by Germany's 'father of Pietism', the Lutheran writer Johann Arndt (1555–1621), whose own masterwork was also entitled *True Christianity* (published between 1605 and 1610 in four volumes). The thrust of Arndt's work was a prolonged critique of religious nominalism, a sterile head-knowledge of Christian truth among Lutherans, and a counter-emphasis on a personally authentic Christianity of the heart, a lived and experienced faith. It has frequently been observed that a keynote in Arndt's teaching was to warn against a merely notional belief in salvation through Christ's atoning death, if this was divorced from the transformative sanctification that flowed from participation in His risen life.[10] At any rate, there can be no over-stressing the spiritually fertilising influence

10. For Arndt, see Volume 4, Chapter 1, Part 4, section 1.

that Arndt and his treatise had on Tikhon. In advising a young Russian noble on his religious reading, Tikhon said of Arndt's *True Christianity*: 'Always, morning and night, study the Bible and Arndt; you should only skim other books.' Plainly Tikhon found in Arndt a source of spiritual wisdom and inspiration second only to the Bible.

If we ask how Lutheran Pietist literature came into Tikhon's possession, the answer is found in the Pietist 'headquarters' of Halle in Saxony-Anhalt in eastern-central Germany, by the River Saale. In Halle, a special printing press had been set up to print translations into Russian of Pietist writings, including Arndt's *True Christianity*. Some of these Russian translations may have found their way into Russia through Radical Pietists, German Lutherans who had broken away from the state-established Lutheran Churches of Germany, some of whom emigrated and settled in southern Russia.

Much more definitely, we know that the translator of Arndt into Russian was actually a Russian Orthodox bishop – Simon Todorsky (d.1754), Bishop of Pskov – who belonged to the school of Prokopovich, and would later catechise none other than Catherine the Great, persuading the young German Lutheran princess (as she then was) to embrace Orthodoxy.[11] Todorsky was well-versed in Lutheranism, a fluent German-speaker who had spent four years as a student at the Pietist Foundation in Halle: the ideal translator of Arndt's seminal treatise into Russian. Indeed, Arndt in Russian turned out to be very popular among pious Russian Orthodox; four Russian translations were printed to meet popular demand, in 1735, 1784, 1790, and 1800. It is not therefore something odd or unusual that Arndt's *True Christianity* found its way into Tikhon's hands. The only remarkable thing is the sheer depth of its impact on him, and how he creatively wove that impact into his own epoch-making treatise on Orthodox spirituality.[12]

11. Catherine became Orthodox in 1744 in preparation for her marriage to the future Tsar Peter III.

12. Tikhon may also have made use of a Latin translation of Arndt.

Tikhon's treatise could be seen as an adaptation of Arndt's teachings on authentic heart-piety to an Orthodox setting. The core message is much the same: the rejection of religious nominalism, and the vital necessity of a lived, experienced faith, that bears fruit in a life of ongoing spiritual struggle and sanctification. In communicating this message, Tikhon proved unusually eloquent. The great 20th Century Orthodox theologian, Georges Florovsky (1893–1979),[13] commented that Tikhon's great literary gift was his transparent clarity, coupled with an unusually vibrant and pervasive sense of being a pilgrim through the world, not its citizen or inhabitant. To whatever we might attribute it, Tikhon's *True Christianity* was a runaway success, becoming a set text in many seminaries, and widely read by spiritually minded Orthodox people across Russia.

In addition to his message about living, sanctifying faith, Tikhon reproduced Arndt's Lutheran perspective on justification through that faith alone:

> It is impossible to become justified before God, and thus saved, without Christ and outside Christ, but only by faith in Christ. The sinner is like a little child standing naked before his mother, asking for clothing, and receiving as a garment the clothes of justification, namely, the righteousness of Christ, which he receives by faith.

Among Tikhon's other great treatises on practical Christianity was his *A Spiritual Treasure Collected from the World* (1770). This is an adaptation of a 17th Century work by Anglican Calvinist Joseph Hall (1574–1656), Bishop of Exeter: another example of Tikhon's readiness to appreciate what he felt was good in Western Christian literature. After Tikhon's death, the Holy Synod produced an anthology of his writings with the title *Counsels on the Particular Duties of Every Christian,* later known as *Journey to Heaven.* This anthology achieved phenomenal popularity in Russia, going through scores of editions.[14]

---

13. 'Georges' is correct, not George.

14. The forty-ninth edition of 1870 was translated into Greek. This then formed the basis for an English translation, under the title *Journey to*

3. Tikhon's death and legacy

By the time Tikhon's life was drawing to an end, he had become a spiritual guide to multitudes, whether through his letters to individuals or his widely circulated writings. It is recorded that three years before his death in 1783, he had been praying earnestly, 'Tell me, Lord, of my end,' when he dreamed that he was standing beside a large and beautiful field, on which stood palaces of marvellous appearance. He desired to enter the field, but angelic voices told him, 'You will be allowed to enter in three years' time. For the time being, though, carry on with your labours.' So profound was this dream, Tikhon responded by hiding himself away even more totally in his cell, letting only a few select friends enter. He was a relatively young fifty-nine when he died.

For the next one hundred and fifty years, Tikhon was the most read and best-loved saint in all Russia – the Russian Church officially declared him a saint in 1861. His writings were often reprinted, continually winning fresh hosts of admirers. Other great Russian saints, notably the renowned Theophan the Recluse (1815–94), were humble disciples of Tikhon. But perhaps the most famous tribute was paid to him by the celebrated Russian novelist Dostoevsky, one of Tikhon's most ardent devotees. In weaving a literary portrait of Tikhon in his fiction, Dostoevsky said, 'I will not be creating something from nothing, but simply revealing the real Tikhon, whom I fervently embraced in my heart a long time ago.'[15]

Heaven, in 1991, published by Holy Trinity Monastery, Jordanville, in the state of New York.

15. See the introduction to Part 2 above for Dostoevsky and his fiction.

3
The Greek Philokalia: Macarios of Corinth and Nicodemos the Hagiorite

The *Philokalia* is today widely known and acknowledged, across all the historic Christian traditions, as one of the key texts on Orthodox spirituality. 'Philokalia' is Greek for 'love of the good'.[1] It took some time, however, after its initial publication to achieve this recognition among Greek-speaking Orthodox. Oddly, it was more swiftly received among Russians through the translational work of Paisius Velichkovsky (see Part 4 below). Even so, the *Philokalia* won its way among Greek-speakers, and there is no disputing its permanent worth in the longer perspective of history. A scholarly compilation of what its editors regarded as the best historic Orthodox texts on the practice of a spiritually oriented life, especially through the disciplines of prayer enshrined in hesychasm and the 'Jesus Prayer' (see section 3), the *Philokalia* has become essential reading for anyone who wants to understand (and even embrace) the tradition of Orthodox spirituality. Its two compilers were Macarios of Corinth and Nicodemos the Hagiorite.

1. Macarios of Corinth (1731–1805)

The birth name of Macarios was Michael Notaras, born in 1731 in Corinth, the Greek city of New Testament fame. The

1. The Greek word *kalos* (good) also has strong connotations of 'the beautiful'.

son of George Notaras, a man of great wealth, Michael showed no interest in his father's money-making activities, much to George's disgust; the heart of Macarios was only interested in spiritual riches. We are informed by early sources that as a youngster he ran away from home, secluding himself in the Monastery of the Great Cave, west of Corinth – but his father found him and dragged him back home. As Michael grew, his father tried to throw him in the deep end of a business life by giving him a supervisor's job, in which opportunities abounded for the pursuit and accumulation of wealth. But once again, the son gravely disappointed the father by giving all his money away to the disadvantaged. Meanwhile, Michael's chief delight was the study of the Bible and the literature of piety. He also distinguished himself by tutoring students in the Corinthian school for six years without demanding any salary.

In 1764 the Archbishop of Corinth, Parthenios, died. By this time, Michael had become so well-liked in Corinth as a Christian man that the Corinthians petitioned Patriarch Samuel I of Constantinople to ordain Michael as their new Archbishop, even though he held no rank (not even the most junior) within the Church hierarchy. The Patriarch consented, and Michael was rapidly ordained in Constantinople to each successive stage in the ecclesiastical 'chain of command', until at last he arrived at the high dignity of Archbishop. It was now that he took the name Macarios. For the next four years, Archbishop Macarios distinguished himself as a preacher and reformer, in the latter capacity introducing new measures to make certain that those who offered themselves for the priesthood were effectively trained. However, his Episcopal vocation was cut short by the outbreak of war between the Ottoman Empire and Russia in 1768 – the war lasted until 1774, with Russia annexing substantial amounts of Ottoman land. To escape the hostilities, Macarios fled, taking refuge in a monastery in Hydra. When the war was over in 1774, the Patriarchate would not allow him to resume his duties in Corinth (some conjecture that Macarios' flight from his diocese was held against him as unbecoming of a pastor), but rather than being cast aside he was appointed as a kind of itinerant preacher, with freedom to preach wherever he wished.[2]

Macarios finally ended up on Mount Athos in 1777, where he lived in the Cell of St Anthony. At that juncture in history, controversy raged on Athos over the question of when religious services commemorating the departed should be celebrated. Macarios championed the traditional practice, according to which these services should be held on Saturdays, and that it was contrary to tradition to hold them on Sundays or Feast Days (as some were then doing). The controversy became so fierce, provoking riots, that Macarios decided to leave Athos – not the haven of peace he had been expecting. He found his way at length to the island of Patmos, in whose Monastery of St John he discovered a vast library of Greek manuscripts which included many treatises by Eastern writers on prayer. Macarios copied these, and then passed them on to Nicodemos the Hagiorite (see below): these copies became a treasured public possession when the *Philokalia* was published. In 1782 – under the auspices of the St John Monastery – Macarios established a hermitage and church on Mount Koumana.

From 1793 until his death, Macarios lived on the island of Chios with some other monks who had fled from the 'memorial service wars' on Mount Athos. His influence as a spiritual guide spread across the whole island, so that he became known as 'the spiritual father of Chios'. One of his most delicate labours here was to counsel apostates – Orthodox Christians who (for whatever reason) had converted to Islam, but now wished to return to Orthodoxy. Some of these died as martyrs, executed by the Ottoman authorities for the Islamic crime of having forsaken Islam.

Macarios died on Chios in 1805, after suffering a stroke the previous year. A contemporary account summed up his life thus:

---

2. Another theory is that the Turkish authorities believed Macarios had encouraged the Greeks to rebel against Ottoman rule during the war, demanding his replacement as Archbishop, and that the Patriarchate acquiesced.

Macarios lived his life in a state of peace, without worldly pleasures, and far away from the sounds of the cities. His life was one of continual fasting, without much sleep, and with continual prayer. Together with this, he also lived with practical love toward his fellow man, in keeping with the Lord's command, 'Love your neighbour as yourself.'

2. Nicodemos the Hagiorite (1749–1809)[3]

Nicodemos was born in 1749 as Nicholas Kallivourtzis, in Naxos, Greece, the son of pious Orthodox parents. He became a student at the then celebrated Greek School of Smyrna[4] when he was sixteen, immersing himself in theology and linguistic studies (classical Greek, Latin, French, Italian). However, harassment from the Ottoman authorities compelled his return in 1770 to Naxos. Inspired by some Athonite monks to love the monastic life, Nicholas journeyed to Mount Athos in 1775, becoming a monk at the St Dionysios Monastery and taking the name Nicodemos. He remained on Athos for thirteen years. His decisive personal development here was learning the theory and practice of hesychasm – inner prayer of the heart, with its use of the Jesus Prayer as a special aid. Western readers may perhaps need a reminder that the Jesus Prayer consists of the words 'Lord Jesus Christ, Son of God, have mercy on me, the sinner,' impressed so deeply into the heart that the prayer goes on at all times inwardly, whatever a person might be doing outwardly.

Nicodemos left the actual mountain of Athos in 1788, and ended up living as a hermit in the wilderness region of Kapsala, an area close to Athos into which many Athonite monks withdrew to practise a more solitary life, either alone or in groups of two or three. In Kapsala, Nicodemos attracted a host of visitors, both monks and laymen, as his reputation for holiness and spiritual insight began to spread. One of his first biographers said:

---

3. 'Hagiorite' means 'of the Holy Mountain' (Mount Athos). Sometimes he is called 'Nicodemos of the Holy Mountain'.

4. Known from 1808 until its closure in 1922 as the Evangelical School (nothing to do with Western Evangelicalism).

> All of those who had been injured by their sins took themselves, not to the Hierarchs and Spiritual Fathers for relief, but all went running to Nicodemos, clothed in tattered rags as he was, in order to find spiritual healing and strength in their trials. They came to him, not only from the monasteries, sketes, and cells, but a multitude of Christians journeyed from various countries to visit him, receiving encouragement in their misfortunes from Nicodemos.

Nicodemos' own spiritual writings got him into some trouble from critics, who accused him of plagiarising Western source material: in Nicodemos' case, not the Lutheran sources utilised by Platon Levshin and Tikhon of Zadonsk, but Roman Catholic sources, such as Ignatius Loyola (founder of the Jesuit order), the Theatine priest Lorenzo Scupoli (1530–1610), whose *The Spiritual Combat* had been a Roman Catholic best-seller in its day, and the Jesuit Paolo Segneri (1624–94) who wrote a notable handbook on confession. The controversy surrounding this issue is ongoing. Nicodemos' defenders have argued that he simply and successfully adapted his Roman Catholic source material to an Eastern Orthodox theological and spiritual mindset.[5] His own freedom from heresy was resoundingly asserted by the Athonite monks in 1801:

> We all together declare and acknowledge him as truly godly and truly Orthodox, nurtured on the doctrines of Christ's Church, which is proved by his holy and widely useful treatises, none of which contain any heretical teachings. For this reason we bear witness that he is Orthodox, in order that all may know him to belong to the truth.

Nicodemos' most respected and often reprinted work was his *The Rudder of the Ship of Knowledge*, a commentary on the canon law of Greek Orthodoxy. Other than the *Philokalia*, his greatest

---

5. Much as Protestant writers had adapted Roman Catholic treatises like Thomas à Kempis' *The Imitation of Christ*, or Francis de Sales' *Introduction to a Devout Life*, to a Protestant theological and spiritual mindset. There were, for instance, two English Protestant versions of *Introduction to a Devout Life* in the 17th Century.

work of compilation from the writings of earlier Orthodox teachers was *The Evergetinos*, a treasury of wisdom on how to live the monastic or more generally Christian life and avoid its spiritual pitfalls. The original version had been compiled in the 11th Century by the monk Paul Evergetinos (d.1054).[6] By Nicodemos' time there were several conflicting manuscripts of *The Evergetinos*; Nicodemos gathered and compared them, preparing and publishing a new standard edition in 1783. The *Evergetinos* today is, along with the *Philokalia*, a cherished collection of texts on living a spiritually minded Christian life.

Nicodemos died on July 14th 1809. Other monks, seeing his physical weakness, had asked him the previous day whether he was at peace. He answered, 'I have put Christ within me: how can I not be at peace?' Among the earliest of the 'lives of Nicodemos' we find this description of his earthly end:

> On July 14th, as the visible sun was rising on the earth, the spiritual sun of Christ's Church [Nicodemos] was setting. The new Israel's pillar of guidance to godliness was among us no longer; he who had been the cloud of refreshment to those liquefying in sin's furnace is now hidden from sight. His friends, his acquaintances, indeed all Christians wept. Among these was an uneducated Christian, who said: 'My fathers, how much better it would have been for a thousand Christians to die today, and not Nicodemos.' Yet the shining splendour of his teachings remains with us, and they give us light, and shed light within the Church.

3. The Philokalia

It is not entirely clear precisely how (and when) Macarios and Nicodemos collaborated in producing the Greek *Philokalia*. As a broad principle, however, we can say that it was generally Macarios who unearthed the manuscripts, and Nicodemos who prepared them for ultimate publication. The two monks

---

6. Evergetinos means 'benefactress' in Greek, and refers to the fact that the original compiler Paul had belonged to the Monastery of the Benefactress (the Theotokos, Mary) in Constantinople.

seem to have met on Athos and remained in touch with each other thereafter.

The first edition of the *Philokalia* was published by Nicodemos in 1782. Its overall aim was to reintroduce Greek readers to the largely forgotten teachings of previous generations of Greek spiritual writers on inner spiritual 'watchfulness', focused through the practice of prayer, especially the Jesus Prayer. The goal of such watchfulness and prayer was to overcome sinful passions, arrive at inner peace, and through constant prayer to seek the vision of God as eternal light (the light that shone from Jesus on the Mount of Transfiguration). In a general sense, this body of teaching can be summed up under the name *hesychasm* (from the Greek *hesychia*, peace, stillness, silence). The doctrine and the disciplines of hesychasm were described in some detail in Volume Two of this series; it was a major ingredient in the spiritual outlook of Simeon the New Theologian (949–1022), one of the Byzantine Empire's foremost practitioners and communicators of spiritually minded Orthodoxy.[7] However, the underlying and essential principles of hesychasm should not be exclusively restricted to Simeon and his successors, and Macarios found treatises by Eastern fathers long pre-dating Simeon that contained the core of hesychasm, such as Mark the Ascetic (5th Century) and Hesychios the Priest (8th/9th Century) – see extracts in the Primary Historical Sources section below.

It took a good while for the *Philokalia* to establish itself among Greek-speaking Orthodox as an accepted anthology of piety (although the intention was never that the individual should read and practise its teachings without the oversight of a living spiritual father). By the close of the following century, the *Philokalia* seems to have made some genuine impact; we may discern this from the publication of a new and slightly enlarged edition in 1893 in Athens. Today most readers are familiar with a five-volume edition, published again in Athens between 1957 and 1963, which was the basis for an English translation. The

7. For Simeon see Volume 2, Chapter 3, section 5. For later hesychasm, see Volume 2, Chapter 9, section 3. The great vindicator of a more developed hesychasm was Gregory Palamas (1296–1359).

true 'success story' of the *Philokalia* was much more among the Slavs through the translation by Paisius Velichkovsky, published in 1793 (see Part 4). Today, the *Philokalia* is very widely known, studied, and appreciated as embodying the spiritual heart of the Eastern tradition on the divine mystery and practice of inner prayer.

4
Paisius Velichkovsky

Another spiritual giant of 18th Century Slavic Orthodoxy was the scholar-monk Paisius Velichkovsky (1722–94). His work lay in transmitting to the Slavic world the monastic piety found in the collection of source materials on the spiritual life (originally in Greek) which came to be known as the *Philokalia,* as we have just seen in Part 3, and especially in reviving interest in the 'Jesus Prayer' of the hesychasts.

1. The early life of Paisius

The eleventh of twelve children, and bearing the birth name Peter, Velichkovsky was a native of Poltava in Ukraine, the son of John Velichkovsky, a priest who served in the city's cathedral. Ukraine at that time was part of the Commonwealth of Poland-Lithuania, a union between the Kingdom of Poland and the Grand Duchy of Lithuania, which endured from 1569 to 1795. After his father's death when Peter was only four years old, the child's mother Irene nurtured him spiritually; he tells us that he developed an 'unquenchable love' for reading the Bible, the lives of the saints, and the works of John Chrysostom and Ephrem the Syrian.[1] As a young teenager he became a student in 1735 at Kiev's Theological Academy (Kiev, as Ukraine's historic chief city, was also then in Poland-Lithuania). He did not, however, find that the Academy's teaching exerted any abiding grip on

1. For John Chrysostom, see Volume 1, Chapter 9, section 1. For Ephraim the Syrian, see Volume 1, Chapter 10, section 5.

his mind and heart, owing to his ever-deepening yearning for the life of a monk. In 1741, therefore, he took the first steps into monastic life, receiving the new name Platon at the St Nicholas Medvedovsky Monastery beside the River Chasmin. Soon, however, this monastery was shut down by the Uniate hierarchy of Poland-Lithuania – Uniates were former Eastern Orthodox who had submitted to the authority of the pope whilst retaining the Eastern liturgy.

This event threw Platon off into a quest for a new monastery where he could settle and learn how to be the best Christian and monk. The search was proving difficult, even futile, when he met two Romanian monks who were just preparing to leave Kiev and go back to their homeland. Platon joined them. As they passed through Moldavia, on the southern border of Poland-Lithuania and adjacent to the Black Sea coast, they stopped at the St Nicholas Skete in Vlachia.[2] Here Platon found what he was seeking, settling in the Skete in 1743. Among other disciplines, he learned here the hesychastic Jesus Prayer, as it was still known and practised by some on Mount Athos. Much of this wisdom he gathered from the renowned elder or *starets* Basil of Poiana Mărului (d.1767), who taught Platon the traditions of hesychasm and the inner prayer of the heart.

After some five years in the St Nicholas and other sketes in the Buzău region, home to some forty monastic communities (Russian, Serbian, and Bulgarian), Platon's longing to visit Mount Athos overcame him. With his skete's blessing, in 1746 he journeyed to Athos with another monk, Tryphon, and there joined the Pantokrator Monastery, which allowed Platon to live in comparative solitude. He sat at the feet of various spiritual masters, but none of them decisively spoke to his condition. Still, Platon had enough regard for his former teacher Basil of Poiana Mărului to receive at his hands, when Basil visited Athos in 1750, his next step forward on the monastic path as a fully committed monk with the badge of the monastic tonsure. It was

2. In Eastern monasticism a skete is something in between the hermit's way of life and the full monastic community.

now that he took the name for which he is remembered, Paisius. Basil also counselled him to emerge from his near-solitude into a more public life, and so Paisius became the leader of a skete community of Slavs and Romanians on Athos, the Skete of the Prophet Elias. The skete flourished, and Paisius' disciples began to clamour for his ordination to the priesthood, which however he resisted as long as he felt able. In 1758 he gave in, and was ordained a priest, thus becoming a hieromonk (priest-monk).

2. The spiritual teaching of Paisius: The Slavonic Philokalia

In Paisius' own mind, his mission had now crystalised: he was to base his teaching on the spiritual life on a painstaking study of the patristic Greek texts in which that life had first received its classic formulation. The ancient writers would become living teachers again, speaking through their writings. Paisius thereupon learned Greek, and began translating what he believed were the key writings into Slavonic, assisted by two Romanian monks, Macarios[3] and Hilarion, who had acquired a good knowledge of Greek in their studies at the St Sabbas Academy in Bucharest. Paisius expressed his outlook thus to his earliest disciple on Athos, the Romanian Bessarion:

> How hard it is to guide a soul along ways one does not personally know. Only someone who has carried on a lengthy warfare against sinful passions, and with Christ's aid has overcome sensual desires, anger, pride, covetousness; who has found healing for his soul through humility and prayer, and who has loved and followed his Saviour in all things – only such a person can show all the commands and virtues of Christ to his disciple, without pretence. But where shall we discover such a guide? In our day especially, there are not many of them. There is only one answer left: by day and by night to study the Holy Scriptures and the treatises of the fathers, seeking the advice of like-minded brothers and elder fathers, so that we might learn how to fulfil God's commands, and follow in the footsteps of the ancient ascetics.

---

3. Not to be confused with Macarios of Corinth (Part 3).

In his ongoing translational work, Paisius' source material at length came to include the Greek collection of texts by Macarios of Corinth and Nicodemos the Hagiorite on the spiritual life, the *Philokalia*, published in 1782.[4] Paisius rapidly translated a huge chunk of Macarius' and Nicodemos' compilation into Slavonic – specifically the type of Slavonic used in the liturgy ('Church Slavonic'). Perhaps confusingly, Paisius' own work was also entitled the *Philokalia*, which we might distinguish from its Greek equivalent by referring to it as the *Slavonic Philiokalia*. Paisius' version of the *Philokalia* was at length translated from Church Slavonic into Russian in 1857 by Ignatius Brianchaninov, and Theophan the Recluse then produced another translation in 1877. The fact that Theophan was a devoted disciple of Tikhon of Zadonsk shows that there was no necessary inconsistency between Tikhon's and Paisius' spirituality. The English Anglo-Catholic scholar and poet, T. S. Eliot, sponsored a partial translation from Theophan's version into English in 1951; this sold so well that fuller English translations were then made.

The keynote of Paisius' teaching, originally learned from his mentor Basil of Poiana Mărului, and now mediated to others through Paisius' translations of older texts, can usefully and concisely be summed up under the term 'hesychasm'. As we saw in Part 3 in looking at Macarios of Corinth and Nicodemos the Hagiorite, hesychasm was the practise of concentrated inner prayer as instrumental in conquering sinful passions and fostering fellowship with God in Christ, especially though not exclusively through the Jesus Prayer. The underlying spiritual philosophy, embraced by Paisius, was a belief that notional knowledge of biblical and theological truths was insufficient for salvation; a living communion with the triune God was necessary, and this could be attained only through the disciplined practice of prayer as taught by the acknowledged 'masters' of the spiritual life in the Eastern tradition, whose writings Paisius devoted himself to collecting and translating.

4. See Part 3.

This whole rich phase in Paisius' life – his journey out of Moldavia to Athos where he became a spiritual leader, who would then go on to return to Moldavia, renewing its monastic traditions and spreading the knowledge of hesychastic spirituality – was summarised thus by one of his earliest biographers:

> Who can discern the Lord's ways? Who knows His plans? By His heavenly Providence, He took St Paisius out of his native country, and led him through many other lands, so that he might collect great treasures for his soul as he acquired these by spiritual application. Then at last He conducted him to Holy Mount Athos, so that he might carry on accumulating his spiritual riches, and then impart them to everyone who sought his guidance. The Lord turned him into an imitator of St Anthony of the Caves, who was also born in Ukraine. St Paisius followed in the steps of St Anthony, a wanderer who at length found a home on Mount Athos, where he took upon himself the angelic dignity of monk, and after many years of toil on Athos, obtaining great spiritual gifts, then went back to his fatherland to sow the fruitful seeds of monastic life. Likewise did St Paisius, gathering heavenly riches, go back to his home in Moldavia, to revitalise the monks, to raise up again their fallen cenobitic[5] life, and to plant within its bosom a thrice-blessed obedience, shedding light through his teaching, and thus driving away the darkness of ignorance, bestowing wisdom through the correction and the new translations from Greek into Slavonic of the treatises of the Holy Fathers, and other texts of theology.

Unfortunately for Paisius, his teaching and translational work on Athos ran into stiff opposition from another abbot, Athanasius of the Kavsokalyvia Skete, who accused Paisius of disseminating an 'untraditional innovation'. Even on Athos, it seems that a knowledge of hesychasm had fallen on hard times, and many did not know their own history or traditions. Not

5. Cenobitic = monastic community life, in contrast with the life of a hermit.

one to take such a criticism lying down, Paisius fought back, vindicating the soundness of his teachings in a treatise entitled *Letter of Apologia*, in which he demonstrated Athanasius' ignorance, and the indisputable historic basis of Paisius' own teachings, via quotations from the Orthodox sources.

In 1764, the Prince of Moldavia, Grigore III Ghica (reigned 1764–67, and again 1774–77, with an interlude in which he had been toppled from the throne) invited Paisius to settle in Moldavia, with a view to revitalising the country's Orthodox monastic life and witness. Paisius complied, relocating with sixty-four disciples to the Monastery of the Descent of the Holy Spirit in Dragomirna. The new venture prospered, soon growing to around three hundred and fifty monks. The translational work continued unabated. International politics intervened when Catholic Austria seized the Moldavian territory where Dragomirna was situated, resulting in its Orthodox monastic community relocating first to Sekul, and then to Neamț in 1779. The community continued to increase, eventually comprising some seven hundred monks. It was in Neamt that Paisius finished his translation of the *Philokalia* into Slavonic.

At first, Paisius had intended the work for use only in Russia's Optina Monastery, south-west of Moscow, which had become a sort of unofficial nerve centre for the revival and teaching of the hesychastic spirituality advocated by Paisius. (Many who had learned hesychasm from Paisius had spread the teaching in Russia, and the Optina Monastery had proved unusually receptive in embracing, cultivating, and further propagating Paisian spirituality.) Paisius' great concern was that if people tried to practise the spiritual disciplines of the *Philokalia* by themselves as 'lone ranger' Christians, without the direction of the gifted elders of Optina, they would unavoidably misunderstand and misapply the disciplines, falling into a state of delusion (in Russian, *prelest*). However, in 1793 the Metropolitan of St Petersburg prevailed upon Paisius to overcome his scruples and permit the general publication of the work.

The *Slavonic Philokalia* soon became essential spiritual reading for Russian Orthodox who were intent on a committed approach to the practice of their faith. Another illustrious Slavic saint and *starets*, Seraphim of Sarov (1759–1833), 19th Century Russia's greatest 'mystic', was a keenly devoted reader of Paisius' *Philokalia*. There is also an intriguing American connection in the person of Herman of Alaska (d.1836), Russian Orthodox missionary to the Aleuts of Alaska (at a time when Alaska was part of the Russian Empire – Russia sold it to America in 1867). Herman had been schooled in Paisian spirituality, and took his copy of the *Slavonic Philokalia* with him to Alaska. The Optina Monastery was another vibrant and effective transmitter of Paisius' teachings, especially in its heyday in the 19th Century, when Optina became the informal spiritual 'capital' of Russian Orthodox spirituality. Lastly, one should note the impact of another seminal Russian devotional work, the 19th Century classic *The Way of a Pilgrim*, which in the 20th Century burst the bounds of its Orthodox origins, becoming globally known and appreciated. The anonymous pilgrim's most treasured source-book of spiritual teaching and practice was Paisius' *Philokalia*.

We have the following account of the aged Paisius from someone named Constantine Caragea who met him:

> I have seen holiness living in the flesh, and not play-acted, for the first time in my life. I am very struck by his shining, pastel, and pallid looks, his long bushy beard, as bright as silver, and the neatness of his clothing and his cell. His words were mild and truthful. He had the appearance of someone who existed totally apart from the flesh.

As he drew near his death (of which he might have had preternatural knowledge, according to some traditions), Paisius began work on an autobiography, although it remained unfinished. He entitled it *Narrative of the Holy Community of my Beloved Fathers, Brothers, and Spiritual Sons, who in the Name of Christ have Come to me, the Unworthy one, for the Salvation of their Souls*. Its central theme was the various sketes and monasteries he had established. After Paisius' death in 1794, several lives of the saint were written that helped fill in the gaps in his own narrative. His legacy in the Russian version of the *Philokalia* was to transform the spiritual life of Russian Orthodoxy in the following century.

5
Cosmas the Aetolian

Cosmas the Aetolian (d.1779) was probably the nearest counterpart in 18th Century Orthodoxy to George Whitefield or John Wesley: an itinerant preacher whose work throughout Greece attracted vast crowds of enthusiastic hearers, and helped to put fresh fire, at grass-roots level, into the sputtering flame of Greek Orthodox church life. His reputation stands high among Orthodox today. Cosmas was 'glorified' (declared a saint) in 1961, and he is nicknamed 'equal to the apostles' for his widespread preaching labours.

1. The early life of Cosmas

Cosmas was a native of Mega Dendron, a Greek village in the region of Aetolia (hence 'Cosmas the Aetolian'). We are unsure of his birth date – somewhere between 1700 and 1714. He was the son of parents who were both weavers by profession. They had fled from local anti-Christian harassment in Epirus by the local authorities representing the Ottoman Empire of the Muslim Turks, to re-settle in Mega Dendron. It should be remembered, however, that the whole of Greece at this historical juncture was within the Islamic embrace of the Ottoman Empire. There was no guaranteed freedom from all forms of religious discrimination against Orthodox Christians, in whichever part of Greece one lived.

Cosmas worked alongside his parents as a weaver in the village for a long time. Eventually, however, as a young man, he became a student in one of the Aetolian monasteries, where all the basics of education (not just theology) were taught. Then he progressed to a school in the Aetolian village of Lombotina. In keeping with normal practice in Greek schools in Cosmas' day, he was soon assigned to teach his fellow students, where the traditional account of his life tells us that he was remarkable for not using physical punishment on his pupils. Inspired by a thirst for knowledge, Cosmas continued his education in the St Parasceve Monastery in Mandra, near Athens, which had established a school under its direction. His delight here was to plunge himself in study in the huge monastic library; it housed a treasure-trove of precious copies of Greek theological writings, some of them known to exist only in one or two manuscripts.

In 1749, Cosmas went to Mount Athos, where he kept up his studies at the school in the Vatopedi Monastery, the Athoniada. Among his tutors was the famous Orthodox philosopher Eugenios Voulgaris (1716–1806), who was steeped in the literature of the Enlightenment, and had exchanged a long series of letters with France's foremost Enlightenment thinker, Voltaire. Yet Voulgaris had come to repudiate the Enlightenment as inconsistent with Orthodox faith. He and others had committed themselves to a war against illiteracy among Greeks: how could the riches of Orthodoxy be communicated successfully, if people could not even read the Bible or the Fathers?[1] Cosmas absorbed this vision, and began studying rhetoric to gain the skill of imparting the knowledge of Orthodoxy most effectively as a teacher and/or preacher. It was also on Athos that Cosmas became a monk, at the Philotheos Monastery.

2. Cosmas the preacher

In 1760, Cosmas left Athos after a decade of study, relocating to Constantinople, capital city of the Ottoman Empire. He hoped there to receive the blessing of his ecclesiastical superiors to begin a life of preaching, thereby to spread a well-grounded

1. This was coupled with a desire to see the re-creation of the Byzantine Empire as the political expression of Orthodoxy.

understanding of the Orthodox faith to his Greek compatriots. One of his earliest biographers relates:

> Cosmas frequently remarked, 'My fellow Christians have a deep need for the Word of God! For this reason, those among us who possess education should not aim our endeavours at royalty, nor at the courts of the aristocracy, nor should we spread abroad our education to obtain money and fame; rather, that we might gain a reward in heaven and the glory that never fades away, those who are learned should, above all, teach the ordinary people, who are living in terrible ignorance and crudeness.' However, despite his desire to do this, and despite his burning ardour that his brothers should be blessed, Cosmas could also envisage the problems involved in apostolic preaching. Therefore, possessing the lowly-mindedness that flows from wisdom and modesty, he did not launch out to commence this labour guided only by his own will, unless he was first certain of God's will. Therefore, desiring to discern if his purpose met with God's approval, he opened the Divine Scripture, and his eyes miraculously fell upon the words of the apostle: 'Let no one seek his own interests, but let everyone seek the interests of others' (1 Cor. 10:24); that is, everyone should seek, not the things that merely benefit himself, but the things that bring benefit to his brother.

Cosmas found a positive response to his missionary ideals in Patriarch Seraphim of Constantinople. In 1760, therefore, with Seraphim's blessing, Cosmas began his preaching, at first among the Greeks of Thrace, the area of Europe just west of Constantinople, and later throughout Greece proper. His purpose was twofold. On the one hand, he sought to deliver the ordinary masses of Greeks from an ignorant religious nominalism – people for whom Orthodoxy had become little more than a dead formalism of attending Sunday worship, devoid of any real understanding of the actual meaning of the faith they outwardly professed. Such nominalism made them all too ripe for conversion to Islam, a process that was ongoing at a somewhat concerning rate, enough to worry Patriarch Seraphim. On the other hand, Cosmas also sought to deepen the faith of the spiritually minded, leading them on into the treasures of patristic teaching, thereby to upbuild church life at the local level. Cosmas' biographer again tells us:

> So it was that the blessed Cosmas began to preach the Gospel of the Heavenly Kingdom, originally in the churches and villages on the edges of Constantinople, after which he journeyed further afield to Nafpaktos, Vrachochori, Mesolongi, and other localities. He then once more went back to Constantinople, where he sought the counsel of Sophronios, who was then Patriarch; having been granted his consent and blessing, Cosmas set out again, with even greater fervour and zeal, preaching the teachings of the Gospels without any thought of self. He journeyed through all the Dodecanese Islands, instructing the Christians to show forth a true change of heart, and to do those works that bring pleasure to God and are in harmony with repentance. He then once more went back to the Holy Mountain [Athos] in 1775. He visited its monasteries and sketes, exhorting the fathers, and dedicating a portion of his time to studying patristic literature. However, his heart was overflowing with love for Christians and a desire to bring help to his brethren, about which he frequently spoke to many monastic fathers; and thus he could delay no longer. Leaving the Holy Mountain, Cosmas re-commenced his preaching in the nearby villages, and carried on preaching in Thessalonica, Berea, and the whole of Macedonia. He journeyed through the territory of Kimarou, Acarnania, Aetolia, even as far as Arta and Preveza; and from there, he set sail for the islands of St. Maura and Cephalonia.

It was not as though other zealots had not tried to preach the faith to the nominal Orthodox of Thrace and Greece. They, however, had met with no positive response. Why then did Cosmas prove so triumphantly effective? A large element in his success lay in the style of language he adopted. Where other preachers had spoken in a stiff, formal, scholarly manner, Cosmas used popular language – the idiom of the home and the marketplace. We might call him an Orthodox John Bunyan in this respect. Such employment of the vernacular enabled

Cosmas to win a much easier hearing, especially after people became convinced of his sincerity. He often encountered initial apathy and antagonism; but he persevered, and the villages that had at first been hostile soon welcomed him warmly, with a willingness to hear his preaching and learn from it. From the accounts, another secret of Cosmas' success was that he did not 'speak down' to people as a superior, or as a lofty lecturer, but as a brother and an equal.

As his reputation spread, it was not long before huge crowds numbered in the tens of thousands were gathering to listen to Cosmas. This of course meant that he could no longer preach in constricted places (churches, village squares), but in fields large enough to accommodate the enthusiastic multitudes. The place chosen for his sermon would be announced in advance; a big wooden cross would be planted there, and a bench for Cosmas to stand upon in order to preach. The wooden cross afterwards would be left standing in its place, as a memorial of where God's Word had sounded forth. It was later reported that many miracles occurred at these crosses. However, Cosmas did not rely on preaching alone; rather like John Wesley, he gathered those his preaching had positively affected in each community into small groups, instructing them to meet often and sustain the flame of heavenly life by discussing spiritual matters among themselves.

Another central aspect of Cosmas' work was to ensure the future education of those communities where he preached. He laid upon all his hearers the sacred obligation to build schools for their children, who would then be instructed not only in the rudiments of literacy but in Orthodox faith as well. These schools were funded by donations, and they sprang up wherever Cosmas went. The mushrooming of Cosmas' schools took place not only in Greece but in the Balkans too, where he also preached, and the example seems to have caught on in other parts of the Orthodox world, e.g., among the Eastern Orthodox of Egypt. When someone from England journeyed through Greece in 1808, the account of that experience included the following observation: 'From Wallachia and Moldavia all the way to Egypt, from Smyrna to Kerkera, there is not a single town, not a single island where you will not find a school providing free education, functioning on the community's funds.' The writer, perhaps without realising it, was describing the legacy of Cosmas. This side of his labour to educate a nominally Orthodox people in a well-informed understanding of their faith helped to pave the way for the successful Greek War of Independence against the Ottoman Empire in 1821–29. Greek national morale had been so boosted by Cosmas' educational work, it fed into a wider desire among Greeks to throw off the alien Islamic yoke of their Ottoman conquerors, and once more enjoy their own self-governing Greek Christian civilisation.

3. Cosmas' martyrdom

Although Cosmas' preaching and educational labours enjoyed such widespread success for a period of some twenty years, he also stirred up powerful enemies. Some of the wealthier Greeks did not like him; they functioned as village and town elders, and they felt their social authority undermined by Cosmas' popularity. Jewish businessmen had a strong grudge against him for his having persuaded the Greek population to shut down all Sunday markets – Cosmas had a lofty view of the sacredness of the Lord's Day, which must not be disturbed or defiled by the everyday activity of buying and selling. Some local Turkish governors also disliked him for strengthening the Christian faith of their Orthodox subjects, thus making them less likely to convert to Islam (although it should be noted that other Turkish governors revered and protected Cosmas as a 'holy man', recognising his sanctity despite his non-Islamic faith).

The exact circumstances are uncertain, but it seems that some combination of Cosmas' enemies brought about his downfall in August 1779. He was arrested by the Ottoman authorities, and – without trial – executed by hanging at Kolkondas, in what is now Albania. His remains were later relocated to a monastery in Ioaninna, a city in north-western Greece; the occasion brought Greeks out in countless numbers to honour the cherished memory of the evangelist. Although Cosmas left no written texts, the content of many of his sermons was preserved by others, who wrote down what they remembered. Many of his prophecies were preserved in the same way. These sermons and prophecies had a very wide circulation for a long time in Greece. He was also venerated as a saint and martyr on Mount Athos – one of the 'new martyrs of the Turkish yoke'.

6
Missionary expansion

Russian Orthodoxy experienced significant missionary growth in the 18th Century, especially in Siberia, a vast area stretching from the Ural Mountains of western Russia to the Pacific Ocean. This missionary growth was partly owing to Tsar Peter the Great (1689–1725) and his desire to bind the peoples of Siberia to the Russian way of life, and hence to his own authority as ruler of Russia. Whatever Peter's motivations may have been, he found a man of religious integrity and evangelistic commitment to spearhead the spread of Orthodoxy among the Siberians – Filofei Leschinsky (1650–1727).[1]

Leschinsky belonged to the lesser (somewhat impoverished) Russian nobility, born in Ukraine and educated at its Kiev Theological Academy. After his training he was ordained to the priesthood, but his priestly service was cut short by the death of his wife,[2] an event that led him in a new direction – monastic life. It was on becoming a monk that he took the name Filofei,[3] joining the Kiev-Pechersk Lavra.

In 1700, Peter the Great decided that Filofei was the person to head the Siberian mission, and the monk was appointed Metropolitan of Tobolsk and all of Siberia. There had been an

1. Or Leszczynski.
2. Perhaps the Western reader may need reminding that the Orthodox priesthood is ordinarily married.
3. Filofei is Russian for Philotheos. There is more than one St Philotheos after whom Filofei might have been named – possibly the 10th Century St Phliotheos the Wonderworker of Bithynia.

Archbishop of Tobolsk since 1620, and the first man to occupy the post, Cyprian, had undertaken missionary work with considerable success; Filofei was to build on this and extend the work. Arriving in Tobolsk with several monks, Filofei focused his evangelistic efforts (although not exclusively) on the Ostayak and Vogul tribes. It was physically demanding work; travel over long distances was necessary, a squad of soldiers was sometimes required to protect Filofei from violence, and he was dogged by ill health. Occasionally he gave up in despair. Nonetheless, his labours ultimately bore notable fruit. The number of Orthodox Siberian churches grew from one hundred and sixty to four hundred and forty-eight. In obedience to Tsar Peter's remit, Filofei also presided over the demolition of Pagan idols and temples. He gained the distinction of erecting the first stone building outside of St Petersburg, the Holy Trinity Monastery at Tyumen, beside the River Tura east of the Ural Mountains (up until then, stone buildings outside of St Petersburg had been prohibited by imperial decree). His missionary journeys took him as far east as Mongolia and Lake Baikal, north of Mongolia, the world's largest freshwater lake.

By the time Filofei retired in 1721 in order once again to practise a less peripatetic piety in a monastery, his twenty years of labour had seen the Orthodox faith achieve a striking penetration into Siberia. Even though the next twenty years saw some setbacks, with a number of villages and tribal chieftains lapsing back into Paganism, this trend was again reversed in the 1740s, under a new Bishop, Silvester Golovacky, who occupied the position from 1746 to 1758.

Another missionary development in the vastness of Siberia came in 1727, when the city settlement of Irkutsk on the Angara River, which had been within the diocese of Tobolsk, was given its own bishop. Irkutsk had previously been known as a place of exile and imprisonment for Russian criminals and political dissidents. Now, however, the centre of the new diocese rapidly became a vital base of evangelistic activity, especially in the establishment of a new seminary for training priests, where the native languages of the region – Mongolian and Chinese

– were taught to the seminarians. The most significant Irkutsk missionary was Cyril Vasilyevich Suchanov (1741–1815). He began as a lay evangelist, working with the Tungus (or Tungusic) people-group situated in the Dauria region.[4] Dauria is a vast area of flat grassland, punctuated by pine forests, low-lying hills, and warm salt-water lakes; it lies in the middle of Eurasia, connecting Russia, Mongolia, and China. Journeying around the entire region in apostolic poverty (his only possessions were what he carried with him in a bag), Cyril's saintliness conquered the hearts of the Tungus people. The first Orthodox church building was erected among them in 1776, where Cyril not only catechised them in the Eastern faith but instructed them in the scientific principles of agriculture. Thereafter he was (finally) ordained by Michael Mitkevich (Bishop of Irkutsk from 1782 until 1789), continuing his labours thereafter as a priest.

The Kamchatka peninsula was successfully evangelised by Ioasaf Chotunshevsky, a former preacher in Moscow's Theological Academy. He set up his base of operations in the peninsula in 1745. Nor was he alone, but the head of a mission team comprising six students from the Academy, two monks and a deacon from Moscow, and a further seven clergymen from Tobolsk. Kamchatka is in the far east of Russia, its coastline washed by the Pacific Ocean, its land formed largely by volcanic rock. It had both a native and a Russian population, and it was among the latter, at first, that Chotunshevsky and his team worked. They found, according to their own reports, a Russian population scarcely Orthodox in religion and held in the grip of deep moral depravity. The mission team laboured, successfully, to make Orthodox faith a lived reality among the Russians, and soon embraced the native Kamchatka people in their endeavours, resulting in numerous professions of faith and baptisms. Chotunshevsky reported in 1747 that the converted Kamchatka natives were morally far superior to the Russian settlers. This success story, however, was not without its costs:

---

4. Tungusic was not a name native to the people, but created by Russians in an attempt to classify the group of languages spoken in the region.

one of the monks and one of the students from Moscow were murdered during a native insurrection against Russia. Later on, in 1766–67, a smallpox epidemic ravaged the peninsula, killing half or more of the population and most of the Orthodox clergy. It would take several generations for the Church to get fully back on its feet in Kamchatka after this calamity.

There was a small but scholarly Russian Orthodox congregation in Peking, capital city of the Chinese Empire. Up until 1727, China had resolutely closed its doors to foreign influence; however, the Russian and Chinese Empires signed a new peace treaty in 1727, the Treaty of Kyakhta, in which Russia – under Tsar Peter II – acknowledged China's authority over Mongolia. In return, China now allowed a Russian Orthodox congregation to be established in Peking, under the care of four priests. By 1732, nine Chinese converts had been baptised, and there was a steady trickle of conversions for the rest of the century, although never in sufficient numbers to produce a large congregation. Perhaps the truest significance of the Orthodox community in Peking lay in its powerful contributions to Western scholarly study of China and its culture.

One less than happy missionary policy pursued in some parts of Russia involved offering tax concessions to Pagans who embraced Christianity. This, of course, resulted in a rash of economically driven professions of faith, where many of the converts (it was later reported) remained in fairly profound ignorance of what it meant in practice to be Christians. This tax-concession policy was tried out, notoriously, in the early 1700s in Russia's Middle Volga region, stretching from the mouth of the Oka River to that of the Kana River. A great deal of strict order was introduced into the evangelistic laxity by Archbishop Luke Konashevich (the ruling Bishop of Kazan from 1738 to 1755), who took very seriously his duty to bring Orthodoxy to the tribes under his jurisdiction – the Chuvash, Tchermiss, and Ostiak tribes. He built up the Kazan Seminary, making it a respectable house of learning. However, even Archbishop Luke was found to be using inappropriate strong-arm methods (such as forcibly placing Pagan children in Orthodox schools, against their parents' wishes). The Holy Synod diplomatically transferred him from Kazan to Belgorod, an ethnically Russian region, in 1755, where he could reform the local seminary without having to force Orthodoxy on a people who already accepted it.

PRIMARY HISTORICAL SOURCES

Platon Levshin on the atonement

The death of Christ is the true sacrifice, by which we have become reconciled to God, justified, and saved, through faith toward this divine Mediator.

We have repeatedly alluded to the necessity of satisfying divine justice for the sin committed, and that it was impossible to avoid the effects of God's justice by an expiation of our own. It is also evident that the sacrifice of the Old Testament (which consisted in the offering of animals) was equally insufficient. The Son of God, and our Mediator, has therefore assumed all to Himself, His passion, the shedding of His blood, and His painful death, viewed in the sight of His Father as if the sinner had suffered them all; and the punishment of the innocent Saviour, according to the inscrutable counsel of God, was counted instead of the punishment due to us. Thus the Apostle thinks when he says, 'For the love of Christ constrains us; because we thus judge, that if one died for all, then all died' (2 Cor. v. 14), and in verse 21, 'For God has made Him who knew no sin to be sin for us, so that we might be made the righteousness of God in Him.' And thus it is that we read in Isaiah, 'But he was wounded for our transgressions, he was bruised for our iniquities; the chastisement of our peace was upon him, and by his wounds we are healed.'

The death of Christ is a sacrifice, since He offered Himself as a sacrifice on the cross, and as an innocent lamb was slain, in order to make peace with God, burning with the desire to save mankind, and thus becoming an acceptable offering to God His Father, and a pattern of love. The sacrifice of Christ was a true sacrifice, as all those that preceded it were but the foreshadowings and types. Only such a one could satisfy the justice of God and become a worthy vessel of His mercy, so as to cleanse mankind from their sins, and return them to their former happiness, as the Scripture says: 'But Christ has come a high priest of good things to come, by a greater and more perfect tabernacle, not made with hands, that is to say, not of this building; neither by the blood of goats and calves, but by His own blood, He entered once and for all into the holy place, having obtained eternal redemption for us. For if the blood of bulls and of goats, and the ashes of a heifer, sprinkling the unclean, sanctify for the purifying of the flesh, how much more shall the blood of Christ, who through the eternal Spirit offered Himself without spot to God, purge your consciences from dead works, to serve the living God?' (Heb. ix. 11–14).

By this sacrifice, an end was put to the sacrifice of Aaron, that is, of the Old Testament, and Christ has become the only eternal High Priest; for besides His, there can be no other sacrifice, and according to the Apostle, 'This man, because he abides forever, has an unchangeable priesthood. Therefore He is able also to save to the uttermost those who come to God through Him, since He ever lives to make intercession for them' (Heb. vii. 24). This great High Priest has been called by God Himself 'Priest', yet not of the order of Aaron, but according to the order of Melchizedek (Heb. v. 10). Whoever wishes to understand the mysterious meaning of these words, let him read the following remarks on Melchizedek, in the Appendix to this Treatise.

In this great work of redemption are manifested the following infinite qualities of God, that is, His mercy, justice, and wisdom. His compassion has been so great, as to give over to death His Only-begotten Son who is of one substance with Him, for us His enemies. His justice remained so intact, that our fault has not been forgiven except through the most perfect atonement. His wisdom became manifest in that He found such an astonishing means for pouring forth (so to say) the whole flood of His benevolence, without tainting in the least

His justice. 'O the depth of the riches both of the wisdom and knowledge of God!' (Rom xi. 33). This great mystery is 'to the Jews a stumbling-block, and to the Greeks foolishness, but to those who are called, the power and the wisdom of God' (1 Cor. i. 23, 24). And we boast of nothing, with Paul, 'save in the cross of our Lord Jesus Christ' (Gal. vi. 14) by whose death we expect everything good from the mercy of God; for as 'He did not spare His own Son, but gave Him up for us all, how will He not, together with Him, also freely give all things to us?' (Rom. viii. 32). As therefore the death of Christ guarantees that His heavenly Father will show mercy and love to those who believe in His Son, so on the other hand it binds His believing ones to be always grateful to God, and to fulfil His holy will.

Platon Levshin
Orthodox Teaching: or, A Short Compendium of Christian Theology (1765)

Platon Levshin on personal salvation

ARTICLE I – *What is Faith*

The Creed begins from that very faith which consists in the hearty reception of the Gospel. The Creed very appropriately begins from faith; for faith alone teaches man how he be reconciled to God, and, as the Apostle says, 'Without faith it is impossible to please God.' (Heb. xi. 6.) By *Gospel* we understand the glad tidings of man's salvation, through the Only-begotten Son of God, and our Mediator, Jesus Christ. He only is a believer who receives this doctrine with a repenting heart; every other man, differently disposed, is an unbeliever. The acknowledgment of this sublime doctrine is called faith, because we do not comprehend this doctrine by the power of our natural reason, as we have proved in the First Part of this Treatise, but by an immediate and direct revelation from God Himself in the Holy Scriptures. When our Saviour says to His disciples, 'Go into all the world, and preach the Gospel to every creature' – 'he who believes and is baptised shall be saved; but whoever does not believe shall be damned' – He means by this that the adoption of the Gospel is faith, as the rejection of it is unbelief.

What is Necessary to True Faith

For embracing the Gospel, two things are requisite. *First,* The knowledge that man is wretched and poor in the sight of God; that he is subject to His just wrath, and that he cannot justify himself before His righteous judgment. Hence John the Baptist (Matt. iii. 2) as well as our Saviour (Matt. iv. 17) and the Apostle Peter (Acts ii. 38) invariably began their preaching by saying, 'Repent.' *Secondly,* To embrace unhesitatingly the doctrine of the Prophets and Apostles, and firmly believe that Jesus Christ, by them proclaimed, is the Saviour of mankind. This is chiefly the substance of Gospel faith, as Paul's Epistles plainly testify: 'Even the righteousness of God, which is by faith in Jesus Christ to all and upon all who believe' (Rom. iii. 22). The same is asserted in the whole of the succeeding chapter, as well as in Gal. i. 16, 'We have believed in Jesus Christ, that we might be justified by faith in Christ, and not by the works of the law.'

Of Justifying Faith

It is called justifying faith, since by faith man becomes justified before God, even without the works of the law, as Paul says in his Epistle to the Romans, xi. 6; for how can human actions justify man, when he cannot be justified except after acknowledging that he is a sinner, and worthy of Divine wrath? But as soon as man is justified by faith, he is bound to show this faith by his works, and hold fast to the obtained justification by the observance of the Divine Commandments; for 'faith,' according to the Apostle, must be such 'as works by love' (Gal. v. 6).

What is Living Faith

Such faith as we have described is called 'living faith', because the spark of sincere faith is constantly enlivened by continual progress to virtue. But when man does not confess his own wretchedness before God, neither is willing to place all the hope and confidence of his salvation in Christ, nor leads a Christian life, the faith of such a man is dead, hypocritical, and vain.

Platon Levshin
Orthodox Teaching: or, A Short Compendium of Christian Theology (1765)

Tikhon of Zadonsk: The nature of the Gospel

Beloved Christians! There is nothing so delightful, so lovely, and so sweet to us sinners than the Gospel. For sinners who know their misery, the Gospel is more welcome than bread to those who hunger, drink to those who thirst, liberty to prisoners and those locked away. 'The Son of Man has come to seek and save what is lost' (Luke 19:10). Such is the extremely sweet voice of the Gospel. And who is this Son of Man? The Son of God, King of Heaven, sent from His Heavenly Father! He is the One who chose for our sakes to be known as the Son of Man. And why did He come? In order to seek us out and save us, who are lost, and bring us into His everlasting Kingdom. Could there be anything more welcome, anything more attractive to us who are lost? But now let us consider what the Gospel is, what it asks of us, and those to whom it is fittingly proclaimed.

1. The Gospel, from its very name, is the happiest of news. To all the world, it proclaims Christ the world's Saviour, who came to seek out the lost and save them. Listen, then, all you lost sinners! Listen to that extremely sweet voice of the Gospel! It loudly declares to us all, 'The Son of Man has come to seek and save what is lost.' It is a dreadful thing for us to be found in a state of sin in God's sight. But the Gospel proclaims that our sins are forgiven on account of Christ's name, and that Christ is our justification in God's sight. In You, O my Saviour, Jesus Christ, God's Son, I am justified! You are my truth, You are my illumination!

It is a dreadful thing for us to be found the enemies of God. But the Gospel proclaims that Christ has reconciled us to God! Having come, He preached peace to all who were both near and far off.

The curse of the Law is a dreadful thing for us, since we are all sinners. That curse brings punishment upon the sinner both in time and eternity. But the Gospel proclaims that Christ has redeemed us from the curse of the Law, having been made a curse for us!

Death is a dreadful thing for us. But the Gospel proclaims that Christ is our resurrection and life!

Gehenna and hell are dreadful things for us. But the Gospel proclaims that Christ has rescued us from hell and all its misfortunes!

Separation from God is a dreadful thing for us. But the Gospel proclaims that we will be forever with the Lord in His Kingdom without end!

This, O blessed Christians, is the Gospel's most sweet voice! Therefore, 'Taste and see that the Lord is good!' (Ps. 34:8). 'For God so loved the world, that He gave His Only- Begotten Son, so that whoever believes in Him might not perish, but have everlasting life. For God did not send His Son into the world to condemn the world, but that the world might be saved through Him. Whoever believes in Him is not condemned' (John 3:16-18). 'Blessed be the Lord God of Israel, for He has visited and redeemed His people, and raised up a horn of salvation for us in the house of His servant David' (Luke 1:68-69).

2. And what is required of us? O Christians, our part is to receive these heavenly and sweetest tidings thankfully, as sent from Heaven, and from a pure heart always to give thanks to God our Benefactor, who so freely has had mercy on us, and to show forth a holy obedience and submission with all gratefulness. Conscience itself teaches and persuades us to be grateful to one who is our Benefactor. For He loved us when we were unworthy. Now let us also love Him, for He is worthy of all love! Love asks that we should never offend the Beloved. And God finds all sin offensive. Thus let us keep ourselves away from every sin, and do His holy will, that we may not offend our compassionate Father and Benefactor. 'Our Father in heaven, hallowed be Your name, Your kingdom come, Your will be done on earth as it is in heaven,' and so forth (Matt. 6:9-10).

3. And to whom is the Gospel proclaimed? We have our answer from Christ: 'The Spirit of the Lord is upon me, because

He has anointed Me to preach Good News to the poor; He has sent Me to heal the broken-hearted' (Luke 4:18). In other words, the Gospel is fittingly proclaimed to those who, recognising their sins, knowing their destitution, misfortune, and misery, and having a sorrowful, contrite heart that feels awe toward God's judgement – to such is the Gospel fittingly preached as a healing salve is poured upon injured flesh. Hear, then, O sorrowful and contrite souls, hear the sweetest voice of the Gospel! 'The Son of Man has come to seek and save what is lost!' This healing salve of the most sweet Gospel is spread over your wounded souls. By this medicine of salvation, therefore, heal your broken hearts! 'The Son of Man has come to seek and save what is lost,' He seeks you and He saves you, for you are one of those He came to seek. Accept that you are sinners before God; confess it! Your sins are forgiven on account of Christ's name. Therefore, repent of your sins and weep before God, since He has prepared salvation even for you!

Tikhon of Zadonsk

Journey to Heaven, Part II: The Way of Salvation

Tikhon of Zadonsk: How to combat the spirit of dejection

I understand from the letter you sent me that you have been assaulted by the spirit of dejection. This is a dreadful passion of the mind, and Christians working out their salvation must strive against it forcefully. Dejection attacks even those who have food and the other necessities of life ready before them; how much more does it assault those who dwell in solitude. I recommend the following exercises to ward off dejection:

1. Put forth your efforts! Force yourself to pray and to carry out every good work, no matter how opposed these might be to your inclination. A man with a whip forces a lazy horse to walk and gallop. In the same way, we have to force ourselves to carry out every kind of spiritual labour, especially to pray. When God sees your efforts and labour, He will bestow zeal and a good inclination upon you. Habit has the power to create inclination,

and (we might say) allures us toward prayer and good works. Therefore, learn to develop the habit, and it will lead you on to practise prayer and good works.

2. We also obtain zeal by varying our occupations – by turning aside from one activity in order to carry out another. Consequently, you should do the following. Pray; then carry out some physical task; then read a book; then ponder your spiritual state, thinking about everlasting salvation, and so forth. Do these things one after the other. If dejection gets a savage hold upon you, get out of your room, walk up and down, meditate on Christ, uplift your mind to God and pray. In this way, dejection will depart from you

3. These also will deliver you from dejection: the thought of death, which might perhaps enter your mind, the thought of Christ's judgement, of everlasting misery and everlasting blessedness. Meditate on these things!

4. Pray and sigh to God, beseeching that He Himself would bestow zeal and a good inclination upon you; for without God, we are not fit for any spiritual task at all.

If you obey these four rules, then trust me that, by degrees, you will acquire both zeal and a good inclination. God lays upon us the duty of labouring and of working with fortitude, and He has promised His aid to those who labour. Labour, then, so that God might give you His help! He helps people who strive, not those who lie down and slumber. Satan waits in ambush to achieve our destruction. Let us not slumber, then, but stand upright and engage in conflict with so extreme an enemy! We can do this only through prayer, and spiritual reading, and every kind of good work. Then, when the evil one comes upon us, he will find no place for him. Resist the devil and he will flee from you!

Tikhon of Zadonsk

Letter to a monk suffering from the spirit of dejection

Tikhon of Zadonsk: Glory to God for everything!

Glory to God for everything! Glory to God for making me in His image and likeness! Glory to God for redeeming me, the fallen one! Glory to God extending His care to me, the unworthy one! Glory to God for leading me, the sinner, to repentance! Glory to God for giving me His holy words, shining like a lamp in a dark place, thereby setting my feet on the way of righteousness! Glory to God for shedding light upon the eyes of my heart! Glory to God for having revealed His holy name to me! Glory to God for washing away my sins through the cleansing of baptism! Glory to God for showing me the way to everlasting blessedness! The way is Jesus Christ Himself, God's Son, who says of Himself, 'I am the way, the truth, and the life.'

Glory to God that He has not delivered me up to destruction on account of my sins, but shown such patience toward them, on account of His lovingkindness! Glory to God for making known to me the nothingness and emptiness of this world! Glory to God for His helping hand amid all manner of temptations, trials, and disasters! Glory to God for keeping me safe me when accidents and mortal perils came upon me! Glory to God for shielding me against the devil, the adversary! Glory to God for lifting me up me when I was in the dust! Glory to God for comforting me when I was sorrowful! Glory to God for converting me when I was wandering! Glory to God for chastening me as a Father! Glory to God for declaring to me His final judgement, that I might tremble and turn away from my sins! Glory to God for making known to me everlasting misery and everlasting blessedness, that I might fly from the one and seek the other! Glory to God for giving me, the unworthy one, food to strengthen my body, clothes to cover my nakedness, a house to provide shelter! Glory to God for all the other blessings He gave me to comfort and uphold me! I received blessings from Him as often as I drew breath. Glory to God for everything!

From Tikhon's *Last Will and Testament*

Paisius Velichkovsky: A brief exposition of thoughts which dispose to repentance

O my soul! Call to mind the dread and fearful wonder: for your sake, your Creator became Man, and chose to suffer to bring you salvation. His angels tremble at the sight, the Cherubim are awe-struck, the Seraphim are confounded, and all the powers of heaven utter endless praise; and yet you, hapless soul, remain bound in sloth!

From now onward, rise up, O my beloved soul, and do not delay the practice of a holy change of heart, inward remorse, and repentance for your sins. If you delay these for year upon year, month upon month, and day after day, you will no longer desire to undergo a full change of heart, and you will find no one to show you pity.

In that case, it shall be with great anguish that you will then begin to repent, without any effect. But since you have the opportunity today to do something good, do not delay a holy change of heart until tomorrow, O my beloved soul, since you do not know what a day may bring forth, or what misfortune may befall you this very night. For you have no knowledge of what the day or night will bring; you do not know whether a long life awaits you, or if you will suddenly and without warning undergo a swift and wretched death.

Now, O my beloved soul, is the time for patient endurance; now is the time for bearing sorrow; now is the time for keeping the commands and fulfilling the virtues; now is the time for the sweetness of lamentation and mournful weeping. If you genuinely desire salvation, my soul, take delight in sorrow and groaning, as beforehand you took delight in indolence. Pass your life as if you were dying each day; for soon your life will flee away like the shadow of clouds in the face of the sun, and no one will remember you. So to express it, the days of our life are cast forth into the air! Therefore do not hold back, even when confronted by the most testing sorrow.

In relation to other people: let us not speak about pointless sorrow, but even in temperate sorrow, do not surrender yourself to grief, do not be shaken, do not flee; but regard yourself as dust under the feet of others. Without this humility, you cannot be saved nor escape everlasting torment. For our earthly life soon comes to an end, and vanishes in a single day. If a man will not crush his ego in a godly way through practising the virtues, or will not sacrifice his own life in order to fulfil God's commands and the traditions of the Fathers, he cannot be saved.

Therefore, O my beloved soul, call to mind all the Saints: the Prophets, the Apostles, the Martyrs, the Hierarchs, the Holy Monks and Righteous Men, the Fools-for-Christ, and all who have pleased God down through the ages. Where have you ever discovered Saints who did not subject the flesh to the spirit, who did not suffer in hard trials, also suffering hunger and thirst, keeping vigil and praying day and night, possessing humility and heartfelt repentance, a childlike absence of malice, mercy to all, offering help in every sadness and need, giving various gifts and charity, as much as they were able? To sum up, they possessed all the virtues, together with love devoid of pretence. Whatever they did not desire or hated, they did not do this to others. And they did everything with obedience, like purchased slaves, working not as unto man, but unto God, with a wise simplicity. Yet they did not appear wise, but counted themselves insignificant, only giving attention to their own salvation. O man! Death is standing before you. If you labour heavenward, you will be crowned with life eternal life in the age to come.

We acquire virtue by forcing ourselves in every way. So if you want to vanquish the sinful passions, cut yourself off from delight in pleasure! For if you are devoting yourself to material food, your life will be spent in passions; your soul will never be humbled as long as your flesh remains attached to bread. The soul cannot be saved from destruction while the body is being kept safe from everything unpleasant.

Let us then go back to what is fundamental. If you desire to be saved, O my soul, to walk along on the painful pathway I have just sketched, and thus to find entrance into the Kingdom of heaven and know the reality of eternal life, then you must discipline your flesh, experience voluntary hardship, and undergo trying sorrows, even as all the Saints have experienced and undergone. When someone is making himself ready for this, and commits himself to the command to endure all things for God's sake – all the troubles and pain that will befall him – then all troubles, bitter experiences, and the attacks of demons and men, will seem to him light and easy. Such a person is not afraid of death, and nothing will be able to separate him from the love of Christ!

O my beloved soul, have you heard how the Holy Fathers spent their lives? O my soul! Follow their example, at least a little. Did they not shed tears? Alas, my soul! Were they not sorrowful, thin, physically worn out? Alas, my soul! Did they not suffer illnesses of body, and deep heart-wounds and mourning of soul with tears? Alas, my soul! Were they not garbed in the same weak flesh that we have? Alas, my soul! Did they not wish for delightful, sweet, and easy rest in this world, and every kind of physical rest?

Yes, they desired such things, and they experienced bodily distress. But these desires they traded for endurance, and their present sorrow for a future joy. They severed themselves once and for all from everything unprofitable. They counted themselves as dead men, and troubled themselves without self-pity in spiritual toils. O my soul, do you see how the Holy Fathers toiled, without any rest, suffering all manner of hardship? They made the flesh subordinate to the spirit, and fulfilled all the other commands of God, and thus were saved.

And yet you, O wretched soul, do not in the least desire to force yourself to virtue, and you become weak from the littlest labours. You become downhearted, not remembering in the slightest the hour of death, nor weeping over your sins. O my wretched soul, you have gotten used to eating your fill, drinking your fill, and being languid about spiritual things. Do you not understand that you are summoned to impose deliberate hardship on yourself? And yet you endure nothing! If so, how can you really want to be saved?

From now onward, then, rise up, O my beloved soul, and do what I tell you. If you are unable to toil as the Holy Fathers toiled, then at least make a beginning according to your strength. Serve others with lowliness and simplicity of heart! Confess your weakness and bring yourself down in your own estimation! Say: 'Alas for you, my wretched soul; alas for you, sinful one; alas for you, O totally defiled one! You are lazy, thoughtless, sluggish, and unsympathetic. Alas for you, you have already perished!' And so, by small degrees, your soul will grow in tenderness of feeling, shed tears, come to its senses, and repent.

Paisius Velichkovsky

***Field Flowers, or Lilies of the Field, Gathered from the Divine Scripture, Concerning God's Commands and the Holy Virtues,* Chapter 1**

The Greek Philokalia: Hesychios the Priest on spiritual watchfulness

[Hesychios the Priest lived sometime in the 8th or 9th Century. He was the abbot of the Monastery of the Theotokos of the Burning Bush on Mount Sinai. Macarios and Nicodemos greatly admired his treatise on spiritual watchfulness.]

St Hesychios the Priest, On Watchfulness and Holiness, written for Theodoulos.

1. We can describe watchfulness as a spiritual practice which, if undertaken diligently over a lengthy period of time, purifies us (with God's assistance) from the thoughts, words, and evil deeds inspired by evil passion. It brings us to an assured knowledge of the unknowable God, to the extent that such a thing is possible, helping us to enter into divine mysteries concealed from human sight. It empowers us to carry out all God's commands in the Old and New Testaments, showering us with all the blessings of the future life. It is that purity of heart (in the genuine sense) that Christ blessed when He said: 'Blessed are the pure in heart, for they shall behold God' (Matt. 5:8). This purity is now very rare among monks, on account of its spiritual dignity and loveliness, or rather on account of our own laziness. This being the case, such watchfulness is purchased only at a high cost. And yet, once it has taken root in us, it leads us to an authentic and holy manner of life ...

2. The famous lawgiver Moses – or we should say, the Holy Spirit Himself – shows us the pure, all-embracing, and edifying nature of this watchfulness, instructing us how we can obtain

it and bring it to perfection, saying, 'Take heed to yourself, in case there should arise a secret thing in your heart, even an iniquity' (Deut. 15:9, Septuagint). This phrase 'a secret thing' is speaking of the situation when an evil thought first springs up. The Fathers refer to this as a provocation which the devil puts into our hearts. The moment this thought arises in our minds, our thoughts begin pursuing it, establishing a passion-driven fellowship with it.

3. Through watchfulness we can fulfil every virtue, every command. Watchfulness is stillness of heart; when it is pure from mental images, it also preserves the intellect.

4. A man born blind does not behold the light of the sun; likewise, whoever neglects to cultivate watchfulness does not behold the abundant brightness of God's grace. Nor is he able to purify himself from sinful thoughts, words, and deeds. On account of these thoughts and deeds, such a man will not be able to evade the clutches of the princes of hell, when he leaves this life.

5. Attentiveness is stillness of heart, which no thought disturbs. In this stillness, the heart breathes and calls upon the name of Jesus Christ alone, who is God's Son and Himself God, ceaselessly and without interruption. It acknowledges Him who has sole power to pardon our sins; with His help, it faces its foes undaunted. Through this calling upon Him, and being embraced continually in Christ, who secretly knows the secrets of all hearts, the soul does all it can to ensure that its spiritual sweetness and its interior struggle remain hidden from human sight. Thus the devil, coming upon the soul furtively, does not carry it into evil and wreck its precious labour.

6. Watchfulness is an incessant fastening and fixing down of thought at the heart's gateway. Destructive and deadly thoughts are thus detected as they draw near, and their words and deeds are taken note of. We are then able to see the false and deceptive shape in which the demons are attempting to mislead the intellect. If we are industrious in this activity, we can reap a good deal of experience and knowledge concerning spiritual conflict.

7. When someone is endeavouring to block up the fountain of sinful thoughts and deeds, constancy of vigilant watchfulness in the intellect is fostered by the following: trembling before hell and before God, God hiding Himself from the soul, and the coming of trials that both chasten us and teach us. These losses and unlooked-for trials aid us in rectifying our way of life, particularly when we become negligent concerning the peace brought by being watchful, after we have once tasted it. Constancy of attention fosters an interior firmness; interior firmness, by its own nature, fosters a deepening of watchfulness; this deepening, by degrees and in its own way, bestows spiritual insight into the unseen warfare of the soul. This is then itself followed by perseverance in the Jesus Prayer, and by the spiritual condition granted to us by Jesus. In this condition, the intellect is purified from all mental images, and experiences a complete stillness and tranquillity.

8. When the mind flees to Christ for protection, calls upon Him, stands its ground, and drives off its invisible foes, like a wild animal in a favourable situation of defence before a pack of dogs, then the mind foresees their spiritual ambushes long before they can attack. By means of a continual calling upon Jesus the Peacemaker against these enemies, the mind abides in a totally secure condition.

9. If you are spiritually skilful, having entered into the mysteries of God, and standing in His presence at daybreak (cf. Ps. 5:3), you will understand what I am saying. If you do not understand, practise watchfulness; and then you will grasp it.

10. A great quantity of water gives you an ocean. Intense watchfulness and the Prayer of Jesus Christ, undisturbed by distracting thoughts, form the indispensable foundation for spiritual attentiveness and profound inner stillness, for the depths of personal meditation (unseen by men), for the lowliness of heart that understands and judges, for uprightness and love. We must practise this watchfulness and the Jesus Prayer in a forceful, focused, and unfailing way.

11. Scripture says: 'Not everyone who says to Me, "Lord, Lord", will enter the kingdom of heaven, but only he who does

the will of My Father' (Matt. 7:21). The Father's will is shown in these words: 'Whoever loves the Lord, hate evil' (Ps. 97:10). Therefore, we ought to do both of these things – pray the Prayer of Jesus Christ, and also hate our sinful thoughts. This is how we do God's will.

Hesychios the Priest
On Watchfulness and Holiness
In *The Philokalia*

The Greek Philokalia: Mark the Ascetic on the right balance between faith and works, God's grace and human striving

[Mark the Ascetic was a 5th Century Athenian monk, perhaps a disciple of John Chrysostom, whose work below was deemed worthy of inclusion in the Greek *Philokalia* of Macarios of Corinth and Nicodemos the Hagiorite]

Two Hundred and Twenty-Six Texts, On Those who Think They are Justified by Works

1. In these chapters, those with exact faith, who know the truth, show the emptiness and poverty of faith of those who lead a righteous life merely outwardly.

2. The Lord wished to show that the fulfilment of every command is a duty, whereas sonship is a gift freely bestowed on men through His own blood. Therefore He said: 'When you have done everything that has been commanded to you, you shall say: We are unprofitable servants: we have only done that which was our duty' (Luke 17:10). Thus the kingdom of heaven is not a reward given to works, but a gift of grace made ready by the Master for His servants who believe in Him.

3. No slave demands his freedom as though it had been owed to him as a reward. Rather he performs his obligations as one who is in debt; and it is as a gift that he receives his freedom.

18. Some think that they believe correctly, while they do not practise God's commands; others, while practising the commands, expect the kingdom to be given to them as a deserved reward. Both sin against the truth.

20. If 'Christ died for us in accordance with the Scriptures' (1 Cor. 15:3), and we do not 'live for ourselves, but for Him who died for us and rose again' (2 Cor. 5:15), it is plain that we are Christ's debtors, so that we should serve Him unto death. If we are His debtors, how then can we look upon sonship as something He owed to us, as though He were our debtor?

21. Christ is our Master by virtue of His own nature and by virtue of the life He lived in the flesh. For He created humankind out of nothing, and through His own blood He redeems humanity when it lies dead in sin; and to those who trust in Him, He has given His grace.

22. When Scripture says, 'He will reward everyone according to their works' (Matt. 16:27), do not think that our works in themselves will merit either hell or the heavenly kingdom. On the contrary, Christ rewards each one according to whether that person's works are done with faith or without faith in Himself. He is not a merchant bound by a contract, but God who creates us and redeems us.

Mark the Ascetic
On Those who Think They are Justified by Works
In *The Philokalia*

The Evergetinos

From St. Ephrem [the Syrian][1]

My brothers and sisters, the time given to us for our repentance is this our present life, here on earth. We count as truly blessed the soul that has not ever fallen, not even a single time, into the snares of the Adversary. Still, if a soul that has been trapped in the Adversary's snares has found the strength to tear free of those snares, thus escaping his bondage to the Evil One, then such a soul must likewise count himself blessed. Even though we now live in the flesh, we are delivered from the assault of our souls' Adversary by escaping from his snares, in the same

1. Ephrem or Ephraim the Syrian (306–73), one of the most revered Eastern fathers for his many hymns and his teaching on the Christian life.

way that a fish escapes from the fishnet. If a fish is ensnared, but manages to tear the fishnet and rush off down into the deep waters, we know that the fish is saved, so long as he remains in the water. However, when the fisherman drags the fish in the fishnet up onto the dry land, then the fish is no longer able to save itself.

We ourselves experience the very same thing. Throughout the period when we are living in this present life, God has bestowed on us authority and strength in ourselves to shatter the fetters of the Adversary's wicked purposes, and by means of repentance to throw off the weight of our sins. Without any doubt, this brings us salvation and the inheritance of God's Kingdom! On the other hand, should the dread decree of death descend upon us, and the soul depart from the body, the body being deposited in the depths of the grave, then none of us can help himself any longer. We are like the fish, removed from the water, seized fast by the fisherman, deposited securely in his fishing basket: that fish can in no way be saved anymore!

O brother, never say to yourself, 'Today I shall sin, and I will repent of it tomorrow.' You do not even know if tomorrow will come! Tomorrow lies only in the hands of God.

Ephrem the Syrian

The Evergetinos, Book 1, Hypothesis 2: Throughout the time of this present life, we must do what is good here and now, and not put it off until tomorrow. Once we have died, we shall be unable to put things right.

Cosmas of Aetolia: Some of his preserved teachings

Let us nurture love for God and for our neighbour. If we do this, God will come to us, bringing us joy, and planting the life that is eternal life within our hearts. Then we shall flourish in this life, and also enter Paradise, where we shall rejoice for all eternity.

Blessed is the one in whose heart these two loves abide: love for God and love for his brothers and sisters. Such a one truly possesses God; and whoever possesses God has every blessing, and cannot bear to practise sin. Again, miserable is one man who lacks these two loves. Truly such a one has the devil and evil with him, and he always sins. O my brothers and sisters, God asks us to abide in these two loves! He Himself says so in His Holy Gospel: 'On these two commands hang all the Law and the Prophets.' Through these two loves, all the Saints of our Church, both men and women, fulfilled holiness and entered Paradise. Whoever has this blessed love, for God first of all and then for his fellow Christian, becomes a fit vessel to receive the Holy Trinity into his heart.

If you desire to walk in the path of salvation, then as long as you are here in this world, above all things seek love.

If we want to flourish in this life and to enter Paradise, and to call our God 'Love' and 'Father', we must abide in the two loves: love for God and love for our neighbour. It is natural for Christians to abide in these two loves, and contrary to our nature not to have them. Just as a swallow requires two wings if it is to fly through the air, so we require these two loves, because without them we cannot tread the way of salvation.

My brothers and sisters, understand that love has two attributes, or two gifts. One is to make man strong in what is good; the other is to make him weak in what is evil. I have a loaf of bread to eat; you have none. Love says to me: do not eat the loaf by yourself, give some of it to your brothers and sisters, and then you eat what is left. Or I have clothes. Love says to me: give one of your garments to your brother, and then you can wear the other one. Or I open my mouth to condemn you, to lie to you and deceive you; but immediately I remember love, and it makes my mouth dead, not allowing me to tell you lies. Again, I reach out with my hands to steal what is yours, your money, even all your belongings. But love does not allow me to steal them. Do you see, my brothers and sisters, the gifts love brings?

The Martyrs received their welcome into Paradise through their blood; the Ascetics, through their ascetic life. Now you, my brothers and sisters, who have families, how will you receive a welcome into Paradise? Through hospitality, by sharing with your brothers and sisters who are destitute, blind, or crippled.

If you are earning your bread through toil and sweat, you should rejoice, because such bread is blessed; and if you give away some of it as charity, it is counted as a great amount. But those who live through injustice and stealing should weep, because what you obtain in this way is under a curse; and if you give charity out of such ill-gotten gains, it will not benefit you at all – it will be a fire that consumes you.

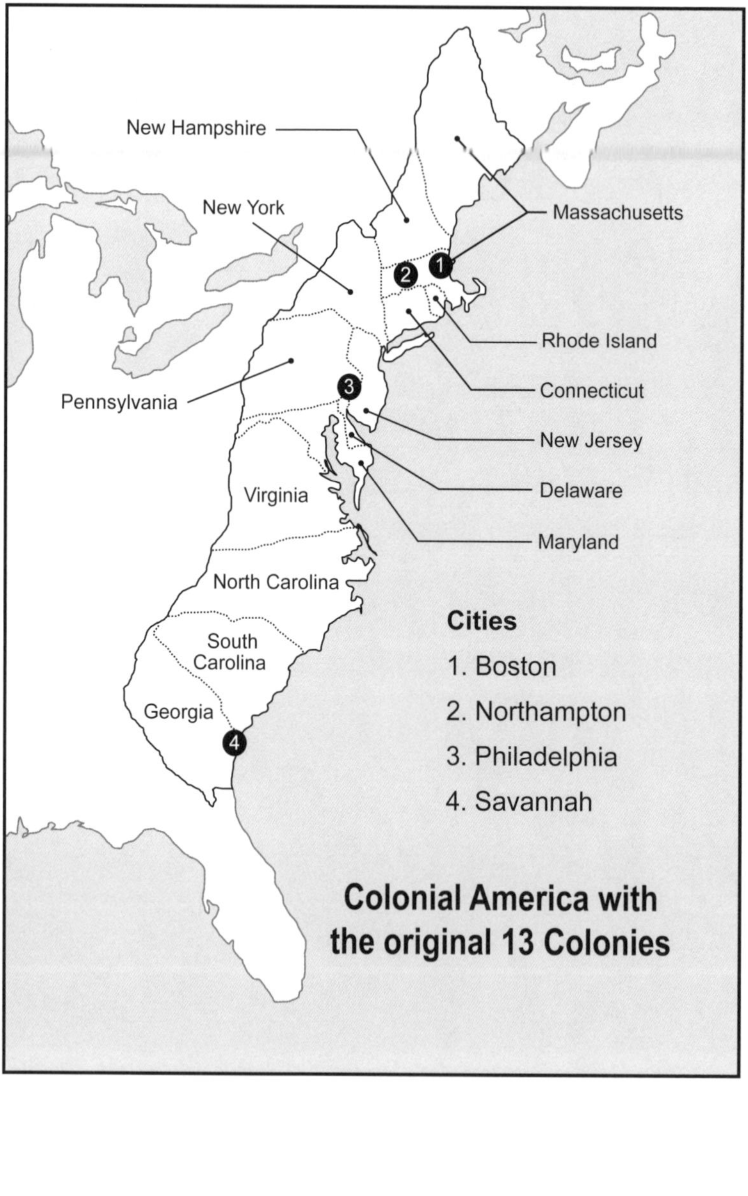
New Hampshire
New York
Massachusetts
Rhode Island
Connecticut
Pennsylvania
New Jersey
Delaware
Maryland
Virginia
North Carolina
South Carolina
Georgia
1
2
3
4
Cities
1. Boston
2. Northampton
3. Philadelphia
4. Savannah
Colonial America with the original 13 Colonies

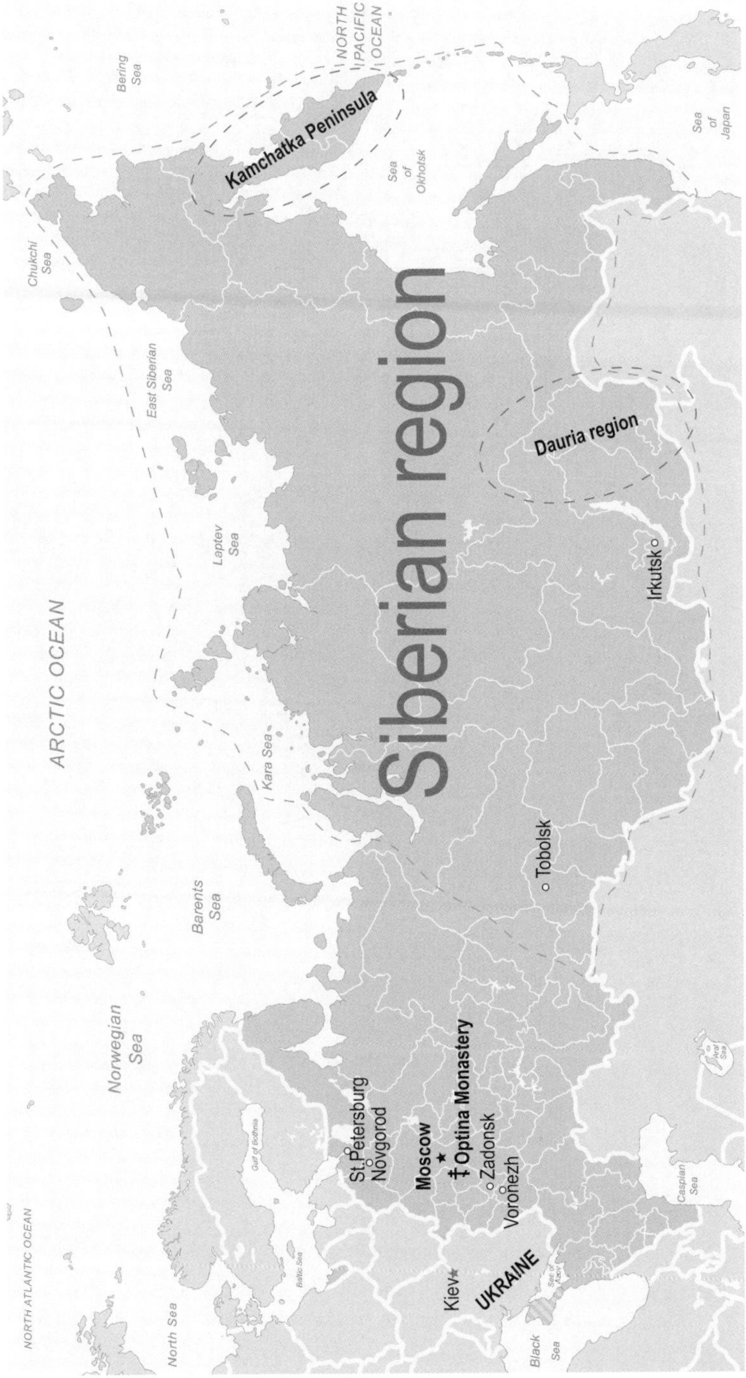
Siberian region
Kamchatka Peninsula
Dauria region
ARCTIC OCEAN
NORTH PACIFIC OCEAN
NORTH ATLANTIC OCEAN
Bering Sea
Chukchi Sea
East Siberian Sea
Laptev Sea
Kara Sea
Barents Sea
Norwegian Sea
North Sea
Baltic Sea
Gulf of Bothnia
Sea of Okhotsk
Sea of Japan
Black Sea
Sea of Azov
Caspian Sea
Aral Sea
Irkutsk
Tobolsk
St. Petersburg
Novgorod
Moscow
Optina Monastery
Zadonsk
Voronezh
Kiev
UKRAINE

SELECT BIBLIOGRAPHY

This is a selection of some of the books and articles found useful in writing this volume.

Cynthia Y. Aalders, '"In Melting Grief and Ardent Love": Anne Steele's Contribution to 18th Century Hymnody', in *The Hymn* vol.60, No.3, Summer 2009

Robert Merrihew Adams, 'Leibniz's Examination of the Christian Religion', in *Faith and Philosophy: Journal of the Society of Christian Philosophers*, Vol.11, Issue 4

Margaret Allen, *Fletcher of Madeley* (St Albans: Salvation Army, 1905)

Gerald H. Anderson (ed.), *Biographical Dictionary of Christian Missions* (New York: Erdmans, 1998)

Johann Arndt, *True Christianity* (trans. and introduction by Peter Erb. New York: Paulist Press, 1979)

Francis Bacon, *Novum Organum* (ed. Lisa Jardine and Michael Silverthorne, CUP 2000)

Josiah Henry Barr, *Early Methodists Under Persecution* (New York: The Methodist Book Concern, 1916)

Karl Barth, *Protestant Theology in the Nineteenth Century* [good chapters on the 18th as well] (London: SCM Press, 2001)

Hugh Blair, *Sermons* (5 volumes, London 1802)

Thomas Bokenkotter, *A Concise History of the Catholic Church* (New York: Doubleday, 1990)

David Brainerd, *Life and Diary* (New York: Cosimo Classics, 2007)

J. H. S. Burleigh, *A Church History of Scotland* (London: Oxford University Press, 1960)

Nigel Cameron (ed.), *Dictionary of Scottish Church History and Theology* (Edinburgh: T & T Clark, 1993)

Joseph Carmichael, *The Hymns of Anne Steele in John Ripon's Selection of Hymns: A Theological Analysis in the Context of the English Particular Baptist Revival* (Dissertation, Southern Baptist Seminary 2012)

Pierre de Caussade, *Abandonment to Divine Providence* (Mineola NY: Dover Publications, 2008)

Archbishop Chrysostomos and Hieromonk Patapios (trans. and ed.), *The Evergetinos* (Center for Traditionalist Orthodox Studies, 2008)

John Coffey, 'Evangelicals, Slavery & the Slave Trade: From Whitefield to Wilberforce', in *Anvil* vol. 24:2, 2007

Frank J. Coppa, *The Modern Papacy* (Abingdon OXON: Routledge, 1998)

William Cowper, *Poetical Works* (OUP 1934)

G. R. Cragg, *The Church and the Age of Reason 1648–1789* (Harmondsworth: Penguin Books, 1966)

F. L. Cross and E .A. Livingstone, *The Oxford Dictionary of the Christian Church* (New York: Oxford University Press, 1997)

H. Daniel-Rops, *The Church in the Eighteenth Century* (London: J. M. Dent & Sons, 1964)

Arnold Dallimore, *George Whitefield* (2 volumes, Edinburgh: Banner of Truth Trust, 1970)

Andrew Davies, *The Moravian Revival of 1727* (Evangelical Library lecture for 1977)

Samuel Davies, *Letters from the Rev. Samuel Davies, &c, Shewing the State of Religion in Virginia, Particularly Among the Negros* (London 1757)

—— Arthur P. Davis, *Isaac Watts* (London: Independent Press, 1948)

Rene Descartes, *Discourse on Method* (trans. F.E.Sutcliffe, London: Penguin Books, 1968)

Philip Doddridge, *The Life of Colonel James Gardiner* (Nabu Press, 2012)

Gordon Donaldson, *The Faith of the Scots* (London: Batsford, 1990)

Tim Dowley (editor), *The Lion Handbook on the History of Christianity* (Oxford: Lion, 1996)

Anne Dutton, *Letters on Spiritual Subjects* (Bottom of the Hill Publishing, 2013)

Jonathan Edwards, *Distinguishing Marks of a Work of the Spirit of God* (available in *Jonathan Edwards on Revival,* Edinburgh: Banner of Truth Trust, 1984)

—— *Narrative of Surprising Conversions* (available in *Jonathan Edwards on Revival,* Edinburgh: Banner of Truth Trust, 1984)

—— *Treatise Concerning Religious Affections* (available in vol.1 of *The Works of Jonathan Edwards,* Edinburgh: Banner of Truth Trust, 1974)

Peter C. Erb (ed.), *Pietists: Selected Writings* (New York: Paulist Press, 1983)

G. P. Fedetov (ed.), *A Treasury of Russian Spirituality* (Gloucester MASS: Peter Smith, 1969)

Sinclair Ferguson and David F. Wright (eds.), *New Dictionary of Theology* (Leicester: IVP, 1988)

Edward Fisher, *The Marrow of Modern Divinity* (Tain, Ross-shire: Christian Heritage, 2015)

Andrew Fuller, *Works* (Edinburgh: Banner of Truth Trust, 2007)

John Gillies, *Historical Collections of Accounts of Revival* (Edinburgh: Banner of Truth Trust, 1981)

Eric W. Gritsch, *A History of Lutheranism* (Minneapolis: Fortress Press, 2002)

George E. Handley, 'The Ministerium of Pennsylvania, From 1748', in *Lutheran Quarterly*, vol.10, 1996

Robert T. Handy, *A History of the Churches in the United States and Canada* (Oxford: Clarendon Press, 1976)

J. Derek Holmes and Bernard W. Bickers, *A Short History of the Catholic Church* (Tunbridge Wells: Burnes and Oates, 1983)

Samuel Hopkins, *Works* (3 volumes, Boston MA: Doctrinal Book and Tract Society, 1852)

David Hume, *An Enquiry Concerning Human Understanding* (OUP 2007)

Francis Hutcheson, *A Short Introduction to Moral Philosophy* (Miami, FL: HardPress, 2017)

J. E. Hutton, *History of the Moravian Church* (New York, private printing 1922)

George H. Ingram, 'Biographies of the Alumni of the Log College: 3. Rev. William Robinson', in *Journal of the Presbyterian Historical Society* (1901-1930), Vol. 13, No. 6 (June, 1929).

Robert W. Jenson, *America's Theologian: A Recommendation of Jonathan Edwards* (OUP 1988)

John Morgan Jones and William Morgan, *The Calvinistic Methodist Fathers of Wales* (trans. John Aaron, Edinburgh: Banner of Truth Trust, 2008)

F. Kadloubovsky and G. E. H. Palmer (trans.), *Writings from the Philokalia on Prayer of the Heart* (London: Faber and Faber, 1993)

Immanuel Kant, *Religion Within the Bounds of Reason Alone* (trans. Allen Wood, CUP 2018)

J. N. D. Kelly, *Oxford Dictionary of Popes* (Oxford: Oxford University Press, 1986)

John Lancaster, *The Life of Darcy, Lady Maxwell, of Pollock* (Methodist Episcopal Church, 1848)

K. S. Latourette, *A History of the Expansion of Christianity. Three Centuries of Advance: 1500-1800* (Exeter: The Paternoster Press, 1971)

Platon Levshin, *The Orthodox Doctrine of the Apostolic Eastern Church* (London: Whitaker and Co., 1857)

____ *The Present State of the Greek Church in Russia* (New York, Collins & Co., 1815)

Carter Lindberg (ed.), *The Pietist Theologians. An Introduction to Theology in the Seventeenth and Eighteenth Centuries* (Oxford: Blackwell, 2005)

John A. McGuckin, 'The Life and Mission of St. Paisius Velichkovsky. 1722-1794. An Early Modern Master of The Orthodox Spiritual Life', in *Spiritus*, vol.9:2, 2009

R. L. Mackie, *A Short History of Scotland* (ed. Gordon Donaldson. Edinburgh: Oliver and Boyd, 1962)

George A. Maloney, *A History of Orthodox Theology Since 1453* (Belmont, Massachusetts: Nordland Publishing Company, 1976)

Frank Edward Manuel, *The Changing of the Gods* (Providence RI: Brown University Press, 1983)

The Memorial Days of the Renewed Church of the Brethren (London: Moravian Publication Office, 1895)

Iain Murray, *Jonathan Edwards* (Edinburgh: Banner of Truth Trust, 1987)

Stephen Neill, *A History of Christian Missions* (Harmondsworth: Penguin, 1991)

Kenneth Newport, *Charles Wesley in Perspective: Poet, Priest and Theologian*, Gresham College lecture, Thursday, 13 December 2007

John Newton, *Works* (4 volumes, Edinburgh: Banner of Truth Trust, 2015)

Harold Nicholson, *The Age of Reason* (Garden City, NY: Doubleday & Company, 1960)

Mark Noll, *A History of Christianity in the United States and Canada* (London: SPCK, 1991)

Thomas Paine, *The Age of Reason* (New York: Citadel Press, 1974)

Roy Porter, *Enlightenment* (Penguin Press: London, 2000)

Henry D. Rack, *Reasonable Enthusiast: John Wesley and the Rise of Methodism* (London: Epworth Press, 1989)

James Robe, *Narrative of the Extraordinary Work of the Spirit of God at Kilsyth* (Miami FL: HardPress, 2020)

Jean-Jacques Rousseau, *Emile: or, On Education* (trans. Barbara Foxley, Project Gutenberg https://gutenberg.org/ebooks/5427)

J. C. Ryle, *Christian Leaders of the 18th Century* (Edinburgh: Banner of Truth Trust, 1978)

Simon Schama, *Citizens: A Chronicle of the French Revolution* (London: Penguin Books, 2004)

William Sprague, *Lectures on Revival* (London: Banner of Truth Trust, 1959)

Douglas H. Shantz, *An Introduction to German Pietism* (Baltimore: Johns Hopkins University Press, 2013)

August Gottlieb Spangenberg, *The Life of Nicolas Lewis Count Zinzendorf* (London: Holdsworth, 1838)

Harry S. Stout, *The Divine Dramatist: George Whitefield and the Rise of Modern Evangelicalism* (Grand Rapids MICH: Eerdmans, 1991)

Robert Strivens, *The Thought of Philip Doddridge in the Context of Early Eighteenth-Century Dissent* (PhD, University of Stirling 2011)

Frank Tallett and Nicholas Atkin, *Priests, Prelates, and People* (London: I.B.Tauris & Co., 2003)

Tikhon of Zadonsk, *Journey to Heaven* (Jordanville NY: Holy Trinity Publications, 1991)

Augustus C. Thompson, *Moravian Missions: Twelve Lectures* (New York; Charles Scribner's Sons, 1882)

W. Townsend, H. Workman, and G. Eayrs, *New History of Methodism* (London: Hodder and Stoughton, 1909)

Joseph Tracy, *The Great Awakening* (Edinburgh: Banner of Truth Trust, 1976)

Paisius Velichkovsky, *Little Russian Philokalia* (Alaska: New Valaam Monastery, 1994)

Alec Vidler, *The Church in an Age of Revolution* (London: Penguin Books, 1990)

Voltaire, *Candide* (trans. Theo Cuffe, London: Penguin Books, 2005)

Robert Wallace, *The Rise of Russia* (Netherlands: Time/Life, 1967)

Timothy Kallistos Ware, *The Orthodox Church* (London: Penguin Books, 1997)

John Wesley, *Journal* (London: Epworth Press, 1960)

George Whitefield, *Journals* (London: Banner of Truth Trust, 1960)

C. T. Collins Winn, Christopher Gehrz, G. William Carlson, and Eric Holst, *The Pietist Impulse in Christianity* (Cambridge: James Clarke & Co., 2012)

A. Skevington Wood, *Inextinguishable Blaze: Spiritual Renewal and Advance in the Eighteenth Century* (Exeter, Devon: Paternoster Press n.d.)

Nicolas Zernov, *Eastern Christendom* (London: Weidenfeld and Nicolson, 1963)

INDEX to NAMES

INDEX to SUBJECTS

E

F

G

H

I

J

K

Grace
Publications

Grace Publications Trust

Grace Publications Trust is a not-for-profit organisation that exists to glorify God by making the truth of God's Word (as declared in the Baptist Confessions of 1689 and 1966) clear and understandable, so that:

- Christians will be helped to preach Christ
- Christians will know Christ better and delight in Him more
- Christians will be equipped to live for Christ
- Seekers will come to know Christ

From its beginning in the late 1970s the Trust has published simplified and modernised versions of important Christian books written earlier, for example by some of the Reformers and Puritans. These books have helped introduce the riches of the past to a new generation and have proved particularly useful in parts of Asia and Africa where English is widely spoken as a second language. These books are now appearing in editions co-published with Christian Focus as *Grace Essentials*.

More details of the Trust's work can be found on the web site at *www.gracepublications.co.uk.*